D1569740

2020
The Supreme Court Review

"Judges as persons, or courts as institutions, are entitled to no greater immunity from criticism than other persons or institutions ...
[J]udges must be kept mindful of their limitations and of their ultimate public responsibility by a vigorous stream of criticism expressed with candor however blunt."
—*Felix Frankfurter*

"... while it is proper that people should find fault when their judges fail, it is only reasonable that they should recognize the difficulties. ... Let them be severely brought to book, when they go wrong, but by those who will take the trouble to understand them."
—*Learned Hand*

THE LAW SCHOOL

THE UNIVERSITY OF CHICAGO

Volume 2020

The Supreme Court Review

EDITED BY

DAVID A. STRAUSS

GEOFFREY R. STONE

AND JUSTIN DRIVER

 THE UNIVERSITY OF CHICAGO PRESS

CHICAGO AND LONDON

The Supreme Court Review, Volume 2020

Published annually by The University of Chicago Press.
www.journals.uchicago.edu/SCR/

Subscriptions: Individual subscription rates are $84 print + electronic and $67 e-only. Institutional print + electronic and e-only rates are tiered according to an institution's type and research output: $113 to $198 (print + electronic), $98 to $172 (e-only). For additional information, including back-issue sales, classroom use, rates for single copies, and prices for institutional full-run access, please visit www.journals.uchicago.edu /SCR/. Free or deeply discounted access is available in most developing nations through the Chicago Emerging Nations Initiative (www .journals.uchicago.edu/ceni/).

Please direct subscription inquiries to Subscription Fulfillment, 1427 E. 60th Street, Chicago, IL 60637-2902. Telephone: (773) 753-3347 or toll free in the United States and Canada (877) 705-1878. Fax: (773) 753-0811 or toll-free (877) 705-1879. E-mail: subscriptions@press .uchicago.edu.

Standing orders: To place a standing order for this book series, please address your request to The University of Chicago Press, Chicago Distribution Center, Attn. Standing Orders/ Customer Service, 11030 S. Langley Avenue, Chicago, IL 60628. Telephone toll free in the U.S. and Canada: 1-800-621-2736; or 1-773-702-7000. Fax toll free in the U.S. and Canada: 1-800-621-8476; or 1-773-702-7212.

Single-copy orders: In the U.S., Canada, and the rest of the world, order from your local bookseller or direct from The University of Chicago Press, Chicago Distribution Center, 11030 S. Langley Avenue, Chicago, IL 60628. Telephone toll free in the U.S. and Canada: 1-800-621-2736; or 1-773-702-7000. Fax toll free in the U.S. and Canada: 1-800-621-8476; or 1-773-702-7212. In the U.K. and Europe, order from your local bookseller or direct from The University of Chicago Press, c/o John Wiley Ltd. Distribution Center, 1 Oldlands Way, Bognor Regis, West Sussex PO22 9SA, UK. Telephone 01243 779777 or Fax 01243 820250. E-mail: cs-books@wiley.co.uk.

The University of Chicago Press offers bulk discounts on individual titles to Corporate, Premium, and Gift accounts. For information, please write to Sales Department—Special Sales, The University of Chicago Press, 1427 E. 60th Street, Chicago, IL 60637 USA or telephone 1-773-702-7723.

This book was printed and bound in the United States of America.

ISSN: 0081-9557
E-ISSN: 2158-2459
ISBN: 978-0-226-80321-0 (cloth)
E-ISBN: 978-0-226-80335-7 (ebook)

IN MEMORIAM

JUSTICE RUTH BADER GINSBURG

CONTENTS

CRISTINA M. RODRÍGUEZ

READING REGENTS AND THE POLITICAL SIGNIFICANCE OF LAW

When the Supreme Court handed down its decision in *Department of Homeland Security v. Regents of the University of California*, in June 2020, advocates celebrated. DACA—an acronym that no longer requires definition—lived to see another day.[1] Newspaper headlines marked the decision as a decisive rebuff of the Trump administration's efforts to end the Obama-era program that shielded so-called Dreamers from deportation while authorizing them to work in the United States.[2]

Cristina M. Rodríguez is Leighton Homer Surbeck Professor of Law, Yale Law School.

AUTHOR'S NOTE: I am enormously grateful for the outstanding research assistance of Callie Bruzzone, Kayla Crowell, Daniel Esses, and Becca Steele.

[1] For the sake of precision, DACA is the acronym for an Obama-era initiative called Deferred Action for Childhood Arrivals, which invited non-citizens lacking lawful immigration status who met certain criteria to apply for relief, which entailed extending the deferral of their removal for two years and rendered them eligible to apply for work authorization and other discrete benefits tied to "lawful presence" as recognized by the Attorney General. *See* Memorandum from Janet Napolitano, Sec'y, U.S. Dep't of Homeland Sec., to David V. Aguilar, Acting Comm'r, U.S. Citizenship & Immigr. Servs., et al. (June 15, 2012), https://www.dhs.gov/xlibrary/assets/s1 -exercising-prosecutorial-discretion-individuals-who-came-to-us-as-children.pdf (hereinafter Napolitano memorandum).

[2] *See, e.g.*, Robert Barnes, *Supreme Court Blocks Trump's Bid to End DACA, a Win for Undocumented 'Dreamers,'* WASH. POST (June 18, 2020), https://www.washingtonpost.com/politics /courts_law/supreme-court-rules-against-trump-administration-attempt-to-end-daca-a-win -for-undocumented-immigrants-brought-to-us-as-children/2020/06/18/4f0b6c74-b163-11ea -8758-bfd1d045525a_story.html; Alan Gomez, *'We Won': DACA Recipients Overwhelmed by Surprise Supreme Court Victory Over Trump*, USA TODAY (June 18, 2020), https://www.usatoday

The Supreme Court Review, 2021.

Initiated in 2012, the Deferred Action for Childhood Arrivals program had survived almost four years of a presidential administration
overtly hostile to immigrants and immigration—a government bent
on unraveling as much of the administrative and political legacy of its
immediate predecessors as possible.[3] The Supreme Court largely
affirmed the Ninth Circuit's holding that efforts by the Department
of Homeland Security (DHS) to rescind DACA were arbitrary and
capricious and therefore invalid, sending DHS back to the drawing
board to accomplish its objectives.[4] With the 2020 presidential election less than five months away and the very real possibility of regime
change in the air, the decision seemed decisive. The Supreme Court
had saved DACA, at least for the time being.

On the other side of the presidential election, we can now say that
the Dreamers and their lawyers succeeded in using the courts to run
out the clock on one of the more high-profile efforts of the Trump
presidency. This success calls for an explanation. The original legal
theory of DACA was predicated on its discretionary and therefore
defeasible character. The government justified DACA as a series of
individual acts of prosecutorial discretion, defined as the inherent
discretion law enforcement officials possess to forbear from enforcement, at their convenience, in order to prioritize enforcement resources.
DACA's founding document—a memorandum issued by the Secretary
of Homeland Security—included the disclaimer standard in Executive
orders and agency guidance documents: "this memorandum confers

---

.com/story/news/nation/2020/06/18/dreamers-daca-recipients-celebrate-rare-supreme-court
-win-over-trump/3213617001. The appellation "Dreamer" long predates DACA and has been
self-consciously adopted by immigrant youth mobilized to claim a legal status that matches their
felt sense of belonging—a status that would be made available by the DREAM Act (an acronym
for Development, Relief, and Education for Alien Minors), which was first introduced in
Congress in 2001 and has remained a mainstay of immigration reform proposals that have attracted support from both major parties but have yet to be enacted.

[3] No court has yet declared DACA to be illegal. During the Obama years, both ICE agents and
other enforcement-minded officials at the state level challenged DACA's legality, but the
lawsuits were all dismissed. *See* Crane v. Napolitano, No. 3:12-CV-03247-0, 2013 WL 8211660,
at *2 (N.D. Tex. July 31, 2013) (concluding that the Civil Service Reform Act provides "comprehensive and exclusive procedures for settling work-related controversies between federal civil
-service employees and the federal government"), *aff'd sub nom.* Crane v. Johnson, 783 F.3d 244
(5th Cir. 2015); Arpaio v. Obama, 797 F.3d 11, 14 (D.C. Cir. 2015) (holding that Maricopa
County Sheriff Joe Arpaio lacked standing to challenge DACA). One lawsuit challenging the
legality of DACA, brought by the state of Texas, remains pending in the Southern District of
Texas. *See infra* notes 48 and 84 and accompanying text.

[4] Dep't of Homeland Sec. v. Regents of the Univ. of Cal., 140 S. Ct. 1891 (2020).

no substantive right."[5] DACA's promise, then, lasted as long as the Executive wanted it to. The promise was durable as long as President Obama remained in office but unenforceable should the Executive branch fall into the hands of officials hostile to the program.

Given the apparently weak anchor DACA provided, why was it so difficult for a new administration, whose enforcement priorities did not include categorical forbearance for Dreamers, to reorient the enforcement system in its preferred direction? A conventional answer, repeated as a description of many of the Trump administration's stumbles across regulatory arenas, was that officials were incompetent, sloppy, and disingenuous. The myriad court opinions in the DACA rescission litigation of the Trump years, from across the country and up and down the judicial hierarchy, reflected a version of this thesis. No court concluded that DACA was required by law. All parties, including the Supreme Court, seemed to agree that an administration could end the program.[6] But despite efforts to respond to the demands and criticisms of the lower courts, the Trump administration could not find its way to its desired conclusion.

But if the Court has implicitly acknowledged that DACA is not legally required and expressly stated that the government has the authority to wind it down, in what sense was *Regents* a major victory? In this essay, I argue that *Regents* is not a triumph in immigration law or even a decision of immigration law; far from it, the opinion contains a roadmap to DACA's demise. The decision's salutary outcome for immigrants also distracts us from a more ominous turn in the Roberts Court toward a reading of the immigration laws that empowers both Congress and the President to do as they please—a reading exemplified by one of the Term's other decisions, *Department of Homeland Security v. Thuraissigiam*, in which the Court rejects a Suspension Clause challenge to expedited removal proceedings.[7] *Regents* does reflect a kind of political triumph, however, not just because DACA was

---

[5] Napolitano memorandum, *supra* note 1. This framing arguably reflected the administration's desire to proceed quickly, not its intention for DACA status to be unstable or unreliable for its participants. By casting it as an exercise of discretion, DHS could avoid the notice and comment requirements applicable to the promulgation of a binding legislative rule under the Administrative Procedure Act.

[6] *See Regents*, 140 S. Ct. at 1905 ("The dispute before the Court is not whether DHS may rescind DACA. All parties agree that it may. The dispute is instead primarily about the procedure the agency followed in doing so.").

[7] 140 S. Ct. 1959 (2020).

saved but because the Court calls attention to the profound interests its recipients have in remaining in the United States and thus to their new social status, separate and apart from their legal status. And yet, within the *Regents* decision itself, as well as in the legal claims made against the Trump administration, are the very tools with which courts might again stymie political change designed to advance immigrants' rights, relying on the exacting procedural regularity championed in *Regents* by Chief Justice Roberts.

I. The Trump Administration's Failed Rescission

Chief Justice Roberts opened his opinion in 2012, at the moment of DACA's inception. But to understand what DACA sought to achieve as a matter of administration, it is important to understand what it replaced. As most every court to have heard a DACA-related dispute has recognized, implicit in the operation of an immigration enforcement regime is the authority of Executive officials to set priorities for law enforcement agents. Those priorities can encourage agents to forbear from arresting or deporting otherwise removable non-citizens as part of a larger systemic interest in channeling resources toward removals in the government's highest interests. Beginning in 2010, Obama-era DHS officials articulated a set of priorities in guidance documents (known as the Morton Memos) in an effort to encourage line-level officials to consider non-enforcement against certain types of individuals, including those who met the criteria that would eventually define DACA – the hundreds of thousands of non-citizens lacking immigration status who had been brought to the United States as youth.[8] After two years of trying to steer the enforcement system with these exhortations, DHS officials determined that few obvious or publicly visible changes to enforcement practices had occurred. The Department's political leadership, in conjunction with the White House, thus devised DACA to protect Dreamers from deportation. The program, adopted by what came to be known as the Napolitano memorandum, invited applications for forbearance from

---

[8] Adam Cox and I have recounted this story in detail, explaining how the Morton Memos departed in important respects from previous administrations' prioritization memos, and situating DACA in a long history of presidential control over immigration law and developing practices of political officials supervising the bureaucracy. *See* Adam B. Cox & Cristina M. Rodríguez, The President and Immigration Law 162–90 (2020).

those who satisfied carefully drawn eligibility criteria, virtually ensuring, though not guaranteeing, protection and work authorization for
Dreamers.[9]

By the time President Donald Trump took office, more than
750,000 Dreamers had been granted DACA status,[10] which provided
them actual and psychological relief from removal and enabled them
to enter the workforce and live as if their immigration status were im-
material. As a candidate, Donald Trump vowed to rescind DACA immediately, but in his initial months in office, President Trump himself
expressed ambivalence and even reservations.[11] In September 2017,
however, Attorney General Jefferson Sessions sent a one-page, four-
paragraph letter to Acting DHS Secretary Elaine Duke to "advise"
that DHS should rescind the Napolitano memorandum initiating
DACA on the ground that DACA was "an open-ended circumvention
of immigration laws" and "an unconstitutional exercise of the authority of the Executive Branch."[12] The next day, in what had to have
been a coordinated decision within the administration, Secretary Duke
released her own memorandum terminating DACA,[13] citing the Attorney General's letter and the litigation that had called into question
the legal authority for a second but now moribund Obama-era deferred
action policy (Deferred Action for Parents of Americans and Lawful

---

[9] The eligibility criteria for DACA applied to non-citizens without immigration status who
were under age 31 in 2012; had continuously resided in the United States since 2007; were current students, high school graduates, or honorably discharged veterans; had not been convicted
of serious crimes; and did not present national security or public safety threats. *See* Napolitano
memorandum, *supra* note 1, at 1. In November 2014, DHS attempted to expand these criteria as
part of the Deferred Action for Parents of Americans and Lawful Permanent Residents (DAPA)—
an expanded deferred action policy quickly enjoined by the courts and later abandoned by the
Trump administration. *See* Memorandum from the Office of Legal Counsel to the Sec'y of
Homeland Sec. and the Counsel to the President 10 (Nov. 19, 2014), http://www.justice.gov
/sites/default/files/olc/opinions/attachments/2014/11/20/2014-11-19-auth-prioritize-removal
.pdf [http://perma.cc/85Y5-N94M] [hereinafter OLC Memorandum Op.].

[10] *See Number of Form I-821D, Consideration for Deferred Action for Childhood Arrivals, Fiscal
Year 2012-2017*, U.S. Citizenship & Immigration Servs. (Sept. 30, 2017), https://www.uscis
.gov/sites/default/files/document/data/daca_performancedata_fy2017_qtr4.pdf.

[11] *See, e.g.*, Gregory Krieg, *Trump's Many Shifting Positions on DACA, from the Campaign to
Right Now*, CNN (Jan. 25, 2018), https://www.cnn.com/2018/01/25/politics/donald-trump
-positions-daca.

[12] Letter from Jefferson B. Sessions, Att'y Gen., U.S. Dep't of Just., to Elaine Duke, Acting
Sec'y, Dep't of Homeland Sec. (Sept. 4, 2017), https://www.dhs.gov/sites/default/files/pub
lications/17_0904_DOJ_AG-letter-DACA.pdf [hereinafter Sessions Letter].

[13] Memorandum from Elaine Duke, Acting Sec'y, U.S. Dep't of Homeland Sec., to James
W. McCament, Acting Dir., U.S. Citizenship & Immigr. Servs., et al. (Sept. 5, 2017), https://
www.dhs.gov/news/2017/09/05/memorandum-rescission-daca.

Permanent Residents (DAPA)).[14] The timing and content of each of these two administrative documents became central to the Supreme Court's resolution of the legal question before it—whether the Trump administration's efforts to rescind DACA had been lawful.

The court case began in three different circuits, where an array of plaintiffs raised numerous substantive claims, two of which ended up before the Supreme Court: that the rescission of DACA was arbitrary and capricious in violation of the Administrative Procedure Act and that the rescission violated the Equal Protection Clause of the Constitution. In its culminating opinion, the Supreme Court first concluded that DACA did not fall into the class of non-enforcement decisions long held to be unreviewable by courts on the authority of *Heckler v. Chaney*.[15] DACA amounted, instead, to a full-blown program for granting immigration relief and attendant benefits, justifying judicial review—review that jurisdiction-stripping provisions of the Immigration and Nationality Act (INA) also did not preclude. The Court then proceeded to hold that the rescission of DACA in its entirety was indeed inconsistent with the requirements of the APA but that none of the plaintiffs' allegations established a "plausible" claim of racial animus under the Equal Protection Clause.

But DACA was a discretionary program that the administration should have been able to undo easily, not a program that should have survived more than three years of a concerted rescission effort (assuming Trump officials' hearts were in it). Why did a clearly permissible outcome evade the Trump administration? Though incompetence has been charged repeatedly in public commentary, the explanations offered by Chief Justice Roberts underscore that the federal courts' conceptualization of the administration's fault changed throughout the litigation.

In his letter to Secretary Duke, Attorney General Sessions justified the rescission as legally required, in part citing the litigation risk that maintaining the program posed, given that the Fifth Circuit had

[14] Texas v. United States, 809 F.3d 134, 166, 179-81 (2015) (affirming a lower court preliminary injunction, concluding that DAPA was "much more than nonenforcement: It would affirmatively confer 'lawful presence' and associated benefits on a class of unlawfully present aliens" and that plaintiffs were likely to succeed on their claim that DAPA should have gone through notice and comment rulemaking and that the APA required DAPA's invalidation because it was "manifestly contrary" to the INA).

[15] *Regents*, 140 S. Ct. 1905-07 (citing Heckler v. Chaney, 470 U.S. 821 (1985)).

invalidated President Obama's similarly structured DAPA initiative.[16] At the time, Adam Cox and I argued that the administration was hiding behind flimsy legal arguments to duck political responsibility and accountability for ending a widely popular and successful program.[17] The lower courts quickly put a stop to this evasion by demanding that the Trump administration provide reasons for the rescission beyond what the courts viewed to be erroneous legal claims.[18] Judge John Bates in the District for the District of Columbia actually gave the administration an opportunity to remedy the APA violation by providing the court with a more extended rationale for the rescission.[19] The administration obliged with a memorandum from a new DHS Secretary, Kirstjen Nielsen, in which she purported not to disturb the Duke memorandum and its legal conclusions but added multiple policy reasons to justify the rescission.[20] By elaborating on its legal reasoning and offering a policy rationale for ending DACA that could justify the rescission if the court continued to find the legal reasoning wanting—just the sort of rationale courts typically do not second-guess—the path to rescission seemed to have been cleared.

And yet, at the Supreme Court, the sufficiency of the Nielsen memo went untested. In its opinion, the Court dismisses the memo's relevance because it had been framed as an elaboration of the Duke memo and yet bore "little relationship" to the original purported basis for the agency action.[21] Under hornbook administrative law, then, the Nielsen

---

[16] *See Texas*, 809 F.3d at 181–82 (concluding that DAPA was "manifestly contrary to the INA" because it "would make 4.3 million otherwise removable" non-citizens eligible to apply for work authorization and receive other benefits).

[17] Adam B. Cox & Cristina M. Rodríguez, *Don't Let Trump Hide Behind the Constitution in Ending DACA*, JUST SECURITY (Sept. 6, 2017), https://www.justsecurity.org/44735/dont-trump-hide-constitution-daca. In the wake of the *Regents* decision, Benjamin Eidelson has characterized the litigation and the Court's decision as accountability forcing. *See* Benjamin Eidelson, *Reasoned Explanation and Political Accountability in the Roberts Court*, 130 YALE L.J. 1748 (2021).

[18] *See, e.g.*, Batalla Vidal v. Nielsen, 279 F. Supp. 3d 401, 437–38 (E.D.N.Y 2018) (granting plaintiffs' motion for preliminary injunction); *but see* Casa De Md. v. Dep't of Homeland Sec., 284 F. Supp. 3d 758 (D. Md. 2018) (concluding that it was reasonable for DHS to have concluded that DACA was unlawful and should be wound down in orderly manner).

[19] NAACP v. Trump, 298 F. Supp.3d 209 (D.D.C. 2018).

[20] The policy reasons included that DHS should exercise prosecutorial discretion on a case-by-case basis, leaving categorical relief to Congress, and that it was important for DHS to "project a message" that the immigration laws were to be enforced against all categories of violators. Memorandum from Kirstjen M. Nielsen, Sec'y, U.S. Dep't of Homeland Sec. (June 22, 2018), https://www.dhs.gov/sites/default/files/publications/18_0622_S1_Memorandum_DACA.pdf.

[21] Dep't of Homeland Sec. v. Regents of the Univ. of Cal., 140 S. Ct. 1891, 1908 (2020).

memo constituted an irrelevant post hoc rationalization. In support of this conclusion, the Court lists the familiar case law, for which the standard citation is *SEC v. Chenery Corp.*[22], and the reasons for rejecting an elaborated justification and insisting that the agency start a new policy process or issue a new decision to invoke new reasons: that such requirements promote accountability, ensure the parties and public can respond to the agency's authority, preserve the orderly process of review, and constrain the agency from making its reasons and therefore its policy a moving target.[23]

Thus focused on the Duke memo, the Supreme Court offers a two-part reason for finding the rescission procedurally flawed, each part of which I consider in more detail in Part II. The first is a legal rationale not yet hit upon by the federal courts but offered by the respondents from the District of Columbia: according to the Court, the Sessions letter had concluded that DACA was unlawful because it contained the same legal defects the Fifth Circuit had found in DAPA. Because the Fifth Circuit focused its analysis on the benefits DAPA conferred (primarily eligibility for work authorization), the Secretary failed to appreciate that the Sessions letter left her with discretion to decouple the two parts of DACA and consider whether its forbearance policy standing alone, without benefits, passed legal muster.[24] The second of the Court's rationales also sounds in basic administrative law—that when it changes a policy, an agency must consider the reliance interests engendered by that policy, not because those interests are necessarily legally dispositive, but because they are always substantively relevant.[25] Leaving aside the puzzlement expressed by Justice Thomas in his partial dissent—why should these reliance interests matter if some or

---

[22] 332 U.S. 194 (1947).

[23] 140 S. Ct. at 1908–09 (citing Chenery, 332 U.S. at 201 (1947), and D.C. Circuit precedent establishing that on remand, an agency can either amplify its original reasons or take new agency action that complies with the procedural requirements for new action).

[24] *Id.* at 1912 ("The Attorney General neither addressed the forbearance policy at the heart of DACA nor compelled DHS to abandon that policy. . . . Duke's memo offers no reason for terminating forbearance. She instead treated the Attorney General's conclusion regarding the illegality of benefits as sufficient to rescind both benefits and forbearance, without explanation."). What the Court characterized as a "unique statutory provision," *id.* at 1910, made the Attorney General's legal conclusions binding on the Secretary. See 8 U.S.C. § 1103(a)(1) (2018).

[25] *Regents*, 140 S. Ct. at 1913–15 (citing Encino Motorcars, LLC v. Navarro, 136 S. Ct. 2117, 2126 (2016), and FCC v. Fox Television Stations, Inc., 556 U.S. 502, 515 (2009)).

all of the program itself was without legal foundation?—the Court gave the administration two clear assignments on remand if it hoped to continue the rescission effort.

With this move, Chief Justice Roberts found a political sweet spot for someone hoping not to take sides on the merits. He did not allow the rescission to proceed, but he also avoided concluding that DACA was lawful. He thus did not close the door to an eventual gutting of DACA through elimination of the path to work authorization that made it so valuable. But whether *Regents* amounts to a "win" depends both on whose perspective we take and the timeframe we adopt. In the months after the decision, DACA recipients had clearly triumphed. The story's denouement unfolded in a courtroom in the Eastern District of New York. After *Regents*, the government did indeed return to the drawing board. Attorney General William Barr rescinded all DOJ authorities relevant to the case, including a 2014 memorandum from the Office of Legal Counsel elaborating why the much larger DAPA program was consistent with the INA and within the Secretary's authority.[26] At DHS, Acting Secretary Chad Wolf rescinded the Nielsen and Duke memoranda and styled his own memo as beginning the process of considering DACA anew. He pledged that, while DHS conducted its fresh process, the agency would honor existing DACA grants but would no longer adjudicate new or pending applications. In his memorandum explaining these steps, Acting Secretary Wolf acknowledged the reliance interests of existing DACA holders by repeating back the Supreme Court's articulation of those interests. But he then offered: "[w]hatever the merits of these asserted reliance interests on the maintenance of the DACA policy, they are significantly lessened, if not entirely lacking" for those who had never received deferred action in the first place.[27]

Litigants immediately challenged this new quasi-rescission. But rather than determine if DHS had properly adhered to the procedural path cleared by the Supreme Court, Judge Nicholas Garaufis found

---

[26] Letter from William P. Barr, Att'y Gen., to Chad F. Wolf, Acting Sec'y, U.S. Dep't of Homeland Sec. (June 30, 2020), https://www.dhs.gov/sites/default/files/publications/20_0630_doj_aj-barr-letter-as-wolf-daca.pdf.

[27] Memorandum from Chad F. Wolf, Acting Sec'y, U.S. Dep't of Homeland Sec., to Mark Morgan, Senior Off. Performing the Duties of Comm'r, U.S. Customs & Border Prot. (July 28, 2020), https://www.dhs.gov/sites/default/files/publications/20_0728_s1_daca-reconsideration-memo.pdf.

Wolf's appointment to have been unlawful, thus invalidating his actions as lacking authorization—a conclusion reached by numerous courts reviewing various DHS actions in the waning days of the Trump administration.[28] Whether DHS could correct this structural defect and try yet again to rescind DACA became moot with the election of Joseph R. Biden to the presidency in November 2020. Biden pledged during the campaign to shore up DACA. Not long after his inauguration, he followed through by declaring his intention to "fortify" the program.[29]

But even though the election brought the rescission saga to an end, a deeper, more speculative strain of *Regents* is now in play. Despite being a procedural decision on its surface and in its holdings, Chief Justice Roberts's novel reasoning forecasts still more legal wrangling over both DACA's validity and, more generally, the capacity of a new president to chart a different path on immigration policy.

II. Immigration and the Roberts Court

Regents ensured that DACA would survive into a new administration determined to preserve it. But the decision itself is neither a victory for immigrants' rights in a jurisprudential sense nor a particularly probative data point in a more holistic account of immigration law in the Roberts era. Most immediately, the opinion provides a

---

[28] *See, e.g.*, Pangea Legal Servs. v. U.S. Dep't of Homeland Sec., No. 20-CV-09253-JD, 2021 WL 75756, at *4-5 (N.D. Cal. Jan. 8, 2021) (enjoining a rule altering procedures for asylum and withholding of removal); Batalla Vidal v. Wolf, No. 16CV4756NGGVMS, 2020 WL 6695076, at *9 (E.D.N.Y. Nov. 14, 2020) (granting summary judgment for plaintiffs in challenge to memorandum effectively suspending DACA program pending DHS review); Nw. Immigrant Rts. Project v. U.S. Citizenship & Immigration Servs., No. CV 19-3283 (RDM), 2020 WL 5995206, at *24 (D.D.C. Oct. 8, 2020) (enjoining a rule requiring first-time asylum applicants to pay a fee and reducing the availability of fee waivers), *appeal dismissed*, No. 20-5369, 2021 WL 161666 (D.C. Cir. Jan. 12, 2021); Immigrant Legal Res. Ctr. v. Wolf, 491 F. Supp. 3d 520, 533 (N.D. Cal. 2020) (enjoining rule implementing fee changes for immigrant benefit requests); Casa de Md., Inc. v. Wolf, 486 F. Supp. 3d 928, 960 (D. Md. 2020) (enjoining rules overhauling an employment authorization scheme for asylum seekers). This improper installation of Wolf and the subsequent invalidation of numerous administration policy initiatives may be the best candidate for the award of administrative incompetence during the Trump years. At the same time, it may have been that the virtue of avoiding the scrutiny of confirmation and the ease of installing preferred agents as acting officials outweighed whatever discrete policy losses the administration suffered. In the case of DACA, unwinding it may have mattered less to the officials most focused on immigration policy than simply signaling hostility to even the most publicly sympathetic immigrants.

[29] *See* Memorandum of January 20, 2021, 86 Fed. Reg. 7053 (Jan. 25, 2021); *Statement by Homeland Security Secretary Mayorkas on DACA*, Dep't of Homeland Sec. (Mar. 26, 2021), https://www.dhs.gov/news/2021/03/26/statement-homeland-security-secretary-mayorkas -daca.

roadmap to DACA's demise by inviting litigants and judges to separate its two pillars—categorical forbearance from removal on the one
hand and eligibility for work authorization and benefits tied to deferred action status on the other—and to invalidate the latter. Beyond
DACA, the prospects for a jurisprudence that restrains the coercive
power of the government against non-citizens grew even dimmer this
Term, despite *Regents*. In the unrelated *Thuraissigiam* decision, the Roberts Court rejected yet another rights-based challenge to the assertion
of a sweeping enforcement and removal power expressly authorized
by Congress, continuing what increasingly appears to be the Court's
steady departure from its prior practice of infusing interpretations of
the INA with a concern for basic due process principles. This opinion
attracted much less interest from the media and general public than
the fate of DACA, but it is of far greater importance to the future of
immigration law qua law.

The first step to dismantling DACA through the courts is establishing its justiciability, which the *Regents* Court appears to do defini-
tively. As originally conceived, DACA was an exercise of the Secretary's enforcement discretion—a form of decision-making typically
insulated from judicial review.[30] The so-called benefits features of
DACA merely flowed from the decision to forbear from removal in
light of regulations and administrative policies, dating back decades,
that linked those benefits to a grant of deferred action.[31] Indeed, it
seems quite plausible that the Obama administration chose deferred

---

[30] As the Court in *Regents* notes, the basic presumption of judicial review embodied in the
Administrative Procedure Act "can be rebutted by a showing that the relevant statute 'preclude[s]'
review, § 701(a)(1), or that the 'agency action is committed to agency discretion by law,' § 702
(a)(1)." 140 S. Ct. at 1905. Under the Court's precedent in *Heckler v. Chaney*, 470 U.S. 821, 831–
32 (1985), a decision not to bring an otherwise authorized enforcement action is ordinarily not
subject to judicial review because the decision requires balancing a number of factors "peculiarly
within [the agency's] expertise," mirrors the decision of a prosecutor not to indict, and "as a
practical matter" provides no action to focus judicial review. *Regents*, 140 S. Ct. at 1906 (citing
Chaney, 470 U.S. at 831–32).

[31] *See* 8 C.F.R. § 274a.12(c)(14) (2020) (establishing that deferred action recipients are eligible
to apply for employment authorization); 8 C.F.R. §1.3(a)(4)(vi) (establishing that recipients
of deferred action are "lawfully present" for the purposes of receiving certain Social Security
benefits). In addition to these federal regulations, in many states, recipients of deferred action
or holders of EADs are eligible under state law to acquire driver's licenses. Again, this eligibility flows from the deferral of removal and is not part of a holistic regulatory scheme to
confer a status on certain non-citizens. *See, e.g.*, Wis. Stat. § 343.14 (2020); Ind. Code § 9-
24-9-2.5 (2020); Kan. Stat. Ann. § 8-240 (2019); Tex. Transp. Code § 521.142 (2019);
Ariz. Rev. Stat. Ann. § 28-3158 (2020); S.D. Codified Laws §32-12-3.1 (2021); Fla. Stat.
§ 322.08 (2020); 75 Pa. Cons. Stat. § 1506 (2019).

action as the vehicle through which to provide Dreamers some relief because of these legal parameters—unreviewable discretion connected to an already established regulatory structure, complete with a ready-made and routine process by which recipients of forbearance could apply for employment authorization documents (EADs).

But in various instantiations of the litigation over both DACA and DAPA, the Supreme Court and the lower courts have rebuffed the government's argument (common across administrations) that the policies are unreviewable exercises of enforcement discretion.[32] In *Regents*, the Court declines to apply *Heckler v. Chaney* and its holding that the decision to decline to enforce the law is not subject to judicial review because it is committed to agency discretion, emphasizing that "DACA is not simply a non-enforcement policy."[33] By erecting an application process to identify individuals who met enumerated criteria, the administration created a "program for conferring affirmative immigration relief," not a "passive non-enforcement policy."[34] By reframing DACA as a program with component parts, each subject to legal review, the Court thus raises the stakes for the government by redefining the nature of what the administration seeks to accomplish in a way that imposes more procedural obligations and heightens the threat of judicial surveillance.[35]

---

[32] For the government's position on reviewability in the litigation surrounding DAPA, see Brief for Petitioner at 36, United States v. Texas, 136 S. Ct. 2271 (2016) (No. 15-674) (arguing that DAPA was "an unreviewable exercise of enforcement discretion with unreviewable consequences" under the APA). The Fifth Circuit viewed DAPA as "much more than nonenforcement," saying that the program would "affirmatively confer 'lawful presence' and associated benefits on a class of" unlawfully present noncitizens. *Texas v. United States*, 809 F.3d 134, 166 (5th Cir. 2015), *as revised* (Nov. 25, 2015), *aff'd by an equally divided court*, 136 S. Ct. 2271 (2016). The Fifth Circuit stated that "to be reviewable agency action, DAPA need not directly confer public benefits—removing a categorical bar on receipt of those benefits and thereby making a class of persons newly eligible for them 'provides a focus for judicial review.'" *Id.* at 167 (citing *Chaney*, 470 U.S. at 832). It referred to "DAPA's issuance of lawful presence and employment authorization" as "affirmative agency action" and concluded that the INA provided enough of a framework that judicial review to determine whether the agency had exceeded its statutory powers was appropriate. *Id.* at 168.

[33] 140 S. Ct. at 1906.

[34] *Id.*

[35] Even though this conceptualization of DACA as non-enforcement "plus" seems to constrain the Executive, it also in some sense raises the Executive's stature by treating enforcement judgments as a form of policymaking. This move is of a piece with the way Justice Kennedy treated enforcement priorities as a form of federal policymaking that could preempt state-level enforcement laws that might conflict or interfere with the scope of federal law as defined by Executive enforcement judgments in *Arizona v. United States*, 567 U.S. 387 (2012). It also accords

But despite finding DACA to be reviewable, the Court does not purport to evaluate the legality of its component parts on the merits. Instead, the Court finds fault with the Secretary's own failure to de-couple DACA's two pillars—forbearance and benefits—and then eval-uate the legality and viability of a forbearance-only policy.[36] In finding this avenue legally available to the Secretary, Roberts is arguably under-reading the Sessions letter to Secretary Duke, which, as the Chief Justice himself emphasizes, binds the Secretary's discretion. That letter—one page in length—does not clearly draw the distinction Roberts iden-tifies and arguably casts legal doubt on DACA as a whole.[37] But Rob-erts seizes on the letter's statement that "the DACA policy has the same legal . . . defects that the courts recognized as to DAPA" to chart his course through the fraught case. In the litigation over DAPA, the Fifth Circuit, in *Texas v. United States*,[38] had determined the relevant legal question to be whether the Secretary had authority to make DAPA recipients eligible for benefits, not whether he had authority to forbear from removing the class of people who fit into the program's criteria. In other words, even under Sessions's letter and the specter of litigation risk raised by the Fifth Circuit, the Secretary could have considered a forbearance-only version of DACA. And under bedrock administrative law—*Motor Vehicle Manufacturer's Association v. State*

---

with the theory of policymaking through enforcement that Adam Cox and I have developed, through which we emphasize how history, legal structure, and administrative practice have trans-formed supposedly one-off discretionary judgments into a form of systematic policymaking. See Cox & Rodríguez, *supra* note 8, at 103-32, 191–214.

[36] *See supra* note 24.

[37] If we read the Sessions letter as impugning the legality of DACA as a whole, that is, as foreclosing the bifurcation of its parts to save forbearance from a conclusion of legal invalidity, then the Secretary truly would have been required to end DACA altogether in light of that letter, given the Attorney General's authority to determine the scope of the immigration laws—an authority the Court recognizes. The Court's options for disposition would then have changed and perhaps become politically less comfortable for the Chief Justice, because it would have been impossible to avoid taking a position on DACA's legality. As Justice Thomas notes in his partial dissent and concurrence in the judgment, if DACA was not lawful, then reliance interests, no matter how strong, could not have justified keeping it in place. And thus, to send DHS back to the drawing board to better justify its decision to rescind DACA would have required Roberts implicitly to accept DACA's legality as a whole and to demand a better policy rationale for the rescission, including an explanation for disrupting the reliance interests. By instead bifurcating DACA, Roberts is able to remain agnostic on DACA's legality, leaving open the possibility of narrowing the Executive's authority in the future, while rebuffing the Trump administration's effort to disrupt the lives of the enormously sympathetic Dreamers.

[38] 809 F.3d 134 (5th Cir. 2015), *as revised* (Nov. 25, 2015), *aff'd by an equally divided court*, 136 S. Ct. 2271 (2016).

Farm[39]—an agency seeking to rescind a policy must consider in its "reasoned analysis" whether alternatives "within the ambit of the existing policy" might be viable. Because forbearance was at the very core of DACA, DHS ought to have considered a policy of "forbearance without benefits,"[40] and the Sessions letter simply did not foreclose that possibility.

The *Regents* opinion thus gave the Trump administration a roadmap, albeit a lengthy one, to rescinding DACA once and for all. The agency could return to the drawing board, find the benefits prongs to be legally unfounded while maintaining a forbearance-only policy, which it then could have phased out if it had articulated policy reasons for abandoning this particular form of enforcement prioritization—reasons that adequately took into account reliance interests (more on which soon). And as noted above, in what turned out to be the waning months of the Trump administration, Chad Wolf formally started the rescission process anew, appearing to adopt a posture that threaded the Court's needle before Judge Garaufis found his authority wanting.

Today, the Court's roadmap is no longer of use to the administration itself. But it does steer litigants (the state of Texas, for example) seeking to challenge DACA's very legality down a clear path that the Court already understands. Despite not addressing DACA's legality squarely, the construction and reasoning of the Court's opinion are both highly suggestive: whereas forbearance seems safe, the future of work authorization and other benefits is in doubt. This prediction flows in part from the extensive use, bordering on adoption, by the Chief Justice of the Fifth Circuit's reasoning in *Texas v. United States*, which was, after all, a lower court decision concerning an immigration relief program not actually at issue in *Regents* and that did not culminate in a Supreme Court decision on the merits. To be sure, Attorney General Sessions put the Fifth Circuit opinion at issue by seeming to rely on it in his DACA letter to the Secretary. But not only does Chief Justice Roberts fold *Texas v. United States* and the fate of DAPA into his discussion of the history of the DACA rescission, he engages in an extended exposition of the Fifth Circuit's analysis when evaluating Secretary Duke's determination that she had no legal discretion to continue DACA. In his explication of the decision, Chief Justice Roberts ends

---

[39] 463 U.S. 29 (1983).

[40] Dep't of Homeland Sec. v. Regents of the Univ. of Cal., 140 S. Ct. 1891, 1913 (2020).

up making a persuasive case for the bifurcation of the program. And
by suggesting that the Secretary consider this alternative, he is at the
very least implying that it may well be legally available, if not legally
advisable.

Or put slightly differently, if the Chief Justice thought it likely that
a DACA-style forbearance policy contravened the Executive's legal
duties, it would have been curious for him to send the matter back to
the agency for consideration of an option doomed to fail. When the
litigation over DAPA began, its challengers, not to mention critical
commentators, raised doubts about the categorical forbearance it embodied—the same legal concerns Justice Thomas highlights in his *Regents* opinion dissenting from the APA holding, in which he emphasizes
Congress has not authorized categorical exemptions to the INA's removal requirements.[41] But by the time the DAPA case had reached
the Fifth Circuit, that court seemed to have accepted forbearance only
as a manifestation of the Executive's authority to prioritize removal
resources.[42] Indeed, for a court to reject the forbearance component of
DACA truly would be a rejection of a very basic enforcement practice.[43] As Adam Cox and I have argued, DACA is no less enforcement

---

[41] *Id.* at 1921 (Thomas, J., concurring in the judgment in part and dissenting in part). Citing
both the reasoning of the elephants-in-mouseholes canon and the major-questions doctrine,
Justice Thomas, with whom Justices Alito and Gorsuch join, concludes "the detailed statutory
provisions governing temporary and lawful permanent resident status, relief from removal, and
class-wide deferred-action programs lead ineluctably to the conclusion that DACA is 'inconsistent with the design and structure of the statute as a whole.'" *Id.*

[42] According to the Fifth Circuit, Texas and the other litigating states "do not challenge the
Secretary's decision to 'decline to institute proceedings, terminate proceedings, or decline to
execute a final order of deportation,'" and nothing in its decision "requires the Secretary to
remove any alien or to alter" the agency's class-based "enforcement priorities." *Texas*, 809
F.3d at 168, 166, 169.

[43] In his partial dissent, Justice Thomas takes precisely this position. He would have called
into question not just the legal authority for DACA but also for other categorical grants of
deferred action that defenders of DACA have cited as evidence of past and probative administrative practice. *Regents*, 140 S. Ct. at 1924, n.6 (Thomas, J., dissenting) ("In the DAPA
litigation, DHS noted that some deferred action programs have been implemented by the
Executive Branch without explicit legislation. But 'past practice does not, by itself, create
[Executive] power. . . . Moreover, if DHS has the authority to create new categories of new
aliens eligible for deferred action, then all of Congress' deferred-action legislation was but a
superfluous exercise." (citations omitted)). The district court in the DAPA litigation took a
similar position. "Instead of merely refusing to enforce the INA's removal laws against an
individual, the DHS has enacted a wide-reaching program that awards legal presence . . . to
individuals Congress has deemed deportable or removable." Texas v. United States, 86 F.
Supp. 3d 591, 654 (S.D. Tex. 2015), *aff'd*, 809 F.3d 134 (5th Cir. 2015), *as revised* (Nov. 25,
2015), *aff'd by an equally divided court*, 136 S. Ct. 2271 (2016). Some commentators have
maintained this position, too. *See, e.g.*, Zachary Price, *Enforcement Discretion and Executive
Duty*, 67 VAND. L. REV. 671, 688–96 (2014).

discretion for having shifted the locus of discretion to the Secretary level and away from individual agents, even as individual agents continue to make decisions.[44]

Now that we have a presidential administration that intends to fortify rather than wind down DACA, the central note of doubt in the *Regents* opinion comes into play: will the courts permit the Biden administration to continue extending eligibility for work authorization (and other benefits) to recipients of deferred action under the DACA program?[45] DACA's value to its beneficiaries turns on the answer to this question. Though a promise of forbearance diminishes the uncertainty and psychological anxiety associated with the threat of deportation, eligibility for work authorization is what has made DACA truly transformative for hundreds of thousands of non-citizens without legal status who are fundamentally American. Again, Chief Justice Roberts does not address on the merits whether DHS has the authority to extend eligibility for work authorization. But he also does not take the approach of several of the lower courts, which outright rejected the Trump administration's conclusion that DACA was unlawful. He offers as an alternative for the agency a position that jettisons work authorization for being illegal (as Sessions had concluded) but continues on with forbearance. Perhaps if the administration had gone through with such an approach and it had reached the Supreme Court a second time, Roberts and his fellow justices, upon closer inspection, would have concluded, in fact, that extension of work authorization was perfectly legal. After all, the regulations making deferred action recipients eligible to apply for EADs date back to the Reagan era.[46] The administration would then have had to rescind or modify those regulations (possibly after having gone through notice

---

[44] Cox & RODRÍGUEZ, *supra* note 8, at 178–79.

[45] Adam B. Cox & Cristina M. Rodríguez, *The Supreme Court's Ominous DACA Decision: Perils for Dreamers in What Comes Next*, JUST SECURITY (June 22, 2020), https://www.justsecurity.org/70956/the-supreme-courts-ominous-daca-decision-perils-for-dreamers-in-what-comes-next.

[46] The rationale for these longstanding notice-and-comment rules was to ensure that recipients of deferred action, whose presence the government had chosen to tolerate for some period of time, would have the means to sustain themselves while the government tolerated their presence in the country despite their lack of lawful status. An animating concern of the courts that have rejected categorical work authorization is that DACA seemed to go beyond what was intended by the work authorization originally—it's one thing to say small numbers can be authorized to work, quite another to do so for hundreds of thousands when Congress has clearly prohibited employers from hiring people not authorized to work.

and comment) and explain why it was doing so – something that, as even Justice Thomas's dissent recognized, would be no easy task.[47] But would the Chief Justice really have sent the Trump administration back for more likely fruitless memoranda drafting? Perhaps he expected them to once and for all come up with sufficiently articulated policy reasons for rescinding all of DACA, obviating the need for the Court to address the legality of DACA on the merits.

If the Court was seeking to avoid a decision on the merits, the 2020 election may have foiled its plans. Again, the Biden administration has announced its intention to fortify DACA through notice and comment rulemaking. This move seems intended to add more procedural armor to the program in the hopes of preserving it through what may be a lengthy legal battle already begun by the state of Texas and some of its allies in the Southern District of Texas, where the district judge who invalidated DAPA now sits on the case.[48] If and when DACA returns to the Court under this new guise, no one should be surprised if only forbearance stands at the end, leaving it to Congress to provide a meaningful anchor of belonging for the Dreamers.[49] The way the Chief Justice in *Regents* presents the work authorization question as potentially expendable for legal reasons, and the incredulity expressed

---

[47] *See Regents*, 140 S. Ct. at 1929 n.14 (Thomas, J., concurring in the judgment in part and dissenting in part).

[48] When DACA was first announced in 2012, legal challenges to it quickly emerged, but none of them gained traction. One lawsuit by ICE officials who claimed that the policy required them to violate their oaths to protect and defend the Constitution was dismissed for lack of subject-matter jurisdiction on the ground that this personnel complaint had to proceed through an alternate administrative system. And in a second lawsuit brought by Sheriff Joseph Arpaio of Maricopa County, Arizona, the D.C. Circuit also rejected the case on justiciability grounds, finding that Arpaio lacked standing to challenge the federal policy. Perhaps because the litigation over DAPA consumed the attention of litigants hostile to immigration relief (and to the Obama administration) for a period of years, Texas and the other usual suspects at the state level did not organize to challenge DACA until the Trump administration showed early ambivalence about whether to rescind it. *See supra* note 3.

[49] As was predicted and hoped, DACA has had substantial stabilizing benefits for its recipients. *See* Tom K. Wong et al., *DACA Recipients' Livelihoods, Families, and Sense of Security Are at Stake This November*, CTR. FOR AM. PROGRESS (Sept. 19, 2019), https://www.americanprogress.org /issues/immigration/news/2019/09/19/474636/daca-recipients-livelihoods-families-sense -security-stake-november (reporting on results of a survey of over 1,000 DACA recipients that documents their improved lives, including that 59 percent of respondents moved to a job with better pay, 48 percent to a job with better working conditions, 53 percent to a job that better fits their education and training, and 53 percent to a job with health insurance or other benefits). And yet it remains a contingent and precarious status, as the rescission effort and ongoing lawsuits challenging its legality underscore. *See* COX & RODRÍGUEZ, *supra* note 8, at 241–42 (citing studies highlighting the precarity of discretionary statuses).

by some of the Justices at oral argument in the DAPA case back in 2015, justify characterizing the litigation risk associated with DACA as high.[50]

If the Court does indeed come to rest on a forbearance-only version of DACA, its decision will stand alongside *Regents* as an example of the Court's skepticism of administrative innovation and perhaps an insistence that expansive Executive policymaking be supported by clear and even express statutory authority. In so doing, the Court would hamstring the ability of the Executive branch to introduce humanity and stability into its management of a massive deportation regime that Congress thus far has been unable or unwilling to reform. This form of disabling the Executive in the name of accountability and the separation of powers would in turn exacerbate another feature of today's immigration law that the Supreme Court slowly but surely has been re-enforcing in recent years, including during the October 2019 Term.

In a string of decisions over the last several years, the Court has taken the inverse approach of its opinion in *Regents*, finding that DHS has robust power to choose how to enforce the immigration laws in light of expansive statutory delegations. In at least two startling cases, the Court outright rejects the application of meaningful and direct constitutional limits on the political branches themselves, in ways that depart from past precedent.[51] And in other cases, the Court increasingly reads statutory provisions with strenuous resistance to interpretive

---

[50] As Justice Kennedy put it at oral argument, DAPA turns the Constitution "upside down," because the Executive has claimed authority that belongs only to Congress. Transcript of Oral Argument at 24, United States v. Texas, 136 S. Ct. 2271 (2016) (No. 15-674). One feature of the DAPA litigation that did not arise in *Regents* but may complicate the government's defense of DACA moving forward is that the extension of Social Security benefits, in particular, arises by virtue of an Attorney General decision in the 1990s to treat recipients of deferred action as having "lawful presence" for the purposes of certain benefits under a 1996 companion law to the public benefits reforms of that era known as the Personal Responsibility and Work Opportunity Reconciliation Act (PRWORA). Unlike the 2012 DACA memorandum issued by Secretary Napolitano, the memorandum from Secretary Jeh Johnson announcing DAPA adverted to this term of art and as a result sowed massive confusion and consternation in the lower courts, as well as at oral argument at the Supreme Court. How could the government maintain that deferred action recipients had lawful presence for one purpose but were not given lawful status more generally, something only Congress has the authority to do? In fact, the issue is a red herring: the term "lawful presence" as used in DAPA and DACA means eligibility for benefits, not lawful immigration status.

[51] In the case of DACA, invalidating it on legal grounds could call into question longstanding Executive branch practice through which administrations have developed case-management and programmatic techniques to manage the massive amount of enforcement discretion the law effectively delegates to the Executive by virtue of rendering so many millions of non-citizens deportable. *See* Cox & Rodríguez, *supra* note 8, at 198–201.

possibilities that would be protective of immigrants' interests, including in ways that sound in basic fairness. In other words, the real story of the Roberts Court's immigration jurisprudence has been to empower the political branches working in tandem, with waning interest in scrutinizing how the Executive wields the power Congress has delegated to it.

Three data points are especially worth noting as part of an initial sketch of judicial review and immigration in the Roberts era: *Trump v. Hawaii, DHS v. Thuraissigiam,* and *Jennings v. Rodriguez.* These other jurisprudential developments help to put *Regents* in a more holistic perspective. The contrast underscores that *Regents'* rigorous review of Executive action that advances the interests of immigrants cannot be generalized. To the contrary, the government's interest in the enforcement of the immigration laws, not the interests and rights of non-citizens, remains at the heart of modern immigration law and policy.

The clearest example of a Roberts-era decision that reads a statutory mandate to authorize sweeping Executive power with minimal to no constitutional constraint is *Trump v. Hawaii,*[52] in which the Court effectively upholds President Trump's proclamation barring the entry of nationals from several Muslim-majority countries on the ostensible ground that their governments could not provide adequate security information.[53] Two of that opinion's features bear mention as signals of the direction of the Roberts Court on immigration law.[54] First, the Court, in an opinion by Chief Justice Roberts, offers an uncomplicated, neatly textualist reading of the specific statutory provision at issue, which is indeed straightforward and clearly grants the president the power to deny entry to "any aliens or class of aliens" whose entry would be "detrimental to the United States."[55] More important, the Court rejects the complex arguments grounded in the INA's structure offered by challengers, who attempted to read subsequent additions to

---

[52] 138 S. Ct. 2392 (2018).

[53] Presidential Proclamation No. 9645, 82 Fed. Reg. 45,161 (Sept. 24, 2017).

[54] I have written about this case at length elsewhere. *See* Cristina M. Rodríguez, Trump v. Hawaii *and the Future of Presidential Power over Immigration,* AM. CONST. SOC'Y SUP. CT. REV., 2017–2018, at 161 (2018), https://www.acslaw.org/wp-content/uploads/2019/01/ACS-Supreme-Court-Review-2018-Revised.pdf.

[55] 8 U.S.C. § 1182(f) (2018).

the INA focused on national security screening as limiting the suspension power first adopted in 1952.[56]

Second, and still more important, even as Chief Justice Roberts got the statutory arguments correct, he offered a startling vision of the (lack) of constitutional scrutiny of the president's actions pursuant to his clear authority. Not only does the opinion apply a highly deferential standard of review that requires the government to provide only a "facially legitimate and bona fide reason" for its actions, it purports to apply a heightened version of rational basis review for the sake of argument and concludes that even an "established discriminatory motive would not have warranted invalidation of the government's actions, as long as another, facially legitimate reason for the exclusion existed."[57] Instead of attempting to contextualize, diminish, or otherwise cabin the anti-Muslim statements of the president, which Justice Sotomayor powerfully recounts in dissent, Chief Justice Roberts concludes that those statements, and the motivations they arguably reflect, are beside the point. For the first time since the notorious cases of the Chinese exclusion era, the Court upholds an action by the political branches that could reasonably be characterized as a violation of ordinary domestic constitutional law, in this case government action predicated on grounds ordinarily considered illicit.[58] In other words, the president not only has power (delegated by Congress), the Court will impose almost no constraint on its exercise (under the Constitution).

But at least *Trump v. Hawaii*, when it was decided, could be cabined in various ways. Its constitutional analysis addressed a specific sort of intent-based antidiscrimination claim, and its national security-infused deference involved non-citizens on the precipice of entry, outside the custody and control of the United States.[59] But this past Term, the Court issued a decision that signaled that these implicit limits on the government's power might be hard to maintain. *Thuraissigiam v.*

---

[56] Among the problems with these sorts of arguments is that they embody a logic that would invalidate a raft of Executive branch practices of the last several decades undertaken to enforce the INA, including, arguably, DACA itself. *See* Rodríguez, *supra* note 54, at 170–73.

[57] *Id.* at 179.

[58] For development of this argument, see Adam B. Cox, Ryan Goodman & Cristina Rodríguez, *The Radical Supreme Court Travel Ban Opinion—But Why It Might Not Apply to Other Immigrants' Rights Cases*, JUST SECURITY (June 27, 2018), https://www.justsecurity.org/58510/radical-supreme-court-travel-ban-opinion-but-apply-immigrants-rights-cases.

[59] Rodríguez, *supra* note 54, at 166.

Department of Homeland Security[60] rejects a Suspension Clause challenge to a provision of the system of expedited removal—a statutory scheme that authorizes the government to remove in summary fashion, without a hearing, certain categories of non-citizens seeking admission, subject to a staged screening process for migrants who express the intention to seek asylum.[61] The Court overturns a Ninth Circuit decision that had invalidated the provision at issue. That provision authorized a non-citizen to obtain review via a writ of habeas corpus in only three discrete circumstances, none of which applied to Mr. Thuraissigiam, an ethnic Tamil who crossed the southern border unlawfully and indicated to an immigration officer his fear of persecution if returned to Sri Lanka.[62] In his habeas petition, Thuraissigiam challenged the officer's determination that he lacked a credible fear of persecution, contending that the officer had not given him a meaningful opportunity to establish his claim. Had he succeeded in establishing credible fear, he would have been entitled to a full asylum hearing before an immigration judge followed by judicial review, rather than to summary removal.

Justice Samuel Alito's majority opinion prompted a lengthy concurrence and dissent and involves technical details of immigration and habeas law, the ins and outs of which deserve a treatment all their own.[63] For present purposes, the opinion's marked departure in tone

---

[60] 140 S. Ct. 1959 (2020).

[61] Under a statutory provision enacted in 1996, an applicant for admission is subject to expedited removal if the applicant is inadmissible for lacking a valid entry document, has not been physically present in the United States for more than two years, or has been designated by the Secretary for expedited removal. 8 U.S.C. § 1225(b)(1)(A)(i), (iii)(I)-(II) (2018). If an immigration officer determines that the person is inadmissible, the officer must order the non-citizen removed without "further hearing or review." *Id.* § 1225(b)(1)(A)(i). An applicant who expresses an intention to apply for asylum is referred to a screening to determine if he has a "credible fear of persecution." *Id.* § 1225(b)(1)(B)(v). If the screening officer finds no credible fear, the non-citizen is subject to expedited removal. A non-citizen who shows a credible fear is referred for full consideration of the asylum claim. 8 C.F.R. § 208.30(f) (2020).

[62] 8 U.S.C. § 1252(e)(2) (limiting habeas review to "whether the petitioner is an alien," was ordered removed, or already was granted entry as a lawful permanent resident).

[63] For three excellent treatments of the case, see Gerald Neuman, *The Supreme Court's Attack on Habeas Corpus in* DHS v. Thuraissigiam, Just Security (Aug. 25, 2020), https://www.justsecurity.org/72104/the-supreme-courts-attack-on-habeas-corpus-in-dhs-v-thuraissigiam (noting, in particular, how the Court departs from its seminal habeas decision in *Boumediene v. Bush*); Ahilan Arulanantham & Adam Cox, *Immigration Maximalism at the Supreme Court*, Just Security (Aug. 11, 2020), https://www.justsecurity.org/71939/immigration-maximalism-at-the-supreme-court (describing *Thuraissigiam* as demonstrating the Court's immigration maximalism, in contrast to *Regents*, and showing how the case reflects disregard for the interests of non-citizens in ways that deviate from past precedent); and Amanda L. Tyler, Thuraissigiam

and substance from some of the Court's major precedents concerning not only habeas, but also the Due Process Clause, make it noteworthy. The decision represents another installment—perhaps the most important yet—in the Roberts Court's resistance to reading immigration statutes to advance rights-based constitutional goals. It also shows the Court in a tightening embrace of a regulatory scheme created by Congress that dramatically empowers the Executive to enforce the immigration laws without meaningful judicial scrutiny.

Whereas Roberts's voice in *Regents* channels the aspirations of DACA recipients and acknowledges their connection to American communities, Justice Alito's voice in *Thuraissigiam* is suspicious of noncitizens and friendly to the government's interests in efficiency.[64] In the exposition of the case, for example, he laments the amount of time removal cases take to be adjudicated, noting the considerable expense to the government of detaining the non-citizen or the "attendant risk" that someone released might not ever be found again.[65] He refers to the "burdens" asylum screenings pose by "overwhelming our immigration system."[66] This sort of framing may not be outlandish (the backlog of immigration cases is real), or even tendentious, but it does reflect a valuation of the efficiency that the system of expedited removal prioritizes as opposed to a robust consideration of potential

---

and the Future of the Suspension Clause, LAWFARE (July 2, 2020), https://www.lawfareblog.com /thuraissigiam-and-future-suspension-clause (noting how the opinion calls into question aspects of *Boumediene v. Bush* and expresses a more narrow view of the Suspension Clause than embodied in that case).

[64] Justice Alito increasingly has become the voice of the conservative majority of a sharply divided Court on immigration, having authored five significant opinions in the last three years. In addition to *Thuraissigiam*, most notable are *Nielsen v. Preap*, 139 S. Ct. 954 (2019), in which the Court holds that the INA's mandatory-detention provision applies to all non-citizens convicted of predicate crimes and not just to those immediately taken into custody from the state by DHS, and *Jennings v. Rodriguez*, 138 S. Ct. 830 (2018), in which the Court declines to read the INA's mandatory-detention provisions as time-limited or necessitating bond hearings. As a judge on the Third Circuit, Alito took a "harder line" on criminal and immigration cases than even other Republican appointees on the courts of appeals. *See* Amy Goldstein & Sarah Cohen, *Alito, In and Out of the Mainstream: Nominee's Record Defies Stereotyping*, WASH. POST (Jan. 1, 2006), https:// www.washingtonpost.com/archive/politics/2006/01/01/alito-in-and-out-of-the-mainstream -span-classbankheadnominees-record-defies-stereotypingspan/2ba042c7-773e-48da-9056 -14300cea054e; CONG. RSCH. SERV., RL33218, IMMIGRATION: SELECTED OPINIONS OF JUDGE SAMUEL ALITO (2006) (offering an extensive survey of then-Judge Alito's majority and dissenting opinions in immigration cases heard by the Third Circuit).

[65] 140 S. Ct. at 1964–65.

[66] Justice Alito notes that there has been an almost 2,000 percent increase in credible-fear claims and that the majority of them have "proven to be meritless." He also characterizes expedited removal as "protecting" the Executive's discretion from "undue" interference by the courts. *Id.* at 1966.

asylum claims that the system arguably underplays. And Alito's rhetoric borders on sarcasm as he dismisses Thuraissigiam's habeas claim
by saying that the government "is happy to release him—provided the
release occurs in the cabin of a plane bound for Sri Lanka."[67]

The core holding of the case was that the Suspension Clause as
understood in 1789 does not reach the sort of claim Thuraissigiam
sought to raise – a challenge to his credible fear screening and the
chance to make his asylum claim anew. That holding may not obviously strain credulity. As the Court put it, "the historic role of habeas
is to secure release from custody," but Thuraissigiam sought "the
opportunity to remain lawfully in the United States" through an application for asylum and other relief, the rejection of which he claimed
was flawed.[68] Justices Breyer and Ginsburg concur that the section of
the INA at issue was not unconstitutional as applied to the respondent,
agreeing that Congress has the power to foreclose habeas review of
the sort of claim Thuraissigiam raised – one that sought to challenge
the immigration officer's factual findings.[69] But Breyer and Ginsburg
depart from the majority's opinion because it calls into question the
availability of habeas to challenge removal orders at all. As Gerald
Neuman noted powerfully in the aftermath of the decision, Justice
Alito's opinion "eviscerates the Suspension Clause" and departs from
the Court's seminal habeas decisions in *Boumediene v. Bush* and *INS v.
St. Cyr.*[70] And as Justice Sotomayor emphasizes, in a dissent joined

---

[67] *Id.* at 1970.

[68] *Id.* at 1970–1971.

[69] *Id.* at 1990 (Breyer, J., concurring) ("Respondent, to be sure, casts the brunt of his challenge
to this adverse credible fear determination as two claims of legal error. But it is the factual
findings underlying that determination that respondent, armed with strong new *factual* evidence,
now disputes.").

[70] *See* Neuman, *supra* note 63 ("The expectation that the court would give DHS a second
chance to decide petitioner's case lawfully, rather than ordering his immediate release, follows
longstanding practice in immigration law and other fields."). Alito addresses *Boumediene* simply
by noting that it "is not about immigration at all," and that nothing in the Court's decision
suggests those held at Guantanamo could have used a petition in the way Thuraissigiam sought
to—in order to gain entry into the United States. *Thuraissigiam*, 140 S. Ct. at 1981. He similarly
dismisses the relevance of *St. Cyr* in three paragraphs as not addressing the sort of claim respondent sought to raise. *Id.* For an outstanding treatment of *St. Cyr* in the larger context of
habeas jurisprudence, see Richard H. Fallon, Jr. & Daniel J. Meltzer, *Habeas Corpus Jurisdiction,
Substantive Rights, and the War on Terror*, 120 HARV. L. REV. 2029, 2099 (2007) ("In *St. Cyr*, the
Court came close to holding that the petitioner, an alien seized and detained within the United
States, was entitled to review not merely of constitutional but also statutory questions underlying
his claim of unlawful detention. . . . *St. Cyr's* understanding that the core function of habeas
review is to ensure judicial determination of fundamental legal issues—statutory as well as
constitutional—is not unique."). *See also* Gerald H. Neuman, *Habeas Corpus, Executive Detention,*

Justice Kagan, the implication of the majority opinion is that "expedited removal proceedings shall be functionally unreviewable through the writ of habeas corpus, no matter whether the denial is arbitrary or irrational or contrary to governing law"—an implication that runs counter to a century of the Court's precedents.[71]

The fact that Justice Alito reached still further to address a due process claim not clearly raised by respondent—a reach wholly unnecessary to resolve the case—expands the opinion's remarkable breadth and further announces the Court's intention to retreat from constitutional review of congressional schemes to enforce the immigration laws. Alito disclaims that that the Due Process Clause applies to Thuraissigiam simply because he set foot into US territory; he remained "on the threshold," which meant that he had only those rights Congress saw fit to give him. Though Alito does not explain whether and how far this reasoning extends beyond an individual like Thuraissgiam, who has just entered the country, the stunning implications of his reasoning become apparent when he underscores that being stopped at the border is in fact a term of art and that someone "paroled elsewhere in the country for years pending removal" would also appear to be at the threshold.[72] Not only does this reference suggest that Congress's authorization of expedited removal for any non-citizen who has not been admitted and has been in the United States for fewer than two years is perfectly constitutional[73]—an authorization no Executive until the Trump administration had sought to utilize—it also suggests Congress may go still further.

With its due process analysis, *Thuraissigiam* fits together with the Court's 2017 detention decision in *Jennings v. Rodriguez*, which also revealed the Roberts Court's skepticism that the Due Process Clause meaningfully restrains Congress from authorizing extraordinary enforcement measures. In that case, the Court declined to read several of the INA's mandatory detention provisions as containing either an implicit time limit or the requirement of a bond hearing out of respect for

---

and the Removal of Aliens, 98 Colum. L. Rev. 961, 967-1021, 1044–45 (1988) (arguing that historical evidence supports the interpretation of the Suspension Clause as extending to proceedings for the removal of aliens from the United States by immigration officials and that "habeas corpus does aim at detentions ancillary to other deprivations [removal orders], and not only at pure detention orders").

[71] *Thuraissigiam*, 140 S. Ct. at 1993 (Sotomayor, J., dissenting).

[72] *Id.* at 1982 (majority opinion).

[73] *See* 8 U.S.C. § 1225(b)(1)(A)(iii)(II) (2018).

underlying due process rights of those detained.[74] Also written by Justice Alito, *Jennings* signaled the Court's departure from an important jurisprudential predisposition of the early 2000s—the application of principles of constitutional avoidance to temper the reach of enforcement statutes, particularly those authorizing detention and the deprivation of the core liberty interest to be free from it. The lodestar in this turn-of-the-century jurisprudence has been the Court's decision in *Zadvydas v. United States*, which energetically reenforced the principle that the Due Process Clause applies to non-citizens and then proceeded to read a detention statute that could have given rise to indefinite detention as containing an implicit six-month limit on detention, subject to the government establishing anew that detention still served its purposes and was justified.[75] *Zadvydas* has had an enormous influence in the way lower courts have read detention statutes as well as on government detention practices. The decision has come under fair criticism for relying on the avoidance canon to rewrite Congress's statute rather than directly confronting the constitutional question raised by potentially indefinite detention. But it has also come to stand for the Court's willingness to cautiously superintend the massively coercive powers of the immigration system. It may be possible to reconcile cases like *Trump v. Hawaii* and *Thuraissigiam* with the *Zadvydas* holding. But the Court's inclinations have very clearly changed with respect to both detention itself and challenges by non-citizens more generally to the enforcement apparatus authorized by Congress and mobilized by DHS.[76]

---

[74] 138 S. Ct. 830 (2018). At issue were 8 U.S.C. § 1125(b) (applying to individuals arriving at the border who seek admission to the United States); 8 U.S.C. § 1226(c) (applying to non-citizens convicted of enumerated crimes); and 8 U.S.C. § 1231(a) (applying to non-citizens who have been ordered removed and "shall" be detained for up to ninety days while government effectuates their removal).

[75] Zadvydas v. Davis, 533 U.S. 678, 692 (2001) ("The serious constitutional problem arising out of a statute that, in these circumstances, permits an indefinite, perhaps permanent, deprivation of human liberty without any such protection is obvious.").

[76] This is not to say that the Court's opinions in recent years have blithely accepted every last government argument about the scope of its authority under the INA. In *Sessions v. Dimaya*, 138 S. Ct. 1204 (2018), for example, the Court found a provision of the INA unconstitutionally vague. In an opinion written by Justice Kagan, the Court rejected the government's argument that a more lenient form of the void for vagueness doctrine should apply in this civil context. In his concurrence, Justice Gorsuch writes a kind of treatise on the importance of the vagueness doctrine and the provision of clear notice by the law to avoid arbitrary power, *id.* at 1223–34 (Gorsuch, J., concurring in part and concurring in the judgment), and in so doing he rejects a conclusion embraced by Justice Thomas, *id.* at 1245–48 (Thomas, J., dissenting), that non-citizens at the time of the Founding did not possess rights under the Due Process Clause.

As *Zadvydas* fades further back in time, its hold on the Court's approach to constitutional review appears to be weakening.[77]

III. REGENTS AND THE POLITICS OF JUDICIAL REVIEW

Even if DHS had not run afoul of *State Farm* and *Chenery* in its attempts to rescind DACA, the Court identifies another flaw in the Duke memorandum. The claim emerged early in the litigation and reflected the moral heart of the DACA recipients' case, translated into the language of administrative law. The Duke memorandum was arbitrary and capricious for failure to take into account the reliance interests that DACA had generated.[78] As a legal matter, the Court's recognition of these has limited significance; the Court makes clear that reliance interests are not dispositive, only that they must be taken into account and explained away as less significant that the administration's policy goals. But the Court presents the interests not only as serious and weighty, but also as "radiating outward" from the recipients themselves to the economic and social institutions with which they have become intertwined.[79] Also important, the Court rejects the government's argument, echoed by the dissent, that because DACA never promised an entitlement, no reliance interests could be said to have arisen.[80] The Court here privileges a social fact over a legal construct—what we all know to be true about DACA's implicit promise to forbear and include, even as the express trappings of the initiative

---

For a reading of *Jennings* and other cases that suggest a possible "new era for immigration exceptionalism" that does not bode well for immigrant interests, see David Rubenstein, *The Future of Immigration Exceptionalism*, SCOTUSBLOG (June 29, 2017, 2:29 PM), https://www .scotusblog.com/2017/06/immigration-symposium-future-immigration-exceptionalism. For a more extended discussion of these themes, see David S. Rubenstein & Pratheepan Gualsekaram, *Immigration Exceptionalism*, 111 Nw. U. L. Rev. 583 (2017), which synthesizes the courts' treatment of immigration exceptionalism with respect to rights, federalism, and the separation of powers and argues that the Court sometimes but not always treats immigration as exceptional, and that litigants sometimes, but not always, want it that way, but that this approach is unstable and requires coming to terms with trade-offs.

[77] I have explored the arc of the Court's treatment of due process claims in immigration cases elsewhere. See Rodríguez, *supra* note 54, at 198–208.

[78] Dep't of Homeland Sec. v. Regents of the Univ. of Cal., 140 S. Ct. 1891, 1913 (2020).

[79] *Id.* at 1914 (noting that the rescission would radiate outward to DACA recipients' families, their U.S.-citizen children, the schools where they study and teach, to their employers and the labor force more generally, resulting in the loss of billions of dollars in economic activity and tax revenue).

[80] *Id.* at 1913. The Court does note that this feature of DACA might go to the weight the agency gives to the reliance interests.

disclaimed any sense of obligation. Though the reliance passage is brief, it underscores that the agency cannot elide the way DACA has changed the social world, immediately raising the political costs to the agency and the administration of abandoning DACA altogether.

This remarkable passage connects, in a way, to the unsuccessful equal protection claims made in the case. Only Justice Sotomayor credits those claims formally, concluding (in an opinion concurring in part and dissenting in part) that President Trump's statements denigrating Mexican immigrants, both during the campaign and once in office, created the "strong impression" that the attempted rescission of DACA was "contaminated by impermissible animus."[81] The Court dismisses these claims in two pages, concluding that none of the plaintiffs' arguments, "either singly or in concert, establishes a plausible equal protection claim."[82] This debate echoes the exchange between these two justices in *Trump v. Hawaii*, but here the majority opinion at least communicates that the rescission would have been unfair or disruptive, even if legally unavoidable or within the government's discretion.

Regents thus offers us an example of a phenomenon that abounds in immigration law and other domains where substantive constitutional claims have become elusive due to doctrinal development—the use by litigants and courts of structural doctrines as de facto stand-ins for rights claims.[83] The typical lament heard about this turn to structure over substance is that it precludes the development of the substance or otherwise occludes the malign motives of the government, which in turn compounds societal failure to grapple with anti-Muslim, anti-immigrant, and anti-Latino sentiment. But at least in the case of DACA, the evidence cited of anti-Mexican or anti-immigrant sentiment seemed

---

[81] *Regents*, 140 S. Ct. at 1917 (Sotomayor, J., concurring in part, concurring in the judgment, dissenting in part).

[82] *Id.* at 1915 (majority opinion).

[83] *See, e.g.,* Jennifer M. Chacón, *The Inside-Out Constitution:* Department of Commerce v. New York, 2019 Sup. Ct. Rev. 231, 236 (noting that the litigation over the 2020 census exemplifies how "substantive-rights claims are increasingly being vindicated, if they are vindicated at all, through procedural channels"); Jenny-Brooke Condon, *The Preempting of Equal Protection for Immigrants?*, 73 Wash. & Lee L. Rev. 77, 84 (2016) (arguing that federalism has transformed "equal protection doctrine involving state alienage classifications into a preemption-like inquiry"); Geoffrey Heeren, *Persons Who Are Not the People: The Changing Rights of Immigrants in the United States*, 44 Colum. Hum. Rts. L. Rev. 367, 375 (2013) (describing the shift away from jurisprudence assessing laws regulating migrants under a rights-based analysis to "one focused on the rights and responsibilities of the federal government").

far off of what would have been required to establish an equal protection claim, even as it does not seem controversial to cite racial resentment and nativism as factors relevant to the whole of the Trump administration's immigration policies.

More to the point, despite being focused on structural questions, both DACA itself and the litigation surrounding its rescission have been political projects to entrench the Dreamers' claims in public perception and in our governing institutions.[84] In retrospect, we may see both DACA and the rescission litigation as bridges to legalization. Both have bought time for DACA recipients, and both have highlighted the simultaneous desert and precarity of the Dreamers and others like them, underscoring the urgency of legalization.[85] Chief Justice Roberts's recitation of the individual and social reliance interests generated by DACA certainly highlights how non-citizens, advocates, and determined officials, through legal forms and legal contestation, have changed the social meaning of unlawful status.[86] This sociological development arguably brings us closer to a political transformation of the immigration laws—a transformation that eludes the increasingly unsuccessful constitutional litigation discussed in Part II. Perhaps one day we will be able to characterize the strong assertion of Executive authority in DACA as having disrupted the political economy of immigration lawmaking that for the last generation has given

[84] DACA's structural move is to emphasize the proper supervision and the distribution of enforcement resources, and the litigation focused on how the government organizes its policy process. The long arc of the DACA and DAPA litigation may even have changed the perceptions of some of the judicial participants. When grappling post-*Regents* with the challenge to DACA's legality brought by the state of Texas, Judge Andrew Hanen of the Southern District of Texas, who emphatically found DAPA unlawful, appeared reticent, at least for a time, to apply the same analysis to DACA. At one point in the litigation, he called for a status conference on the impact of the American Dream and Promise Act, a bill introduced in the House of Representatives that contained a path to legal status for DACA recipients, on the litigation. American Dream and Promise Act of 2021, H.R. 6, 117th Cong. (2021), https://www.congress.gov/bill/117th-congress/house-bill/6/text. This move seemed at the time like a delay tactic. At the conference Judge Hanen asked for further submissions with a deadline of April 9, 2021. As this essay went to press, Judge Hanen issued his decision, citing *Regents* and concluding that DACA violated the Administrative Procedure Act and exceeded DHS's statutory authority. Texas v. United States, No. 18–cv–00068, 2021 WL 3025857, at *20 (S.D. Tex. July 16, 2021), appeal filed, No. 21–40680 (5th Cir. Sept. 16, 2021).

[85] Even in dissent, Justice Kavanaugh adverts to the uncertainty Dreamers face and presumes that the solution would be action by Congress to address their uncertainty. Even though he leaves it to Congress to decide their fate "one way or another," this passage evokes sympathy rather than suspicion. *Regents*, 140 S. Ct. at 1935 (Kavanaugh, J., concurring in the judgment in part and dissenting in part).

[86] *Id.* at 1913–15 (majority opinion).

rise mostly to the sorts of punitive, anti-due process enforcement schemes to which the justices increasingly defer.

But even if *Regents* embodies this kind of triumph for immigrant advocacy, we might still cast a skeptical eye on the way the Court reaches its conclusion precisely because of the way it constrains the government. Had the 2020 election turned out differently, it seems probable that DHS would have jumped through the additional procedural hoops required by the Court and pursued the policy goals it had all along. The question would have become what value those extra procedural steps had, other than inhibiting policy change that everyone in the litigation agreed was legally permissible because DACA was not legally required. Justices Thomas and Kavanaugh, in their separate dissents, make the point that insistence on exacting procedural regularity is at odds with the discretionary nature of the DACA program and what courts ought to expect of agencies seeking to make changes in policy.

In his partial concurrence and partial dissent, Justice Kavanaugh provides an alternate account of *Chenery* that may not be true to what the decision requires but that provides a more sensible approach to evaluating government action. He would have evaluated the government's actions based on the Nielsen memorandum, which expressly addressed the reliance interests generated by DACA, provided policy reasons for the rescission alongside the legal ones, and was in fact invited by a district court judge in the litigation. Kavanaugh criticizes what he describes as the Court's distortion of *Chenery*, which he characterizes as a constraint on the government's ability to justify its actions in litigation, not on the agency's authority to supplement or develop its reasons for a policy through other forms of final agency action.[87] As he points out, the Court's decision seems to permit the agency on remand to "relabel and reiterate" the contents of the Nielsen memo, so what function other than delay (for the agency and the Court's own reckoning with DACA's legality) does the decision perform?[88] Chief Justice Roberts rejects Justice Kavanaugh's view, offered by the government, too, that requiring a formally new policy process would be "an idle and useless formality," arguing that procedural requirements can serve "important values of administrative law," including giving the

---

[87] *Id.* at 1934 (Kavanaugh, J., concurring in the judgment in part and dissenting in part).
[88] *Id.* at 1935.

parties and the public the opportunity to "respond fully and in a timely manner to an agency's exercise of authority."[89]

In our consideration of whether and how courts might discipline the Executive's enforcement powers, Adam Cox and I have emphasized the value of importing reason-giving requirements from the mainstream of administrative law but also warned against the imposition of overly wooden procedural requirements that "stand in the way of an incoming regime's ability to better tailor policy to its own political views."[90] Some scholars have begun to interpret *Regents* as standing on the right side of this line—as promoting accountability in government.[91] Others have suggested that the decision distorts the policy process, making what should otherwise be swift and decisive policy change subject to a slog in the courts.[92] In a contemporary context in which the administrative state itself and the deference doctrines that sustain it are under concerted challenge, from both opponents of regulation and proponents of certain formal conceptions of the

---

[89] *Id.* at 1909 (majority opinion).

[90] Cox & RODRÍGUEZ, *supra* note 8, at 230; *see also id.* ("An expectation of reason giving could prompt courts to ask various questions of an enforcement policy. Does the policy reflect deliberation within the agency or the administration, such that the outcome reflects considered judgments...? Was an agency's choice to shift its enforcement strategy based on values that can be defended as public-regarding and legitimate? ... [T]his reason-giving approach should re-enforce the complexity of governance to the Executive, helping to sustain its culture of deliberation grounded in evidence and sound judgment.").

[91] Benjamin Eidelson, for example, argues that the Court "recast *Chenery* as an accountability-forcing tool" in response to the agency's post-hoc rationalizations in the Nielsen memo. *See* Eidelson, *supra* note 17, at 1768. He posits that the Administration's handling of the rescission, including by issuing the Nielsen memo as a follow-on to the Duke memo rather than a new agency action, *id.* at 1765–66, was motivated by a desire to avoid public consequences of an unpopular policy choice. He notes that although the policy statements in the Nielsen memo gave the Court reason to believe that the agency would not reach a different decision if it redid the action properly, the Court nevertheless chose to force the agency to face public scrutiny. *Id.* at 1769–70. Other commentators have suggested that the decision is democracy forcing. *Regents*, in particular, implicates an anti-regulatory strategy one scholar has called statutory abnegation, according to which agencies disclaim statutory authorities on which they had previously relied—a strategy courts typically resist in order to promote various forms of political accountability. *See* William W. Buzbee, *Agency Statutory Abnegation in the Deregulatory Playbook*, 68 DUKE L.J. 1509 (2019); *see also* Eidelson, *id.* at 1777–81 (arguing that *Regents* does not let the Trump administration claim Congress has made the decision that the administration itself is making).

[92] *See* Zachary Price, *Symposium: DACA and the Need for Symmetric Legal Principles*, SCOTUSBLOG (June 19, 2020, 3:51 PM), https://www.scotusblog.com/2020/06/symposium-daca-and-the-need-for-symmetrical-legal-principles (arguing that *Regents* engages in ad hoc reasoning driven by a strategic judgment that departs from courts' typical reluctance "to recognize any estoppel based on government assurances . . . and claims of reliance based on forbearance," which also has the effect of freezing policies in place).

separation of powers, we have every reason to be skeptical of procedural doctrines that make change within government cumbersome or
difficult.[93] Indeed, because just about every agency action generates
reliance interests of some kind, the way the Court deploys them
in *Regents* could undermine the very act of policy change. And in this
particular case, the Court's accountability rhetoric comes up somewhat empty. Neither DACA itself nor any new policy process adopted
to rescind it would have entailed opportunity for public comment or
participation. If Secretary Nielsen's primary mistake was in treating
her memo as an outgrowth of the Duke memo, forcing DHS back to
the drawing board to start anew is arguably overkill, given that the
Nielsen memo from the Secretary more fully elaborated a policy
position that in the first instance should have been sufficient to pass
court review. Any suggestion to the contrary that the reasons given in
her memo if presented in the proper procedural posture would not
have been sufficient to justify the government's policy choice would
be ratcheting up the power of the courts to inhibit policy change.

Thus far in the lower courts, *Regents* has taken its place alongside
canonical administrative law cases such as *State Farm* and *Overton
Park* as a citation for the proposition that an agency must take account
of the alternatives available to it.[94] But one key litigant—the state
of Texas—is behaving predictably, seizing the *Regents* rationale to
attempt to stymie every effort of the new Biden administration to
change course from its predecessor. One court in Texas, for example,
greeted the new administration with a preliminary injunction of its
efforts to shift immigration enforcement policy by pausing removals
in order to take stock of what the Trump administration had done
to the system.[95] Partisan litigants may well find partisan courts to use

---

[93] *See* Gillian Metzger, *The Supreme Court, 2016 Term – Foreword: 1930s Redux: The Administrative State Under Siege*, 131 Harv. L. Rev. 1 (2017).

[94] *See, e.g.*, Invenergy Renewables LLC v. United States, 476 F. Supp. 3d 1323, 1344–45
(Ct. Int'l Trade 2020) (relying on *Regents* as an outline of the established principles courts
should focus on when they analyze agency explanations of their actions); MediNatura, Inc. v.
FDA, No. CV 20-2066 (RDM), 2020 WL 6262121, at *27–28 (D.D.C. Oct. 23, 2020)
(making ample use of *Regents* for analyzing the FDA's change in position and its impact on
homeopathic drug companies' reliance interests).

[95] Texas v. United States, No. 6:21-CV-00003, 2021 WL 723856 (S.D. Tex. Feb. 23,
2021). For critical commentary warning that this case is an opening salvo in an effort to use
administrative law to stymie the Biden administration, see Noah Feldman, *Biden Didn't
Deserve to Lose That Immigration Case*, Bloomberg Opinion (Jan. 27, 2021, 12:30 PM EST),

arbitrary and capricious review to demand ever clearer and more elaborate explanations for their positions – in turn pushing the government into ever more elaborate policy processes – when it arguably ought to be enough for an administration to offer that it was elected to implement a new set of policy views.[96] Whether this exacting proceduralism contributes to good and accountable government ought to be an ongoing debate and a point of true reflection for the courts called upon to referee our political disputes.

CONCLUSION

Despite surviving the concerted efforts of the Trump administration to rescind it, the future of DACA remains uncertain—a state that arguably befits a status that is itself temporary and provides no path to permanent membership, even as it mitigates the unfairness and stress of unlawful status. The optimistic version of the future culminates in the achievement of legalization for the Dreamers and perhaps still others, a political outcome that DACA and the activist energy that produced it will have helped make possible. If these events come to pass, they will in one sense prove DACA's detractors correct: that with its adoption, President Obama and Secretary Napolitano transformed immigration law by grounding the Dreamers' claims to membership in official policy. By prompting Executive action, the Dreamers expanded the limits of the law in a way even the most determined of opponents could not undo, even once they controlled the enforcement power. The pessimistic end of the story is of endless conflict and permanent instability, not just for the Dreamers, but across the regulatory state, as the structural tools honed in litigation against the Trump administration are used to stymie the attempts at change by all of its successors, through courts that have become players

---

https://www.bloomberg.com/opinion/articles/2021-01-27/biden-s-immigration-order-lost
-in-court-but-didn-t-deserve-to.

[96] This development also underscores how the DAPA litigation changed the landscape by recognizing states' standing to sue the federal government for its enforcement policies—a development that commentators at the time warned would open the government up to vexatious litigation and stymie policy change. For excellent examples of the growing literature on how state attorneys general have been using their litigating and enforcement powers to shape national policy, see Jessica Bulman-Pozen, *Federalism All the Way Up: State Standing and "The New Process Federalism,"* 105 CALIF. L. REV. 1739 (2017); and Mark L. Earley, *"Special Solicitude": The Growing Power of State Attorneys General,* 52 U. RICH. L. REV. 561, 564–65 (2018).

in the political scrum. It is too early to say that the courts' vaunted insistence on reasoned decision-making has thrown sand into the government's gears. But neither *Regents* nor the Roberts Court's immigration jurisprudence will fix our immigration system to make it more humane, and we can only hope that the Court will not stand in the way of the political actors seeking to do just that.

MARTHA MINOW

NOT IN THE ROOM WHERE IT HAPPENS: ADVERSARINESS, POLITICIZATION, AND LITTLE SISTERS OF THE POOR

"The art of the compromise/hold your nose and close your eyes/we want our leaders to save the day/but we don't get a say in what they trade away."[1] What happens when some people are singularly not in "the room where it happens," where laws are passed, regulations are devised, and lawsuits are argued and decided? Participation, individual rights, and democratic accountability are supposed to be central in a constitutional democracy but can be elusive in practice, as any member of any kind of minority knows. The gap between the ideal and the reality of constitutional democracy is especially challenging where different groups claim competing rights and interests. On the one hand, the case of *Little Sisters of the Poor Saints Peter and Paul Home v Pennsylvania*[2] emerged from decades of political and legal struggles over religious accommodation and employer coverage

Martha Minow is 300th Anniversary University Professor, Harvard University.

AUTHOR'S NOTE: Thanks to the Harvard Law School faculty workshop participants and the Public Law Workshop students and faculty for valuable insights and comments; thanks to Kim Foreiter, Blessing Jee, Jenny Samuels, Mariah Smith, and James Stramm for invaluable research and editorial assistance and to David Strauss for wise advice of many kinds.

[1] Lin-Manuel Miranda, *The Room Where It Happens, on* HAMILTON: VOCAL SELECTIONS (Hal Leonard 2016).

[2] 140 S. Ct. 2367 (2020).

The Supreme Court Review, 2021.

of contraceptive services under publicly mandated health plans. On the other hand, the convergence of debates over birth control, religious exercise, and healthcare provision leaves in its wake concerns over who has been heard and how justifiable interests can all be recognized.

Respect for individuals' free exercise of religion lies at the heart of narratives of American values and of pivotal constitutional and human rights. Yet unlimited deference to individual free exercise of self-professed beliefs would destroy shared laws and benefits. Because the Supreme Court has extended religious freedom to closely held private corporations, employers who have religious objections to some healthcare benefits may demand accommodation. And because the United States relies on private employers as a key vehicle for providing health insurance, public policies governing health insurance can collide with private employer views. If government healthcare policies do not attend to the independent interests of employees—here, notably, women employees—will their otherwise-assured healthcare coverage be subordinated to the religious views of the employers? This question presses to the limits of adjudication. It forces complex issues into either/or, yes/no questions, obscuring both the impact on unrepresented parties and options offering a third way.[3] And simplistic answers would imperil decades of arduous efforts by many people tackling three areas critical to people's daily lives: 1) access to birth control and related protection for women's health, 2) accommodating religious exercise in a pluralistic world that has other competing values, and 3) bringing the United States closer to the standards of universal healthcare coverage dominant in other advanced democracies.

Meeting at the crossroads of these issues is *Little Sisters of the Poor Saints Peter and Paul Home v. Pennsylvania*. Even a casual observer will notice there is trouble going on when the nine-member Supreme Court breaks into four distinct opinions. For those watching more closely, the Court's majority opinion is striking in how few of the larger conflicts surface. Comparing that opinion with the three

---

[3] Courts can try to attend to the interests of individuals and groups not parties to the litigation, but with limited and fragile protections. *See* Note, *Reframing the Harm: Religious Exemptions and Third-Party Harm after* Little Sisters, 134 HARV. L. REV. 2186 (2021), https://harvardlawreview.org/2021/04/reframing-the-harm-religious-exemptions-and-third-party-harm-after-little-sisters [hereinafter cited as *Reframing the Harm*]. Courts and legislatures have grappled with such issues in contract law. *See* Melvin Aron Eisenberg, *Third-Party Beneficiaries*, 92 COLUM. L. REV. 1358 (1992); David M. Summers, *Third Party Beneficiaries and the Restatement (Second) of Contracts*, 67 CORNELL L. REV. 880 (1982).

others exposes diverging views about the questions before the Court. This contrast becomes even sharper with close examination of each opinion, with a look into the distinct and disconnected histories of the key issues addressed and with attention to how the framing of the case affects who can be seen and heard. Litigation transmutes complex issues into questions that can at least seem to be answered. One frame asks: did Congress give an agency the power to adopt a rule? Another asks, has the agency acted arbitrarily and capriciously? And still another asks, how has the government accommodated free exercise of religious exercise while also ensuring that women employees receive full and equal health coverage?

This third frame is the one used by Justice Ruth Bader Ginsburg. Her searing dissent spoke for women employees missing as parties but objects of the decision at hand. The dissent also spoke for the conception of law that seeks to solve problems, not just win battles. That this was her last opinion in a case on the merits is particularly poignant, given her pathbreaking work advancing gender equality. The passing of Justice Ginsburg in 2020 casts deep doubt on the likelihood that the Supreme Court, anytime soon, will ensure consideration of unrepresented parties or resist simplistic all-or-nothing decisions in the face of religious accommodation claims.[4] Such work now falls to others; this essay is a small effort in that spirit.

I. Nine Justices, Four Opinions, and Seven Issues (At Least)

In his opinion for the Court, Justice Clarence Thomas wrote for Chief Justice John Roberts, Justice Samuel Alito, Justice Neil Gorsuch, and Justice Brett Kavanaugh and addressed two issues, reversed the Court of Appeals for the Third Circuit, and remanded "for further proceedings consistent with this opinion."[5] Justice Alito wrote a concurring opinion, joined by Justice Gorsuch. After noting that the Court actually reversed on three issues, Justice Alito addressed yet another issue, and on that basis, called for an outright reversal with no remand and complete and final victory for Little Sisters. Writing for herself and Justice Stephen Breyer, Justice Elena

---

[4] On her passing, see *Ruth Bader Ginsburg, Supreme Court's Feminist Icon, Is Dead at 87*, N.Y. Times (Sept 18, 2020), https://www.nytimes.com/2020/09/18/us/ruth-bader-ginsburg-dead.html. On her legacy, see *Memoriam: Justice Ruth Bader Ginsburg* 134 Harv. L. Rev. 882 (2021).

[5] *Little Sisters*, 140 S. Ct. at 2386.

Kagan agreed with the majority on one of its conclusions but not on its reasoning and endorsed the remand but with a call for consideration of yet another issue, with extensive reasons for why the further proceedings should produce a result diametrically opposed to the one favored by Justices Alito and Gorsuch and implied by the majority. Justice Ruth Bader Ginsburg, joined by Justice Sonia Sotomayor on the basis of still another issue, argued for affirming the decision of the court of appeals—and no remand.

Now, a little more slowly in detail: The case actually was a consolidation of two cases, one brought in 2013 by the Little Sisters, a Roman Catholic religious nonprofit organization that operates homes for the elderly poor, against the federal government during the presidency of Barack Obama. This suit challenged a 2013 final rule, issued pursuant to the Affordable Care Act (ACA), that required coverage for contraceptive services but provided an accommodation that allowed eligible, objecting religious organizations to avoid offering such coverage and instead trigger the group health plan's separate provision of such a benefit. That suit had been stayed pending other litigation.[6]

The second suit started after several intervening Supreme Court decisions on related issues and after the election of Donald Trump. His administration issued first one and then a second interim final rule allowing employers with sincere religious or moral objections to be exempted from the ACA's obligation to provide contraceptive coverage in their employee health plans. The Commonwealth of Pennsylvania filed an action alleging that these interim rules were procedurally and substantively invalid. Pennsylvania expressed its interests both in helping its residents avoid undesired pregnancies and in limiting financial exposures to greater public expenses for women unable to secure insurance coverage for contraceptive services from their employers. The district court granted Pennsylvania's motion for a preliminary injunction. In the meantime, the federal government finalized the interim rules. One rule governs organizations with religious objections—hence, organizations that are not themselves religious organizations and may instead be organized as for-profit entities and

---

[6] Represented by a religious liberty organization, BECKET, the Little Sisters' cases include *Zubik v. Burwell*, 136 S. Ct. 1557 (2016), and *California v. Azar*, 911 F.3d 558 (9th Cir. 2018). For more information on Becket, see *Becket Case Detail*, BECKET, https://www.becketlaw.org /case/commonwealth-pennsylvania-v-trump/, last visited June 18, 2021.

publicly traded for-profit entities.[7] The second creates a "moral exemption" for employers that are nonprofit organizations and for-profit companies with no publicly traded components.[8] New Jersey joined Pennsylvania in its challenge, the Little Sisters intervened to defend the rules, the federal district court issued a nationwide preliminary injunction, and the Court of Appeals affirmed.

The ACA requires that an employer-sponsored group health plan cover "preventive care and screenings" without "cost-sharing" by the employee, meaning the employee should face no out-of-pocket copays or bill for the covered services.[9] Further, the law requires that those "preventive care and screenings" with respect to women must cover care "provided for in comprehensive guidelines supported by" the Health Resources and Services Administration (HRSA), a sub-agency of the Department of Health and Human Services (HHS).[10] After the ACA was adopted, this agency consulted with the Institute of Medicine and, in the 2013 Obama Administration rule that was the subject of the Little Sisters' first suit, directed that women's preventive services be insured under employer-sponsored group health plans and include all contraceptive methods, sterilization procedures, and patient education and counseling for all women with reproductive capacity.[11] Some religious organizations raised objections as employers; the administration responded with an accommodation procedure: a "self-certification" rule for objecting religious organizations.[12] The Obama Administration's rule, unlike its Trump-era replacement, was designed to ensure that employees under employer-sponsored health plans had no-cost contraceptive coverage even if they worked at objecting religious organizations.

Under the accommodation of the Obama-era rule, an employer would self-certify that it opposed coverage for a particular contraceptive service; then the insurance issuer or third-party administrator would exclude coverage for that contraceptive method or

---

[7] *Little Sisters*, 140 S. Ct. at 2377 (quoting 82 Fed. Reg. 47,812 (2017)); *Little Sisters*, *Id.* at 2378 (quoting 82 Fed. Reg. 47,850, 47,861–62 (2017)).

[8] *Id.* at 2378 (quoting 82 Fed. Reg. 47,813, 47,854 (2017)).

[9] 42 U.S.C. § 300gg–13(a).

[10] *Id.* § 300gg–13(a)(4).

[11] *Little Sisters*, 140 S. Ct. at 2402 (Ginsburg, J., dissenting) (quoting 77 Fed. Reg. 8725 (2012)).

[12] *See Id.* at 2375.

methods from the group plan and instead provide separate payments for any contraceptive services required to be covered, without any cost-sharing imposed on the employer.[13] Thus, the rule as promulgated would:

1. Accommodate eligible religious organizations that oppose coverage for all or some of the contraceptive services due to religious objections;
2. If the organization was a nonprofit;
3. If it held itself out as a religious entity; and
4. If it self-certified that it satisfied 1, 2, and 3.[14]

In their challenge to the Obama-era rule, the Little Sisters objected that participating in this self-certification process would make them complicit with contraception and/or contraceptive coverage contrary to their sincere religious faith. Outsiders might be perplexed about how the request for a religious accommodation constitutes complicity in the alternative mechanism for contraceptive health insurance coverage.[15] Does complicity arise with a refusal to participate? Or does the objection represent the Little Sisters' larger concern that the coverage is being provided at all? The Little Sisters in their reply brief indicated that "tak[ing] affirmative steps to execute paperwork ... necessary for the provision of 'seamless' contraceptive coverage to their employees" implicates them in providing the services that violate their beliefs.[16] The tradition of judicial deference to sincerely expressed religious belief halts further inquiry into these issues.

---

[13] *Id.* at 2402 (Ginsburg, J., dissenting) (quoting *Burwell v. Hobby Lobby*, 573 U.S. 682, 698–99 (2014)).

[14] *Id.* at 2410 ("Under the self-certification accommodation, then, the objecting employer is absolved of any obligation to provide the contraceptive coverage to which it objects; that obligation is transferred to the insurer. This arrangement 'furthers the Government's interest [in women's health] but does not impinge on the [employer's] religious beliefs.'" (quoting *Hobby Lobby*, 573 U.S. at 698–99)).

[15] *See* Douglas NeJaime & Reva B. Siegel, *Conscience Wars: Complicity-Based Claims in Religion and Politics*, 124 YALE L. J. 2516, 2519–21 (2015) (describing the rise of complicity-based conscience claims and the particular dangers of such claims in a pluralistic society); Nomi Maya Stolzenberg, *It's About the Money: The Fundamental Contradiction of* Hobby Lobby, 88 S. CAL. L. REV. 727 (2015).

[16] Reply Brief of Petitioner, at 7, *Little Sisters*, 140 S. Ct. 2367 (Apr. 24, 2020) (No. 19-431).

The Supreme Court found plenty of other issues to address, issues that can be summarized with these seven questions:

1. Did the Little Sisters have appellate standing to intervene even though a related suit in the District Court of Colorado had already issued a permanent injunction that applied to the plans in which Little Sisters participate?[17]

2. Did the federal government, under the Trump administration, have authority to issue rules exempting any organization, non-profit or for-profit, religious or secular, from mandated employer health insurance contraception coverage if they have either religious or moral objections?

3. Did the final rules issued by the Trump administration have fatal procedural defects because both the interim and final rules failed to comply with the Administrative Procedure Act's requirements for notice and comment?

4. Did the Court of Appeals correctly impose an additional new procedural requirement that the federal government Departments maintain "an open mind" toward comments received after the issuance of the interim final rules?[18]

5. Does the Religious Freedom Restoration Act (RFRA) bear on the federal government's rule, i.e., may—or must—the federal government consider that law? How does the RFRA inquiry into whether a government action imposes a substantial burden on a religious belief apply, and does RFRA require the federal government's exemptions?

6. Do the exemptions embodied in the rules fail the APA requirement that federal government agency action not be "arbitrary, capricious, an abuse of discretion, or otherwise not in accordance with law"?

7. Does §300gg–13(a) of the ACA, which specifies that group health plans "shall ... provide" certain services, authorize federal agencies to exempt certain employers and, if so, establish that services

---

[17] The Court of Appeals ruled that the Little Sisters lacked appellate standing to intervene; the Supreme Court majority found this in error as another party—the federal government—had appellate standing, and the intervenor as of right—seeking no broader relief—did not need to establish standing. *Little Sisters*, 140 S. Ct. at 2379 n.6.

[18] This is the characterization of the majority opinion; the issue is not addressed by the other opinions. The Third Circuit held that the agencies' notice and comment procedures were procedurally defective due in part to the agencies' lack of an open mind. *Pennsylvania v. President United States*, 930 F.3d 543, 568–69 (3d Cir. 2019).

must continue to be provided even if particular employers are exempted?[19]

Taking the issues one by one not only shows the complexity in each, but also shows how each justice's selected framework reflects whose interests and voices inform the analysis.

A. DID THE LITTLE SISTERS HAVE APPELLATE STANDING TO INTERVENE?

Only the majority opinion, answering affirmatively, addressed this first question that concerns standing of an intervenor to appeal.[20] None of the opinions addressed a related procedural question about the propriety of the Little Sisters seeking further review: arguably, their claim was moot, because a related suit in the District Court of Colorado had already issued a permanent injunction barring application of the Obama-era rule to the plans in which the Little Sisters participate.[21] Allowing the Little Sisters to continue in the Pennsylvania case, however, meant giving the justices in the majority the ability to put this religious organization, rather than the Trump administration, as the face of the litigation. Both the majority opinion and Justice Alito's concurring opinion offered commendations to the Little Sisters for their charitable work and expressed sympathy for the burdens of litigation and related uncertainty spread over several years.[22]

---

[19] The fifty-five amicus briefs not only offered different versions of these seven questions but also provided new questions, including: whether the district court lacked legal authority to issue a nationwide preliminary injunction halting the new rules; whether the new rules unconstitutionally established religion or impermissibly deprived employees of a previous benefit; whether the new rules endangered children's health, gender health and equity, or the rule of law; and whether consideration of harm to third parties can supply a compelling government interest under RFRA. Thanks to Kimberly Foreiter for analysis of these briefs.

[20] *Little Sisters*, 140 S. Ct. at 2379 n.6.

[21] Initially the Tenth Circuit held that preliminary injunctive relief was not warranted as the religious accommodation scheme relieved the plaintiffs of the contraceptive mandate. *See Little Sisters of the Poor v. Burwell*, 794 F.3d 1151 (10th Cir. 2015), *vacated and remanded*, 136 S. Ct. 1557 (2016). The Supreme Court granted certiorari on the Tenth Circuit's decision and consolidated it with cases from the Third, Fifth, and District of Columbia Circuits; after hearing these cases, under the name of *Zubik v. Burwell*, 136 S. Ct. 1557 (2016), the Court remanded these cases, without reaching the merits, to consider an argument that emerged in supplemental briefs. *Zubik*, 136 S. Ct. at 1561. See the discussion of *Zubik* below.

[22] *See Little Sisters*, 140 S. Ct. at 2386; *id.* at 2396 (Alito, J., concurring).

B. DID THE FEDERAL GOVERNMENT, UNDER THE TRUMP
   ADMINISTRATION, HAVE AUTHORITY TO ISSUE RULES EXEMPTING
   ANY ORGANIZATION, NONPROFIT OR FOR-PROFIT, RELIGIOUS OR
   SECULAR, FROM MANDATED EMPLOYER HEALTH INSURANCE
   CONTRACEPTION COVERAGE IF THEY HAVE RELIGIOUS OR MORAL
   OBJECTIONS?

Seven members of the Court—those in the majority and those concurring in the result—agreed that Congress granted expansive authority allowing the issuance of the Trump-era rules exempting employer organizations with religious or moral objections. The justices in
the majority emphasized the breadth of the delegation—the majority
opinion calls it "sweeping"—and pointedly observed that no party in
the case questioned the constitutionality of such a broad delegation,
leaving that avenue for objection open for another day.[23] One might
have thought that, since at least four members of the majority have
suggested that broad delegations are unconstitutional,[24] the majority
might apply the canon of constitutional avoidance and construe the
delegation narrowly to limit the power of the agencies in this case. But
the majority showed no inclination to do that.

The crucial language was "as provided for." Adopted in the context
of an amendment to the original draft of the ACA to address women's
healthcare needs, the provision in its broader terms states that "with
respect to women" a "group health plan and a health insurance issuer
offering group or individual health insurance coverage shall, at a minimum, provide ... such additional preventive care and screenings ...
as provided for in comprehensive guidelines supported by [HRSA.]"[25]
Does this language allow HRSA to mandate some but not other preventive services or to exempt some plans from the specified coverage?
The dissenters argued no on both issues and emphasized that any other
reading would thwart Congress's intention to provide women equal
access to healthcare without extra costs, and that would include, as
HRSA specified, contraceptive coverage to employees through the
plans governed by the ACA.[26] In particular, argued the dissent, the

---

[23] *Id.* at 2380, 2382.

[24] *See Gundy v. United States*, 139 S. Ct. 2116, 2130–31 (Alito, J., concurring); *id.* at 2131–48 (Gorsuch, J., dissenting).

[25] 42 U.S.C. § 300gg–13(a)(4) (emphasis added).

[26] *See Little Sisters*, 140 S. Ct. at 2401, 2404 (Ginsburg, J., dissenting).

relevant language did not grant authority to HRSA to decide who should provide coverage for the services it specifies, nor to interfere with the statutory instruction that the group health plans "shall … provide" the preventive services identified for coverage by HRSA.[27] The dissent argued that the agency in question—HRSA—has no authority or expertise relevant to crafting exemptions and only has expertise in improving healthcare outcomes among those experiencing disparities.[28] The majority read the language more broadly to allow the agency to exempt employers from the requirement to provide the covered preventive services.[29]

Justice Kagan's opinion, concurring in the result, viewed the disagreement among the majority and the dissenters about how broad Congress meant to make the delegation as evidence of the statute's ambiguity. Under the *Chevron* doctrine, calling for deference to a reasonable interpretation by the implementing agency in the face of statutory ambiguity, she said she would defer to the agencies' determination that they could exempt particular employers from the requirement.[30]

C. DID THE FINAL RULES ISSUED BY THE TRUMP ADMINISTRATION HAVE FATAL PROCEDURAL DEFECTS BECAUSE BOTH THE INTERIM AND FINAL RULES FAIL TO COMPLY WITH THE ADMINISTRATIVE PROCEDURE ACT'S REQUIREMENTS FOR NOTICE AND COMMENT RULEMAKING?

The same seven justices rejected claims by Pennsylvania and New Jersey that the Trump-era rules had fatal procedural defects because they were issued without following the notice and comment requirements

---

[27] *Id.* at 2405.

[28] *Little Sisters*, 140 S. Ct. at 2406 (Ginsburg, J., dissenting); *see About HRSA*, https://www.hrsa.gov/about/index.html, last visited June 18, 2021.

[29] *Little Sisters*, 140 S. Ct. at 2381–82.

[30] *Id.* at 2397 (Kagan, J., concurring) (relying on *Chevron USA, Inc. v. Nat. Res. Def. Council*, 467 U.S. 837, 842–43 (1984)). The doctrine of "*Chevron* deference" is subject to considerable criticism. *See, e.g., Baldwin v. United States*, 140 S. Ct. 690, 690–91 (2020) (Thomas, J., dissenting from the denial of certiorari) (arguing that the *Chevron* doctrine is unconstitutional); *Pereira v. Sessions*, 138 S. Ct. 2105, 2121 (2018) ("[I]t seems necessary and appropriate to reconsider, in an appropriate case, the premises that underlie *Chevron* and how courts have implemented that decision."); *Gutierrez-Brizuela v. Lynch*, 843 F.3d 1142, 1149 (10th Cir. 2016) (Gorsuch, J., concurring) ("[T]he fact is *Chevron* and *Brand X* permit executive bureaucracies to swallow huge amounts of core judicial and legislative power and concentrate federal power in a way that seems more than a little difficult to square with the Constitution of the framers' design. Maybe the time has come to face the behemoth.").

for rulemaking under the APA. The majority characterized this as an argument that there was a fatal flaw because the final rules followed a document entitled "Interim Final Rules with Request for Comments" instead of "General Notice of Proposed Rulemaking."[31] The majority did not address the argument that the agencies had failed to justify the decision to make the rules effective before, rather than after, notice and comment.

D. DID THE COURT OF APPEALS CORRECTLY IMPOSE AN ADDITIONAL
   NEW PROCEDURAL REQUIREMENT THAT THE FEDERAL GOVERNMENT
   DEPARTMENTS MAINTAIN "AN OPEN MIND" TOWARD COMMENTS
   RECEIVED AFTER THE ISSUANCE OF THE INTERIM FINAL RULES?

The fourth question turned to the approach taken by the Third Circuit, which, the Supreme Court said, had viewed the small degree of change between the interim and final rules as evidence of a procedural flaw in the final rules. The Supreme Court majority described the appellate court's analysis as adding a new procedural requirement of "open-mindedness" by an agency and rejected any judicial addition of procedures beyond those specified by the APA.[32] This characterization seems at odds with the actual ruling of the court of appeals. That court pointed to the fact that the Interim Final Rules were made effective before any opportunity for comment; Pennsylvania brought suit at that point and amended its complaint when, despite subsequent comments, the government issued "virtually identical" final rules.[33] Authority granted by another statute to issue interim rules does not obviate the requirement of notice and comment, reasoned the appellate court.[34]

Then, the court of appeals asked whether the government had satisfied the APA's provision that an agency must have "good cause" to bypass the notice and comment requirements that ordinarily must be satisfied before a rule becomes effective.[35] The court reviewed and

---

[31] *Little Sisters*, 140 S. Ct. at 2384–85. On the use of such interim final rules, see generally Michael Asimow, *Interim-Final Rules: Making Haste Slowly*, 51 ADMIN. L. REV. 703 (1999).

[32] *Little Sisters*, 140 S. Ct. at 2385–86.

[33] *Pennsylvania v. President United States*, 930 F.3d 543 at 558–59.

[34] *Id*. at 565–66.

[35] *Id*. at 565, 567. Thanks to Matthew Stephenson for elucidating the "good cause" issue. For a thoughtful consideration of whether moral and religious objections should provide "good cause" to dispense with notice and comment process, see generally Miriam R. Stiefel,

found insufficient the government's assertion that it had "good cause": "(1) the urgent need to alleviate harm to those with religious objections to the current regulations"; (2) the need to address "continued uncertainty, inconsistency, and cost" arising from "litigation challenging the previous rules"; and (3) the fact that "the Agencies had already collected comments" on prior related regulations, and cited precedent for the inadequacy of obtaining comments after the adoption of a rule.[36] The court used the phrase "open-mindedness" in discussing the reasons for the notice and comment requirements and the benefits of public participation.[37] And the court of appeals relied on prior decisions to highlight the importance of notice and comment prior to adopting a rule.[38] Hence, rather than imposing new procedural requirements, arguably the court of appeals applied existing requirements and rejected the government's arguments for bypassing them. Nonetheless, the majority treated the matter as an impermissible addition of new procedures by the courts, and the other justices did not discuss the issue in detail.[39]

E. HOW, IF AT ALL, DOES THE RFRA BEAR ON THE FEDERAL
   GOVERNMENT'S RULE; MAY—OR MUST—THE FEDERAL
   GOVERNMENT CONSIDER THAT LAW?

The fifth question involves the relevance of RFRA to the treatment of employer objections to contraceptive coverage in employee health plans. As *Employment Division v. Smith* still places most religious exemption claims outside the purview of the First Amendment, none of the opinions pursued constitutional religious free exercise

Comment, *Invalid Harms: Improper Use of the Administrative Procedure Act's Good Cause Exemption*, 94 WASH. L. REV. 927 (2019).

[36] *Pennsylvania v. President United States*, 930 F.3d at 567–68. Good cause for dispensing with notice of proposed rulemaking and comments could include demonstrating that the usual procedures are impracticable, unnecessary, or not in the public interest because of an emergency or other reasons. *See* JARED P. COLE, THE GOOD CAUSE EXCEPTION TO NOTICE AND COMMENT RULEMAKING: JUDICIAL REVIEW OF AGENCY ACTION, CONG. RSCH. SERVS, R44356, 4 (2016); GAO FEDERAL RULEMAKING: AGENCIES OFTEN PUBLISHED FINAL RULEMAKING WITHOUT PROPOSED RULES, GEN. ACCOUNTING OFFICE 30, 32 (1998).

[37] *President United States*, 930 F.3d at 568–69.

[38] *Id.* at 569.

[39] The dissent noted that it had no need to consider procedural flaws because of its conclusion that the government lacked authority to enact the rules. *Little Sisters*, 140 S. Ct. 2367 at 2411 n.27 (Ginsburg, J., dissenting). Justice Kagan simply observed that she "agree[s] with the Court that the final rules issuing the exemptions were procedurally valid." *Id.* at 2398 n.2 (Kagan, J., concurring).

dimensions in depth,[40] although both Justice Kagan's opinion and Justice Ginsburg's dissent included brief rejections of the claim that the First Amendment would justify the exemptions. The dissent asserted that "all agree" that the exemption is not supported by the First Amendment and found no basis in the ACA for exemption beyond what the First Amendment requires.[41] Justice Kagan stressed that prior First Amendment cases have never reached all employees of a private organization.[42] Justice Alito's concurring opinion gave no analysis of the First Amendment issues and explicitly emphasized such issues were not raised and not addressed by the Court.[43]

Some of the opinions discussing the matter asked whether and how the government should consider RFRA in this context. Others asked whether RFRA requires the accommodation represented by the Trump-era rules. The majority opinion treated this second question as unnecessary given its decision to uphold the rules, though it concluded that it is not only appropriate for the government to consider RFRA here but it might be arbitrary and capricious under the APA not to do so.[44] Justice Alito's concurring opinion emphasized that the government is obligated to consider RFRA and proceeded to apply it, concluding that requiring Little Sisters or employers with similar objections to comply with the requirement to include contraception in their health plans would impose a substantial burden on their religious belief because noncompliance triggers financial penalties and self-certification could still implicate the employer in the contested coverage.[45] Hence, because Little Sisters objected to self-certifying and triggering separate coverage of employees' contraceptive services, an accommodation beyond what the Obama-era rule prescribed would be required.[46]

---

[40] *See infra* pages 32–34 (discussing *Employment Division v. Smith* and enactment of the Religious Freedom Restoration Act).

[41] *Little Sisters*, 140 S. Ct. at 2400 (Ginsburg, J., dissenting).

[42] *Id.* at 2397–98 n.1 (Kagan, J., concurring). Justice Kagan's opinion offered a few sentences on the "ministerial exception" protecting religious institutions from employment discrimination laws as applied to particular employees, and firmly asserted "there is no general constitutional immunity over and above the ministerial exception, that can protect a religious institution from the law's operation." *Id.*

[43] *Id.* at 2394 n.11 (Alito, J., concurring).

[44] *Id.* at 2382–84.

[45] *Id.* at 2389.

[46] *Id.* at 2389–91.

Justice Alito's opinion rejected the counterargument invited by RFRA: that RFRA would allow assertion of the compelling governmental interest in ensuring contraceptive coverage with no additional expense for covered employees. Justice Alito asserted that even though Congress required preventive services "with respect to women," Congress did not treat such a requirement as compelling, for several reasons: 1) there is no national legislative requirement of contraceptive coverage (or any healthcare coverage) for individuals who do not work outside their homes; 2) the ACA does not itself specify coverage of contraceptive services and instead left specification of coverage scope to the sub-agency, HRSA; 3) many employers are exempted from the ACA altogether; 4) the ACA gave discretion to craft even further exemptions; 5) the Trump administration's exemptions shows that the government itself did not find contraceptive coverage compelling; and 6) just asserting a desirable state of affairs—such as seamless coverage for all forms of medical care—is not a compelling governmental interest.[47]

Further, going well beyond a matter directly posed in the case, the concurring opinion attacked the no-longer-existing Obama-era rule as failing to provide the least-restrictive means to accomplish an allegedly compelling interest. Justice Alito reasoned that a less intrusive means would provide direct government payment for contraceptives for any person unable to obtain them from their health insurance plans.[48] Rather than confine itself to the case before the Court, Justice Alito's opinion seems to extend to past and future cases. Reaching even further, the concurring opinion maintains that while a government intrusion on a religious belief must be the "least restrictive" needed to implement a compelling governmental interest, the government's accommodation under RFRA need not be the least restrictive needed to accommodate that interest. Thus, extending an exemption to employers with moral instead of religious beliefs, and to publicly traded companies, poses no legal problem.[49] Intrusion on interests of the women employees of exempted employers does not warrant concern. Nor, according to Justice Alito, does the Trump-era rules' failure to provide alternative avenues for cost-free contraceptive coverage,

---

[47] *Id.* at 2390–94.

[48] *Id.* at 2394–95.

[49] *Id.* at 2395–96.

despite the constitutionally recognized right to purchase and use contraceptives.[50] That the women employees are receiving less compensation than they were promised and less than their counterpart male employees is not considered by the concurring opinion by Justice Alito. Perhaps because the women employees of exempted employers were not parties to the suit, their interests receive little attention from the majority or Justice Alito's concurrence.

The opinions by Justices Kagan and Ginsburg both raised the concerns of women employees of exempted employers but in different ways. Justice Kagan focused on judicial review of administrative rulemaking. Calling for a vigorous review on remand of potential ways in which the Trump-era rules are arbitrary and capricious, Justice Kagan's opinion implicitly questioned much of Justice Alito's treatment of RFRA. Concurring in the majority's results only, Justice Kagan explicitly noted that RFRA does not govern moral concerns, only religious ones. Her opinion further emphasized that RFRA does not alter the government's duty to weigh the benefits of exempting more employers against the harm of depriving more women of contraceptive coverage.[51]

Justice Ginsburg's dissenting opinion framed the case as unavoidably presenting the legal obligation to attend to religious freedom and to gender equality. Her dissent noted how the Supreme Court in prior decisions in related cases "repeatedly assumed that any religious accommodation would preserve women's continued access to seamless, no-cost contraceptive coverage." Justice Alito's concurring opinion responded by stressing that those statements were mere assumptions made in the course of analyzing other issues and as a result are not legal holdings or conclusions; the concern of the women can disappear from the Court's review just as they did in the Trump regulations.[52] The dissent acknowledged that the government does not need to wait for a lawsuit alleging a violation of RFRA before addressing any such violations, yet the dissent nonetheless stressed that religious

---

[50] *Id.* at 2396. *But see Reframing the Harm, supra* note 3, between text at n.105 and text at n.106 (explaining that the government's interest was not in providing free contraceptives but in "ensuring that if an employer offers health insurance to employees as a form of compensation, the employer-sponsored plan may not exclude from coverage a service that only women and non-cis male people use.")

[51] *Id.* at 2399–2400 (Kagan, J., concurring).

[52] *Compare id.* at 2407–08 (Ginsburg, J., dissenting), *with id.* at 2393–94 (Alito, J., concurring).

accommodations should not override other interests. Before accommodations are made for employers' religious or moral concerns, reasoned Justice Ginsburg, the administrative process is obliged to consider the interests of third parties—such as employees of organizations with religious or moral objections to contraceptive coverage.[53] Documenting the impact of the Trump-era exemptions on such employees, the dissent underscored how the rules before the Court failed to satisfy the explicit Congressional commitment to ensure gender equality in preventive services. Alternatives to insurance coverage would be insufficient to meet this commitment. Thus, to the dissent, it is not sufficient for the government to direct employees, as it did, to try other government-funded programs. Such an alternative requires women employees to undertake research, to navigate providers other than their own healthcare professionals and insurers, to satisfy income-restricted eligibility requirements for services for low-income women, or to pay for the services out of their own pockets.[54] None of these alternatives has a counterpart for preventive health services needed by men, and, in the dissent's view, they depart from Congressional policy.

The dissent, like Justice Alito's concurring opinion, goes on to apply RFRA to the Obama-era policy. Justice Ginsburg concluded that the policy imposed no substantial burden and therefore raised no issue under RFRA, while the Trump-era rules were directly inconsistent with the ACA and judicial precedent and not required by RFRA. Mere financial expenses have not counted as "substantial burdens" in prior religion cases, and entitlement to religious accommodation for an individual is not an entitlement to "insist that . . . *others* must conform their conduct" to the religious demand.[55] The Little Sisters indicated that they do not oppose "registering their objections" to the contraceptive coverage requirement or notifying the government of their request for exemption; hence, their concern instead seems to involve connecting with insurance issuers to convey their objection. The problem appears that those insurers then would take steps to provide the contraceptive coverage outside the plan used by Little Sisters.[56]

---

[53] *Id.* at 2407 n.17, 2408.

[54] *Id.* at 2408–09.

[55] *Id.* at 2410 (quoting *Estate of Thornton v. Caldor, Inc.*, 472 US. 703, 710 (1985) (quoting *Otten v. Baltimore & Ohio R. Co.*, 205 F.2d 58, 61 (2d Cir. 1952)) (emphasis added).

[56] *Id.* at 2411.

Would adding yet another step—having the objecting employer notify yet another actor, who in turn would notify the insurer—help, or would this too represent a substantial burden? Prior precedents rejected this potentially infinite regress: the Court denied an accommodation under the Free Exercise Clause of the First Amendment for a Native American father concerned that his daughter's spirit would be harmed by government use of her social security number given such concerns.[57] The dissent underscored that there is no disrespect for the sincerity of proffered religious beliefs in resisting a demand that the government conduct its own internal affairs to comport with those beliefs..[58] To the potential claim of complicity, then, the dissent emphasized that no action by the objecting employer—but instead the ACA and the Obama-era rule—created that link to the insurers.[59]

F. DO THE EXEMPTIONS EMBODIED IN THE GOVERNMENT RULES FAIL
   THE ADMINISTRATIVE PROCEDURE ACT'S REQUIREMENT THAT
   AGENCY ACTION NOT BE "ARBITRARY, CAPRICIOUS, AN ABUSE OF
   DISCRETION, OR OTHERWISE NOT IN ACCORDANCE WITH LAW"?

This sixth question concerns a matter to be addressed on remand: are the Trump-era rules arbitrary and capricious under the APA? This is the central focus of Justice Kagan's opinion. This was the only opinion to note that the lawsuit framed by Pennsylvania and New Jersey actually challenged these rules on this ground. That challenge remains alive because the district and appellate courts in this case did not reach the issue after finding the rules invalid on other grounds.[60] Justice Kagan devoted the bulk of her opinion to outlining considerations for the court on remand; she stated that the Trump-era rules "give every appearance of coming up short."[61] She specified three causes for concern. First, the Trump-era rules clash with government's continuing commitment to minimize the impact on contraceptive coverage. Second, the exemptions extend further than justified by RFRA or the First Amendment as they encompass

---

[57] *Id.* at 2410 (Ginsburg, J., dissenting) (citing *Bowen v. Roy*, 476 U.S. 693 (1986)).

[58] *Bowen*, 476 U.S. at 699–700. A question for another day: does RFRA point to a different result?

[59] *Little Sisters*, 140 S. Ct. at 2411–12 (Ginsburg, J., dissenting).

[60] *Id.* at 2398 (Kagan, J., concurring).

[61] *Id.*

publicly traded companies, employers who did not object to Obama-era rule, and employers with moral objections, not just those with re-ligious claims. And third, the rules impose real costs on employees.[62] Each of these concerns could, after inquiry, show that the rules fail the requisite standard of reasonableness encompassed by "arbitrary and capricious" review.

Justice Thomas's opinion for the majority remanded with no further comment about what could or should happen on remand beyond calling for "proceedings consistent with this opinion."[63] That opinion simply rejected the appellate opinion rulings that the federal government lacked authority to issue the two Trump-era rules. It found no proce-dural defects in the issuance of these rules. It gave no mention of issues for the court of appeals or district court to consider on remand. The majority opinion's only reference to the "arbitrary and capricious" standard explored by Justice Kagan's opinion came in the suggestion that an agency's failure to consider RFRA—not a problem here—would be susceptible to a claim that its action was arbitrary and capricious.[64]

Justice Alito's concurring opinion opposed a remand and any fur-ther consideration of the remaining challenges framed by Pennsyl-vania. The case should end without any further steps because the government was "required by RFRA to create the religious exemption (or something very close to it)"[65] Justice Alito also remarked that no employee of the Little Sisters has raised concerns about their treat-ment.[66] Justice Ginsburg's dissent agreed that no remand was needed, but for the opposite reason: she would have affirmed the holding of the court of appeals that the government lacks authority under RFRA, the ACA, or any other grant of power to enact the exemptions.[67]

G. DOES THE AFFORDABLE CARE ACT AUTHORIZE THE EXEMPTION
   OF PARTICULAR EMPLOYERS AND DENIAL OF BENEFITS
   TO COVERED EMPLOYEES?

The final of the seven questions brings to the fore concerns of the people affected but not parties to the suit and is the heart of the

---

[62] *Id.* at 2398–40.

[63] *Id.* at 2386.

[64] *Id.*

[65] *Id.* at 2396 (Alito, J., concurring).

[66] *Id.* at 2387.

[67] *Id.* at 2411–12 (Ginsburg, J., dissenting).

dissent by Justice Ginsburg. Does the ACA require continuing coverage of contraceptive services or does it permit particular employers to be exempted from including such coverage in their health plans
for their employees? The dissent relies on text, legislative history, and
the structure of the statute as a whole to answer that the law requires
continuing coverage for the women employees. The textual basis of
the dissent's argument was section 300gg–13(a)(4) of the ACA: "with
respect to women," group health plans "*shall ... provide* coverage for ...
preventive care and screenings ... as provided for in comprehensive
guidelines" issued by HRSA.[68] In the legislative history, Congress discussed and intended equal treatment of preventive services without additional costs to women when compared with men.[69] Neither the text
nor the legislative history, Justice Ginsburg said, provided any authority to sacrifice entitlements that were otherwise guaranteed in order
to accommodate particular employers' religious or moral concerns.[70]

The Obama-era accommodation absolved the objecting employers
of an obligation to provide contraceptive coverage while still ensuring
such coverage from the insurer itself.[71] Because the objections persist
despite the availability of win-win solutions, the dissent suggested, the
real objection of the Little Sisters is not to the obligation of registering
their objections or seeking an accommodation but to the fact that their
employees would still obtain contraceptive services.[72] In the eyes of the
dissent, this crosses over from the claim of freedom of belief and
practice according to one's religion into the desire to impose one's
views on others; here, the objectors seem to shift from seeking government help to ensure space to exercise their own religion to instead
seeking authority from the government to govern others.[73] An exemption for the Little Sisters need not deprive their employees from
the coverage intended under the law. Seemingly conflicting interests

---

[68] *Id.* at 2405 (citing 42 U.S.C. § 300gg–13(a) (emphasis added)).

[69] *Little Sisters*, 140 S. Ct. at 2405 (Ginsburg, J., dissenting)

[70] *Id.* at 2406 & n.14.

[71] *Id.* at 2410–11.

[72] *See id.* at 2411.

[73] Carol Weisbrod, *Family, Church and State: An Essay on Constitutionalism and Religious Authority*, 26 J. FAM. L. 741, 749 (1988).

can converge with the assistance of careful regulations; decisionmakers need not pit one interest against the other in a zero-sum game.[74]

The interests of women employees who seek access to contraceptives are outside any requisite concern, according to the majority opinion. Congress itself did not explicitly mention contraceptive coverage and instead used the phrase "preventive care and screenings"—and assigned the task of specifying covered preventive services to a sub-agency.[75] The Court's majority also suggests that the dissent's view of the ACA would not permit any religious accommodation and therefore would call into question the Obama-era rules, despite the dissent's defense that those rules meet the claims and interests of both religious objector employers and their employees and are justified on First Amendment grounds.[76]

On one point, the opinions of Justice Ginsburg and Justice Alito agreed. They both noted that Little Sisters want no part, however remote, in conduct that makes contraceptives available to their employees. In his concurring opinion, Justice Alito acknowledged that Little Sisters and other employers "objected to engaging in any conduct that had the effect of making contraceptives available to their employees."[77] Justice Alito accepted this objection as meeting the test for a substantial burden on religious claims. Accordingly, because RFRA requires accommodating religious employers substantially burdened by government action, and because no accommodation could be found, the objecting employers win. Moreover, Justice Alito asserted, the government could not have a compelling interest that overrode the burden on the objecting employers because it does not provide contraceptive coverage to women who do not have employers at all and because it allowed employers with fewer than fifty employees to avoid the requirements.[78]

The opinions contrast thus not only in their answer to questions but in which questions to ask. The clashes among the justices reflect different starting points. The starting point for the dissent is the ACA coverage requirements while the starting point for Justice Alito is the

---

[74] *See generally* Martha Minow, *Is Pluralism an Ideal or a Compromise: An Essay for Carol Weisbrod*, 40 Conn. L. Rev. 1287 (2008).

[75] *Little Sisters*, 140 S. Ct. at 2381–82.

[76] *Compare id*. at 2382 n.9, *with id*. at 2406–07 (Ginsburg, J., dissenting).

[77] *Id*. at 2388 (Alito, J., concurring).

[78] *Id*. at 2392.

freedom of religious employers. The majority and Justice Kagan both start with the scope of authority granted to administrative agencies, but they interpret the statute differently and consider different factors in their analyses.

In no small way, this state of affairs reflects the truncation of highly complex and multidimensional issues resulting from the structure of the litigation. The Court did not have before it objecting employees; the Court did not have as parties any women seeking contraceptive services.[79] The Court did have fifty-five briefs from friends of the Court—twenty-four supporting Little Sisters, and thirty-one supporting Pennsylvania—but the core litigation was not structured to take into account the effects of the rules on employees except as indirect results of the claims of religious employers, states, and the federal government.[80]

These varied briefs bring distinct ideas about who is involved in the matter before the Court and who should attend to contrasting interests. Justice Ginsburg's opinion proceeds with the view that both religious employers and their employees have interests at stake in scope of the insurance coverage requirements—and both kinds of interests are compatible with statute—while Justice Alito's opinion treats any such conflicts as a matter for resolution in political processes.[81] For the dissent, if there is no way to resolve the problem to meet both the claims of religious objectors and of those seeking equal healthcare benefits for women, then religious accommodation should not be done at the expense of third parties, nor should it require the government to alter its internal operations.[82] The concurring opinion sees no conflict—and hears no concerns raised by employees of the Little Sisters.

Justice Kagan's opinion initially seems agnostic on the question whether the ACA requires insurance to cover contraception services for employees whose employers have been exempted, by regulations, from ensuring such coverage. Actually, her opinion offers constant attention to the issue, though as a factor requiring consideration under the arbitrary and capricious inquiry coming on remand rather

---

[79] Amicus briefs included national advocacy organizations and scholars, but not employees facing loss of contraceptive coverage.

[80] *Reframing the Harm*, *supra* note 3.

[81] *Compare Little Sisters*, 140 S. Ct. at 2409–11 (Ginsburg, J., dissenting), *with id.* at 2392–93 (Alito, J., concurring).

[82] *Id.* at 2409–12 (Ginsburg, J., dissenting).

than as a matter of statutory interpretation for the Court. Emphasizing that the government left in place the finding that contraceptive coverage "is necessary for women's health and well-being," Justice Kagan's opinion stresses that the government has committed itself to "minimizing the impact on contraceptive coverage. . . . but they failed to fulfill that commitment to women."[83] Moreover, in calling for review of the exemption for employers with moral rather than religious objections, "a careful agency would have weighed anew, in this different context, the benefits of exempting more employers from the mandate against the harms of depriving more women of contraceptive coverage."[84] Indirectly, then, Justice Kagan shows how judicial review of administrative agencies' actions will address Justice Ginsburg's concern about the impact of religious free exercise claims on third parties. These efforts to elevate concerns of unrepresented parties point to issues abbreviated by the litigation.

II. Saying What Was Barely Seen

Underneath the explicit questions and lines of analysis in *Little Sisters* and barely discussed by any of the justices are still further questions: Should birth control be understood as a controversial feature of women's changing status or as an element of basic healthcare? Should religious freedom claims trump general legal provisions? Does the reliance on employers as key distributors of health insurance coverage authorize employers' views to override those of their employees or of public policy and healthcare experts? How can judicial action be compatible with the decades of hard work accommodating and reconciling competing interests? And should accommodation of different religious views allow imposition of those views on others?

Seeking ways to avoid religious conflict in no small measure fueled the movement of White Europeans to colonize America at the expense of its own inhabitants. In her illuminating typology of conflicts between a religious group and a secular state, Carol Weisbrod contrasted two approaches: in the first, a religious group "tries to 'co-opt' the state and persuade it to adopt and impose a religious norm as universal," while in the second, the religious group seeks "simply to preserve

---

[83] *Id.* at 2398–99 (Kagan, J., concurring).

[84] *Id.* at 2400.

singularity and create space for its alternative."[85] These alternatives are easier to imagine when the issue involves a practice of the adherents than when it involves financial contributions to the practices of others. Accommodation can often be achieved by ensuring separation of the religious objectors from what contravenes their religious views without imposing those views on others.

Behind *Little Sisters of the Poor v. Pennsylvania*, employers—with the aid of the Trump administration—seek to impose their view on their employees. This contravenes the federal policy of ensuring access to contraception under a federally compliant health insurance plan. It also in no small way involves the government in the act of imposing religious views of employers on their employees. Obviously not at issue is the employees' own decisions about whether to use contraceptives. The result can be framed in terms of sex discrimination—impairing specifically the access to a healthcare service used by female employees—or in terms of deprivation of a portion of earned employee compensation.[86]

The Obama administration's plan also broke the link between the employer and the employees' access to contraceptive services by shifting coverage to the insurer itself. The Little Sisters did not argue to the Court that the Obama approach would indirectly raise employers' contributions to health plans or otherwise produce some contagion or connection as the Trump administration rule, exempting them and other objectors altogether, seems to presuppose.[87] Members of the Trump administration pursued the issues due either to their own beliefs or to their political calculus about preferring religious views of some supporters to the rights and interests of female employees.

In the meantime, the Supreme Court has been cast in a role defined by others to support the elevation of religious views of some employers over Congressional intent and the self-determination

---

[85] Weisbrod, *supra* note 73, at 747.

[86] See *Reframing the Harm*, *supra* note 3 at notes 106 and 124. The sex discrimination issues involve not only differences in covered healthcare benefits but also in relation to women's effective ability to participate in the paid workforce. On the first, see Comm'n Decision on Coverage of Contraception (EEOC, Dec. 14, 2000), https://www.eeoc.gov/commission-decision-coverage-contraception}. On the second, see American College of Obstetricians and Gynecologists Committee on Health Care for Underserved Women, *Committee Opinion No. 615: Access to Contraception*, 125 *Obstetrics & Gynecology*, 250, 251 (2015) (recommending contraceptive services that address pain, excessive bleeding, risks of cancer, and unintended pregnancies).

[87] For consideration of the facilitation of sin, see Stolzenberg, *supra* note 15, at 749.

represented by access to contraceptive services. Advocates engaged in the litigation for the Little Sisters showed persistence and foresight. In seeking and obtaining intervention for the Little Sisters in the lawsuit Pennsylvania brought against the Trump administration rule, Becket positioned Little Sisters to appeal and ultimately to become the face—and name—of the lawsuit, allowing members of the Court to commend the mission of the organization and to criticize the burdens of the litigation.[88] The rhetorical power of this framing apparently obscured the fact that the Little Sisters organization itself had long before obtained relief from any duty to include contraceptive coverage in insurance for its employees—both under the Obama rule and continuing with the Trump rule. The Little Sisters either would seem to demand that contraceptive service coverage be denied for their employees—even if Little Sisters themselves did not provide that coverage and did not expend resources on that coverage—or to assert that simply asking for exemption would violate their beliefs.[89] They or their lawyers proceeded with an approach seeking to allow any employer to avoid providing such coverage, and with the Trump administration rule, they succeeded—pending the remand to the district court for further proceedings.

More significant than the details of this particular litigation is its transmutation of complex negotiations over public values into a few either-or questions. The issues are multifaceted, involving moral and political arguments and many different areas of law. In questions involving religion or women's bodies, American political parties and their fundraising machines for the past several decades have contributed massively to this either-or framing. Over one 150 years of work on birth control and women's health, over sixty years of changes in legal and political treatments of religion, and a similarly long and often fraught political and economic contest over healthcare provision come together in the *Little Sisters* case. It is also stands at the intersection of multiple generations of movements for women's rights and the emergence of Christian fundamentalism as a major

---

[88] See text accompanying note 21, *supra*. Little Sisters initially lost a motion to intervene but by the time the case reached the Supreme Court had become the face of the litigation.

[89] Reply Brief for Petitioner, *supra* note 16, at 7–8; see also Zalman Rothschild, *Judges' Politics Absolutely Sway How They Decide Cases*, Guardian (Oct. 12, 2020), https://www.theguardian.com/commentisfree/2020/oct/12/supreme-court-judges-amy-coney-barrett.

force in the Republican Party and hence in American politics, and the uniquely complex form of American healthcare and health insurance.

Legislative, administrative, and contractual contests have produced nuanced accommodations that could not emerge from the plaintiff-vs-defendant, win-or-lose structure of lawsuits. What follows is a brief history of the complex arguments, strategies, and negotiations leading to the treatment of contraceptive coverage in the ACA; a discussion of the roles of institutions outside of courts in accommodating multiple parties and interests especially in politically charged issues joining religious and women's interests; and a cautionary word about potential consequences of further judicial rulings in complex matters with more than two sides.

A. CONVERGING AND CONFLICTING MOVEMENTS FOR CONTRACEPTIVE
    ACCESS AND WOMEN'S HEALTH, FOR RELIGIOUS FREE EXERCISE,
    AND FOR HEALTH CARE GUARANTEES

Political debates over birth control have produced regulations and clashes for some 150 years in the United States despite the long-standing use of methods to control fertility in other societies.[90] Abortion has drawn particular opposition in the United States, although this is a relatively recent phenomenon, tied to political mobilization by right-wing and Republican groups since the 1970s.[91] Although there

---

[90] Controversies over birth control are frequently linked with controversies over abortion. *See* Joseph G Schenker & Vicki Rabenou, *Contraception: Traditional and Religious Attitudes*, 49 EUR. J. OBSTETRICS GYNECOLOGY REPROD. BIO. 15, 16 (1993).

[91] Soon after the Supreme Court announced in *Roe v. Wade*, 410 U.S. 113 (1972), constitutional protection for a woman's right to choose an abortion, Congress adopted the Hyde Amendment, blocking use of federal funds for abortion costs unless the pregnancy endangers the woman's life or resulted from rape or incest. Hyde Amendment, Pub. L. No. 103–112 107 Stat. 1082 (1993). The Hyde Amendment has been approved as a temporary rider to the annual Congressional appropriations bill for the Department of Health and Human Services ever since. Insurance plans covered by the Affordable Care Act are not required to offer abortion services, and twenty-six states exclude such coverage. *Regulating Insurance Coverage of Abortion*, GUTTMACHER INST. (Dec. 1, 2020), https://www.guttmacher.org/state-policy/explore/regulating-insurance-coverage-abortion. The Supreme Court rebuffed challenges to the Hyde Amendment and reasoned that constitutional protection for freedom of choice does not entail entitlement to financial services. See *Harris v. McRae*, 448 U.S. 297 (1980); *Maher v. Roe*, 432 U.S. 464 (1977). Some courts have ruled to the contrary under state constitutions. *See, e.g.*, *Planned Parenthood of the Great NW. v. Streur*, No. 3AN-14-04711-CI, 2015 WL 9898581, at *1–2 (Ala. Sup. Ct., Aug. 1, 2015) (finding that criteria for Medicaid coverage of abortions not imposed on other services covered by Medicaid violated the state constitution's equal protection guarantee). In July 2020, however, a judge halted a Trump administration rule that would have required marketplace insurers to send a separate and additional invoice for abortion services, compounding financial and administrative burdens on both insurers and consumers. *Planned*

are some religious groups opposed to contraception, the anti-abortion movement has targeted contraception as well, in part by confusing the distinction between the two.[92] This has complicated access to contraception despite opinion polls showing that even people who identify as pro-life predominantly do not oppose contraception and significant majorities across the country support insurance coverage for contraception.[93] Indeed, the vast majority of American women (regardless of religious or political affiliation) have obtained and used highly effective forms of birth control.[94]

Although the Supreme Court's opinions in *Little Sisters* framed the relevant issues in terms of fairly narrow legal questions, the case stands at the crossroads of three significant, distinct movements and public controversies involving birth control, the scope of enforceable religious free exercise claims, and government involvement in health insurance. Yet the Supreme Court's opinions in *Little Sisters* give little evidence of these often fierce debates coursing through the nation over the past 150 years.

Birth control: Moral, medical, gender, and religious frames have come together in political and legal debates and reforms addressing birth control. During the 1870s, the American women's movement pursued reforms of laws governing marriage, suffrage, education, ownership, employment—and especially birth control, as a key to

---

Parenthood of Maryland, Inc. v. Azar, No. CCB-20-00361, 2020 WL 3893241, at *1 (D. Md. July 10, 2020). Government funding and insurance coverage of abortion remains subject entirely to political forces.

During the presidential campaigns Joseph Biden favored ending the Hyde Amendment. With the results of the 2020 election finally clear, the availability of federal funding for abortions will likely become a focus for legal and political debate.

[92] Joerg Dreweke, *Contraception Is Not Abortion: The Strategic Campaign of Antiabortion Groups to Persuade the Public Otherwise*, 17 GUTTMACHER POL. REV. 14, 15 (2014); *Is Antiabortion Movement Undermining Contraception?*, CONTRACEPTIVE TECH. UPDATE 133 (1999).

[93] William Saletan, *Do Pro-Lifers Oppose Birth Control?*, SALON, Jan. 15, 2014, https://slate.com/news-and-politics/2014/01/do-pro-lifers-oppose-birth-control-polls-say-no.html (citing Gallup poll of 2012); *Use A Scalpel, Don't Amputate Obamacare, U.S. Voters Tell Quinnipiac University National Poll; Voters Oppose Fund Cut For Planned Parenthood 7–1 Quinnipiac University*, QUINNIPIAC POLL, (Jan. 27, 2017), https://poll.qu.edu/national/release-detail?ReleaseID =2421. On public attitudes about insurance coverage for contraception, see *generally* Robert P. Jones et al., *The State of Abortion and Contraception Attitudes in All 50 States*, PUB. RELIG. RSRCH. INST. (2019). In the early 1970s, even those opposed to premarital sexual activity showed widespread support for access to contraception. Richard Pomeroy & Lynn C. Landman, *Public Opinion Trends: Elective Abortion and Birth Control Services to Teenagers*, 4 FAM. PLAN. PERSPS. 44, 45, 52 (1972).

[94] *Contraceptive Use in the United States*, GUTTMACHER INSTS. (May 2021), https://www.guttmacher.org/fact-sheet/contraceptive-use-united-states.

personal autonomy and equality.[95] The slogan "voluntary motherhood" embraced conventional female roles remade in the conceptions of personal choice and equality forged after the Civil War.
These movements, over time, led to significant changes in the lives of
individual women, women as a group, and society at large. Current
research shows that women's access to birth control is a top driver of
women's increased economic success and also one of the largest influences in transforming businesses.[96]

Access to birth control required political movements, scientific
research, and judicial action. Invented in 1839, the diaphragm joined
other birth control methods, and by the 1980s, pharmacists, dry
goods stores, and catalogues made condoms, sponges, douching sy-
ringes, diaphragms, cervical caps, and folk remedies widely available
in the United States.[97] Birth control also received support during and
after the 1870s with the rise of the "social purity" movement, which
sought to confine sex within marriage as a matter of public policy.[98]
Although not couched as a matter of religious freedom, this movement actually reinforced arguments for contraceptive access as a
matter for the marital couple. Support for access to contraceptives
also came from the eugenics movement, while opposition grew in the
wake of President Theodore Roosevelt's characterization of women's
choosing smaller families as "race suicide."[99]

Although that movement was compatible with contraception, the
public morals movement also spawned the public career of Anthony
Comstock, head of the philanthropically funded New York Society for
the Suppression of Vice. Comstock successfully lobbied Congress to
criminalize the sale or distribution of materials that could be used for
contraception or abortion. Many states enacted their own versions of
the law, banning or tightly regulating sale, distribution, and use of
contraceptive materials. The Comstock Law of 1873 was highly

---

[95] LINDA GORDON, THE MORAL PROPERTY OF WOMEN: A HISTORY OF BIRTH CONTROL
POLITICS IN AMERICA 55–71 (2002).

[96] Gini Ehrlich, *Birth Control Gives Women Power to Decide*, NBC (Mar. 8, 2017), https://
www.nbcnews.com/news/latino/opinion-birth-control-gives-women-power-decide-n730751
(opinion piece citing research from University of Michigan and Bloomberg Businessweek).

[97] *American Experience: A Timeline of Contraception*, PBS, https://www.pbs.org/wgbh/american
experience/features/pill-timeline/.

[98] GORDON, *supra* note 95, at 72–85.

[99] *Id.* at 86–104.

influential and led to the prosecution of Margaret Sanger for distributing birth control information in a newsletter. She continued her advocacy, especially for working women seeking ways to manage their risk of pregnancies and of bearing children they could not support.[100] Sanger formed alliances with social workers, founded birth control clinics despite legal prohibitions, and created organizations (including one that became Planned Parenthood). The efforts succeeded in allowing distribution of birth control materials to women for therapeutic and medically prescribed contraceptive use.[101] Nonetheless, the Comstock Law treatment restricting the mailing of birth control information remained on the books until 1983.[102]

Birth control techniques in the meantime continued to be developed; the Food and Drug Administration (FDA) approved as safe and effective the first oral contraceptive in 1960. This development actually addressed women's health issues far beyond birth control: with regular use, it assists with the timing and scale of menstrual bleeding; reduces cramps, mood swings, weight gain, and anemia associated with periods; relieves painful symptoms of endometriosis (when the lining grows outside rather than inside of the uterus); can prevent ovarian cysts and polycystic ovarian syndrome; can reduce the risk of some cancers, and have other health benefits.[103] Many women have sought access to this medication in part or wholly for these reasons unrelated to birth control.[104]

Nonetheless, legal restrictions remained. Connecticut's version of the Comstock laws banned use, counseling, or assistance in conception, and persisted until a test case initiated by Estelle Griswold, executive director of the local Planned Parenthood office, and C. Lee Buxton, the Chair of the Yale Medical School's Department

---

[100] *See* PETER C. ENGELMAN, A HISTORY OF THE BIRTH CONTROL MOVEMENT IN AMERICA (2011); Dorothy Wardell, *Margaret Sanger: Birth Control's Successful Revolution*, 70 AM. J. PUB. HEALTH 736, 740 (1980).

[101] *Bolger v. Youngs Drug Prods. Corp.*, 463 U.S. 60 (1983); *United States v. One Package of Japanese Pessaries*, 86 F.2d 737 (2d Cir. 1936); Lakshmeeramya Malladi, *The People of the State of New York v. Margaret H. Sanger (1918)*, EMBRYO PROJECT ENCYC. (Jan. 22, 2018), https://embryo .asu.edu/pages/people-state-new-york-v-margaret-h-sanger-1918.

[102] *Bolger*, 463 U.S. 75.

[103] *Birth Control: Benefits Beyond Pregnancy Prevention*, WEBMD, https://www.webmd.com /sex/birth-control/other-benefits-birth-control.

[104] *Id.*

of Obstetrics and Gynecology.[105] This effort, at the dawn of the second-wave women's movement, emerged before the abortion fights and emphasized the rights of married couples rather than the rights of women.[106] The litigation started before the 1964 Civil Rights Act and before the founding of the National Organization for Women—but after approval of an oral contraceptive known as "the pill."[107] The Supreme Court in 1965 voted 7–2 to strike down the Connecticut law, although the majority differed over how to articulate the constitutional infringement. Justice Douglas, for the majority, relied on a construct of infringement of privacy rights implied by various parts of the Constitution and particularly connected with marital unions.[108] Justice Goldberg offered instead the Ninth Amendment's protection of rights not enumerated but nonetheless preserved by the Constitution.[109] Justice Harlan rejected those arguments and instead embraced a due process protection for values "implicit in the concept of ordered liberty." Justice White particularly stressed that the law intruded impermissibly on marital relationship and the privacy and association it involves.[110]

The Court in 1972 extended the scope of constitutional protection to unmarried individuals, and in 1977, with some restrictions, to minors.[111] Protections against gender discrimination in employment, over time, were interpreted to include some access to birth control materials. The Equal Employment Opportunity Commission concluded that a company providing prescription drug coverage to employees without including birth control violated Title VII of the 1964 Civil Rights Act, and a federal court agreed.[112] Birth control

---

[105] Nancy Finlay, *Taking on the State*: Griswold v. Connecticut, CONN. HIST.ORG (Nov. 9, 2016), https://connecticuthistory.org/taking-on-the-state-griswold-v-connecticut/.

[106] BONNIE J. MORRIS & D-M WITHERS, THE FEMINIST REVOLUTION: THE STRUGGLE FOR WOMEN'S LIBERATION (2018). *See generally* Reva Siegel, *The Unfinished Story of* Roe v. Wade, *in* REPRODUCTIVE RIGHTS & JUSTICE STORIES (Melissa Murray, Kate Shaw & Reva Siegel eds., 2019) (tracing legislative debates before and after *Roe v. Wade*).

[107] ELAINE TYLER MAY, AMERICA AND THE PILL: A HISTORY OF PROMISE, PERIL, AND LIBERATION (2011).

[108] *Griswold v. Connecticut*, 381 U.S. 479, 484 (1965).

[109] *Id.* at 487.

[110] *Id.* at 502–03.

[111] *Eisenstadt v. Baird*, 405 U.S. 428 (1972); *Carey v. Population Servs. Int'l*, 431 U.S. 678 (1977).

[112] *Erickson v. Bartell Drug Co.*, 141 F. Supp. 2d 1266 (W.D. Wash. 2001).

and reproductive choice became a critical focus for the growing movement for women's rights in education, employment, politics, and law.[113]

The development of the "morning after" pill, introduced for medical use in 1970, led to prompt scientific findings of safety and effectiveness but political pressures against government approval and consumer access.[114] Although the FDA is authorized only to consider a limited number of expert issues (safety and effectiveness, quality of manufacturing and processing, and accuracy of labels), the agency's leaders during the administration of President George W. Bush delayed the process, overruled the recommendation of expert advisors, and invented an unprecedented requirement of age-specific research concerning seventeen- and eighteen-year-olds, producing more delays.[115]

Susan Wood resigned her post as assistant commissioner for women's health at the FDA and director of the FDA Office of Women's Health because of the continued delay of approval of the emergency contraceptive product Plan B for over-the-counter sale.[116] She later described that ongoing and unprecedented political interference stalled approval and distribution of this contraceptive drug. The head of the Department of HHS appointed by President Barack Obama overruled the decision of the Food and Drug Administrator as to seventeen- and eighteen-year-olds (the FDA is a component of HHS) but caused further delay by raising new concerns about eleven- and twelve-year-olds and their abilities to understand the label and use the drug as directed. This presidential election season event (occurring in late 2011) was the first time a HHS Secretary overruled

---

[113] *See* LINDA KERBER ET AL., WOMEN'S AMERICA: REFOCUSING THE PAST (8th ed. 2015).

[114] The prevention of fertilization is purpose of medication used as emergency contraception within seventy-two hours after the relevant sexual act; some other medications can be effective to prevent convention if used within five days. On political interference with approval and access, see Susan F. Wood, *Inappropriate Obstructions to Access: The FDA's Handling of Plan B*, 16 AM. MED. ASSOC. J. ETHICS 295, 296 (2014). Contraceptive medicines differ from RU-486—"the abortion pill"—which operates on a fertilized egg that has attached to a uterine wall. *Morning After Pill*, MAYO CLINIC (June 19, 2020), https://www.mayoclinic.org/tests-procedures/morning-after-pill/about/pac-20394730.

[115] Wood, *supra* note 114, at 295, 297. Wood points to the Food, Drug and Cosmetic Act, 21 U.S.C. 505 (1938).

[116] Wood, *supra* note 114, at 297; *5 Questions: Susan Wood on Quitting the FDA*, STAN. NEWS, May 10, 2006, https://news.stanford.edu/news/2006/may10/med-wood-051006.html.

a FDA decision about a medical product approval.[117] Ultimately, after litigation and a court order, the drug was approved for over-the-counter sale without prescriptions.[118] Political controversy and legal action thus has surrounded and at times impeded access to birth control materials for women in different episodes over the past 100 years. The recent opposition to Plan B may reflect the belief that it induces abortions rather than prevents conception—but that belief is simply mistaken.[119]

Having made promises to evangelical supporters, the Trump administration slashed portions of President Richard Nixon's Public Health Services Act, marking the dramatic shift from a Republican Party supporting family planning services to one forbidding medical personnel from even telling patients about where to find abortion services.[120] Birth control access for women thus reflects complex interactions across political conflicts, scientific and regulatory developments, and judicial decisions.

By the time the ACA was enacted, an estimated ninety-nine percent of American women used birth control at some time during their lives.[121] This choice to use birth control is a recognized constitutional

---

[117] Wood, *supra* note 114, at 298. When the FDA granted Plan B OTC status in 2006, states were allowed to revise their coverage to exclude non-prescription Plan B. This was because of a 1990 amendment to the Medicaid Act that allowed states to "exclude or restrict coverage of certain outpatient drugs, including nonprescription drugs." Hence, before the ACA but after Plan B was available OTC, states' coverage of emergency contraception varied even more widely. Camille Fischer & Jaye Kasper, *Access to Contraception*, 15 GEO. J. GENDER & L. 37, 53 (2014).

[118] Wood, *supra* note 114, at 297–98 (citing *Tummino v. Hamburg*, 936 F. Supp. 2d 162 (E.D.N.Y. 2013)); *Tummino v. Hamburg*, No. 13-1690, 2013 WL 2435370 at *1 (2d. Cir. June 5, 2013). Jennifer Levin, *FDA Approves Plan B One-Step Emergency Contraceptive for Use Without a Prescription for all Women of Child-Bearing Potential*, FIERCE PHARM., June 21, 2013), https://www.fiercepharma.com/pharma/fda-approves-plan-b-one-step-emergency-contraceptive -for-use-without-a-prescription-for-all.

[119] Carly Vandergriendt, *Is Plan B the Same Thing as an Abortion Pill?*, HEALTHLINE (Sept. 10, 2019), https://www.healthline.com/health/healthy-sex/is-plan-b-abortion#why-people-confuse-the -two.

[120] Kinsey Hasstedt & Ruth Dawson, *Title X Under Attack—Our Comprehensive Guide*, GUTTMACHER INST. (Mar. 22, 2019), https://www.guttmacher.org/article/2019/03/title-x-under -attack-our-comprehensive-guide. Court challenges to these cuts are ongoing. See Andrew Hamm, *Petitions of the Week: Three Cases Testing the Legality of a Federal ban on Abortion Referrals*, SCOTUSBLOG (Nov. 6, 2020), https://www.scotusblog.com/2020/11/petitions-of-the-week-three -cases-testing-the-legality-of-a-federal-ban-on-abortion-referrals/.

[121] Lara Cartwright-Smith & Sara Rosenbaum, *Controversy, Contraception, and Conscience: Insurance Coverage Standards Under the Patient Protection and Affordable Care Act*, 127 PUB. HEALTH REP. 541, 541 (2012).

right, even though its exercise remains unavailable to many. Despite some movement toward male contraceptive medication and responsibilities, women continue to bear the major financial, health, and social responsibilities associated with conception.[122] The ACA expanded access to birth control—or at least, that is what its drafters tried to do.

Enforceable religious exercise claims. For nearly 100 years after its enactment, the Constitution's guarantee of free exercise of religion, like the rest of the Bill of Rights, did not give rise to federal enforcement actions.[123] Even as litigation emerged, general neutral rules until the 1960s overrode claims of free exercise of religion except when combined with claims of freedom of expression.[124] In a case seeking access to unemployment benefits, the Supreme Court in 1963 held that the government must show a "compelling interest" in order to deny accommodation to someone asserting interference with a religious practice.[125] After that, courts determined whether accommodations were required on the basis of the actual burdens a government regulation imposed on religious beliefs or practices, the compelling, or not, nature of the government's interest, and whether the regulation was narrowly tailored to achieve that interest.[126] The Court found occasions not to find substantial burdening of an individual's free exercise or otherwise to limit accommodations for free exercise claims. And some accommodation arguments ran into the risk of governmental establishment of one religious view over others or over a secular position.[127] Then in 1990, the Court removed the requirement that the government show a compelling interest to justify burdens on

---

[122] Lisa Campo-Engelstein, *Contraceptive Justice: Why We Need a Male Pill*, 14 Am. Med. Assoc. J. Ethics 146, 146 (2012).

[123] *See* Sarah Barringer Gordon & Arlin M Adams, *The Doctrine of Accommodation in the Jurisprudence of the Religion Clauses*, 37 DePaul L. Rev. 317, 317 (1988).

[124] *See, e.g., W.V. State Bd. of Educ. v. Barnette*, 319 U.S. 624 (1943); *Cantwell v. Connecticut*, 310 U.S. 296 (1940); *Schneider v. New Jersey*, 308 U.S. 147 (1939); *Lovell v. City of Griffin*, 303 U.S. 444 (1938).

[125] *Sherbert v. Verner*, 374 U.S. 398, 403 (1963) (quoting *NAACP v. Button*, 371 U.S. 415, 438 (1963)). *See* Michael W. McConnell, *Justice Brennan's Accommodating Approach Toward Religion*, 95 Calif. L. Rev. 2187, 2188 (2007) (detailing Justice Brennan's accommodation approach to the Free Exercise Clause); Kathleen M. Sullivan, *The New Religion and the Constitution*, 116 Harv. L. Rev. 1397, 1403–11 (2003) (comparing approaches to the religion clauses).

[126] Gordon & Adams, *supra* note 123, at 319.

[127] *Id.* at 319–322.

religion exercise.[128] In *Employment Division v Smith*,[129] the Court ruled that free exercise claims would fail in the face of a law of general applicability that did not target a particular religious practice.[130]

As courts then repeatedly rejected claims for accommodation of religious exercise, more than sixty civil liberties and religious organizations worked together to press for legislative reform.[131] Congress promptly responded by seeking to reinstate the compelling interest test through RFRA, but the Supreme Court rejected that statute's application to state laws and practices as going beyond the power of Congress under section five of the Fourteenth Amendment.[132] That was a setback for supporters of accommodations for religious exercise. (Showing the broad support for reviving the earlier stringent constitutional protections for religious exercise, nearly half the states have enacted laws modeled on RFRA which could protect objecting parties from having to pay for contraceptives for their employees.[133]) The federal RFRA remains applicable, however, to actions by the federal government—including the ACA.[134]

Whether private companies can successfully assert claims under the federal RFRA has only been partially addressed by the Supreme Court. In *Burwell v Hobby Lobby*,[135] the Court approved the request for exemption from the contraception mandate of the ACA made by a closely held private company.[136] Confining its decision, though, to

---

[128] *Employment Division v. Smith*, 494 U.S. 872 (1990).

[129] *Id.*

[130] *Id.* at 872–73.

[131] Claire Mullally, *Free Exercise Clause Overview*, FREEDOM F. INST. (Sept. 16, 2011), https://www.freedomforuminstitute.org/first-amendment-center/topics/freedom-of-religion/free-exercise-clause-overview/.

[132] *City of Boerne v. Flores*, 521 U.S. 507, 536 (1997); *see Gonzales v. O Centro Espirita Beneficente Uniao Do Vegetal*, 546 U.S. 418, 418–19 (2006) (holding the RFRA remains applicable to federal actions).

[133] *State Religious Freedom Restoration Acts*, NAT'L CONF. STATE LEGISLATURES (May 4, 2017), https://www.ncsl.org/research/civil-and-criminal-justice/state-rfra-statutes.aspx. The remaining scope of a compelling interest test under federal law is limited to land use and institutional persons' claims. See *Religious Land Use and Institutionalized Persons Act of 2000*, 42 U.S.C. § 2000cc et seq. (protecting individuals, houses of worship, and other religious institutions from discrimination in zoning and landmarking laws).

[134] Victoria L. Killion, *The Federal Contraceptive Coverage Requirement: Past and Present Legal Challenges*, CONG. RSCH. SERV., 28–30 (Apr. 28, 2020).

[135] 573 U.S. 682 (2014).

[136] *Id.*

closely held companies as extensions of their owners, the Court did not reach the further question about whether publicly traded companies enjoy the same constitutional rights to assert free exercise of religion claims. It is a further question precisely because the ownership group includes a potentially wide variety and large number of individuals, organized not by religious belief but by investment priorities.

In *Hobby Lobby*, the federal government in some ways impaired its arguments against accommodating the closely held private company's religious exemption claims by acknowledging that religious nonprofits could be accommodated with no inconvenience to the covered employee. Hence both the majority and Justice Kennedy's opinions noted that Hobby Lobby's employees could receive full contraceptive coverage under the same accommodation, if it were extended to them, without requiring the employer to pay for it.[137] With the change of administration and policies, the Trump-era rule rejected any effort to ensure coverage without out-of-pocket expense for employees whose employers are granted exemption from the contraceptive mandate; the Trump rule also extends that exemption to all companies and to objections on grounds of conscience as well as religion.

These federal legal developments cannot be fully understood without the context of the changing role of Christian fundamentalism in the Republican Party and hence in American politics. White American Christian fundamentalism arose around 1919 in reaction to the teaching of evolution, the League of Nations, emerging women's suffrage, and threats to rights and freedoms perceived by particular Protestant leaders.[138] The theological and social movement turned to literal interpretations of the Bible with militancy and fervor in apparent reaction to modernization, urbanization, and other social changes.[139] A long period of removal from public and political worlds

---

[137] See *id.* at 730–31; *id.* at 738–39 (Kennedy, J., concurring). *But see* Andrew Koppelman & Frederick M. Gedicks, *Is* Hobby Lobby *Worse for Religious Liberty than* Smith?, 9 Univ. St. Thomas J.L. & Pub. Pol'y 223, 234–39 (2015).

[138] Matthew Avery Sutton, American Apocalypse: A History of Modern Evangelicalism (2014).

[139] Martin E. Marty & R. Scott Appleby, Fundamentalisms Observed 22–23 (1991); Michael Adger Smith, Christian Fundamentalism: Militancy and the Scopes Trial 2 (2010) (M.A. thesis, Clemson University) (on file with author), https://tigerprints.clemson.edu/cgi/viewcontent.cgi?article=1962&context=all_theses; see Echo E. Fields, *Understanding Activist Fundamentalism: Capitalist Crisis and the "Colonization of the LifeWorld,"* 52 Socio. Analysis 175, 188 (1991) (depicting the fundamentalist movement as a response to contradictions in social systems and struggles over control).

followed the trial of John Scopes, although attacks on Al Smith's 1928 presidential campaign and the New Deal included voices from fundamentalist communities.[140] Charismatic evangelical Protestant ministers created television shows in the 1950s and 1960s, taking advantage of cheap Sunday morning airtime made available as television stations could fulfill their "public service" obligations with religious programming.[141] Reverend Jerry Falwell reported a change from a theological view calling religious people to separate from political engagement to instead a vigorous embrace of politics.[142] Political campaigns around the Equal Rights Amendment, abortion, gay rights, and vouchers for religious schools followed, with vocal involvement of Falwell and other evangelical Christian leaders. And conservative political organizers for the Republican Party came to view fundamentalist ministers as promising participants in building a new right-wing movement. After 1978, Jerry Falwell, Pat Robertson, and a few other leaders forged a bold and aggressive role for Christian fundamentalists in political campaigns and fundraising, litigation strategies, and national discussions.[143] In recent years, reflections on how evangelicals reshaped elections have become familiar in mainstream media.[144] A period of intense partisanship emerged and a transformation of the Republican Party from one that supported family planning to one fiercely opposed to abortion, reproductive choice, and gay rights—even as Americans reported disagreement with these views and also revealed declining religious affiliation.[145] Republican "capture" by the religious

[140] SUTTON, *supra* note 138.

[141] Frances FitzGerald, *A Disciplined, Charging Army*, NEW YORKER (May 18, 1981), https://www.newyorker.com/magazine/1981/05/18/a-disciplined-charging-army.

[142] *Id.*

[143] *See, e.g.*, JONATHAN J EDWARDS, SUPERCHURCH: THE RHETORIC AND POLITICS OF AMERICAN FUNDAMENTALISM (2015); DANIEL K. WILLIAMS, GOD'S OWN PARTY: THE MAKING OF THE CHRISTIAN RIGHT (2010); SUSAN FRIEND HARDING, THE BOOK OF JERRY FALWELL: FUNDAMENTALIST LANGUAGE AND POLIT. 189–94 (2001); John C. Green & James L. Guth, *The Christian Right in the Republican Party: The Case of Pat Robertson's Supporters*, 50 J. POL. 150 (1988).

[144] Clyde Haberman, *Religion and Right-Wing Politics; How Evangelicals Reshaped Elections*, N.Y. TIMES (Oct. 28, 2019), https://www.nytimes.com/2018/10/28/us/religion-politics-evangelicals.html; Alex Morris, *Donald Trump, The End-Times President*, ROLLING STONE, Oct. 30, 2020, https://www.rollingstone.com/politics/politics-features/donald-trump-christians-fundamentalists-end-times-rapture-1083131/.

[145] Tim Rymel, *The Fundamentalist Christian Chokehold on America*, HUFFPOST (Aug. 7, 2017), https://www.huffpost.com/entry/the-fundamentalist-christian-chokehold-on-america_b_598109dae4b02be325be0206; Katherine Stewart, *How Christian Fundamentalism Feeds the Toxic*

right changed the party's positions on abortion and reproductive issues.[146] The movement of Catholics toward the Republican Party is another part of the story.[147]

Because religious claims can be raised against laws addressing public health, employment conditions, criminal laws, and civil rights, exemptions for any who asserts a sincere religious belief puts the values behind those laws in jeopardy. Religious claims have not succeeded in gaining exemptions from legal protections against racial discrimination, although new judicial and legislative patterns may emerge.[148] Religious views of course also anchored the civil rights movement. And for many, protections against discrimination on the basis of race, gender, and sexual orientation are essential. Legislatures and executive branch leaders—and the courts—have often worked to respect religious liberty while effectuating other similarly significant goals. Although the population of the United States has grown less Christian and less religiously affiliated over time, the Congress is out of step. Looking at the Congress elected in 2020, researchers reported recently, "eighty-eight percent of Congress is Christian, while sixty-five percent of US adults are Christian."[149] The Supreme Court's nine members included five Catholics, one Protestant, and three Jews, while the American people are approximately twenty percent Catholic,

---

Partisanship of U.S. Politics, Guardian (Oct. 26, 2012), https://www.theguardian.com/commentis free/2012/oct/26/religious-fundamentalism-toxic-partisanship-us-politics.

[146] Michele McKeegan, *The Politics of Abortion: A Historical Perspective*, 3 Women's Health Issues 127, 127 (1993); Scarlet Neath, *There's a Long History of Republicans Supporting Planned Parenthood—Why Is No One Talking About It?*, Marie Claire (Oct. 1, 2015), https://www.marieclaire.com/politics/news/a16149/planned-parenthood-republicans/. See also Catholics for Choice, *The Secret History of the GOP and Choice*, 3 Conscience Mag. (Dec. 8, 2011) (tracing the earlier Republican support for birth control).

[147] Steven P. Millies, Good Intentions: A History of Catholic Voters' Road from *Roe* to Trump (2018).

[148] Martha Minow, *Should Religious Groups Be Exempt from Civil Rights Laws?*, 48 B.C. L. Rev. 781 (2007) (exploring cooperative solutions to religious and equality claims). Thus far, religious exemption claims have failed to justify exemptions from protections against racial discrimination, perhaps because political as well as legal decisions settled that question. *Id. See Reframing the Harm, supra* note 3 at (tan 69–70) ("[N]either the Court nor those seeking exemptions [in oral argument in *Fulton v. City of Philadelphia*] seem willing to stretch religious exemption doctrine so far as to allow racially discriminatory exemptions. Aggressive interpretation of religious freedom claims by the Supreme Court will put this settlement in question.").

[149] *Faith on the Hill: The Religious Composition of the 117th Congress*, Pew Rsch. Ctr. (Jan 4, 2021), https://www.pewforum.org/2021/01/04/faith-on-the-hill-2021/.

forty-six percent Protestant, and two percent Jewish.[150] There is an outsized influence of religious groups in politics in general, and some religious interests in particular. Legal protection for religious freedom is a hallmark of America, but now, as at other times, such protection risks conforming public policies to the religious views of some at the expense of other religious or secular commitments.[151]

Government and Access to Health Care. Nearly unique among advanced industrialized democracies, the United States has historically failed to develop a system of healthcare access to include all or even most of its population. As recently as 2012, forty-two million people in the country lacked health insurance.[152] Even with extraordinary medical facilities and procedures, American healthcare is characterized by massive inequalities in access, higher expenses, and worse outcomes than other high-income countries.[153] It is also characterized by private sector provision and private insurance, with employer-based insurance providing ninety percent of the private insurance market and covering sixty percent of the non-elderly population.[154] An implicit contract distributes responsibilities for social provision; as a result, across families and businesses, the government steps in for the elderly and the poor.[155] This fundamental feature of American healthcare provision, reflecting incremental developments and failures

[150] *Religious Landscape Study*, PEW RSCH. CTR. https://www.pewforum.org/religious-landscape -study/, last accessed June 18, 2021.

[151] The continuing controversy over prayer in public schools reflects disagreements over religious liberty and government establishment of religion. *See* FRANK RAVITCH, SCHOOL PRAYER AND DISCRIMINATION: THE CIVIL RIGHTS OF RELIGIOUS MINORITIES AND DISSENTERS (2001); *Religion in the Public Schools*, PEW RSCH. CTR. (Oct. 3, 2019), https://www.pewforum.org /2019/10/03/religion-in-the-public-schools-2019-update/.

See also FRANK RAVITCH, FREEDOM'S EDGE: RELIGIOUS FREEDOM, SEXUAL FREEDOM, AND THE FUTURE OF AMERICA (2016) (evaluating tensions between religious exercise and individual sexual expression in America). For a survey of rising religiously based restrictions around the globe, see *A Closer Look at How Religious Restrictions Have Risen Around the World*, PEW RSCH. CENTER, (July 15, 2019), https://www.pewforum.org/2019/07/15/a-closer-look-at-how-religious -restrictions-have-risen-around-the-world/.

[152] Goran Ridic et al., *Comparisons of Health Care Systems in the United States, Germany and Canada*, 24 MATERIA SOCIO MEDICA 112, 117 (2012).

[153] Roosa Tikkanen & Melinda K. Abrams, *U.S. Health Care From a Global Perspective, 2019: Higher Spending, Worse Outcomes*, COMMONWEALTH FUND (Jan. 30, 2020), https://www.common wealthfund.org/publications/issue-briefs/2020/jan/us-health-care-global-perspective-2019.

[154] Thomas C. Buchmueller & Alan C. Monheit, *Employer-Sponsored Health Insurance and the Promise of Health Insurance Reform*, Nat'l Bureau of Econ. Rsch. (Working Paper No. 14839, Apr. 2009).

[155] Naomi Cahn & June Carbone, *Uncoupling*, ARIZ. ST. L. J. (forthcoming).

of healthcare reform initiatives rather than a deliberate design, opens the avenue for private religious views of some to impede access to contraceptive care for others. With so many people reliant on their own, their spouse's, or their parents' employers for healthcare coverage, the vagaries of particular employer preferences produce the gaps and differences in coverage and expenses that have made efforts toward universal coverage particularly challenging in the United States.

Health care costs historically required patients to pay for each service, but as health insurance emerged, it prompted first state and now federal regulation. Failed efforts to secure a federal health insurance program reflected an ethos of volunteerism, suspicion of government, a medical profession organized as small business, wage freezes during World War II (which prompted employer competition around other forms of compensation), tax policies, and perhaps also social and political divisions and exclusions along lines of race and class.[156] Presidents Franklin D. Roosevelt, Harry Truman, and Bill Clinton each made substantial efforts to change the situation, only to face several obstacles and achieve limited success.[157] Hoping to achieve bipartisan support, President Obama pursued a model relying on private health insurance coverage, developing state-level markets for health insurance, and seeking to improve the quality of care while reducing costs. The ACA was enacted, but without support from Republicans, and has faced repeated legal and political challenges since its enactment.[158] Even this transformative legislation rests on an assumption that patients should bear a substantial portion of healthcare costs in order to encourage efficiency and defend against misuse of resources—and large numbers of individuals and families continue to lack health insurance or healthcare access and to face financial ruin when severe health needs rack up bills.[159]

---

[156] David J. Rothman, *A Century of Failure: Health Care Reform in America*, 18 J. HEALTH POLITICS POL. & L. 271 (1993); Aaron E. Carroll, *The Real Reason the U.S. Has Employer-Sponsored Health Insurance*, N.Y. TIMES (Sept. 5, 2017), https://www.nytimes.com/2017/09/05/upshot/the-real-reason-the-us-has-employer-sponsored-health-insurance.html.

[157] D. W. Brady & D. P. Kessler, *Why is Health Reform So Difficult?*, 35 J HEALTH POLITICS POL. & LAW 161 (2010); *see* John E McDonough, *Medicare for All: What History Can Teach U.S. About Its Chances*, Health Affairs, (Feb. 21, 2020), https://www.healthaffairs.org/do/10.1377/hblog20200218.541583/full/.

[158] Laxmaiah Manchikanti et al., *A Critical Analysis of Obamacare: Affordable Care or Insurance for Many and Coverage for Few?*, 20 PAIN PHYSICIAN 111 (2017).

[159] CHRISTOPHER T. ROBERTSON, EXPOSED: WHY OUR HEALTH INSURANCE IS INCOMPLETE AND WHAT CAN BE DONE ABOUT IT (2020).

Contrasting views about birth control entered into arguments over health insurance. By the mid-1990s, twenty-eight states required coverage of prescription contraceptives in the health insurance plans they regulated.[160] Thus, in the past few decades, intense political mobilization around healthcare, birth control, and religious free exercise has shaped the context for the challenge ultimately reaching the Supreme Court in *Little Sisters of the Poor*.

B. BIRTH CONTROL, RELIGIOUS FREE EXERCISE,
  AND THE AFFORDABLE CARE ACT

The ACA seeks to make health insurance more affordable and available while lowering healthcare costs and advancing innovations in delivering healthcare. It facilitates the purchase and sale of qualified health coverage in the individual market and provides options for small businesses through "exchanges" established by states or by the federal government.[161] The law allows states to open access to Medicaid to adults having incomes below 138 percent of the federal poverty level; it also provides subsidies that lower health insurance premiums for households with incomes between 100 percent and 400 percent of the federal poverty level.[162] The Act expanded oversight to include most private health insurance plans across the country, including the plans provided by employers that self-insure (which affects some sixty percent of employees).[163] The Act covers preventive services. An employer-sponsored "group health plan" must cover specified "preventive health services" without "cost-sharing."[164]

As initially drafted, the law did not give specific mention to contraceptives or related services; in its original form, the bill did not include

---

[160] *Insurance Coverage of Contraceptives*, GUTTMACHER INST. (Jan. 1, 2020), https://www.guttmacher.org/state-policy/explore/insurance-coverage-contraceptives#.

[161] *National Conference of State Legislatures, Federal Health and Human Services Guidance and Regulatory Activity*, NAT'L CONF. STATE LEGISLATURES (May 4, 2017), https://www.ncsl.org/research/health/federal-guidance-and-regulatory-actions.aspx#:~:text=The%20Affordable%20Care%20Act%20(ACA)%20builds%20on%20the%20Mental%20Health,ten%20essential%20health%20benefits%20categories.

[162] Patient Protection and Affordable Care Act of 2010, 26 U.S.C. § 36(c)(1)(A).

[163] 42 U.S.C. § 18031. Many states amended their laws to match the federal requirements, and some go further, requiring coverage for contraceptive methods available without a doctor's prescription. *Id.*

[164] *Id.* § 300gg–13 (preventive services covered without such out-of-pocket costs as copays or deductibles).

specific preventive services used by women at all until Senator Barbara Mikulski introduced the Women's Health Amendment.[165] Studies showed that compared with men, women need more healthcare services between the ages of eighteen to forty-five even as they face higher out-of-pocket medical costs with lower average incomes.[166] When women forgo mammograms and reproductive services, they face larger health risks—and investment in preventive services is cheaper than the costs involved in treating more severe problems. As enacted, the Women's Health Amendment delegates the identification of the specific covered services to the HRSA, an agency within the HHS. This was most likely an effort to avoid contentious fights over right to life/reproductive choice and meant to turn the scope of covered services to experts within an administrative process. Mere mention of contraception seemed such a lightning rod for some religious objectors that Congress used the label "preventive care" to ensure gender equity in the ACA and kicked it over to experts in a specialized administrative agency the specification of contraception as part of women's preventive medical needs. Perhaps for similar reasons, the statute provided for the involvement by three different administrative agencies to oversee the relevant rules.[167]

After the adoption of the Act, an expert advisory panel to the Institute of Medicine recommended the services to be covered. [168] That expert advice is what produced the resulting "Women's Preventive Services Guidelines" requiring cost-free access for all contraceptive methods approved by the FDA; annual checkups and screenings for breast cancer, cervical cancer, postpartum depression, and gestational diabetes; and approved contraceptive methods, sterilization procedures, and patient education and counseling for all women with reproductive capacity.[169] Nothing in the rulemaking process that produced the Trump administration's exemptions for employers with

---

[165] *Breast Cancer Group Honors Sen. Mikulski*, Balt. Sun (June 11, 2003), http://articles.baltimoresun.com/2003-06-11/news/0306110166_1_breast-cancer-women-with-breast-mikulski.

[166] Sheila Rustgi et al., *Women At Risk: Why Many Women Are Foregoing Needed Health Care*, Commonwealth Fund 1 (2009).

[167] *See Little Sisters*, 140 S. Ct. 2367, 2402 (Ginsburg, J., dissenting) (noting that the rulemaking involving the IRS, the Employee Benefits Security Administration, and the Center for Medicare and Medicaid Services behind 76 Fed. Reg. 46623 (2011)).

[168] Institute of Medicine, Clinical Preventive Services for Women: Closing the Gaps (2011).

[169] See text accompanying note 19, *supra*.

religious or conscientious objections raised questions about the expert judgments regarding women's health needs and the cost-savings from preventive services.

Anticipating religious objections to the coverage of contraception methods and services, the regulators initially during the Obama administration planned only for exemptions for houses of worship.[170] The interim final rule defined a religious employer eligible for exemption as "one that (1) has the inculcation of religious values as its purpose; (2) primarily employs persons who share its religious tenets; (3) primarily serves persons who share its religious tenets; and (4) is a non-profit organization under the Internal Revenue Code." It faced immediate objections from some religiously affiliated schools and hospitals.[171] The Obama administration requested comments on how to accommodate self-insured religious institutions while still providing female employees access to contraceptive coverage and proposed a third-party administrator to handle accommodation of religious employers. After receiving comments, the Obama administration announced an eight-month reprieve from the rule for nonprofit employers with religious objections to providing contraceptive coverage.[172]

Critics objected that this approach merely forestalled requirements that would violate the consciences of religious employers.[173] One month later, the Obama administration provided further accommodation, exempting from the mandate not-for-profit employers such as hospitals, universities, and charities with religiously based objections to the provision of contraceptive services. This effort sought nonetheless to meet the requirements of the Women's Health Amendment by providing coverage for contraceptive services through the insurance

---

[170] Lauren Sydney Flicker, *Religious Employers and Exceptions to Mandated Coverage of Contraceptives*, 15 Am. Med. Assoc. J. Ethics 220, 220 (2013).

[171] Internal Revenue Service, Department of the Treasury, Employee Benefits Security Administration, Department of Labor; Centers for Medicare & Medicaid Services, Department of Health and Human Services, Group health plans and health insurance issuers relating to coverage of preventive services under the Patient Protection and Affordable Care Act. Interim Final Rules with Request for Comments, 76 Fed. Reg. 46,621–46,626 (2011).

[172] *Statement by U.S. Department of Health and Human Services Secretary Kathleen Sebelius*, FIERCE HEALTHCARE (Jan. 20, 2012), https://www.fiercehealthcare.com/payer/a-statement-by-u-s-department-health-and-human-services-secretary-kathleen-sebelius.

[173] *Times Topics: Contraception and Insurance Coverage* (Religious Exemption Debate), N.Y. TIMES (Feb. 20, 2021), http://topics.nytimes.com/top/news/health/diseasesconditionsandhealthtopics/health_insurance_and_managed_care/health_care_reform/contraceptionindex.html [hereinafter *Times Topics*].

companies used by objecting employers. This revised approach to accommodate religious objections from employers invited an objecting
employer to "self-certify"[174] its opposition, which in turn would automatically exclude the contraceptive coverage from the employers'
group health insurance coverage. Then, the insurance issuer would
provide separate payments for contraceptive services for relevant employees without making the employees share the cost.[175] Objecting
employers viewed this approach as making them complicit in the
behavior to which they objected.[176]

Dozens of lawsuits, including *Hobby Lobby*, followed. When the
Court decided that a closely held for-profit corporation could assert
religious beliefs and show a substantial burden from the contraceptive
coverage requirement, it specifically reserved for another day assessment of whether the Obama administration's accommodation would
comport with RFRA. But Justice Alito, for the Court, did observe: "At
a minimum, however, it does not impinge on the plaintiffs' religious
belief that providing insurance coverage for the contraceptives at issue
here violates their religion, and it serves HHS's stated interests equally
well."[177] Due to the passing of Justice Scalia, the Supreme Court's
membership was down to eight justices, who were likely evenly divided
about these and other matters.

The Court remanded seven further cases brought by religious nonprofits objecting to the contraceptive coverage accommodation. Collected under the name *Zubik v Burwell*,[178] this remand included the
instruction to try to negotiate an "approach going forward that accommodates petitioners' religious exercise while at the same time ensur[es]

---

[174] *Burwell v. Hobby Lobby Stores*, 573 U.S. 682, 731 ("Under th[e] accommodation, [an em-
ployer] can self-certify that it opposes providing coverage for particular contraceptive services. If
the organization makes such a certification, the organization's insurance issuer or third-party
administrator must expressly exclude contraceptive coverage from the group health insurance
coverage provided in connection with the group health plan and [p]rovide separate payments for
any contraceptive services required to be covered without imposing any cost-sharing requirements ... on the eligible organization, the group health plan, or plan participants or beneficiaries." (internal quotations and citations omitted)).

[175] *Id.*

[176] *Times Topics, supra* note 124; Administration Releases Advance Notice of Proposed
Rulemaking on Preventive Services Policy [news release], Washington, DC: Department of
Health and Human Services, March 16, 2012; Laurie Goodstein, *Bishops Reject White House's
New Plan on Contraception*, N.Y. TIMES (Feb. 11, 2012), https://www.nytimes.com/2012/02/12
/us/catholic-bishops-criticize-new-contraception-proposal.html.

[177] *Hobby Lobby*, 573 U.S. at 731.

[178] 136 S. Ct. 1557 (2016).

that women covered by petitioners' health plans 'receive full and equal health coverage, including contraceptive coverage.'"[179] The Court also made a point to state that nothing in its decision to remand "'precludes the Government from relying on this notice, to the extent it considers it necessary, to facilitate the provision of full contraceptive coverage' going forward."[180] Those negotiations continued through the election season of 2016, apparently until the last day of President Obama's term in office. No doubt deeply affected by the results of the 2016 election, the Obama administration concluded in January 2017 that it found "no feasible approach" acceptable to objecting religious employers under which women of child-bearing age—including employees of religious employers—were assured of access to contraceptives.[181]

Having no feasible approach to this problem puts in severe jeopardy what the Centers for Disease Control and Prevention (CDC) views as one of the ten great public health achievements of the twentieth century: women's access to safe and effective contraception.[182] Evaluations of the ACA included assessments of the contraceptive mandate during the Obama administration. One study concluded, "the share of women of reproductive age with out-of-pocket spending on oral contraceptive pills plummeted from 20.9 percent in 2012 to 3.6 percent in 2014, corresponding to the timing of the ACA provision."[183] Moreover, cost-sharing for contraceptives can lead women to choose less effective contraceptive methods or forgo the use of contraceptives altogether.[184]

Expanding exemptions from contraceptive coverage became a priority as Donald Trump ran for and became president; Republican candidates in the 2012 and 2016 presidential election spotlighted the issue and promised relief for employers and schools with religious

---

[179] *Id.* at 1560 (quoting Supplemental Brief for the Respondents, at 1, *Zubik v. Burwell*, 136 S. Ct. 1557 (Apr. 12, 2016)).

[180] *Zubik*, 136 S. Ct. at 1561 (quoting *Wheaton College v. Burwell*, 134 S. Ct. 2806, 2807 (2014)).

[181] Lyle Denniston, *New Limits on Birth Control Blocked*, NAT'L CONST. CTR., (Jan. 14, 2019), https://constitutioncenter.org/blog/new-limits-on-birth-control-blocked.

[182] The American College of Obstetricians & Gynecologists, *supra* note 86, at 251.

[183] Gary Claxton et al., *Examining High Prescription Drug Spending for People with Employer Sponsored Health Insurance*, KAISER FAM. FOUND. (Oct. 27, 2016), https://www.healthsystemtracker.org /brief/examining-high-prescription-drug-spending-for-people-with-employer-sponsored-health -insurance/#item-start.

[184] *See Little Sisters*, 140 S. Ct. 2367, 2409 (Ginsburg, J., dissenting).

objections. In 2017, the Trump administration decided to automatically exempt most private employers from the coverage requirement,
despite objections raised in comments by women's health and civil
rights groups. President Trump issued an executive order, and the
rulemaking process delivered the change.[185] The administration treated
the matter as a campaign promise.[186] In announcing the change, the
administration asserted its protection of religious liberty while also
claiming that the rule would affect very few people.[187] It also settled remaining lawsuits challenging the Obama rule and, in some instances,
paid attorneys' fees.[188]

Over fifteen states filed or joined lawsuits challenging the expanded
exemption.[189] The Supreme Court combined several challenges under
the name *Little Sisters of the Poor v. Pennsylvania*—a step that itself
reflects savvy lawyering and perhaps some unusual reaching by the
Court itself. The actual case involving the Little Sisters of the Poor
stemmed from a challenge to the Obama-era rule; the Little Sisters
actually had several such challenges, and one led to an injunction
protecting them from compliance. By the time of the Trump-era
ruling, the Little Sisters of the Poor not only had the injunctive relief
but also benefited from a rule widely granting the exemption they
sought, which suggests the challenge was moot.[190] Their counsel, the
Becket Fund for Religious Liberty, nonetheless argued for their
continued involvement.[191] Using the "Little Sisters of the Poor" name
for combined cases also gave sympathetic justices a vivid and appealing

[185] Press Release, Dep't of Health & Human Servs., Trump Administration Issues Rules
Protecting the Conscience Rights of All Americans, (Oct. 6, 2017), public3.pagefreezer.com
/browse/HHS.gov/31-12-2020T08:51/https://www.hhs.gov/about/news/2017/10/06/trump
-administration-issues-rules-protecting-the-conscience-rights-of-all-americans.html.

[186] Amy Goldstein et al., *Trump Administration Narrows Affordable Care Act's Contraception
Mandate*, WASH. POST (Oct. 6, 2017), https://www.washingtonpost.com/national/health-science
/trump-administration-could-narrow-affordable-care-acts-contraception-mandate/2017/10/05
/16139400-a9f0-11e7-92d1-58c702d2d975_story.html.

[187] Dep't of Health & Human Servs., *supra* note 185 ("out of millions of employers in the
US, these exemptions may impact only about 200 entities, the number that that filed lawsuits
based on religious or moral objections. These rules will not affect over 99.9 percent of the
165 million women in the United States.").

[188] Laurie Sobel & Alina Salganicoff, *Round 3: Legal Challenges to Contraceptive Coverage at
SCOTUS*, KAISER FAM. FOUND. (May 4, 2020), https://www.kff.org/womens-health-policy/issue
-brief/round-3-legal-challenges-to-contraceptive-coverage-at-scotus/.

[189] *Id.* ("Seventeen states and DC have challenged the Trump regulations.").

[190] See text accompanying note 21, *supra*.

[191] *See Victory for the Little Sisters of the Poor*, BECKET, http://thelittlesistersofthepoor.com
/#back-to-supreme-court.

party as a focus. [192] As counsel, the Becket Fund for Religious Liberty reported the Court's decision with these lessons: "Religious communities have the right to organize and operate according to their beliefs without the government discriminating among sincere religious [sic]" and "Religious individuals and organizations are free to follow their faith in all aspects of their lives, including in the workplace and not just in houses of worship."[193]

From the vantage point of those seeking to ensure gender equity in health insurance, different lessons emerge. One lesson is the power of particular religiously guided advocates in politics. Another is deployment of religious arguments to enlarge exemptions from health insurance obligations even for people and organizations without religious claims. The three justices nominated by President Trump now serving on the Supreme Court already demonstrate a shift toward greater concern for religious claims.[194]

III. Unraveling Longstanding Negotiations and Accommodations

The denouement of the Little Sisters case has not arrived. Preserving as it did broad federal regulatory power to interpret the contraception mandate under the ACA, the Supreme Court has paved the way for the replacement of the Trump-era regulation by new rules pursued by the incoming administration of President Joe Biden. Justice Kagan's concurring opinion lays out one path for the remand, while pointing to potential rulings that failing to preserve coverage for employees departs from rational rulemaking.[195] Future regulations will no doubt be challenged by the Little Sisters of the Poor and other groups asserting claims of religious freedom and perhaps, inspired by the Trump rule, claims of conscience even for

---

[192] See text accompanying note 17, *supra*.

[193] *Little Sisters of the Poor v. Commonwealth of Pennsylvania*, Becket, https://www.becketlaw.org/case/commonwealth-pennsylvania-v-trump/.

[194] Ariane de Vogue, *Supreme Court Backs Religious Groups Against Covid-19 Restrictions in Colorado and New Jersey*, CNN (Dec. 15, 2020), https://www.cnn.com/2020/12/15/politics/supreme-court-colorado-new-jersey-covid/index.html; see *Reframing the Harm, supra* note 3, text at n.128 ("With the passing of Justice Ginsburg and the confirmation of Justice Barrett... it seems nearly inevitable that the Court's trajectory on religion will be toward granting more and more extreme religious exemptions.... The balance that once existed now seems ready to tip entirely to the side of religious objectors, largely at the expense of society's most marginalized populations.").

[195] *See Little Sisters*, 140 S. Ct. at 2398–2400 (Kagan, J., concurring).

those who are not religious. Conflicts over religion, birth control, gender equality, and health insurance provision will persist. But the cramped view of the issues that was imposed by the adversarial structure of litigation led to a decision that ignored the delicate processes of negotiations that over time produced birth control access, religious accommodation, and insurance coverage. The majority and concurring opinions in *Little Sisters* treated as unimportant the task that Congress and the Obama administration had embraced: how to ensure equal access to health services for women, accommodation for religious exercise, and a workable health insurance scheme.

In her last opinion written as a Supreme Court justice, Justice Ruth Bader Ginsburg tried to preserve the complex balance of many interests and voices. She worked to bring the voices and concerns of women employees present alongside those of employers and religious groups. She reminded the Court of its own multiple acknowledgments that this was the task. She pointed to the Court's own directive that the diverging parties (in related cases) should have the chance "to arrive at an approach ... that accommodates petitioners' religious exercise while ensuring that women covered by petitioners' health plans receive full and equal health coverage, including contraceptive coverage."[196] And she quoted the Court's prior recognition of ways for Congress and the regulators to ensure that everyone has cost-free access to approved contraceptives while also respecting the religious liberties of employers.[197] Justice Ginsburg urged the Court to remember that "[w]hile the government may 'accommodate religion beyond free exercise requirements' ... when it does so, it may not benefit religious adherents at the expense of the rights of third parties."[198] Doing so subordinates and even taxes one group to the benefits of others.[199] If there were a soundtrack, it would echo here Lin-Manuel Miranda's haunting lyric about the "The Room Where it Happened": who deserves a say in what is traded away?[200]

---

[196] *Id.* at 2407–08 (Ginsburg, J., dissenting) (quoting *Zubik*, 136 S. Ct. at 1560).

[197] *Id.* at 2408 (Ginsburg, J., dissenting) (citing *Hobby Lobby*, 573 U.S. at 692).

[198] *Id.* at 2408 (Ginsburg, J., dissenting) (quoting *Cutter v. Wilkinson*, 544 U.S. 709, 713 (2005)).

[199] *Id.* at 2408 (Ginsburg, J., dissenting).

[200] LIN-MANUAL MIRANDA, *supra* note 1 ("The room where it happens/ The art of the compromise/ Hold your nose and close your eyes/ We want our leaders to save the day/ But we don't get a say in what they trade away.") Legislative, judicial, and administrative processes often exclude those without the resources or knowledge to participate.

It may seem that courts are poorly constructed to attend to multiple voices, and that is a deeper issue.[201] One of the problems with the Little Sisters case is that the parties and their lawyers framed the case, pitting governments facing more healthcare costs against religious employers—without the female employees or their families as parties. Other actors—legislatures, majors, employers, civic leaders—might be able to devise collaborative, win-win solutions even in challenging conflicts over religious freedom and other societal commitments. Yet even trial courts have structural capacities for multiparty litigation and appellate courts can hear from large numbers of friends of the court, including some promoting the interests of women employees who risk loss of contraception coverage.[202] Proportionality review, common in other countries, offers ways to accommodate multiple interests and points of view even in constitutional litigation.[203] The more serious problem, greater than even getting in the room, is being heard—and ensuring the search for win-win rather than win-lose answers to competing values and rights.[204] At stake are not just the rights of some but the fabric of a society, resting on so many decades of work by so many people to distribute rights and duties in a complex and conflictual society.[205] Remembering Justice Ginsburg, others will have to pick up the fight.

---

[201] See MARY ANN GLENDON, RIGHTS TALK (2008) (examining problems with all-or-nothing reasoning); MARY ANN GLENDON, ABORTION AND DIVORCE IN WESTERN LAW (1987) (comparing legislative compromises to judicial all-or-nothing rulings); Minow, *supra* note 148 at 843–47 (exploring cooperative solutions to religious and equality claims).

[202] Abram Chayes, *The Role of the Judge in Public Law Litigation* 89 HARV. L. REV. 1281 (1976). Fifty-eight amicus briefs were filed in the *Little Sisters* case alone. On the growing importance and number of amicus briefs, see Anthony J. Franze & R. Reeves Anderson, *Amicus Curiae at the Supreme Court: Last Term and the Decade in Review*, NAT. L.J. (Nov. 18, 2020)

[203] See Jamal Greene, *Foreword: Rights as Trumps?*, 132 HARV. L. REV. 30, 56–60 (2018); *see generally* Vicki C. Jackson, *Constitutional Law in an Age of Proportionality*, 124 YALE L. J. 3094 (2015).

[204] See generally LAWRENCE SUSSKIND, GOOD FOR YOU, GREAT FOR ME: FINDING THE TRADING ZONE AND WINNING AT WIN-WIN NEGOTIATION (2014); ROGER FISHER ET AL., GETTING TO YES: NEGOTIATING AGREEMENT WITHOUT GIVING IN (1981).

[205] See Cahn & Carbone, *supra* note 155 (naming alterations in the implicit arrangements across governments, families, and corporations to ensure the social safety net and provision for families and children).

CASS R. SUNSTEIN AND
ADRIAN VERMEULE

THE UNITARY EXECUTIVE:

PAST, PRESENT, FUTURE

I. A Bracingly Simple Idea

It is a bracingly simple idea.

Article II, section 1 of the U.S. Constitution vests the executive power in "a president of the United States." Those words do not seem ambiguous. Under the Constitution, the President, and no one else, has executive power. The executive is therefore "unitary."[1] It follows, as the night follows the day, that Congress lacks the power to carve up the executive—to say, for example, that the Secretary of Transportation is a free agent, immune from presidential control, or that the Secretary of Commerce can maintain their job unless the President is able to establish some kind of "cause" for removing them.[2]

Cass R. Sunstein is the Robert Walmsley University Professor, Harvard University. Adrian Vermeule is the Ralph S. Tyler, Jr. Professor of Constitutional Law, Harvard Law School.

Authors' note: We are grateful to David Strauss for excellent comments and to Eli Nachmany for exceptional research assistance and valuable comments.

[1] See Steven Calabresi and Christopher Yoo, The Unitary Executive (2008).

[2] We are speaking here only of the removal power, not the directive power, that is, the power to issue orders to those who implement the law.

The Supreme Court Review, 2021.

On this view, the Supreme Court's unambiguous embrace of the idea of the unitary executive in *Myers v. United States*[3] was a golden moment in constitutional law, a ruling on which diverse people ought to be able to agree, and indeed one that they should enthusiastically embrace. And on this view, the Court's messy, confusing, neologism-based, indefensible rejection of the unitary executive in *Humphrey's Executor v. Federal Trade Commission*,[4] upholding the independence of the Federal Trade Commission, was a dark stain, one of the lowest moments in the Court's history and a prime candidate for inclusion in the "anticanon" of constitutional law. If that is so, the only serious question in the removal debate, for many decades, has been simple: Should *Humphrey's Executor* be flatly overruled, or should it be confined as much as possible simply in deference to a longstanding precedent on which much of American government has been built?

A. MINIMALISM AND MAXIMALISM

In *Seila Law LLC v. Consumer Financial Protection Bureau*,[5] the Court invalidated the provision guaranteeing that the Director of the CFPB could not be removed by the President except for cause. But the Court did not overrule *Humphrey's Executor*; it distinguished it, confining it to its facts. The resulting opinion, however, is deeply ambiguous, because it is not obvious what the legally relevant description of *Humphrey's Executor* should now be taken to be.

On one reading, which we will call the "minimalist reading," the Court's opinion might be read to say: "We have made some mistakes in the past, and we may or may not overrule them, but if we can find any minimally plausible ground for distinguishing them, that is exactly what we will do." On this view, the Court distinguished *Humphrey's Executor* principally on the ground that the CFPB is headed by a single person, not a multimember commission, along the lines of then-Judge Kavanaugh's earlier opinion for a D.C. Circuit panel.[6] In simpler words: "Go forth, and sin no more."

---

[3] 272 U.S. 52 (1926). We believe that the phrase "unambiguous embrace" is accurate, but as we shall see, the Court did not conclude that all those who operate within the executive branch are unequivocally subject to the President's will.

[4] 295 U.S. 602 (1935).

[5] Seila Law v. Consumer Fin. Protection Bureau, 140 S. Ct. 2183 (2020).

[6] PHH Corp. v. Consumer Fin. Protection Bureau, 839 F.3d 1 (D.C. Cir. 2016), *vacated and remanded on rehearing en banc*, 881 F.3d 75 (D.C. Cir. 2018).

But in fact, there are significant strands of the Court's opinion that seem far more ambitious; call these "the maximalist reading." This reading arises because the Court repeatedly described the exception derived from *Humphrey's Executor* as not extending to independent agencies that exercise significant executive power, as by rulemaking or enforcement in internal agency proceedings. In a crucial passage, the Court said that the baseline rule of *Myers*, granting the President at-will removal authority for all officers exercising executive power, is subject to "two exceptions—one for multimember expert agencies that do not wield substantial executive power, and one for inferior officers with limited duties and no policymaking or administrative authority."[7] The Court continued that these two exceptions "represent what up to now have been the outermost constitutional limits of permissible congressional restrictions on the President's removal power"[8] and refused to expand or add to them. Justice Thomas, who joined the majority opinion in relevant part, also wrote a separate opinion, joined by Justice Gorsuch, saying unambiguously that *Humphrey's Executor* was wrong and that he would overrule it.[9] In his words, "*Humphrey's Executor* does not comport with the Constitution."[10]

The maximalist reading, if pursued in future cases, would effect radical changes in administrative law and indeed the fabric of modern government. The main independent agencies with multiple heads wield broad rulemaking and enforcement powers; the Court's ruling thus casts a legal cloud over the removal provisions for the commissioners and heads of the FTC, the FCC, the SEC, the NRC, the NLRB, and others. The constitutionality of those removal provisions would seem to depend on what, particularly, those agencies are authorized to do. Whether the maximalist reading is in fact pursued depends on many contingencies, but it is nonetheless significant that the Court read *Humphrey's Executor* so narrowly that it might well be taken to have thrown the independence of most of the current independent agencies, and longstanding understandings of that decision, into grave doubt.

---

[7] *Seila Law*, 140 S. Ct. at 2199–2200.

[8] *Id.* at 2200 (internal quotation marks and citation omitted).

[9] *See Seila Law*, 100 S. Ct. at 219–21 (Thomas, J., concurring in part and dissenting in part).

[10] *Id.* at 2216.

B. ORIGINALISM AND DWORKINISM

There is also a major methodological ambiguity in *Seila Law*. Some of its defenders are likely to understand the ruling as a clear vindication of the Constitution itself, understood in terms of the original understanding of the text. Indeed, we predict that the decision will be taken as an originalist triumph and in two different ways: as an enthusiastic embrace of originalism as the proper method of constitutional interpretation and as an unquestionably proper use of originalism. *Seila Law* might even take its place with *District of Columbia v. Heller*[11] as a defining example of originalism at work and as a vindication of that method.

We shall explore that possibility and raise some doubts about it. Taken in purely originalist terms, the decision might or might not be correct. For our purposes, the more fundamental point is that in our view, the Court's opinion is not only, or not principally, an originalist one. The Court does not refer to the "original public meaning," as many originalists do, and it does not work hard with the text and the history to show that in 1789, a widely shared understanding of the executive power would compel its conclusion. Indeed, there are major nonoriginalist strands to the opinion. To put things in slightly provocative terms, one might even call the majority's opinion frankly Dworkinian, in the sense that it rests on an effort to put the existing fabric of law in the best constructive light by reference to considerations of political morality.[12]

In that respect, *Seila Law* can be illuminatingly understood as a form of constitutional common law[13] and as responsive to emphatically contemporary concerns. The decision reflects anxiety about the powers of unaccountable bureaucrats freed from the constraining arm of the President (and hence We the People). Even while confining *Humphrey's Executor* to its facts, it appeals throughout to high-level principles, such as "liberty" and "accountability," to decide which of those facts are legally relevant. Is the number of agency heads, one versus many, relevant? The Court sometimes says it is not only relevant, but crucial; elsewhere, as we have described, the Court's focus is

---

[11] 554 U.S. 570 (2008).

[12] *See* Ronald Dworkin, Law's Empire (1986).

[13] *See* David A. Strauss, The Living Constitution (2010).

on whether agencies wield executive power. The important thing is
that on the terms of the Court's own analysis, emphasizing those high-
level principles—that is, which features of the history and caselaw are
critical—is not simply read off from any previous precedent or from
the original understanding. Rather, the Court arrives at its conclusions through high-level structural reasoning from what it sees as defining constitutional principles, and it expressly defends that structural
reasoning as such.[14]

In other words, the conclusion and the analysis in *Seila Law* are
rooted in large part in rich interpretations of abstract, contested principles of self-government and liberty. That is why the decision can be
understood not only in originalist terms but also as a species of constitutional common law, or, more precisely, as a reflection of Dworkin's
notion of law as "integrity," by which judges attempt both to "fit"
existing legal materials and to "justify" them by making them the
best that they can be.[15] So understood, *Seila Law* is an exercise in fit,
and an unusually creative one; it is also an exercise in justification, and
an especially bold one.

In what follows, we explore these two ambiguities about the opinion, which involve respectively the scope of its holding and its methodology. Our exposition comes in four parts. Part II explores the idea
of a unitary executive with reference to text and history and also with
reference to changed circumstances. We attempt to show the ambiguities in the founding era that gave rise to reasonable, competing
understandings of what was and was not settled. We also attempt to
show that the emergence of the modern administrative state can be
taken both to fortify and to undermine the argument for the idea of a
strongly unitary executive. Part III discusses the Court's disparate,
inconclusive encounters with that idea. Part IV turns to *Seila Law* and
its striking treatment of *Humphrey's Executor*, which it simultaneously
preserves (for now) and perhaps hollows out, thus endangering many
contemporary independent agencies. Part V discusses implications and
constitutional method, showing that the decision rests crucially on
contested normatively laden views about the meaning of high-level
principles. In the end, *Seila Law* is best seen as part of a much broader
effort, in prominent circles, to constrain the operation of the regulatory

---

[14] *See Seila Law*, 140 S. Ct. at 2202–04.

[15] *See* DWORKIN, *supra* note 12.

state in general and of apparently unaccountable institutions in particular by referencing a distinctive understanding of constitutional principles.

II. Two Kinds of Unitariness

In a sense, everyone agrees that the Constitution creates a "unitary executive."[16] There is one President, not an executive council, and the President is broadly in charge of the executive branch. But reasonable people strenuously disagree about what a unitary President entails.[17] We begin by distinguishing two ways of thinking about the unitary executive and then we turn, respectively, to originalist and nonoriginalist disputes about which way is best. The result is a map with four possible positions.

A. STRONG AND WEAK

Some people believe in a strongly unitary presidency; others believe in a weakly unitary presidency. The former insist that at a minimum, the President has the constitutional authority to remove all noninferior policymaking officials who exercise executive power (and also to control their decisions).[18] On this view, the executive power is the President's alone, and any congressional effort to compromise that principle by limiting the President's ability to fire executive branch officials is forbidden. All those who implement the law, including all those who exercise administrative authority, must be controlled by the President, at least in the sense of being at-will employees.[19] The

---

[16] *See* Calabresi and Yoo, *supra* note 1; Lawrence Lessig & Cass R. Sunstein, *The President and the Administration*, 94 Colum. L. Rev. 1 (1994).

[17] For different views, *see, e.g.*, Elena Kagan, *Presidential Administration*, 114 Harv L. Rev. 2245 (2001); Steven Calabresi & Saikrishna Prakash, *The President's Power to Execute the Laws*, 104 Yale L.J. 541 (1994).

[18] *See* Calabresi & Prakash, *supra* note 17. We are bracketing here the definition of "inferior officers" and the precise relationship between them and the President. As noted, an important issue, not explored here. is whether the President is able to control them by issuing directions they are obligated to obey, even if they are not his at-will employees.

[19] As discussed below, those who believe in a strongly unitary President might accept some limits on this principle; they might not believe in the directive power. On that issue, *see* Cass R. Sunstein and Adrian Vermeule, *Presidential Review: The President's Statutory Power Over Independent Agencies*, Geo. L. J. (forthcoming 2021); Robert V. Percival, *Who's In Charge? Does the President Have Directive Authority Over Agency Regulatory Decisions?*, 79 Fordham L. Rev. 2487 (2011).

Court's opinion in *Seila Law* seems to embrace this view, certainly as a matter of constitutional text and history.

By contrast, those who believe in a weakly unitary presidency insist that under the Necessary and Proper Clause, Congress has significant authority to limit the President's authority of removal (and also supervision).[20] They are likely to agree that with respect to some executive officers—the Secretary of Defense, the Secretary of State, the Attorney General—the President must have plenary removal authority. The President must have that authority where specific constitutional texts that make grants of power to the President, such as the Commander-in-Chief Clause, are implicated, and where tradition holds that core executive powers and prerogatives involving war, diplomacy, and foreign affairs are at issue. But they also believe that as a general matter, Congress has considerable room to structure the administrative state as it sees fit, especially where tradition suggests that agency independence is essential, as with respect to agencies that engage in financial regulation.[21] Justice Kagan's dissenting opinion in *Seila Law* embraces this position.[22]

Those who believe in a weakly unitary executive insist that Congress is able to immunize adjudicative officers from presidential control[23]; they add that some administrative functions might be exercised by people who are not subject to the President's policy preferences.[24] They believe that multiple authorities, including rulemaking and even prosecution, might be taken out of plenary presidential control so long as doing so does not prevent the President from exercising constitutionally specified functions, defined not broadly to mean control of all executive or administrative powers but more narrowly to include specific ones, such as the Commander-in-Chief power.[25] Of course it is true that those who believe in a weakly unitary executive have to do considerable work to spell out what their position particularly entails. The general point is that under the Necessary and

---

[20] *See* Gerhard Casper, *An Essay in Separation of Powers: Some Early Versions and Practices*, 30 Wm. & Mary L. Rev. 211 (1989); Lessig & Sunstein, *supra* note 16.

[21] *See id.*

[22] *See Seila Law*, 140 S. Ct. 2224–45 (Kagan, J., concurring in the judgment with respect to severability and dissenting in part).

[23] Wiener v. United States, 357 U.S. 349 (1958).

[24] Morrison v. Olson, 487 U.S. 654 (1988).

[25] *Id.* at 691.

Proper Clause, Congress is permitted to carve out some important functions from presidential control.

Some participants in these debates speak in originalist terms; others do not.[26] We can therefore identify four positions:

	Originalist	Non-Originalist
Strongly unitary	(1)	(2)
Weakly unitary	(3)	(4)

B. TEXT AND HISTORY

1. *Strongly unitary: the original meaning.* Seeking to uncover the original public meaning of the founding document, those in Cell (1) begin with the text.[27] Article II vests the executive power in "a President of the United States."[28] It also grants the President the power to "take Care that the Laws be faithfully executed."[29] On one view, these terms are exceedingly clear.[30] They demonstrate that the President, and no one else, is in charge of execution of the laws. Invoking history, those in Cell (1) add that the contemporaneous debates show that the strongly unitary view reflects the original public meaning.[31] In their view, those debates demonstrate that the framers and ratifiers sought to ensure that the executive branch would be accountable, coordinated, and energetic.[32] The concentration of the relevant authorities in a single person was deemed necessary to achieve those goals. On this view, the original public meaning of the constitutional text compels Cell (1).

Cell (1) is often thought to have compelling structural justifications, as emphasized in the founding period. As Hamilton put it in The Federalist No. 70: "Decision, activity, secrecy, and dispatch will

---

[26] Some influential and informative work on this topic distinguishes between "formal" and "functional" approaches, where the former term refers to constitutional text and the latter term refers to constitutional goals and purposes. *See* Peter L. Strauss, *Formal and Functional Approaches to Separation of Powers Questions: A Foolish Inconsistency*, 72 CORNELL L. REV. 488 (1987). It is not clear that this distinction easily maps onto recent decisions, discussed below.

[27] *See* Calabresi & Prakash, *supra* note 17, at 551.

[28] U.S. CONST. art. II, § 1.

[29] U.S. CONST. art. II. § 3.

[30] *See* Calabresi & Prakash, *supra* note 17, at 576–77.

[31] *See id.* at 617.

[32] *See* JOSEPH POSTELL, BUREAUCRACY IN AMERICA 49–57 (2017).

generally characterize the proceedings of one man in a much more eminent degree than the proceedings of any greater number."[33] In addition, "one of the weightiest objections to a plurality in the executive ... is that it tends to conceal faults, and destroy responsibility."[34] A unitary executive is more clearly subject to the people and therefore well-suited to a self-governing nation. If Congress were authorized to divide the executive power—for example, by creating independent officials charged with implementing important aspects of federal law— all of the Constitution's structural commitments, as specified by Hamilton, would be gravely undermined.

If there were any doubts (the Cell (1) view asserts), the Decision of 1789, as it is called, resolves them.[35] In that year, an early Congress debated the President's removal power and the unitariness of the executive at great length in the context of determining the legal relationship between early cabinet heads (Treasury, War, and Foreign Affairs) and the President.[36] Various views were represented in that debate, but Congress ultimately concluded that, by Constitutional compulsion, those who execute the laws must be at-will employees of the President, at least if they work at sufficiently high levels.[37] That conclusion, clearly emerging from the historical materials, is, on this view, authoritative with respect to the original public meaning of the Constitution.[38]

2. Weakly unitary: the original public meaning. Those in Cell (3) respond either that the text is murky and inconclusive or that it rejects the strongly unitary view.[39] In their view, the original understanding

---

[33] The Federalist No. 70 (Alexander Hamilton).

[34] *Id.*

[35] *See* Myers v. United States, 272 U.S. 52 (1926); Free Enter. Fund v. Pub. Co. Accounting Oversight Bd., 561 U.S. 477, 492 (2010); Saikrishna Prakash, *New Light on the Decision of 1789*, 91 CORNELL L. REV. 1021 (2006).

[36] *See id.* at 1026.

[37] *See* Geoffrey P. Miller, *Independent Agencies*, 1986 S. CT. REV. 41, 47.

[38] See Prakash, *supra* note 35, at 1026 ("In passing three acts in 1789 that assumed the President enjoyed a preexisting removal power, majorities in the House and Senate affirmed the executive power theory on three separate occasions. Members of Congress understood that votes in favor of the acts were votes favoring the executive power theory. Following these votes, members of Congress and newspaper accounts repeatedly described the final acts as endorsing the theory that the Constitution granted the president a removal power").

[39] *See* Casper, *supra* note 20; JERRY MASHAW, CREATING THE ADMINISTRATIVE CONSTITUTION (2012); Peter Shane, *The Originalist Myth of the Unitary Executive*, 19 U. PA. J. CONST. L. 322 (2016).

does not call for Cell (1). With respect to the text itself, Justice Holmes put it briskly but memorably: "The arguments drawn from the executive power of the President, and from his duty to appoint officers of the United States (when Congress does not vest the appointment elsewhere), to take care that the laws be faithfully executed, and to commission all officers of the United States, seem to me spider's webs inadequate to control the dominant facts."[40] Justice Holmes did not spell that out, but on one view, the vesting of executive power in a President says essentially nothing about Congress' capacity to insulate certain officials from presidential control. (It is a spider's web.) The general idea that there is one President, and the general idea that the President has the executive power, need not be taken to resolve the specific question whether Congress can declare that some officials, executing the laws, are not his at-will employees.

If this proposition seems puzzling or provocative, those in Cell (3) add that tellingly, Hamilton himself, a strong believer in a unitary executive, specifically rejected Cell (1) in *The Federalist* and concluded that the removal power followed from the Appointments Clause. In his view, that meant that officials who were subject to advice and consent for their appointment could be made removable only with the consent of the Senate.[41] In his words, "the consent of [the Senate] would be necessary to displace as well as to appoint."[42] Remarkably, he added this, in a passage that is much less well-known than it ought to be:

> A change of the Chief Magistrate, therefore, would not occasion so violent or so general a revolution in the officers of the government as might be expected, if he were the sole disposer of offices. Where a man in any station had given satisfactory evidence of his fitness for it, a new President would be restrained from attempting a change in favor of a person more agreeable to him, by the apprehension that a discountenance of the Senate might frustrate the attempt, and bring some degree of discredit upon himself. Those who can best estimate the value of a steady administration, will be most disposed to prize a provision which connects the official existence of public men with the approbation or disapprobation of that body which, from the greater permanency of its own composition, will in all probability be less subject to inconstancy than any other member of the government.[43]

---

[40] *Myers*, 272 U.S. at 177 (Holmes, J., dissenting).

[41] The Federalist No. 77 (Alexander Hamilton).

[42] *Id.*

[43] *Id.*

Thus far, the claim is not that Hamilton necessarily had the original public meaning right. It is only that the textual vesting of the executive power in the President, by itself, need not be taken to resolve the question at hand. Hamilton's views would seem to be decisive on that particular question—and a strong point in favor of Holmes's claim that the relevant words of the constitutional text are "spider's webs inadequate to control the dominant facts."[44]

The same conclusion holds for the Take Care Clause.[45] One can wholeheartedly agree that the President is authorized and obliged to execute the laws faithfully while also insisting that Congress has the capacity to immunize some officials from the President's plenary control. The duty of faithful execution need not entail the conclusion that the President can discharge law-implementing officials in the President's discretion. On one view, the laws that limit their power to do that must themselves be faithfully executed.[46] In any case, the Clause can be taken as a statement of a duty, phrased in the passive voice, not speaking to the particular question whether Congress can limit the President's removal power. Hamilton's views are relevant here as well. Hamilton had no problem with the Take Care Clause, but he also believed that Congress could condition removal of cabinet officials on the advice and consent of the Senate.

Consider in this regard the Opinions in Writing Clause: "The President ... may require the Opinion, in writing, of the principal Officer in each of the executive Departments, upon any Subject relating to the Duties of their respective Offices."[47] On one view, this clause is hard textual evidence against the strongly unitary view, taken as an originalist matter. If the President is fully in control of the operations of all those who administer federal law, why would the framers and ratifiers deem it necessary to specify this particular power? The question might be taken to be rhetorical. Though the Opinions in Writing Clause raises many questions and can be understood in different ways, it takes some work to explain how it sits comfortably with the strongly unitary view of the presidency.[48]

---

[44] *Myers*, 272 U.S. at 177 (Holmes, J., dissenting).

[45] *See* Andrew Kent et al., *Faithful Execution and Article II*, 132 Harv. L. Rev. 2111 (2019).

[46] *See id.*

[47] U.S. Const. art. II, § 2.

[48] *See* Akhil Reed Amar, *Some Opinions on the Opinions Clause*, 82 Va. L. Rev. 647 (1996); *see also* Peter L. Strauss, *Overseer, or "The Decider?": The President in Administrative Law*, 75 Geo. Wash. L. Rev. 696 (2007).

As for post-ratification history, the Decision of 1789 contained a range of competing strands, with influential figures explicitly rejecting the strongly unitary view.[49] The debates were complicated and messy—far more so than they might initially appear.[50] Those outcomes, and the Decision itself, could be read in different ways. It would be possible to read them as rejecting the proposition that the strongly unitary view is constitutionally mandatory and instead as revealing a discretionary congressional *choice*, not compelled by the Constitution, to confer unrestricted removal authority over particular officials. After a careful study of the debates, for example, Jed Shugarman refers to "the legend of the Decision of 1789," and concludes, "A majority of the first Congress opposed the powers cited by unitary theorists . . . On whether the president had exclusive removal power, the first Congress decisively answered no."[51]

On another view, also based on a careful analysis of the debates, there was no clear Decision of 1789 that authoritatively settled the question whether Article II establishes a strongly or weakly unitary executive. On that view, "the outcome was not nearly as decisive as later actors would claim. The process by which the removal issue was settled produced only a murky, very tenuous precedent in favor of the president's constitutional removal power."[52] Note too that any settlement, if it even counts as one, involved just three departments (State, War, and Treasury), whose particular functions might be thought to be essentially indistinguishable from the President's own.[53] If so, the Decision of 1789 might have no bearing on congressional efforts to immunize from presidential control the decisions of agencies with other sorts of authorities; consider the Federal Reserve Board, the Securities and Exchange Commission, the National Labor Relations Board, the

---

[49] This point is acknowledged in Prakash, *supra* note 35, at 1024–25, 1039 even though he finds the general conclusion authoritative. For a rejoinder, *see* POSTELL, *supra* note 32, at 84–89.

[50] See Jed Shugarman, The First Congress Rejected Unitary Presidentialism: The Indecisions of 1789: Strategic Ambiguity and the Imaginary Unitary Executive (June 22, 2020) (unpublished manuscript), https://papers.ssrn.com/sol3/papers.cfm?abstract_id=3596566; Jed Shugarman, The Decisions of 1789 Were Non-Unitary: Removal by Judiciary and the Imaginary Unitary Executive (June 22, 2020) (unpublished manuscript), https://papers.ssrn.com/sol3/papers.cfm?abstract_id=359656.

[51] *Id.* at 3, 1.

[52] See POSTELL, *supra* note 32, at 84. Note, however, that Postell adds that "the practice of removals largely followed the Decision of 1789 during the first several decades of American history." *Id.* at 89.

[53] For discussion on some of the complexities with the example of the Treasury Department, *see* Lessig & Sunstein, *supra* note 16.

Social Security Administration, and the Nuclear Regulatory Commission. Even if there was a Decision of 1789, it might not speak to the question whether Congress can immunize those agencies, and assorted others, from plenary presidential removal authority.

In addition, prominent legal historians have read both theory and practice during the founding era as an endorsement of the weakly unitary view, at least in some form.[54] Some historians have agreed that first, some department heads (such as the Secretaries of State and Defense) must be subject to presidential control, so that the President can exercise their own constitutional authority but that others need not be, and second, that the Necessary and Proper Clause gives Congress considerable discretion to decide on the appropriate allocation of authority between the President and the administrative state.[55] Those in Cell (3) can easily insist that their opponents in Cell (1) turn out to be living constitutionalists, motivated by emphatically present-day concerns and fears (about, say, accountability and liberty) while proclaiming a clear constitutional settlement that cannot, in fact, be traced to the original understanding and the founding generation.

C. NONORIGINALIST APPROACHES

For various reasons, many people are not originalists.[56] They do not believe that the original public understanding is binding. They too commit to following the text, of course, but they insist that structural principles and inferences, institutional roles, changed circumstances, unanticipated problems, judicial precedents, longstanding practices, the views of Congress and the President, and new or emerging values are a legitimate part of constitutional interpretation, part of how the text's meaning is best understood.[57]

In the context at hand, the rise of the modern administrative state, arguably an unanticipated development, might be taken to motivate nonoriginalist approaches to separation of powers questions.[58] Nonoriginalist approaches can of course take diverse forms. In the context

---

[54] See MASHAW, supra note 39; Casper, supra note 20.

[55] Casper, at 235.

[56] See STRAUSS, supra note 13; STEPHEN BREYER, ACTIVE LIBERTY (2006); DWORKIN, supra note 12; JOHN HART ELY, DEMOCRACY AND DISTRUST (1980).

[57] See BREYER, supra note 56; NLRB v. Noel Canning, 573 U.S. 513 (2014).

[58] On the relevance of changing circumstances in general, see STRAUSS, supra note 13; LAWRENCE LESSIG, FIDELITY AND CONSTRAINT (2019).

at hand, one form involves constitutional common law.[59] Another form involves "translation": efforts to understand the Constitution's commitments in circumstances that the founding generation could not have anticipated.[60] Yet another form, elaborated by Dworkin, suggests that constitutional interpretation requires judges to put the existing legal materials in the best constructive light.[61]

Cell (2) can be seen as an exercise in constitutional common law in translation[62] or in Dworkinian law-as-integrity. The basic idea is that in a period in which the executive branch is wielding unanticipatedly expansive power that touches so many domains of domestic affairs, the founding commitments to accountability, dispatch, coordination, and energy call for strong unitariness, even if those commitments authorized weak unitariness two centuries earlier.[63] It is one thing to say that in (say) 1800, Congress had the constitutional authority to immunize certain agencies and institutions, not so fundamental to national life, from plenary presidential control. It is quite another to say that Congress can carve out an assortment of crucial agencies affecting the economy in multiple ways, such as the Federal Communications Commission, the Federal Trade Commission, the Nuclear Regulatory Commission, and the CFPB, and let them do their work without control from the constitutionally specified executor of the laws. In the modern era, fidelity to constitutional commitments calls for insistence on presidential primacy, even if it did not quite do that in the founding era, when the administrative state was so much smaller and less central to people's lives.

It is true that this approach to constitutional interpretation might seem looser and more speculative than originalism, supposing, quite controversially, that the latter yields straightforward answers. But because many areas of constitutional law have unmistakable common-law features, with new judgments emerging from the case-by-case process,[64] we might want to insist that careful attention to the most central founding commitments, as opposed to particular founding-era

---

[59] See STRAUSS, *supra* note 13.

[60] *See* LESSIG, *supra* note 58.

[61] *See* DWORKIN, *supra* note 12.

[62] *See* Lessig & Sunstein, *supra* note 16, at 88.

[63] *See id.* at 101.

[64] *See* STRAUSS, *supra* note 13.

understandings and practices, is an honorable way to engage in constitutional interpretation. And if we attend to those commitments, strong presidential oversight of the administrative state, including agencies now characterized as independent, might seem essential if we are to avoid devastating damage to the very principles invoked by Hamilton in defense of a unitary presidency.

The ironic conclusion, embraced by those in Cell (2), is that even if the founding generation did not believe that a strongly unitary presidency was necessary to promote their own deepest commitments, such a presidency is necessary now, given the sheer size and nature of the contemporary administrative state. Those in Cell (2) think that those in Cell (1) do not have the original understanding right. But for reasons of principle, they are happy to make common cause with them.

A firm rejoinder comes from Cell (4).[65] Perhaps Cell (2) gets it exactly wrong. If fidelity is the goal, perhaps we should emphasize the risks of concentrated power and the importance of checks and balances—and the need to allow Congress to have some flexibility given the diversity of circumstances that give rise to new agencies. Perhaps the real concern, highlighted by changed circumstances, is the capacity of just one person, acting on their own, to move the government in their preferred direction. It should not be necessary to mention that that capacity is anathema to founding commitments; it raises the specter of monarchy.[66] As James Landis put it in a famous translation-based defense of expert administrative tribunals:

> The administrative process is, in essence, our generation's answer to the inadequacy of the judicial and the legislative processes. It represents our effort to find an answer to those inadequacies by some other method than merely increasing executive power. If the doctrine of the separation of power implies division, it also implies balance, and balance calls for equality. The creation of administrative power may be the means for the preservation of that balance, so that paradoxically enough, though it may seem in theoretic violation of the doctrine of the separation of power, it may in matter of fact be the means for the preservation of the content of that doctrine.[67]

---

[65] *See* Abner S. Greene, *Checks and Balances in an Era of Presidential Lawmaking*, 61 U. Chi. L. Rev. 123 (1994).

[66] On that specter, *see* Cass R. Sunstein, Impeachment: A Citizen's Guide (2017).

[67] James Landis, The Administrative Process 46 (1925). For discussion, *see* Adrian Vermeule, *Bureaucracy and Distrust: Landis, Jaffe and Kagan on the Administrative State*, 130 Harv. L. Rev. 2463 (2017).

Or, as Abner Greene puts it in a sustained modern defense of Cell (4), "if we accept sweeping delegations of lawmaking power to the President, then to capture accurately the framers' principles—principles that deserve our continuing adherence—we must also accept some (though not all) congressional efforts at regulating presidential lawmaking."[68]

To compress what might be turned into a lengthy argument: If executive power is concentrated in the President, and if they are able to oversee everything now included in the immensely broad category of administration, we would see a kind of Madisonian nightmare.[69] Given the risk of a discretion-wielding, immensely powerful set of administrative authorities concentrated in a single person, Congress should have the authority to insulate at least some such authorities from presidential control, simply in order to preserve diffusion of power.

The strongest example may well be the Federal Reserve Board: If Presidents could control it, they could promote their own short-term political interests by reducing interest rates to the detriment of the economy's long-term health. In the year before an election, for example, the President might manipulate the Board's decisions in such a way as to promote the President's own prospects for reelection. A similar argument might apply to the Federal Communications Commission, whose independence might be deemed necessary to prevent a situation in which the President is punishing their political enemies and rewarding their political friends. After all, the FCC has the authority to give out and to renew licenses to radio and television stations. If the President is entitled to control its decisions, the President could manipulate the speech market in such a way as to promote their own political interests. These arguments could easily be generalized—for example, to the FTC, which has the authority to approve or disapprove mergers, and to a range of financial authorities whose decisions might bear on the short-term political prospects of the President.

To reach a conclusion on the underlying questions, it would be necessary to begin by deciding on the right approach to constitutional interpretation—that is, to choose between Cells (1) and (3) or Cells (2) and (4). Those who embrace originalism would have to

[68] Greene, *supra* note 65, at 124.

[69] *See* The Federalist No. 51 (James Madison).

3]   THE UNITARY EXECUTIVE   99

undertake a careful investigation of history in order to choose between Cell (1) and Cell (3). If one rejects originalism, an assessment
of how best to fit with founding commitments would determine the
choice between Cell (2) and Cell (4). Our goal here is not to resolve
those questions. At the same time, we agree that on originalist grounds,
some executive officers—including the Secretary of State, the Secretary of Defense, the Secretary of the Treasury, and the Attorney General—must be at-will employees of the President. But we are not
originalists, and we would give substantial weight both to judicial precedents and institutional practices over time, which means that we land
in Cell (4), which can easily fit, broadly speaking, with judicial decisions since 1926.[70]

To be sure, general cells do not decide concrete cases,[71] including *Seila Law*. Thus far, our more modest goal has been to offer a
concrete sense of why many people believe that a strongly unitary
executive is constitutionally mandatory and why many people reject
that proposition.

III. THE UNITARY EXECUTIVE IN THE SUPREME COURT

Before *Seila Law*, the Court's decisions, often adopting the
weakly unitary position,[72] are best understood as falling within Cell (4),
though they could be defended by reference to Cell (3), and though
Cells (1) and (2) make prominent appearances (and very much have
come to the fore as a result of *Seila Law*). Here again, our goal is to give
a brisk sense of the constitutional background rather than to offer a
comprehensive treatment.

---

[70] The reference is to *Myers v. United States*, 272 U.S. 52 (1926), taken up below. Many years
ago, one of the present authors (Sunstein) argued in favor of Cell (2). *See* Lessig & Sunstein, *supra*
note 16. He remains there, with the proviso that he would not overrule *Humphrey's Executor* and
that the statutory standard—inefficiency, neglect of duty, malfeasance—can be interpreted to
give the President the requisite authority. *See* Cass R. Sunstein & Adrian Vermeule, *Presidential
Review*, 109 GEO. L.J. 637 (2021). But candor compels an acknowledgement that he now believes
that the historical evidence on behalf of the strongly unitary executive is somewhat stronger than
he once thought and that the structural argument, emphasizing changed circumstances, on behalf
of the strongly unitary argument is somewhat weaker than he once thought.

[71] We are playing, of course, on Justice Holmes's famous formulation: "General proposi-
tions do not decide concrete cases." Lochner v. New York, 198 U.S. 45, 76 (1905) (Holmes, J.,
dissenting).

[72] *See* Humphrey's Executor v. United States, 295 U.S. 602 (1935); Morrison v. Olson, 487
U.S. 654 (1988); Free Enter. Fund v. Pub. Co. Accounting Oversight Bd., 561 U.S. 477 (2010).

A. THE EARLY ERA

Myers v. United States,[73] the Court's first sustained encounter with the issue, is essentially Cell (1), urging that the text and the original understanding call for broad presidential control over the executive branch, above all through plenary removal authority. *Myers* offers an elaborate discussion of text, structure, and history, including the Decision of 1789, and thus provides the foundation for much of contemporary analysis.[74] For modern defenders of a strongly unitary executive, *Myers* is the shining and fixed star[75] even though it was written by a former President, Chief Justice Taft, who might be expected to be particularly insistent on presidential prerogatives. It could even be said that for those who believe in a strongly unitary presidency, all of subsequent constitutional theory has been a series of footnotes to *Myers*.[76]

By contrast, the widely reviled opinion in *Humphrey's Executor*,[77] generally understood to validate the independent agency form, deals not at all with constitutional history and barely at all with constitutional text. Mounting a fundamental attack on the very idea of agency independence and asserting a strongly unitary view, President Franklin Delano Roosevelt asserted that the "inefficiency, neglect of duty, and malfeasance in office" standard, which restricted his power to discharge members of the Federal Trade Commission, was an unconstitutional restriction on his Article II authority to discharge them on whatever grounds he chose.[78] Insofar as the Court unanimously rejected that argument, it made no effort to ground its analysis in something akin to Justice Holmes's skepticism about the supposed

---

[73] 272 U.S. 52 (1926).

[74] *See generally id.*

[75] *See* CALABRESI & YOO, *supra* note 1, at 18.

[76] *Cf.* ALFRED NORTH WHITEHEAD, PROCESS AND REALITY 39 (1978) ("The safest general characterization of the European philosophical tradition is that it consists of a series of footnotes to Plato.").

[77] 295 U.S. 602 (1935). On the reviling, *see, e.g.*, Miller, *supra* note 37, at 93. In stating that the opinion in *Humphrey's Executor* is widely reviled, we do not mean to suggest that *Myers* is without its critics, certainly of its sheer breadth. *See, e.g.*, Casper, *supra* note 20. And despite the reviling, it is important to emphasize that *Humphrey's Executor* has had a constitutive effect on the structure of the administrative state, arguably more so than *Myers*. We are grateful to Daphna Renan for pressing this point.

[78] 295 U.S. at 618.

clarity of the text, in constitutional structure, in changed circumstances, or in the ambiguities of the Decision of 1789. Instead, the Court emphasized the need to specify the relevant administrative functions. It held that Congress has the power to immunize members of independent agencies from plenary presidential removal authority insofar as such agencies exercise "quasi-judicial" functions (namely, adjudication) and "quasi-legislative" functions (namely, compiling reports for Congress).[79]

Thus understood, the actual decision was far more modest than it has long been taken to be;[80] as we shall see, *Seila Law* corrects the historical record. *Humphrey's Executor* was hardly a broad endorsement of the independent agency form as it is now understood. Because the Federal Trade Commission made policy only through adjudication (and lacked the authority to issue binding orders at that)[81] and did not even try to exercise rulemaking authority until the 1970s,[82] *Humphrey's Executor* was very limited indeed. It does not hold that Congress may restrict the President's ability to control the exercise of the authority to make rules. Its narrow holding, focused on the distinctive functions of the FTC in 1935, can in fact be defended on originalist grounds.[83] Insofar as it allows Congress to immunize purely adjudicative officials from plenary presidential control, it did not even depart radically from *Myer*s. In that case, the Court had stated:

> Then there may be duties of a quasi-judicial character imposed on executive officers and members of executive tribunals whose decisions after hearing affect interests of individuals, the discharge of which the President cannot in a particular case properly influence or control. But even in such a case, he may consider the decision after its rendition as a reason for removing the officer, on the ground that the discretion regularly entrusted to that officer

---

[79] *Id.* at 629.

[80] Peter L. Strauss, *The Place of Agencies in Government: Separation of Powers and the Fourth Branch*, 84 COLUM. L. REV. 573, 615 (1984) (noting that President Roosevelt "had given Commissioner Humphrey no particular directive; he had asked no advice that Humphrey then refused to give; he did not, perceiving insubordination, direct [Humphrey] to leave" and therefore the Court did not resolve the question "whether the President could give the FTC Commissioners binding directives . . . or what might be the consequences of any failure of theirs to honor them").

[81] *See* pages 29–30 *infra.*

[82] *See* Nat'l Petroleum Refiners Ass'n v. Fed. Trade Comm'n, 482 F.2d 672 (D.C. Cir 1973).

[83] *See* MASHAW, *supra* note 39.

by statute has not been, on the whole, intelligently or wisely exercised. Otherwise, he does not discharge his own constitutional duty of seeing that the laws be faithfully executed.[84]

In this passage, the *Myers* Court recognized that adjudicatory authority is distinctive, in the sense that its exercise might be immunized from presidential influence or control. To be sure, *Humphrey's Executor* goes further than *Myers* insofar as it rejects the idea that as a matter of constitutional right, the President may discharge adjudicatory officials simply on the ground that the President does not like their decisions. But that is not exactly a radical shift from *Myers*.

Insofar as the Court ruled that Congress can immunize from presidential control those who compile reports to inform legislation, the Article II objection is hardly at its strongest. After all, Congress can have its own staff; perhaps it can also say that certain officials, compiling those reports within an executive agency, are not at-will employees of the President.[85] Recall *Humphrey's Executor* has absolutely nothing to say about whether Congress has the authority to make rulemaking agencies independent of the President. As of 1935, then, and for the following decades as well, we might say that the Court held that the Constitution allows Congress to immunize adjudicative officers from at-will discharge by the President but did essentially nothing more than that to authorize Congress to exempt policymaking officials from plenary presidential control. This is so even if actual practice by independent agencies, including the Securities and Exchange Commission, the Federal Reserve Board, and the Federal Communications Commission, went far beyond what was necessarily authorized by *Humphrey's Executor*.

B. MODERNITY

Until *Seila Law*, the modern era had been largely defined by a continued endorsement of Cell (4), fortified by longstanding practice and *Humphrey's Executor* as currently understood, butting up hard against Cell (1) and perhaps Cell (3), and on occasion Cell (2) as

---

[84] 272 U.S. at 135.

[85] The reason for the word "perhaps" is that a court could say (1) Congress can have its own staff while also saying (2) Congress cannot immunize executive branch officials, compiling reports for it, from the plenary control of the President.

well. In *Free Enterprise Fund v. Public Company Oversight Board,*[86] for example, the Court clearly accepted *Humphrey's Executor* even as it also signaled a lack of enthusiasm for its decisions authorizing Congress to create independent agencies: "The parties do not ask us to reexamine any of these precedents, and we do not do so."[87] Its holding, invalidating two tiers of insulation from the President (an independent agency within an independent agency), was relatively narrow. But in reaching that holding, the Court also offered a degree of support for strong unitariness, not on originalist grounds but largely by reference to structural principles associated with the Take Care Clause:

> The President cannot "take Care that the Laws be faithfully executed" if he cannot oversee the faithfulness of the officers who execute them. Here the President cannot remove an officer who enjoys more than one level of good-cause protection, even if the President determines that the officer is neglecting his duties or discharging them improperly. That judgment is instead committed to another officer, who may or may not agree with the President's determination, and whom the President cannot remove simply because that officer disagrees with him. This contravenes the President's "constitutional obligation to ensure the faithful execution of the laws."[88]

Invoking text and history but also speaking broadly in terms of basic principle, the Court stated plainly: "It is *his* responsibility to take care that the laws be faithfully executed. The buck stops with the President, in Harry Truman's famous phrase."[89] In words that could easily be invoked to challenge the very idea of independence, the Court added: "By granting the Board executive power without the Executive's oversight, this Act subverts the President's ability to ensure that the laws are faithfully executed—as well as the public's ability to pass judgment on his efforts. The Act's restrictions are incompatible with the Constitution's separation of powers."[90] By emphasizing the need for the President to have the tools with which to take care that the laws be faithfully executed, the Court planted a seed that could grow over time. The central idea is that unitariness within the executive operates mainly through the particular obligation reflected in the Take Care

---

[86] 130 S. Ct. 3138 (2010).

[87] *Id.* at 3174. A valuable treatment is Peter L. Strauss, *On the Difficulties Of Generalization – PCAOB in the Footsteps of Myers, Humphrey's Executor, Morrison and Freytag,* 32 CARDOZO L. REV. 2255 (2011).

[88] 130 S. Ct. at 3174.

[89] *Id.* at 3152.

[90] *Id.* at 3155.

Clause, which ensures that the President is ultimately responsible for faithful execution and which means that the President must have the tools to carry out that responsibility. That idea is very different from, or at least more specific than, any organizing principle that the Court had offered before.

Decided decades earlier, *Morrison v. Olson*[91] is by contrast a clear Cell (4) case, allowing Congress to create an independent prosecutor who is empowered to investigate and prosecute wrongdoing on the part of high-level executive branch officials. In *Morrison*, the Court did not much engage constitutional text and history. Instead it spoke in pragmatic and functional terms, emphasizing that so long as the President could carry out their constitutionally assigned tasks, Congress could establish an office with a degree of independence from the President.[92] The Court went out of its way to emphasize that the statutory restriction on the President's removal power—"good cause"—left the President with a great deal of authority:

> This is not a case in which the power to remove an executive official has been completely stripped from the President, thus providing no means for the President to ensure the "faithful execution" of the laws. Rather, because the independent counsel may be terminated for "good cause," the Executive, through the Attorney General, retains ample authority to assure that the counsel is competently performing his or her statutory responsibilities in a manner that comports with the provisions of the Act. Although we need not decide in this case exactly what is encompassed within the term "good cause" under the Act, the legislative history of the removal provision also makes clear that the Attorney General may remove an independent counsel for "misconduct."[93]

Here, then, is an emphasis on the centrality of the Take Care Clause, and an insistence that the "good cause" standard was compatible with it.

Even before *Seila Law*, it would have been fair to say that the view associated with Cell (1) enjoyed strong support on the current Court.[94]

---

[91] 487 U.S. 654 (1988).

[92] *Id.* at 691.

[93] *Id.* at 692.

[94] *See* In re Aiken County, 645 F.3d 428, 440 (D.C. Cir. 2011) (Kavanaugh, J., concurring in the judgment). Consider in particular this passage:

> Reading only the text of Article II, one would assume that the Nuclear Regulatory Commission would report to the President, not the President to the Nuclear Regulatory Commission. If two agencies in the Executive Branch were not on the same

It would have been fair to speculate that a majority believed that the independent agency form is constitutionally illegitimate and that *Humphrey's Executor* was wrongly decided, at least as it is currently understood.[95] For such justices, the only question is whether it should be overruled—which brings us directly to the case at hand.

IV. Strongly Unitary

In some ways, the problem in *Seila Law* was straightforward. The Director of the CFPB was protected from presidential removal by the same statutory formula that was at issue in *Humphrey's Executor*: inefficiency, neglect of duty, or malfeasance in office.[96] The most obvious difference between the CFPB and the vast majority of independent agencies is that the former is headed by a single person whereas the latter are headed by multimember commissions.

A. OPTIONS

In these circumstances, the Court had four principal options:

1. It could have upheld the provision apparently guaranteeing independence to the CFPB on the grounds that the number of heads was constitutionally irrelevant and that *Humphrey's Executor* essentially settled the constitutional issue.
2. It could have interpreted the provision apparently guaranteeing independence to the CFPB so as to allow the President to have considerable authority over the bureau's policymaking and concluded that, so interpreted, the provision is constitutionally unobjectionable. An interpretation that would allow the president that authority would have meant that the CFPB was not really

---

page (as may happen in this case if the Nuclear Regulatory Commission rejects the Department of Energy's withdrawal application), the President presumably would have the authority to resolve that disagreement. If an agency were departing from the President's preferred course (as the Nuclear Regulatory Commission may do), the President presumably would have the authority to prevent that. And if an agency were taking too long to make a critical legal or policy decision (as appears to be the case with the Nuclear Regulatory Commission), the President presumably would have the authority to fix that as well.

[95] Recall the Court's pointed statement in *Free Enterprise Fund*: "The parties do not ask us to reexamine any of these precedents, and we do not do so." Free Enter. Fund v. Pub. Co. Acct. Bd., 561 U.S. 477, 483 (2010).

[96] *See Humphrey's Executor*, 295 U.S. at 623.

independent at all—and hence could have weakened and perhaps met the constitutional objection.
3. It could have overruled *Humphrey's Executor* and thus struck down the independent agency form.
4. It could have struck down the provision apparently guaranteeing independence to the CFPB on the ground that independence is permissible only for agencies headed by a multimember commission and not for agencies headed by a single person.

Each of these options could be accompanied, of course, by opinions with very different emphases. Option (2) is evidently attractive, and it could be written in numerous ways that allowed the President more or less in the way of policy control.[97] The Court chose Option (4), but not with a minimalist opinion that strongly affirmed *Humphrey's Executor*, and concluded, modestly and narrowly, that independence was unacceptable when the agency was headed by a single person. Instead, the Court offered the most forceful embrace of the strongly unitary view since *Myers* itself. In the process, the Court's opinion seems to have gutted *Humphrey's Executor* and in a sense to have confined it to its facts in a way that opens up a great deal of room for contemporary challenges to independent agencies.

B. NOT MINIMALIST

Toward the very beginning, the Court's opinion, by Chief Justice Roberts, signaled the sheer magnitude of the issue in the case: "Under our Constitution, the 'executive Power'—all of it—is 'vested in a President,' who must 'take Care that the Laws be faithfully executed.'"[98] Just a few paragraphs thereafter, the Court declared categorically, "The President's power to remove—and thus supervise—those who would wield executive power on his behalf follows from the text of Article II, was settled by the First Congress, and was confirmed in the landmark decision *Myers v. United States*."[99] As the Court explained, "[L]esser officers must remain accountable to the President, whose authority they wield."[100] Emphasizing what it saw as the Decision of

---

[97] *See* Sunstein & Vermeule, *supra* note 19.

[98] *Seila Law*, 140 S. Ct. at 2191.

[99] *Id.* at 2191–92 (citation omitted).

[100] *Id.* at 2197.

1789, the Court explicitly and fully endorsed the analysis in *Myers*; it put a kind of halo around both the holding and the analysis. By contrast, it did not have a favorable word to say about *Humphrey's Executor*.

With *Myers* as the defining case, the Court said that it had recognized only two exceptions to the strongly unitary executive. The first is "expert agencies led by a *group* of principal officers removable by the President only for good cause"; the second is "certain *inferior* officers with narrowly defined duties."[101] The Court said that it would not "extend these precedents to . . . an independent agency that wields significant executive power and is run by a single individual."[102] Pointedly, it said that it "need not and do[es] not revisit our prior decisions"[103]—which is not the most enthusiastic endorsement.

At this point, it would have been possible for the Court to avoid the constitutional question and to embrace Option (2). The Court might have said that the statutory standard allows the President the kind of policymaking control that Article II requires. That conclusion would have had large implications for the President's relationship to a host of independent agencies and the Court refused to offer it. On this count, at least, the Court's analysis is a ringing endorsement of agency independence—as a statutory matter. More specifically:

> *Humphrey's Executor* implicitly rejected an interpretation that would leave the President free to remove an officer based on disagreements about agency policy. In addition, while both *amicus* and the House of Representatives invite us to adopt whatever construction would cure the constitutional problem, they have not advanced any workable standard derived from the statutory language. *Amicus* suggests that the proper standard might permit removals based on *general* policy disagreements, but not *specific* ones; the House suggests that the permissible bases for removal might vary depending on the context and the Presidential power involved. They do not attempt to root either of those standards in the statutory text. Further, although nearly identical language governs the removal of some two-dozen multimember independent agencies, *amicus* suggests that the standard should vary from agency to agency, morphing as necessary to avoid constitutional doubt. We decline to embrace such an uncertain and elastic approach to the text.[104]

---

[101] *Id.* at 2192 (emphasis in original).

[102] *Id.*

[103] *Id.*

[104] *Id.* at 2206 (citations omitted).

The Court added, "Without a proffered interpretation that is rooted in the statutory text and structure, and would avoid the constitutional violation we have identified, we take Congress at its word that it meant to impose a meaningful restriction on the President's removal authority."[105] These words may or may not mean that the President entirely lacks policymaking control over independent agencies. But they certainly mean that the statutory provision that grants independence is a "meaningful restriction"— which means, in the Court's view, that the constitutional issue could not be avoided.

In an important sense, however, the Court did revisit *Humphrey's Executor*, if only by interpretation. The Court took that decision in accordance with its historical context rather than with modern-day understandings of the authorities of the FTC (including rulemaking). In 1935, it would have been plausible to say that the agency did very little that would qualify as narrowly "executive," and insofar as it engaged in quasi-adjudicative and quasi-legislative actions, its powers were sharply limited (and quasi!). As the *Seila Law* Court had it, all that was central to the Court's ruling.[106] On this count, *Seila Law* is exceedingly important; even in the modern era, the Court had never interrogated or narrowed *Humphrey's Executor* in this way.

The Court emphasized that the FTC had several features: it consisted of five members; it had bipartisan membership; and its members had staggered, seven-year terms.[107] And the Court did not stop there. It added that the agency's functions were quasi-judicial and quasi-legislative and in distinctive ways.[108] They were quasi-judicial insofar as the FTC acted as an adjudicator.[109] They were quasi-legislative insofar as the FTC undertook investigations and compiled reports for Congress.[110] Hence the *Humphrey's Executor* exception was strictly limited to "multimember expert agencies that do not wield substantial executive power."[111] If taken at face value, this reading

---

[105] *Id.* at 2207.

[106] *See id.* at 2198.

[107] *See id.* at 2198–99

[108] *See id.*

[109] *See id.*

[110] *See id.*

[111] *Id.* at 2199–2200. The Court added this qualification in a footnote:

> The Court's conclusion that the FTC did not exercise executive power has not withstood the test of time. As we observed in *Morrison* v. *Olson*, 487 U. S. 654

of *Humphrey's Executor*, while historically accurate, is astonishing, because the major multimember independent agencies assuredly do wield "substantial executive power," however defined, and because the passage seems to raise the possibility that their independence is unconstitutional to that extent. Pointedly, the Court declined to embrace the view that *Humphrey's Executor* allows Congress to make agencies independent because and when they engage in rulemaking.[112]

The second exception, stemming above all from *Morrison*, merely said that Congress can protect an inferior officer "lacking policy-making or significant administrative authority" with a for-cause provision.[113] So understood, that exception seems quite narrow. (It is also puzzling; the power to initiate criminal prosecutions might well be taken to qualify as "significant administrative authority." But we bracket that point.)

By contrast, the Director of the CFPB "is hardly a mere legislative or judicial aid."[114] On the contrary, the Director "possesses the authority to promulgate binding rules fleshing out 19 federal statutes, including a broad prohibition on unfair and deceptive practices in a major segment of the U.S. economy."[115] Nor does the Director merely submit "recommended dispositions to an Article III court."[116] It is worth emphasizing this point; unlike the FTC, "the Director may unilaterally issue final decisions awarding legal and equitable relief in administrative adjudications."[117] In addition, the Director's "enforcement authority includes the power to seek daunting monetary penalties against private parties on behalf of the United States in federal

---

(1988), "[I]t is hard to dispute that the powers of the FTC at the time of *Humphrey's Executor* would at the present time be considered 'executive,' at least to some degree." *Id.*, at 690, n. 28. See also *Arlington v. FCC*, 569 U. S. 290, 305, n. 4 (2013) (even though the activities of administrative agencies "take 'legislative' and 'judicial' forms," "they are exercises of—indeed, under our constitutional structure they *must be* exercises of—the 'executive Power'" (quoting Art. II, §1, cl. 1)).

Id. at 2198 n.2. The relationship between this paragraph and the Court's main analysis is puzzling. One way to square the two is to say that even if the FTC's adjudicative-type functions and legislative-type functions "must be" executive, they are not the kinds of functions that must be subject to plenary presidential control.

[112] *See id.* at 2200.

[113] *Id.* at 2199 (quoting *Morrison*, 487 U.S. at 691).

[114] *Id.* at 2200.

[115] *Id.*

[116] *Id.*

[117] *Id.*

court—a quintessentially executive power not considered in *Humphrey's Executor*."[118]

In refusing to extend its prior rulings to this new situation, the Court did not speak in originalist terms. Instead, it worked by reference to historical practice and to high-level principles. Thus, the Court emphasized that the CFPB's structure "is almost wholly unprecedented."[119] Single-headed independent agencies have been very rare. The most prominent example is the Social Security Administration, whose independence "is comparatively recent and controversial." Further, the Social Security Administration "lacks the authority to bring enforcement actions against private parties" and is largely an adjudicative agency.[120]

Even more fundamentally, the Court held that the CFPB's structure was incompatible with the constitutional design, understood in the large, which "scrupulously avoids concentrating power in the hands of any single individual," except in the case of the President, "the most democratic and politically accountable official in Government . . . elected by the entire nation."[121] By contrast, the "single-Director structure contravenes this carefully calibrated system by vesting significant governmental power in the hands of a single individual accountable to no one."[122] The result is to threaten, at once, the core structural principles of self-government and liberty.

Importantly, and in a bow to Cell (4), the Court showed that it was not oblivious to the rise of "'a vast and varied federal bureaucracy.'"[123] In light of that size and variety, the Court said that it had a sharpened "duty to ensure that the Executive Branch is overseen by a President accountable to the people."[124] This is not quite a point about translation, but it is not so far from it, and it can be readily seen as Dworkinian or a form of constitutional common law. The basic idea is that the structural argument for presidential control is strengthened, rather than weakened, by the existence of the modern administrative state.

---

[118] *Id.* (footnote omitted).

[119] *Id.* at 2201.

[120] *Id.* at 2202.

[121] *Id.* at 2203.

[122] *Id.*

[123] *Id.* at 2207 (quoting *Free Enterprise Fund*, 561 U.S. at 499).

[124] *Id.* at 2207.

V. New Doubts, In Brief

It is clear that the CFPB is permitted to continue in operation, now as an executive agency.[125] A noteworthy implication is that it can now be made subject to the review process that is overseen by the Office of Information and Regulatory Affairs, which includes a complex process of interagency review and various analytical requirements, including cost-benefit analysis.[126] For better or for worse, it is permissible to require CFPB regulations to be submitted to OIRA for application of the standard process. It is therefore subject to the control of the Executive Office of the President and ultimately to the judgments of the President personally.

But some fundamental questions are now suddenly open. We have seen that the Court adopted an extremely narrow reading of *Humphrey's Executor*, emphasizing that the FTC (1) did not issue binding rules; (2) merely submitted recommended dispositions to federal courts; and (3) did not wield substantial executive power, which would be wielded if, for example, the FTC were authorized to seek monetary penalties against private parties.[127] Many contemporary independent agencies, including the FTC, exercise much broader powers than that. If the narrow reading of *Humphrey's Executor* is correct, then many of those agencies are in serious constitutional trouble. And indeed, the Court went out of its way to invite that conclusion. In an important footnote, it said that "we take the decision on its own terms, not through a gloss added by a later Court in dicta."[128] It added that "what matters is the set of powers the Court considered as the basis for its decision, not any latent powers that the agency may have had not alluded to by the Court."[129] The Court need not have said all of this, or any of it. It could easily have relied solely on the single fact that the CFPB was a single-headed agency. It could have been silent on the precise authorities of the FTC as the Court understood them in 1935 and thus left the independent status of the multimember commissions unquestioned.

---

[125] This much follows from the Court's analysis of the severability question. That analysis warrants a detailed discussion, but it would take us beyond our topic here.

[126] *See* Cass R. Sunstein, *The Office of Information and Regulatory Affairs: Myths and Realities*, 126 Harv. L. Rev. 1838 (2013).

[127] *See Seila Law*, 140 S. Ct. at 2198.

[128] *Id.* at 2200 n.4.

[129] *Id.*

In this light, it would be possible to mount a serious challenge to many of the current independent agencies, including the Securities and Exchange Commission, the Federal Communications Commission, the Federal Reserve Board, the Nuclear Regulatory Commission, and even the Federal Trade Commission in its current form. The work of each of these agencies—and all other independent agencies—must now be scrutinized to see if they (1) issue binding rules, (2) issue final decisions, in adjudications, ordering relief, (3) seek monetary penalties against private parties, and (4) display other features of concern to the *Seila Law* majority, such as independent budgetary authority. The relationship among these factors is unclear. Perhaps the presence of all four is enough to require an agency to be subject to presidential removal at will; perhaps the presence of even one is enough. It is easily imaginable, at least in principle, that hardly any independent agencies would survive.

We suspect that a majority of the Court would not be prepared to be so aggressive. If it were, the Court would wreak havoc on institutions that have been central to the U.S. government for many decades. But for the first time in decades, the constitutional status of the independent agencies has become insecure.

VI. The Living Constitution

Seila Law claims to be an originalist and textualist opinion—and in some respects, it is. But the Court did not spend a great deal of time on the original public meaning of Article II; it did not engage the competing historical accounts. As is not infrequently the case with originalism, at critical points, the analysis turns to contestable interpretations of abstract principles to decide what the Constitution means. As far as express text is concerned, we have explored the view that the Vesting Clause and the Take Care Clause grant the President unrestricted removal power. But the Constitution says essentially nothing specific about removal as such, and it offers only a few sideways glances at what would today be considered administrative officers. But even if one is inclined to read the Vesting Clause and the Take Care Clause to create a strongly unitary executive, to extrapolate from Article II very specific and reticulated rules—for example, that multimember independent agencies are constitutionally tolerable while single-member independent agencies are intolerable, or that two levels of for-cause removal are intolerable even if one level is tolerable—requires additional premises. The Court finds such premises in "structural inferences" that yield high-level abstract "principles" such as "liberty," "accountability" and "separation of powers." As Justice Kagan wrote in dissent, acutely on this methodological point[130]:

> It is bad enough to "extrapolat[e]" from the "general constitutional language" of Article II's Vesting Clause an unrestricted removal power constraining Congress's ability to legislate under the Necessary and Proper Clause. It is still worse to extrapolate from the Constitution's general structure (division of powers) and implicit values (liberty) a limit on Congress's express power to create administrative bodies. And more: to extrapolate from such sources a distinction as prosaic as that between the SEC and the CFPB—*i.e.*, between a multi-headed and single-headed agency. That is, to adapt a phrase (or two) from our precedent, "more than" the emanations of "the text will bear." By using abstract separation-of-powers arguments for such purposes, the Court "appropriate[s]" the "power delegated to Congress by the Necessary and Proper Clause" to compose the government.

Our point here is not that Justice Kagan is necessarily right or the majority necessarily wrong. It is that the majority is engaged in a process of reasoning from abstract principles of constitutional-political morality—what the Court calls "first principles"[131]—and adopting contested conceptions of those principles in ways that can reasonably be called Dworkinian. If this is originalism, one wonders what is not originalism.[132] It is not surprising, therefore, that the dissent discusses at some length Dean John Manning's argument[133] that the Constitution contains no general, abstract principles such as "the separation of powers." Nor is it surprising that the Court squarely rejected that argument, stating that although "there [is not a] a 'separation of powers clause' or a 'federalism clause' [in the express constitutional text, t]hese foundational doctrines are . . . evident from the Constitution's vesting of certain powers in certain bodies."[134] For the Court,

---

[130] *Seila Law*, 140 S. Ct. at 2243–44 (Kagan, J., concurring in the judgment with respect to severability and dissenting in part) (internal citations omitted).

[131] *Seila Law*, 140 S. Ct. at 2206.

[132] We are bracketing, and not necessarily rejecting, the proposition that the strongly unitary understanding, in its purest form, can be justified on originalist grounds; see above for competing views on that proposition. Our claim here is the Court's analysis, and the distinctions that the Court deems critical, cannot be defended simply by reference to originalism.

[133] *See* John Manning, *Separation of Powers as Ordinary Interpretation*, 124 Harv. L. Rev. 1939 (2011).

[134] *Seila Law*, 140 S. Ct. at 2205.

the text's distribution of certain powers to certain bodies are in fact evidence of true, underlying, subsistent constitutional principles that are themselves part of "the law." If this is not a form of structural analysis, and Dworkinian, it isn't clear what would be.

Consider the Court's most critical legal move, seemingly confining *Humphrey's Executor* to its facts and then declaring that new "exceptions" to presidential removal will not be allowed. This turns out to be a normatively complicated exercise, one resolvable only by arguments about the best interpretation of abstract principles of political morality, such as "liberty" and "accountability." The problem is that which facts are legally relevant cannot be read off from *Humphrey's Executor*, let alone from the vesting of the "executive power" or the Decision of 1789, in any simple way. *Humphrey's Executor* happened to involve an agency whose name begins with an "F"; is that legally relevant? Why not? Or to take a somewhat less random fact: *Humphrey's Executor* happened to involve an agency that was concerned with monopoly and fair competition. Is that relevant? Certainly the fact that the agency's name began with F, and that the FTC dealt with monopoly and fair competition, formed no part of the Court's rationale in 1935. Likewise, *Humphrey's Executor* also happened to involve an agency headed by multiple members, but the difference between multiple heads and a single head was also not a part of the Court's rationale in 1935.[135] If that feature is to make a difference, unlike the myriad of other features one might discern in "the facts," there will have to be a normative argument to that effect.

The Court certainly does offer such arguments; it is not true that the Court simply declares, by fiat, that *Humphrey's Executor* is different. It suggests that in a multimember agency, the members check each other in some way, and that this produces a kind of mutual accountability, an additional safeguard for constitutional liberty[136]:

> The CFPB's single-Director structure contravenes this carefully calibrated system by vesting significant governmental power in the hands of a single individual accountable to no one. . . . [T]he Director may *unilaterally*,

---

[135] It is true that the Court referred on several occasions to the fact that the FTC was a multimember commission—by way of description, not legal argument. *Humphrey's Executor* did in fact make the point about the seven-year terms of the several commissioners as "necessary to the effective and fair administration of the law" in the sentence just before discussing the insulation from complete change in the leadership. See Humphrey's Ex'r v. United States, 295 U.S. 602, 624 (1935). But that was no part of its holding or rationale, and it would be a stretch even to consider the references to be dicta.

[136] *Seila Law*, 140 S. Ct. at 2203–04.

without meaningful supervision, issue final regulations, oversee adjudications, set enforcement priorities, initiate prosecutions, and determine what
penalties to impose on private parties. With no colleagues to persuade, and
no boss or electorate looking over her shoulder, the Director may dictate and
enforce policy for a vital segment of the economy affecting millions of
Americans. . . . [T]he agency's single-Director structure means the President
will not have the opportunity to appoint any other leaders— such as a chair
or fellow members of a Commission or Board—who can serve as a check on
the Director's authority and help bring the agency in line with the President's preferred policies.

The point of these arguments is not that, somewhere in the text
or original understanding of Article II, a distinction is drawn between
single-member-headed agencies and multiple-member-headed agencies. It is that the Court is attributing to the "structure" of the whole
Constitution broad principles and then arguing for a particular conception of those principles. Justice Kagan characterized the Court's conception of "liberty," for example, as one of "anti-power-concentration."[137]
The Court's particular conception is not some straightforward exercise in originalism; it is closer to political philosophy. It is contestable
and premised on a thick, normative view of constitutional liberty.

On the merits, it is hardly obvious, of course, that the Court in fact
has the right conceptions of these contested principles. It is hardly
obvious that the Court was right to say that a single-headed independent agency is worse, from the constitutional point of view, than
an independent agency headed by a multimember commission. Justice
Kagan offered a forceful response, based on different conceptions of
the same principles[138]:

If a removal provision violates the separation of powers, it is because the
measure so deprives the President of control over an official as to impede
his own constitutional functions. But with or without a for-cause removal
provision, the President has at least as much control over an individual as
over a commission—and possibly more. That means the constitutional concern is, if anything, ameliorated when the agency has a single head.

Ultimately, however, the merits are not the point. The key thing
is that the Court's "originalism" ends up deeply engaged in arguments about competing conceptions of abstract principles of political
morality.

[137] *Id.* at 2243 (Kagan, J., concurring in the judgment with respect to severability and
dissenting in part).
[138] *Id.* at 2255.

In this light, *Seila Law* is best understood not as a vindication of the original understanding, and hence as a Cell (1) case, but in terms of Cell (2), as a response to contemporary fears and concerns, expressed in terms of political morality. Many observers, and several of the justices themselves, have expressed grave concerns about the rise of a powerful administrative apparatus that often exercises broad discretion.[139] Those concerns have been manifested in multiple domains, including heightened interest in the nondelegation doctrine[140] and intense skepticism about judicial deference to agency interpretations of law.[141] Serious concerns about the administrative state seem to define the modern era.[142]

On one view, the rise of the modern administrative state is a kind of constitutional barnacle, raising real threats to core constitutional values. That view could be founded in Cell (2), not Cell (4). The idea of a strongly unitary executive might seem a necessary corrective.[143] If administrative agencies are going to have a great deal of discretion and wield awesome power, a minimal requirement might be that they must act under the constraining arm of an elected President. Perhaps that is an essential way of maintaining continuity with core constitutional commitments under unanticipated circumstances. On this view, *Seila Law* can be seen as the culmination (thus far) of a sustained and emphatically modern effort to insist on the strongly unitary executive as a response to the problem of administrative discretion.[144] Indeed, it can be taken as a close sibling to *District of Columbia v. Heller*,[145] also written in originalist terms but plausibly taken as a response to contemporary concerns.

Here is another way to put the point. We have noted that in his work on legal reasoning, Dworkin urged that judges have a duty to fit the existing legal materials and also to justify them, in the sense of putting them in the best constructive light.[146] *Seila Law* can easily be

---

[139] For a summary, *see* Cass R. Sunstein & Adrian Vermeule, Law and Leviathan (2020).

[140] *See, e.g.*, Gundy v. United States, 139 S. Ct. 2116, 2131–48 (2019) (Gorsuch, J., dissenting).

[141] *See, e.g.*, Kisor v. Wilkie, 139 S. Ct. 2400, 2425–48 (2019) (Gorsuch, J., dissenting).

[142] *See generally* Philip Hamburger, Is Administrative Law Unlawful? (2014).

[143] *See* Mistretta v. United States, 488 U.S. 361, 422–27 (1989) (Scalia, J., dissenting).

[144] *See* Miller, *supra* note 37.

[145] 554 U.S. 570 (2008).

[146] *See* Dworkin, *supra* note 12.

seen as a case for which the existing legal materials were indeterminate. As we have seen, plausible opinions could take multiple forms. In choosing the approach it did, the majority claimed to speak in originalist terms, but it quickly turned to judgments, grounded in abstract principles, about what would make the constitutional order the best that it could be. On that view, the Court's emphasis on accountability and liberty, and its sharpened duty under contemporary circumstances, were not throwaway lines. They were essential.

VII. Conclusion

For many decades, there has been a sharp dispute between those who believe in a strongly unitary presidency, in accordance with the idea that the President must have unrestricted removal power over high-level officials entrusted with implementation of federal law, and those who believe in a weakly unitary presidency, in accordance with the view that Congress may, under the Necessary and Proper Clause, restrict the President's removal power so long as the restriction does not prevent the President from carrying out the President's constitutionally specified functions.

Both positions can claim some support from the original understanding of relevant clauses; both can also claim to keep faith with constitutional commitments in light of dramatically changed circumstances, above all the rise of the modern administrative state. In *Seila Law*, the Court wholeheartedly accepted the strongly unitary position, in an opinion that appeared to accept *Humphrey's Executor* but that read the case so narrowly that it left a great deal of room for constitutional challenges to many independent regulatory commissions in their present form. The Court's analysis purports to be rooted in the original understanding of the constitutional text, and its conclusion can certainly claim support from that understanding. But that conclusion might also be understood and defended as a response to contemporary fears and concerns about a powerful, discretion-wielding administrative state—and as reflective of a judgment that a necessary response to those concerns is a firm insistence on firm presidential control.

CARY FRANKLIN

LIVING TEXTUALISM

In 2020, the Court held in *Bostock v. Clayton County* that discrimination on the basis of sexual orientation and gender identity is discrimination "because of sex" and therefore violates Title VII of the 1964 Civil Rights Act.[1] That landmark holding extended federal antidiscrimination protection to millions of gay and transgender workers.[2] But that is not the only axis on which *Bostock* was transformative. For the past twenty-five years, the Court has adopted a living constitutionalist approach to gay rights—an approach that takes account of "evolving understanding[s] of the meaning of equality" in interpreting old laws.[3] *Bostock* rejects living constitutionalism in favor of

Cary Franklin is McDonald/Wright Chair of Law, UCLA School of Law.

AUTHOR'S NOTE: I am deeply grateful to Reid Coleman, Justin Driver, Katie Eyer, Joey Fishkin, Tara Leigh Grove, Will Leathers, Richard Re, and Reva Siegel for their helpful comments and suggestions. My thanks also to Jill Applegate, Julia Camp, Sarah Fernandez, and Zoraima Pelaez for excellent research assistance.

[1] 140 S. Ct. 1731, 1737 (2020).

[2] *See* KERITH J. CONRON & SHOSHANA K. GOLDBERG, LGBT PEOPLE IN THE U.S. NOT PROTECTED BY STATE NON-DISCRIMINATION STATUTES 1, WILLIAMS INST., UCLA SCH. L. (Apr. 2020), https://williamsinstitute.law.ucla.edu/wp-content/uploads/LGBT-ND-Protections-Update -Apr-2020.pdf (reporting, just prior to *Bostock*, that there were 8.1 million LGBT workers in the U.S. over the age of 16, and that nearly half lived in states without statutory protections against anti-LGBT discrimination in the workplace).

[3] Windsor v. United States, 570 U.S. 744, 769 (2013); *see also* Obergefell v. Hodges, 576 U.S. 644, 664 (2015) (observing that "[t]he nature of injustice is that we may not always see it in our own times" and asserting that the scope of concepts like liberty and equality will evolve "as we learn [their] meaning"); *Obergefell*, 576 U.S. at 673 ("[T]he Court has recognized that new insights and societal understandings can reveal unjustified inequality within our most fundamental institutions that once passed unnoticed and unchallenged."); Lawrence v. Texas,

The Supreme Court Review, 2021.

textualism—an approach that eschews "evolving understandings" and seeks to enforce a law's original public meaning: the meaning the "words on the page [would] have conveyed to the reasonable speaker of English in the relevant audience at the time of enactment."[4] As a result, *Bostock* engages in a very different sort of analysis from the Court's other gay rights decisions. It does not rely on the "new insights and societal understandings"[5] that played a central role in the same-sex marriage decisions. In fact, the Court in *Bostock* blames "societal understandings" over the past half-century for clouding our vision and preventing us from recognizing that, as a matter of ordinary meaning, Title VII's prohibition on sex discrimination has always barred discrimination against gay and transgender people.

Commentators have hailed *Bostock* as a "triumph for textualism"[6]; "a new highwater mark for textualism, as *District of Columbia v. Heller* was for originalism"[7]; confirmation of Justice Elena Kagan's endlessly quoted observation that "[w]e're all textualists now."[8] This assessment stems in part from the fact that all of the opinions in *Bostock*—the majority and the two dissents—embrace textualism. Not too long ago, textualism was an insurgent methodology. It took shape alongside its close cousin, originalism, as part of a campaign by Reagan-era conservatives to develop "antidotes to the 'judicial activism' of the Warren and Burger Courts."[9] Those early conservative

---

539 U.S. 558, 579 (2003) ("[T]imes can blind us to certain truths and later generations can see that laws once thought necessary and proper in fact serve only to oppress. As the Constitution endures, persons in every generation can invoke its principles in their own search for greater freedom.").

[4] Randy E. Barnett, *The Gravitational Force of Originalism*, 82 FORDHAM L. REV. 411, 417 (2013).

[5] *Obergefell*, 576 U.S. at 673.

[6] Jonathan Skrmetti, *Symposium: The Triumph of Textualism: "Only the Written Word is the Law,"* SCOTUSBLOG (June 15, 2020, 9:04 PM), https://www.scotusblog.com/2020/06/symposium-the-triumph-of-textualism-only-the-written-word-is-the-law/; *see also* Daniel Hemel, *The Problem with That Big Gay Rights Decision? It's Not Really About Gay Rights*, WASH. POST (June 17, 2020, 5:00 AM), https://www.washingtonpost.com/outlook/2020/06/17/problem-with-that-big-gay-rights-decision-its-not-really-about-gay-rights/; Ezra Ishmael Young, *Bostock is a Textualist Triumph*, JURIST (June 25, 2020, 3:53 PM), https://www.jurist.org/commentary/2020/06/ezra-young-bostock-textualist-triumph/.

[7] Skrmetti, *supra* note 6.

[8] Justice Elena Kagan, *The Scalia Lecture: A Dialogue with Justice Kagan on the Reading of Statutes*, at 8:29 (Nov. 17, 2015), http://today.law.harvard.edu/in-scalia-lecture-kagan-discusses-statutory-interpretation.

[9] Margaret H. Lemos, *The Politics of Statutory Interpretation*, 89 NOTRE DAME L. REV. 849, 853 (2013).

adopters argued that other modes of statutory interpretation (purposivism, pluralism) do not yield determinate answers and thus invite "judges to imbue authoritative texts with their own policy preferences"[10]—preferences that inevitably reflect contemporary (elite) social values and not the values of the people who democratically enacted the law.[11] Textualism was intended to combat judicial presentism and policymaking by providing judges with a "single truthmaker"[12]: original public meaning. When judges apply this meaning, they are—on the textualist's view—applying the law as written, the law that satisfied the requirements of bicameralism and presentment,[13] the law that reflects the will of the people and not the preferences of today's judiciary.[14]

For many, the fact that *Bostock*'s uniquely high-profile application of textualism resulted in a victory for gay and transgender people cemented its triumph. Textualism has long been associated with political conservatism: it is the Federalist Society's methodology of choice[15]; its most prominent champions include Justice Antonin Scalia and other

---

[10] Antonin Scalia & Bryan A. Garner, Reading Law: The Interpretation of Legal Texts at xxviii (2012).

[11] *See, e.g.*, Obergefell v. Hodges, 576 U.S. 644, 718 (2015) (Scalia, J., dissenting) ("[T]o allow the policy question of same-sex marriage to be considered and resolved by a select, patrician, highly unrepresentative panel of nine is to violate a principle even more fundamental than no taxation without representation: no social transformation without representation."); Lawrence v. Texas, 539 U.S. 558, 603–04 (2003) (Scalia, J., dissenting) ("It is indeed true that 'later generations can see that laws once thought necessary and proper in fact serve only to oppress' . . . But . . . those judgments are to be made by the people, and not imposed by a governing caste that knows best." (internal citations omitted)); Romer v. Evans, 517 U.S. 620, 636 (1996) (Scalia, J., dissenting) ("This Court has no business imposing upon all Americans the resolution favored by the elite class from which the Members of this institution are selected, pronouncing that 'animosity' toward homosexuality, is evil.").

[12] William Baude, *Originalism as a Constraint on Judges*, 84 U. Chi. L. Rev. 2213, 2227 (2017).

[13] *See* Bostock v. Clayton County, 140 S. Ct. 1731, 1755 (2020) (Alito, J., concurring) (arguing that only sections of text that have satisfied Article I requirements of "passage in both Houses and presentment to the President" count as law).

[14] *See* Neil Gorsuch, A Republic, If You Can Keep It 132 (2019) ("Textualism honors only what's survived bicameralism and presentment and not what hasn't. The text of the statute and only the text becomes law. Not a legislator's unexpressed intentions, not nuggets buried in the legislative history, and certainly not a judge's policy preferences.").

[15] Donald B. Ayer, 2019 Higgins Distinguished Visitor Lecture: The Subversive Side of Textualism and Original Intent (Mar. 11, 2019), *in* 24 Lewis & Clark L. Rev. 1049, 1054 (2020) (attributing the rise of textualism to the Reagan Administration's effort to restrain perceived judicial activism and the Federalist Society's "coordinated support and evangelism" for this project on law school campuses); Senator Ted Cruz, Second Annual Gregory S. Coleman Memorial Lecture (Sept. 14, 2019), *in* 24 Tex. Rev. L. & Pol. 283, 286 (2019) (describing textualism and originalism as "the two legal principles . . . at the heart of the founding of The Federalist Society").

famous conservative jurists[16]; and, in practice, it tends to produce legal outcomes consistent with conservative policy preferences.[17] For a theory whose claim to fame is its objectivity and political neutrality, these associations are discomfiting. Thus, when Republican Senator Josh Hawley responded to *Bostock* by publicly denouncing textualism for failing to produce reliably conservative results,[18] it was like winning all over again. Proponents of textualism took to the media, declaring that *Bostock* "shore[s] up textualism's bona fides"[19] and proves "that textualist methodology . . . can yield progressive or conservative results, depending on what the text says."[20] "If what matters most to you are the results in specific cases," proponents exulted, "you may want non-originalist judges."[21] But if you would prefer an objective and politically neutral methodology that enables judges "to transcend our moral disagreements" and simply apply the rule of law, textualism is the approach for you.[22]

---

[16] Orin S. Kerr, *Shedding Light on Chevron: An Empirical Study of the Chevron Doctrine in the U.S. Courts of Appeals*, 15 YALE J. ON REG. 1, 28 (1998) (observing that "textualism is strongly associated with Reagan and Bush judges"); Thomas J. Miles & Cass R. Sunstein, *Do Judges Make Regulatory Policy? An Empirical Investigation of Chevron*, 73 U. CHI. L. REV. 823, 828–29 (2006) ("[A]s an empirical matter, the more conservative justices (Justices Antonin Scalia and Clarence Thomas) have embraced 'plain meaning' approaches and the more liberal justices have not."); Caleb Nelson, *What Is Textualism?*, 91 VA. L. REV. 347, 373 (2005) (observing that "today's textualists tend to be politically conservative").

[17] *See* Neil H. Buchanan & Michael C. Dorf, *A Tale of Two Formalisms: How Law and Economics Mirrors Originalism and Textualism*, 106 CORNELL L. REV. (forthcoming 2020) (manuscript at 37–42) (on file with author) (observing that judges applying textualist and originalist methods of interpretation reach conservative results in the vast majority of cases); Lemos, *supra* note 9, at 901 ("[T]extualism has become a conservative brand. . . . The strength of the brand is reinforced by what we observe in the practice of textualism: we see conservative judges advocating the methodology, and we see those same judges reaching conservative results in most cases.").

[18] Senator Josh Hawley, *Was It All for This? The Failure of the Conservative Legal Movement*, PUB. DISCOURSE (June 16, 2020), https://www.thepublicdiscourse.com/2020/06/65043/.

[19] Young, *supra* note 6.

[20] Lawrence B. Solum, *Judge Barrett Is an Originalist. Should We Be Afraid?*, L.A. TIMES (Oct. 14, 2020, 1:31 PM), https://www.latimes.com/opinion/story/2020-10-14/amy-coney-barrett -supreme-court-originalism-conservative; *see also* Damon Root, *How Gorsuch Took a Page from Scalia in an LGBT Employment Discrimination Case*, REASON (June 15, 2020, 4:15 PM), https://reason.com /2020/06/15/how-gorsuch-took-a-page-from-scalia-in-an-lgbt-employment-discrimination -case/ (citing *Bostock* as evidence that textualism is objective and politically neutral and allows judges to set aside personal policy preferences and simply apply the rule of law).

[21] William Baude, *Conservatives, Don't Give Up on Your Principles or the Supreme Court*, N.Y. TIMES (July 9, 2020), https://www.nytimes.com/2020/07/09/opinion/supreme-court-originalism -conservatism.html.

[22] *Id.*; *see also* George F. Will, *The Supreme Court's LGBTQ Decision Shows the Conflicting Ideas of Textualism*, WASH. POST (June 16, 2020), https://www.washingtonpost.com/opinions

It is certainly true that textualism can yield progressive or conservative results.[23] *Bostock* demonstrates as much—but not, this Article argues, for the reasons textualism's proponents claim. *Bostock* does not demonstrate that textualism is neutral or objective, that textualism enables judges to put aside contemporary social values and simply apply the rule of law, or that textualism provides a means of "transcend[ing] our moral disagreements." What it demonstrates is that textualism is no more capable of providing a neutral truthmaker or of cabining the influence of evolving social values than any other leading method of statutory interpretation. All three of the opinions in *Bostock* purport to apply Title VII's original public meaning. But *Bostock* is not a product of 1964. It is a product of 2020. It reflects today's moral values and partakes in current forms of legal and social contestation—over same-sex marriage, gender identity, and religious liberty—and that is just as true of the dissenting opinions as it is of the majority opinion.

The problem is not that the Justices in *Bostock* were insufficiently disciplined or did not try hard enough to eradicate present-day understandings from their interpretation of the law. The problem is that textualism does not actually provide judges with a means of excising current "value judgments about persons or policies"[24] from the interpretation of contested legal texts. This Article examines some of the reasons why, starting with the fact that, as Justice Gorsuch observes, "the cases that land in the Supreme Court are the hardest ones in our legal system."[25] On a granular level, there may be various factors specific to a given case that make statutory interpretation hard. The meaning of a contested text might be particularly ambiguous or particularly standard-like. However, what is generally true of the cases that reach the Court is that they are strongly contested. They are the site of significant, often sustained, legal conflict, and—especially now that we're all textualists—they are the subject of multiple, competing textual interpretations. It would be surprising if text alone clearly and

---

/the-supreme-courts-decision-on-lgbtq-protections-shows-the-conflicting-ideas-of-text ualism/2020/06/16/c6979b76-aff8-11ea-8758-bfd1d045525a_story.html (asserting that "the unchanged meaning of the 1964 language entails the conclusion that the court's majority reached," and gently chiding "Gorsuch's conservative critics [for] reasoning backward from a policy outcome of which they disapprove, thereby embracing the result-oriented jurisprudence they usually associate with judicial liberalism").

[23] Lemos, *supra* note 9, at 906–07.

[24] GORSUCH, *supra* note 14, at 130.

[25] *Id.* at 112.

unambiguously resolved such cases with any degree of frequency. As Victoria Nourse puts it: "If grammar alone were enough, the case would never have ended up in the Supreme Court."[26]

Textualism and originalism—or, at least, the increasingly dominant version of originalism that shares textualism's focus on original public meaning—start from the opposite premise. Justice Scalia acknowledged that seekers of original public meaning might occasionally disagree with one another, but he argued that "usually . . . [original public meaning] is easy to discern and simple to apply."[27] Justice Gorsuch argues the same: that "texts are not . . . usually indeterminate" and that "'[s]tatutory ambiguities are less like dandelions on an unmowed lawn than they are like manufacturing defects in a modern automobile: they happen, but they are pretty rare.'"[28] The claim is that "statutes do not change,"[29] original public meaning is fixed at the moment of enactment, and judges in almost all cases can easily locate and apply that meaning using "preexisting, neutral, and objective interpretive tools."[30] On occasion, textualist judges (and somewhat more frequently, textualist academics) acknowledge it might not actually be as simple as that.[31] But Justice Gorsuch insists, "at least when we use the value-neutral tools of textualism the dispute remains a distinctly legal one carried out in legal terms."[32] That is clearly preferable to living or

---

[26] Victoria Nourse, *Textualism 3.0: Statutory Interpretation After Justice Scalia*, 70 ALA. L. REV. 667, 681 (2019).

[27] ANTONIN SCALIA, A MATTER OF INTERPRETATION: FEDERAL COURTS AND THE LAW 45 (1997).

[28] GORSUCH, *supra* note 14, at 136 (quoting Judge Raymond Kethledge).

[29] SCALIA, *supra* note 27, at 40.

[30] GORSUCH, *supra* note 14, at 132.

[31] *See, e.g.*, GORSUCH, *supra* note 14, at 135 (acknowledging the criticism "that textualism does not yield determinate answers . . . and that meaning is always and ultimately controlled by the interpreter, not the text itself," and suggesting "this argument perhaps contains a nugget of truth" before generally rejecting it); Antonin Scalia, *Originalism: The Lesser Evil*, 57 U. CIN. L. REV. 849, 863–64 (1989) (acknowledging that the search for original meaning is "sometimes inconclusive"; asserting "that one cannot realistically expect judges (probably myself included) to apply [originalist methods] without a trace of constitutional perfectionism"; and "fall[ing] back upon G.K. Chesterton's observation that a thing worth doing is worth doing badly"). For a discussion of textualist scholars' various concessions and acknowledgements that this methodology does not always deliver on its promises, see Dorf & Buchanan, *supra* note 17 (manuscript at 34–37); Jeremy K. Kessler & David E. Pozen, *Working Themselves Impure: A Life Cycle Theory of Legal Theories*, 83 U. CHI. L. REV. 1819, 1848–54 (2016); Jonathan T. Molot, *The Rise and Fall of Textualism*, 106 COLUM. L. REV. 1 *passim* (2006).

[32] GORSUCH, *supra* note 14, at 136.

dynamic approaches that have no fixed rules, that are "fickle"[33] and unpredictable, and that allow judges to pick and choose from among different forms of evidence depending on what they think the law "*ought* to mean."[34]

Textualism and public meaning originalism do not offer more objectivity or determinacy than their more explicitly dynamic counterparts, however. What they offer is the illusion of those characteristics. At the core of the illusion is the premise that original public meaning is something fixed and determinate that judges merely uncover by consulting period sources. In reality, original public meaning is a judicial construct. It is not something judges find, but something they produce—and something they need to produce because, in the kind of conflicts that reach the Court, there generally is not a single truth of the matter from a semantic standpoint. That may be because the meaning of the statutory text is particularly underdetermined, but it is also because the meaning of that text has been put in contest. And, particularly over time, that contest changes the terrain on which we argue about the statute's meaning and alters the parameters of what counts as a plausible interpretation of the text. The title *Living Textualism* is meant to capture this evolutionary process, and to suggest that, at its core, textualism is no less "living" than any other leading method of statutory interpretation. Indeed, this Article shows that textualism is a form of dynamic statutory interpretation—one that proceeds by making and remaking the original public meaning of contested statutory text over time.[35]

---

[33] *Id*. at 112.

[34] SCALIA, *supra* note 27, at 18; *see also* Baude, *supra* note 12, at 2229 ("[I]t remains of some importance that originalism operates as an internal constraint. . . . That fact sets originalism aside from what has been called its greatest competitor—constitutional pluralism, most forms of which fail to contain a single 'truthmaker.'").

[35] My project differs in this way (and others) from Jack Balkin's "living originalism." *See* JACK M. BALKIN, LIVING ORIGINALISM (2011). My aim is not to construct a new hybrid theory of textualism or to expand the parameters of textualism to incorporate some of the insights or mechanisms of other, more explicitly dynamic interpretative methodologies. Fidelity to "original semantic meaning," *id*. at 37, is a key component of Balkin's theory; that concept is precisely what this Article critiques. What I mean to convey by the term "living textualism" is that textualism is itself a "living" form of interpretation. In this sense, my argument is closer to the one Reva Siegel makes when she frames originalism as a form of living constitutionalism in *Dead or Alive: Originalism as Popular Constitutionalism in* Heller, 122 HARV. L. REV. 191, 192 (2008); *id*. at 192 (aiming to "show how *Heller*'s originalism enforces understandings of the Second Amendment that were forged in the late twentieth century through popular constitutionalism").

Of course, this claim runs directly counter to textualist theory. The textualists on the Court insist that, by consulting a dictionary or a corpus linguistics database and examining the text in context, they can easily discern the single, unambiguous meaning of Title VII's sex provision and then apply that meaning in an entirely text-driven, value-free way. One result of this simultaneous need to rely and deny reliance on extratextual considerations is that much of the work in *Bostock*—and in textualist opinions more generally—takes place at what this Article calls *shadow decision points*: generally unacknowledged, often outcome-determinative choices about how to interpret statutory text that are framed as methodological but that are typically fueled by substantive extratextual concerns.

Examples of such shadow decision points include, but are not limited to: which bits of statutory text to subject to textualist analysis; whether to consult a dictionary or a corpus linguistics database or both; which dictionary and/or database to use; which definition to select, if, as often occurs, there are several to choose from; how literally to take that definition; whether to deem the text "ambiguous" and what quantum of ambiguity is sufficient to permit the consultation of some wider unspecified set of extratextual sources; how strongly to weigh original expected applications in determining original public meaning; when to deem a statute amended in a relevant way, potentially substantially altering the appropriate date for determining its original meaning; whether to consult and what significance to attach to earlier versions of a statute, including earlier drafts of the bill that ultimately became law or the original version of a statute that has since been amended[36]; and because textualists acknowledge that "statutory prohibitions often go beyond the principal evil to cover reasonably comparable evils,"[37] what is the "principal evil" the statute addresses and what sorts of conduct are sufficiently comparable to that evil to also violate the statute.

There is a growing literature showing how textualist and originalist judges' choices at such points have influenced the outcome of high-stakes cases and how dependent those choices have been on

---

[36] *See* Anita S. Krishnakumar, *Statutory History*, 108 Va. L. Rev. (forthcoming 2022) (manuscript at iii, 4) (on file with author) (finding that "the Justices on the Roberts Court exercise significant discretion when drawing inferences from statutory history" and that a substantial majority "of the statutory history inferences the Court employs conflict in some way with the parameters textualists have articulated to distinguish statutory history from traditional legislative history").

[37] Oncale v. Sundowner Offshore Servs., Inc., 523 U.S. 75 (1997).

unacknowledged extratextual considerations.[38] Victoria Nourse has
an astute article entitled *Picking and Choosing Text*, which demonstrates, by examining a series of textualist decisions, that the choice to
focus on "one piece of text over another can amount to assuming that
which one is trying to prove" and "can put the thumb on the scales of
any interpretation."[39] Justice Kavanaugh has made the same point
about the choice of whether to label a text ambiguous—a key and potentially outcome-determinative step in textualist analysis because it
determines whether a judge may look to sources beyond the text—such
as legislative history—to decipher its meaning. "[D]eterminations of
ambiguity dominate statutory interpretation in a way that few people
realize,"[40] Justice Kavanaugh writes, and such determinations "matter[]
in a huge way in many cases of critical importance to the Nation."[41] But,
he contends, "[t]he simple and troubling truth is that there is no definitive guide for determining whether statutory language is clear or
ambiguous"[42] and "often no good or predictable way" to make this
determination.[43] Much of the time, "there is no right answer."[44] This,
he argues, "is a major problem for the Scalia vision of constraining the
discretion of judges and for the corresponding Roberts vision of the
judge as umpire."[45]

---

[38] Some major works questioning the determinacy and objectivity of textualist analysis include
William N. Eskridge, Jr., Interpreting Law: A Primer on How to Read Statutes and the
Constitution (2016); Robert A. Katzmann, Judging Statutes (2014); and Victoria F.
Nourse, Misreading Law, Misreading Democracy (2016). All of these authors have numerous
other pieces on this subject as well, as do Richard Fallon, Abbe Gluck, Anita Krishnakumar, Kevin
Tobia, and others.

[39] Victoria Nourse, *Picking and Choosing Text: Lessons for Statutory Interpretation from the
Philosophy of Language*, 69 Fla. L. Rev. 1409, 1412, 1409 (2017).

[40] Brett M. Kavanaugh, Keynote Address: Two Challenges for the Judge as Umpire: Statutory
Ambiguity and Constitutional Exceptions, *in* 92 Notre Dame L. Rev. 1907, 1913 (2017).

[41] *Id.* at 1910; *see also* Brett M. Kavanaugh, *Fixing Statutory Interpretation*, 129 Harv. L. Rev.
2118, 2140 (2016) (reviewing Katzmann, *supra* note 38 ("A number of important Supreme
Court decisions have implicated the clarity versus ambiguity problem.").

[42] Kavanaugh, *supra* note 40, at 1910.

[43] Kavanaugh, *supra* note 41, at 2136.

[44] Kavanaugh, *supra* note 40, at 1910 ("Here's my biggest problem. . . . [H]ow do courts
know when a statute is clear or ambiguous? . . . Judges go back and forth. One judge will say it
is clear. Another judge will say, 'No, it's ambiguous.' Neither judge can convince the other.
Why not? The answer is that there is no right answer. There are two separate problems here.
First, how much clarity is enough? Sixty-forty? Eighty-twenty? Who knows. Second, let's
imagine we can agree on eighty-twenty. How do we apply that? How do we know whether
and when a statute is eighty percent clear?").

[45] *Id.* at 1913; *see also id.* at 1911 (arguing that the fact that "there is no coherent way to
determine whether a statute is clear or ambiguous . . . is a problem for the goal of neutral

Textualism has risen to prominence on this vision of judges as umpires—on the claim that it provides a way of keeping values and other extratextual considerations out of judging by enabling judges to enforce the law as written and nothing more. But textualism does not exclude such considerations from judicial decision-making, it simply makes judges' reliance on those considerations harder to see. This Article shines a light on this dynamic by examining the Justices' various accounts of original public meaning in *Bostock* and in anti-discrimination law more generally. It shows: a) how much of the work involved in identifying and applying the original public meaning of a contested law occurs at shadow decision points; b) how infrequently textualist judges acknowledge they are even making choices at these points; and c) how consistently extratextual considerations are smuggled in at these points to enable textualist judges to reach conclusions not clearly required by the text. In sum, this Article shows how judges working at shadow decision points produce the original public meaning textualist methodology purports to discover. Textualism does not eliminate judicial discretion, but it does mask it. That, this Article argues, is primarily what sets textualism apart from other dynamic interpretive approaches: not the degree to which it constrains judicial discretion, but the degree to which it renders the exercise of that discretion visible and thus professionally and democratically accountable.

Part I analyzes the mechanics of the Justices' textualist analysis in *Bostock*. It shows that they barely acknowledge and do not justify the ostensibly methodological choices they make—and that they make different methodological choices in closely related contexts, sometimes within the same opinion or in other opinions interpreting the same piece of statutory text. Upon examination, it is apparent that their forays into dictionaries and corpora are not the real drivers of the legal conclusions in *Bostock*. The real drivers lie elsewhere—not in clashes over the finer points of textualism but in unstated extratextual judgments about the proper scope of Title VII. Those same judgments fuel the Justices' application of (their preferred version of) the statute's original public meaning. Part I ends by showing that

---

statutory interpretation"); Kavanaugh, *supra* note 41, at 2138–39 (arguing that "[b]ecause judgments about clarity versus ambiguity turn on little more than a judge's instincts," policy preferences inevitably seep in, and that such "preferences can seep into ambiguity determinations in subconscious ways" because "judges don't make the clarity versus ambiguity determination behind a veil of ignorance" (footnotes omitted)).

applying even the majority's "simple" anticlassificationist under-standing of Title VII requires significant extratextual judgment. Part II shows that the same is true of the dissenters' more overtly culturally-attuned antisubordinationist understanding of the law, and that the dissenting Justices apply that understanding in a blatantly inconsistent manner, jettisoning it altogether when it comes to race despite the fact that Title VII bars race discrimination and sex discrimination in the same sentence using the same words.

Progressives often fault interpretive methodologies that privilege original public meaning for tethering us to old understandings un-suited to the modern era: the dead hand problem. That criticism is not entirely fair. As this Article shows, textualism does not neces-sarily bind us to the past. Original public meaning is a moving target; it evolves over time, in part through the very sort of contestation that occurs in *Bostock*. The more substantial problem with textualism, from a democratic perspective, is that it vastly aggrandizes judicial power. It enables judges to rely on normative and other forms of extratextual judgment while denying that they are doing so; it enables them to decide matters of paramount social importance without providing the people and their elected representatives with a complete account of their reasoning. That creates democratic accountability problems, and it also creates rule-of-law problems. It liberates judges from the burden of demonstrating that their conclusions are based in law and it deprives those governed by law of any real sense of the principles guiding judicial interpretation and of the likely implications of legal precedent. *Bostock* exemplifies these problems. The Justices contend they are simply obeying the dictates of a long-ago public. But the real work in their opinions happens in the shadows. That is different from the dead hand problem. It is the Court exerting its own will, making its own inevitably value-laden choices, falsely claiming its hands were tied.

I. SHADOW DECISION POINTS IN THE MAKING OF TITLE VII'S ORIGINAL PUBLIC MEANING

Commentators have already begun to cast *Bostock* as this gen-eration's equivalent of *Texas v. Johnson*,[46] the case in which Justice Scalia agreed that the First Amendment protects flag burning: a

---

[46] 491 U.S. 397 (1989).

decision that purportedly cuts against a Justice's policy preferences
and therefore proves the objectivity of his interpretive methodology.[47]
Justice Scalia rarely missed an opportunity to emphasize how much he
hated the outcome in the flag burning case and how quickly he would
throw the flag burner, whom he referred to as a "bearded weirdo," in
jail if he were king.[48] The point he was trying to make (and that many of
his fellow textualists have made subsequently) is that he could not do
as he liked because he "ha[d] . . . rules that confine[d]" him: Once he
"f[ound] . . . the original meaning" of a legal text, he was "handcuffed"
and could not "do all the mean conservative things [he] would like."[49]
After *Bostock*, some conservative commentators asserted that, once
again, "[p]rogressive critics" who portray textualist Justices as "result-
oriented reactionaries have egg on their face."[50] By siding with the
LGBT plaintiffs, Justice Gorsuch demonstrated that he too was handcuffed by the text and would not allow policy preferences to hamper
his enforcement of original public meaning.

    As a preliminary matter, it is not at all clear that Justice Gorsuch
dislikes gay and transgender people and wishes he could do to them
what Justice Scalia wanted to do to the flag burner. Approximately

[47] *See, e.g.*, Akhil Reed Amar, *Justices Shrug Off Politics*, N.Y. Times, July 15, 2020, at A23 (citing Justice Gorsuch's decision in *Bostock* as evidence that "there is no aisle on the Supreme Court bench"); Noah Feldman, *The Supreme Court Is Still Capable of Shocking the Nation* (July 14, 2020), https://www.bloombergquint.com/opinion/justices-roberts-gorsuch-show-supreme-court -can-still-surprise ("Justice Neil Gorsuch revealed himself as so highly principled in his com- mitment to textualist statutory interpretation that he will carry its logic to conclusions that liberals love. . . . Now liberal academics like me have to admit that he is a serious justice with a serious judicial philosophy that he follows where it logically goes.").

[48] Erin Fuchs, *Justice Scalia Says He Would Jail This "Bearded Weirdo" If He Were King*, Bus. Insider (Mar. 26, 2014, 3:38 PM), http://www.businessinsider.com/scalia-talks-texas-v-johnson -at-brooklyn-law-2014-3; *see also, e.g.*, James F. McCarty, *Scalia Says His Beliefs, His Feelings Can Differ: He Tells How He Had to Side with Flag Burner*, Plain Dealer, Mar. 20, 2003, at B4; Frank Sikora, *Justice Scalia: Constitution Allows 'Really Stupid' Things*, Birmingham News, Apr. 14, 1999, at 3D; Margaret Talbot, *Supreme Confidence: The Jurisprudence of Justice Antonin Scalia*, New Yorker, Mar. 28, 2005, at 40, 43.

[49] Justice Antonin Scalia, Constitutional Interpretation the Old Fashioned Way, Remarks at the Woodrow Wilson International Center for Scholars (Mar. 14, 2005), http://www.cfif .org/htdocs/freedomline/current/guest_commentary/scalia-constitutional-speech.htm.; *see also, e.g.*, Steven G. Calabresi & Justin Braga, *The Jurisprudence of Justice Antonin Scalia: A Response to Professor Bruce Allen Murphy and Professor Justin Driver*, 9 N.Y.U. J.L. & Liberty 793, 805 (2015); Diarmuid F. O'Scannlain, *"We Are All Textualists Now": The Legacy of Justice Antonin Scalia*, 91 St. John's L. Rev. 303, 312–13 (2017); John C. Yoo, *Choosing Justices: A Political Appointments Process and the Wages of Judicial Supremacy*, 98 Mich. L. Rev. 1436, 1451 n.25 (2000).

[50] Ilya Shapiro, *After* Bostock, *We're All Textualists Now*, Nat'l. Rev. (June 15, 2020), https://www.nationalreview.com/2020/06/supreme-court-decision-bostock-v-clayton-county -we-are-all-textualists-now/.

ninety percent of Americans believe gay and transgender people should be protected from discrimination in the workplace[51] and there is no reason to believe Justice Gorsuch isn't among them.[52] But the more important point is the one Judge Richard Posner made about the discrepancy between Justice Scalia's "personal and judicial positions" in the flag burning case.[53] Judge Posner observed that:

> the judicial position may be supporting a more important, though not necessarily less personal, agenda of the Justice.... One of the things that is important to Justice Scalia is promoting a textualist approach to the Constitution that would, if adopted, entail the eventual overruling of *Roe v. Wade* and other decisions of which he deeply disapproves.... In effect, [by ruling in favor of the flag burner] Justices Scalia . . . trades a minor preference for a major one.[54]

It is not clear that *Bostock* even required such a trade-off. What is clear is that Justice Gorsuch's ruling enabled him to advance his major preference for textualism. Viewed from that perspective, it is not clear that the outcome in *Bostock* proves textualism's objectivity and its disregard for extratextual concerns.

This Part shows that *Bostock* proves nothing of the sort. It starts by situating the decision in the context of the Court's other recent gay rights decisions and showing that *Bostock*'s pathbreaking conclusions about Title VII's original public meaning were driven by the same forms of legal contestation and change that have fueled explicitly dynamic forms of doctrinal evolution in the constitutional context. Those extratextual influences become even more apparent in subsequent sections of this Part, which examine how the Justices actually determine Title VII's original public meaning and how the Court applies its understanding of that meaning in *Bostock* and other cases. The idea that textualism enabled the Court to interpret and apply

---

[51] *Large Majorities, Including Republicans, Oppose Discrimination Against Lesbian, Gay, Bisexual and Transgender People by Employers and Health Care Providers*, KAISER FAM. FOUND. (June 24, 2020), https://www.kff.org/other/press-release/poll-large-majorities-including-republicans-oppose-discrimination-against-lesbian-gay-bisexual-and-transgender-people-by-employers-and-health-care-providers.

[52] Richard Primus, *A Weak Assumption in the Discussion of Gorsuch in* Bostock, BALKINIZATION (July 30, 2020), https://balkin.blogspot.com/2020/07/a-weak-assumption-in-discussion-of.html ("'[H]e followed his principles and not his preferences' only makes sense here if we think that Gorsuch would prefer a world in which employers were free to discriminate on the basis of sexual orientation and gender identity.... I don't see why I should assume it of Gorsuch.").

[53] Richard A. Posner, *Foreword: A Political Court*, 119 HARV. L. REV. 31, 50 (2005).

[54] *Id.* at 50–51.

this endlessly contested, highly culturally salient civil rights statute in a completely neutral and objective way, without relying on any extratextual judgments, does not withstand such scrutiny.

A. TEXTUALISM AS A FORM OF DYNAMIC INTERPRETATION

Defenders of the Court's use of textualism in *Bostock* see it differently. Shortly after *Bostock* came down, Tara Grove published an article in the *Harvard Law Review* arguing that the decision vindicates claims of textualism's objectivity and ability to screen out extratextual considerations.[55] Grove argues that, after decades of purposivist precedent denying sex-based Title VII claims by LGBT workers, the Court's embrace of textualism enabled it to look beyond social prejudice and finally apply the statute's true semantic meaning.[56] Grove also argues that purposivism's relative porousness to social values means that it may act as an impediment to the realization of civil rights where disfavored groups are concerned—whereas textualism, which puts aside such values, may enable the enforcement of those rights. Indeed, the article suggests that if the Court had embraced textualism fifty years ago, gay and transgender workers might not have had to wait so long to gain protection under Title VII. Although "[i]t is impossible . . . to say for sure how" a textualist court would have ruled fifty years ago if confronted with the claims in *Bostock*, the article asserts, "there is at least some evidence that a textualist approach would have benefitted the plaintiffs."[57]

In fact, the evidence points strongly in the other direction: The adoption of textualism would have done nothing to alter the fate of gay and transgender workers in the early Title VII cases. One reason it is possible to say this with near certainty is that courts in those cases actually paid a substantial amount of attention to Title VII's text. They observed, with great frequency, that

> [i]t is a maxim of statutory construction that, unless otherwise defined, words should be given their ordinary, common meaning. The phrase in Title VII prohibiting discrimination based on sex, in its plain meaning, implies that it is unlawful to discriminate against women because they are women and against men because they are men. The words of Title VII do

---

[55] Tara Leigh Grove, *Which Textualism?*, 134 HARV. L. REV. 265 (2020).

[56] *Id.* at 274–78.

[57] *Id.* at 278.

not outlaw discrimination against a person who has a sexual identity disorder....[58]

Courts made the same observation in cases with gay plaintiffs, finding that "sexual preference" did not fall within the ordinary meaning of Title VII's text.[59] Like today's textualists, courts in the early cases sometimes quoted the dictionary as part of their analysis of the "ordinary, common meaning"[60] of sex discrimination.[61] Unlike the Court in *Bostock*, however, courts in the decades after Title VII's enactment viewed the dictionary definition of "sex" as clearly excluding sexual orientation and gender identity.

---

[58] Ulane v. E. Airlines, Inc., 742 F.2d 1081, 1085 (7th Cir. 1984); *see also, e.g., id.* at 1087 ("[I]f the term 'sex' as it is used in Title VII is to mean more than biological male or biological female, the new definition must come from Congress."); Sommers v. Budget Mktg., Inc., 667 F.2d 748, 750 (8th Cir. 1982) (asserting that "for the purposes of Title VII the plain meaning must be ascribed to the term 'sex,'" and "that the word 'sex' in Title VII is to be given its traditional definition, rather than an expansive interpretation"); DeSantis v. Pac. Tel. & Tel. Co., 608 F.2d 327, 330 n.3 (9th Cir. 1979) (noting approvingly that, based in part on "the principle that 'words used in statutes are to be given their ordinary meaning,' the EEOC has concluded 'that when Congress used the word sex in Title VII it was referring to a person's gender' and not to 'sexual practices'" (quoting EEOC Decision No. 76-75, Emp. Prac. Guide (CCH) ¶ 6495, at 4266 (1976))); Holloway v. Arthur Andersen & Co., 566 F.2d 659, 662 (9th Cir. 1977) (rejecting a transgender woman's Title VII claim after finding "that the term sex should be given the traditional definition based on anatomical characteristics"); Oiler v. Winn-Dixie La., Inc., No. Civ.A. 00-3114, 2002 WL 31098541, at *4 (E.D. La. Sept. 16, 2002) (citing the "maxim of statutory construction that, unless otherwise defined, words should be given their ordinary, common meaning," and asserting that "discrimination on the basis of *sex* means discrimination on the basis of the plaintiff's biological sex" (internal quotation marks omitted)); Powell v. Read's, Inc., 436 F. Supp. 369, 371 (D. Md. 1977) (granting relief to a transgender woman would be "inconsistent with the plain meaning of the words" of Title VII); Voyles v. Ralph K. Davies Med. Ctr., 402 F. Supp. 456, 457 (N.D. Cal. 1975), *aff'd*, 570 F.2d 354 (9th Cir. 1978) ("[Title VII] speaks of discrimination on the basis of one's 'sex.' No mention is made of change of sex or of sexual preference.").

[59] *See, e.g., DeSantis*, 608 F.2d at 329–30 (noting that "Congress has not shown any intent other than to restrict the term 'sex' to its traditional meaning," and declining to "judicially extend[]" that statutory term "to include sexual preference such as homosexuality") (internal quotation marks omitted)); *cf.* DeCintio v. Westchester Cnty. Med. Ctr., 807 F.2d 304, 306–07 (2d Cir. 1986) ("[T]he other categories afforded protection under Title VII refer to a person's status as a member of a particular race, color, religion or nationality. 'Sex,' when read in this context, logically could only refer to membership in a class delineated by gender, rather than sexual activity...."); *id.* at 306 (declining to expand the definition of sex "to include 'sexual liaisons' and 'sexual attractions'").

[60] *Oiler*, 2002 WL 31098541, at *4.

[61] *See, e.g., Holloway*, 566 F.2d at 662 n.4 (quoting the 1970 edition of WEBSTER'S SEVENTH NEW COLLEGIATE DICTIONARY's definition of sex as "either of two divisions of organisms distinguished respectively as male or female," and citing this definition as evidence that Title VII does not bar discrimination on the basis of "transsexualism"); *cf. In re* Estate of Gardiner, 42 P.3d 120, 135 (Kan. 2002) (quoting the same definition—in a case involving marriage and inheritance—and concluding that "[t]he plain, ordinary meaning" of the word "sex" refers to "a biological man and a biological woman and not persons who are experiencing gender dysphoria"); *id.* ("The word[] 'sex' . . . in everyday understanding do[es] not encompass transsexuals.").

It is true that judges in those early cases did not consider themselves textualists. They often professed their readiness to depart from the ordinary meaning of the text if plaintiffs could show that Congress "intended that this 1964 legislation apply to anything other than the traditional concept of sex."[62] Such evidence was not forthcoming, however, so courts tended to fall back on the text, concluding "that for the purposes of Title VII the plain meaning must be ascribed to the term 'sex.'"[63] In light of courts' insistence that they were merely enforcing the ordinary meaning of Title VII's sex provision, it is difficult to see how a more formal embrace of textualism would have altered the outcome of those early cases.[64] If courts in the 1970s and 1980s had decided to eschew consideration of purpose and intent and focus only on Title VII's semantic meaning, LGBT plaintiffs would almost always still have lost their claims.

This is because antidiscrimination law is not "autonomous from the beliefs and values" of the society it regulates.[65] Those beliefs and values will always influence judicial interpretations of the meaning

---

[62] *Ulane*, 742 F.2d at 1085.

[63] *Sommers*, 667 F.2d. at 750; *see also Ulane*, 742 F.2d at 1085 ("The dearth of legislative history on [Title VII's sex provision] strongly reinforces the view that that section means nothing more than its plain language implies."); *Holloway*, 566 F.2d at 662–63 (discussing the "dearth of legislative history" and concluding that "Congress has not shown any intent other than to restrict the term 'sex' to its traditional meaning"); Grossman v. Bernards Twp. Bd. of Educ., No. 74-1904, 1975 WL 302, at *4 (D.N.J. Sept. 10, 1975) ("In the absence of any legislative history indicating a congressional intent to include transsexuals within the language of Title VII the Court is reluctant to ascribe any import to the term 'sex' other than its plain meaning.").

[64] There were one or two exceptions in these early years in which judges suggested that "transsexuals"—but not gays and lesbians—could state a claim under "the language of the statute itself," despite the fact "that Congress probably never contemplated that Title VII would apply to transsexuals." *Holloway*, 566 F.2d at 664 (Goodwin, J., dissenting); *see also Ulane v. E. Airlines, Inc.*, 581 F. Supp. 821, 823 (N.D. Ill. 1983), *overruled by Ulane v. E. Airlines, Inc.*, 742 F.2d 1081 (1984) ("I have no problem with the idea that the statute was not intended . . . to cover the matter of sexual preference. . . . It seems to me an altogether different question as to whether the matter of sexual identity is comprehended by the word, 'sex.'"); *Ulane*, 581 F. Supp. at 825 (concluding "that working with the word that the Congress gave us to work with," Title VII covers "transsexuals"). But these rare instances in which judges concluded that the word "sex" applies to transgender people are not evidence that the adoption of textualism would have altered the fortunes even of transgender plaintiffs. All of the other judges that weighed in on the question of whether the ordinary meaning of sex encompasses transgender people answered in the negative. The nearly universal view in this era was that "[a] reading of the statute to cover [a transgender] plaintiff's grievance would be impermissibly contrived and inconsistent with the plain meaning of the words." *Powell*, 436 F. Supp. at 371.

[65] Robert Post, *Foreword: Fashioning the Legal Constitution: Culture, Courts, and Law*, 117 HARV. L. REV. 4, 7 (2003).

(semantic or otherwise) of Title VII's ban on sex discrimination. As Justice Alito observes in his dissenting opinion in *Bostock*, gay and transgender people were social pariahs at the time of Title VII's enactment and for decades thereafter.[66] They were viewed as mentally diseased and their relationships were criminalized; federal agencies were permitted to fire them; some states barred them from teaching and denied them occupational licenses necessary to work in a range of fields, including law; the military barred them from service; and they were denied entry into the country.[67] The story with respect to transgender people is similar. In the 1960s, Americans were barely cognizant of that category,[68] but growing social awareness was not accompanied by acceptance: transgender people were viewed as ill and faced tremendous prejudice, social exclusion, and even violence in the decades after Title VII's enactment.[69]

It would be an understatement to say that the social status of LGBT people in this period made it difficult for them to win antidiscrimination claims. Courts routinely characterized transgender identity as a "mental disorder,"[70] insisted that "nature's choice of his or her . . . sex" (by which courts meant sex assigned at birth) was an individual's true sex,[71] and expressed skepticism that, even with gender-affirming surgery, "a woman can be so easily created from what remains of a man."[72] In 1967, the Court affirmed the deportation of a gay man, holding that he was excludable under the Immigration and Naturalization Act as a person "afflicted with psychopathic personality."[73]

---

[66] Bostock v. Clayton County, 140 S. Ct. 1731, 1769–71 (2020) (Alito, J., dissenting).

[67] *Id.*

[68] *Id.* at 1773 (observing that "transgender" was "a concept that was essentially unknown to the public" at the time Title VII was enacted).

[69] For more on the emergence of social awareness of transgender identity, see generally JOANNE MEYEROWITZ, HOW SEX CHANGED: A HISTORY OF TRANSSEXUALITY IN THE UNITED STATES (2004). For more on the violence transgender people faced as they became more visible, listen to *A History of Violence in the Fight for Trans Rights*, WYNC STUDIOS: TAKEAWAY (June 15, 2015), https://www.wnycstudios.org/podcasts/takeaway/segments/struggle-transgender -acceptance.

[70] *See, e.g.*, Ulane v. E. Airlines, Inc., 742 F.2d 1081, 1083 n.3 (1984); *cf. Bostock*, 140 S. Ct. at 1773 (Alito, J., dissenting) (noting that "the great majority of physicians surveyed in 1969 thought that an individual who sought sex reassignment surgery was either 'severely neurotic' or 'psychotic'" (citation omitted)).

[71] *Ulane*, 742 F.2d at 1083 n.3.

[72] *Id.*; *id.* at 1087 (expressing skepticism "that post-operative male-to-female transsexuals do in fact qualify as females and are not merely 'facsimiles'").

[73] Boutilier v. INS, 387 U.S. 118, 118 (1967).

Two decades later, the Ninth Circuit upheld the Department of Defense's refusal to grant security clearances to "known or suspected gay applicants" in a decision that linked homosexuality with necrophilia, pedophilia, voyeurism, and other "deviant conduct."[74] In 1986, when a gay man challenged the constitutionality of his arrest under Georgia's anti-sodomy statute, the Court characterized as "facetious" the notion that the Constitution protects gay people and condoned the legal enforcement of "majority sentiments about the morality of homosexuality."[75]

As long as courts viewed gay and transgender people as dangerous and deviant or sick and sad, no interpretive methodology was going to come to their rescue. Courts were not going to find that their exclusion from the central institutions of American society constituted discrimination—on any ground. So gay and transgender people lost their claims. They lost under the Constitution and under Title VII; they lost whether they framed their claims in terms of sex or in terms of sexual orientation or gender identity; they lost regardless of the interpretive methodology courts applied. Courts held in the early cases that Title VII's purpose was to protect biological women and men, that Congress did not intend the statute to cover gay and transgender people, and that the statute's original public meaning did not apply to individuals with "unusual and untraditional"[76] sexual orientations and gender identities. All of those holdings were informed by prevailing social values, the textualist ones no less than the purposivist and intentionalist ones.

Since that time, however, advocates of LGBT rights have worked to change these values and the law that polices sexual orientation and gender identity. Partially as a result of these efforts, public support for gay people has increased more rapidly than for any other group in recent decades.[77] This tremendous social change has spurred, and

---

[74] High Tech Gays v. Def. Indus. Sec. Clearance Off., 895 F.2d 563, 567–68 (9th Cir. 1990). The Department of Defense also denied clearance for "misconduct" such as "transsexualism," which it said "may indicate a mental or personality disorder." Id.; see also Dronenburg v. Zech, 741 F.2d 1388, 1398 (D.C. Cir. 1984) (upholding the Navy's discharge of an accomplished gay linguist on the ground that the Navy's anti-gay policy advances "crucial[] interest[s] common to all our armed forces," including upholding "discipline and good order," preserving morale, and protecting young recruits from "homosexual seduction").

[75] Bowers v. Hardwick, 478 U.S. 186, 194, 196 (1986).

[76] *Ulane*, 742 F.2d at 1086.

[77] ANDREW R. FLORES, NATIONAL TRENDS IN PUBLIC OPINION ON LGBT RIGHTS IN THE UNITED STATES, WILLIAMS INST., UCLA SCH. L. 5 (Nov. 2014), https://williams\institute.law

been spurred by, legal contestation over LGBT rights.[78] In recent years, these interrelated social and legal developments have begun to yield new interpretations of antidiscrimination law—most prominently, prior to *Bostock*, in the constitutional context. Over the past generation, the Court has issued a groundbreaking series of decisions—including *Romer v. Evans*, *Lawrence v. Texas*, *Windsor v. United States*, and *Obergefell v. Hodges*—holding that discrimination against gays and lesbians violates due process and equal protection. Those decisions were avowedly living-constitutionalist. Particularly in the later cases, the Court acknowledged the revolution in attitudes toward gay people and embraced the idea "that new insights and societal understandings can reveal unjustified inequality within our most fundamental institutions that once passed unnoticed and unchallenged."[79]

Protections for gay and transgender people under Title VII have evolved in tandem with these new constitutional protections. In 2012, the year the Court decided *Windsor*, the EEOC held that discrimination against transgender people violates Title VII.[80] In 2015, the year the Court decided *Obergefell*, the EEOC reached the same conclusion with respect to discrimination against gays and lesbians.[81] Courts also began to extend the statute's protections to LGBT people. Prior to *Romer*, there was virtually no movement on this front, but then—particularly as same-sex couples began to rack up victories in marriage cases—judges began to hold that Title VII bars discrimination against gay and transgender people in the workplace.

The courts that issued those holdings applied a range of interpretive methodologies; textualism was not the dominant approach. Indeed, the three most important decisions extending Title VII's coverage to gay and transgender workers prior to *Bostock* were written by

.ucla.edu/wp-content/uploads/Public-Opinion-LGBT-US-Nov-2014.pdf (reporting that "[p]ublic support for lesbians and gay men has doubled in the past three decades, more so than for any other group surveyed over the same time period," and that with respect to transgender people, there was "a 40% increase in support between 2005 and 2011").

[78] *See* Douglas NeJaime, *Winning Through Losing*, 96 Iowa L. Rev. 941, 945–46 (2011) (describing "law and social change as a dialogical process in which social movement actors seize on judicial decisions and activate legal norms across a variety of institutional settings," and showing how even litigation loss may "result in productive social movement effects and lead to more effective reform strategies").

[79] Obergefell v. Hodges, 576 U.S. 644, 673 (2015).

[80] Macy v. Holder, Appeal No. 0120120821, 2012 WL 1435995, at *11 (E.E.O.C. Apr. 20, 2012).

[81] Baldwin v. Foxx, Appeal No. 0120133080, 2015 WL 4397641, at *5 (E.E.O.C. July 15, 2015).

Judge Robert Katzmann of the Second Circuit, Judge Karen Nelson Moore of the Sixth Circuit, and Judge Diane Wood of the Seventh Circuit,[82] none of whom are textualists, and at least two of whom are outspoken critics of the methodology.[83] These judges accorded great weight to the fact that, "[s]ince 1964, the legal framework for evaluating Title VII claims has evolved substantially."[84] They argued that the appropriate question is "what the correct rule of law is now in light of the Supreme Court's authoritative interpretations, not what someone thought it meant" in the past.[85]

These judges cited *Price Waterhouse v. Hopkins*[86] and *Oncale v. Sundowner Offshore Services*[87] in particular as bases for extending the law's protections to LGBT people.[88] *Price Waterhouse* held that Title VII constrains the practice of sex stereotyping, as "we are beyond the day when an employer could evaluate employees by assuming or insisting that they matched the stereotype associated with their group."[89] *Oncale* held that same-sex sexual harassment is a cognizable form of sex discrimination under Title VII.[90] The Court acknowledged that "male-on-male sexual harassment in the workplace was assuredly not the principal evil Congress was concerned with when it enacted Title VII,"

---

[82] *See* Zarda v. Altitude Express, Inc., 883 F.3d 100 (2d Cir. 2018); EEOC v. R.G. & G.R. Harris Funeral Homes, Inc., 884 F.3d 560 (6th Cir. 2018); Hively v. Ivy Tech Cmty. Coll., 853 F.3d 339 (7th Cir. 2017).

[83] Judge Katzmann is one of the nation's leading proponents of purposivism. His 2014 book, *Judging Statutes*, critiques textualism, argues that courts should interpret statutory text in light of congressional purpose, and strongly advocates the consultation of legislative history. KATZMANN, *supra* note 38. Judge Wood is also a forceful proponent of dynamic forms of interpretation. *See, e.g.,* Diane P. Wood, Madison Lecture, Our 18th Century Constitution in the 21st Century World, *in* 80 N.Y.U. L. REV. 1079, 1079 (2005) (addressing "the classic question of whether courts should interpret the United States Constitution from an originalist or dynamic approach" and "argu[ing] for the dynamic approach"); *cf.* Karen Nelson Moore, *The Supreme Court's Role in Interpreting the Federal Rules of Civil Procedure*, 44 HASTINGS L.J. 1039, 1109 (1993) ("The rigidity and ultimate futility of the plain meaning analysis must be recognized. What is plain to one person . . . is not necessarily plain to another. It is misleading to pretend that language is plain.").

[84] *Zarda*, 883 F.3d at 131.

[85] *Hively*, 853 F.3d at 350; *id.* at 350–51 ("The . . . Court's decisions, as well as the common-sense reality that it is actually impossible to discriminate on the basis of sexual orientation without discriminating on the basis of sex, persuade us that the time has come to overrule our previous cases that have endeavored to find and observe that line.").

[86] 490 U.S. 228 (1989).

[87] 523 U.S. 75 (1998).

[88] *See Zarda*, 883 F.3d at 111–23; *Harris Funeral Homes*, 884 F.3d at 571–81; *Hively*, 853 F.3d at 342–47.

[89] 490 U.S. at 251.

[90] 523 U.S. at 79.

but observed that "statutory prohibitions often go beyond the principal evil to cover reasonably comparable evils."[91] Congress likewise did not have LGBT people in mind when it enacted Title VII. But the law now protects workers against a wide range of gender conformity demands. Against this doctrinal backdrop, these judges reasoned, allowing employers to require such conformity with respect to gender identity and sexual orientation creates an unjustified loophole in the law's coverage.

Indeed, Judge Wood argued, the ongoing exclusion of gays and lesbians from Title VII's protections appears particularly unwarranted when viewed "against the backdrop of the Supreme Court's decisions, not only in the field of employment discrimination, but also in the area of broader discrimination on the basis of sexual orientation."[92] She argued that the LGBT loophole in contemporary Title VII doctrine ran contrary to the teachings of *Romer*, *Lawrence*, *Windsor*, and *Obergefell*.[93] She and Judge Katzmann both observed that continuing to exempt gays and lesbians from Title VII's coverage after those constitutional decisions generated a "paradoxical legal landscape" in which a person could "be married on Saturday and then fired on Monday for just that act."[94] They argued this "bizarre" state of affairs ran contrary to modern precedent.[95]

How, then, are we to understand *Bostock*? The Court in *Bostock* affirmed the outcome of these appellate court decisions but insisted that all of this discussion of the law's development was unnecessary, as gay and transgender workers have been protected under Title VII's sex provision from the start. But if that is so, why did the Court only discover this in 2020, in the wake of the same-sex marriage decisions? Fifty years ago, LGBT plaintiffs lost antidiscrimination cases regardless of the legal provision they invoked, the interpretive method courts applied, or whether they framed their claims in terms of sex or in terms of sexual orientation or gender identity. Today, LGBT plaintiffs are winning cases. But, as before, legal and social conceptions of the licitness of anti-LGBT discrimination—and not anything to do with

---

[91] *Id.*

[92] *Hively*, 853 F.3d at 349.

[93] *Id.*

[94] *Id.* at 342; *see also Zarda*, 883 F.3d at 131 (quoting this passage in *Hively*).

[95] *Hively*, 853 F.3d at 342; *see also Zarda*, 883 F.3d at 131 (observing that interpreting Title VII in a manner consistent with "the modern constitutional framework" eliminates this paradox).

the interpretive method courts apply—seem to be playing a primary role in the outcomes of these cases. The new understandings that animated the Court's decisions in the marriage cases—and the new understandings those decisions themselves helped to forge—have radically altered the legal terrain on which we fight about LGBT rights.

The Court in *Bostock* makes no mention of the ongoing legal and social revolution of which its decision is a part. But the claim cannot be that it is simply a coincidence that the Justices discovered the gay- and trans-protective nature of Title VII's sex provision in the midst of this revolution. The best textualist claim has to be that this revolution caused the scales to fall from the Justices' eyes—that all of this change swept away the distorting effects of prejudice and enabled them to recognize for the first time the statute's true semantic meaning.[96] A concession of this sort acknowledges the reality that *Bostock* is part of a broader legal and social revolution while holding onto the idea that the decision itself is textualist.

However, to concede that our understanding of ordinary public meaning is evolutive in this way—that it evolves along with society and may be altered by contestation inside and outside of courts—saps textualism of much of its purported distinctiveness as an interpretive methodology. It belies the central textualist claim that it is possible to identify ordinary public meaning in a manner that is "largely removed from the most salient moral issues of the day."[97] It acknowledges that ongoing legal and social conflict will shape, and eternally reshape, judicial perceptions of a statute's semantic meaning. There is already a robust debate among legal scholars about whether textualism retains any analytical distinctiveness in the face of concessions of this general sort.[98] *Bostock* would seem to provide additional cause for skepticism.

B. ORDINARY PUBLIC MEANING IS MADE, NOT FOUND

That is far from the biggest problem *Bostock* poses for textualism, however. A close reading of the decision reveals deeper methodological

---

[96] For scholars making versions of this claim, see Jessica Clarke, *How the First Forty Years of Circuit Precedent Got Title VII's Sex Discrimination Provision Wrong*, 98 Tex. L. Rev. Online 83, 112–13 (2019); Katie Eyer, *Statutory Originalism and LGBT Rights*, 54 Wake Forest L. Rev. 63, 83–86 (2019); Grove, *supra* note 55, at 278 n.82.

[97] Baude, *supra* note 12, at 2226.

[98] *See, e.g.*, Dorf & Buchanan, *supra* note 17 (manuscript at 34–37); Kessler & Pozen, *supra* note 31, at 1848–54; Molot, *supra* note 31 *passim*.

trouble. The majority and the dissenting opinions in *Bostock* do not simply track evolving understandings of equality. They are actively engaged in the construction of various original public meanings for Title VII through the choices they make at shadow decision points. The textualist rhetoric of the decision suggests otherwise. The Justices claim they are simply enforcing "legal terms with plain and settled meanings."[99] They all agree that a quick consultation of a dictionary or corpus linguistics database is sufficient to yield a determinate answer in this case and that the original public meaning of Title VII's bar on sex discrimination unambiguously protects (or does not protect) LGBT workers.

As this section shows, however, the original public meaning of Title VII's sex provision is not something the Justices discover; it is something they produce. As is often the case in the kind of statutory interpretation disputes that arrive at the Court, there are several plausible ways to interpret the statutory language at issue in *Bostock*. Just about the only thing that is unambiguous in this case is that the meaning of Title VII's sex provision is not unambiguous. That raises questions about how the Justices arrive at the conclusions they do about the statute's meaning. This section looks beneath the Justices' textualist rhetoric and examines how their analysis actually works. What it finds is a series of unacknowledged, often outcome-determinative choices unbound by any kind of methodological rule or requirement of consistency. On the surface, the opinions in *Bostock* confidently assert that the phrase "discriminate . . . because of . . . sex" has a determinate meaning that obviously resolves the case. Underneath the surface, the Justices make choices that steer the analysis inexorably toward a particular conclusion.

1). *Defining Discrimination.* Here is the core of the Court's textualist analysis in *Bostock*:

> What did "discriminate" mean in 1964? As it turns out, it meant then roughly what it means today: "To make a difference in treatment or favor (of one as compared with others)." *Webster's New International Dictionary* 745 (2d ed. 1954). To "discriminate against" a person, then, would seem to mean treating that individual worse than others who are similarly situated. . . . [A]n employer who intentionally treats a person worse because of sex—such as by firing the person for actions or attributes it would tolerate

---

in an individual of another sex—discriminates against that person in violation of Title VII.[100]

The Court makes numerous choices in this passage that it does not
acknowledge making, let alone offer any reasons for making. It chooses
to rely on a dictionary rather than one of the new corpus linguistics
databases. It chooses to rely on *Webster's New International Dictionary*.
It chooses to analyze the word "discriminate" in isolation from the rest
of the statutory text. Most importantly, it selects this particular anticlassificationist definition of "discriminate" from among the several
definitions of that word contained in period dictionaries. To discriminate can mean to differentiate. One might discriminate in this sense
between different shades of blue. But as Judge Gerald Lynch observed
in his dissenting opinion for the Second Circuit in *Zarda* (one of the
cases consolidated in *Bostock*), that is not the only meaning of the word.
Judge Lynch acknowledged that "there are recognized English uses of
'discriminate' . . . that imply nothing invidious, but merely mean 'to
perceive, observe or note [a] difference.'"[101] But, he argued, "in the
language of civil rights, a different and stronger meaning applies, that
references invidious distinctions: 'To treat a person or group in an
unjust or prejudicial manner, esp[ecially] on the grounds of race, gender,
sexual orientation, etc.; frequently with *against*.'"[102]

In his dissenting opinion in *Bostock*, Justice Alito—joined by Justice
Thomas—endeavors to prove that Judge Lynch is right by bypassing
the dictionary and relying instead on the tools of corpus linguistics.
Justice Alito cites a legal corpus linguistics study that "searched a vast
database of documents from [the 1950s and 1960s] to determine how
the phrase 'discriminate against . . . because of [some trait]' was used."[103]

---

[100] *Id.* at 1740.

[101] *Zarda v. Altitude Express, Inc.*, 883 F.3d 100, 149 (2d Cir. 2018) (Lynch, J., dissenting)
(quoting "*The Oxford English Dictionary Online*, http://www.oed.com (search for 'Discriminate,'
verb, definitions 2a and 2b"). Judge Lynch uses a contemporary dictionary to analyze the ordinary public meaning of "discriminate," which is not the preferred textualist approach—although in practice, there is considerable variation regarding choice of appropriate dictionary
publication date. *See* James J. Brudney & Lawrence Baum, *Oasis or Mirage: The Supreme Court's
Thirst for Dictionaries in the Rehnquist and Roberts Eras*, 55 Wm. & Mary L. Rev. 483, 483 (2013)
(arguing that the Justices "lack a coherent position on citing to editions from the time of statutory
enactment versus the time the instant case was filed"); Brudney & Baum, *supra*, at 533–35
(discussing the issue at greater length, with empirical evidence).

[102] *Zarda*, 883 F.3d at 149.

[103] *Bostock*, 140 S. Ct. at 1769 n.22 (Alito, J., dissenting) (citing James C. Phillips, The Overlooked Evidence in the Title VII Cases: The Linguistic (and Therefore Textualist) Principle of
Compositionality 3 (May 11, 2020) (second alteration in original)). The cited manuscript—which was

As Judge Lynch noted, midcentury American writers sometimes used the word "discriminate" to mean differentiate. But, the study concluded, writers in that period used the phrase "discriminate against" differently—to refer not to "*any* adverse treatment that even *adverts* to [the protected trait]," but "only to adverse treatment that rests on *prejudice or bias.*"[104] Thus, Justice Alito and Justice Thomas argue, as a matter of original public meaning, Title VII's prohibition on discrimination does not bar all forms of differential treatment based on protected traits, but only "discrimination against 'someone . . . motivated by prejudice, or biased ideas or attitudes . . . directed at people with that trait in particular.'"[105]

The choice between these definitions is highly consequential; for some of the Justices in *Bostock*, it may be outcome-determinative. There are various ways one can reach the conclusion that discrimination against LGBT people violates Title VII's prohibition on sex discrimination. But the particular path Justice Gorsuch chooses is entirely dependent on his conclusion in the passage quoted above: that discrimination means differentiation rather than prejudice and subordination.[106] It is similarly important to Justice Alito and Justice Thomas that Title VII's bar on sex discrimination *does* entail prejudice and subordination; the claim that the statute bars only "sexist"[107] practices is a central component of their argument that it does not protect gay and transgender people. Thus, it is worth examining the various (unacknowledged and extratextual) choices the Justices make in deciding to define discrimination as they do in *Bostock*.

---

available at https://ssrn.com/abstract=3585940 while *Bostock* was under consideration by the Court, but which was pulled by its author after the decision came down—is on file with this author.

[104] Phillips, *supra* note 103, at 3.

[105] *Bostock*, 140 S. Ct. at 1769 n.22 (citing Phillips, *supra* note 103, at 7).

[106] As an analytical matter, victory for the plaintiffs in *Bostock* did not depend on the Court adopting an anticlassificationist definition of sex discrimination. It is quite plausible to argue that discrimination against gay and transgender people is a form of sex-based subordination and sex-role stereotyping; in fact, Part II argues it is implausible to suggest otherwise. *See infra* text accompanying notes 273–284. But these antisubordinationist and anti-stereotyping arguments necessitate more analytical work than the simple anticlassificationist argument, and conservatives generally reject them. Indeed, the dissenting Justices in *Bostock* treat it as axiomatic that the plaintiffs lose under the antisubordinationist definition. *See, e.g., Bostock*, 140 S. Ct. at 1765 (Alito, J., dissenting) ([D]iscrimination because of sexual orientation is not historically tied to a project that aims to subjugate either men or women. An employer who discriminates on this ground might be called 'homophobic' or 'transphobic,' but not sexist.").

[107] *Bostock*, 140 S. Ct. at 1765 (Alito, J., dissenting).

It is relatively easy to see the choices Justice Gorsuch makes. Dictionaries from the time of Title VII's enactment contain multiple definitions of the word "discriminate." In fact, Bill Eskridge notes that "dictionaries of the 1960s, when Title VII was enacted, often gave the prejudice meaning as the first definition of discrimination"[108]—which may be why Justice Gorsuch chooses (otherwise seemingly inexplicably) to rely on the one particular dictionary he does, which was published in 1954[109]: It leads with an anticlassificationist definition. There are plenty of other dictionaries from this period that do not lead with that definition.[110] Consulting the dictionary does not clarify which definition captures Title VII's original public meaning any more than reading the text of the statute does.

The dissenting Justices' decision-making about the meaning of discrimination is no less reliant on extratextual considerations, but their use of corpus linguistics makes it harder to see. Advocates of this technology—including a substantial and growing number of textualists—portray it as a reliable, objective, and scientific approach to determining original public meaning.[111] The idea is that by harnessing the power of big data, interpreters can gain insight into how a word or phrase was actually used and would have been understood by people in a particular era.[112] Without getting too deep into the weeds, it is worth

---

[108] William N. Eskridge, Jr., *All About Words: Early Understandings of the "Judicial Power" in Statutory Interpretation, 1776–1806*, 101 COLUM. L. REV. 990, 1101 n.538 (2001).

[109] Justice Gorsuch's choice of a 1954 dictionary is particularly puzzling in light of the scholarly argument that textualists must "search out dictionaries published . . . a few years *after* the date of the statute" because meanings current at the time of the statute's enactment will not be captured in dictionaries until a few years later. Ellen P. Aprill, *The Law of the Word: Dictionary Shopping in the Supreme Court*, 30 ARIZ. ST. L.J. 275, 332 (1998) (emphasis added). Justice Gorsuch's decision to use a dictionary that *predates* Title VII by a decade seems especially odd given that Americans' understanding of "discrimination" may have been especially subject to change in that particular ten-year period. Then again, there are few rules governing textualist's dictionary usage; it is not clear there is an objectively correct way to do this. *See* Brudney & Baum, *supra* note 101, at 537 ("The Justices' choices in citing dictionary definitions seem to be largely ad hoc, based on the appeal of particular dictionaries in particular cases."); Stephen C. Mouritsen, *The Dictionary Is Not a Fortress: Definitional Fallacies and a Corpus-Based Approach to Plain Meaning*, 2010 B.Y.U. L. REV. 1915, 1915–46 (2010) (arguing that dictionary usage creates the illusion of objectivity but does not actually provide objective answers, especially in hard cases).

[110] For example, the 1963 edition of *Funk & Wagnalls Standard College Dictionary* defines discrimination as "prejudice or partiality in attitudes, actions, etc.: *discrimination* against minorities"—and then, also, as "the power or ability to perceive distinctions or differences; discernment." FUNK & WAGNALLS STANDARD COLLEGE DICTIONARY 380 (10th ed. 1963).

[111] *See, e.g.,* Thomas R. Lee & Stephen C. Mouritsen, *Judging Ordinary Meaning*, 127 YALE L.J. 788 (2018).

[112] *See* Lee J. Strang, *How Big Data Can Increase Originalism's Methodological Rigor: Using Corpus Linguistics to Reveal Original Language Conventions*, 50 U.C. DAVIS L. REV. 1181 (2017).

taking a look at how Justice Alito and Justice Thomas use corpus linguistics in *Bostock*, both because it bears directly on the question of whether textualism is able to resolve the questions at issue in this case and because corpus linguistics is quickly becoming the gold standard in textualist analysis.[113] This will not be the last time it features in a Supreme Court opinion.

The corpus linguistics study on which Justices Alito and Thomas rely purports to prove that Title VII defines discrimination in an anti-subordinationist way. Here is how the study reaches that conclusion. First—using the Corpus of Historical American English (COHA), a database containing approximately 48 million words from the 1950s and 1960s, with texts drawn from popular magazines, newspapers, and fiction and non-fiction books—the study shows that the word that most commonly follows the word "discriminate" is "against."[114] The database generates 236 hits for the word "discriminate" (and various versions of it) in those decades, and the word "against" follows it approximately half of the time, and five times more frequently than any other word.[115] On this basis, the study concludes that "discriminate against" is a "linguistic unit" that must be analyzed as a whole,[116] and that analyzing the meaning of "discriminate" in isolation, the way Justice Gorsuch does, will not yield accurate results. The study then searches for "collocates"—or words that appear within some (unspecified) number of words of the phrase "discriminate against"—and finds that "among the top five collocates are *negro(es)*, *Jews*, *group(s)*, *women*."[117] The study interprets the frequent proximity of the term "discriminate against" to these group names as "evidence of a semantic focus on bias or prejudice against members of a group."[118]

---

[113] *See* Lee & Mouritsen *supra* note 111, at 796 n.23 (discussing judges' increasingly frequent use of corpus linguistics); Kevin Tobia, *Testing Ordinary Meaning*, 134 HARV. L. REV. 726, 733 (2020) (observing that "[l]egal corpus linguistics . . . has . . . grown in use and esteem" and that this growth "is likely to continue"); Tobia, *supra*, at 733 n.43 (citing examples of increasing judicial reliance on corpus linguistics in recent years); Amanda Kae Fronk, *Big Lang at BYU*, BYU MAG., Summer 2017, https://magazine.byu.edu/article/big-lang-at-byu/ (quoting the prominent textualist scholar Lawrence Solum predicting that "corpus linguistics will revolutionize statutory and constitutional interpretation").

[114] Phillips, *supra* note 103, at 4.

[115] *Id.* (reporting that the word "against" follows the word "discriminate" five time more often than the next most frequent word).

[116] *Id.* at 3.

[117] *Id.* at 5.

[118] *Id.*

This enterprise is wildly subjective and generates a veritable avalanche of shadow decision points. As a preliminary matter, the conclusion that "discriminate against" is a "linguistic unit," i.e., that it has a specialized meaning distinct from the word "discriminate," is highly dubious.[119] As the study itself observes, "[p]arties on both sides [in *Bostock*] refer to *discrimination because of sex*. . . . Everyone seems to drop the word 'against' and focus just on 'discriminate.'"[120] Indeed, they do. That is because everyone has always done this; from the time of Title VII's enactment through the present day, the terms "discriminate" and "discriminate against" have been used interchangeably. The congresspeople who enacted Title VII used "discriminate" and "discriminate against" interchangeably,[121] as did the EEOC, from the moment it began to interpret the statute.[122] The *text of Title VII itself* uses those

---

[119] The study is not clear about precisely what qualifies "discriminate against" as a "linguistic unit." It might be the fact that "against" follows "discriminate" half the time; it might be the fact that "against" follows "discriminate" more frequently than any other word; it might be these factors in conjunction, weighted equally, or not. If there was any rule established prior to obtaining the results for identifying a "linguistic unit"—or even any rule established once the results were in—the study does not mention it.

[120] Phillips, *supra* note 103, at 2–3.

[121] It is difficult to capture, in a footnote, the constant interchangeable use of the terms "discriminate" and "discriminate against" over hundreds of pages of the 1964 Civil Rights Act's legislative history; but I will try, using three illustrations. 1) Opponents of the 1964 Act complained endlessly about the fact that it did not define "discrimination." They argued that "[t]he language of the bill is so uncertain, indefinite, imprecise, and vague, that it is subject to an almost unlimited variety of interpretations and constructions." 110 Cong. Rec. 5432 (1964) (statement of Sen. Thurmond). While the Senate was debating the bill, opponents took out a full-page advertisement in newspapers across the country that devoted an entire section—entitled *"The Mystery Word: Discrimination"*—to this argument. *See* 110 Cong. Rec. 5931–32 (1964) (reprinting an advertisement by the Coordinating Committee for Fundamental American Freedoms, Inc.). These attacks spurred extensive congressional discussion about the definition of "discrimination," and never once, over the course of many months of debate, did anyone suggest that the phrase "discriminate against" had any kind of specialized meaning or that it meant anything different from the word "discriminate." 2) In fact, Senator Hubert Humphrey, the Democratic whip who shepherded the bill through Congress, argued that the bill defined discrimination in the same way as the Hill-Burton Act, the Interstate Commerce Clause, and the Federal Aviation Act—all of which barred "discrimination" but did not include the word "against." 110 Cong. Rec. 5863–64 (1964) (statement of Sen. Humphrey). 3) Even more to the point: some sections of the 1964 Civil Rights Act use the word "discriminate" and other sections use the phrase "discriminate against"— and no one, including the lawmakers who passed the Act, has ever attached any significance to this fact. Indeed, when those lawmakers discussed Title VII, they regularly omitted the word "against" and described Title VII as barring *"discrimination because of* race, [etc.]." 110 Cong. Rec. 2719 (1964) (statement of Rep. Cellar) (emphasis added); *see also* 110 Cong. Rec. 2719 (stating that Title VII would make it unlawful "to *discriminate among* applicants for employment" (emphasis added)). There is no evidence that the lawmakers who enacted Title VII understood the phrase "discriminate against" to have any special semantic significance; indeed, the evidence points very strongly in the other direction.

[122] The EEOC issued its first set of guidelines interpreting Title VII's sex provision shortly after it went into effect and omitted the word "against" from its discussion of the law. *See*

terms interchangeably.[123] Textualist Justices have always done so as well. In one of his most famous and important textualist opinions, Justice Scalia repeatedly omitted the word "against" and described Title VII as "prohibit[ing] discrimination on the basis of race or sex."[124] Indeed, Justice Scalia explicitly declined to attach any semantic significance to the word "against," arguing that Title VII (which contains the word "against") must be interpreted the same way as Title VI (which does not contain the word "against") because these two provisions of the 1964 Act contain "virtually identical categorical language" barring discrimination.[125] Justice Thomas has also consistently taken this position (until now). He has argued that Title IX of the Education Amendments of 1972 and Title II of the Americans With Disabilities Act define discrimination in the same way as Title VII—despite the fact that the former two statutes do not contain the word "against."[126]

EEOC Guidelines on Discrimination Because of Sex, 30 FED. REG. 14,926, 14,926 (1965) (characterizing Title VII as prohibiting "discrimination in employment on account of sex").

[123] Section 703(a)(1) of Title VII, the provision at issue in *Bostock*, bars employers from "discriminat[ing] against any individual . . . because of . . . sex." 42 U.S.C. § 2000e–2(a)(1). Numerous other sections of Title VII also use that language. But some sections—including those that address, *inter alia*, seniority and merit systems, and the law's application to the federal government—omit the word "against" and simply prohibit "discrimination based on race [etc.]" or "discriminat[ion] because of race [etc.]" 42 U.S.C. § 2000e–2(h); 42 U.S.C. § 2000e–16(a). Textualists have long observed that "[w]here Congress includes particular language in one section of a statute but omits it in another section of the same Act, it is generally presumed that Congress acts intentionally and purposely in the disparate inclusion or exclusion." Olmstead v. L.C. *ex rel.* Zimring, 527 U.S. 581, 622 (1999) (Thomas, J., dissenting; joined by Scalia, J.) (internal quotation marks omitted). If one accepts the claim that "discriminate against" is a "linguistic unit" with a particular meaning, it would appear that Title VII veers from one definition of discrimination to another, from section to section, and that everyone has failed to appreciate the significance of this for over half a century. Indeed, antidiscrimination laws in general appear to use the terms "discriminate" and "discriminate against" interchangeably. *See infra* notes 125–126 and accompanying text. If Congress has been sending a clear signal about which of these laws is to be interpreted in an anticlassificationist way and which in an antisubordinationist way through its decision to include or omit the word "against," why has nobody noticed this? Why have legislators—or textualist judges—never mentioned it? In reality, there is not some important, yet heretofore unnoticed, information about the meaning of "discrimination" being communicated through this word choice. This argument reveals far more about corpus linguistics, and textualism in general, than it does about the meaning of "discrimination."

[124] Johnson v. Transp. Agency, 480 U.S. 616, 675 (1987) (Scalia, J., dissenting); *see also, e.g., id.* at 670.

[125] *Id.* at 665 n.3; *see also id.* (instructing the reader to "[c]ompare 42 U.S.C. § 2000d ('No person . . . shall, on the ground of race, color, or national origin, be . . . subjected to discrimination'), with § 2000e–2(a)(1) (no employer shall 'discriminate against any individual . . . because of such individual's race, color, religion, sex, or national origin,')" and observing that these two provisions contain "virtually identical" language regarding discrimination).

[126] Olmstead v. L.C. *ex. rel.* Zimring, 527 U.S. 581, 616 n.1 (1999) (Thomas, J., dissenting; joined by Chief Justice Rehnquist and Justice Scalia). In another, more recent, case involving

One might have thought this material—particularly the material from the 1960s—was solid evidence that the phrase "discriminate against" does not have some distinct and specialized significance as a matter of original public meaning. But multiple leading textualists— Randy Barnett, Josh Blackman, Robert George—have weighed in on precisely this point, insisting along with Justice Alito (and Justice Thomas in *Bostock*) that the corpus linguistics evidence is conclusive: the fact that the word "against" follows the word "discriminate" about half the time, and more frequently than any other word, in the small number of results the COHA churns out, proves that "discriminate against" is a "linguistic unit" with a specialized meaning.[127] Why this very limited data set trumps the countless instances in which "discriminate" and "discriminate against" were used interchangeably in the 1960s is difficult to understand. None of these textualists explain the rule that yields this conclusion, and the study itself does not provide one. But that is of no matter; I have no interest in establishing that "discriminate against" is not a "linguistic unit," or that whatever rule textualists are using to reach the opposite conclusion is wrong.

---

the interpretation of a law that prohibits states from imposing a "tax that discriminates against a rail carrier," Justice Thomas engaged in a lengthy textualist analysis of the meaning of the word "discriminates" and never suggested that the word "against" had any semantic significance or bearing on the law's meaning. Ala. Dep't of Revenue v. CSX Transp., Inc., 575 U.S. 21, 32–42 (2015); CSX Transp., Inc. v. Ala. Dep't of Revenue, 562 U.S. 277, 297–306 (2011).

[127] *See* Josh Blackman & Randy Barnett, *Justice Gorsuch's Halfway Textualism Surprises and Disappoints in the Title VII Cases*, NAT'L REV. (June 26, 2020), https://www.nationalreview.com /2020/06/justice-gorsuch-title-vii-cases-half-way-textualism-surprises-disappoints/ ("Professor James Phillips conducted a thorough study of how the phrase 'discriminate against' was used in the 1950s and 1960s. That phrase did not merely refer to differential treatment. Rather, 'discriminate against' referred to differential treatment 'based on some trait [that is] motivated by prejudice, or biased ideas or attitudes.' . . . Had Justice Gorsuch relied on the ordinary meaning of 'discriminate against' in 1964, he would have recognized that bias or prejudice had to play some role in the differential treatment."); Josh Blackman, *Justice Gorsuch's Textualism Has a Precedent Problem*, ATLANTIC (July 24, 2020), https://www.theatlantic.com/ideas/archive/2020/07/justice -gorsuch-textualism/614461/ ("[T]he phrase 'discriminate against' must inform the meaning of 'because of.' In the 1960s, that phrase formed a single linguistic unit. . . . [T]he phrase discriminate against because of sex references discrimination based on bias or prejudice about a person's sex."); *id.* ("Justice Gorsuch relied on decades of precedents that focused primarily on 'because of' and not the entire clause. Doing so eliminated the requirement that some sort of bias or prejudice exists based on a person's sex. In effect, he severed the statute in half, and concluded that if sex plays any role in the discrimination, the employers' actions are unlawful."); Robert George, *Further Thoughts on the Title VII Cases and Textualism*, MIRROR JUST. (June 16, 2020), https:// mirrorofjustice.blogs.com/mirrorofjustice/2020/06/further-thoughts-on-the-title-vii-cases -and-textualism.html (arguing that textualists must analyze "the ordinary meaning of th[e] phrase ['discrimination against' individuals 'because of' sex] taken as a whole"; holding out "Professor James Phillips' recent study relying on linguistic principles and systematic data" as a model for how to do this analysis; and endorsing the study's conclusions).

The real problem—and my real focus here—is the enterprise of textualism itself, which enables all of this highly subjective, highly contestable, potentially outcome-determinative decision-making to occur, unacknowledged, in the shadows.

That is only the start of it. Even if one accepts that "discriminate against" is a "linguistic unit," one still has to determine what it means—a process that involves yet another round of shadow decision points. The study on which Justice Alito and Justice Thomas rely treats the fact that the phrase "discriminate against" often appears in close proximity to the names of protected groups as evidence that midcentury Americans understood that phrase in an antisubordinationist way. But that is a highly questionable, if not entirely tautological, approach—not least because some of the results the COHA generates simply reproduce the text of antidiscrimination provisions. Consider this result from a 1956 book by Justice William O. Douglas quoting the Indian Constitution: "'ARTICLE 15: (1) The State shall not discriminate against any citizen on grounds only of religion, race, caste, sex, place of birth or any of them.'"[128] Another one of the results quotes the EEOC discussing Title VII itself![129] Under the study's methodology, these

---

[128] WILLIAM O. DOUGLAS, WE THE JUDGES: STUDIES IN AMERICAN AND INDIAN CONSTITUTIONAL LAW FROM MARSHALL TO MUKHERJEA 301 (1956).

[129] The passage discusses the EEOC's initial guidelines for interpreting Title VII, which characterize the law as barring "separate seniority lists that discriminate against either men or women." *When Is the Difference Unequal?*, TIME, Dec. 10, 1965, at 36. The study counts this usage as antisubordinationist because the term "discriminate against" appears in close proximity to the name of a protected group. But that is the very question we are trying to answer.

These passages reveal an additional set of issues (and shadow decision points) that I will simply note in passing. First, it is surprising that conservative textualists view foreign laws and sources as relevant to determining the semantic meaning of American laws when those laws and sources happen to be included in a corpus linguistics database. Justice Scalia and others have strenuously objected to the consultation of foreign laws and sources in the interpretation of American law, *see, e.g.*, Lawrence v. Texas, 539 U.S. 558, 598 (2003) (Scalia, J, dissenting; joined by Chief Justice Rehnquist and Justice Thomas), and it is difficult to understand why inclusion in a database alters that analysis. Second, and relatedly, some COHA results include quotations from Supreme Court opinions reproduced in popular publications. The study's author suggests it is inappropriate to consult the corpus of Court opinions to determine a law's ordinary public meaning unless the law employs a "legal term of art." James Phillips, *A Response to Ryan Nees on Textualism and Title VII*, ORIGINALISM BLOG (May 17, 2020), https://originalismblog.typepad.com/the-originalism-blog/2020/05/a-response-to-ryan-nees-on-textualism-and-title-viijames-phillips .html. But if passages from Court opinions happen to be included in a corpus linguistics database, they then become relevant to the law's meaning, even if the law does not contain a "legal term of art." This is undertheorized (and what counts as a "legal term of art" is yet another shadow decision point). Third, texts in the COHA often contain quotes from other texts produced at earlier time periods (e.g., the section from the Indian Constitution quoted above was written prior to 1950, which the study identifies as the relevant starting point for assessing Title VII's meaning—but it was picked up because it was quoted in Justice Douglas's book, which was

results count as evidence that Title VII defines discrimination in an antisubordinationist way. Indeed, the study would count all of the following (hypothetical) results as evidence supporting an antisubordinationist interpretation: a) "Women are asking, what does it mean to discriminate against someone because of sex?"; b) "Discrimination against Negroes consists in deviating from a strict colorblind regime."; c) "Americans understand the phrase 'discriminate against women' in an exclusively anticlassificationist way."[130]

Analyzing the results qualitatively, rather than in this mechanistic way, does not generate any reliable answers either. I found, in my own corpus linguistics experiments on the phrase "discriminate against," that different interpreters characterize results differently; that it is very often unclear, or at least debatable, how to categorize a particular result; and that this uncertainty is dramatically compounded by the fact that anticlassificationist and antisubordinationist definitions of discrimination were not understood to be in tension with one another in midcentury America the way they are today.[131] There is no way, when coding these results, to avoid projecting contemporary categorizations of discrimination (anticlassificationism *v.* antisubordinationism) back onto writers who came of age in the first half of the twentieth century, before battles over affirmative action and disparate impact drove a hard wedge between these conceptualizations of discrimination.[132] Proponents of textualism have billed it as a selling point of the

---

published after 1950). Again, this is undertheorized (and what time period is relevant for assessing a statute's original meaning is yet another shadow decision point).

[130] The study does not rely exclusively on collocate data. It also notes that "the most common form of the binomial prejudice and [WORD] was prejudice and discrimination, appearing twice as often as any other word following the phrase prejudice." Phillips, *supra* note 103, at 5. The study cites this as "further evidence of a semantic link" between prejudice and discrimination. *Id.* But nobody disputes that discrimination can entail prejudice. Showing that midcentury Americans often associated those two words with one another does not prove that Title VII defines discrimination in an antisubordinationist way. The study also claims that period dictionaries support its interpretation. But textualists have been citing dictionary definitions of the word "discriminate" for decades and this has not resolved the question of Title VII's meaning. Indeed, textualist judges almost always agree with Justice Gorsuch that the dictionary supports an anticlassificationist reading of the statute. *See infra* notes 335–339 and accompanying text.

[131] *See* Reva B. Siegel, *Equality Talk: Antisubordination and Anticlassification Values in Constitutional Struggles Over* Brown, 117 HARV. L. REV. 1470, 1474–75 (2004) (observing that in the 1950s and 1960s, "talk of classification and subordination did not have the same significance it now has" and that "[t]he understanding that anticlassification and antisubordination are competing principles that vindicate different complexes of values and justify different doctrinal regimes is an outgrowth of decades of struggle over *Brown*").

[132] *Id.* at 1534–44.

methodology that "you don't need a PhD. in history to discover [ordinary public meaning]."[133] But one reason paying attention to history is helpful is that it can reveal problems like the deep anachronism involved in trying to code snippets of text from over half a century ago using contemporary conceptualizations of discrimination.

What this foray into the search for Title VII's original public meaning ultimately demonstrates is the deep subjectivity of textualism. The objective, data-driven veneer of this methodology disguises a wealth of unacknowledged and potentially outcome-determinative and outcome-driven decision-making. Neither the dictionary nor corpus linguistics can resolve deep disputes over what counts as sex discrimination. Courts interpreting Title VII must look beyond the statute's text in order to determine the kinds of conduct it bars.

Proponents of textualism sometimes respond to criticism of this sort by arguing that the failure of dictionaries and corpus linguistics databases to produce determinate results in hard cases is not a reason to abandon textualism. In fact, they argue, this is textualism functioning as it should, yielding determinate results in cases where such results are available, and proving ambiguity where ambiguity exists. Thus, they argue, "even an avowed 'anti-textualist' should be attracted to corpus linguistics . . . for an instrumental or strategic reason"[134]:

> A key move for the anti-textualist is to challenge the purported determinacy of statutory text (or fixation of constitutional language). Corpus analysis can often help in that endeavor. Where the data show that there is no ordinary meaning, or that there is a wide range of ordinary meanings, the interpreter will be free to dismiss the notion of determinacy (or fixation) and turn to other theories or tools of interpretation.[135]

Here is the problem with that argument: It is radiantly clear, to me, that the corpus linguistics data (and the dictionary) strongly support the proposition "that there is no ordinary meaning, or that there is a wide range of ordinary meanings" of Title VII's prohibition on discrimination—and that, consequently, we should "be free to dismiss the notion of determinacy (or fixation) and turn to other theories or tools of interpretation." In the past—prior to the rise of textualism—the

---

[133] Randy E. Barnett, *Another Oblivious Critique of Neil Gorsuch and Originalism*, Wash. Post, (Mar. 14, 2017), https://www.washingtonpost.com/news/volokh-conspiracy/wp/2017/03/14/another-oblivious-critique-of-neil-gorsuch-and-originalism/.

[134] Lee & Mouritsen, *supra* note 111, at 877.

[135] *Id.*

Court shared this view, treating it as a matter of fact that "the word "discrimination" is inherently . . . [ambiguous],"[136] and that "[t]he concept of 'discrimination' . . . is susceptible of varying interpretations."[137] Even today, *outside the context of civil rights*, textualist Justices acknowledge that "the meaning of 'discriminates' is ambiguous"[138]; that there is an inherent "ambiguity in the word 'discriminates'"[139]; and that Court was right to conclude that "'the word "discrimination" is inherently [ambiguous]'"[140] and "'susceptible of varying interpretations.'"[141]

In the domain of civil rights, however, most, if not all, textualists now firmly reject the idea that there is anything ambiguous about the meaning of discrimination. Indeed, the rejection of the idea that there is any ambiguity about the meaning of discrimination is deeply bound up with the development of textualism itself. When Justice Scalia was beginning to develop the new textualism in the late 1980s, he held up Title VII's bar on sex discrimination as "a model of statutory draftsmanship" and argued that the law defined discrimination with crystalline "clarity"[142] (Justice Scalia argued in that case—which involved affirmative action—that Title VII unambiguously defines discrimination in a thin, anticlassificationist way.[143]) The conservative Justices who embrace textualism in *Bostock* all agree with Justice Scalia's assessment that the statute's meaning is unambiguous—though they vehemently disagree about what that meaning is. All of the textualist scholars who have weighed in on *Bostock* (of whom I am aware) have also endorsed the idea that the statute's meaning is unambiguous, though they too disagree about what that meaning is.[144]

---

[136] Guardians Ass'n v. Civ. Serv. Comm'n, 463 U.S. 582, 592 (1983) (interpreting Title VI of the 1964 Civil Rights Act).

[137] Regents of Univ. of Cal. v. Bakke, 438 U.S. 265, 284 (1978) (Powell, J.).

[138] Ala. Dep't of Revenue v. CSX Transp., Inc., 575 U.S. 21, 37 (2015) (Thomas, J., dissenting) (interpreting the Railroad Revitalization and Regulatory Reform Act of 1976, which, *inter alia*, bars states from imposing a "tax that discriminates against a rail carrier").

[139] CSX Transp., Inc. v. Ala. Dep't of Revenue, 562 U.S. 277, 303 (2011) (Thomas, J., dissenting).

[140] *Id.* at 298–99 (quoting *Guardians Ass'n*, 463 U.S. at 592).

[141] *Id.* at 299 (quoting *Bakke*, 438 U.S. at 284); *see also id.* (discussing the multiple ambiguities in the meaning of the word "discriminates" in the phrase "tax that discriminates against a rail carrier").

[142] Johnson v. Transp. Agency, 480 U.S. 616, 657 (1987) (Scalia, J., dissenting).

[143] *See infra* notes 196–199 and accompanying text for a discussion of the way textualist judges toggle between different definitions of discrimination in different contexts.

[144] For textualist arguments that Title VII unambiguously protects gay and transgender workers, see, e.g., Eyer, *supra* note 96, at 72–80; Grove, *supra* note 55, at 274–82; Ilya Somin,

It is not a coincidence that all, or nearly all, textualists insist that Title VII's meaning is unambiguous.[145] Textualists have a strong incentive to deny ambiguity. If one concedes that there is often a need to look beyond the text and rely on extratextual sources to determine statutory meaning, many of the arguments regarding the special objectivity and value-free nature of textualist methodology lose their force.[146] Thus, the argument that non-textualists ought to embrace corpus linguistics because it can reveal ambiguity and thereby justify reliance on non-textualist methodologies rests on a faulty premise: that determining whether a statute is ambiguous is itself a value-free, text-driven enterprise.[147] In fact, as *Bostock* shows, that determination is itself a major shadow decision point, and one that is deeply reliant on extratextual considerations (including the desire to bolster the practice of textualism itself). In this way, the ambiguity determination is

---

Textualism and Purposivism in Today's Supreme Court Decision on Discrimination Against Gays, Lesbians, and Transsexuals, VOLOKH CONSPIRACY (June 15, 2020, 5:43 PM), https://reason.com /2020/06/15/textualism-and-purposivism-in-todays-supreme-court-decision-on-discrimination -against-gays-lesbians-and-transsexuals/. For textualist arguments that Title VII unambiguously does not protect gay and transgender workers, see, e.g., Nelson Lund, *Unleashed and Unbound: Living Textualism in* Bostock v. Clayton County, 21 FED. SOC'Y REV. 158 (2020); Blackman & Barnett, *supra* note 127; Blackman, *supra* note 127; George, *supra* note 127; John O. McGinnis, *Errors of Will and of Judgment*, L. & LIBERTY (June 25, 2020), https://lawliberty.org/errors-of-will -and-of-judgment/; Phillips, *supra* note 103.

[145] *See* Kavanaugh, *supra* note 41, at 2129 (observing that a "critical difference between textualists and purposivists is that, for a variety of reasons, textualists tend to find language to be clear rather than ambiguous more readily than purposivists").

[146] Admitting ambiguity may also require textualist judges to cede some of their power, as Justice Scalia observed. *See* Antonin Scalia, *Judicial Deference to Administrative Interpretations of Law*, 1989 DUKE L.J. 511, 521 ("One who finds *more* often (as I do) that the meaning of a statute is apparent from its text . . . thereby finds *less* often that the triggering requirement for *Chevron* deference exists. It is thus relatively rare that *Chevron* will require me to accept an interpretation which, though reasonable, I would not personally adopt.").

[147] *See supra* notes 40–45 and accompanying text (Justice Kavanaugh disputes this premise). Justice Scalia himself recognized the faultiness of this premise—at least when it came to the " 'rule of lenity,' which says that any ambiguity in a criminal statute should be resolved in favor of the defendant," and the "rule which says that ambiguities in treaties and statutes dealing with Indian rights are to be resolved in favor of the Indians." SCALIA, *supra* note 27, at 27. Justice Scalia rejected these rules because it was "virtually impossible to expect uniformity and objectivity" while according judges so much flexibility. *Id.* at 28. He wrote: "Every statute that comes into litigation is to some degree 'ambiguous'; how ambiguous does ambiguity have to be before the rule of lenity or the rule in favor of Indians applies?" *Id.*; *see also* United States v. Hansen, 772 F.2d 940, 948 (D.C. Cir. 1985) (Scalia, J.) ("[The rule of lenity] provides little more than atmospherics, since it leaves open the crucial question—almost invariably present—of how much ambiguousness constitutes an ambiguity."). But presumptions in favor of vulnerable groups are not *sui generis* in requiring judges to make determinations about ambiguity: *textualism itself* requires judges to make such determinations. It is not clear why Justice Scalia found the ambiguity determination to be a major, problematic shadow decision point in one context but not the other.

like every other textualist choice the Justices make in *Bostock*. It demonstrates that textualism does not eradicate extratextual considerations but simply pushes those considerations underground, making it
appear that the Justices are having a fight about methodological matters when they are in fact engaged in value-laden arguments about how
to implement Title VII's deeply underspecified antidiscrimination
guarantee.

One of the most striking aspects of *Bostock* is how little any of
the Justices say about any of their ostensibly methodological choices.
Justice Gorsuch offers no explanation for eschewing corpus linguistics
and relying on the dictionary, for analyzing the word "discriminate"
in isolation, or for selecting the thin, anticlassificationist definition
of that word. Nor does he explain how he concluded—in the face of
enormous disagreement and his own assertion at oral argument that
this "case is really close, really close, on the textual evidence"[148]—that,
actually, "no ambiguity exists about how Title VII's terms apply to the
facts."[149] Justice Alito likewise offers no justification for relying on
corpus linguistics or for the various highly contestable choices underlying his conclusion that corpus linguistics proves that Title VII
bars only discrimination motivated by "prejudice, or biased ideas or
attitudes."[150] Nor does he offer any justification for eschewing corpus
linguistics and reverting to the dictionary when it comes to defining
the word "sex."[151] Shifting between textualist tools in this manner
enables Justice Alito to pick his friends out of the crowd. (The corpus
linguistics data presented to the Court on the word "sex" suggests its
original meaning was broad enough to encompass sexual orientation
and gender identity.[152]) This kind of cherry-picking of textualist tools
and definitions offers significant reason to doubt the objectivity of the

[148] Transcript of Oral Argument at 25, R.G. & G.R. Harris Funeral Homes, Inc. v. EEOC, 140 S.
Ct. 1731 (2020) (No. 18-107), https://www.supremecourt.gov/oral_arguments/argument_tran
scripts/2019/18-107_c18e.pdf.

[149] *Bostock v. Clayton County*, 140 S. Ct. 1731, 1749 (2020).

[150] *Id.* at 1769 n.22 (Alito, J., dissenting).

[151] *Id.* at 1756, 1784–91.

[152] *See* Brief for Corpus-Linguistics Scholars Professors Brian Slocum, Stefan Th. Gries,
and Lawrence Solum as Amici Curiae in Support of Employees, *Bostock v. Clayton County*,
140 S. Ct. 1731 (2020) (No. 17-1618) (using corpus linguistics to show that the term "sex"
was used far more capaciously in the 1960s than it is today, in ways that could have encompassed
contemporary conceptions of sexual orientation and gender identity).

textualist enterprise, and the Justices offer no arguments for their methodological choices that would in any way allay those doubts.

The larger point here is that the Justices in *Bostock* are not actually engaged in a value-neutral dispute over textualist methodologies. They do not have—or, at least, chose not to explain or to implement—any sustained commitments to particular means of assessing original public meaning. Textualism offers a variety of tools to pick and choose at key points, and the Justices in *Bostock* take full advantage of that flexibility. But even if the Justices had clear and articulated transcontextual methodological commitments regarding the practice of textualism, implementing those commitments would not yield determinate answers. The meaning of Title VII's bar on discrimination is simply underdetermined from a textualist standpoint. Congress did not define the key words of the statute, those words are susceptible of multiple interpretations, and their meaning is constantly being contested. The Justices are thus required to make a series of interpretive choices based on extratextual considerations in order to resolve disputes over its meaning. But something—perhaps textualism itself—appears to preclude them from acknowledging (or perhaps even recognizing) when they are looking outside the text for guidance in making those choices.

The next section shows that the need to look beyond the text does not end once the Justices select their preferred definitions of discrimination. It is also necessary to look beyond the text in order to *apply* those definitions to the facts in *Bostock*. All of the Justices act as though determining the semantic meaning of Title VII's prohibition on sex discrimination automatically resolves the question of whether that prohibition extends to discrimination on the basis of sexual orientation and gender identity. It does not. Determining the statute's semantic meaning is only the start of the analysis. Part II examines the extratextual judgments that guide the dissenters' application of their preferred antisubordinationist understanding of the statute. The next section shows that the majority too engages in extratextual judgments in applying its preferred anticlassificationist understanding. There is no way to apply even this "simple" definition of discrimination absent the kind of value judgments textualism supposedly excludes.

2). *Applying Bostock's "Simple Test" for Discrimination.* The Court in *Bostock* asserts, based on its textualist analysis, that Title VII establishes a "simple test" for detecting sex discrimination: "ask[] whether an individual female employee would have been treated the same regardless of her sex"[153] (or, if the plaintiff is male, whether he would have been treated the same regardless of his sex). If the answer is no, sex discrimination has occurred.

Visit almost any American workplace, however, and you will find employees being subjected to this kind of sex-based differential treatment on a daily basis, with no relief in sight from Title VII. For example, there is a near-universal consensus among courts that sex-differentiated grooming codes and sex-segregated bathrooms do not violate Title VII, even though a woman who is fired for refusing to wear make-up or for entering the men's bathroom can argue, quite persuasively, that her employer would not have fired a man for engaging in those acts. In these contexts, however, courts do not "buy[] into th[e] [literalist] approach."[154] They routinely hold that such policies do not discriminate on the basis of sex, but rather require male and female employees alike to comply with basic social norms. In *Willingham v. Macon Telegraph Publishing*, probably the most cited case in this area, the Fifth Circuit explained that when an employer institutes a sex-specific grooming policy, "each sex is treated equally" because "both sexes are being screened with respect to a neutral fact, i.e., grooming in accordance with generally accepted community standards of dress and appearance."[155] This reasoning has also been used to justify sex-segregated bathrooms—the idea being that "'[e]very student can use a restroom associated with their physiology, whether they are boys or girls.'"[156] As long as the burdens on the sexes are equal, in the courts' view, such "generally applicable, gender-specific policies"[157] are not understood to "'discriminate' on the basis of sex within the meaning of Title VII."[158]

---

[153] *Bostock*, 140 S. Ct. at 1743.

[154] *Cf. id.* at 1824 (Kavanaugh, J., dissenting) (criticizing the Court for "buy[ing] into this approach" in *Bostock*).

[155] 507 F.2d 1084, 1092 (5th Cir. 1975).

[156] G.G. *ex rel.* Grimm v. Gloucester Cnty. Sch. Bd., 972 F.3d 586, 624 (4th Cir. 2020) (Wynn, C.J., concurring) (quoting the school board's explanation for why its exclusion of a transgender boy from the boys' bathroom did not discriminate on the basis of sex).

[157] Schroer v. Billington, 577 F. Supp. 2d 293, 304 (D.D.C. 2008).

[158] Viscecchia v. Alrose Allegria LLC, 117 F. Supp. 3d 243, 253 (E.D.N.Y. 2015) (finding that a policy requiring male but not female employees to have short hair did not discriminate on the basis of sex); *see also* Jespersen v. Harrah's Operating Co., 444 F.3d 1104, 1110 (9th Cir. 2006) ("We have long recognized that companies may differentiate between men and women in appearance and grooming policies, and so have other circuits. The material issue under

Until very recently, courts characterized discrimination against gay and transgender people in this same sex-neutralizing way. They rejected the argument that discrimination against gays and lesbians is sex-based, reasoning that "whether dealing with men or women the employer is using the same criterion: it will not hire or promote a person who prefers sexual partners of the same sex."[159] Courts adopted a parallel sex-neutralizing characterization of discrimination against transgender people, finding that it was based on employers' objection to "*change* in sex," a form of conduct in which both men and women engage.[160] This was the core of the dissenting Justices' argument in *Bostock*. Justice Alito asserted that "[i]n cases involving discrimination based on sexual orientation or gender identity, the grounds for the employer's decision—that individuals should be sexually attracted only to persons of the opposite biological sex or should identify with their biological sex—apply equally to men and women."[161]

The Court in *Bostock* decided to stop characterizing discrimination against gay and transgender people in this sex-neutralizing way. It rejected the approach of the grooming cases and likened anti-LGBT discrimination instead to a policy under which "an employer eager to revive the workplace gender roles of the 1950s. . . . enforces a policy that he will hire only men as mechanics and only women as secretaries."[162] The employer could argue that this policy does not discriminate on the basis of sex because it requires men and women alike

---

our settled law is . . . whether the policy imposed on the plaintiff creates an 'unequal burden' for the plaintiff's gender." (citations omitted)); Harper v. Blockbuster Ent. Corp., 139 F.3d 1385, 1389 (11th Cir. 1998) (holding that the permissibility of sex-differentiated grooming codes is so well-established that plaintiffs could not have had an objectively reasonable belief that their employer's grooming policy discriminated against them on the basis of sex); Tavora v. New York Mercantile Exch., 101 F.3d 907, 908 (2d Cir. 1996) (upholding a policy that barred male but not female employees from having long hair in part because "such employment policies have only a *de minimis* effect"); Boyce v. Gen. Ry. Signal Co., No. 99-CV-6225T, 2004 WL 1574023, at *1 (W.D.N.Y. 2004) ("[A]llegations based upon a male employee's hair length do not give rise to a sustainable claim under Title VII.").

[159] DeSantis v. Pac. Tel. & Tel. Co., 608 F.2d 327, 331 (9th Cir. 1979); *id.* ("[T]his policy does not involve different decisional criteria for the sexes").

[160] Grossman v. Bernards Twp. Bd. of Educ., No. 74-1904, 1975 WL 302, at *4 (D.N.J. Sept. 10, 1975); *id.* ("No facts are alleged to indicate, for example, that plaintiff's employment was terminated because of any stereotypical concepts about the ability of females to perform certain tasks, nor because of any condition common only to woman." (internal citation omitted)).

[161] *Bostock v. Clayton County*, 140 S. Ct. 1731, 1764 (2020) (Alito, J., dissenting).

[162] *Id.* at 1748.

to conform to traditional gender roles. But, the Court declared, "No one thinks *that*."[163]

But why do we think what we think about these various examples? How do courts decide which policies to characterize in sex-neutralizing ways and which policies to characterize as sex discrimination? For that matter, why do courts think it is permissible for employers to require female but not male lifeguards to wear bathing suit tops,[164] but not to require female but not male employees to wear uniforms?[165] Why do courts think it is permissible to have a men's basketball team but not a men's law firm? Why do courts think it is permissible for employers hiring in male-dominated fields to engage in the targeted recruitment of women but not of men? The American workplace is replete with sex-based differential treatment and Title VII constrains only some of it. The text of the statute is of very limited use in helping to make or to explain legal determinations about the licitness of various sex-conscious practices.[166]

Against this backdrop, it is possible to see more clearly what *Bostock* did and did not do. *Bostock* rejected courts' long-standing practice of erasing the sex-dependent judgments constitutive of antigay and

---

[163] *Id.* at 1749.

[164] *See* Zarda v. Altitude Express, Inc., 883 F.3d 100, 150 (2d Cir. 2018) (Lynch, J., dissenting) (assuming widespread judicial agreement with the proposition "that a pool that required both male and female lifeguards to wear a uniform consisting only of trunks would violate Title VII, while one that prescribed trunks for men and a bathing suit covering the breasts for women would not").

[165] Carroll v. Talman Fed. Sav. & Loan Ass'n of Chicago, 604 F.2d 1028, 1029 (7th Cir. 1979) (finding a Title VII violation because the company "requires all of its female tellers, office and managerial employees to wear a uniform, whereas male employees in the same positions need wear only customary business attire").

[166] Richard Primus and Reva Siegel, among others, have made a similar point in the context of race, showing that what counts as an "express racial classification" is, at least in part, a normative question. Richard A. Primus, *Equal Protection and Disparate Impact: Round Three*, 117 HARV. L. REV. 493, 509 (2003) (arguing that courts "decide whether to apply strict scrutiny based on a normative sense that a statute is constitutionally problematic and then, reasoning backwards, announce that something in the statute constitutes an express classification"); *id.* at 505–06 ("[M]any practices that do involve government actors' identifying people by race are not always subject to strict scrutiny. Examples include the police use of racial descriptions of criminal suspects, the Census Bureau's collection of demographic data, state legislatures' race-based redistricting practices, and social service agencies' race-conscious adoption placements.... [N]ot all instances in which the government explicitly considers the race of individuals are 'express racial classifications' for purposes of equal protection doctrine. Some are, and some are not."); Reva B. Siegel, *Foreword: Equality Divided*, 127 HARV. L. REV. 1, 59–67 (2013) (comparing and contrasting judicial stances toward race-conscious affirmative action policies with judicial stances toward race-conscious stop-and-frisk policies).

antitrans discrimination by characterizing such discrimination in sex-neutralizing terms. It did not develop an objective, text-driven way to determine what counts as sex discrimination. The Court declared in *Bostock* that "an employer who intentionally treats a person worse because of sex ... discriminates against that person in violation of Title VII."[167] But there is no way to implement that rule without looking beyond the text of the statute. As the examples cited above demonstrate, it is impossible to determine when employers are treating an individual of one sex "worse" than an individual of another without considering the social context and making a normatively inflected judgment.

In fact, it is not even possible to determine when employers are treating the sexes *differently* without engaging in such judgment. Consider the case of the would-be FBI agent who flunked out of the FBI Academy after falling one push-up short of the number required of men to progress to the next stage of training.[168] He filed a Title VII claim against the Bureau, correctly claiming that if he were a woman, the number of push-ups he completed would have satisfied the test. But the Fourth Circuit rejected his claim. It held that the Bureau's sex-differentiated standards treat men and women the same because they demand the same level of fitness of both sexes. Indeed, the court suggested that *equalizing* the raw scores required of applicants would *discriminate* against women because it would require them to be considerably more fit than their male counterparts to pass the test.[169] The court explained that "[w]hether physical fitness standards discriminate based on sex ... depends on whether they require men and women to demonstrate different levels of fitness."[170] This decision was not an outlier: the Fourth Circuit noted that no court has found sex-differentiated physical fitness standards to be discriminatory under Title VII.[171]

---

[167] Bostock v. Clayton County, 140 S. Ct. 1731, 1740 (2020).

[168] Bauer v. Lynch, 812 F.3d 340 (4th Cir. 2016).

[169] *Id.* at 349 (suggesting "that some differential treatment of men and women based upon inherent physiological differences is not only lawful but also potentially required" under Title VII (quotation marks omitted)); *see also* Powell v. Reno, No. 962743, 1997 U.S. Dist. LEXIS 24169, at **10–11 (D.D.C. July 24, 1999) (finding that "physical tests in which women are compared against women and men are compared against men do not discriminate against either sex," and that, in fact, "physical fitness tests that have the same standards for men and women may discriminate against women in violation of Title VII").

[170] *Bauer*, 812 F.3d at 351.

[171] *Id.* at 348. For other decisions upholding sex-differentiated physical fitness standards, see, e.g., *In re* Scott, 172 Vt. 288 (2001) (upholding as non-discriminatory sex-differentiated

Our legal system does not generally treat sex-differentiation in sports as violating prohibitions on sex discrimination either. Here too, it is often unclear what counts as treating the sexes the same or differently. Title IX of the 1972 Education Amendments bars discrimination on the basis of sex under any education program or activity that receives federal funds.[172] The law contains several exemptions, but it does not exempt athletics from its antidiscrimination mandate. The regulations implementing Title IX affirm that "[n]o person shall, on the basis of sex, ... be treated differently from another person or otherwise be discriminated against."[173] Then, in the next sentence, those regulations begin to lay out rules for establishing sex-segregated teams.[174] Indeed, the agency that first produced these regulations specifically stated that if a school opens its teams to members of both sexes and girls do not make the teams, sex-segregated teams might be required under the law.[175] That remains true today.[176] There are a million questions (and lawsuits) about what constitutes discrimination on the basis of sex in this context, where the baseline is for making that determination, and how to treat male and female athletes the same, or equally. Even assuming we all accepted Justice Gorsuch's understanding of sex discrimination, the law's text—and the "simple test"— wouldn't get us very far in many of these cases.

Examples of and variations on these problems abound in the employment context. What about the "female lineman" who filed a Title VII claim after complaining about the absence of bathroom facilities and being told she should just urinate outside like all the other

---

standards designed "to hold males and females to *the same level of fitness* based on their aerobic capacity" in Vermont State Police examination); Hale v. Holder, EEOC Decision No. 570-2007-00423X, at *4 (2010) (holding that FBI established sex-differentiated but "equivalent relative fitness standards for males and females and thereby applied nondiscriminatory fitness requirements to its trainees").

[172] 20 U.S.C. §1681(a) (2000) ("No person in the United States shall, on the basis of sex, be excluded from participation in, be denied the benefits of, or be subjected to discrimination under any education program or activity receiving Federal financial assistance. . . .").

[173] 34 C.F.R. § 106.41(a) (2020).

[174] *Id.* § 106.41(b) (2020).

[175] *See* Off. for Civil Rights, U.S. Dep't of Educ., Letter to Chief State School Officers, Title IX Obligations in Athletics (Nov. 11, 1975), https://www2.ed.gov/about/offices/list/ocr/docs/holmes.html (stating that a school would not be in compliance with Title IX if it disbanded "its women's teams and opened up its men's teams to women, but only a few women were able to quality for the men's teams").

[176] *See* 34 C.F.R. § 106.41(c) (2020).

(male) linemen do?[177] Or the female firefighter who was required to sleep in the men's bunk room, which technically became a unisex bunk room once she was hired?[178] Were these women being treated the same as their male counterparts, or differently?

The point here is that applying the "simple test" for discrimination is nowhere near as simple as the Court in *Bostock* suggests. Even if a judge tried to apply the "simple test" across the board, in an entirely text-driven way, the need to consult extratextual sources and make normative choices would still arise. Textualism can mask those choices. But it is of little help when it comes to actually making choices about what forms of regulation violate the law's prohibition on discrimination.

3). *Context Matters: Textualists' Disparate Treatment of Sex and Race.* The underlying normativity of textualist decision-making becomes particularly apparent if we look beyond the interpretation of legal prohibitions on sex discrimination alone and compare it with the interpretation of legal prohibitions on race discrimination. Antidiscrimination doctrine—in both the constitutional and the statutory contexts—only partially constrains sex-based classifications but adopts a considerably stricter stance toward race-based classifications. In fact, sex-based Title VII doctrine has more in common with sex-based equal protection doctrine in this regard than it does with race-based Title VII doctrine—and that is true even (maybe even especially) in textualist jurisprudence. The fact that textualist judges define discrimination differently where sex and race are concerned—even though Title VII does not—is a pretty fair indication that textualist decision-making in these contexts is not based on text alone.

In *Bostock*, the Court insists it can determine what counts as sex discrimination without looking beyond Title VII's text. But in the constitutional context, the Court has long insisted on the need for socially

---

[177] *See* DeClue v. Cent. Ill. Light Co., 223 F.3d 434, 438 (7th Cir. 2000) (Rovner, C.J., dissenting in part) ("[R]efusal to provide female employees with restrooms can be understood as creating a hostile work environment" under Title VII's sex provision; *see also id.* at 439–40 ("Discrimination in the real world many times does not fit neatly into the legal models we have constructed. . . . Because prejudice and ignorance have a way of defying formulaic constructs, the lines with which we attempt to divide the various categories of discrimination cannot be rigid.").

[178] *See* Epps v. City of Pittsburgh, 33 F. Supp. 2d 409, 410 (W.D. Pa. 1998). The plaintiff refused to sleep in the station's bunk room, where the male firefighters typically wore few clothes. She "initially slept on an old couch in the . . . garage . . . behind a fire engine," but then a captain destroyed it and informed her "she must sleep in the bunk room with the men." *Id.* at 410–11.

attentive judgments in determining what counts as sex discrimination. *United States v. Virginia,*[179] the leading constitutional sex discrimination decision, holds that the question of whether a sex-based practice is discriminatory depends on whether it perpetuates traditional social hierarchies or reinforces conventional sex-role stereotypes. The Court explains that "[s]ex classifications may be used to compensate women 'for particular economic disabilities [they have] suffered,' to 'promot[e] equal employment opportunity,' [and] to advance full development of the talent and capacities of our Nation's people."[180] But, the Court holds, "such classifications may not be used, as they once were, to create or perpetuate the legal, social, and economic inferiority of women."[181]

All of the Justices, liberal and conservative alike, embrace the idea that sex classifications are sometimes permissible under the Fourteenth Amendment and that determining the constitutionality of such classifications requires an inquiry into their social purposes and effects. For instance, Justice Scalia would have upheld the exclusion of women from the Virginia Military Institute on the ground "[t]hat single gender education at the college level is beneficial to both sexes," and that the facts "utterly refute the claim that VMI has elected to maintain its all male student body composition for some misogynistic reason."[182] In *Nguyen v. Immigration and Naturalization Service,* Justice Kennedy upheld a law that made it harder for American fathers to transmit their citizenship to children born overseas than it was for American mothers after finding that the disparate treatment reflected real biological differences and did not reinforce sex stereotypes.[183] Justice Kennedy explained in *Nguyen* that sex classifications are discriminatory only when they are "marked by misconception and prejudice" or when they "show disrespect for either class."[184] Conservative Justices have rejected anticlassificationist approaches to sex discrimination since the 1970s, arguing that courts should not "treat gender classification as a talisman . . . without regard to the rights involved or the persons affected."[185]

---

[179] 518 U.S. 515 (1996).

[180] *Id.* at 533 (citations and footnote omitted) (second and third alterations in original).

[181] *Id.* at 534.

[182] *Id.* at 580 (Scalia, J., dissenting).

[183] Tuan Anh Nguyen v. INS, 533 U.S. 53, 68 (2001).

[184] *Id.* at 73.

[185] Craig v. Boren, 429 U.S. 190, 220 (1976) (Rehnquist, J., dissenting); *id.* at 219 (arguing against heightened scrutiny of a law enabling young women to buy low-alcohol beer at a

But this is not how conservative Justices approach the issue of classification in the context of race. At the same time these Justices were developing the argument that courts should not treat sex classification as a talisman of illegality, they were starting to argue the opposite in the context of race, under both Title VII and the Fourteenth Amendment. In 1979, the Court issued a landmark decision, *United Steelworkers of America v. Weber*,[186] upholding an affirmative action program against a race-based Title VII challenge. That decision elicited a forceful dissent from Justice Rehnquist (who three years earlier warned against treating sex classification as a talisman), arguing that racial classification *is* a talisman of illegality. He argued that "[t]he operative sections of Title VII prohibit racial discrimination in employment *simpliciter*," and that the "normal meaning" of the statute's bar on discrimination categorically "prohibits a covered employer from considering race when making an employment decision."[187] In fact, the massive conservative backlash to the Court's decision in *Weber* helped to fuel the rise of textualism in the 1980s.[188] Justice Scalia had been on the Court for less than a year when he issued one of the boldest dissenting opinions of his career, demanding that *Weber* be overruled.[189] Justice Scalia argued in that opinion that Title VII's prohibition on discrimination was "a model of statutory draftsmanship" and that it defined discrimination—with crystalline "clarity"—in strict anticlassificationist terms.[190]

Conservative Justices in this period also began to interpret the Fourteenth Amendment's bar on race discrimination in this way, arguing that all race-based classifications should be subject to strict scrutiny and almost always invalidated.[191]

---

younger age than young men because there is no evidence "males in this age group are in any way peculiarly disadvantaged, subject to systematic discriminatory treatment, or otherwise in need of special solicitude from the courts").

[186] United Steelworkers of America v. Weber, 443 U.S. 193 (1979).

[187] *Id.* at 220; *id.* at 254 (arguing that "the cold words of the statute itself" bar racial classifications of any kind, including affirmative action).

[188] Philip P. Frickey, John Minor Wisdom Lecture: Wisdom on *Weber*, *in* 74 Tul. L. Rev. 1169, 1184 (2000) (suggesting "the conservative reaction to *Weber*[] has provided much fuel for the remarkable evolution in conservative statutory methodology we have seen since the early 1980s").

[189] Johnson v. Transp. Agency, 480 U.S. 616, 657 (1987) (Scalia, J., dissenting).

[190] *Id.*

[191] Conservative Justices argued then, and argue today, that all racial classifications are subject to strict scrutiny, but, as noted above, the question of what counts as a classification

Justice Scalia argued that "to classify and judge men and women on the basis of . . . the color of their skin. . . . is illegal, immoral, unconstitutional, inherently wrong, and destructive of democratic society."[192] Justice Thomas has suggested that only the need to prevent imminent "anarchy" or "violence" could ever justify race-based state action.[193] He has explained that "[t]he Constitution abhors classifications based on race . . . because every time the government places citizens on racial registers and makes race relevant to the provision of burdens or benefits, it demeans us all."[194] That was also the logic behind Chief Justice John Roberts' plurality opinion in *Parents Involved in Community Schools v. Seattle School District No. 1*: "racial classifications are simply too pernicious to permit"[195] in almost all circumstances, regardless of their social purposes or effects.

What is important for purposes of this Article—and a serious challenge to explain from a textualist perspective—are the substantial continuities between Fourteenth Amendment doctrine and Title VII doctrine when it comes to defining discrimination in the contexts of race and sex. The text of Title VII's prohibition on discrimination is identical with respect to race and sex: It states that employers may not "discriminate against any individual . . . because of such individual's race . . . [or] sex."[196] But as in the equal protection context, courts in Title VII cases have treated race discrimination and sex discrimination differently: they have adopted a more anticlassificationist approach in the context of race and a more antisubordinationist approach in

---

remains a major shadow decision point. *See supra* note 166. The Court has yet to provide an adequate account of what counts as a classification.

[192] City of Richmond v. J.A. Croson Co., 488 U.S. 469, 520–21 (1989).

[193] Grutter v. Bollinger, 539 U.S. 306, 353 (2003) (Thomas, J., dissenting).

[194] *Id.*

[195] Parents Involved in Cmty. Sch. v. Seattle Sch. Dist. No. 1, 551 U.S. 701, 702 (2007).

[196] 42 U.S.C. § 2000e(k) (2012); *see also* Johnson v. Transp. Agency, 480 U.S. 616, 665 (1987) (Scalia, J., dissenting) (observing that "the portions of Title VII at issue here [including the statute's core antidiscrimination provision] treat race and sex equivalently"). Title VII does treat race and sex differently with respect to the bona fide occupational qualification (BFOQ) exception. The law states that in certain instances a person's religion, sex, or national origin may be reasonably necessary to carrying out a particular job function; in those exceptional instances, the law permits employers to discriminate on the relevant basis. 42 U.S.C. § 2000e-2(e) (2012). The statute does not permit race to function as a BFOQ. *Id.* This does not, however, provide a sound textualist justification for courts' differing interpretations of race and sex discrimination outside the BFOQ context, and I am not aware of any textualist who argues that the existence of the BFOQ exception means that Title VII defines discrimination in an antisubordinationist way with respect to most of the covered categories—including national origin—but adopts an exceptional anticlassificationist definition in the context of race.

the context of sex.[197] Judge Lynch very matter-of-factly references the differential treatment of race and sex in Title VII jurisprudence in his dissenting opinion in *Zarda*. He observes that in race-based Title VII cases, "courts have taken the view that to distinguish *is*, for the most part, to discriminate."[198] But in sex-based Title VII cases, they have held that "not every distinction between men and women in the workplace constitutes discrimination against one gender or the other."[199]

The difference in the law's treatment of race-segregated and sex-segregated bathrooms and locker rooms illustrates this phenomenon in a particularly stark way. Race-segregated facilities are now illegal, of course, while sex-segregated bathrooms and locker rooms remain ubiquitous. Courts offer a variety of reasons for the differential treatment: there are real biological differences between the sexes; "many people . . . are reticent about disrobing or using toilet facilities in the presence of individuals" of the opposite sex; "[f]or women who have been victimized by sexual assault or abuse, the experience of seeing an unclothed [male] person . . . in a confined and sensitive location such as a bathroom or locker room can cause serious psychological harm."[200] But those are all extratextual considerations. Title VII bars discrimination because of race and sex. The idea that segregated bathrooms are stigmatizing and discriminatory in one of those contexts and innocuous or even desirable in the other does not come from the text.[201] It is a product of evolving social values.[202]

---

[197] *See* Reva B. Siegel, *Pregnancy as a Normal Condition of Employment: Comparative and Role-Based Accounts of Discrimination*, 59 Wm. & Mary L. Rev. 969, 987–90 (2018) (discussing the differing conceptions of discrimination conservatives apply in the contexts of race and sex); *id.* at 988 (noting the frequency with which advocates of anticlassificationism in the race context make "substantive judgments about which kinds of sex distinctions are sex discriminatory"). In fact, it is the conservative textualist judges who toggle most insistently between different definitions of discrimination in the contexts of race and sex. Liberal judges generally apply an antisubordinationist understanding across the board.

[198] Zarda v. Altitude Express, Inc., 883 F.3d 100, 149 (2d Cir. 2018) (Lynch, J., dissenting).

[199] *Id.*

[200] Bostock v. Clayton County, 140 S. Ct. 1731, 1778–79 (2020) (Alito, J., dissenting).

[201] Indeed, when it comes to bathrooms, conservative textualist judges, such as Judge William Pryor of the Eleventh Circuit, argue that "context matters." Adams *ex rel.* Kasper v. Sch. Bd. of St. Johns Cnty., 968 F.3d 1286, 1311 (11th Cir. 2020) (Pryor, C.J., dissenting); *id.* ("As the late Justice Thurgood Marshall once put it, 'A sign that says "men only" looks very different on a bathroom door than a courthouse door.'"). Needless to say, this is not the stance conservative textualists take when it comes to affirmative action.

[202] If the result of *Bostock* is that Title VII now bars employers from requiring transgender employees—but not cisgender employees—to use bathrooms associated with their birth sex, that will be yet another example of the influence of extratextual considerations on textualist

4). *Textualism's Democratic Deficit.* Robert Post has argued that a necessary consequence of the fact that "constitutional law could not plausibly proceed without incorporating the values and beliefs of non-judicial actors" is that "constitutional law will be as dynamic and as contested as the cultural values and beliefs that inevitably form part of the substance of constitutional law."[203] The same is true of Title VII law. Like the equal protection clause, Title VII was enacted prior to the women's rights and LGBT rights movements. The changes those movements have wrought, and the legal and social conflicts they continue to engender, have powerfully shaped the law's meaning over the past half-century. Textualist rhetoric might lead one to assume that textualism would act as a drag on this process, eternally confining Title VII to what it meant at the time of its enactment. But the ascendance of textualism has not resulted in a noticeably less dynamic antidiscrimination jurisprudence than the jurisprudence produced by more explicitly dynamic methodologies. Decisions framed in textualist terms have been just as responsive to developments fueled by social mobilizations and legal contestation as decisions adopting other methodological approaches. *Oncale* and *Bostock* are paradigmatic examples: they are both textualist, but also doctrinally innovative, and they both build on, and in turn shape, important ongoing processes of legal and social change.

This dynamism and responsiveness to cultural and doctrinal evolution raises important and difficult questions about textualism that have thus far gone unaddressed by the Court. There is one point in *Bostock* where the Court appears to tee up such questions: It acknowledges toward the end of its opinion that Title VII was not always interpreted as it is now. In the 1960s and 1970s, judges held that "Title VII did not prevent an employer from firing an employee for refusing his sexual advances," and that the practice of "hiring mothers but not fathers of young children wasn't discrimination because of sex."[204] Indeed, the Court observes that, "[i]n the years immediately following Title VII's passage, the EEOC officially opined that listing men's

---

interpretation. That result may reflect the best reading of current legal doctrine, and it may track emerging majoritarian social values, but it does not spring unambiguously from the text of the law.

[203] Post, *supra* note 65, at 4, 10.

[204] Bostock v. Clayton County, 140 S. Ct. 1731, 1752 (2020).

positions and women's positions separately in job postings was simply helpful rather than discriminatory."[205] No one thinks any of *this* today, so what changed?

The Court drew these examples from a law review article I wrote on the meaning of Title VII's sex provision.[206] That article quotes an EEOC Commissioner who observed in the mid-1960s that "the sex provision of Title VII is mysterious and difficult to understand and control."[207] The widely acknowledged ambiguity of the sex provision at the time of its enactment meant that legal actors had to consult extratextual sources as guides to its meaning. Women's rights advocates especially helped to shape popular and judicial conceptions of the provision's meaning—in some cases inventing new conceptual tools that extended the law's reach to practices previously viewed as distinct from sex discrimination. By the early 1980s, courts and the EEOC had reversed themselves in all of the instances the Court cites. My article shows that those reversals—of which all the Justices in *Bostock* approve—were driven by social and legal contestation that shaped the statute's meaning.

The Court, however, makes no mention of that history. It (partially) reproduces the quote from the EEOC Commissioner but omits the part where he says that Title VII's sex provision is "mysterious and difficult to understand." The Court instead characterizes him as saying that "the words of 'the sex provision of Title VII [are] difficult to . . . control'"[208]—a form of selective editing that obscures the fact that there was explicit discussion of the law's ambiguity at the time of its enactment. The Court also omits any mention of the legal feminists who exerted such a substantial influence on the law's development (including those who founded the National Organization for Women in 1966 explicitly in order "to effect 'a public redefinition of discrimination based on sex'" under Title VII[209]). The Court instead explains

---

[205] *Id.*

[206] *Id.* (citing Cary Franklin, *Inventing the "Traditional Concept" of Sex Discrimination*, 125 Harv. L. Rev. 1307, 1338, 1340, 1345 (2012)).

[207] Franklin, *supra* note 206, at 1338 & n.153 (quoting Federal Mediation Service to Play Role in Implementing Title VII, [1965–1968 Transfer Binder] Empl. Prac. Dec. (CCH) P8046, at 6074 (Feb. 7, 1966) (internal quotation marks omitted)).

[208] *Bostock*, 140 S. Ct. at 1752 (quoting Franklin, *supra* note 206, at 1338, quoting the Commissioner (internal quotation marks omitted)).

[209] *See* Franklin, *supra* note 206, at 1345 (quoting Nat'l Org. for Women, The First Five Years 1966–71, at 16 (1971) (on file with the Schlesinger Library, Radcliffe Institute, Harvard University)); *id.* at 1340–47 (discussing this campaign and the legal results it yielded).

the major interpretive changes that occurred in Title VII jurisprudence in the 1970s and 1980s by claiming that "[o]ver time, the breadth of the statutory language proved too difficult to deny."[210]

This is textualism at its most aggressive: denying the problem of underdeterminacy and the corresponding need to consult extratextual sources even in the face of deeply ambiguous statutory text. The Court in *Bostock* claims that all the change that has occurred in Title VII's meaning over the past half-century, and all the change that occurs in *Bostock* itself, is the product of judges' increasing willingness to heed the unambiguous semantic meaning of Title VII's text; there has never been any "construction"[211] involved. The Court insists that the text alone is and always has been capable in this context of resolving our deepest legal and cultural conflicts.[212]

This approach gives rise to a serious democratic accountability problem. When the Court engages in statutory construction without admitting it, it fails to provide the American people and the coordinate branches of government with a full account of how it is actually constructing the law's meaning: what extratextual sources it is relying on and what rules or principles it is applying to reach the outcomes it does. That is a problem for a host of reasons. For a start, it undermines the democratic dialogue textualism is supposed to enable between the Court and Congress if the Court is not communicating to lawmakers the principles it is actually using to interpret the laws. Interpretive methodology is increasingly at the center of judicial confirmation battles, but elected leaders and the people they represent can hardly object or engage in any real discussion of this topic if judges obscure the methods they actually use. On the most basic level, textualism relieves judges of their obligation to provide a complete and honest

---

[210] *Bostock*, 140 S. Ct. at 1752.

[211] *See* KEITH E. WHITTINGTON, CONSTITUTIONAL INTERPRETATION: TEXTUAL MEANING, ORIGINAL INTENT, AND JUDICIAL REVIEW 7 (1999) (explaining that sometimes, even after all interpretive tools have been applied, "there will remain an impenetrable sphere of meaning that cannot be simply discovered," and asserting that in such cases "[t]he specification of a single governing meaning . . . requires an act of creativity beyond interpretation," which he refers to as "the construction of meaning").

[212] Justice Gorsuch cites key Title VII precedents in his opinion, and some have argued that his opinion actually relies more heavily on those (non-textualist) precedents than on the original meaning of Title VII's text. *See, e.g.*, Blackman, *supra* note 127. That may be so. But Justice Gorsuch insists it is not. He argues that the outcome in *Bostock* is determined entirely by Title VII's ordinary public meaning circa 1964 and that he is merely "confirming [his] work against th[e] Court's precedents" when he cites them. *Bostock*, 140 S. Ct. at 1739.

accounting of their reasoning and alleviates the need for them to demonstrate that their opinions are based in law—in the way Judge Katzmann, Judge Moore, and Judge Wood do in the cases leading up to *Bostock*.

This lack of reason-giving also gives rise to a significant rule-of-law problem. The Court in *Bostock* declares that after fifty years of applying Title VII one way, the tools of textualism have now revealed that it ought to be applied another way. Justice Alito ends his dissenting opinion with what he considers a parade of horribles: predictions about where the law will go after *Bostock*.[213] But it is very hard to predict, based on the majority's opinion, whether he is right or what other implications this decision may have. All the Court tells us in *Bostock* is that the dictionary has revealed that gay and transgender workers are covered by Title VII. It is not at all clear, based on this assertion, what the dictionary will reveal next.

In fact, if one wanted to predict where the Court will next find textualist support for a previously losing argument in the context of antidiscrimination law, the best approach would likely be to identify other social mobilizations and kinds of discrimination claims that have recently gained ground at the Court. That seems one of the clearest lessons of *Bostock*, although it is precisely what the Court seeks to deny. That denial does little work, however. It does not actually insulate the Justices from the moral disagreements of the day or eradicate the influence of fifty years of legal and social contestation on the interpretation of Title VII. It simply makes the outcome in *Bostock*—highly justifiable on other, non-textualist legal grounds—more susceptible to accusations that it came about through judicial fiat.

II. The Inevitability of Extratextual Judgments and the Problem of Judicial Accountability

Part I shows that the Court in *Bostock* made a number of critical choices at shadow decision points guided by unacknowledged extratextual considerations. By denying that it was consulting anything other than the text of Title VII, the Court sought to position itself as a wholly independent and autonomous actor: outside politics, above democratic debate, and impervious to legal and social change. That image of courts has considerable popular appeal, but it is an

---

[213] *Bostock*, 140 S. Ct. at 1778–83.

inadequate and misleading model of how courts operate, and it masks the interactive and iterative process through which legal meaning is made and evolves over time. This model also aggrandizes judicial power in antidemocratic ways, enabling judges to respond selectively to favored social mobilizations while claiming absolute neutrality and to make consequential decisions without giving a complete account of their reasons.

The dissenting Justices—Justice Alito, Justice Thomas, and Justice Kavanaugh—argue that the problem in *Bostock* lies not with textualism itself, but with the way the Court does textualism. They accuse the Court of interpreting Title VII's antidiscrimination provision in an overly literal way, for results-oriented reasons. The vast majority of Americans today support antidiscrimination protections for gay and transgender workers. The dissenting Justices argue that the right way to create such protections is by persuading lawmakers to take action, not by using the power of judicial review to write such protections into a statute that was enacted a long time ago and that unambiguously lacks such protections. They argue that textualism done right reveals that the ordinary meaning of sex discrimination in 1964 "was as clear as clear could be,"[214] and that it did not extend to discrimination on the basis of sexual orientation and gender identity. In fact, they argue that the semantic meaning of discrimination "because of sex" has remained constant since the late nineteenth century, when states began to enact early sex-based antidiscrimination provisions,[215] and that none of the Court's precedents prior to *Bostock* did anything to alter that meaning. They argue that, even today, "Title VII's prohibition of discrimination because of 'sex' still means what it has always meant"[216] and that discrimination against LGBT people simply does not fall within this meaning.

This Part shows that the problem does lie with textualism. The outcome the dissenting Justices reach in *Bostock* may hew more closely to the original expected applications of Title VII's sex provision, but their conclusions about the statute's semantic meaning are no more objective or exclusively text-driven than those of the majority. The dissenting Justices make just as many choices at shadow decision

---

[214] *Id.* at 1756.

[215] *Id.* at 1768–69.

[216] *Id.* at 1755.

points as their colleagues, and they too necessarily rely on extratextual considerations, both in deciding how to define sex discrimination and in deciding how to apply that definition.

When it comes to defining discrimination "because of sex," the dissenting Justices claim that the meaning of that phrase has remained constant since the late nineteenth century—or more boldly still, that that phrase has "always" meant the same thing. Examining these claims, one appreciates why the original public meaning methodology causes historians such deep consternation.[217] The idea that the meaning of sex discrimination (semantic or otherwise) has remained unchanged throughout American history is wildly inaccurate. Indeed, much of the historical evidence Justice Alito adduces in support of this proposition actually serves to undermine it. This Part examines popular and judicial understandings of sex discrimination over time in various contexts, including marriage, parenthood, pregnancy, and sexual harassment. It shows that what sex discrimination means— not simply in terms of expected applications but also on a definitional level—has changed substantially over the past century as courts have grappled with claims challenging the legality of various sex-respecting practices. The dissenting Justices accept some of this change without acknowledging that it has occurred; some of it they reject. The text of Title VII, even in context, cannot explain why they draw the lines where they do.

This variability substantially undermines the dissenting Justices' claim that their preferred outcome in *Bostock* reflects a neutral, entirely text-driven interpretation of Title VII. The dissenters contend that only "some exotic understanding of sex discrimination" could lead to the conclusion that discrimination against gay and transgender people falls within the confines of that term.[218] In fact, this Part shows, the idea that opposition to LGBT people reflects and reinforces traditional sex stereotypes is common knowledge, in all senses of that term. One need not read gender theory to know it. In fact, outside the context of this particular litigation, conservatives, no less than liberals,

---

[217] *See, e.g,* Jack N. Rakove, *Joe the Ploughman Reads the Constitution, or, the Poverty of Public Meaning Originalism,* 48 SAN DIEGO L. REV. 575, 584–88 (2011) (enumerating the faults of public meaning originalism from a historian's standpoint); Jonathan Gienapp, *Constitutional Originalism and History,* PROCESS: A BLOG FOR AMERICAN HISTORY (Mar. 20, 2017), https://www.processhistory.org/originalism-history/ (arguing that the search for original public meaning "repel[s] historical expertise" and "is an affront to *all* historians").

[218] *Bostock,* 140 S. Ct. at 1767 (Alito, J., dissenting).

often insist upon it. As was the case with the majority, it is only extratextual considerations that lead the dissenting Justices to reach the
conclusions they do in *Bostock*. But in the dissenting opinions, those
extratextual considerations yield an outcome less supported by law.

A. "HISTORY WILL BE HEARD"[219]

To support his argument that sex discrimination "was a familiar and
well-understood concept"[220] at the time of Title VII's enactment and
that its meaning has remained unchanged throughout American history, Justice Alito includes a long historical section in his opinion
discussing prohibitions on sex discrimination dating back to the nineteenth century. "Long before Title VII was adopted," he observes,
"many pioneering state and federal laws had used language substantively indistinguishable from Title VII's critical phrase, 'discrimination
because of sex.'"[221] He notes, for instance, that "the California Constitution of 1879 stipulated that no one, '*on account of sex*, [could] be dis-
qualified from entering upon or pursuing any lawful business, voca-
tion, or profession.'"[222] Wyoming, Montana, Washington, and Utah
had similar constitutional provisions, all dating back to the late nineteenth century, the most expansive of which stated that male and female citizens "'shall equally enjoy all civil, political and religious rights
and privileges.'"[223]

Justice Alito's aim, in citing these early constitutional provisions, is
to demonstrate that "discrimination because of sex" has always meant
the same thing. But even a brief look at the history of sex-based antidiscrimination law reveals that this is not true. The meaning of this
phrase has always been under negotiation and there are numerous
historical precedents for the kind of conceptual shift that occurred in
Bostock.

1). *The "Traditional Concept" of Sex Discrimination.* The dissenting Justices are right to suggest that the Court's determination that
Title VII protects gay and transgender workers would have surprised

[219] Parents Involved in Cmty. Sch. v. Seattle Sch. Dist. No. 1, 551 U.S. 701, 746 (2007).

[220] *Bostock*, 140 S. Ct. at 1768 (Alito, J., dissenting).

[221] *Id.* Note that Justice Alito here omits the word "against" from his characterization of
Title VII's operative language and suggests that "discriminate against" is not a linguistic unit
with a distinct meaning after all. *See supra* notes 116–25 and accompanying text.

[222] *Id.* (alteration in original).

[223] *Id.* (quoting "Wyoming's first Constitution . . . Art. VI, § 1 (1890)").

midcentury Americans.[224] But that is not the only aspect of *Bostock* that would have generated surprise. Americans half a century ago would have been surprised by much of what the Justices say—and perhaps even more by what they take for granted. One aspect of *Bostock* that reflects its contemporary provenance is the absolute certainty with which all of the Justices assume and assert that an employment practice need not affect all women (or all men) in order to qualify as discrimination "because of sex."[225] The notion that an employment practice can count as sex discrimination if it targets only a subset of one sex was not at all clear at the time of Title VII's enactment. In fact, many courts in the 1960s rejected that conceptualization as obviously erroneous, holding that—by definition—only practices that divide men and women into two groups perfectly differentiated along biological sex lines qualify as sex discrimination and that discrimination against subsets of men or women obviously rest on factors other than sex.[226]

That understanding, which courts in the 1960s and 1970s often referred to as the "traditional concept of sex discrimination," doomed all sorts of claims that would count as sex discrimination claims under Title VII today, including claims involving marriage, motherhood, pregnancy, and sexual harassment. The next sections of this Article address pregnancy and sexual harassment; this section focuses on marriage and motherhood.

Discrimination against married women and mothers in the workplace was ubiquitous in the nineteenth and early twentieth centuries and remained common at the time of Title VII's enactment. Some employers fired women when they married, others drew the line at motherhood, refusing to hire mothers and terminating the employment of women who became mothers. Today, workplace policies explicitly barring the employment of married women or mothers (but not married men and fathers) would generally be understood to violate Title VII. In fact, such policies so obviously violate Title VII, on today's understanding of the law, that contemporary employers rarely implement such policies. But when Title VII was enacted, such policies were common, and courts generally upheld them against sex-based Title VII challenges.

---

[224] *Id.* at 1767.

[225] *Id.*

[226] For a more extensive discussion of this history, see Franklin, *supra* note 206.

Courts in early Title VII cases found that claims challenging discrimination against married women and mothers unambiguously fell outside the ordinary meaning of the law's prohibition on sex discrimination. Those courts observed "that the words of the statute are the best source from which to derive the proper construction,"[227] and that from this textualist perspective, policies that discriminate against subsets of women, based on characteristics not shared by all women, clearly fall outside the law's scope. Courts responded to claims by married women by observing that Title VII bars only five categories of discrimination and that simply "[b]y reading the act it is plain that Congress did not ban discrimination in employment due to one's marital status."[228] On this view, the fact that employers were willing to hire single women proved that their objection was not sex-based, i.e., to women *per se*. It was to the fact that the plaintiffs were married—and, courts held, "the law does not prevent discrimination against married people in favor of single ones."[229]

That interpretation seemed plausible in the 1960s because policies barring married women had a long history and had coexisted for many decades with laws barring sex discrimination in employment.[230] It was not until after the rise of the women's movement in the late 1960s and the development of a new conceptual tool that expanded the parameters of what counted as sex discrimination under Title VII that courts finally began to strike down policies barring the employment of married women on the ground that those policies discriminated on the basis of sex. The movement in those years worked to persuade courts—and ordinary Americans—that laws and policies that enforce traditional sex and family roles are not benign reflections of the natural order, but rather, unfair limitations on opportunity. Policies regulating married women and mothers were among the movement's prime targets—and the campaign against those policies helped to spur the development of "sex-plus" doctrine. Under this doctrine, employers may not treat female employees differently than male employees

---

[227] Phillips v. Martin Marietta Corp., 411 F.2d 1, 3 (5th Cir. 1969) (making this argument about a policy—structurally identical to policies barring the employment of married women— that barred the employment of mothers, but not fathers, with young children).

[228] Cooper v. Delta Airlines, Inc., 274 F. Supp. 781, 783 (E.D.La. 1967).

[229] *Id.*

[230] For more on the history of these laws, see Claudia Goldin, *Marriage Bars: Discrimination Against Married Women Workers, 1920's to 1950's* (Nat'l Bureau of Econ. Rsch., Working Paper No. 2747, 1988), https://www.nber.org/papers/w2747.

on the basis of sex "plus" some facially neutral characteristic, such as the fact that they are married or have young children.[231] This new conceptual tool helped courts to reconceptualize longstanding policies barring the employment of wives and mothers as sex discrimination. In 1971, the Seventh Circuit deployed sex-plus doctrine in *Sprogis v. United Airlines* to invalidate a policy that barred stewardesses from marrying.[232] That same year, the Supreme Court deployed the same tool in *Phillips v. Martin Marietta* to invalidate a policy barring the employment of mothers, but not fathers, with young children.[233]

Today, this understanding of sex discrimination is firmly rooted in Title VII doctrine. All of the Justices in *Bostock* take it for granted that policies affecting only a subset of women (or men) can qualify as discrimination because of sex—although, it is worth noting that, even today, the parameters of this rule remain unclear. Many courts have held that workplace practices count as sex discrimination only when the plus factor is an immutable characteristic or a fundamental right.[234] On this definition, firing women but not men who have children would count as discrimination because of sex, but firing men but not women who wear skirts would fall outside the parameters of that term.[235]

Justice Alito characterizes *Bostock*'s holding that Title VII's ordinary meaning bars discrimination against gay and transgender people as "breathtaking" in its "arrogance," because it suggests that, for half a century, legal actors "did not grasp what discrimination 'because of . . . sex' unambiguously means" and were "not smart enough" to appreciate the "obvious."[236] But Justice Alito's attempt to differentiate *Bostock* from, say, *Martin Marietta* by insisting that the latter case *really*

---

[231] For more on the development of sex-plus doctrine, see Reva B. Siegel, *Introduction: A Short History of Sexual Harassment*, in DIRECTIONS IN SEXUAL HARASSMENT LAW 13–17 (Catharine A. MacKinnon & Reva B. Siegel eds., 2004); Franklin, *supra* note 206, at 1374–78.

[232] Sprogis v. United Airlines, Inc., 444 F.2d 1194, 1198 (7th Cir. 1971). Future Supreme Court Justice John Paul Stevens dissented in this case. *See id.* at 1202 (Stevens, J., dissenting). He argued that the marriage bar, as applied to stewardesses, could not logically constitute sex discrimination because United employed only women in this job category—proving that the discrimination was not on the basis of sex but on the basis of marriage. *Id.* at 1205.

[233] Phillips v. Martin Marietta Corp., 400 U.S. 542, 543 (1971).

[234] *See* Kimberly A. Yuracko, *Trait Discrimination as Sex Discrimination: An Argument Against Neutrality*, 83 TEX. L. REV. 167, 204–07 (2004).

[235] *See* Regina E. Gray, *The Rise and Fall of the "Sex-Plus" Discrimination Theory: An Analysis of* Fisher v. Vassar College, 42 HOW. L.J. 71, 84 (1998) ("The requirement that the 'plus' in a 'sex-plus' case consist of an 'immutable characteristic' or a 'fundamental right' was established in cases challenging employers' grooming/dress code regulations.").

[236] Bostock v. Clayton County, 140 S. Ct. 1731, 1757 (2020) (Alito, J., dissenting).

was enforcing the original public meaning of sex discrimination[237] would seem to be equally susceptible to these charges. On his textualist understanding, policies barring the employment of married women and mothers (as well as sexual harassment, including the male-on-male kind) have unambiguously violated prohibitions on sex discrimination not simply since 1964, but presumably since the time such prohibitions became part of American law in the late nineteenth century. The implication of this is that for nearly a century, Americans were simply "not smart enough" to realize it.

The problem here does not lie with our ancestors and their purported lack of intelligence. The problem lies with textualism and its utterly unrealistic account of how language and law work. Within the field of linguistics, it is uncontroversial that "[j]ust about all words in any language have different meanings now than they did in the past."[238] This is especially true of words such as "discrimination," "sex," and "discrimination because of sex," which have been subject to strong and sustained evolutionary pressure. Prior to the rise of textualism, courts and other legal actors routinely acknowledged that the meaning of those words is ambiguous; that ambiguity arises in part from ongoing contestation over their meaning. For decades, even centuries, social movements have worked tirelessly to alter people's understanding of those words and the phenomena they seek to describe. Textualists and originalists criticize proponents of dynamic statutory interpretation and living constitutionalism for suggesting that the meaning of legal provisions may evolve over time and that judges may properly enforce new meanings. Justice Alito and Justice Thomas accuse the majority in *Bostock* of doing this and excoriate them for it. Justice Scalia reserved some of his harshest criticism for adherents of dynamic interpretive approaches, whom he accused of "deprecating the closed-mindedness of our forebears" and arrogantly assuming their own superiority.[239]

But that is an odd criticism for a textualist to make. The basic premise of textualism, as applied in *Bostock*, is that discrimination because of sex has only one meaning, that this meaning has never changed, and that it has always been completely unambiguous. The necessary implication of this premise is that Americans in the past were so blinded

[237] *Id.* at 1775.

[238] JOHN McWHORTER, WORDS ON THE MOVE: WHY ENGLISH WON'T—AND CAN'T—SIT STILL (LIKE, LITERALLY) 59 (2016).

[239] United States v. Virginia, 518 U.S. 515, 566 (1996) (Scalia, J., dissenting).

by the prejudices of their day that they consistently misinterpreted sex-based antidiscrimination laws to permit conduct that obviously violated them—but that now, textualist judges (who do textualism right) can access the true and eternal meaning of those laws and apply that meaning unencumbered by the kinds of cultural considerations that blinded our forebears. Now, the dissenting Justices contend, they (although not the Justices in the majority) have been able to transcend the situatedness that plagued judges in the past and to apply the ordinary meaning of legal prohibitions on sex discrimination in an entirely text-driven and value-free way.

The remainder of this Part demonstrates that the dissenting Justices have not actually managed this feat—because no judge could. Judges are inescapably part of the culture in which they judge; they are not impervious to social influences, and thus, the law is not either. On this understanding, to say that *Bostock* incorporates "2020 values"[240] is not, as Justice Alito imagines, to accuse the majority of arrogance and lawlessness. It is to note something obviously and unavoidably true: the fact that all of us—even judges—are creatures of our time. It is not clear that an interpretive methodology that ignores, or claims to be able to transcend, that fact is a study in humility.

2). *The Regulation of Pregnancy.* The issue of pregnancy arises only once in *Bostock*, in a footnote.[241] Justice Alito adverts in that footnote to the fact that Congress amended Title VII in 1978 to define pregnancy discrimination as sex discrimination. He argues that "[t]his definition should inform the meaning of 'because of sex' in Title VII more generally" because it shows that the statute, at its most expansive, covers "conditions that are biologically tied to sex"—and, he asserts, sexual orientation and gender identity fall outside even that expansive definition.[242] Justice Alito suggests in this footnote that pregnancy discrimination did not fall within the original public meaning of Title VII's prohibition on sex discrimination but that its later inclusion in that prohibition makes sense (in a way that the inclusion of sexual orientation and gender identity would not).

That is one way of understanding the relationship between pregnancy discrimination and sex discrimination, but it is not the only

---

[240] *Bostock*, 140 S. Ct. at 1761 (Alito, J., dissenting).

[241] *Id.* at 1761 n.16.

[242] *Id.*

way. Contestation over whether Title VII's prohibition of sex discrimination covered pregnancy discrimination—including as a matter of semantic meaning—began almost immediately after the statute's enactment. Even after Congress amended Title VII to cover pregnancy discrimination, contestation over whether pregnancy discrimination constitutes sex discrimination *as a semantic matter* continued. Indeed, it continues to this day. This section examines this contestation, not in an attempt to resolve the question of whether pregnancy discrimination is sex discrimination but to demonstrate that the tools of textualism are utterly inadequate to that task. Textualist argument over the question of whether pregnancy discrimination is sex discrimination illustrates in a particularly clear way the role that extratextual values inevitably play in textualist interpretation of Title VII's sex provision. Particularly when juxtaposed with textualist reasoning about whether Title VII covers gay and transgender people, textualist argument over pregnancy discrimination reveals that all of these questions are part of a broader textualist jurisprudence saturated with normative judgments about gender and sexuality.

The basic outline of pregnancy discrimination's fate under Title VII is familiar. In 1976, the Court held in *General Electric v. Gilbert* that Title VII's bar on sex discrimination did not extend to discrimination on the basis of pregnancy.[243] That decision followed *Geduldig v. Aiello*, in which the Court held that a state-run disability insurance program that exempted pregnancy and no other disabilities from coverage did not violate constitutional protections against sex discrimination.[244] The core reasoning in the two cases was the same: The challenged conduct "'divides potential recipients into two groups—pregnant women and nonpregnant persons. While the first group is exclusively female, the second includes members of both sexes.'"[245] In 1978, however,

---

[243] Gen. Elec. Co. v. Gilbert, 429 U.S. 125, 136 (1976) (concluding "that an exclusion of pregnancy from a disability-benefits plan providing general coverage is not a gender-based discrimination at all"); *id.* at 140 ("[T]here is no facial gender-based discrimination . . . here.").

[244] Geduldig v. Aiello, 417 U.S. 484, 496 n.20 (1974) ("Absent a showing that distinctions involving pregnancy are mere pretexts designed to effect an invidious discrimination against the members of one sex or the other, lawmakers are constitutionally free to include or exclude pregnancy from the coverage of legislation such as this on any reasonable basis. . . .").

[245] *Gilbert*, 429 U.S. at 135 (quoting *Geduldig*, 417 U.S. at 496–97 n.20); *id.* (finding no evidence that "'the program worked to discriminate against any definable group or class in terms of the aggregate risk protection derived by that group or class. . . . There is no risk from which men are protected and women are not. Likewise, there is no risk from which women are protected and men are not.'" (quoting *Geduldig*, 417 U.S. at 496–97); *see also*

Congress responded to this ruling by enacting the Pregnancy Discrimination Act. The PDA states that under Title VII "[t]he terms 'because of sex' or 'on the basis of sex' include, but are not limited to, because of or on the basis of pregnancy, childbirth, or related medical conditions."[246]

How should we understand this history from a textualist perspective? One possibility is that *Gilbert* got it wrong. The ordinary public meaning of Title VII's sex provision obviously encompasses pregnancy discrimination and the PDA simply clarified what was true all along. On this view, pregnancy discrimination has been illegal since 1964 (or perhaps, in some Western states, since the late nineteenth century). Another possibility is that *Gilbert* got it right and the PDA altered the law's definition of sex discrimination to include pregnancy. On this view, pregnancy discrimination became illegal under Title VII starting in 1978 and did not fall within the ordinary public meaning of sex discrimination circa 1964.

Numerous courts have taken the former position, that the original public meaning of Title VII's sex provision covers pregnancy discrimination. These courts have observed that dictionaries from the time of Title VII's enactment define "sex" as, among other things, "'[t]he sum of the structural, functional, and behavioral peculiarities of living beings that subserve reproduction by two interacting parents and distinguish males and females.'"[247] They have explained that "[t]he common thread running through these definitions is a focus on reproduction, including the 'structural' and 'functional' differences between typical male and female bodies."[248] On this basis, they have concluded

---

Deborah Dinner, *Strange Bedfellows at Work: Neomaternalism in the Making of Sex Discrimination Law*, 91 WASH. U.L. REV. 453, 484–86 (2014) (showing that the Court in these cases adopted the approach to pregnancy discrimination advocated by business associations and employers and rejected the approach advocated by legal feminists).

[246] Pregnancy Discrimination Act of 1978, Pub. L. No. 95-555, 92 Stat. 2076 (codified at 42 U.S.C. § 2000e(k) (2018)).

[247] Conley v. N.W. Fla. State Coll., 145 F. Supp. 3d 1073, 1077 (N.D. Fla. 2015) (quoting WEBSTER'S SEVENTH NEW COLLEGIATE DICTIONARY 795 (1967)); *see also id.* (quoting BLACK'S LAW DICTIONARY 1541 (4th rev. ed. 1968), which "defin[es] 'sex' as '[t]he sum of the peculiarities of structure and function that distinguish a male from a female organism'"); *id.* at 1076 (quoting MERRIAM-WEBSTER'S COLLEGIATE DICTIONARY 1140 (11th ed. 2003), which defines sex as "'the sum of the structural, functional, and behavioral characteristics of organisms that are involved in productive behavior marked by the union of gametes and that distinguish males and females'"); *id.* at 1076 n.6 (quoting the online version of the COLLINS AMERICAN ENGLISH DICTIONARY (2015), which defines "sex" as "'either of the two divisions, male or female, into which persons, animals, or plants are divided, with reference to their reproductive functions' and 'anything connected with sexual gratification or reproduction'").

[248] *Id.* at 1077.

that "by virtue of common usage," prohibitions on sex discrimination unambiguously encompass pregnancy discrimination.[249]

Evidence strongly suggests that a number of progressive Supreme Court Justices would also have taken this position if asked to assess the question of whether pregnancy discrimination is sex discrimination from a textualist perspective. In fact, Justice John Paul Stevens made something resembling a textualist argument in his dissenting opinion in *Gilbert*. He argued that pregnancy discrimination *"[b]y definition . . .* 'discriminates' on account of sex; for it is the capacity to become pregnant which primarily differentiates the female from the male."[250] Justice Brennan made a similar argument in his dissenting opinion in *Geduldig*, claiming that pregnancy discrimination applies "one set of rules . . . to females and another to males," and that "[s]uch dissimilar treatment of men and women, on the basis of physical characteristics inextricably linked to one sex, inevitably constitutes sex discrimination."[251] Justice Ginsburg frequently argued that *Gilbert* and *Geduldig* were wrongly decided[252] and routinely cited Justice Stevens' assertion that pregnancy discrimination is "[b]y definition" sex discrimination.[253]

---

[249] *Id.*; *see also, e.g.*, Glass v. Captain Katanna's, Inc., 950 F. Supp. 2d 1235, 1245 (M.D. Fla. 2013) (concluding on the basis of various dictionary definitions of the word "sex" that "a plain reading" of the Florida Civil Rights Act's prohibition on sex discrimination leads unambiguously to the conclusion that pregnancy discrimination falls within that prohibition); *id.* (explaining that the semantic meaning "of the phrase . . . 'discriminate against any individual . . . because of such individual's . . . sex' should be understood to ban discrimination against any individual 'because of such individual's reproductive functions (*e.g.*, pregnancy)"); *Mass. Elec. Co. v. Mass. Comm'n Against Discrimination*, 375 Mass. 160, 167–68 (1978) (holding that "any classification which relies on pregnancy as the determinative criteria is a distinction based on sex" and citing in support of this holding Justice Stevens' assertion in *Gilbert* that pregnancy discrimination is " '[b]y definition' " sex discrimination (quoting *Gilbert*, 429 U.S. at 167 (Stevens, J., dissenting)).

[250] *Gilbert*, 429 U.S. at 167–68 (Stevens, J., dissenting) (emphasis added).

[251] Geduldig v. Aiello, 417 U.S. 484, 501 (1974) (Brennan, J., dissenting).

[252] *See, e.g.*, Coleman v. Court of Appeals of Md., 556 U.S. 30, 56–57 (2012) (Ginsburg, J., dissenting) ("Because pregnancy discrimination is inevitably sex discrimination, and because discrimination against women is tightly interwoven with society's beliefs about pregnancy and motherhood, I would hold that *Aiello* was egregiously wrong to declare that discrimination on the basis of pregnancy is not discrimination on the basis of sex."); AT & T Corp. v. Hulteen, 556 U.S. 701, 728 (2009) (Ginsburg, J., dissenting) ("I would . . . explicitly overrule *Gilbert* so that the decision can generate no more mischief.").

[253] *Coleman*, 556 U.S. at 55 (alteration in original) (quoting *Gilbert*, 429 U.S. at 161–62); *cf. id.* (arguing that, " '[a]s an abstract statement,' it is 'simply false' that 'a classification based on pregnancy is gender neutral' " (quoting Bray v. Alexandria Women's Health Clinic, 506 U.S. 263, 327 (1993) (Stevens, J., dissenting) (alteration in original)). Note that when Justice Ginsburg quoted Justice Stevens, she was in a sense quoting herself, because she had pressed this argument

She characterized the PDA as ending "any pretense that classification on the basis of pregnancy can be facially nondiscriminatory."[254]

The textualist case for interpreting Title VII's prohibition on sex discrimination to cover pregnancy discrimination seems strong. Yet the dominant view among leading textualist judges today seems to be that the ordinary meaning of sex discrimination *does not* encompass pregnancy discrimination. Judge William Pryor, a prominent conservative proponent of textualism, recently endorsed this view in an opinion dissenting from an Eleventh Circuit decision holding that a policy barring a transgender student from using bathrooms corresponding to his gender identity discriminated on the basis of sex.[255] In his opinion, Judge Pryor quoted a number of dictionaries that define sex in the manner we have just seen.[256] But Judge Pryor viewed those definitions as evidence that *Gilbert* was rightly decided. Because pregnancy discrimination creates two categories—pregnant people and non-pregnant people—and the non-pregnant category includes members of both sexes, he argued, there is a clear "'lack of identity' between pregnancy and sex."[257] On his account, "sex," by definition, "refers 'only to biological distinctions between male and female,'"[258] and pregnancy is not such a distinction.[259]

---

in a series of Supreme Court briefs in the 1970s. For more on these briefs, see Reva B. Siegel, *The Pregnant Citizen, from Suffrage to the Present*, 108 GEO. L.J. 167, 197 (2020).

[254] *Hulteen*, 556 U.S. at 721 (internal quotation marks omitted).

[255] Adams *ex rel.* Kasper v. Sch. Bd. of St. Johns Cnty., 968 F.3d 1286, 1315 (11th Cir. 2020) (Pryor, C.J., dissenting).

[256] *Id.* at 1320 ("*See, e.g., Sex, The American Heritage Dictionary of the English Language* (1979) ('The property or quality by which organisms are classified according to their reproductive functions.'); *Sex, The Random House College Dictionary* (1980) ('either the male or female division of a species, esp. as differentiated with reference to the reproductive functions'); *see also* Am. Psychiatric Ass'n, *Diagnostic and Statistical Manual of Mental Disorders* 451 (5th ed. 2013) ('This chapter employs constructs and terms as they are widely used by clinicians from various disciplines with specialization in this area. In this chapter, *sex* and *sexual* refer to the biological indicators of male and female (understood in the context of reproductive capacity). . . .')").

[257] *Id.* at 1315 (quoting Geduldig v. Aiello, 417 U.S. 484, 496 n.20 (1974)). Judge Pryor argues that pregnancy thus provides an "instructive" analogue for cases in which plaintiffs argue that discrimination against transgender students in the context of bathrooms constitutes sex discrimination. *Id.* ("The bathroom policy creates two groups—students who can use the boys' bathroom and students who can use the girls' bathroom. Both groups contain transgender students and non-transgender students, so a 'lack of identity' exists between the policy and transgender status. *Geduldig*, 417 U.S. at 496 n.20.").

[258] *Id.* at 1311 (quoting Bostock v. Clayton County, 140 S. Ct. 1731, 1739 (2020)).

[259] *Id.* at 1320 (arguing that "[a]s used in Title IX and its implementing regulations, 'sex' unambiguously is a classification on the basis of reproductive function," and that pregnancy, sexual orientation, and gender identity unambiguously fall outside that definition).

Ricky Polston, then-Chief Justice of the Florida Supreme Court, reached the same conclusion in a recent opinion dissenting from his court's holding that pregnancy discrimination constitutes sex discrimination under the Florida Civil Rights Act.[260] Justice Polston is also a prominent conservative proponent of textualism, and he too argues that the Court in the 1970s got it right with respect to pregnancy discrimination.[261] He cites a number of dictionaries defining sex in the familiar way and concludes that "pursuant to [its] plain meaning," the Florida Civil Rights Act's "prohibition of sex discrimination does not encompass discrimination on the basis of pregnancy."[262]

The most prominent textualist of all, Justice Scalia, would almost certainly have taken this position as well. In a 1993 opinion holding that the harassment of "women seeking abortions" does not constitute discrimination "against women as a class" under § 1985(3), Justice Scalia endorsed the Court's reasoning in *Geduldig*, explaining that pregnancy discrimination, which targets only a subset of women on the basis of their reproductive choices, does not constitute discrimination on the basis of sex.[263] Justice Thomas joined that opinion. He also joined a more recent opinion by Justice Scalia endorsing *Geduldig*'s reasoning (in a sex-based Title VII case, no less).[264] Justice Scalia, Justice Thomas, and Justice Alito also joined the majority in *AT & T v. Hulteen*, in which the Court concluded, among other things, that pregnancy discrimination prior to the PDA did not violate Title VII's prohibition on sex discrimination.[265] It would be difficult to square that conclusion with a textualist interpretation finding that Title VII unambiguously barred pregnancy discrimination starting in 1964.

What are we to make of this ongoing conflict within textualism over whether legal provisions barring discrimination because of sex encompass pregnancy discrimination? Textualists' standard response

---

[260] Delva v. Cont'l Grp., Inc., 137 So. 3d 371, 376 (Fla. 2014).

[261] *Id.* (noting that at the time *Gilbert* was decided, Title VII "included language very similar to Florida's current statute").

[262] *Id.*

[263] Bray v. Alexandria Women's Health Clinic, 506 U.S. 263, 269 (1993).

[264] Young v. United Parcel Serv., Inc., 575 U.S. 206 (2015).

[265] AT & T Corp. v. Hulteen, 556 U.S. 701, 705 (2009) (stating that "[i]n the 1960s and early to mid–1970s, . . . [the] differential treatment of pregnancy leave . . . was lawful"); *id.* at 710 ("As a matter of law, at that time, an exclusion of pregnancy from a disability-benefits plan providing general coverage [was] not a gender-based discrimination at all." (internal quotation mark omitted) (alteration in original)).

when confronted with conflicts of this sort is to accuse critics of at-tacking a straw man. Of course textualism will not produce uniform results in every case, they argue; no theory could.[266] Textualism does not eliminate the need for judgment, so we should expect "the occa-sional disagreement" among its practitioners, especially in the kind of "cases that land in the Supreme Court . . . the hardest ones in our legal system."[267] The superiority of textualism, relative to other methods of statutory interpretation, is not that it relieves judges of the difficult work of judging. It is that, although textualist judges "may some-times disagree on outcomes, they are at least constrained by the same value-neutral methodology and the same closed record of historical evidence."[268]

But that defense is its own kind of straw man argument. The point of examining the ongoing conflict over whether the ordinary public meaning of sex discrimination encompasses pregnancy discrimination is not to suggest that the fact that judges reach different outcomes undermines the legitimacy of textualism. The point is to show that this conflict and these different outcomes are not fueled by value-free disagreements about the finer points of textualist interpretation. The fight over whether pregnancy discrimination is sex discrimination is not a fight over whether to rely on a dictionary or a corpus linguistics database, how to apply one of Justice Scalia's fifty-seven canons of tex-tualist interpretation, or any other value-neutral methodological rule. No judge in any of these cases even purports to be engaged in this sort of argument or tries to adduce this sort of methodological justification for his conclusions.

That is because the question of whether pregnancy discrimination is sex discrimination is part of a longstanding, transcontextual, and pitched ideological battle over the application of antidiscrimination law in contexts involving women's sex and family roles that encom-passes conflict over abortion, birth control, family leave, pregnancy disability leave, and sexual orientation and gender identity. Every one of the textualist judges cited above who purports to reject on semantic

---

[266] See Judge Amy Coney Barrett, 2019 Sumner Canary Lecture: Assorted Canards of Contemporary Legal Analysis: Redux, in 70 CASE W. RES. L. REV. 855, 859 (2020) ("Those who take an oversimplified view of textualism imagine that it works like Google Translate: a judge punches in words, and—voila!—out pops the result. If that were how interpretation worked, one could expect every textualist judge to interpret text in exactly the same way.").

[267] GORSUCH, supra note 14, at 112.

[268] Id.

grounds the idea that pregnancy discrimination falls within the ordinary public meaning of sex discrimination is a committed conservative, a frequent attendee at Federalist Society events, and a staunch opponent of expansive conceptions of women's rights in all of the contexts listed above. I have no doubt that if the late Justice Ginsburg, a fierce advocate of women's rights, had been required to write a textualist opinion on whether pregnancy discrimination is sex discrimination, she would have reached a different conclusion from these conservative judges. It strains credulity beyond the breaking point to suggest that what is driving this disagreement over the ordinary meaning of sex discrimination with respect to pregnancy is an unarticulated, value-neutral, outcome-determinative disagreement about how to apply a particular textualist rule.

Proponents of textualism often respond to this sort of critique by contending that it is not the fault of the methodology if judges allow themselves to be influenced by extratextual considerations; few if any interpretive methodologies can "constrain the wayward judge" who refuses to put such considerations aside when interpreting the law.[269] Here too, however, the fault does not lie with errant humanity. The fault lies with textualism, which does not actually provide judges with a means of putting aside social values and substantive jurisprudential commitments, particularly in the hard cases that arrive at the Court. What generally makes a case hard, in the context of antidiscrimination law, is that it involves a matter over which Americans are deeply divided. The spare and Rorschach-like text of our landmark antidiscrimination laws cannot itself resolve such conflict. Determining what such laws mean requires more and different kinds of knowledge than textualism can provide.

B. SAILING UNDER A TEXTUALIST FLAG

The dissenting Justices in *Bostock* vehemently reject that contention. They argue that textualism easily resolves the question of whether Title VII prohibits discrimination against gay and transgender workers, relieving judges of the need to consult extratextual sources. As with pregnancy discrimination, however, any guidance provided by the text of Title VII stops well short of resolving the question of whether

---

[269] Baude, *supra* note 12, at 2223.

discrimination on the basis of sexual orientation and gender identity is sex discrimination. The dissenting Justices' determination that Title VII does not bar anti-LGBT discrimination is based just as much on "2020 values,"[270] and is just as responsive to current contestation over LGBT rights, as the Court's determination to the contrary. In fact, this section shows, the dissenting opinions in *Bostock* find more support in social values than they do in law.

1). *The Strange Career of the Sex Discrimination Argument.* Twice in his dissenting opinion in *Bostock*, Justice Alito alleges that the Court's holding that Title VII's prohibition on sex discrimination extends to gay and transgender people reflects an "exotic understanding of sex discrimination."[271] The implication is that although this understanding might hold sway among queer theorists and graduate students at Ivy League universities today, it is not an idea to which regular Americans would have subscribed fifty years ago. When Americans in the 1960s heard the term sex discrimination, they thought of employers who paid women less than men or refused to hire them at all: discrimination against people because of their sex, not because of their sexual orientation or gender identity.[272]

By this point, the various arguments in support of the idea that anti-LGBT discrimination is sex discrimination are familiar. There's the formalistic argument the Court endorses in *Bostock*: refusing to hire women, but not men, who date women treats employees differently on the basis of sex. There's the antistereotyping argument, which suggests that gay and transgender workers face discrimination in part because they fail to conform to sex stereotypes about who men and women should date and how they should express their gender identity. There's a related antisubordinationist argument, which focuses on the fact that sex-based social hierarchy depends on sex-differentiated sex and family roles for men and women, and gay and transgender people are perceived as threats to this traditional sex-role system. None of these arguments strikes me as particularly exotic. But

---

[270] Bostock v. Clayton County, 140 S. Ct. 1731, 1761 (2020) (Alito, J., dissenting).

[271] *Id.* at 1767.

[272] *Id.* at 1769 (arguing that "the concept of discrimination 'because of,' 'on account of,' or 'on the basis of' sex was well understood" in 1964, and that "[i]t was part of the campaign for equality that had been waged by women's rights advocates for more than a century, and what it meant was equal treatment for men and women").

that is the label the dissenting Justices assign them. So perhaps it would be useful to start with something humbler.

When I was a child, girls and boys did not play together on the playground. The boys played kickball, and I am not sure what the girls played because I too played kickball. The other kids generally tolerated this, but sometimes they called me a lesbian. It would be years before any of us, or most of us anyway, would learn the definition of that term the Court employs in *Bostock*. We understood the word "lesbian" to mean "a boyish girl," a girl who fails to do what girls are expected to do. We were not unique in this understanding. Sociologists have documented American schoolchildren's widespread understanding of homosexuality as a form of sex-role transgression. One sociologist, who spent two years embedded in an American high school, reported that in the students' eyes, being "a fag has as much to do with failing at the masculine tasks of competence, heterosexual prowess, and strength or in any way revealing weakness or femininity as it does with a sexual identity."[273] She concluded that although homophobia certainly played a role in the constant anti-gay discourse at this school, the kids themselves understood that discourse as part of a larger project of enforcing normative conceptions of masculinity. Indeed, a substantial number of them insisted that their use of antigay slurs had "'nothing to do with sexual preference at all.'"[274] It was about policing "any sort of behavior defined as unmasculine."[275]

In addition to being common knowledge, the idea that discrimination against gay people is, in part, a response to perceived sex-role transgressions is old knowledge. In the nineteenth century, the term "[s]exual inversion referred to a broad range of gender deviant behavior, of which homosexual desire was only a logical but indistinct aspect."[276] Later conceptions of "'homosexuality' focused on the narrower issue of sexual object choice,"[277] but the idea that homosexuality was a form of gender deviant behavior lived on. It is why gay men were, and sometimes still are, called sissies, fairies, pansies, and

---

[273] C.J. PASCOE, DUDE, YOU'RE A FAG: MASCULINITY AND SEXUALITY IN HIGH SCHOOL 53–54 (2011).

[274] *Id.* at 57.

[275] *Id.*

[276] George Chauncey, Jr., *From Sexual Inversion to Homosexuality: Medicine and the Changing Conceptualization of Female Deviance*, 58–59 SALMAGUNDI 114, 116 (1983).

[277] *Id.*

nancy boys. It is why, even today, discrimination against gay men in the workplace so often involves gendered insults, women's clothing and accessories, and the color pink. Sometimes workplace harassers just come right out and call the gay employee a woman.[278]

These insults are all perfectly culturally legible and have been for many decades. They do not rest on "some exotic understanding of sex." They rest on the pervasive and long-standing perception that LGBT people violate normative conceptions of how men and women should be. If anything, the charge of exoticism would seem to apply more readily to the dissenting Justices' more contemporary notion that sexual orientation and gender identity are completely distinct from sex. If you asked regular Americans in the 1960s whether identifying as a man and being sexually attracted to women are a core part of what it means to be a man, would they all have responded with a resounding no?

In fact, outside the legal context in which *Bostock* is set, it has often been social conservatives and opponents of LGBT rights who have advanced the argument that prohibitions on sex discrimination cover LGBT people. In the 1970s, one of the central arguments against the Equal Rights Amendment—which prohibits the government from denying or abridging "[e]quality of rights under the law . . . on account of sex"[279]—was that it would outlaw discrimination on the basis of sexual orientation. Phyllis Schlafly, leader of the prominent and successful campaign to defeat the ERA, argued throughout the 1970s that "[i]t is precisely 'on account of sex' that a state now denies a marriage license to a man and a man, or to a woman and a woman.'"[280] She claimed that if the ERA became law, "[a] homosexual who wants

---

[278] *See, e.g.*, Prowel v. Wise Bus. Forms, Inc., 579 F.3d 285, 287 (3d Cir. 2009) (noting that gay employee was called "Princess" and "Rosebud," and that "a pink, light-up, feather tiara" was left at his desk); Rene v. MGM Grand Hotel, Inc., 305 F.3d 1061, 1064 (9th Cir. 2002) (noting that gay plaintiff's co-workers "call[ed] him 'sweetheart' and 'muñeca' (Spanish for 'doll')" and "that his coworkers would 'touch [his] body like they would to a woman.'" (alteration in original)); Spearman v. Ford Motor Co., 231 F.3d 1080, 1084 (7th Cir. 2000) (reporting that the gay plaintiff was called a "'bitch,' which, according to another utility worker . . . meant . . . a 'woman,' . . . that his co-workers perceived him to be too feminine to work at Ford," and that he was assigned to "window-washing . . . which is a function 'traditionally reserved for women'"); see also Eginton v. Fla. State Univ., 111 F. Supp. 3d 1263, 1267 (M.D. Fla. 2015) (describing harassment of a lesbian employee who was called a "dyke" and "completely unfeminine").

[279] H.R.J. Res. 208, 92d Cong., 2d Sess. (1972); S.J. Res. 8, 92d Cong., 1st Sess. (1971).

[280] PHYLLIS SCHLAFLY, THE POWER OF THE POSITIVE WOMAN 90 (1977).

to be a teacher could argue persuasively that to deny him a school job would be discrimination 'on account of sex.'"[281]

The Catholic Church today continues to frame its opposition to expansions of LGBT rights in terms of sex. The Church's central justification for opposing same-sex marriage is that such partnerships violate principles of gender complementarity: the idea that men and women are fundamentally different, biologically and psychologically, and that "[a] mother and father each bring something unique and irreplaceable to child-rearing that the other cannot."[282] The Church opposes the expansion of transgender rights for the same reason, arguing that "Pope Francis has rightly rejected an ideology of gender that denies the difference and reciprocity in nature of a man and a woman," and noting that "Pope Benedict XVI criticized gender ideology in similar terms."[283] The Church argues against legal recognition of transgender kids' rights in bathroom cases on the ground that "being created by God as male and female pertains to the essence of the human creature" and that "[t]his duality is an essential aspect of what being human is all about."[284] The Church insists in all these cases—the marriage cases and the bathroom cases—that its opposition to LGBT rights does not stem from any animus against LGBT people but entirely from its fundamental commitment to traditional ideas about the nature of men and women.

Justice Alito portrays this kind of thinking as "exotic," but it isn't. It is common, it is deeply rooted in American culture, and it cuts across political and social divisions. Thus, Justice Alito and the other

---

[281] *Id.* For more on ERA opponents' use of the argument that prohibitions on sex discrimination bar discrimination on the basis of sexual orientation, see Cary Franklin, *Marrying Liberty and Equality: The New Jurisprudence of Gay Rights*, 100 Va. L. Rev. 817, 846–48 (2014); Reva B. Siegel, *Constitutional Culture, Social Movement Conflict and Constitutional Change: The Case of the De Facto ERA*, 94 Calif. L. Rev. 1323, 1389–1402 (2006).

[282] Brief Amicus Curiae of United States Conference of Catholic Bishops in Support of Respondents, Obergefell v. Hodges, 2015 WL 1519042, Nos. 14-556, 14-562, 14-571, 14-574 (Apr. 2, 2015), at **7–8; *id.* at *7 (quoting Pope Francis, Address to Participants in the International Colloquium on the Complementarity Between Man and Woman (Nov. 17, 2014), http://www.vatican.va/content/francesco/en/speeches/2014/november/documents/papa -francesco_20141117_congregazione-dottrina-fede.html ("Children have a right to grow up in a family with a father and a mother capable of creating a suitable environment for the child's growth and emotional development.")).

[283] Brief of Major Religious Organizations as Amici Curiae Supporting Petitioner, Gloucester County Sch. Bd. v. G.G., 2017 WL 192761, No. 16-273 (Jan. 10, 2017), at *8; *id.* at **6–7 (discussing the centrality of these ideas about gender in Catholic doctrine).

[284] *Id.* at *9 (internal quotation marks omitted).

dissenters in *Bostock* get it precisely backwards. What it means to discriminate because of sex has changed significantly over time. What has remained constant across the decades is the understanding that gay and transgender people violate conventional gender norms.

2). *How Precedent is Folded Into Original Public Meaning.* The idea that discrimination against gay and transgender people is a form of sex discrimination has deep roots in American history and culture. Even small children understand it, and it cuts across political and ideological lines. So what is the argument against it? The core of the dissenting Justices' argument in *Bostock* is that Americans in the early 1960s did not understand Title VII's bar on sex discrimination to extend to anti-LGBT discrimination, either as a matter of expected application or as a matter of semantic meaning—that, in fact, "any such notion would have clashed in spectacular fashion with the societal norms of the day."[285] Discrimination against gays and lesbians was widespread and accepted in the 1960s, and Americans were not even familiar with the category "transgender." "While it is likely true that there have always been individuals who experience what is now termed 'gender dys-phoria,'" Justice Alito writes in *Bostock*, "the current understanding of the concept postdates the enactment of Title VII."[286] He argues that "[i]t defies belief to suggest that the public meaning of discrimination because of sex in 1964 encompassed discrimination on the basis of a concept that was essentially unknown to the public at that time."[287]

This core claim runs into trouble, however, when juxtaposed with the dissenting Justices' insistence that sexual harassment (including same-sex sexual harassment) unambiguously falls within the original public meaning of Title VII's prohibition on sex discrimination.[288] Like discrimination against gays and lesbians, sexual harassment was pervasive at the time of Title VII's enactment. Like the category "transgender," the category "sexual harassment" had not yet come into being.[289] While there have always been individuals who experienced

---

[285] Bostock v. Clayton County, 140 S. Ct. 1731, 1769 (2020) (Alito, J., dissenting).

[286] *Id.* at 1773.

[287] *Id.*

[288] *Id.* at 1773–74; *id.* at 1834–35 (Kavanaugh, J., dissenting).

[289] The "terminology [of sexual harassment] made its public debut in 1975," in testimony before the New York City Commission on Human Rights by Lin Farley, who developed the term while teaching at Cornell University. *See* Kyle Swenson, *Who Came Up with the Term 'Sexual Harass-ment'?*, WASH. POST (Nov. 22, 2017), http://www.washingtonpost.com/news/morning-mix/wp /2017/11/22/who-came-up-with-the-term-sexual-harassment/?noredirect = on&utm_term

what is now termed "sexual harassment," the current understanding of that concept postdates the enactment of Title VII. Prior to the late 1970s, many women and some men were subjected to unwanted sexual advances, touching, teasing, demeaning comments, bullying, roughhousing, and rape in the workplace. The very substantial contribution of thinkers and advocates such as Lin Farley and Catharine MacKinnon was to reconceptualize (a still evolving set of) those behaviors as "sexual harassment" and to argue that this practice is a form of sex discrimination.[290]

Courts initially rejected the argument that sexual harassment is sex discrimination.[291] They held that "loss of employment as the result of rejection of sexual advances is not the same thing as discrimination based on sex."[292] They held that harassing behavior is "nothing more than a personal proclivity, peculiarity or mannerism," and that an employer who engages in such behavior is simply "satisfying a personal urge."[293] They held that Title VII does not "provide a federal tort remedy for what amounts to a physical attack motivated by sexual desire on the part of a supervisor and which happened to occur in a corporate corridor."[294] But by the 1980s, feminists' reconceptualization of the conduct at issue in those cases had begun to take root. Practices that had long been understood to fall outside the scope of

=.3b14f3d8bbcf; *see also* Enid Nemy, *Women Begin to Speak Out Against Sexual Harassment at Work*, N.Y. Times, Aug. 19, 1975, at 38 ("Although the issue of sexual harassment is still a comparatively new one, it is being treated with increasing seriousness by government agencies."). Catharine MacKinnon's classic 1979 book on sexual harassment played a major role in popularizing the term and developing the legal theory that conceptualized this kind of harassment as sex discrimination. *See* Catharine A. MacKinnon, Sexual Harassment of Working Women: A Case of Sex Discrimination (1979).

[290] For more on the development and early history of the concept of "sexual harassment," see Siegel, *supra* note 231, at 8–26; *see also* Sheelah Kolhatkar, *How Two Legal Cases Established Sexual Harassment as a Civil Rights Violation*, Bloomberg (Dec. 4, 2014), https://www.bloomberg.com/news/articles/2014-12-04/sexual-harassment-naming-it-paved-the-way-to-legal-victories (quoting Catharine MacKinnon's observation that "[s]exual harassment law is the first law written by women about our own condition").

[291] Siegel, *supra* note 231, at 11 (observing that, when women first began to challenge this conduct under Title VII, "the central ground on which courts resisted the claim was simply that sexual harassment was not discrimination 'on the basis of sex'").

[292] Seritis v. Lane, 30 Fair Empl. Prac. Cas. (BNA) 423 (Cal. Super. Ct. 1980).

[293] Corne v. Bausch & Lomb, Inc., 390 F. Supp. 161, 163 (D. Ariz. 1975).

[294] Tomkins v. Pub. Serv. Elec. & Gas Co., 422 F. Supp. 553, 556 (D.N.J. 1976); *id.* at 557 ("The abuse of authority by supervisors of either sex for personal purposes is an unhappy and recurrent feature of our social experience. . . . It is not, however, sex discrimination within the meaning of Title VII even when the purpose is sexual.").

Title VII came to be seen—by Americans generally and by courts interpreting the law—as discrimination "because of sex."[295]

This process repeated itself a decade later in the context of male-on-male harassment. Even some courts that had come to accept sexual harassment as a form of sex discrimination when perpetrated by men against women continued to hold well into the 1990s that the harassment of men by other men did not—and by definition could not—constitute discrimination because of sex. In 1994, the Fifth Circuit held that, by definition, "'[h]arassment by a male supervisor against a male subordinate does not state a claim under Title VII even though the harassment has sexual overtones'" because "'Title VII addresses gender discrimination.'"[296] When an oil rig worker named Joseph Oncale filed a Title VII lawsuit alleging he had been sexually harassed by male co-workers, his employer's (intelligent and accomplished) lawyers made the same argument.[297] They argued that accepting Oncale's claim "would write the 'because of sex' language out of the statute" because "all same-gender sexual harassment has only sexual content, and nothing to suggest discrimination because of gender."[298] But by 1998, that argument no longer prevailed; the Court held in *Oncale*

---

[295] In 1986, the Supreme Court held for the first time that "sexual harassment" is a cognizable form of sex discrimination under Title VII. See Meritor Sav. Bank, FSB v. Vinson, 477 U.S. 57, 65–67 (1986). The Court reaffirmed and expanded on that holding seven years later in Harris v. Forklift Systems, Inc., 510 U.S. 17 (1993)—and it is now an established part of Title VII law.

[296] Garcia v. ELF Atochem N. Am., 28 F.3d 446, 451–52 (5th Cir. 1994) (quoting Giddens v. Shell Oil Co., 12 F.3d 208 (5th Cir. 1993)) (alteration in original). For other decisions concluding that same-sex sexual harassment is not discrimination because of sex under Title VII, see, e.g., Ashworth v. Roundup Co., 897 F. Supp. 489, 493–94 (W.D. Wash. 1995); Myers v. City of El Paso, 874 F. Supp. 1546, 1548 (W.D. Tex. 1995); Oncale v. Sundowner Offshore Servs., Inc., Civ. A. No. 94-1483, 1995 WL 133349, at **1–2 (E.D. La. Mar. 24, 1995); Fleenor v. Hewitt Soap Co., No. C-3-94-182, 1995 WL 386793, at **2–3 (S.D. Ohio Dec. 21, 1994); Hopkins v. Balt. Gas & Elec., 871 F. Supp. 822, 834 (D. Md. 1994); Vandeventer v. Wabash Nat'l Corp., 867 F. Supp. 790, 796 (N.D. Ind. 1994).

[297] Sundowner's lawyers were serious people: Harry M. Reasoner, managing partner at Vinson & Elkins and one of Texas's most celebrated attorneys, and Samuel Issacharoff, a prominent constitutional law professor then at the University of Texas. See Brief for Respondents, Oncale v. Sundowner Offshore Servs., Inc., 523 U.S. 75 (1997) (No. 96-568), 1997 WL 634147.

[298] *Id.* at *16, *23. They also argued, with some foresight, that recognizing male-on-male harassment claims under Title VII would effectively extend the law's protection to gays and lesbians because such "claims invariably devolve into allegations of conduct that conflates gender with sexual orientation." *Id.* at *7; *id.* at *43 (arguing that courts "meld gender discrimination and discrimination because of sexual orientation when they conclude that gender stereotyping in the context of same-gender harassment amounts to discriminatory sexual harassment in violation of Title VII").

that Title VII's prohibition on sex discrimination extends to male-on-male sexual harassment as well.[299]

The dissenting Justices in *Bostock* embrace *Oncale* and endorse the idea that Title VII has prohibited sexual harassment—including the male-on-male sort—since 1964.[300] (Indeed, Justice Alito and Justice Thomas suggest such conduct has been prohibited in some Western states since the late nineteenth century.) But, as noted above, sexual harassment and anti-LGBT discrimination are quite similar with respect to characteristics the dissenters identify as important to determining whether a practice falls within Title VII's original public meaning. Neither sexual harassment nor anti-LGBT discrimination was understood to violate Title VII in 1964—in part because the concept of "sexual harassment," like the concept of "transgender," had yet to enter public consciousness. Like anti-LGBT discrimination, sexual harassment came to be defined as sex discrimination only after decades of sustained legal and social contestation and substantial doctrinal evolution in constitutional and statutory sex discrimination law. The dissenting Justices do not provide any justification for treating these practices differently, other than falling back on the tautological and presentist claim that sexual harassment just obviously is discrimination because of sex and anti-LGBT discrimination is not.

The dissenting Justices' embrace of other Title VII precedents, such as *Manhart* and *Price Waterhouse*, causes similar problems.[301] As Judge Wood and Judge Katzmann observed in the federal appeals court cases that preceded *Bostock*, once one accepts *Manhart*, *Price Waterhouse*, and *Oncale*, there is not a strong basis in law for excluding gay and transgender workers from Title VII's protections.[302] *Manhart* states "that employment decisions cannot be predicated on mere 'stereotyped' impressions about the characteristics of males or females."[303] *Price Waterhouse* declares that "we are beyond the day when an employer could evaluate employees by assuming or insisting that they matched the stereotype associated with their group,"[304] and that Title VII "'strike[s] at the entire spectrum of disparate treatment of

---

[299] Oncale v. Sundowner Offshore Servs., Inc., 523 U.S. 75, 78–80 (1997).

[300] Bostock v. Clayton County, 140 S. Ct. 1731, 1774 (2020) (Alito, J., dissenting).

[301] *Id.* at 1774–75.

[302] *See supra* text accompanying notes 86–95.

[303] Los Angeles Dep't of Water & Power v. Manhart, 435 U.S. 702, 707 (1978).

[304] Price Waterhouse v. Hopkins, 490 U.S. 228, 251 (1989).

men and women resulting from sex stereotypes.' "[305] For years, courts
tied themselves in knots trying to explain why traditional gendered
expectations that women will date men and that people labeled female
at birth will assume a female gender identity were not rooted in sex
stereotypes but instead reflected a distaste for gay and transgender
people.[306] As if those things could be teased apart. As if being a lesbian
or a transgender man is not in fact "the ultimate case of failure to
conform to the female stereotype (at least as understood in a place such
as modern America, which views heterosexuality [and cisgenderedness]
as the norm …)."[307] Once one accepts all the precedents that have
extended Title VII's reach over the past fifty years, it becomes very
difficult to justify drawing the line where the dissenting Justices do in
Bostock on anything other than normative grounds.

The more consistent approach, for the *Bostock* dissenters, would
have been to call for the overruling of these precedents: to argue that
the Court got it wrong and that sexual harassment, for example, does
not fall within the original public meaning of sex discrimination. Josh
Blackman, a prominent textualist scholar, has suggested that this is
precisely what the Justices in *Bostock* should have done, because by
accepting "precedents [that] were inconsistent with textualism," they
"undermined textualism's justification."[308] Blackman asserts: "One
can't profess to follow the original meaning of a text while in fact following precedents that ignored that meaning."[309]

---

[305] *Id.* (quoting *Manhart*, 435 U.S. at 707 n.13).

[306] *See* Zarda v. Altitude Express, Inc., 883 F.3d 100, 121–22 (2d Cir. 2018) (observing that
courts "have long labored to distinguish between gender stereotypes that support an inference of impermissible sex discrimination and those that are indicative of sexual orientation
discrimination," and that "many courts have found these distinctions unworkable, admitting
that the doctrine is illogical, and produces untenable results" (internal citation and quotation
marks omitted)); *id.* at 122 ("In the face of this pervasive confusion, we are persuaded that the
line between sex discrimination and sexual orientation discrimination is difficult to draw because that line does not exist save as a lingering and faulty judicial construct." (internal quotation
marks omitted)); Hively v. Ivy Tech Cmty. Coll., 853 F.3d 339, 342 (7th Cir. 2017) (discussing
"how difficult it is to extricate the gender nonconformity claims from the sexual orientation
claims" and asserting that "[t]hat effort … has led to a confused hodge-podge of cases" (internal
quotation marks omitted)).

[307] *Hively*, 853 F.3d at 346; *id.* at 342 ("[A]ll gay, lesbian and bisexual persons fail to comply
with the *sine qua non* of gender stereotypes—that all men should form intimate relationships
only with women, and all women should form intimate relationships only with men.").

[308] Blackman, *supra* note 127. Blackman aims his criticism at Justice Gorsuch, but it applies
equally to the dissenting Justices, who accepted the same precedents.

[309] *Id.*

That may be true. But as a practical matter, the Justices could not seriously have pursued this more consistent interpretive approach. The problem is not only that it would mean calling for the overruling of decades of precedent, which some textualists may be hesitant to do (another shadow decision point).[310] The more substantial problem is that for the lawyers and other twenty-first century Americans across the political spectrum who will read their opinions, the truth of the proposition that sexual harassment is sex discrimination is so obvious that to deny it would call into question the credibility of everything else the Justices argue. Arguing that sexual harassment is not sex discrimination today would be outlandish. As Justice Gorsuch observes in a parallel context in *Bostock*: "nobody believes *that*."

The incorporation of legal precedent into mainstream legal understandings is one important way in which original public meaning evolves. The American people, and the courts, have had many "new insights" with respect to gender and sexuality since the time of Title VII's enactment, and some of these insights have become so deeply embedded in legal doctrine and legal culture that it would now be "off-the-wall" to argue for their rejection. In this way, sexual harassment is like school segregation. When courts first began to hold such segregation illegal, supporters of the old regime made (quite plausible) textualist and originalist arguments against those rulings.[311] But it

---

[310] The question of whether or not to follow precedent when it conflicts with original public meaning is another major shadow decision point. Some textualists take a hard line, arguing that original public meaning always trumps precedent, regardless of how deeply that precedent has been woven into the fabric of the Court's jurisprudence and the reality of American life. *See, e.g.*, Randy E. Barnett, Response, *It's a Bird, It's a Plane, No, It's Super Precedent: A Response to Farber and Gerhardt*, 90 MINN. L. REV. 1232 (2006) (rejecting stare decisis when it would require infidelity to original public meaning); Gary Lawson, *The Constitutional Case Against Precedent*, 17 HARV. J.L. & PUB. POL'Y 23, 25–28 (1994) (arguing that it is unconstitutional to adhere to precedent that conflicts with the Constitution's text). Justice Scalia, on the other hand, referred to himself (at least early in his career) as a "faint-hearted originalist" due to his willingness to uphold some precedents that depart from the original public meaning of constitutional text. *See* Antonin Scalia, *Originalism: The Lesser Evil*, 57 U. CIN. L. REV. 849, 864 (1989). Some speculate that Justice Barrett may share this "moderate" stance toward precedent and praise this approach. *See, e.g.*, Solum, *supra* note 20. Blackman suggests that the faint-hearted "approach has the virtue of humility, even if it [sometimes] reaches the 'wrong' result, at least by a textualist standard." Blackman, *supra* note 127. But it is not clear that a textualist judge who picks and chooses when to abide by a text's original public meaning and when to depart from it demonstrates "humility." That approach could be characterized as a rather bold judicial assertion that original public meaning is law, except when I decide it is not.

[311] *See* Michael J. Klarman, Brown, *Originalism, and Constitutional Theory: A Response to Professor McConnell*, 81 VA. L. REV. 1881 (1995) (discussing the history on which originalist arguments against *Brown* were based); Siegel, *supra* note 166, at 28 n.39 (citing examples of those arguments).

would be surprising, even shocking, for a textualist or originalist to argue that school segregation is consistent with the original public meaning of the Fourteenth Amendment today. The idea that this practice violates the law has become so ingrained in twenty-first century legal culture that nobody makes—or even wants to make—arguments to the contrary. In fact, the idea that this practice is illegal is such a fixture of the contemporary legal landscape that it may be difficult, or even impossible, for people to believe, or to accept, that it was once licit under the ordinary public meaning of our laws. It is quite possible, perhaps even likely, that this is what the future holds for *Bostock*: If textualism remains a dominant interpretive approach fifty years from now, the consensus among its practitioners will be that the Court got it right in this case.

The linguist John McWhorter has written: They tell you "that a language is something that *is*, when it is actually something always *becoming*. They tell you a word is a thing, when it's actually something going on."[312] McWhorter was not talking about textualism, but these lines capture the dynamic this Article describes. Textualism portrays original public meaning as something frozen in time, preserved in period dictionaries or corpora. But it is actually something forged, over time, through legal and social contestation. We shape and reshape the original public meaning of legal provisions as we argue about what those provisions mean. The problem with textualism is not that it tethers us to old meanings, but that it enables courts to respond to legal and social change selectively and from a normative perspective while denying that that's what they're doing. It enables judges to decide the most significant questions in our legal system—including questions about who counts as a full and equal member of the American polity—without showing their work. So much of the decision-making in a textualist opinion happens in the shadows, out of view of the people and the elected branches. That is the opposite of judicial humility and deference: it is an assertion of judicial power.

CONCLUSION

In his book, *A Republic, If You Can Keep It*, Justice Gorsuch contends that one of the advantages of textualism is that it enables judges to tell litigants: "'I didn't rule against you because I disagree

---

[312] McWHORTER, *supra* note 238, at 3.

with your values and goals, but because the law required me to.'"[313] For this reason, Justice Gorsuch argues that textualism is better than other interpretive methodologies at protecting the rights of "minorities and disfavored groups"[314]: "Judges are more likely to fulfill their assigned mission of protecting disfavored persons from intemperate majorities when they can . . . say . . . the law required" them to reach the outcome they did.[315]

Of course, textualist judges can and do make this assertion in every case—those that extend legal protections to minorities as well as those that dismantle such protections. The latter sort of decision can also be unpopular, and the argument that "the law required me to" can be deployed as a shield against criticism of that sort of decision too. Indeed, the ability to say "the law required me to" would seem to embolden textualist judges to make countermajoritarian decisions of all kinds. Justice Gorsuch foregrounds cases in which textualist judges use original public meaning to thwart the oppression of minorities, but that is only one kind of judicial countermajoritarianism. The claim that "the law required me to" helps to justify and defend all decisions that thwart the will of majorities and the work of the elected branches.

It is not difficult to understand the appeal of the claim that "the law required me to." That claim taps into a persistent and widespread desire to view judges as umpires, calling balls and strikes, applying the law, not making it. Textualism has risen to great prominence promising to operationalize that vision of judging, in which law is fully and comfortingly separate from politics—and even from judges' own substantive constitutional and jurisprudential views. But, in reality, "we are long past the day when we can plausibly imagine judicial work as merely ministerial and mechanical, . . . [b]ecause everyone knows that judges have discretion in their interpretation of the law."[316] The adjudication of disputes over contested legal texts is not, and cannot be, insulated from extratextual considerations. As Justice Kavanaugh observes, judges do not interpret legal texts behind a veil of ignorance.[317] When they interpret words like "commerce" and "discrimination,"

---

[313] GORSUCH, *supra* note 14, at 134.

[314] *Id.* at 139.

[315] *Id.* at 134.

[316] Robert Post, *Theorizing Disagreement: Reconceiving the Relationship Between Law and Politics*, 98 CALIF. L. REV. 1319, 1331 (2010).

[317] Kavanaugh, *supra* note 41, at 2139; *see also supra* note 45.

when they decide what to make of the Second Amendment's invocation of militias,[318] they do so in the full knowledge of the consequences of their decisions, and their interpretations reflect their understanding of those consequences. Textualism does not enable judges to put such considerations aside; it disguises those considerations under a veneer of scientism and filters them through shadow decision points. This enables judges to act on substantive values and commitments without acknowledging that they are doing so or taking responsibility for the consequences of their decisions. When textualist judges insist that disputed bits of text compel them to reach the results they do, that is not, as Justice Gorsuch suggests, an expression of judicial humility. It is an assertion of judicial authority without accountability.

There is no better place to witness this dynamic playing out right now than in the context of affirmative action—a subject that arose frequently in the aftermath of *Bostock* and that provides an apt setting for some closing reflections on the themes of this Article. Numerous commentators have declared that *Bostock* "spells the end of affirmative action."[319] The majority in *Bostock* defined discrimination in a thin, anticlassificationist way, suggesting that any time an employer treats one employee worse than another on the basis of a protected trait, that differential treatment violates Title VII, regardless of its purposes or effects. Opponents of affirmative action have long embraced this anticlassificationist account of discrimination in the context of race, arguing that Title VII mandates race blindness and that any racial

---

[318] *See* Siegel, *supra* note 35, at 197–201, 239–40 (discussing the *Heller* Court's characterization of the Second Amendment's first clause, which discusses the necessity of "a well regulated Militia," as "prefatory," and its second clause, which discusses the right of the people to keep and bear Arms, as "operative": a textbook instance of shadow decision-making that has an substantial impact on the case's resolution but that isn't clearly compelled by the text itself or unambiguously part of the Amendment's original public meaning).

[319] Cass R. Sunstein, *Gorsuch Paves Way for Attack on Affirmative Action*, Bloomberg (June 17, 2020, 10:00 AM), https://www.bloomberg.com/opinion/articles/2020-06-17/gorsuch-gay-rights-opinion-targets-affirmative-action; *see also* Jeannie Suk Gersen, *Could the Supreme Court's Landmark L.G.B.T.-Rights Decision Help Lead to the Dismantling of Affirmative Action?*, New Yorker (June 27, 2020), https://www.newyorker.com/news/our-columnists/could-the-supreme-courts-landmark-lgbt-rights-decision-help-lead-to-the-dismantling-of-affirmative-action (arguing that "there is reason to think that *Bostock*'s formalist articulations on discrimination will bolster a conservative decision to dismantle race-conscious admissions policies"); Jason Mazzone, Bostock: *Were the Liberal Justices Namudnoed?*, Balkinization (July 6, 2020), https://balkin.blogspot.com/2020/07/bostock-were-liberal-justices-namudnoed.html (asserting that "[i]n *Bostock*, the absolutist language in Gorsuch's opinion . . . about Title VII is readymade for a future ruling that Title VII prohibits . . . affirmative action").

preference is suspect regardless of the motivation underlying it. Conservative textualists have already begun to argue that "logic, consistency, [and] fidelity to the rule of law" require the Court, post-*Bostock*, to declare affirmative action illegal.[320] And they have already begun to construct a narrative portraying the invalidation of affirmative action as a neutral, value-free choice—one that is unambiguously mandated by Title VII's text and impervious to charges that it is part of a conservative political agenda, given that it rests on a definition of discrimination taken directly from *Bostock*.[321]

The problem with this argument is that any decision interpreting Title VII to bar affirmative action would almost certainly require the assent of some or all of the dissenting Justices in *Bostock*. Those Justices vehemently reject the Court's anticlassificationist interpretation of Title VII in *Bostock*, portraying it as overly "literal," "legalistic," and "wooden."[322] Justice Alito and Justice Thomas insist, on the basis of purportedly unambiguous corpus linguistics evidence, that Title VII prohibits only practices "motivated by prejudice, or biased ideas or attitudes."[323] They argue that to determine whether a practice "discriminates" in the eyes of the law, it is necessary to attend to its social history, to assess whether it is "historically tied to a project that aims to subjugate" on the basis of a protected trait.[324]

This is the basis on which the dissenting Justices reject the *Bostock* plaintiffs' attempts to analogize anti-LGBT discrimination to antimiscegenation laws. Advocates of LGBT rights have long argued that if it is illegal for the state/an employer to police the race of one's romantic partner it should also be illegal for the state/an employer to police the sex of one's romantic partner. But the dissenters in *Bostock* reject that reasoning as overly formalistic, arguing that it "totally ignores the historically rooted reason why discrimination on the basis of an

---

[320] Lund, *supra* note 144, at 167.

[321] *See, e.g., id.* ("Although *Bostock*'s particular application of textualist principles is fatally flawed, those principles can and should be faithfully applied in other cases. Title VII's antidiscrimination language does not apply . . . to discrimination on the basis of sexual orientation. . . . But [its] application . . . to preferences based on race or sex is indisputably clear.").

[322] Bostock v. Clayton County, 140 S. Ct. 1731, 1745 (2020) (Justice Gorsuch's characterization of the dissenting Justices' critique).

[323] *Id.* at 1769 n.22 (Alito, J., dissenting).

[324] *Id.* at 1765.

interracial relationship constitutes race discrimination."[325] Bars on
interracial marriage violate the law because "history tells us" they are
"a core form of race discrimination."[326] The dissenters argue that anti-
LGBT discrimination does not have the same historical and sociological relationship to sex discrimination. Discrimination against gay
and transgender people may treat men and women differently as a
formal matter,[327] but, the dissenters argue, it is not "sexist."[328] It is not
the kind of practice that contravenes "the campaign for equality . . .
waged by women's rights advocates for more than a century."[329]

Conservative textualist federal appeals court judges have also embraced this socially attentive, antisubordinationist approach to Title VII
in LGBT rights cases. They too have advocated taking history and context into account in antidiscrimination law and explicitly condemned
the kind of formalism that sometimes prevails in this area of law. Judge
James Ho, a staunchly conservative textualist on the 5th Circuit, railed
against "the blindness theory of Title VII"[330] in a decision just prior to
Bostock in which he rejected a sex-based claim by a transgender plaintiff. He argued that Title VII does not categorically bar all classifications on the basis of protected traits but only those that constitute
"invidious . . . discrimination."[331] Judge William Pryor echoed this con-
demnation of anticlassificationism in his own recent textualist opinion
rejecting a sex-based claim by a transgender student. Judge Pryor argued that "context matters" in antidiscrimination law—a proposition
for which he cited the great antisubordinationist Justice, Thurgood
Marshall.[332] Judge Pryor is not an outlier. Much conservative textualist

---

[325] *Id.*

[326] *Id.; see also id.* (explaining that antimiscegenation laws were "grounded in bigotry against a particular race and w[ere] an integral part of preserving the rigid hierarchical distinction that denominated members of the black race as inferior to whites").

[327] *Id.* at 1824 (Kavanaugh, J., dissenting).

[328] *Id.* at 1765 (Alito, J., dissenting).

[329] *Id.* at 1769; *see also id.* at 1828 (Kavanaugh, J., dissenting) (asserting that "Seneca Falls was not Stonewall" and that such historical and sociological evidence is relevant to the question of whether anti-LGBT discrimination qualifies as discrimination because of sex).

[330] Wittmer v. Phillips 66 Co., 915 F.3d 328, 337 (5th Cir. 2019) (Ho, J., concurring); *id.* at 334 ("The blindness theory . . . would hold that Title VII prohibits both transgender and sexual orientation discrimination. Because under that theory . . . [a]ll that matters is that company policy treats people differently based on their sex. . . .").

[331] *Id.* at 340 (internal quotation marks omitted).

[332] *See* Adams *ex rel.* Kasper v. Sch. Bd. of St. Johns Cnty., 968 F.3d 1286, 1311 (11th Cir. 2020) (Pryor, C.J., dissenting).

commentary in recent sex-based LBGT rights decisions echoes anti-subordinationist arguments generally associated with Justice Marshall and other progressive Justices. These Justices have always argued that context matters—particularly in affirmative action cases, where they have observed that "[a]ctions designed to burden groups long denied full citizenship stature are not sensibly ranked with measures taken to hasten the day when entrenched discrimination and its aftereffects have been extirpated."[333]

One would think, based on conservative textualists' rejection of anticlassificationism and embrace of antisubordinationism in these recent LGBT rights cases, that affirmative action's future under Title VII would be fairly secure. But the commentators who predicted in the wake of *Bostock* that affirmative action was "doomed"[334] may very well be right. Because, in reality, and contrary to what the Justices suggest in *Bostock*, the meaning of Title VII's prohibition of discrimination is underdetermined; it admits of multiple interpretations. There is very little to prevent textualist judges from picking and choosing from among the different definitions of discrimination to reach results that best accord with their extratextual commitments in different legal contexts.

Indeed, *textualist judges already toggle between different definitions of discrimination in different Title VII contexts.* In *Bostock*, Justice Thomas endorses corpus linguistics evidence purporting to show that Title VII's original public meaning does not bar all discrimination, but only discrimination motivated by prejudice or bias. But in *Olmstead v. Zimring*, a case involving disability discrimination, Justice Thomas adopted Justice Gorsuch's approach in *Bostock*: He turned to the dictionary and concluded that the word "discriminate" "means to 'distinguish,' to 'differentiate,' or to make a 'distinction . . .'" between individuals on the basis of a protected trait.[335] Justice Thomas explicitly

---

[333] Gratz v. Bollinger, 539 U.S. 244, 301 (2003) (Ginsburg, J., dissenting); *see also id.* at 301–02 ("[A] classification that denies a benefit, causes harm, or imposes a burden must not be based on race. In that sense, the Constitution is color blind. But the Constitution is color conscious to prevent discrimination being perpetuated and to undo the effects of past discrimination." (internal quotation marks omitted)); Adarand Constructors, Inc. v. Peña, 515 U.S. 200, 245 (1995) (Stevens, J., dissenting) (criticizing rulings invalidating affirmative action on equality grounds for "disregard[ing] the difference between a 'No Trespassing' sign and a welcome mat").

[334] Sunstein, *supra* note 319.

[335] Olmstead v. L.C. *ex rel.* Zimring, 527 U.S. 581, 616 (1999) (Thomas, J., dissenting) (quoting RANDOM HOUSE DICTIONARY 564 (2d ed. 1987)); *see also id.* (quoting WEBSTER'S

stated in *Olmstead* that this thin, anticlassificationist definition of discrimination is the one that captures Title VII's original public meaning,[336] and he cited constitutional decisions prohibiting race-based affirmative action as evidence that the word discrimination always carries this same formalistic meaning.[337] Justice Thomas made the same argument a few years after *Olmstead* in an age discrimination case called *General Dynamics Land Systems, Inc. v. Cline*, in which he excoriated his colleagues for attending to "social history" in interpreting antidiscrimination laws[338] and once again characterized Title VII as adopting a strictly anticlassificationist definition of discrimination.[339]

One response to these shifting and context-dependent interpretations of Title VII's original public meaning might be to say it's just bad textualism. But there is a reason judges keep failing at this, which is that textualism does not actually enable them to do what it promises. It does not actually provide a means of cabining all knowledge of history and social values and resolving highly contested issues in a neutral and value-free way. There are too many shadow decision points; the meaning of words is too varied and dynamic; and the kinds of cases that reach the Court are too contested for the search for original public meaning to yield determinate answers. What textualism provides instead is a string of superficially appealing assertions that its practitioners cannot hear or will not attend to democratic debate over the issues of the day. Textualism promises that arguments involving matters of deep moral and political significance to the American people can be transformed into, and resolved through, value-free arguments over technical methodological questions. But that is not possible and pretending otherwise is not democracy-enhancing. In fact, it is the big

---

THIRD NEW INTERNATIONAL DICTIONARY 648 (1981), which defines "'discrimination' as 'the making or perceiving of a distinction or difference' or as 'the act, practice, or an instance of discriminating categorically rather than individually'").

[336] *Id.* at 616–17.

[337] *Id.* at 620 ("This same understanding of discrimination also informs this Court's constitutional interpretation of the term."); *id.* (citing Adarand Constructors, Inc. v. Peña, 515 U.S. 200, 223–24 (1995) and Richmond v. J.A. Croson Co., 488 U.S. 469, 493–94 (1989) (plurality opinion)).

[338] Gen. Dynamics Land Sys., Inc. v. Cline, 540 U.S. 581, 606–13 (2004) (Thomas, J., dissenting).

[339] *Id.* at 608–12; *id.* at 608 (observing that "[t]here is little doubt that the motivation behind the enactment of the Civil Rights Act of 1964 was to prevent invidious discrimination against racial minorities, especially blacks," but arguing that it does not matter which social group Congress intended to protect because, as a semantic matter, Title VII bars all differential treatment on the basis of race).

lie, in the judicial realm for the coming generation: that judicial elites, trained in the practice of textualism and originalism, can unlock the one true and eternal meaning of our deepest legal commitments, unburdened by history, politics, social change, and the substantive constitutional visions that so profoundly influence how we all understand those commitments.

DAVID A. STRAUSS

SEXUAL ORIENTATION AND THE
DYNAMICS OF DISCRIMINATION

In *Bostock v. Clayton County*[1] the Supreme Court held that the Title VII ban on employment discrimination "because of sex" forbids discrimination on the basis of sexual orientation or transgender status. The majority said that that outcome was dictated by "the express terms of [the] statute" interpreted according to the "ordinary public meaning of its terms at the time of its enactment." It also said that the answer was "clear."[2]

The Court reached the right result, but it got many things wrong along the way. It understated the difficulty of the issue presented by the case. It inverted the importance of text and precedent in resolving that issue. The majority did not adequately respond to a competing, plausible understanding of sex discrimination that the dissenters embraced. The majority also did not really come to grips with the fact that neither the Congress that enacted Title VII, nor any court for a half-century afterward, understood Title VII in the way it did. And the

David A. Strauss is the Gerald Ratner Distinguished Service Professor of Law, University of Chicago.

AUTHOR'S NOTE: I thank Jennifer Nou, Jonathan Masur, Eric Posner, Brian Leiter, and the participants in the University of Chicago Law School Work in Progress Workshop for comments on an earlier draft, and the Burton and Adrienne Glazov Faculty Fund for financial support.

[1] Bostock v. Clayton Cnty., 140 S. Ct. 1731 (2020).

[2] *Id.* at 1737–38.

The Supreme Court Review, 2021.

Court's narrow focus on the words of Title VII meant that it never considered the relationship between the issue in *Bostock* and the substantial body of constitutional law concerning sex discrimination, or the more recently developed constitutional protections for gay and lesbian people.

The main source of these problems was the claim that the case could be decided on the basis of the words of the statute alone—as if the answer has been there ever since 1964, awaiting only the majority's analysis of meaning and syntax to unlock it, and as if we have not learned anything in the intervening years. The Court was right to extend Title VII to discrimination on the basis of sexual orientation not because that conclusion was already contained in the words themselves but because of a decades-long evolution in which courts, and to some extent actors outside the courts, worked out what impermissible sex discrimination is, in interpreting both Title VII and the Equal Protection Clause of the Constitution.

The Court's pretense that the answer was already in the "ordinary public meaning" of the text implicitly discredits efforts to bring about a better understanding of statutes like Title VII or, to the extent a similar approach is taken to the Constitution, of constitutional provisions—the kinds of efforts to which we owe much of the progress we have made in this and other areas. To put the point another way, saying that the only thing we need to do is to examine the words of authoritative texts more carefully is a formula for either quietism or self-deception. If we were to take the majority seriously, there would be little point in trying to engage with the moral and institutional issues involved in deciding questions like those about sex discrimination or LGBT rights under existing provisions, because it is all and only about the text. In fact, though, what will happen is that efforts to engage with those issues will have to masquerade as ever more subtle readings of the language of the texts, when in fact they are something much different from that. That is what happened in *Bostock*.

First, I will describe the different ways that the majority and the principal dissent understood the prohibition against sex discrimination in Title VII. It is actually a disagreement not about the definition of the terms in the statute but about how to apply an agreed-upon definition. That disagreement cannot be resolved by the words of Title VII alone. Then I will explain what resolves that disagreement in the case of discrimination on the basis of LGBT status: the way that the law concerning discrimination has developed over decades. The majority's position, not the dissenters', is consistent with the fabric of antidiscrimination law as it has developed. For purposes of the issue in *Bostock* the most important development, as others have said, is the understanding that requiring conformity to stereotyped gender roles can be a form of impermissible sex discrimination. That understanding, and the way it condemns discrimination against LGBT individuals, developed over time, in constitutional law as well as in the interpretation of Title VII, as a result of a greater understanding of both sex discrimination and discrimination on the basis of sexual orientation.

The Court would have been justified in taking those understandings into account, even though that meant departing from how the statute was understood when it was enacted, and even though the text allows but does not compel the result the majority reached. In fact, it is difficult to avoid the conclusion that those understandings, or something like them, are what really enabled the Court to decide the case the way it did, not the definitional analysis on which the Court claimed to rely.

I. Two Veils of Ignorance

Bostock involved three Title VII suits. Two were brought by gay men who alleged that they were fired because they were gay. A third was brought by a transgender woman who presented as male when she was hired, then was fired when she told her employer of her plan to transition. The Court's opinion mostly discussed discrimination against gays and lesbians; the Court treated its conclusion about the transgender individual as essentially a corollary.

There are substantial arguments that Title VII does not reach discrimination on the basis of LGBT status. For one thing, there does not seem to be any doubt about what Congress thought it was doing, and not doing, with respect to sexual orientation when it enacted Title VII as part of the Civil Rights Act of 1964. At least as compared to the present day, that era was saturated with homophobia, as the dissenters in *Bostock* argued at length.[3] It is hard to believe that any reasonable observer at the time would have thought that the enactment of Title VII immediately outlawed discrimination against gay people and lesbians. And the idea that transgender individuals even

---

[3] *See, e.g.*, 140 S. Ct. at 1769–72 (Alito, J., dissenting).

constituted a group of the kind that might be protected against discrimination was not in wide circulation in 1964.[4]

In addition, there are arguments, derived from the text itself, that discrimination on the basis of "sex" does not include discrimination on the basis of sexual orientation. Title VII forbids employment discrimination on the basis of "[an] individual's race, color, religion, sex, or national origin."[5] Many other jurisdictions' antidiscrimination provisions include "sexual orientation" on their versions of that list.[6] That suggests that the omission of sexual orientation from the Title VII list should count for something. Since Title VII was enacted, there have been proposals to add sexual orientation to the Title VII list, but none has been successful.[7] And the addition of sexual orientation to the list of forbidden bases for discrimination does not seem like the kind of relatively minor adjustment that Congress might have anticipated courts' making for changed circumstances.

These points alone are not conclusive against the Court's interpretation of Title VII, but they are also not easy to rebut. Some lower court judges explicitly said that they would have liked to rule in favor of LGBT employees in Title VII cases but could not overcome those concerns.[8] The majority in *Bostock* acknowledged but discounted all of those things because, it said, only the words of the statute matter, at least if the statute is clear—which, the Court concluded, it was. The dissent, unsurprisingly, asked why, if the text was so clear, no court had accepted the majority's view until very recently, and many had unequivocally rejected it.

The "ordinary public meaning" of Title VII does not answer these objections. The *Bostock* majority's principal argument to the contrary focused on the term "because of," which it interpreted to adopt "the traditional but-for causation standard."[9] "So long as the plaintiff's sex

---

[4] *See id.* at 1772–73.

[5] 42 U.S.C. § 2000e-2(a)(1).

[6] *See* Brief for the United States as Amicus Curiae at 15, Bostock v. Clayton Cnty., 140 S. Ct. 1731 (2020) (No. 17-1618); Hively v. Ivy Tech Cmty. Coll., 853 F.3d 339, 364 (7th Cir. 2017) (en banc) (Sykes, J., dissenting); Zarda v. Altitude Express, 883 F.3d 100, 152 & n.21 (2d Cir. 2018) (en banc) (Lynch, J., dissenting), *aff'd sub nom.* Bostock v. Clayton Cnty., 140 S. Ct. 1731 (2020).

[7] *See Bostock*, 140 S. Ct. at 1755 & nn. 1–4 (Alito, J., dissenting).

[8] *See, e.g., Zarda*, 883 F.3d at 137–67 (Lynch, J., dissenting).

[9] *Bostock*, 140 S. Ct. at 1739. Under Title VII, it is unlawful "to discharge any individual, or otherwise to discriminate against any individual . . . because of such individual's race, color, religion, sex, or national origin." 42 U.S.C. § 2000e-2(a)(1).

was one but-for cause of th[e] decision, that is enough to trigger the law,"[10] the majority said. But that cannot be correct. An employee's sex might be the but-for cause of many attributes that an employer is entitled to take into account. For example, an employee might lack a credential that the employer could legitimately require for a promotion because someone else had treated her differently, on account of her sex, at an earlier point in her career—another employer, a school, or her family. Then her sex might be the but-for cause of her not getting the promotion: if she were not a woman, she would have the necessary credential and she would be promoted. But it would not follow that the employer's failure to promote her violated Title VII; Title VII has never been interpreted to require employers to undo all the consequences of past differential treatment by others.

In fact, the crucial concept in Title VII, for purposes of the issue in *Bostock*, is not causation but discrimination. As a textual matter, this follows from the way the statute links "because of" to "discriminate against,"[11] and in any event there is no doubt that the central concern of Title VII is discrimination. The Court did "[a]ccept[] . . . for argument's sake" that it had to consider the meaning of "discriminate," and that actually led it—by way of precedent more than dictionary definitions—to a common sense definition of sex discrimination: "To 'discriminate against' a person . . . mean[s] treating that individual worse than others who are similarly situated."[12] The majority formulated this test in a variety of ways: "[I]f changing the employee's sex would have yielded a different choice by the employer[,] a statutory violation has occurred."[13] Or, as the Court said elsewhere in the opinion, "an employer who intentionally treats a person worse because of sex—such as firing the person for actions or attributes it would tolerate in an individual of another sex—discriminates against that individual in violation of Title VII."[14]

---

[10] *Bostock*, 140 S. Ct. at 1739.

[11] Title VII makes it unlawful "to discharge any individual, or otherwise to discriminate against any individual . . . because of such individual's" sex. 42 U.S.C. § 2000e–2(a)(1). The use of "otherwise" implies that decisions to "discharge an[] individual . . . because of such individual's sex" are a subset of actions that "discriminate against" that individual. *See Bostock*, 140 S. Ct. at 1740.

[12] *Bostock*, 140 S. Ct. at 1740 (first citing *Burlington N. & S. F. R. Co. v. White*, 548 U.S. 53, 59 (2006); and then *Watson v. Fort Worth Bank & Trust*, 487 U.S. 977 (1988)).

[13] *Bostock*, 140 S. Ct. at 1741.

[14] *Id.* at 1740.

This is a kind of veil of ignorance test; the majority did not use that term, but Justice Alito did, in oral argument, when he asked a question that foreshadowed the way his dissent applied the same definition.[15] The idea is to impose hypothetical information conditions on the decision maker and see if the decision changes. If the employer did not know the employee's sex, would the decision have been different? A veil of ignorance test demands a kind of impartiality, comparable to that required of, say, an umpire in a game, who must act as if she does not know the team affiliations of the players, even though she obviously does. So the causal question under Title VII is not whether the employee's sex is the but-for cause of an adverse employment action; it is whether the employer's *knowledge* of the employee's sex is a but-for cause. To be concrete: if an employer, after being told by a middle manager that he should fire a chronically late employee, asked whether the employee was a man or a woman—and the answer to that question determined the employer's decision— that would be a textbook example of sex discrimination.[16]

This veil of ignorance test is a good account of what Title VII forbids not because it can be deduced from a close reading of the statute but because it is the way most people would intuitively think of discrimination in a run-of-the-mill case. In an earlier decision, the Court characterized it as "the simple test" of what "constitutes discrimination."[17] The Seventh Circuit, in a case that reached the same result about sexual orientation discrimination as *Bostock*, called it "the tried-and-true comparative method."[18]

The issue in *Bostock*, the Court said, is just the same as in the case of an employer whose decision about firing a chronically late employee

---

[15] *See* Transcript of Oral Argument at 51, Bostock v. Clayton Cnty., 140 S. Ct. 1731 (2020) (No. 17-1618).

[16] The question is, or at least can be, hypothetical: whether the employer would have treated the employee differently if she had been male. There is no need for a flesh-and-blood "comparator" who shares all legitimately relevant traits with the plaintiff, although the lack of a comparator might make the evidentiary question more difficult. Having said that, though, the counterfactual inquiry that this test requires will sometimes be unmanageable, when the trait in question is inextricable from one group, as pregnancy is, for example. That draws into question the coherence of this veil of ignorance approach. *See* Cary Franklin, *Inventing the "Traditional Concept" of Sex Discrimination*, 125 HARV. L. REV. 1307, 1366–72 (2012); *see also* David A. Strauss, *Discriminatory Intent and the Taming of* Brown, 56 U. CHI. L. REV. 953, 965–1014 (1989). But neither the majority's nor the dissent's approach in *Bostock* raised that issue.

[17] L.A. Dep't of Water & Power v. Manhart, 435 U.S. 702, 711 (1978).

[18] Hively v. Ivy Tech Cmty. Coll., 853 F.3d 339, 345 (7th Cir. 2017) (en banc).

depends on the employee's sex. Suppose an employer who does not want LGBT people working for him finds out that one of his employees is attracted to men. Will he fire that employee? The answer will depend on whether the employee is a man or a woman. That, the Court said, is sex discrimination, just as in the case of the chronically late employee.

But the dissenters in *Bostock*, using the same definition, made a different veil of ignorance argument.[19] The dissenters' account is not obviously less intuitive, but it leads to the opposite conclusion. Suppose an employer simply announces that it will not consider any LGBT applicants, whatever their sex (as the U.S. military did until relatively recently). Or suppose the employer requires all employees to execute an affidavit about their sexual orientation, without revealing their sex, and fires everyone who is not straight. Obviously in both of these instances the employer has engaged in sexual orientation discrimination. But how can it be discrimination "because of sex"? The employer did not even know the sex of the people he fired or refused to hire. Under the majority's own definition, "changing the employee's sex would [not] have yielded a different choice by the employer"[20]—any LGBT employee, no matter their sex, would be fired. And that employer has not "fir[ed a] person for actions or attributes it would tolerate in an individual of another sex"; it does not tolerate the attribute of being gay or lesbian in any individual.

According to the dissenters' approach, the majority misapplied the "tried-and-true comparative method" because a man who is attracted to men is not "similarly situated" to a woman who is attracted to men. The man is gay, and unless we are going to assume the answer to the question in the case, the employer is allowed to take into account the fact that the man is gay in deciding to fire him, just as the employer would be allowed to take into account the fact that the man is late for work more often. What these hypothetical scenarios show, according to the dissenters, is that discrimination on the basis of sexual orientation is distinct from sex discrimination. Far from the "employee's

---

[19] The principal dissent was by Justice Alito, joined by Justice Thomas. 140 S. Ct. at 1754–1822. Justice Kavanaugh dissented separately. *Id.* at 1822–37. Justice Alito's dissent developed the dissenting version of the veil of ignorance argument in detail, *see id.* at 1758–63 (Alito, J., dissenting), but Justice Kavanaugh took the same approach in substance, *see id.* at 1828 (Kavanaugh, J., dissenting).

[20] *Bostock*, 140 S. Ct. at 1741.

sex play[ing] an unmistakable . . . role in the discharge decision" in *Bostock*, as the majority said,[21] sex played no role, because the employer would have made the same decision in ignorance of the employee's sex.

These are simply two different applications of an agreed-upon veil of ignorance definition of discrimination. Neither is obviously inconsistent with the language of Title VII—that an employer may not "refuse to hire[,] discharge[, or] discriminate against any individual because of such individual's sex."[22] On the majority's view, sex was precisely what caused the employer's decision. The employer fired a man who was attracted to men but would not have fired a woman, indistinguishable in all relevant respects, who was attracted to men. On the dissent's view, sex played no role in the decision; the employee was fired "because of" sexual orientation by an employer who did not even need to know the sex of the employee. If anything, the dissent's account seems better because it reflects the employer's—the alleged discriminator's—self-understanding. The employer could say, without dissembling, that it did not care about the employee's sex, only about sexual orientation. A casual observer who knew all the facts would mostly likely say that the employer discriminated on the basis of sexual orientation, not sex.[23] And the dissent's view is consistent with the way Title VII was understood from its enactment until recently.

One way to understand the difference between these two approaches is that for the dissenters, the crucial factor is what the employer actually cares about. The employer cares about the employees' LGBT status, not their sex. The employer chose a (presumably) sex-neutral criterion—sexual orientation—and applied it without regard to any employee's sex. Applying that criterion in particular cases, like that of the man attracted to men, might involve taking the employee's sex into account. But according to the dissenters' view, that is an incidental, not essential, feature of the employer's decision. Not only will the employer fire, or refuse to hire, both men and women; the employer is indifferent to the employees' sex. It follows, according to the dissenters, that the employer made its decision "because of" the employee's LGBT status, not because of the employee's sex, and the

---

[21] *See Id.* at 1741–42.

[22] 42 U.S.C. § 2000e–(2)(a)(1) (ellipses omitted).

[23] This is a principal theme of Justice Kavanaugh's dissent. *See Bostock*, 140 S. Ct. at 1827–28.

employer discriminated on the basis of sexual orientation but not on the basis of sex.

But for the majority, what the employer supposedly cares about is beside the point. Even if the employer can sometimes enforce its policy without knowing the employee's sex, the employer has adopted a policy that will require the firing of a man who is in a relationship with a man but not an indistinguishable woman who is in a relationship with a man. In any event, often the employer will know the employee's sex and will make the decision on that basis, and there cannot be a different rule for instances in which the employer does not know. And, according to the majority's approach, to say that the man is differently situated because he is gay is just to restate the discriminatory basis of the decision. It is just a way of saying that he is being fired for doing something that a woman would not be fired for doing.

How are we to choose between these competing veil of ignorance arguments about whether discrimination against LGBT people is necessarily sex discrimination? Ordinary linguistic intuitions, on which the *Bostock* majority seemed to rely, are not going to help very much. As a matter of English usage, the terms "because of" and "discrimination" can be understood in either of these ways. But we have more to work with than just linguistic intuitions. The notion of discrimination, in the sense of sex and race discrimination, has been a central feature of U.S. law for a long time, and the difference between these two versions of the veil of ignorance test is, in fact, a fault line that runs through much of antidiscrimination law. The choice between those two versions determined the treatment of rational statistical discrimination.[24] It was implicated in the rejection of the "separate but equal" rationale for racial segregation.[25] And, most directly relevant to the treatment of LGBT individuals, it shaped the general prohibition of laws and employment practices that disadvantage individuals who do not conform to stereotyped gender roles.[26] The way the law has developed in those areas, rather than analysis of the words of Title VII, vindicates the majority's approach in *Bostock*.

---

[24] *See infra* Part II.

[25] *See infra* note 58 and accompanying text.

[26] *See infra* Part III.

II. Statistical Discrimination

In *Los Angeles Department of Water and Power v. Manhart*,[27] an employer required women employees to make larger contributions to the employees' pension fund than men did. The justification was that women tend to live longer than men and therefore receive greater pension benefits. The Court did not question the actuarial premise of that justification: it acknowledged that the employer had acted on the basis not of a "'stereotyped'" or "fictional difference between men and women" but of "a generalization that the parties accept as unquestionably true."[28] But the Court rejected that justification and held that the practice of requiring greater contributions from women employees violated Title VII.

The holding in *Manhart* is an example of a pervasive feature of U.S. antidiscrimination law: rational statistical discrimination on the basis of a characteristic like race or sex—what is sometimes called "profiling"—is impermissible.[29] Rational statistical discrimination, in this context, is the use of a characteristic that a decision maker is ordinarily forbidden to use, like race or sex, as a proxy for a characteristic that it is acceptable to consider. As in *Manhart*, race or sex can be useful as a proxy if it is associated with the acceptable characteristic, like life expectancy, because ordinarily race and sex are easy to ascertain. Employers, like other decision makers, use easily ascertained proxies all the time, of course. An employer might use scores on an aptitude test because they are associated, even if imperfectly, with success on the job, and it is much easier to administer a test than to try to predict job performance in more accurate ways. The fit is

---

[27] 435 U.S. 702 (1978).

[28] *Id.* at 707.

[29] The principle that it is not a defense to a claim of race or sex discrimination to show that one was engaging in rational statistical discrimination is so well established—although there are some complications and qualifications—that it is not easy to find Supreme Court cases that explicitly reject the use of rational statistical discrimination. The peremptory challenge cases, discussed *infra* at text accompanying notes 31–34, are probably the clearest rejection of statistical discrimination that is conceded to be (at least sometimes) rational. In general, it is taken for granted that "profiling" is unacceptable. *See generally* R. Richard Banks, *Beyond Profiling: Race, Policing, and the Drug War*, 56 Stan. L. Rev. 571, 574 & nn.8–10 (2003) (citing statements repudiating "profiling" and statutes outlawing the practice).

Manhart was unusual because the statistical generalization was undisputedly true, so the employer's action looked reasonable—in fact, the Court in *Manhart* conceded as much when it overturned the lower courts' award of compensatory damages. The peremptory challenge cases were unusual because the unrestrained use of peremptory challenges seemed to be so familiar.

imperfect, but the cost savings is worth it. It might be rational to use an individual's race or sex in the same way. But under both Title VII and the Constitution, discrimination cannot be justified in this way, no matter how rational it is.

The *Bostock* majority cited *Manhart* as "confirm[ation]"[30] of the conclusion it purported to derive from the text, but in fact *Manhart*, and the more general prohibition against statistical discrimination, supports the majority's conclusion more strongly than the text does. For one thing, *Manhart* provides a response to the criticism that the majority misapplied "the tried-and-true comparative method" when it compared a man attracted to men to a woman attracted to men. The criticism is that instead of holding constant everything except sex, the majority changed two characteristics: sex and sexual orientation. But the same objection could be made to the holding in *Manhart*. In *Manhart*, the women who were required to make a larger contribution differed from men not only in their sex but in their life expectancy. The Court ruled that treating women differently was, nonetheless, impermissible sex discrimination.

More generally, the prohibition against rational statistical discrimination amounts to a rejection of the dissenters' veil of ignorance approach. The basis of the dissenters' approach was that the employers in *Bostock* did not care about the employees' sex but only about their sexual orientation. Similarly, the employer's concern in *Manhart* was with life expectancy and the associated cost of pension benefits. The dissenters in *Bostock* asserted that the employer did not discriminate on the basis of sex because it would have acted in the same way even if it did not know the sex of the employees. In principle, the employer in a case like *Manhart* would not need to consider sex at all if there were some way for it to identify employees with longer life expectancy that was as accurate as using sex as a criterion and no more costly.

This is not an entirely hypothetical scenario: some uses of artificial intelligence and large data sets might make this a realistic possibility. But in any event, the dissenters in *Bostock* did not limit their disagreement to instances in which the employer actually did not know the sex of an employee. They relied on the hypothetical veil of ignorance definition. Their argument was that as long as the employer knew the employee's sexual orientation, the employee's sex would not

---

[30] Bostock v. Clayton Cnty., 140 S. Ct. 1731, 1743 (2020).

affect the decision. That definition—substituting "life expectancy" for "sexual orientation"—would permit the practice that *Manhart* disapproved.

The Equal Protection Clause, like Title VII, has been interpreted to forbid statistical discrimination.[31] The constitutional prohibition against race- and sex-based peremptory challenges is an especially useful example, because an argument like that of the *Bostock* dissenters was made by the dissent, and rejected by the majority, in the leading case on peremptory challenges, *Batson v. Kentucky*.[32] *Batson* held that it is unconstitutional for a prosecutor to use a peremptory challenge to remove a prospective juror because of the juror's race. Assuming (as the Court in *Batson* did) that prosecutors act in good faith, a prosecutor who uses a race-based peremptory challenge is engaging in rational statistical discrimination. The prosecutor is using race as a proxy for a legitimate criterion—the likelihood that a prospective juror will be a suitable juror from the government's point of view.

Justice Rehnquist's dissent in *Batson* made an argument parallel to the one made by the *Bostock* dissenters: "[T]here is simply nothing 'unequal' about the State's using its peremptory challenges to strike blacks from the jury in cases involving black defendants, so long as such challenges are also used to exclude whites in cases involving white defendants, Hispanics in cases involving Hispanic defendants, Asians in cases involving Asian defendants, and so on."[33] That is, a prosecutor may consider the race of particular prospective jurors in the course of applying a race-neutral criterion about the suitability of the juror, as long as the prosecutor treats prospective jurors of all races that way. The *Bostock* dissenters' argument was the same: an employer does not discriminate on the basis of sex when it applies its criterion—whether an employee is gay or lesbian—to people of both sexes, even if that requires the employer to consider the sex of the employee.

But the Court in *Batson* rejected Justice Rehnquist's argument and concluded that the prosecutor's action constituted impermissible

---

[31] The Court has said that decisions under the Equal Protection Clause are "quite relevant" in determining the meaning of "discrimination" under Title VII. *See infra* notes 39–40 and accompanying text.

[32] 476 U.S. 79 (1986).

[33] 476 U.S. at 137–38 (Rehnquist, J., dissenting).

racial discrimination. The Court has also forbidden sex-based peremptory challenges, while acknowledging that lawyers who use such a challenge might be defending their clients' interests in a way that would otherwise be legitimate[34]—just as an employer who fires men but not women who are attracted to men might be furthering its (assumed) legitimate interest in excluding gay people from its workforce.

In this way, *Manhart* and the general prohibition against statistical discrimination support the *Bostock* majority, rather than the dissent. Having said that, though, there are some disanalogies. Statistical discrimination attributes a characteristic to a group—women in *Manhart*, racial minorities in *Batson*. Discrimination against LGBT people does not (at least not obviously) ascribe a characteristic to men, or to women, in the same way. At least that was not the basis of the decision in *Bostock*.

Also, there is a risk that what purports to be rational statistical discrimination will not, in fact, be based on valid generalizations; it may be the result of prejudice and stereotypes. And the characteristic that statistical discrimination attributes to a group will often be stigmatizing, as in the case of law enforcement officers who "profile" members of racial minorities by attributing to them a propensity to commit crimes. *Manhart* was a particularly dramatic example of the unacceptability of statistical discrimination precisely because the generalization the employer used in that case was neither inaccurate nor stigmatizing. But it is plausible to say that the reason for an across-the-board ban on statistical discrimination is that there is too great a risk of a generalization based on inaccurate or stigmatizing stereotypes.

It is not obvious that there is a parallel concern about discrimination on the basis of sexual orientation. That is, it is not obvious that that form of discrimination differentially stereotypes either women or men. There are arguments to the contrary, but they have not generally persuaded the courts that have forbidden discrimination on the basis of sexual orientation, including the *Bostock* majority. So while the statistical discrimination cases present a clear rejection of the *Bostock* dissent's approach to discrimination, the support that those cases lend to the *Bostock* majority is qualified.

---

[34] *See* J.E.B. v. Alabama *ex rel.* T.B., 511 U.S. 127, 139 n.11 (1994); *id.* at 148–50 (O'Connor, J., concurring).

III. Gender Roles and Sexual Orientation

The most direct support for the majority's conclusion in *Bostock* comes from a different development in antidiscrimination law—the principle that requiring individuals to conform to gender roles is an impermissible form of sex discrimination. This principle—assuming it is an established principle under Title VII, which is in dispute—both implicitly rejects the dissenters' veil of ignorance test, as the statistical discrimination cases do, and more directly supports the conclusion that the Court reached in *Bostock*.

According to this principle, an employer who insists that men act in a stereotypically masculine way and that women act in a stereotypically feminine way is discriminating on the basis of sex. That is true even though there is a sense in which that employer is treating men and women the same—exactly the sense embraced by the dissenters in *Bostock*. The specific argument in support of *Bostock*'s holding is that discrimination against LGBT individuals is discrimination for failure to conform to a stereotyped gender role, because being a gay, lesbian, or transsexual individual is a quintessential example of gender nonconformity.

The argument based on this principle was mentioned only obliquely by the *Bostock* majority, even though it was prominent in court of appeals decisions that reached the same result as *Bostock*. It presents several complexities. For one thing, the *Bostock* dissenters denied that this is an established principle under Title VII. Even if it is established, it does not support the outcome in *Bostock* unless discriminating against an employee because of LGBT status constitutes discrimination on the basis of gender nonconformity. And there is, finally, the question of how to justify a result that would have surprised the Congress that enacted Title VII.

A. THE BASIS OF THE PRINCIPLE

Courts of appeals have consistently cited *Price Waterhouse v. Hopkins*[35] for the proposition that Title VII forbids discrimination against employees, male or female, who fail to conform to traditional gender roles.[36] The *Bostock* dissenters did not accept that reading of *Hopkins*.

---

[35] 490 U.S. 228 (1989).

[36] *See, e.g.*, Hively v. Ivy Tech Comm. Coll., 853 F.3d 339 (7th Cir. 2017) (en banc); Zarda v. Altitude Express, 883 F.3d 100, 119–23 (2d Cir. 2018) (en banc); Lewis v. Heartland Inns, 591

That is not surprising, precisely because this principle relies on the majority's veil of ignorance approach and rejects the dissenters' approach. According to the dissenters' approach, an employer who insists that men and women conform to their respective traditional gender roles is discriminating on the basis of gender nonconformity, not on the basis of sex. That employer does not have to know the sex of any employee in order to enforce its policy—only that the employee is nonconforming.

The plaintiff in *Hopkins* was a woman who was denied a promotion after she had been criticized for not acting in a sufficiently feminine way. The principal issues in the case concerned the burden of proof, not the definition of discrimination. But a majority of the Court appeared to endorse the principle that discrimination against employees who do not conform to gender stereotypes is a form of sex discrimination. The four-Justice plurality opinion said, among other things, that "we are beyond the day when an employer could evaluate employees by assuming or insisting that they matched the stereotype associated with their group."[37] Justice O'Connor's concurring opinion said that the employer's having referred to the plaintiff's "failure to conform to certain gender stereotypes" was a "discriminatory input into the decision[ ]" to deny her a promotion.[38] Justice O'Connor did not suggest that the employer's action would be unobjectionable if the employer required men as well as women to conform. The courts of appeals have relied on these statements in treating *Hopkins* as having established the principle that discrimination on the basis of gender nonconformity constitutes sex discrimination.

Perhaps the strongest support for this principle, though, comes from cases dealing with sex discrimination that were decided under the Equal Protection Clause. While the discriminatory intent standard of Title VII and the Equal Protection Clause are not interpreted *in pari materia*,[39] the Supreme Court has made the commonsense point that "[p]articularly in the case of defining the term 'discrimination,' which Congress has nowhere in Title VII defined," decisions

---

F.3d 1033, 1038–39 (8th Cir. 2010); Smith v. City of Salem, 378 F.3d 566, 572 (6th Cir. 2004); Nichols v. Azteca Rest. Enters., 256 F.3d 864, 874 (9th Cir. 2001).

[37] Price Waterhouse v. Hopkins, 490 U.S. at 251 (Brennan, J., plurality opinion).

[38] *Id.* at 272 (O'Connor, J., concurring).

[39] *See* Johnson v. Transp. Agency, 480 U.S. 616, 627 n.6 (1987) (citing United Steelworkers v. Weber, 443 U.S. 193, 206 n.6 (1979)).

interpreting the Equal Protection Clause "afford an existing body of
law analyzing and discussing that term in a legal context not wholly
dissimilar to the concerns which Congress manifested in enacting
Title VII," so those decisions should be "quite relevant" to the interpretation of Title VII.[40] In addition, the definition of discriminatory intent under the Equal Protection Clause echoes the language of
Title VII.[41] And the veil of ignorance definition on which the *Bostock*
majority and dissenters agreed is a plausible account of what the
Equal Protection Clause forbids.[42] For all of these reasons, the constitutional cases should, at the very least, influence the interpretation
of Title VII.

A central theme of the constitutional cases concerning sex discrimination is that laws may not penalize people, whether they are
men or women, because they fail to conform to gender stereotyped
roles. Many of the plaintiffs in the landmark sex discrimination cases
were men, even though it is not immediately obvious how men are
the victims of sex discrimination; by contrast, few of the cases challenging Jim Crow segregation were brought by white people. The
famous decision to seek out male plaintiffs, by Ruth Bader Ginsburg
and the other leaders of the litigation campaign for women's equality,
is conventionally seen as a tactical decision: a way of enlisting male
judges' sympathy for the plaintiffs. But the effect—and quite possibly
Ginsburg's objective—was that courts concluded that it is unconstitutional to require either men or women to conform to gender
stereotypes.[43]

---

[40] Gen. Elec. Co. v. Gilbert, 429 U.S. 125, 133 (1976).

[41] *Compare* Pers. Adm'r v. Feeney, 442 U.S. 256, 279 (1979) ("'Discriminatory purpose' . . .
implies that the decisionmaker . . . selected or reaffirmed a particular course of action at least
in part 'because of,' not merely 'in spite of,' its adverse effects upon an identifiable group"
(quoting United Jewish Orgs. v. Carey, 430 U.S. 144 (1977))), *with* 42 U.S.C. § 2000e–2(a)(1)
(making it unlawful "to discriminate against any individual . . . because of such individual's
race, color, religion, sex, or national origin").

[42] For an argument to this effect, see Strauss, *supra* note 16, at 956–59. *But see supra* note 16.

[43] The foundational articles on this aspect of the constitutional sex discrimination cases
are Cary Franklin, *The Anti-Stereotyping Principle in Constitutional Sex Discrimination Law*,
85 N.Y.U. L. Rev. 83 (2010); and, on the relationship to Title VII, Mary Anne Case, *Legal
Protections for the Personal Best of Each Employee: Title VII's Prohibition on Sex Discrimination, the
Legacy of* Price Waterhouse v. Hopkins, *and the Prospect of ENDA*, 66 Stan. L. Rev. 1333
(2014); and Mary Anne C. Case, *Disaggregating Gender from Sex and Sexual Orientation: The
Effeminate Man in the Law and Feminist Jurisprudence*, 105 Yale L.J. 1 (1995).

Califano v. Goldfarb[44] is an example. A provision of the social security laws automatically awarded survivors' benefits, which are based on the earnings of the deceased spouse, to widows of employees who had contributed to the system. A widower, by contrast, was not automatically eligible for benefits but had to prove that he had been economically dependent on his wife. The suit was brought by Leon Goldfarb, the widower of Hannah Goldfarb, who had worked outside the home for many years.

The Court held that the sex-based classification was unconstitutional but, puzzlingly, divided on the question of whether the unconstitutional discrimination was against men or women. A plurality of the Court said that the discrimination was against women like Hannah Goldfarb, reasoning that she had paid social security taxes on the same terms as her male coemployees but got a lesser benefit: her surviving spouse, unlike theirs, would not automatically get survivor's benefits. Justice Stevens, concurring, said that the discrimination was against Leon Goldfarb. He had to prove dependency; an identically situated widow would not have to do so. In a later case, presenting a similar provision of a state workers' compensation law, the Court said that the law was unconstitutional sex discrimination because it discriminated against both men and women[45]—again a puzzling conclusion, because one would ordinarily suppose that sex discrimination is a matter of favoring either men over women or vice versa.

What resolves the puzzle is the principle that disadvantaging people who have adopted nonconforming gender roles is a form of sex discrimination. In the then-traditional couple, in which the man worked outside the home, a surviving spouse would automatically receive benefits. In a nontraditional couple, the surviving spouse would have to prove dependency. Both members of the nontraditional couple are victims of unconstitutional sex discrimination.

Many of the constitutional sex discrimination cases can be seen in the same way: laws that disadvantaged individuals who adopted unconventional gender roles were unconstitutional. Some, like *Goldfarb*, involved a married couple who were disadvantaged by a law that

---

[44] 430 U.S. 199 (1977).

[45] Wengler v. Druggists Mut. Ins. Co., 446 U.S. 142, 147 (1980) ("Although the [lower court] was of the view that the law favored, rather than disfavored, women, it is apparent that the statute discriminates against both men and women.").

assumed the stereotypical household division of labor.[46] In a different context, *Mississippi University for Women v. Hogan*[47] held—in a suit brought by a man—that the exclusion of men from the university's all-women nursing school violated the Equal Protection Clause because it "tend[ed] to perpetuate the stereotyped view of nursing as an exclusively woman's job"[48]—a "stereotyped view" that, the Court suggested, disadvantaged both men, like the plaintiff, who wanted to break from the stereotype and women nurses whose job was devalued by the stereotype.[49] In general, laws were unconstitutional if they were based on "the role-typing society has long imposed"[50] on men and women.[51] The Court was untroubled by the fact, pointed out by Justice Rehnquist, that men—who were the plaintiffs in many of the cases—do not constitute the kind of historically disadvantaged group that would ordinarily be entitled to special protection from the courts.[52] That is further evidence that the concern was with gender nonconformity, not simply with the mistreatment of women.

B. GENDER NONCONFORMITY AND SEXUAL ORIENTATION

At least today, it might seem obvious that discrimination against LGBT individuals constitutes discrimination on the basis of a failure to conform to stereotyped gender roles. Attraction to the so-called opposite sex seems like the clearest example of what traditional gender roles entail. Again, though, this is not just an a priori claim about the nature of discrimination; it is borne out by experience.

Specifically, before *Bostock*, lower courts found it very difficult to disentangle claims of discrimination on the basis of gender nonconformity (claims that, on the prevailing interpretation of *Hopkins*, Title VII allowed) from claims of sexual orientation discrimination (when the courts assumed that Title VII did not recognize those

---

[46] *See, e.g.*, Weinberger v. Wiesenfeld, 420 U.S. 636 (1975); Frontiero v. Richardson, 411 U.S. 677 (1973).

[47] 458 U.S. 718 (1982).

[48] *See id.* at 729 & n.15.

[49] *See id.* at 723 & n.8, 729 n.15.

[50] *See, e.g.*, Stanton v. Stanton, 421 U.S. 7, 14–15 (1975).

[51] *See* Mary Anne Case, *"The Very Stereotype the Law Condemns": Constitutional Sex Discrimination Law as a Quest for Perfect Proxies*, 85 CORNELL L. REV. 1447 (2000).

[52] *See* Craig v. Boren, 429 U.S. 190, 217, 219 (1976) (Rehnquist, J., dissenting).

claims). An employer obviously violates the principle of *Hopkins* if it discriminates against men on the ground that they are "effeminate," or otherwise display stereotypically female traits, and against women who are supposedly too "masculine." But "effeminacy" in men is associated with being gay; "masculine behavior" in women is associated with being lesbian. The perverse result, before *Bostock*, was that employers could defend claims brought under *Hopkins* by insisting that when they fired or refused to promote "effeminate" men or "masculine" women, they actually were discriminating on the basis of the sexual orientation they attributed to the employee, not on the basis of gender nonconformity. As a result, courts were in the position—which several courts conceded was untenable—of trying to determine whether the employer was genuinely concerned about sexual orientation or was instead motivated by hostility to some other aspect of gender nonconformity.[53] That is further evidence that discrimination against LGBT individuals is a form of gender nonconformity discrimination that violates the principle associated with *Hopkins*.

But two problems remain. First, *Hopkins* was decided in 1989, more than thirty years before *Bostock*. The evolution of the constitutional cases that condemn discrimination against gender nonconforming individuals was essentially complete by then. Why was it not apparent, long before *Bostock*, that sexual orientation discrimination was illegal? Second, there are generally acknowledged exceptions to the principle that forbids discrimination on the basis of gender nonconformity. The two principal examples are bathrooms (invoked repeatedly in the *Bostock* litigation) and grooming requirements, such as dress codes. Employers can require employees to use the bathroom designated for their sex or comply with a sex-specific dress code. Those certainly seem like clear examples of requiring conformity to traditional gender roles. They appear to rely on the *Bostock* dissenters' definition of discrimination, not the majority's. If employers can require gender conformity in those instances, why can't they discriminate against gender nonconforming LGBT individuals?

These two questions have essentially the same answer. The usual justification for dress codes and sex-segregated bathrooms is that they

---

[53] *See, e.g.*, Hively v. Ivy Tech Cmty. Coll., 830 F.3d 698, 704–13 (7th Cir. 2016) (discussing cases), *vacated and reh'g en banc granted*, 830 F.3d 698 (7th Cir. 2016) (en banc), *rev'd on reh'g*, 853 F.3d 339, 364 (7th Cir. 2017) (en banc).

do not disadvantage anyone.[54] Segregating the sexes is not like segregating the races; it does not necessarily convey the message that women are inferior. Sometimes it just reflects widespread and essentially benign social norms to which any objections would be eccentric and do not have to be taken into account.

Title VII was not interpreted to ban discrimination against LGBT individuals as long as requiring employees to be straight also seemed just to reflect customary social norms and to be as reasonable as dress codes or segregated bathrooms. The claims of LGBT individuals did not have to be taken seriously; in fact, lower courts dismissed the claims of LGBT individuals as the product of deviance or psychopathology.[55] But the law concerning discrimination against gays and lesbians, no doubt influenced by developments outside the courts, evolved in a way that increasingly characterized anti-LGBT attitudes not as unobjectionable social or moral views but as impermissible animus. Because of that evolution, it is no longer plausible to say about excluding LGBT people from the workplace, as one might say about sex-segregated bathrooms, that it is a practice that simply reflects social norms and inflicts no cognizable harm.

The evolution of the law concerning LGBT individuals in some ways recapitulated what happened between *Plessy v. Ferguson*[56] and *Brown v. Board of Education*.[57] The justification for racial segregation, in schools or in intimate relationships, was that it was natural and even benign—a reflection of a familiar and proper social ordering. *Plessy* notoriously dismissed the objections that Black people had to segregation. The progression from *Plessy* to *Brown v. Board of Education* reflected a recognition that segregation was a demeaning practice that damaged people's lives.[58] The same thing happened with

---

[54] The plaintiffs in the *Bostock* litigation made this argument, for example, in explaining why the logic of their position would not prohibit sex-segregated bathrooms. *See* Transcript of Oral Argument at 13–21, Bostock v. Clayton Cnty., 140 S. Ct. 1731 (2020) (No. 17-1618).

[55] *See* Jessica A. Clarke, *How the First Forty Years of Circuit Precedent Got Title VII's Sex Discrimination Provision Wrong*, 98 Tex. L. Rev. Online 83 (2019) (discussing cases).

[56] 163 U.S. 537 (1896).

[57] 347 U.S. 483 (1954).

[58] Not coincidentally, the *Bostock* dissenters' definition of discrimination would also have supported supposedly separate but equal segregation. The competing understandings of discrimination that divided the majority and the dissenters in *Bostock* were, in fact, clearly articulated in the case that marked the final step in dismantling "separate but equal"—*Loving v. Virginia*, 388 U.S. 1 (1967), which struck down Virginia's statute forbidding interracial marriage. Virginia's argument was that the statute did not discriminate on the basis of race; the

discrimination against gay and lesbian people: a practice that was once acceptable came to be recognized as malign. In 1986, in *Bowers v. Hardwick*,[59] the Court dismissed the notion that there was a constitutional right to same-sex intimacy. But ten years later, in *Romer v. Evans*,[60] the Court declared that a state constitutional provision discriminating against gays and lesbians was "born of animosity."[61] The view that forbidding same-sex intimacy was the product of animus, not a legitimate moral judgment, prevailed in *Lawrence v. Texas*,[62] which overruled *Bowers*, and in *Obergefell v. Hodges*,[63] which established a right to same-sex marriage.

Those were, of course, constitutional decisions, not interpretations of Title VII. But the constitutional decisions are "quite relevant" to Title VII, because they "afford an existing body of law analyzing and discussing" the nature of discrimination.[64] And those decisions relied on the judgment that disapproval of LGBT relationships is the product of animus. That judgment cannot be reconciled with a claim that refusing to employ LGBT people is in the same category as arguably reasonable exceptions to the *Hopkins* principle, like segregated bathrooms and dress codes.

Bostock is the product of that understanding. The issue in *Bostock* would not have been decided in the way it was until that understanding

---

only people disadvantaged by the statute were parties to interracial marriages, a group that included both races. That is parallel to the argument that the employers in *Bostock* did not discriminate on the basis of sex but only on the basis of sexual orientation.

The Court in *Loving* rejected that argument. It had to: the same argument would have justified the result in *Plessy v. Ferguson*, which upheld a law that could be described as disadvantaging neither Black nor white people but only people who insisted on mixing with people of a different race. To the extent people voluntarily complied with laws mandating segregation, no government official ever needed to know the race of anyone affected by those laws, just as an employer who announced that it would not hire LGBT would not know the sex of anyone who complied with that policy. The situations are arguably distinguishable, on the ground that segregation enforced white supremacy but discrimination against LGBT individuals does not enforce male supremacy. That distinction is subject to dispute. *See* Andrew Koppelman, *Why Discrimination Against Lesbians and Gay Men Is Sex Discrimination*, 69 N.Y.U. L. REV. 197 (1994). But in any event, this is another instance in which the *Bostock* dissenters' understanding of discrimination does not fit in the fabric of antidiscrimination law.

[59] 478 U.S. 186 (1986).

[60] 517 U.S. 620 (1996).

[61] *Id.* at 634.

[62] 539 U. S. 558 (2003).

[63] 576 U.S. 644 (2015).

[64] *See* Gen. Elec. Co. v. Gilbert, 429 U.S. 125, 133 (1976); *supra* text accompanying notes 39–42.

prevailed, and the best justification for the holding in *Bostock* relies on that understanding.

C. LEGISLATION AND EVOLUTION

The final question is why the *Bostock* Court was entitled to take these evolutionary developments into account itself, instead of leaving to Congress the decision of whether Title VII reached discrimination against LGBT individuals. The *Bostock* dissenters accused the majority of "legislating";[65] in a sense the majority invited that accusation by insisting that the case could be resolved on the basis of the language of the statute alone and that the answer was clear. That attributed to the plain language of the statute an implication that had been generally rejected until recently and made the Court appear to be almost literally rewriting the statute. What was missing from the opinion was an acknowledgment that developments since 1964 also shaped what the statute requires and forbids, an explanation of how those events mattered, and a justification for taking them into account.

This question—whether the Court usurped Congress's role when it held that Title VII extends to discrimination against LGBT individuals—implicates more general, and complex, issues of how far courts can go in interpreting a statute to bring about results that are not foreclosed by the text but that the enacting Congress apparently did not intend. There is a conventional distinction between "common law" statutes that courts treat as if they authorize the development of a body of judge-made law—the Sherman Act is the standard example—and ordinary statutes that should be interpreted in a way that follows the language more closely.[66] One way to understand that distinction is that "common law" statutes are treated as if they were constitutional provisions. The text is a starting point for the development, through precedent, of principles that are generally consistent with the text but that cannot be derived from the text in any simple way and that might not be consistent with how the text was

---

[65] *See* Bostock v. Clayton Cnty., 140 S. Ct. 1731, 1754 (2020) (Alito, J., dissenting) ("There is only one word for what the Court has done today: legislation.").

[66] *See, e.g.,* Margaret H. Lemos, *Interpretive Methodology and Delegations to Courts: Are "Common-Law Statutes" Different?, in* INTELLECTUAL PROPERTY AND THE COMMON LAW 89 (Shyamkrishna Balganesh ed., 2016); Frank H. Easterbrook, *Statutes' Domains,* 50 U. CHI. L. REV. 533, 544 (1983); William N. Eskridge, *Public Values in Statutory Interpretation,* 137 U. PA. L. REV. 1007, 1052 (1989).

originally understood.[67] If Title VII were treated this way, the argument in favor of the result in *Bostock* would be straightforward: that result is consistent with the text and is based on the most plausible reading of precedents like *Hopkins* and *Manhart*. Similarly, because courts play a central role in developing the law under "common law" statutes, even when Congress has not acted, Congress's failure to adopt proposed amendments that would have explicitly prohibited discrimination against LGBT individuals might not preclude the result in *Bostock*[68]—just as the courts will sometimes interpret the Constitution as if it included amendments that were in fact proposed but not adopted.[69]

Title VII is not usually included on the list of "common law" statutes, though, and even other "common law" statutes are not obviously treated in the same way as constitutional provisions.[70] But asking whether Title VII as a whole is a "common law" or quasi-constitutional statute exaggerates the obstacles to concluding that it forbids discrimination against LGBT individuals. First, whatever might be said of the more detailed provisions of Title VII, the notion of "discrimination" seems very well suited to elaboration by the courts, for reasons that the Supreme Court itself has identified. There is no definition of "discriminate" in Title VII; when Congress leaves a crucial term like that undefined, it is plausible to say that it expects the courts to work out the definition. The extensive body of judge-made constitutional law dealing with the notion of discrimination is an obvious source for Title VII, as the Court has recognized.[71]

---

[67] For a defense of this view of constitutional law, see, for example, DAVID A. STRAUSS, THE LIVING CONSTITUTION 33–98 (2010).

[68] One other development that might influence a court's decision not to give much weight to Congress's failure to adopt an amendment to a statute is the apparent difficulty Congress has in enacting major legislation in the current political climate. On this issue, see, for example, Sarah Binder, *The Dysfunctional Congress*, 18 ANN. REV. POL. SCI. 85 (2015). Courts would be unlikely to mention that development explicitly, and whether it *should* influence their interpretation of statutes is a separate issue. But it might influence them nonetheless, perhaps even subconsciously.

[69] The Equal Rights Amendment is an example; arguably the Court has interpreted the Equal Protection Clause in a way that accomplishes what the ERA (which was proposed to the states but not ratified) would have done. There may be other examples as well. *See generally* David A. Strauss, *The Irrelevance of Constitutional Amendments*, 114 HARV. L. REV. 1458, 1475–78 (2001).

[70] *See* Zarda v. Altitude Express, 883 F.3d 100, 163–66 (2d Cir. 2018) (en banc) (Lynch, J., dissenting) (rejecting the view that Title VII should be interpreted in the way a constitutional provision would be).

[71] See *supra* text accompanying notes 39–40.

In addition, courts routinely interpret statutes to reach results that the enacting Congress did not envision. The Court has explicitly recognized that that is true of Title VII; in *Oncale v. Sundowner Offshore Services, Inc.*,[72] which allowed a claim of male-on-male sexual harassment to proceed under Title VII, the Court said: "[M]ale-on-male sexual harassment in the workplace was assuredly not the principal evil Congress was concerned with when it enacted Title VII[, b]ut statutory prohibitions often go beyond the principal evil to cover reasonably comparable evils."[73] And *Oncale* is only one example. The original understandings of what the sex discrimination provision of Title VII prohibited were not well formed; to the extent they can be identified, they are inconsistent with many features of Title VII law that are now settled.[74]

More generally, there is no sharp distinction between "common law" statutes that the courts take the lead in developing and ordinary statutes that are not viewed that way. The Court in *Bostock* was evidently reluctant to admit that the prohibitions in Title VII had evolved over time, but that should not be a controversial point. There is no serious question that precedent plays some role in interpreting all statutes, even if they are not "common law" statutes. Courts faced with a question about the interpretation of a statute do not think they have an obligation to ignore previous interpretations and revert to the text alone as the basis for the decision; even enthusiastic proponents of "textualism" do not go that far. It follows that courts will routinely play a role in developing statutory requirements.

Once precedents are in the picture, they can answer the question of how far the courts may go beyond what Congress contemplated. The precedents give content to the notion of "reasonably comparable evils," the otherwise vague phrase the Court used in *Oncale*. The precedents limit what the courts can do in the name of the statute. By the same token, they also limit the extent to which courts can do what the dissenters did in *Bostock*—to try to recover what the statute meant before two generations of judges, and others, had experience with it.

To be concrete, *Bostock* might not have been a lawful decision without a development like *Hopkins* or the constitutional counterpart. It

---

[72] 523 U.S. 75 (1998).

[73] *Id.* at 79.

[74] *See, e.g.*, Franklin, *supra* note 16, at 1329–73; *see also* Bostock v. Clayton Cnty., 140 S. Ct. 1731, 1752 (2020).

might not have been a lawful decision until the law recognized that disapproval of LGBT individuals was based on animus, not legitimate social or moral judgments. And, by the same token, in order to reach a different result in *Bostock*, the dissenters had to explain away a lot of the law that had developed since 1964. They had to adopt a definition of discrimination—their veil of ignorance approach—that has less support in the antidiscrimination law, as it has developed, than the majority's approach has. The dissenters had to distinguish *Manhart* and the established treatment of statistical discrimination. Then they also had either to reject the consensus view of *Hopkins*—and, inferentially, the constitutional cases that seem to rest on the same principle—or, alternatively, assert that excluding LGBT people from the workplace is on a par with dress codes or sex-segregated bathrooms. The dissenters may have believed, as some lower court judges did,[75] that those were the right positions to take in light of how big a step it is to forbid sexual orientation discrimination. But rejecting the dissent's position is not a matter of "legislating." Once we recognize that the text of the statute does not resolve the question, we can understand what does: a decades-long effort that shaped the law in a way that led to, and that justifies, the result in *Bostock*.

---

[75] *See, e.g., Zarda*, 883 F.3d at 137–67 (Lynch, J., dissenting) and *supra* text accompanying note 8.

SAIKRISHNA BANGALORE PRAKASH

"NOT A SINGLE PRIVILEGE IS ANNEXED TO HIS CHARACTER": NECESSARY AND PROPER EXECUTIVE PRIVILEGES AND IMMUNITIES

By design, the presidency is exceptional. Other branches are plural. Congress, a bicameral legislature, was always meant to have scores of members and now has over 500.[1] Due to Congress exercising the option of creating lower federal courts, the federal judiciary is larger still, with judicial power fractured among more than a hundred federal courts and hundreds of judges.[2] In contrast, one person may command the military, steward foreign affairs, pardon federal offenses, direct the execution of federal law, and superintend the bureaucracy.[3] The presidency is hardly all-powerful, for there are several express and

Saikrishna Bangalore Prakash is James Monroe Distinguished Professor of Law & Miller Center Senior Fellow, University of Virginia.

AUTHOR'S NOTE: Thanks to John Harrison, David Strauss, and Steve Walt for helpful conversations and comments. Gratitude to Janessa Mackenzie and Edward Colombo for excellent research assistance, edits, and comments.

[1] U.S. CONST. art. I, §§ 2–3; *Directory of Representatives*, U.S. HOUSE OF REPRESENTATIVES, https://www.house.gov/representatives (last visited May. 1, 2021).

[2] *Introduction to the Federal Judicial System*, U.S. DEP'T OF JUST., OFF. OF THE U.S. ATT'YS, https://www.justice.gov/usao/justice-101/federal-courts (last visited May 1, 2021).

[3] U.S. CONST. art. 2, §§ 1–2.

The Supreme Court Review, 2021.

implied constraints. But this level of concentrated authority is (and was) unique in the American experience. No other office holds a candle to the presidency's power and responsibilities. The concentration of authority in the hands of one person explains why many read the Constitution and discovered a monarchy in all but name.[4]

But the exceptionality does not end there. A president is the only significant constitutional officer elected in a nationwide contest (the vice president does not count).[5] The presidency is the only office subject to a rule that bars the foreign-born,[6] a telling limit for an immigrant nation. The office has a unique, detailed oath.[7] The presidency has rules designed to ensure immediate succession after death, resignation, or removal.[8] Finally, the office has a special salary privilege, one barring congressional attempts to chasten through cuts or corrupt through increases.[9]

The matter considered here is whether the presidency enjoys additional privileges and immunities, beyond its salary security. Or, put another way, does the Constitution protect that office from certain slings and arrows that individuals, Congress, the courts, or the states might launch toward the incumbent? Is the highest office in the land *that degree of exceptional*?

The Supreme Court has addressed such issues sporadically, in somewhat unsatisfying ways. It first touched upon this area in *Mississippi v. Johnson*, concluding that the president could not be enjoined from enforcing an allegedly unconstitutional law.[10] Among other things, the Court suggested that because it could not compel compliance with an injunction, it could not enjoin him.[11] The next major encounter occurred almost a century later. In *United States v. Nixon* the Court evinced no concerns about compliance, concluding that courts could subpoena a president for documents and tapes in his possession *and*

---

[4] *See* SAIKRISHNA BANGALORE PRAKASH, IMPERIAL FROM THE BEGINNING: THE CONSTITUTION OF THE ORIGINAL EXECUTIVE 1–11 (2015) (recounting how John Adams, Thomas Jefferson, and numerous others regarded the presidency as a limited, elective, republican monarchy of the sort common in Europe).

[5] U.S. CONST. art. 2, § 1.

[6] *Id.*

[7] *Id.*

[8] *Id.*; *Id.* amend. XXV.

[9] *Id.* art. 2, § 1

[10] 71 U.S. (4 Wall.) 475, 501 (1866).

[11] *Id.* at 500–01.

that President Nixon would have to comply.[12] Despite this order, the Court also held that the presidency enjoyed an evidentiary privilege that protected some confidences and secrets.[13] In *Nixon v. Fitzgerald*, the Court concluded that a president could not be sued for damages grounded on his official acts, at least where Congress had not created a cause of action running against the presidency.[14] The risks of policy distortion and presidential distraction were too great.[15] Yet in *Clinton v. Jones* the Court dismissed concerns about distraction. The Court rejected the claim that presidents enjoyed a temporary immunity from suits seeking damages arising out of private acts despite the obvious distraction from their official duties.[16]

The October 2019 term saw the Court weigh in twice on privileges and immunities.[17] Democrats (and many others) wanted to see President Donald Trump's personal documents, including his tax returns.[18] In *Trump v. Vance*, the President's lawyers argued that the presidency was absolutely immune from state criminal process, including grand jury subpoenas.[19] In *Trump v. Mazars USA, LLP*, his attorneys maintained that the House of Representatives lacked a proper legislative purpose in subpoenaing the President's personal documents, and, in the alternative, that the House must meet a heightened need to obtain such papers.[20]

The Court in *Vance* spurned the claim of absolute immunity but said that presidents might contest a state prosecutor's bona fides in various ways.[21] This result seems to offer precious little protection for the presidency. In contrast, the *Mazars* Court held that a chamber of

---

[12] 418 U.S. 683, 706, 712 (1974).

[13] *Id.* at 706.

[14] 457 U.S. 731, 748–49 (1982).

[15] *Id.* at 754.

[16] 520 U.S. 681, 705–06 (1997).

[17] *See* Trump v. Vance, 140 S. Ct. 2412 (2020); Trump v. Mazars USA, LLP, 140 S. Ct. 2019 (2020).

[18] Brian Faler, *To Get Trump's Tax Returns, Democrats Must Show They Have a Good Reason*, POLITICO (Apr. 12, 2019), https://www.politico.com/story/2019/04/12/trump-democrats-tax-returns-1271792.

[19] Reply Brief of Petitioner at 4–9, Trump v. Vance, 140 S. Ct. 2412 (2020) (No. 19-635).

[20] Brief for Petitioners at 35–36, 52–55, Trump v. Mazars USA, LLP, 140 S. Ct. 2019 (2020) (Nos. 19-715, 19-760).

[21] *Vance*, 140 S. Ct. at 2428 ("[W]e cannot ignore the possibility that state prosecutors may have political motivations.").

Congress must make several showings to secure a president's personal documents.[22] As compared to *Vance*, the *Mazars* framework is far more protective of a president's private papers.

Part I argues that the Court's two opinions make little sense as a matter of constitutional policy. As compared to a state prosecutor, Congress should have greater investigatory authority, not less.[23] Part II contends that the Court's jurisprudence in this area relies upon so many factors, distinctions, and intuitions that almost any outcome is possible, something that helps explain the twists and turns in its cases. The Court easily could have rendered *Vance* more protective of the presidency and *Mazars* less so. Part III argues that the Constitution never grants any privileges or immunities to the presidency, other than a salary shield. Instead, the Constitution authorizes Congress to create necessary and proper privileges and immunities for federal officers. Rather than usurping Congress's legislative and public policy roles, the courts should exit the business of crafting dispensations out of whole cloth and then embroidering and trimming them in subsequent cases.[24]

I. Distrust in One Case, Credulousness in Another

In recent memory, presidential candidates released their tax returns.[25] In 2016, candidate Trump assured the public that he would release his returns.[26] But later he said he could not because he was being audited; the implication was that there was some legal bar to disclosure.[27] To many this was suspicious. When there is a culture of disclosure, secrecy seems anomalous. Yet those most mistrustful were

---

[22] *Mazars*, 140 S. Ct. at 2032–33.

[23] Victoria Nourse, *The Dark Side of Mazars—Should a New York Prosecutor Have More Power to Check the President than the House of Representatives?*, Am. Const. Soc'y (Jul. 13, 2020), https://www.acslaw.org/expertforum/the-dark-side-of-mazars-should-a-new-york-prosecutor-have-more-power-to-check-the-president-than-the-house-of-representatives.

[24] I have previously addressed some of these issues in Saikrishna Bangalore Prakash, *A Critical Comment on the Constitutionality of Executive Privilege*, 83 Minn. L. Rev. 1143 (1999) and Prakash, *supra* note 4, at 220–36.

[25] Mitchell Zuckoff, *Why We Ask to See Candidates' Tax Returns*, N.Y. Times (Aug. 5, 2016), https://nytimes.com/2016/08/06/opinion/why-we-ask-to-see-candidates-tax-returns.html.

[26] Jill Disis, *All the Things Donald Trump Has Said about Releasing His Tax Returns*, CNN Money (Apr. 7, 2017), https://money.cnn.com/2017/04/17/news/donald-trump-tax-returns/index.html.

[27] *Id.*

not going to back Trump anyway. So, while Trump's opponents demanded to know more, his supporters seemed unbothered.[28]

Even after Trump entered the White House in 2017, the issue did not quite recede. Upon securing a House majority in 2019, Democrats started investigations.[29] In the scope of a week in April, three House committees issued four subpoenas relating to Trump's finances, his children (and their families), and affiliated organizations. The subpoenas went to the Trump Organization, Mazars, Capital One, and Deutsche Bank.[30] The orders were supposedly issued to further possible legislative reforms related to money laundering, terrorism, and foreign involvement in elections.[31] But one committee chair also mentioned "illegal conduct," along with conflicts of interest, and accuracy in disclosure.[32] Though the subpoenas were principally focused on eight years, they also encompassed earlier documents.[33] Not one subpoena went to Trump or any real person.

In August 2019, a New York grand jury issued a subpoena to Mazars.[34] The grand jury subpoena, presumably issued at the request of the New York County District Attorney, was essentially identical

---

[28] Naomi Jagoda, *House Dem Forces GOP to Take Recorded Vote on Trump Tax Returns*, THE HILL (Feb. 27, 2017), https://thehill.com/policy/finance/321476-house-dem-fails-to-force-release-of-trump-tax-returns.

[29] Manu Raju & Jeremy Herb, *House Democrats Announce Broad Probe into Allegations of Obstruction of Justice*, CNN POLITICS (Mar. 4, 2019), https://www.cnn.com/2019/03/04/politics/congress-investigates-obstruction-justice-jerry-nadler.

[30] Subpoena of the H. of Reps. of the Cong. of the United States of America, Filed April 15, 2019, *reprinted in* Petition for Certiorari app. E at 227a, Trump v. Mazars USA, LLP, 140 S. Ct. 2019 (2020) (Nos. 19-715, 19-760) (Dec. 4, 2019); SDNY Doc. 51-3 (Capital One Subpoena), Filed May 10, 2019, *reprinted in* Joint Appendix app. F at 152a, Trump v. Mazars USA, LLP, 140 S. Ct. 2019 (2020) (Nos. 19-715, 19-760) (Jan. 27, 2020); SDNY Doc. 51-2 (Deutsche Bank Subpoena), Filed May 10, 2019, *reprinted in* Joint Appendix app. E at 128a, Trump v. Mazars USA, LLP, 140 S. Ct. 2019 (2020) (Nos. 19-715, 19-760) (Jan. 27, 2020).

[31] *Mazars*, 140 S. Ct. at 2026.

[32] *Id.* at 2028 (noting that Chairman Elijah Cummings's basis for the subpoena was in part the belief that "[t]he President may have engaged in illegal conduct before and during his tenure in office.").

[33] Subpoena of the H. of Reps. of the Cong. of the United States of America, Filed April 15, 2019, *reprinted in* Petition for Certiorari app. E, *supra* note 30, at 231a; SDNY Doc. 51-3 (Capital One Subpoena), Filed May 10, 2019, *reprinted in* Joint Appendix app. F, *supra* note 30, at 155a; SDNY Doc. 51-2 (Deutsche Bank Subpoena), Filed May 10, 2019, *reprinted in* Joint Appendix app. E, *supra* note 30 at 128a.

[34] William K. Rashbaum & Ben Protess, *8 Years of Trump Tax Returns Are Subpoenaed by Manhattan D.A.*, N.Y. TIMES (Sept. 16, 2019), https://www.nytimes.com/2019/09/16/nyregion/trump-tax-returns-cy-vance.html.

to one issued to Mazars by the House Committee on Oversight and Reform.[35]

Trump instituted three suits to quash the subpoenas.[36] He did not raise executive privilege, as generally understood. Rather, he insisted upon novel shields to protect the private lives of presidents, safeguards that supposedly arose as implied incidents of his unique office. Regarding the House, Trump argued that the committees lacked a legitimate legislative purpose.[37] Going further, he asserted that because committee subpoenas were meant to harass and embarrass him, they violated the separation of powers.[38] The New York subpoenas were even more improper, said Trump, because chief executives were immune from state criminal process.[39] After lower courts rebuffed his claims,[40] Trump filed certiorari petitions.[41] The Court granted three petitions, setting up what seemed to be a constitutional battle royal.[42] Almost every major constitutional issue seemed at stake: executive authority, legislative power, the separation of powers, and federalism.

In the end, the Court somewhat disappointed.[43] In *Vance*, the Court rejected the claim of absolute immunity from state criminal process and the more modest request that the Court impose a "heightened need standard" for state criminal subpoenas.[44] Still, the Court declared that presidents could assert that such subpoenas constituted attempts to interfere with, or influence, their official duties.[45] Additionally, chief

---

[35] Trump v. Vance, 140 S. Ct. at 2420 n.2.

[36] Samantha Fry, *Trump Litigation Round Up*, LAWFARE (Dec. 11, 2019), https://www.lawfareblog.com/trump-litigation-round.

[37] Complaint at 5, Trump v. Comm. on Oversight & Reform of U.S. House of Representatives, 380 F. Supp. 3d 76 (D.D.C Apr. 4, 2019) (No. 1:19-CV-03826).

[38] *Id.* at 10.

[39] Complaint at 3, Trump v. Vance, No. 19 Civ. 8694 (S.D.N.Y. Sept. 19, 2019).

[40] Trump v. Vance, 941 F.3d. 631, 646 (2d Cir. 2019); Trump v. Mazars, 940 F.3d 710, 748 (D.C. Cir. 2019).

[41] Petition for Writ of Certiorari, Trump v. Vance, 140 S. Ct. 2412 (2020) (No. 19-635); Petition for Writ of Certiorari, Trump v. Mazars USA, LLP, 140 S. Ct. 2019 (2020) (No. 19-715).

[42] Amy Howe, *Justices to Take Up Battle over Trump Financial Documents*, SCOTUSBLOG (Dec. 13, 2019), https://www.scotusblog.com/2019/12/justices-to-take-up-battle-over-trump-financial-documents.

[43] *See* Trump v. Vance 140 S. Ct. 2412 (2020); Trump v. Mazars USA, LLP, 140 S. Ct. 2019 (2020).

[44] *Vance*, 140 S. Ct. at 2429.

[45] *Id.* at 2430–31 (citing Clinton v. Jones, 520 U.S. at 710, 714 (1997)).

executives could argue that subpoenas constituted harassment.[46] Finally, under New York law, presidents could allege that subpoenas were overly broad, unduly burdensome, or grounded in bad faith.[47]

While this list suggests some safeguards for presidents, the reality is that they are somewhat exposed. For some protections, presidents are in no better position than any citizen. The portions of *Vance* grounded on the Constitution offer but faint hope. It will be difficult to demonstrate that a prosecutor sought to harass or impede the chief executive or influence executive policy. After all, the Court seemed unmoved by the fact that Vance had cut-and-pasted a subpoena issued by the House, a fact suggesting that his inquiry at least might be political and partisan.[48]

The *Mazars* Court also rejected the President's proposed standard. It denied that Congress must prove a "demonstrated, specific need"[49] or that its subpoenas must be "demonstrably critical"[50] to its legislative purposes. But the Court also spurned the House's argument that the separation of powers had no impact on Congress's authority to demand a president's documents.[51] The Court pointedly remarked that "we would have to be blind not to see what" all others understand— this was not a "run-of-the-mill legislative effort" but a clash between branches over documents that have "intense political interest for all involved."[52] Given such concerns, safeguards were requisite. A court must judge whether the "asserted legislative purpose warrants the significant step of involving the president and his papers."[53] Congress should offer evidence that it actually seeks to further a "valid legislative purpose."[54] If there are other sources of information that could help Congress legislate, it must pursue those sources instead.[55] Moreover, courts should monitor subpoenas to ensure that they are no

---

[46] *Id.* at 2427–28.

[47] *Id.* at 2428.

[48] *Id.* (discussing state prosecutors' possible political motivations).

[49] *Mazars*, 140 S. Ct. at 2032.

[50] *Id.*

[51] *Id.* at 2033–34.

[52] *Id.* at 2034 (internal quotation marks omitted).

[53] *Id.* at 2035–36.

[54] *Id.* at 2031.

[55] *Id.* at 2036.

broader than necessary.[56] Additionally, the courts ought to consider the burden on the president's time and attention.[57] Finally, the Court signaled that it might yet add other considerations, meaning that its list of factors might grow in time.[58]

When read together, the Court privileged state prosecutors over federal legislators. When state or local prosecutors have jurisdiction over a president or his business interest, they can easily convince their grand juries to seek information about a president and, barring some public admission of intent to harass, or other proof of bad faith, these prosecutors should prevail. In contrast, a chamber of Congress must make several heightened showings to receive the material, meaning it will be more difficult for Congress to receive information about the president. In sum, while Congress must surmount several hurdles, prosecutors have a relatively easy path.

Why did the Court favor parochial prosecutors over national legislators? The Court never quite explained. The Constitution's text certainly does not evince any such preference. Congress comes first, suggesting its importance.[59] In contrast, the original Constitution did not even mention grand juries, much less state prosecutors. The Fifth Amendment brought grand juries into the text, requiring grand jury indictment or presentment before trying someone for an "infamous [federal] crime."[60] Even so, the Constitution does not dictate that federal grand juries have greater authority to subpoena information from the president as compared to Congress. The Constitution certainly does not declare that *state* grand juries have broader subpoena authority than Congress, for it never expressly addresses state grand juries, much less their powers.

Perhaps the Court drew this distinction because of putative differences about the proper functions and responsibilities of grand juries and Congress. If we suppose that grand juries, federal and state, may enjoy the powers traditionally associated with grand juries, then it makes sense that they would have the power to seek information about

---

[56] *Id.*

[57] *Id.*

[58] *Id.* ("[O]ne case every two centuries does not afford enough experience for an exhaustive list.").

[59] U.S. CONST. art. I.

[60] U.S. CONST. amend. V.

possible criminal wrongdoing.[61] But what powers does Congress have to seek information? The Court signaled that Congress, because it enjoys limited constitutional authority, has constrained power to subpoena information.[62] It cited several of its own opinions that deny Congress power to investigate mere criminality.[63] It is a legislature and not a crime-fighting institution, said the Court.[64] So every congressional investigation must be in service of a legislative role and not further an ultra vires function (e.g., a criminal inquiry).[65]

But these points hardly yield the conclusion that state prosecutors must enjoy greater authority than Congress vis-à-vis a president's personal papers. First, while Congress has limited authority to make ordinary law, it has comprehensive authority to propose constitutional amendments. If the House had said that it was considering a constitutional requirement for federal candidates to disclose their tax returns, it would have satisfied, it seems to me, the assertion that the chambers can seek information only for "legislative" purposes. Relatedly, nothing prevents a legislator from proposing that Congress be given the broader impeachment powers of ancient legislators, ones that extended to the prosecution of ordinary crimes. The member also can say that she wishes to learn more about actual and alleged crimes, including ones by the incumbent, to better judge whether a broader, more traditional impeachment framework is a good idea. The condition that subpoenas relate to matters within the competence of Congress does little to constrain.

Second, grand juries also serve limited purposes.[66] State grand juries are not meant to be instruments for harassing opponents.[67] If Congress must speak to purpose when it seeks the president's personal

---

[61] *See generally* Comment, *Powers of Federal Grand Juries*, 4 Stan. L. Rev. 68 (1951).

[62] Trump v. Mazars USA, LLP, 140 S. Ct. at 2031.

[63] *Id.* at 2031–32 (citing Quinn v. United States, 349 U.S. 155, 161 (1955), and McGrain v. Daugherty, 273 U.S. 135, 177 (1927)).

[64] *Id.*

[65] The Court did not mention impeachment as grounds for the subpoenas because the House Committees curiously disclaimed impeachment as a reason for issuing the subpoenas.

[66] United States v. Calandra, 414 U.S. 338, 343 (1974) (stating that grand juries determine whether there is probable cause to believe a crime has been committed and protect citizens against "unfounded criminal prosecutions.").

[67] Letter from Thomas Jefferson to Peregrine Fitzhugh (June 4, 1797), *in* 29 The Papers of Thomas Jefferson 415–19 (Barbara B. Oberg ed., 2002) (noting that Jefferson worried about grand juries changing "from a legal to political engine.").

papers, why not the state prosecutor or the grand jury? One might say that state institutions should offer evidence that they have a proper crime-fighting purpose and are not merely seeking to torment or embarrass. Such constraints would have put prosecutors in much the same position as Congress after *Mazars*.

Finally, the Court made it clear that Congress might have a proper legislative purpose but still be unable to secure the information it seeks;[68] the courts might conclude that compliance is unduly burdensome, trim the subpoena, or instruct Congress to look elsewhere for the information.[69] If that is true for Congress, why not state prosecutors? If proper legislative purpose can be insufficient for Congress, the Court might have said the same of prosecutors: a proper investigatory purpose is necessary but hardly sufficient.

If the supposed limits on Congress's investigatory powers cannot explain the Court's divergent approaches, perhaps the separation of powers does the work. One case raised questions of interbranch dynamics (*Mazars*) and the other did not (*Vance*). Though the Constitution never expressly declares that it separates powers, everyone understands that the separation of authority[70] and the Constitution's interbranch provisions signal some concern with the interactions between the three branches.[71] From time to time, the Court has asked whether some statute violates implicit separation of powers principles.[72] Though recourse to these principles did not lead the *Mazars* Court to impose a super-high bar, they did cause it to impose meaningful hurdles nonetheless.

---

[68] *Mazars*, 140 S. Ct. at 2035–36.

[69] *Id.* at 2036.

[70] THE FEDERALIST No. 51, at 288 (James Madison) (Clinton Rossiter ed., 1999) ("But the great security against a gradual concentration of the several powers in the same department, consists in giving to those who administer each department the necessary constitutional means and personal motives to resist encroachments of the others. The provision for defense must in this, as in all other cases, be made commensurate to the danger of attack. Ambition must be made to counteract ambition.").

[71] *See, e.g.*, U.S. CONST. art. I, § 7, cl. 3 (President may veto legislation passed by Congress, but Congress can override the veto); *Id.* at art. II, § 4. (President, Vice President, and civil officers may be removed via impeachment).

[72] INS v. Chadha, 462 U.S. 919, 955–58 (1983) (holding that a single House veto was not "within express constitutional exceptions authorizing one House to act alone" and therefore violated implicit separation of powers principles).

But if the separation of powers was irrelevant to *Vance*, other high constitutional principles were at stake.[73] The Court might have relied upon federalism as a limit on state institutions seeking to acquire information from federal officers, particularly the president. The claim that principles of federalism should constrain a state grand jury would be no less persuasive than the many other decisions that constrained state authority to protect federal institutions. Consider *McCulloch v. Maryland* or *Tarble's Case*. Both involved state attempts to regulate federal entities: in *McCulloch*, a federal bank, and in *Tarble's Case*, federal prison officials.[74] Now *Vance* did not involve an attempt to regulate Donald Trump as president. But to imagine that there are no federalism implications from state institutions demanding private papers from a sitting president is to blink at reality. States can interfere with federal officers by harassing them in their private capacity. From the perspective of a federal officer, any state proceeding might seem a form of persecution, without regard to whether it relates to private or official acts and irrespective of which state institution issues the subpoena.[75] This point might have been more obvious to the Court had a state grand jury sought the private papers of an individual justice in a context of partisan heat and accusations of wrongdoing.

If constitutional fundamentals cannot justify the Court's distinctions, perhaps doctrine can do the work. Maybe *Clinton v. Jones* and *United States v. Nixon* are key. If a private person may sue a sitting president and get discovery, and if a federal grand jury could subpoena official papers of a president,[76] how could a state grand jury lack authority to subpoena a president's private papers?

Nothing in *Jones* or *Nixon* led inexorably to *Vance*. To begin with, federalism concerns were not in play in either of those cases. In contrast, *Vance* posed issues of federalism of the first order because a local prosecutor using a local institution—the grand jury—sought to investigate the federal chief executive, albeit in his private capacity.[77]

---

[73] Trump v. Vance, 140 S. Ct. 2412, 2431 (2020).

[74] McCulloch v. Maryland, 17 U.S. (4 Wheat.) 316 (1819); *In re* Tarble, 80 U.S. (13 Wall.) 397 (1871).

[75] One wonders whether the result would have been different had the New York State Assembly asked for the papers. It has legislative authority over Mazars, Deutsche Bank, and the Trump Organization, as well as over filed tax returns. In the eyes of the Justices, are legislatures categorically more suspect as compared to grand juries led by prosecutors?

[76] *See* Clinton v. Jones, 520 U.S. 681 (1997); United States v. Nixon, 418 U.S. 683 (1974).

[77] *Vance*, 140 S. Ct. at 2420.

A part was attempting to investigate the most consequential instrument of the whole. Further, state institutions arguably pose a greater threat to the executive than does a single litigant, in part because the former are generally better resourced.[78] This suggests that the case for some kind of check on state institutions is relatively stronger. I am not saying that *Jones* and *Nixon* are irrelevant. My limited point is that the Court often draws distinctions that convince some but not others. It surely could have distinguished *Jones* and *Nixon*.

If, however, one supposes that *Jones* or *Nixon* somehow compelled *Vance*, one must wonder why these cases did not likewise compel a similar result in *Mazars*. If Paula Jones could sue and subpoena a sitting president,[79] how can it be that Congress has less authority than Jones? If a federal grand jury can demand documents and tapes with relative impunity, why burden Congress and thereby enfeeble it? No one would have been surprised if the *Mazars* Court had said that *Jones* and *Nixon* help establish that, so long as it cites a proper legislative purpose, Congress can subpoena any sort of personal documents from any federal officer, including the president.

The best explanation for the divergent treatment is that it rests on a certain suspicion, even distrust, of the institution that sits across First Avenue, Northeast. *Mazars* abounds in suggestions that Congress, at least in this context, was especially dubious.[80] It was the patently political nature of these demands (and likely future ones) that necessitated extra burdens on Congress.[81] After all, the chambers are laden with partisan creatures. Further, absent judicial limits on Congress's subpoena of private information, Congress would exert "an imperious control" and "aggrandize itself at the President's expense."[82] As the Court declared, "we would have to be 'blind'" not to perceive what "[a]ll others can see and understand": this was the dirty business of politics.[83]

[78] *E.g.*, Shayna Jacobs & Jonathan O'Connell, *N.Y. Prosecutor Hires Forensic Accounting Firm as Probe of Trump Escalates*, WASH. POST (Dec. 29, 2020), https://www.washingtonpost.com/national-security/trump-tax-returns-new-york-investigation/2020/12/29/11c43a38-43c8-11eb-b0e4-0f182923a025_story.html

[79] *Jones*, 520 U.S. at 695–97.

[80] Trump v. Mazars USA, LLP, 140 S. Ct. 2019, 2031 (2020) (noting the "deeply partisan controversy").

[81] *Id.*

[82] *Id.*

[83] *Id.*

But in a way, the Court suffered from a different blindness. First, as noted earlier, even if the branches were not at war in *Vance*, state and federal authority were. No less than Congress, state prosecutors might be imperious and aggrandize themselves at the executive's expense. Elected state prosecutors are creatures of politics, no less than are members of Congress, and often seek higher office. Indeed, many go on to serve in Congress. In 2016, 11 percent of legislators had served as litigating attorneys in local, state, or federal attorneys offices.[84]

As we consider the motives of prosecutors, the wisdom of Attorney General Robert Jackson is worth bearing in mind:

> The prosecutor has more control over life, liberty, and reputation than any other person in America. His discretion is tremendous. He can have citizens investigated and, if he is that kind of person, he can have this done to the tune of public statements and veiled or unveiled intimations.... While the prosecutor at his best is one of the most beneficent forces in our society, when he acts from malice or other base motives, he is one of the worst.[85]

Because a prosecutor invariably makes choices among possible "cases, it follows that he can choose his defendants. Therein is the most dangerous power of the prosecutor: that he will pick people that he thinks he *should get*. . . ."[86] The New York prosecutor certainly chose a rich, tempting target, a selection that could prove beneficial in future quests for gubernatorial or senatorial office. None of this should have been unfamiliar to the Justices.

Second, in *Mazars*, the Court categorically distinguished judicial subpoenas from legislative ones: congressional subpoenas "bear little resemblance to criminal subpoenas issued to the President in the course of a specific investigation."[87] Yet the *Vance* Court observed that the grand jury subpoena to Mazars had "essentially copied" a congressional subpoena.[88] So far from "bear[ing] little resemblance,"[89] the grand jury subpoena was a clone of a legislative subpoena. Perhaps the

---

[84] David Hawkings, *Yesterday's US Attorneys May Be Tomorrow's Congressional Candidates*, Roll Call (Mar. 16, 2017), https://www.rollcall.com/2017/03/16/yesterdays-us-attorneys-may-be-tomorrows-congressional-candidates.

[85] Robert H. Jackson, *The Federal Prosecutor*, 3 J. Crim. L. & Criminology 3, 3 (1940).

[86] *Id.* at 5 (emphasis added).

[87] *Mazars*, 140 S. Ct. at 2034.

[88] Trump v. Vance, 140 S. Ct. 2412, 2420 n.2 (2020); *Id.* at 2433 (Thomas, J., dissenting) (noting that the subpoena "is nearly identical to a subpoena issued by a congressional Committee").

[89] *Mazars*, 140 S. Ct. at 2034 (2020).

Court was making a prediction about future grand jury subpoenas issued to presidents. They will not be issued in settings fraught with partisanship. But some do not share the Court's confidence.[90]

Finally, and relatedly, the Court was oblivious to the political dimensions of the *Vance* subpoena. Again, they were copied from a House subpoena, issued at the behest of a co-partisan of the House majority,[91] and seemed part of an intense political dispute about Trump and his finances. Indeed, the foremost difference between the subpoenas was the specific demand for tax returns, a detail that laid bare the tight link to the broader political fight.[92] For those willing to open their eyes, it seemed obvious that the New York prosecutor had established another legal/political front against the President. No one familiar with this context could imagine that the "deeply partisan controversy" and "intense political interest" that triggered judicial disquiet in *Mazars* was wholly absent in *Vance*.[93] The Court's distrust in *Mazars* was exceeded by its naiveté in *Vance*.

II. JUDGE-MADE PRESIDENTIAL PRIVILEGES AND IMMUNITIES

None of these criticisms signals how the Court ought to have decided these two cases. I am certainly not asserting that *Mazars* was right and that *Vance* was not. My limited point is that the two opinions, though issued on the same day and written by the Chief Justice, jibe poorly. The Supreme Court distrusts its coordinate branch and simultaneously evinces a credulous faith in state institutions, all in a context where there was ample reason to be dubious about the motives of the House *and* the local prosecutor.

Whatever their tensions, both opinions are part of a larger pattern. Like the previous cases in this area, almost all of which are from the late twentieth century, these two opinions evince a continued willingness on the part of the Justices to draw upon rather debatable

---

[90] *See, e.g., Vance*, 140 S. Ct. at 2447 (Alito, J., dissenting) (citing Thomas Dewey as example of an ambitious prosecutor who became governor and then secured the Republican nomination for President in 1944 and 1948).

[91] David B. Caruso, *DA Seeking Trump's Taxes Cites 'Mountain' of Allegations*, ASSOCIATED PRESS (Sept. 21, 2020), https://apnews.com/article/cyrus-Vance-jr-new-york-subpoenas-man hattan-donald-trump-5e71a8b6c02aa0caf940d775b95ce686.

[92] *Vance*, 140 S. Ct. at 2420.

[93] *Mazars*, 140 S. Ct. at 2031, 2034. Justice Alito made this point. *Vance*, 140 S. Ct. at 2447 (Alito, J., dissenting).

structural inferences to generate and then flesh out the contours of executive privileges and immunities. The Court is engaged in common law reasoning, using a "kind of 'public policy' analysis" to inquire into the "policies and principles that may be considered implicit in the nature of the President's office in a system structured to achieve effective government."[94] In conducting this analysis, the Court is essentially "balanc[ing] the constitutional weight of the interest to be served [via the rejection of an asserted privilege] against the dangers of intrusion on the authority and functions of the Executive Branch."[95] More colloquially, the Court is gauging the costs and benefits of accepting (or rejecting) a claimed executive dispensation in concrete contexts.

There are two dominant themes in this balancing analysis, each of which points in a rather different direction. First is the assessment that presidents are exceptional.[96] Because they are unique and special, they are entitled to singular privileges and immunities. This theory goes back to 1789 when some senators said that every president was a "kind of [s]acred [p]erson," meaning that ordinary courts could not touch them.[97] No judicial process and no trials, civil or criminal. Presidents were touchable only via the arduous impeachment mechanisms.

Though the Court has never wholly endorsed this theory, one finds glimpses of it. In *Mississippi v. Johnson*, the Court seemed to suggest that presidents could not be enjoined because they might refuse to honor any injunction, leaving the courts powerless to enforce their judgments.[98] In other words, because the presidency was powerful and the courts were weak, the Court had to stay its hand. In *Nixon v. Fitzgerald*, the Court endorsed the idea that presidents are somewhat unique, at least concerning their official acts.[99] Allowing suits for damages arising out of official acts would distort their official decisions and distract them from their duties, the Court said.[100]

---

[94] Nixon v. Fitzgerald, 457 U.S. 731, 748 (1982).

[95] *Id.* at 754.

[96] *See* Akhil Amar & Neal Katyal, *Executive Privileges & Immunities: The* Nixon *and* Clinton *Cases*, 108 Harv. L. Rev. 701, 721 (1995).

[97] 9 The Documentary History of the First Federal Congress: The Diary of William Maclay and Other Notes on Senate Debates 168 (Kenneth R. Bowling & Helen E. Veit eds., 1998).

[98] 71 U.S. (4 Wall.) 475, 500–01 (1866).

[99] *Fitzgerald*, 457 U.S. at 748–49.

[100] *Id.* at 753.

The second perspective holds that presidents are (mostly) unexceptional. Or, more precisely, while they have exceptional powers, they lack special dispensations. At the behest of Aaron Burr, Chief Justice John Marshall issued a subpoena to Thomas Jefferson.[101] Marshall said a few words about secret materials, none of which suggested that presidents ought to receive special treatment at least as to issuing subpoenas. *United States v. Nixon* held that courts could subpoena presidents, thereby endorsing Marshall's lower court ruling.[102] The exceptionality of the office did not preclude a judicial subpoena. In *Clinton v. Jones*, the Court held that private parties could sue a sitting president for damages arising out of acts unrelated to the presidency, declaring that presidents are not entitled to a per se rule of temporary immunity.[103]

Most cases feature a mix of these themes. Though Marshall issued the subpoena in *Burr*, he also said that the courts would not have "to proceed against the president as against an ordinary individual. The objections to such a course are so strong and so obvious."[104] Though the *Nixon* Court asserted jurisdiction over the president and enforced a subpoena, it also recognized an executive privilege to withhold intrabranch communications.[105] And in *Jones*, the Court did not wholly close the door to the idea that presidents might have, in certain contexts, some sort of temporary immunity from civil suits brought against them in their personal capacity.[106] If a president truly could not function because of the volume of private suits, he might secure something approaching a temporary immunity.[107]

A. CONTEXTS AND CONSIDERATIONS

The question of presidential privileges and immunities is multifaceted, in part because of the multiplicity of settings, capacities, and claims. For settings, there are two venues in which the executive

---

[101] U.S. v. Burr, 25 F. Cas. 187, 191–92 (C.C.D. Va. 1807) (No. 14,694).

[102] 418 U.S. 683, 712 (1974).

[103] 520 U.S. 681, 692, 705 (1997).

[104] 25 F. Cas. at 192.

[105] 418 U.S. at 706.

[106] 520 U.S. at 708 (observing that if a trial generated additional "civil actions that could conceivably hamper the President in conducting the duties" the trial court might exercise discretion to defer trial").

[107] *Id.*

presses claims that it is entitled to constitutional dispensation, the courts and Congress. By courts, I mean federal and state, for whatever principles the Supreme Court has drawn over recent decades, it has yet to treat the two systems as fundamentally different vis-à-vis the president. Before the courts, presidents press a wide range of claims related to privileges and immunities. But before Congress, presidents are apt to exhibit greater aggression. Chief executives insist upon immunities that they never claim before the courts, like immunity from congressional subpoenas that require their personal testimony.[108]

As to capacities, the Supreme Court has drawn a line between a president's private and official personas. In *Nixon v. Fitzgerald*, the Court held that the president was immune from damages from actions arising out of his acts as President, at least where Congress did not explicitly make the president subject to a damages action.[109] In *Clinton v. Jones*, however, the Court permitted a damages action to proceed because the lawsuit was unrelated to presidential acts.[110] Both *Vance* and *Mazars* likewise drew upon the official-personal distinction, noting that neither New York nor Congress had sought executive branch materials.[111] Because the Court failed to distinguish the documents of Trump-affiliated organizations,[112] lower courts are likely to ignore the separate legal status of corporations and nonprofits when the latter are inextricably tied to the incumbent.

Regarding claims, there are two principal sorts. First is an evidentiary privilege, namely that the president (and the executive) need not provide evidence to the courts or Congress. This includes executive privilege, which is itself dividable into many subparts. The executive branch uses the phrase "executive privilege" to cover at least five types of material: communications with the president, deliberative communications (including agency deliberations), attorney-client communications, law-enforcement communications, and military/national

---

[108] *See, e.g.,* Immunity of Former Couns. to the President from Compelled Cong. Testimony, 31 Op. O.L.C. 191, 192 (2007).

[109] 457 U.S. 731, 749 (1982).

[110] 520 U.S. at 686, 696.

[111] Trump v. Vance, 140 S. Ct. 2412, 2420 (2020); Trump v. Mazars USA, LLP, 140 S. Ct. 2019, 2026 (2020).

[112] *Mazars,* 140 S. Ct. at 2026 ("information about the finances of President Donald J. Trump, his children, and affiliated businesses"); *Vance,* 140 S. Ct. at 2420 ("financial records relating to the President and business organizations affiliated with him").

security communications.[113] The two Trump cases did not involve executive privilege in any of these senses. But they did address assertions that presidents should have evidentiary privileges protecting their personal papers. According to the President's lawyers, any demands for private documents invariably reflect a partisan desire to embarrass and vex the incumbent.[114] So, Trump was seeking judicial recognition of an evidentiary privilege, albeit not one fitting within current conceptions of executive privilege.

The second set of claims consists of supposed constitutional immunities. The argument is that presidents are not subject to the following indignities, intrusions, and impediments: subpoenas, injunctions, damages suits, or indictment, trial, and punishment. Of course, the courts have rejected the idea that the Constitution forbids judicial subpoenas, sanctioning their issuance in *Nixon* and now in *Vance*.[115] Further, the courts suppose that presidents must comply with a lawful judicial subpoena. As to damages suits, the Court has permitted some (*Jones*) and barred others (*Fitzgerald*).[116] For its part, the Justice Department insists that though incumbents can be criminally investigated, they cannot be indicted, prosecuted, or punished.[117]

There are additional dispensations that rise to the surface from time to time. As noted earlier, presidents have long asserted a testimonial immunity vis-à-vis Congress.[118] Presidents have insisted that this immunity extends to high aides not subject to advise and consent, including the Chief of Staff, the White House Counsel, and the National Security Adviser.[119] Further, presidents sometimes make a preliminary

---

[113] John E. Bies, *Primer on Executive Privilege and the Executive Branch Approach to Congressional Oversight*, Lawfare (June 16, 2017), https://www.lawfareblog.com/primer-executive-privilege -and-executive-branch-approach-congressional-oversight.

[114] *Mazars*, 140 S. Ct. at 2026 (House committees "sought these records to harass [the President], expose personal matters, and conduct law enforcement activities beyond its authority").

[115] United States v. Nixon, 418 U.S. 683, 714 (1974).; *Vance*, 140 S. Ct. at 2431; *Mazars*, 140 S. Ct. at 2035–36.

[116] Clinton v. Jones, 520 U.S. 681, 705 (1997); Nixon v. Fitzgerald, 457 U.S. 731, 753 (1982).

[117] *See* Memorandum from Robert G. Dixon, Jr., Assistant Att'y Gen., Office of Legal Couns., Re: Amenability of the President, Vice President and other Civil Officers to Federal Criminal Prosecution while in Office (Sept. 24, 1973), https://fas.org/irp/agency/doj/olc /092473.pdf; A Sitting President's Amenability to Indictment and Criminal Prosecution, 24 Op. O.L.C. 222, 260 (2000).

[118] Immunity of Former Counsel to the President from Compelled Congressional Testimony, 31 Op. O.L.C. 191, 192 (2007).

[119] Assertion of Executive Privilege with Respect to Clemency Decision, 23 Op. O.L.C. 1, 5 (1999) (asserting that "[s]ubjecting a senior presidential advisor to the congressional subpoena

"protective assertion" of privilege to determine which materials within a larger batch are actually privileged.[120] This assertion ensures that the executive has time to separate privileged from unprivileged materials. But it also delays any eventual disclosure.

The question of privileges and immunities is also multifaceted because of the host of policy considerations the Court has drawn upon. The Court has cited judicial impotence in holding that a president cannot be enjoined in his official capacity.[121] It has mentioned the need for candid advice-giving in recognizing executive privilege.[122] It has cited the paramount importance of criminal adjudication in holding that this executive privilege does not apply with full force in the context of a criminal process[123] and that presidents must comply with subpoenas issued in criminal cases.[124] It has mentioned presidential distraction and policy distortion as reasons to reject private damages suits against the president for official acts.[125] It has mentioned the prejudice that would result from delaying damages suits for private acts.[126] And now it has cited the menace of raw politics in deciding to curb congressional investigations of a president's private affairs.[127]

The executive branch has cited additional factors for why it should prevail. This is not surprising because one might suppose that the more factors the executive can adduce in favor of its claimed privileges and immunities, the more likely it is to prevail in court or otherwise. During the Nixon administration, and ever since, the Department of Justice has cited the "stigma and opprobrium" that would result from an indictment, prosecution, or punishment as reasons to bar all three.[128] An indictment would "wound" the incumbent and his or her

---

power would be akin to requiring the President himself to appear before Congress on matters relating to the performance of his constitutionally assigned executive functions").

[120] Protective Assertion of Executive Privilege Regarding White House Office's Documents, 20 Op. O.L.C. 1 (1996).

[121] Mississippi v. Johnson, 71 U.S. 475, 501 (1866).

[122] United States v. Nixon, 418 U.S. 683, 708 (1974).

[123] *Id.* at 707.

[124] Clinton v. Jones, 520 U.S. 681, 704–05 (1997).

[125] Nixon v. Fitzgerald, 457 U.S. 731, 751 (1982).

[126] *Jones*, 520 U.S. at 708.

[127] Trump v. Mazars USA, LLP, 140 S. Ct. 2019, 2031 (2020).

[128] A Sitting President' Amenability to Indictment and Criminal Prosecution, 24 Op. O.L.C. 222, 251 (2000).

ability to exercise the powers of the office.[129] It would play "Russian roulette" and "hamstring" the entire executive branch.[130] In the Clinton administration, the Secret Service cited the need to protect presidents from physical harm as a reason to recognize a protective function privilege, namely a privilege safeguarding whatever information Secret Service agents acquired in the course of protecting the President.[131] Though the latter claim failed in court, that loss did not curb the executive's eagerness for new privileges or immunities or its willingness to expansively construe existing dispensations.

B. THE DOCTRINAL PICTURE

Perhaps due to the multifarious nature of the inquiry, we have a jumble of ill-fitting doctrines. On the one hand, a president cannot be enjoined in his official capacity, at least for executive or political acts, in part because the Court was once worried that he might ignore the injunction. That seems to be a lingering lesson of *Mississippi v. Johnson*.[132] On the other hand, a president can be subpoenaed, can lose a private suit, and perhaps be held in contempt for not honoring subpoenas and failing to comply with judgments. After all, subpoenas and adverse judgments are not invitations but commands,[133] ones backed by the contempt power of the courts. That may be one lesson of *Clinton v. Jones*[134] and *United States v. Nixon*.[135]

Or take another issue, the distraction that comes from being sued. According to *Nixon v. Fitzgerald*, presidents cannot be sued for damages for actions they take as president, at least unless Congress provides otherwise.[136] The risks of policy distortion and presidential distraction are too great.[137] We do not want presidents adopting

---

[129] Dixon, *supra* note 117, at 30 ("To wound him in a criminal proceeding is to hamstring the operation of the whole governmental apparatus, both in foreign and domestic affairs.").

[130] *Id.* at 31.

[131] *In re* Sealed Case, 148 F.3d 1073, 1075 (D.C. Cir. 1998).

[132] 71 U.S. 475, 480 (1866).

[133] Clinton v. Jones, 520 U.S. 681, 704 (1997) (describing *Nixon* as holding that President Nixon "was obligated to comply" with the subpoena).

[134] *Id.*

[135] 418 U.S. 683 (1974).

[136] 457 U.S. 731, 748 (1982) ("Congress [has not] taken express legislative action to subject the President to civil liability for his official acts.").

[137] *Id.* at 751–53.

executive policy with the potential for personal liability looming. Nor do we want them to be distracted by such suits ànd thereby neglect the nation's business. But in *Clinton v. Jones* the Court said that presidents can be sued for damages despite the obvious distraction, asserting that *Fitzgerald* was principally concerned about policy distortion.[138] At the same time, the Court perhaps left open the possibility that future courts might temporarily bar suits from proceeding to trial, saying that "such distractions ... do not *ordinarily* implicate constitutional separation-of-powers concerns."[139]

There are several gaps in the Court's pronouncements. It has yet to say whether the bar against enjoining a president applies to ministerial (nondiscretionary) presidential acts. Nor has the Court discussed whether a president might be enjoined in his private capacity. Further, the Court has never said how executive privilege applies vis-à-vis congressional investigations. It gave hints in *Mazars*, but that case was not about traditional executive privilege.[140] Finally, the Court has not yet disclosed how executive privilege applies to civil suits.[141]

The Court has been even more silent about executive privileges and immunities vis-à-vis crimes. For instance, the Court has not decided precisely how national security secrets interact with a defendant's need for evidence. In particular, it has not decided which is more important, the right of a defendant to a fair trial or the right of the executive to prosecute and simultaneously maintain state secrets. Nor has the Court told us whether a sitting president can be indicted, prosecuted, or punished. The *Vance* Court avoided the question, failing to even mention it.[142] Finally, the Court has not said whether presidents may be criminally prosecuted for their official acts.

The judicial silence extends to the peripheries of *Mazars* and *Vance*. Though I have asserted that the two cases signal that a local grand jury has more authority than Congress, the Court's ability to

---

[138] *Jones*, 520 U.S. at 693–94.

[139] *Id.* at 705 n.40 (emphasis added). *See also id.* at 708 (mentioning deferring trial if there are multiple suits).

[140] Trump v. Mazars USA, LLP, 140 S. Ct. 2019, 2026 (2020) ("Congress and the President ... feature both rivalry and reciprocity.").

[141] In *Cheney v. United States District Court for the District of Columbia*, 542 U.S. 367, 383–84 (2004), the Court claimed that executive privilege was weaker in the civil context. But this was arguably dicta.

[142] Justice Alito, however, focused on this question. *See* 140 S. Ct. at 2443–46.

draw fine distinctions in future cases might mean that I have over-simplified. First, the latitude that grand juries enjoy over the president's private papers after *Vance* might not apply to his official documents. If the grand jury had demanded presidential or executive papers, perhaps the *Vance* Court would have erected all manner of novel hurdles or imposed an absolute bar. Second, and more importantly, the *Mazars* Court did not discuss impeachment as a source of authority, and hence the impediments it imposed may apply only when a chamber seeks information for law reform. In other words, when the House mentions impeachment as a reason for its demands, the Supreme Court might yet reject the notion that the House must make several showings to defend its subpoena. No one can suppose that the Court has uttered its last word on subpoenaing the president, whether the demands come from grand juries, congressional committees, or otherwise.

C. INTERBRANCH DYNAMICS

The executive invariably attempts to enlarge the universe of its dispensations. It has reasons, public-minded and otherwise, for doing so. While investigations may reveal wrongdoing, and lawsuits can compensate victims or right wrongs committed by officials, executive officials know all too well that investigations and lawsuits also have a darker side. Both are often part of the blood sport of Beltway politics, designed to entangle the administration in a web of innuendo, scandal, and public accusations.[143] Given the context they face, little wonder that chief executives (and their aides) seek to expand existing dispensations and establish novel ones.

When confronting the modern presidency, legislators seem at a distinct disadvantage. The underlying disputes, however important they may be, are often viewed through a partisan prism. Legislators keen to investigate an incumbent often do not do themselves any favors, for they often adopt rhetoric steeped in partisanship. This plays into the hands of presidents, who then attack their legislative inquisitors and can count on congressional co-partisans to defend them. Needless to say, the partisan overlay of interbranch disputes

---

[143] Peter Baker, *Trump Is Fighting So Many Legal Battles, It's Hard to Keep Track*, N.Y. Times, (Nov. 6, 2019), https://www.nytimes.com/2019/11/06/us/politics/donald-trump-lawsuits-investigations.html.

strengthens the incumbent, for it means that a good portion of Congress is primed to defend him without regard to the merits.

The *Mazars* Court spoke wistfully of Congress and the president resolving their informational disputes via negotiations.[144] That interplay is likely to be a relic of the past, especially when the executive and the chamber are controlled by different parties. Legislators perhaps understand that negotiation comes with delay and that delay invariably serves the interests of the executive. The greater the delay, the greater the chance that partisan control of a chamber will flip, that the executive's term will expire, or that the fickle minds of legislators will turn elsewhere. Whatever the case may be, the executive generally has the upper hand, and drawing the process out greatly benefits it. More precisely, when the information desired rests solely with the executive, and the opposition demands information or testimony, delay and belated refusals advantage presidents.

Perhaps that explains the relative speed with which the chambers, in modern times, issue subpoenas and hasten to court in a context where they seek information from the executive.[145] Demand information, formally subpoena, quickly negotiate, and then go to court is the new order of the day, at least in cases of partisan divide across the branches. The courts may not rule in favor of the congressional demands, but at least bringing suits demonstrates resolve and action to your partisan base. To be sure, few who go to court ever expect a speedy resolution, for even after the trial court rules, there is an inevitable appeal. But a recourse to the courts might be the eventual outcome anyway. If prolonged negotiations are followed by extended litigation, there is a greater chance that the controversy becomes stale. Quicker recourse to the courts allows Congress to potentially secure a definitive resolution more expeditiously.[146]

---

[144] *Mazars*, 140 S. Ct. at 2031 ("Congress and the President maintained this tradition of negotiation and compromise—without the involvement of this Court—until the present dispute.").

[145] Compare the two-year long negotiations over executive privilege during the Ford-Carter years with the fruitless months of negotiations between Trump and Congress over the testimony of Donald McGahn. *See* MARK ROZELL WITH MITCHELL SOLLENBERGER, EXECUTIVE PRIVILEGE: PRESIDENTIAL POWER, SECRECY, AND ACCOUNTABILITY 82 (4th ed. 2020); Comm. on the Judiciary, U.S. House of Representatives v. McGahn, 415 F. Supp. 3d 148, 153, 157 (2019).

[146] In *Mazars* and *Vance*, President Trump went to court to prevent the private parties from unilaterally complying. In a sense, the executive bought itself time and, at a minimum, delayed any eventual handing over of documents. For their part, the House committees avoided the need for negotiations by demanding information from private parties rather than the President and his family.

The courts are less prone to innovating than the executive branch and are more powerful than Congress in these disputes. The courts sometimes say to the executive that a novel claim has no foundation and hence must be rejected. That is what has happened (thus far) to claims of a protective function privilege.[147] But the courts occasionally do innovate in a way that favors the executive, as they did in *Nixon v. Fitzgerald*, recognizing for the first time a default absolute immunity from damages for actions tied to a president's official acts.[148]

Moreover, because the Court is engaged in a common-law process, it will never utter a final word on these complex matters. Even after it announces a rule or standard, it may distinguish a later case and render a new conclusion in tension with prior pronouncements. The multitude of settings, capacities, claims, and factors ensure that no Court will ever be truly boxed in by prior opinions. For instance, in *Cheney v. United States District Court for the District of Columbia*, the Supreme Court held that district courts may curb expansive and time-consuming discovery requests directed at the executive.[149] This is not executive privilege, properly understood. It was a new privilege designed to protect the executive from even having to assert executive privilege. It also introduced another tool for the executive to shield itself from private litigants.

Presidents are far more apt to honor what courts say than what Congress demands. There is a tradition of long-simmering congressional-executive disagreements and a long practice of executives continuing to reject congressional perspectives on the separation of powers.[150] In contrast, there is a culture of executive deference to Supreme Court opinions, a deep and abiding tradition of executive compliance with judicial judgments, and a rock-solid public expectation that the executive must obey and enforce such judgments.[151]

---

[147] *In re* Sealed Case, 148 F.3d 1073, 1075 (D.C. Cir. 1998).

[148] 457 U.S. 731, 756 (1982).

[149] 542 U.S. 367, 390 (2004).

[150] *See, e.g.*, 4 ANNALS OF CONG. 760–62 (1796) (letter of George Washington) (explaining that because the House was not involved in ratifying treaties, it had no right to inspect treaty instructions given to John Jay).

[151] *See, e.g.*, John C. Yoo, *The First Claim: The Burr Trial*, United States v. Nixon, *and Presidential Power*, 83 MINN. L. REV. 1435, 1474 (1999) (discussing Jefferson complying with Chief Justice Marshall's subpoenas and asserting that the "President publicly accepted the power of the judiciary to summon the executive and his papers").

In the long run, Congress's more frequent and quick recourse to the courts may end up weakening the executive's relative position. First, the executive will be forced to negotiate with Congress in the shadow of the courts. It may sometimes concede more during negotiations rather than face the prospect of losing in court. Second, if compromise proves elusive, Congress may prevail in court, and the incumbent will be chastened. For instance, two district courts have rejected the assertion that high-level executives have complete testimonial immunity before Congress.[152] Even though *Mazars* imposes new burdens on Congress when it seeks personal papers, Congress has much to gain when it seeks judicial assistance in other cases of claimed executive dispensations. Whenever the second branch is recalcitrant, the first branch has much to gain from seeking the assistance of the more esteemed and powerful third branch.

III. No Constitutional Privileges and Immunities for the Chief Executive

It is hard to imagine that the Court will break its habit of drawing distinctions across settings, capacities, and claims. When a case reaches the Court, the Justices may make minor adjustments, elevating new factors and burying others, and draw fine distinctions between cases. Doctrinal fine-tuning is the norm, for fundamental reexaminations are rarities.[153]

A fresh approach would involve stepping back and thinking more deeply about our Constitution. Justice Thomas began this task in *Vance*.[154] A more radical reconsideration would center on two crucial questions: Does the Constitution invite judges to ponder the presidency, speculate about the privileges, immunities, and accouterments that must (or should) inhere in the office, and then impose their intuitions? Or is there another, more grounded means of creating, and fleshing out, executive dispensations? Should the Court ever take up

---

[152] Comm. on the Judiciary v. Miers, 558 F. Supp. 2d 53 (D.D.C. 2008); Comm. on the Judiciary, U.S. House of Representatives v. McGahn, 415 F. Supp. 3d 148 (D.D.C. 2019).

[153] *See* Amy Coney Barrett, *Precedent and Jurisprudential Disagreement*, 91 Tex. L. Rev. 1711, 1728 (2013) ("The Court follows precedent far more often than it reverses precedent.").

[154] *See* Trump v. Vance, 140 S. Ct. 2412, 2434 (2020) (Thomas, J., dissenting) (arguing that "the text of the Constitution … does not support the President's claim of absolute immunity" and citing originalist evidence for the proposition). In *Mazars*, the Justice questioned Congress's power to demand private papers. *See* Trump v. Mazars USA, LLP, 140 S. Ct. 2019, 2038–42 (2020) (Thomas, J., dissenting).

these foundational questions, it may well conclude that there are a host of textual, historical, and structural difficulties with its repeated inference of constitutional privileges and immunities. It may belatedly discover a different solution for the many problems it identifies.

A. TEXT

The Constitution outlines three circumscribed privileges and immunities for senators and representatives. They must receive a federal salary.[155] They have a narrow immunity from civil arrest while in, going to, or coming from a legislative session.[156] This means that these legislators are subject to arrest at all times for any crime, federal and state, including misdemeanors.[157] Indeed, incumbent legislators can be tried, convicted, and jailed.[158] Finally, federal legislators cannot be called to account ("questioned") elsewhere for what they say in either chamber,[159] which amounts to an evidentiary privilege. This privilege is also rather limited because it fairly implies that what legislators say and do elsewhere may be held against them.

In contrast, the presidency has one express privilege, related to salary. Congress can neither raise nor decrease an incumbent's salary.[160] As we have seen, the dearth of express privileges and immunities has not deterred those favoring executive dispensations. While the Constitution's express arrest immunity does not apply to crimes, the supposed presidential immunity against arrest applies to civil and criminal arrests. Further, this supposed immunity applies to the entire criminal process, far beyond arrest. For incumbents, there can be no indictments, no trials, and no punishments, or so the executive believes. Likewise, the inferred executive privilege is far broader than its express legislative counterpart, for it covers statements made wherever and whenever. Executive privilege is not confined to what is said

---

[155] U.S. CONST. art. I, § 6.

[156] Id. art. I, § 6.

[157] See Williamson v. United States, 207 U.S. 425, 438 (1908) (concluding that the exception for "treason, felony, and breach of the peace" applied to all crimes).

[158] This practice goes back to the 18th century. In 1798, a jury convicted Rep. Matthew Lyon of sedition. While in jail, Lyon sought reelection and his constituents rewarded him with another term. See GEOFFREY R. STONE, PERILOUS TIMES: FREE SPEECH IN WARTIME FROM THE SEDITION ACT OF 1798 TO THE WAR ON TERRORISM 51–53 (2004).

[159] U.S. CONST. art. I, § 6.

[160] Id. art. II, § 1.

in the White House. More importantly, executive privilege keeps conversations and documents secret rather than merely preventing legislative statements from forming the basis of a criminal prosecution or civil suit.

Furthermore, certain dispensations protect *former* chief executives, meaning they extend beyond the incumbent's time in office. Executive privilege may last for decades.[161] Similarly, the implied immunity from damages suits arising out of a president's official acts lasts forever.[162] The supposed criminal immunity of presidents is less far-reaching because past presidents cannot assert it. Nonetheless, presidents might be immune from criminal arrest and prosecution for as much as ten years (the maximum amount of time a President may hold office).[163] Importantly, for many crimes the statutes of limitations will expire while the president is in office. Hence in many cases, a supposedly temporary immunity from prosecution may be permanent.

No constitutional text in Article II seems a good vehicle for these myriad privileges and immunities. The grant of "executive power" is a poor candidate, for powers are different in kind from privileges and immunities.[164] For good reason, powers are listed in one section of Article I (Section 8) and privileges and immunities in another (Section 6). Powers are distinct from privileges and immunities in the same way that individual rights are distinct from powers. Further, no other Article II power can be plausibly read as conferring privileges or immunities.[165] Likewise, provisions imposing duties, such as the Presidential Oath, do not grant privileges and immunities.[166] Though the satisfaction of duties may necessitate a concomitant grant of some powers, the mere imposition of obligations does not necessarily convey powers or privileges. The dearth of constitutional text upon which to ground executive privileges and immunities explains why the arguments in favor are structural in nature, resting on intuitions about the Constitution's interstices.

We ought to be loath to infer far-reaching presidential privileges and immunities. The Constitution's structure weighs against the

---

[161] Nixon v. Adm'r Gen. Servs., 433 U.S. 425, 449–51 (1977).

[162] Nixon v. Fitzgerald, 457 U.S. 731, 749 (1982).

[163] U.S. CONST. amend. XXII, § 1.

[164] *Id.* art. II, § 1.

[165] *Id.* art. II, § 2.

[166] *Id.* art. II, §§ 1, 3.

claim of numerous, implied executive dispensations that dwarf the express protections for legislators. Instead, we ought to conclude that when the Constitution intends to grant extraordinary dispensations to high officials, it does so openly, not leaving them to shadowy implications.

B. THE CONTEXT

In the eighteenth century, the British Crown claimed a host of privileges and immunities. Most relevant, no one could sue or prosecute the monarch because, under British law, the monarch could "do no wrong."[167] This, emphatically, was not the theory of American executives. Each of them could do wrong and could be called to account in a host of ways.

Consider the amenability of precursors to the federal executive, namely continental and state executives. At the federal level, members of the plural chief executive—the Continental Congress—had the immunities of Congress today, namely immunity from civil arrest and a privilege against their words on the floor being used against them elsewhere. These two privileges suggest that there were no broader, implied privileges related to crimes or evidence.

The picture in the states also seems consistent with the absence of implied privileges and the principle of enumerated dispensations. For instance, states supplied limited and express executive privileges. Quite a few promised salaries.[168] But a few had broader dispensations. The South Carolina Constitution of 1776 decreed that the "President" would have the "privileges" that the assembly had accorded the royal governor.[169] The 1776 Virginia Constitution provided that its governor could be impeached only "when he is out of office."[170] Because an impeachment conviction could inflict "pains" and "penalties,"[171] Virginia granted a criminal immunity from certain penal proceedings,

---

[167] 1 WILLIAM BLACKSTONE, COMMENTARIES ON THE LAWS OF ENGLAND 238 (Univ. of Chi. 1979) (1765).

[168] *See* PRAKASH, *supra* note 4, at 54 (discussing state governors and pay).

[169] S.C. CONST. of 1776, art. XXXI.

[170] VA. CONST. of 1776 ("The Governor, *when he is out of office* ... shall be impeachable by the House of Delegates.") (emphasis added).

[171] *Id.* (persons found guilty on an impeachment charge may be "subjected to such pains or penalties as the laws shall direct").

namely impeachment.[172] Delaware had a similar provision for its "President."[173] But it also provided that "*all officers* shall be removed on conviction of misbehavior at common law...."[174] This particular clause applied to presidents for they were "officer[s],"[175] meaning that the Delaware Constitution expressly contemplated prosecutions of sitting presidents.

Some foreign constitutions granted immunities as well. The French Constitution of 1791 declared that the king was "inviolable."[176] If a monarch abdicated, however, he could be prosecuted for his post-monarchical acts.[177] In the Polish-Lithuanian Constitution of the same year, the Crown was deemed "sacred and inviolable" and was not "responsible" in any way.[178]

Given the practice of expressly incorporating any desired executive privileges and immunities, the Framers deemed it necessary to incorporate a salary privilege. In the colonies, governors often received pay only after signing various bills. Specifically, executive salaries were often granted to "Purchase [ ] Good laws."[179] Under the federal Constitution, such coercion is impossible because even the most obstructionist president has a guaranteed salary.

The Framers could have granted additional dispensations. Late in the Convention, as delegates considered legislative privileges and immunities, James Madison apparently "suggested also the necessity of considering what privileges ought to be allowed to the Executive."[180]

---

[172] *Id.*

[173] DEL. CONST. of 1776, art. XXIII.

[174] *Id.* (emphasis added).

[175] *Id.* If Delaware presidents could be removed by a conviction for misbehavior, as the text suggests, they could not be impeached but could be criminally prosecuted. This is the inverse of the rule that many find within the federal Constitution.

[176] CONST. OF FR. tit. III, ch. II, § I(II) (1791), *in* BENJAMIN FLOWER, THE FRENCH CONSTITUTION; WITH REMARKS ON SOME OF ITS PRINCIPAL ARTICLES 14, 37 (1792).

[177] *Id.* § I(VIII), at 39.

[178] NEW CONST. OF THE GOV'T OF POLAND, ESTABLISHED BY THE REVOLUTION art. VII, at 21 (1791).

[179] EVARTS BOUTELL GREENE, THE PROVINCIAL GOVERNOR IN THE ENGLISH COLONIES OF NORTH AMERICA 175 (1898).

[180] 2 THE RECORDS OF THE FEDERAL CONVENTION OF 1787, at 503 (Max Farrand ed., 1966). Madison was hardly alone in thinking about executive immunities. Alexander Hamilton's plan from June of 1787 originally provided that "[a]fter removal from office ... The Governor" and perhaps others "could be prosecuted in the ordinary course of law for any crime." He apparently deleted this text before he gave his speech. *See* Hamilton Plan, in 1 THE DOCUMENTARY HISTORY OF THE RATIFICATION OF THE CONSTITUTION 253, 255 (Merrill Jensen ed., 1976).

Madison knew that Virginia and Delaware had some criminal immunities[181] and evidently hoped for some for the new president. His comment on the "necessity" of addressing the subject signaled that the proposed executive lacked generic privileges or immunities. Madison's plea went nowhere. Besides a salary, the delegates never discussed, much less voted upon, any other executive privileges or immunities, suggesting that they never granted any additional shields.

That is largely how people outside the Convention subsequently read the Constitution: the executive generally lacked privileges or immunities. This point was made in three contexts. To begin with, the Constitution's advocates drew a contrast with monarchies, essentially making an ancient version of the modern argument that "no man is above the law." While British sovereigns could "do no wrong," meaning they were immune from all judicial process (both impeachment and ordinary criminal trials), the American president would be different.[182] "Americanus" said that while the king was "above the reach of all Courts of law" and was "sacred and inviolable," presidents would not be.[183] "[N]one of [these immunities] are vested in the President."[184] Another Federalist stated that the president would be "under the immediate controul of the constitution, which if he should presume to deviate from, he would be immediately arrested in his career and summoned to answer for his conduct before a federal court, where strict justice and equity would undoubtedly preside."[185] Finally, "An American Citizen"—Tench Coxe—contrasted the British monarchy and American legislators with the presidency. While the king "could do no wrong," presidents would be different: *His person is not so much protected as that of a member of the House of Representatives; for he may be proceeded against like any other man in the ordinary course of*

[181] *See* THE FEDERALIST No. 39, at 242 (James Madison) (Clinton Rossiter ed., 1961).

[182] BLACKSTONE, *supra* note 167, at 238.

[183] *Americanus II (John Stevens, Jr.)*, N.Y. DAILY ADVERTISER, Nov. 23, 1787, *reprinted in* 19 THE DOCUMENTARY HISTORY OF THE RATIFICATION OF THE CONSTITUTION 287, 288–89 (John P. Kaminski et al. eds., 2009).

[184] *Id.* at 289. *See also Publicola*, STATE GAZETTE N.C., Mar. 27, 1788, *reprinted in* 16 THE DOCUMENTARY HISTORY OF THE RATIFICATION OF THE CONSTITUTION 493, 496 (John P. Kaminski et al. eds., 1986) (While the King can do no wrong and is "not amenable to the courts of justice," the president is impeachable "by the representatives of the people" and can "be tried for his crimes.").

[185] *Cassius, X*, MASS. GAZETTE, Dec. 21, 1787, *reprinted in* ESSAYS ON THE CONSTITUTION OF THE UNITED STATES 38 (Paul Leicester Ford ed., 1892).

law."[186] Coxe understood that presidents have fewer dispensations than federal legislators.

Others emphasized Coxe's last point. These arguments took the form of insisting that presidents were no better, no more privileged, than ordinary citizens. James Wilson asked, "Does even the first magistrate of the United States draw to himself a single privilege or security that does not extend to every person throughout the United States? Is there a single distinction attached to him in this system more than there is to the lowest officer in the republic?"[187] Similarly, a Marylander wrote that executive authority was vested in "a single man, the representative of the people, chosen once in four years, and enjoying no privilege, as an individual, more than his fellow-citizens."[188] In North Carolina, James Iredell assured that

> No man is better than his fellow-citizens, nor can pretend to any superiority over the meanest man in the country. If the President does a single act by which the people are prejudiced, he is punishable himself, and no other man merely to screen him. If he commits any misdemeanor in office, he is impeachable, removable from office, and incapacitated to hold any office of honor, trust, or profit. If he commits any crime, he is punishable by the laws of his country, and in capital cases may be deprived of his life.[189]

One prominent anti-Federalist said the same. *The Federal Farmer* observed that presidents would have "no rights, but in common with the people."[190] In other words, though endowed with momentous powers, presidents had no special dispensations.

Finally, a few Federalists steadfastly insisted the federal officials would enjoy no implied privileges. James Wilson, quoted earlier, also

---

[186] *An American Citizen I, On the Federal Government*, INDEPENDENT GAZETTEER, Sept. 26, 1787, *reprinted in* 2 THE DOCUMENTARY HISTORY OF THE RATIFICATION OF THE CONSTITUTION 141 (Merrill Jensen ed., 1976).

[187] 2 THE DOCUMENTARY HISTORY OF THE RATIFICATION OF THE CONSTITUTION, *supra* note 186, at 579 (comments of James Wilson).

[188] *An Annapolitan*, ANNAPOLIS MD. GAZETTE, Jan. 21, 1788, *reprinted in* 11 THE DOCUMENTARY HISTORY OF THE RATIFICATION OF THE CONSTITUTION 218, 220 (John P. Kaminski et al. eds., 2015).

[189] 4 THE DEBATES IN THE SEVERAL STATE CONVENTIONS ON THE ADOPTION OF THE FEDERAL CONSTITUTION 106, 109 (Jonathan Elliott ed., 1836). *See also* Marcus III, *in* 16 THE DOCUMENTARY HISTORY OF THE RATIFICATION OF THE CONSTITUTION, *supra* note 184, at 322 ("he is not exempt from a trial, if he should be guilty, or supposed guilty, of [treason] or any other offense"). "Marcus" was a pseudonym for James Iredell.

[190] Letters from a Federal Farmer No. XIV (Jan. 17, 1788), *in* 20 THE DOCUMENTARY HISTORY OF THE RATIFICATION OF THE CONSTITUTION 1035, 1042 (John P. Kaminski et al. eds., 2004).

said that though the president is "placed high, and is possessed of power, far from being contemptible, yet not a single privilege is annexed to his character; far from being above the laws, he is amenable to them in his private character as a citizen, and in his public character by impeachment."[191] The president was subject to the laws and bereft of even a "single privilege."[192] Discussing all three branches, one New Yorker rubbished charges of an aristocracy, noting there were no subterfuges regarding powers and privileges. "The Constitution plainly, openly, and without disguise tells us the titles, offices, powers, and privileges of these 'chief agents,' and the purposes of their appointment. What snake in the grass is there here?"[193] Officers only enjoyed express privileges (granted "plainly, openly, and without disguise"). Because the Constitution granted but one executive privilege plainly and openly, it conferred no others.

C. EARLY PRACTICES

In 1789, we spot the claim that the presidency has some privileges and immunities. But the assertions are sweeping, beyond anything anyone advocates today. Several senators read the Constitution and saw a monarch, limited to be sure, but a kingly personage nonetheless. Given their perspective, these senators assumed that presidents must enjoy broad immunity from judicial process. One senator supposedly said that it would be "Sacrilege to touch a [ ] Hair of his head" and that if the president was subject to court process, one might as well put his head on the chopping block.[194] Another said the president was "a kind of [s]acred [p]erson," and hence unreachable by the courts.[195] A third said the President was not "subject to any process whatever, could have no action whatever brought against him [and] was above all the power of [j]udges, [j]ustices, [etc.]"[196] The only exception was

[191] 2 The Documentary History of the Ratification of the Constitution, *supra* note 186, at 487, 495.

[192] *Id.*

[193] *Letter from New York*, Conn. J., Oct. 24 & 31, 1787, *in* 3 The Documentary History of the Ratification of the Constitution 380, 382 (Merrill Jensen ed., 1978).

[194] 9 The Documentary History of the First Federal Congress: The Diary of William Maclay and Other Notes on Senate Debates, *supra* note 97, at 112 (noting a senator's claim that "[i]t is [s]acrilege to touch [a] [h]air [on] [the president's] head").

[195] *Id.* at 168.

[196] *Id.* (recounting arguments that "the President, personally, was not the subject to any process whatever; could have no action whatever brought against him; was above the power

the one that neither they, nor anyone else, could gainsay, namely impeachment.

But these comments were outliers. In response, some senators said the president could "put to [g]aol for [d]ebt,"[197] a comment that implied that presidents had no privileges from civil incarceration, at least. Continuing the point, Senator William Grayson of Virginia insisted that the "President was not above the law," arguing that presidents would be sued and that they might be prosecuted for murder.[198] Grayson thought it particularly absurd to suppose that judicial process should issue in the president's name, as some acolytes of the executive suggested. The following incongruity might result: "The Jurors of our Lord the President, present that the President committed Murder."[199] In other words, Grayson supposed that a president could be prosecuted and concluded that, therefore, judicial process should not issue in his name.

1. *Executive Privilege.* The first President never publicly insisted upon any dispensations. Nonetheless, some assert that his administration marked the beginning of "executive privilege" or the claim that presidents can keep some documents secret.[200] Three incidents are worth considering.

The first episode concerned a potential congressional investigation into the massacre of an army division.[201] The President was worried that "there might be papers of so secret a nature as that they ought not to be given up."[202] Before receiving any request, the cabinet agreed on the following:

1. that the house was an inquest, and therefore might institute inquiries.

---

of all judges, justices, etc. For what, said they, would you put it in the power of a common justice to exercise any authority over him and stop the whole machine of Government?").

[197] *Id.* at 446.

[198] *Id.*

[199] *Id.*

[200] There are several excellent book-length treatments of executive privilege. *See generally* RAOUL BERGER, EXECUTIVE PRIVILEGE: A CONSTITUTIONAL MYTH (1974); DANIEL N. HOFFMAN, GOVERNMENTAL SECRECY AND THE FOUNDING FATHERS: A STUDY IN CONSTITUTIONAL CONTROLS (1981); MARK J. ROZELL, EXECUTIVE PRIVILEGE: THE DILEMMA OF SECRECY AND DEMOCRATIC ACCOUNTABILITY (1994).

[201] HOFFMAN, *supra* note 200, at 70–71.

[202] *See* Memoranda of Consultations with the President (Mar. 31, 1792), *in* 23 THE PAPERS OF THOMAS JEFFERSON 258, 262 (Charles T. Cullen ed., 1990).

2. that it might call for papers generally.
3. that the Executive ought to … refuse those, the disclosure of which would injure the public. Consequently were to exercise a discretion.[203]

The cabinet ultimately resolved that "there was not a paper which might not be properly produced," and thus no withholding of documents was necessary.[204]

Two days later, the House resolved that the President "be requested to cause the proper officers to lay before this House such papers of a public nature, in the Executive Department, as may be necessary to the investigation of the causes of the failure of the late expedition."[205] This eliminated any potential clash because the House conveyed discretion to Washington. For his part, the President never publicly asserted a right to withhold information and, in fact, transmitted all relevant documents.[206] Given the House's qualified request and the fact that Washington conveyed all pertinent documents, the episode is a poor precedent for an *executive right* to withhold papers.[207]

The second incident is not much more instructive. In 1794, the Senate called upon the executive to hand over diplomatic letters related to relations with France.[208] Fearing that disclosure might damage relations, the President sought advice. Again, the cabinet supported a right to withhold documents.[209] Washington transmitted redacted correspondence with an explanation: "After an examination of [the papers], I directed copies and translations to be made; except in those particulars which, in my judgment, for public considerations,

---

[203] *Id.* (Apr. 2, 1792).

[204] *Id.*

[205] 2 ANNALS OF CONG. 536 (1792).

[206] *See* BERGER, *supra* note 200, at 168–69; HOFFMAN, *supra* note 200, at 74–76.

[207] *See* BERGER, *supra* note 200, at 169 n.34.

[208] 3 ANNALS OF CONG. 38 (1794).

[209] Secretary of War Henry Knox said that none of the correspondence should be provided to the Senate. Attorney General Edmund Randolph stated that "all the correspondence proper, from its nature, to be communicated to the Senate, should be sent; but that what the President thinks improper, should not be sent." Hamilton agreed with Knox that the President need not send anything, but that it was fine to send some correspondence. Cabinet Opinion on a Resolution of the U.S. Senate (Jan. 28, 1794), *in* 15 THE PAPERS OF GEORGE WASHINGTON: PRESIDENTIAL SERIES 141 (Christine Sternberg Patrick ed., 2009).

ought not to be communicated."[210] The excisions concerned confidential informants and embarrassing commentary.

The Senate's acquiescence might have signaled an understanding that presidents had a constitutional right to keep certain communications secret. Yet perhaps the Senate found the furnished materials sufficient. More likely, the Senate demand was made in a context where requests for information were read to confer discretion. Indeed, many legislative requests expressly authorized omissions.[211] Given this practice, Attorney General William Bradford argued that every request should be construed to permit "those just exceptions which the rights of the Executive and the nature of foreign correspondence require."[212] The President should not assume that "the Senate intended to include any Letters, the disclosure of which might endanger national honor or individual safety."[213] So what might seem a claim of a privilege may have been reliance on a custom of legislatively authorized withholding.

The third incident, involving a request for an appropriation to implement the divisive Jay Treaty, triggered an open fight. To judge whether the House should pass a law to satisfy a treaty obligation, the House asked for Jay's treaty instructions and authorized Washington to withhold "such of said papers as any existing negotiation may render improper to be disclosed."[214]

Washington flat out refused. To accept "a right in the House of Representatives to demand, and to have, as a matter of course, all the papers respecting a negotiation with a foreign Power, would be to establish a dangerous precedent."[215] He added that "[i]t does not occur that the inspection of the papers asked for can be relative to any purpose under the cognizance of the House of Representatives, except that of an impeachment; which the resolution has not expressed."[216]

---

[210] 3 ANNALS OF CONG. 56 (1794).

[211] ABRAHAM D. SOFAER, WAR, FOREIGN AFFAIRS AND CONSTITUTIONAL POWER: THE ORIGINS 81 (1976).

[212] Letter from William Bradford to George Washington (Jan. 1794), *in* 15 THE PAPERS OF GEORGE WASHINGTON: PRESIDENTIAL SERIES, *supra* note 209, at 166–67.

[213] *Id.* at 167.

[214] 5 ANNALS OF CONG. 759 (1796).

[215] *Id.* at 760

[216] *Id.*

This was no assertion of a privilege. To begin with, Washington's refusal was grounded in the claim that the House lacked the power to demand the papers. Because the House had no role in treatymaking, it had no right to the documents. He buttressed this point by noting that he had provided all the relevant papers to the Senate.[217] Relatedly, he noted that the House had not indicated any interest in impeachment.[218] The only reason to mention this was to signal that he might have complied had the House signaled a possible impeachment. For its part, the House stood its ground. It insisted that so long as the information related to the "Constitutional functions of the House," no additional justification for the demand was necessary.[219]

In sum, though there was a view that the President should be able to withhold documents from Congress, there also was a belief that Congress had a constitutional right to relevant information, particularly where impeachment was a possibility. The first perception hardly established that the President had a *constitutional* right to withhold because most legislative requests expressly permitted the withholding of documents. Moreover, the idea of a congressional right to information, something Washington repeatedly conceded, is in obvious tension with the assertion that presidents have some sort of executive privilege.

Finally, one must underscore that the privilege that was discussed within the confines of the cabinet related to government secrets and not to maintaining the confidentiality of advice. Washington regularly handed over internal executive branch communications to Congress, never saying that he was "waiving" some privilege protecting confidences.[220] In other words, the three episodes, much discussed in the executive privilege literature, are relevant to a *state secrets privilege*, and nothing Washington said, or did, suggested that he had a right to confidential communications with his advisers so that they might give him unvarnished advice.

The first privilege dispute in the courts arose during the third presidency. Facing treason charges, Aaron Burr sought documents in

---

[217] *Id.* at 761.

[218] *Id.* at 760.

[219] *Id.* at 782–83.

[220] *See, e.g.*, To the United States Senate and House of Representatives, Jan. 12, 1790, *in* 4 THE PAPERS OF GEORGE WASHINGTON: PRESIDENTIAL SERIES 567, 568 (Dorothy Twohig ed., 1993) (mentioning that as submitting a report from the War Secretary along with several enclosures, asking that Congress keep the material secret, but not claiming that he was waiving a privilege)

the possession of Thomas Jefferson. The district attorney, George Hay, argued that while the President could be subpoenaed to give testimony, he could not be subpoenaed for his papers.[221] This was an odd argument, for forcing Jefferson to come in person was far more intrusive. In any event, John Marshall famously concluded that presidents could be subpoenaed for testimony *and* documents. In a passage that has been ignored, Marshall wrote that "it is not known ever to have been doubted, but that the chief magistrate of a state might be served with a subpoena ad testificandum."[222] He also observed that the federal and state executives were similarly situated for these purposes and quite different from the British monarch.[223]

Jefferson complained about Marshall's subpoena. Nonetheless, he turned over documents. In so doing, the "President publicly accepted the power of the judiciary to summon the executive and his papers."[224] In handing over papers demanded by Burr, Jefferson never asserted that though he had a constitutional right to ignore subpoenas, he was waiving that right. To the world, it must have seemed that he had conceded that courts could subpoena the executive.[225]

This seemed to be the rule in the British courts as well. In 1789, a judge in the Court of Admiralty said the following: "'In any cause where the crown is a party ... the crown can no more withhold evidence of documents ... than a private person. If the court thinks proper to order the production of any public instrument, that order must be obeyed.'"[226] It seems there might have been no executive privilege vis-à-vis the Crown's courts.

---

[221] United States v. Burr, 25 F. Cas. 30, 34 (C.C.D. Va. 1807) (district attorney admitting that a "general subpoena" could issue to the president but not a "subpoena duces tecum" and Marshall writing that president is no different than an ordinary citizen when called upon to testify personally)

[222] *Id.*

[223] *Id.*

[224] Yoo, *supra* note 151, at 1474.

[225] This is not to say that Jefferson was submissive in complying with the subpoena. Though he fully complied with the first subpoena, in response to the second, he redacted some information from a letter. He was able to do this because Marshall's opinion seemed to contemplate that the executive might make unilateral redactions. These redactions were to stand unless "essential" for the defense. United States v. Burr, 25 F. Cas. 187, 192 (C.C.D. Va. 1807). John Yoo notes that neither Burr nor Marshall objected to the redactions. Yoo, *supra* note 151, at 1463–64. Burr's failure to object suggests that he did not believe the redacted portions were essential.

[226] Chisholm v. Georgia, 2 U.S. (2 Dall.) 419, 430 (1793) (opinion of Wilson, J.) (citing Case of the Ship Columbus (1789), *reprinted in* 1 COLLECTANEA JURIDICA: CONSISTING OF TRACTS RELATIVE TO THE LAW AND CONSTITUTION OF ENGLAND 82, 92 (1791)).

Given that the textual and contextual arguments strongly cut against executive privilege and that the early case for a privilege is rather weak, there is little warrant for supposing that presidents have a constitutional power to shield conversations and documents from either Congress or the courts. While such authority might be useful for the executive and the nation, that hardly proves that presidents have a constitutional right to rebuff attempts to secure information.

2. *Executive Immunity.* As for executive immunity in the courts, I am unaware of any claim by President Washington, or his advisors, that presidents had special civil or criminal immunities in court, much less that they were above judicial process. On the contrary, citizen Washington was something of a regular litigant in court, never asserting any sort of immunity.

In his capacity as an executor for several estates, Washington repeatedly went to court. In 1792, plaintiff Washington secured a judgment against those owing money to an estate.[227] That same year, defendant Washington answered a complaint about a land sale arranged years earlier for a deceased friend.[228] In 1796, Washington was "enjoined" by a court.[229] This was a relief, for as plaintiff he sought to gather all estate claimants before the court. He published the court's mandate in the *London Gazette*, one that "[o]rder[ed]" "George Washington" to deposit funds with the court.[230] To be clear, Washington was hardly delighted with these duties. He complained about his plight: "It is really hard that I am so often called before Courts in matters in which I have no interest; but am continually saddled with the expense of defence."[231] Apparently, state courts bandied the first President from pillar to post. No good deed—serving as an executor—goes unpunished.

---

[227] Court Judgment, *in* 10 THE PAPERS OF GEORGE WASHINGTON: PRESIDENTIAL SERIES 407 (Robert F. Haggard & Mark A. Mastromarino eds., 2002).

[228] Letter from George Washington to John Francis Mercer (July 23, 1792), *in* 32 THE WRITINGS OF GEORGE WASHINGTON 89, 91 (John C. Fitzpatrick ed., 1939). Apparently, Washington had sold the lands as executor to the estate of John Mercer. FRANK E. GRIZZARD JR., GEORGE WASHINGTON: A BIOGRAPHICAL COMPANION 217–18 (2002).

[229] Letter from George Washington to James Keith (July 17, 1796), *in* 35 THE WRITINGS OF GEORGE WASHINGTON 141 (John C. Fitzpatrick ed., 1940).

[230] Notice, London Gazette (Dec. 17, 1796), at 1222.

[231] Letter from George Washington to Bushrod Washington (Apr. 30, 1794), *in* 33 THE WRITINGS OF GEORGE WASHINGTON 347 (John C. Fitzpatrick ed., 1940).

But sometimes Washington was less a victim and more the aggressor. He threatened suits against debtors, squatters, and trespassers. He told one debtor that he would put his bonds "in suit without delay" if the borrower did not pay.[232] On another occasion, he instructed his attorney to sue should a debtor fail to pay.[233] When one person claimed two hundred acres of Washington's land, he warned that any squatting would "be prosecuted as far as right and justice will admit."[234]

While threatening to litigate, bringing lawsuits, facing lawsuits and injunctions, Washington never suggested that he could not be sued or subject to judicial process. He made no such claims because though the Constitution granted him certain monarchical powers, it did not render him "sacred and inviolable."[235] Washington knew that although court proceedings would distract him from the nation's business, the Constitution never granted immunity from suit. Besides, how could he use the courts as a tool or weapon against others while insisting upon an executive shield against their claims? It would have been downright bizarre to sue others and deny them the right to counterclaim.

Though early politicians discussed the possibility that presidents might be prosecuted in the ordinary courts, Washington never was indicted or prosecuted. This reflected his behavior, which was generally above all reproach. But it is worth noting that, so far as I am aware, Washington never claimed immunity from grand jury subpoenas, indictment, prosecution, or punishment. Washington was a majestic figure and held a quasi-regal office, but he understood that his office lacked kingly dispensations.

D. INFERRING THE NECESSARY AND APPROPRIATE INCIDENTS
OF THE OFFICE

The best case for presidential privileges and immunities is not textual, contextual, or grounded on early practice, but structural. Some

---

[232] Letter from George Washington to James Mercer (Apr. 4, 1789), *in* 30 THE WRITINGS OF GEORGE WASHINGTON 270, 271 (John C. Fitzpatrick ed., 1939).

[233] Letter from George Washington to Thomas Smith (Sept. 23, 1789), *in* 30 THE WRITINGS OF GEORGE WASHINGTON, *supra* note 232, at 410.

[234] Letter from George Washington to Reuben Slaughter (Feb. 25, 1792), *in* 31 THE WRITINGS OF GEORGE WASHINGTON 485, 485–86 (John C. Fitzpatrick ed., 1939).

[235] NEW CONST. OF THE GOV'T OF POLAND, *supra* note 178, at 21.

have argued that certain dispensations are inherent in the presidency. Joseph Story argued that some immunity is "necessarily implied from the nature of the [executive's] functions."[236] He argued for immunity from civil arrest. But, of course, others have made similar claims concerning subpoenas, civil immunity, executive privilege, and criminal immunity. All these dispensations, and more, might be "necessarily implied."[237]

If by "necessarily implied," Story meant something like "logically necessary," his argument (and similar ones) is untenable. No one imagines that immunity from subpoena or an executive privilege logically follows from Article II or the rest of the Constitution. We cannot derive either by using deduction or induction. Indeed, we have seen that many Founders denied that the president had any privileges. They too read the Constitution and in concluding that the presidency lacked a single privilege, they judged that immunities were not "necessarily implied" from its functions.

Perhaps Story meant no more than that the high office has implied dispensations regarded as useful to fulfilling the office's many constitutional duties. The office comes with unstated privileges and immunities because, without it, the office cannot function as it must.

This is a more reasonable claim. But it too is flawed, for our Constitution's actual structure cuts decisively against this theory. Start with something basic. Imagine that our Constitution did not guarantee a presidential salary. Would courts deduce a salary as a necessary incident of the office? Would they infer that the separation of powers implicitly demanded a regular salary? I doubt that the courts would manufacture a constitutional salary out of thin air. The argument for various other implied executive dispensations is weaker still.

Consider a related question on a far more important matter. Is any branch entitled to an appropriation for its myriad expenses without regard to the appropriations process spelled out in the Constitution? No. Both branches go to Congress and seek appropriations. In the case of the judiciary, two federal judges often beseech Congress for a suitable appropriation.[238] This is an interesting ritual, especially

---

[236] JOSEPH STORY, 3 COMMENTARIES ON THE CONSTITUTION OF THE UNITED STATES § 1563 (1833).

[237] Id.

[238] BARRY J. MCMILLON, CONG. RSCH. SERV., R45965, Judiciary Appropriations FY2020, at 2 (2020).

when Justices testify, a scene of dignified pleading. The judges doff their robes but typically receive the courtesies befitting federal judges.[239]

The executive branch's requests for funds are often treated less deferentially. In the recent past, executive budget documents have been treated as "dead on arrival." But because the executive has a veto and is willing to use it, members of Congress must negotiate with the executive to strike some sort of compromise. They may give him the money he demands for his branch in return for his agreeing to spending priorities they favor.

The point is that Congress appropriates. The budgets of both branches come from Congress, which wields this power to further the ends of legislators. The president is not constitutionally entitled to a budget of his choosing. Unlike Parliament's granting of a civil list to the Crown, our legislature has never guaranteed a permanent executive appropriation.[240] Further, I do not suppose that anyone has ever read the Constitution as guaranteeing any such appropriation. That is why the Court in *Zivotofsky v. Kerry* declared that though the president had the power to recognize Israel's claim to Jerusalem, the meaningful exercise of that power might require congressional action in the form of an appropriation necessary to move an embassy.[241]

The principle that only Congress can appropriate even extends to guaranteed salaries. While the branches are entitled to salaries for their constitutional officers (presidents and judges), personnel from neither branch can sashay into the Treasury and withdraw funds. Rather, Congress must appropriate and satisfy the Constitution's obligations. Until it does, no monies can be withdrawn from the Treasury,[242] notwithstanding the constitutional guarantees. If the other branches are fully reliant upon Congress for salaries and appropriations, two of the most necessary means of satisfying their respective constitutional duties, it suggests that the other branches are deeply reliant upon Congress for fulfilling their obligations.

---

[239] Todd Ruger, *Justices Break the Ice, Err Glass, at Budget Hearing*, ROLL CALL (Mar. 8, 2019), https://www.rollcall.com/2019/03/08/justices-break-the-ice-err-glass-at-budget-hearing.

[240] *See* Saikrishna Bangalore Prakash, *Some Fragmented Features of the Unitary Executive*, 45 WILLAMETTE L. REV. 701, 703–04, 711–12 (2009) (describing how Parliament would greet each newly crowned monarch with a permanent appropriation to defray the costs of civil executives and administration).

[241] Zivotofsky v. Kerry, 576 U.S. 1, 16 (2015).

[242] U.S. CONST. art. I, § 9.

The dependence on Congress does not end there. It extends to filling out the branches, to structuring and populating them. The chief executive has no branch—no departments, officers, armies, or navies—absent Congress. Congress decides whether there will be a Department of Interior, a Department of Justice, or even an army. Hence Congress decides whether the chief executive will be the sole executive and whether the commander in chief will have anyone to command. Likewise, Congress decides how many Justices will serve on the Supreme Court and whether there will be lower federal courts. Congress has varied the number on the Court as circumstances and perceptions have changed. And as for the lower courts, Congress has always enjoyed discretion and, under the conception promulgated by the Jeffersonians in 1802, might eliminate all inferior federal courts on grounds of unnecessary expense. That is why the great structuralist Charles Black was largely right when he said that Congress could reduce the presidency's staff to one secretary.[243] His only mistake was in assuming that Congress would have to supply a secretary.

My point is that funds, officers, and departments are the muscle, bone, and sinew of the executive. If the executive must rely upon Congress for all three, it is a mistake to imagine that the executive has implied *constitutional* rights to an array of nontextual privileges and immunities, ones that supposedly inhere in the nature of the executive's functions. After all, these inferred accoutrements are far less central to the functioning of the executive branch. Moreover, we must never forget that the presidential salary privilege is wholly dependent upon the independent action of Congress. If that express privilege is utterly dependent on congressional action, why would implied privileges and immunities be more robust and exist without regard to congressional action?

During the term of any president, the ability to ignore a subpoena is positively trivial in comparison to funds, officers, and departments. In the life of a great nation, a president's supposed capacity to be free from private suits or criminal prosecutions is hardly more important than the creation and support of an army or the Department of State. As compared to the flesh and bone of the executive branch, executive privileges and immunities are akin to a shiny trinket: nice to have, but

---

[243] *See* Charles L. Black Jr., *The Working Balance of the American Political Departments*, 1 HASTINGS CONST. L.Q. 13, 15 (1974).

hardly indispensable and certainly not properly inferred from intensely speculative considerations of constitutional structure.

In sum, to say, as Justice Story did, that executive privileges and immunities are "necessarily implied" in the office is to confuse what Story thought would be useful with what the Constitution confers upon the president.[244] But not everything useful and necessary is guaranteed to the executive or, for that matter, any other constitutional officer.

E. LEGISLATING THE NECESSARY AND PROPER ACCOUTREMENTS OF THE OFFICE

Justice Story's quotation contains the seeds of an unexceptional solution to what to my mind is a garden-variety problem. We want executives to focus on their jobs and to receive the most candid advice. If we believe that our chief executives should be able to keep secrets and confidences and that they should not be bothered and harassed by lawsuits and prosecutions, we have a solution at hand that reaches for the Constitution without reading far too much into it.

Even if immunity from subpoenas and lawsuits is not "necessarily implied," it will often be "necessary and proper" to enact immunities into ordinary law. Congress can supply useful and appropriate immunities for our chief executives. By statute, Congress can grant immunity from subpoenas. Congress can keep certain confidences secret by exempting them from the subpoena powers of the courts and Congress. It can shield White House officials from having to testify to Congress. It can bar state and federal investigations of our chief executives, reserving to itself the right to investigate. It can bar state and federal prosecutions of our chief executives.

The advantage of this solution is that it leaves such matters to ordinary legislation and permits Congress to expand, curtail, or adjust the rules as it sees fit. Congress might decide that if the executive invokes executive privilege to shield documents in a criminal investigation, the executive cannot prosecute the defendant whose demands for documents it rebuffed. Executive privilege comes at the expense of the prosecution. Similarly, Congress can conclude that presidents should not be sued for damages or injunctions arising out of some or all of their official acts because it agrees that presidents should not

---

[244] STORY, *supra* note 236, § 1563.

look over their shoulder as they make decisions. Alternatively, Congress can allow the lawsuits to proceed and pass a general indemnification on the theory that lawsuits generate useful information about a president, particularly her willingness to honor the law.[245]

Congress also can ensure a certain level of symmetry and fairness. For instance, it might permit a president to postpone private lawsuits so long as he or she agrees not to sue others. If the president agrees to that, neither the president nor the public may sue one another in their private capacities. Obviously, the incumbent should not have temporary immunity from lawsuits while he privately sues Americans left and right. Concerning crimes, Congress might decide that while the prosecution of relatively trivial crimes should be held in abeyance until after the president leaves office, serious crimes, like murder, can proceed against a sitting chief executive.

There are examples, both contemporary and ancient, of congressional exemptions for important federal personnel. The Servicemembers Civil Relief Act permits members of the military to focus on their duties while staying certain civil proceedings against them.[246] Congress routinely exempts itself from a host of duties and statutes. For instance, members of Congress are exempt from jury service by statute.[247] Congress also exempts itself from laws related to workplace protections. The good government story is that such exemptions ensure a better functioning Congress. There are, of course, more dark reasons for these dispensations.

The history of statutory exemptions dates to early Congresses. The second Militia Act of 1792 provided that every white male ages 18–45 composed the militias within the states. But it also expressly exempted many federal officials. Among those excepted were the vice president, all federal legislators, all federal and judicial personnel, mail carriers, and all mariners, pilots, and ferrymen.[248] The point was to ensure that states did not call forth these males to serve in the state militias because they were busy attending to federal duties or to matters that were of

---

[245] Congress has long indemnified officers owing damages to private parties. *See* James E. Pfander & Jonathan L. Hunt, *Public Wrongs and Private Bills: Indemnification and Government Accountability in the Early Republic*, 85 N.Y.U. L. Rev. 1862 (2010).

[246] *See* 50 U.S.C. §§ 3901–4043.

[247] 2 U.S.C. § 30a.

[248] Act of May 8, 1792, ch. 33, § 1–2, 1 Stat. 271, 271–72.

keen federal interest. An 1800 act exempted those working in federal armories from military (presumably militia) and jury service.[249]

Leaving executive privileges and immunities to ordinary politics may disquiet some, particularly the incumbent president and his lawyers. After all, they may rightly worry that Congress will not supply the needful dispensations, effectively choosing to "punish" the chief executive. This is a legitimate and valid concern. Many legislators adopt aggressive stances toward presidents of the other party even as they roll over for co-partisans.

Yet as disappointing as Congress is, it does not wholly disappoint. To begin with, presidential salaries are left to ordinary politics in two senses: the Constitution does not set the amount, and presidents are wholly reliant upon Congress to appropriate the salary. Congress invariably does the right things concerning presidential salary. Moreover, we must bear in mind that true executive necessities are left to ordinary politics, namely the armed forces, civil executive departments, executive personnel, and funds. Further, if executive dispensations are as needful as executive lawyers are apt to suppose, then Congress will likely supply them because members will acknowledge their benefits. They may not supply them when the incumbent is already in court, in part because of partisan passions. But legislators will supply them when the smoke clears and cooler heads prevail. We need not worry that, should the courts exit the business of creating executive privileges and immunities, our presidents will be left wholly bereft of truly needful dispensations.

A veil of ignorance strategy may serve us all well. Congress can specify a laundry list of executive privileges and immunities for the executive and declare that they will spring into existence after the next presidential inauguration. If legislators agree that presidents merit some dispensations, they will not hesitate to supply them to a future president and can do so without being accused of empowering the incumbent of another party. Congress took this route in the Line-Item Veto Act. Legislators enacted the Act in April of 1996 with a delayed effective date of January 1, 1997.[250] Republicans favored the act and hoped that President Bill Clinton would not be reelected. They were wrong. In any event, delaying the effective date

---

[249] Act of May 7, 1800, ch. 46, 2 Stat. 61, 62.

[250] Line Item Veto Act, Pub. L. No. 104–130, sec. 5, 110 Stat. 1200 (1996).

of legislation for several years makes it more palatable for legislators to do the right thing when it comes to aiding their institutional rival, the executive branch.

CONCLUSION

The Court has long been prone to finding constitutional dispensations when statutory solutions would suffice. The results are sometimes embarrassing. In *McCulloch v. Maryland*, the Court spent pages insisting that Maryland had absolutely no power to tax the Bank of the United States. But the Court concluded by strangely cautioning that its opinion did not address whether Maryland could apply a neutral tax to the Bank.[251] So could states tax a federal instrument after all, at least some of the time? The resulting intergovernmental immunity jurisprudence has waxed and waned, in less than satisfying ways. It would have been better for federal immunities from state taxation to rest upon legislative decisions. The Court might have said that Congress implicitly exempted the Bank from taxation. Or the Court might have concluded that in *discriminating* against the Bank, Maryland was failing to honor the constitutional principle that because federal law is supreme law, it was no less the law of every state. Singling out the Bank treated the federal instrumentality as if it were a foreign creature.

Mazars and *Vance* are the latest cases wrestling with implied immunities. Given *Mazars*, Congress is now shackled by the demand that it make special showings regarding the need for personal documents of presidents. Perhaps the resulting framework is a good one. But it is not one that the Constitution demands. And it is not obvious that the Court can impose the extra limitations on Congress. The third branch has shackled the first branch as it investigates the alleged shenanigans of a citizen-cum-chief executive.[252]

---

[251] *See* McCulloch v. Maryland 17 U.S. (4. Wheat) 316, 317 (1819) ("This [opinion] ... does not extend to a tax paid by the real property of the Bank, in common with the other real property in a particular state, nor to a tax imposed on the proprietary interest which the citizens of that State may hold in this institution, in common with other property of the same description throughout the state.").

[252] The *Mazars* litigation continues into the summer of 2021. At least one House committee reissued a subpoena in March and the *Mazars* litigation continues before the lower courts. *See* Tal Axelrod, *House Oversight Panel Reissues Subpoena for Trump's Accounting Firm*, THE HILL (Mar. 3, 2021), https://thehill.com/regulation/court-battles/541323-house-oversight-committee -reissued-subpoena-for-trumps-accounting.

While in *Vance*, the presidency seemingly lost, the reality is that presidents will latch onto and attempt to expand the case's bits and pieces of pro-executive verbiage. The executive carefully relies upon Supreme Court cases as toeholds to expand presidential dispensations. For instance, the modern executive uses the phrase "executive privilege" to cover contexts never discussed by the Supreme Court, including "law-enforcement communications" and "attorney-client communications." Nothing in *United States v. Nixon* supports any of this. Expect presidents to charge state prosecutors with partisan motivations because this was an avenue left open by *Vance*.[253]

In *Vance*, the Court inadvertently brushed up against the proper inquiry. "[W]e cannot conclude that absolute immunity [from a state grand jury subpoena] is necessary or appropriate under Article II or the Supremacy Clause."[254] This was something like the right analysis conducted by the wrong institution. The question is whether any executive privilege or immunity is necessary and appropriate. But the two cited provisions do not grant the courts a roving commission to bestow whatever privileges they believe are necessary and proper. Rather, Congress enjoys a *necessary and proper power* to implement federal powers and safeguard federal institutions. It is for Congress to decide whether a privilege or immunity for the presidency would be useful and appropriate for implementing federal powers, including the president's constitutional powers.

The judiciary should beat a hasty retreat. They should stop inferring (or manufacturing) executive dispensations. If reliance on Congress works well for salaries, departments, officers, and pretty much everything else, it can work for presidential privileges and immunities as well. Let the first branch decide which dispensations are necessary and appropriate for the second.

---

[253] Trump v. Vance, 140 S. Ct. 2412, 2427–28 (2020). On remand, the president's lawyers argued bad faith and overbreadth. But the lower courts rejected such claims. *See* Trump v. Mazars, 977 F. 3d. 198 (2d Cir. 2020). The Supreme Court refused to intervene. In February of 2021, Mazars handed over millions of pages to the grand jury. Kara Scannell, Shimon Prokupecz & Devan Cole, *Trump's Tax Returns and Related Records Turned over to Manhattan District Attorney*, CNN (Feb. 25, 2021), https://edition.cnn.com/2021/02/25/politics/trump-taxes-mazars-vance/index.html.

[254] *Vance*, 140 S. Ct. at 2429.

REVA B. SIEGEL

WHY RESTRICT ABORTION? EXPANDING
THE FRAME ON JUNE MEDICAL

As the Supreme Court prepares to roll back protections for the abortion right, this Article analyzes the logic of pro-life constitutionalism in *June Medical Services L.L.C. v. Russo*.[1]

I expand the frame on *June Medical* to examine the logic of women-protective health-justified restrictions on abortion.[2] Do these laws protect women or the unborn—and how? By considering the history of the law at issue in *June Medical* and locating it in broader policy context, we can see how legislators who restricted abortion to protect women's health equated women's health with motherhood; they supported laws that push women into motherhood while declining to enact laws that provide for the health of pregnant women and the children they might bear.[3] Expanding the frame on Louisiana's pro-woman

Reva B. Siegel is Nicholas de B. Katzenbach Professor of Law, Yale University.

AUTHOR'S NOTE: For comments on the manuscript, I owe thanks to Cary Franklin, Linda Greenhouse, Melissa Murray, Douglas NeJaime, David Strauss, Geoffrey Stone, Julie Suk, and Bridget Fahey and participants in the University of Chicago Law School Constitutional Law Workshop. I am especially grateful to Duncan Hosie and Chelsea Thompson, as well as to Joshua Feinzig, Jordan Jefferson, Spurthi Jonnalagadda, Zain Lakhani, and Akanksha Shah, for research assistance and conversation about the article.

[1] 140 S. Ct. 2103 (2020).

[2] *See infra* Section II.B.

[3] *See infra* Section II.C.

The Supreme Court Review, 2021.

pro-life law shows us sex-role stereotyping in action, and demonstrates the intersectional injuries it can inflict.

From this vantage point, we can see that judges who refuse to scrutinize pro-life law making—on the grounds that it would involve judges in politics—help legitimate the claims about protecting women's health that supposedly justify the abortion restrictions, while revising the meaning of the Constitution's liberty and equality guarantees.[4] Reading the doctrinal debate in *June Medical* in this context identifies open and hidden efforts to roll back protections for the abortion right—and suggests how the Supreme Court that President Donald Trump helped fashion values women, health, life, truth, and democracy.

At the root of the conflict in *June Medical* is a question we might ask in many contexts. What does it mean to be pro-life? During a 2020 campaign debate, Senator Kamala Harris warned voters that "Donald Trump is in court right now trying to get rid of the Affordable Care Act" "in the midst of a public health pandemic when over 210,000 people have died and 7 million people probably have what will be . . . a preexisting condition because [they] contracted the virus. . . ."[5] Vice President Mike Pence countered this attack on his administration's health care policies by emphasizing its appointment of judges who oppose abortion: "I couldn't be more proud to serve as vice president to a president who stands without apology for the sanctity of human life. I'm pro-life," a claim he substantiated by appeal to the administration's last Supreme Court nomination, "For our part, I would never presume how Judge Amy Coney Barrett would rule on the Supreme Court of the United States, but we'll continue to stand strong for the right to life."[6]

Neither Harris nor Pence connected judgments about abortion and healthcare during the pandemic, but many others have. It is becoming increasingly common to probe commitments in the abortion debate by asking whether they extend to other contexts. Conservatives who oppose mask and shutdown orders have advanced their freedom claims in the abortion rights context by arguing that

---

[4] *See infra* Sections III.A, III.B.

[5] *October 07, 2020 Vice Presidential Debate Transcript*, Comm'n on Presidential Debates (Oct. 7, 2020), https://www.debates.org/voter-education/debate-transcripts/vice-presidential -debate-at-the-university-of-utah-in-salt-lake-city-utah/ (referencing the Patient Protection and Affordable Care Act of 2010, 42 U.S.C. § 18001 (2020)).

[6] *Id.*

liberals are inconsistent in their commitment to liberty. Representative Marjorie Taylor Greene attacked the House's mask rule by tweeting "my body, my choice,"[7] just as chants, signs, and T-shirts at shutdown protests have echoed the abortion rights slogan.[8] Claims about inconsistency run both ways. Critics of the Trump administration's public health response to the pandemic have regularly challenged its claim to be "pro-life." (Try searching "pro-life pandemic.")

We understand Pence's claim that he is "pro-life" and his pride in serving "as vice president to a president who stands without apology for the sanctity of human life" one way when we analyze abortion in a single-issue frame—and in another when we expand the frame to compare the Administration's policy choices about abortion with its other policy choices about life and health.[9] Expanding the frame and comparing the policy choices of pro-life advocates inside and outside the abortion debate can clarify beliefs and values espoused in the

---

[7] Nicole Via y Rada, *Rep.-elect Marjorie Taylor Greene Challenges House Mask Rule with 'My Body, My Choice,'* NBC NEWS (Nov. 13, 2020, 12:57 PM), https://www.nbcnews.com/politics/2020-election/live-blog/2020-11-13-trump-biden-transition-n1247607/ncrd1247735#blog Header (reporting that Greene, known for her "support for the far-right conspiracy theory QAnon," was employing a phrase used to reject mask mandates by "coronavirus protestors who opposed lockdowns and mask usage"). For use of the pro-choice slogan at shut-down protests, see Laura Vozella & Gregory S. Schneider, *With Picnic Baskets and Few Masks, Demonstrators Protest Virginia Stay-at-Home Orders*, WASH. POST (Apr. 16, 2020, 5:45 PM), https://www.washingtonpost.com/local/virginia-politics/with-picnic-baskets-and-few-masks-demonstrators-protest-virginia-stay-at-home-orders/2020/04/16/fe08b016-8016-11ea-8013-1b6da0e4a2b7_story.html, which documents protestors using "my body, my choice" language, and Justin Wingerter, *"My Body, My Choice": Inside Colorado's Growing Anti-Shutdown Movement*, DENVER POST (Apr. 25, 2020, 11:51 AM), https://www.denverpost.com/2020/04/25/coronavirus-shutdown-protests-colorado-politics.

[8] Marcie Bianco, *COVID-19 Mask Mandates in Wisconsin and Elsewhere Spark "My Body, My Choice" Hypocrisy*, NBC NEWS (Aug. 3, 2020, 11:11 AM), https://www.nbcnews.com/think/opinion/covid-19-mask-mandates-wisconsin-elsewhere-spark-my-body-my-ncna1235535.

[9] Pence led the Trump Administration's Coronavirus Task Force, often bending health policy to serve the Administration's political interests but sometimes resisting. *See* Mark Mazzetti et al., *Under Pence, Politics Regularly Seeped into the Coronavirus Task Force*, N.Y. TIMES (Oct. 8, 2020), https://www.nytimes.com/2020/10/08/us/politics/pence-coronavirus-task-force.html. Stories of the Trump Administration's management of the pandemic will take books. For a glimpse of the Task Force during the era of the vice-presidential debate, see Yasmeen Abutaleb et al., *Trump's Den of Dissent: Inside the White House Task Force as Coronavirus Surges*, WASH. POST (Oct. 19, 2020, 6:00 AM), https://www.washingtonpost.com/politics/trumps-den-of-dissent-inside-the-white-house-task-force-as-coronavirus-surges/2020/10/19/7ff8ee6a-0a6e-11eb-859b-f9c27abe638d_story.html; Brett Samuels, *Trump Adviser Scott Atlas Criticizes Plans to Avoid Seeing Elderly for Thanksgiving*, HILL (Nov. 17, 2020, 12:31 PM), https://thehill.com/policy/healthcare/526332-trump-adviser-scott-atlas-criticizes-plans-to-avoid-seeing-elderly-for.

abortion debate, as I have argued in a study of the policy choices of pro-life states.[10]

By expanding the frame on *June Medical Services L.L.C. v. Russo*,[11] this Article analyzes the Supreme Court's emerging approach to restrictions on abortion that claim to be woman-protective and health-justified. These laws, called by critics Targeted Regulations on Abortion Providers (TRAP laws), impose on abortion providers burdensome health and safety regulations not imposed on other medical practices of similar or even greater risk.[12] Health-justified abortion restrictions defy simple characterization, as the laws on their face restrict abortion to protect women rather than the unborn. To analyze the constitutional questions these abortion restrictions pose, I begin inside Supreme Court case law; I then expand the frame to consider the law at issue in *June Medical* in larger historical and policy context, and I then bring this external perspective to bear on the Justices' reasoning in the case. By examining the judgments about women and health driving passage of the law in *June Medical*, we can better assess the practice of constitutionalism that would immunize this exercise of state power from judicial review.

With the Supreme Court's composition transformed by pro-life appointments, the Court seems poised to change its approach to reviewing abortion restrictions, and this change in composition plays a prominent role in *June Medical* itself.[13] In 2016 in *Whole Woman's Health v. Hellerstedt*,[14] the Supreme Court found a Texas law requiring abortion providers to have admitting privileges at a hospital within 30 miles to be an undue burden under *Planned Parenthood v. Casey*,[15] reasoning that the law's health benefits were negligible in comparison to the burdens on access the law imposed by closing many of the state's

[10] *See* Reva B. Siegel, *ProChoiceLife: Asking Who Protects Life and How—and Why It Matters in Law and Politics*, 93 IND. L.J. 207, 207 (2018) ("If we expand the frame and analyze restrictions on abortion as one of many ways government can protect new life, we observe facts that escape notice when we debate abortion in isolation."); *id.* at 209 ("[M]any prolife jurisdictions lead in policies that restrict women's reproductive choices and lag in policies that support women's reproductive choices. Comparing state policies in this way makes clear that the means a state employs to protect new life reflects views about sex and property, as well as life.").

[11] 140 S. Ct. 2103 (2020).

[12] *See infra* notes 133–35 and accompanying text.

[13] *See infra* Section I.A.

[14] 136 S. Ct. 2292 (2016). *See infra* Section I.A.

[15] 505 U.S. 833, 877 (1992).

clinics.[16] In 2020 in *June Medical*, decided after Justice Kennedy re-
tired, the four justices who voted to strike down the Texas law in
Whole Woman's Health voted to strike down the Louisiana law modeled on it under the same standard. Chief Justice Roberts, who dissented in *Whole Woman's Health*, concurred in striking down the
Louisiana law on grounds of stare decisis, but then joined the *June
Medical* dissenters in attacking the plurality's "balancing" standard as
requiring judges to make "legislative" judgments faithless to *Casey*.[17]

As this claim suggests, the fight over balancing is a fight about
whether a Supreme Court transformed by pro-life appointments will
dilute the protections *Casey* provides for decisions about abortion.
The standard that conservatives attacked, which directs judges to
compare the benefits of a health-justified abortion restriction to the
law's burdens in closing clinics, is one way of determining the purpose
of health laws—TRAP laws—that impose burdensome restrictions on
abortion.

Why would legislatures adopt these indirect means of restricting
access to abortion, and why would judges insulate legislative sub-
terfuge from scrutiny? To answer these questions, I expand the frame
and examine the debate over health-justified restrictions on abortion
in wider historical and social context.

To examine the roots and logic of the admitting privileges restrictions at issue in *Whole Woman's Health* and *June Medical*, I return
to the 1990s, a time when the nation was coming to understand
women as constitutional rights holders differently than at the time of
Roe.[18] I show how emergent understandings of women as equal citizens shaped the ways the Supreme Court revised the law governing
abortion in *Casey* and the ways the antiabortion movement struggled
to restrict abortion in *Casey*'s wake. Appropriating feminist frames, the
antiabortion movement called this new generation of health-justified
abortion restrictions pro-woman, pro-life laws. As movement sources
show, pro-woman, pro-life laws restrict abortion to protect a pregnant
woman's health and to protect unborn life, reasoning from the traditional sex-role-based assumption that becoming a mother promotes

---

[16] *Whole Woman's Health*, 136 S. Ct. at 2311, 2313 (noting that the Texas law did not
"advance[] Texas' legitimate interest in protecting women's health" and "led to the closure of
half of Texas' clinics, or thereabouts").

[17] *See infra* Sections I.B, III.B.

[18] Roe v. Wade, 410 U.S. 113 (1973). *See infra* Sections II.A, II.B.

a woman's "health."[19] This historical perspective on the *June Medical* case makes clear why the admitting privileges statute and other health-justified restrictions on abortion implicate both the liberty and equality guarantees of federal and state constitutions.

I then analyze the traditional sex-role-based judgments the admitting privileges law enforced from a second vantage point. I expand the frame and examine how Louisiana protected women's health inside and outside the abortion context. At the same time as advocates for the admitting privileges statute spoke of the importance of protecting women's health and protecting life, the state enforced policies contributing to the state's exceedingly high maternal mortality and infant mortality rates.[20] We can read this disjuncture in policies as evidence that role-based judgments are in play and as an illustration of the harms these judgments can inflict, especially when directed against poor women of color.

Pro-life advocates who act from concern about intentional life-taking without a commitment to support life more generally may be prepared to impose costs on those they see as caregivers that the advocates are not prepared to impose on others or on the community as a whole. As we will see, pro-life advocacy of this kind is suspiciously selective, more concerned with control than care, and susceptible to status-based judgments when aimed at poor women and women of color. Not surprisingly, people and jurisdictions can express pro-life commitments for different reasons, and not all are simple expressions of care.

In short, expanding the frame allows us to be more discriminating in evaluating claims about protecting women and protecting life in the abortion debate. Expanding the frame on Louisiana's pro-woman pro-life law teaches us what sex-role stereotyping looks like in a wider range of contexts and demonstrates the intersectional injuries it can inflict.

It is only after examining the logic of the pro-woman, pro-life law at issue in *June Medical* that we can fully appreciate the doctrinal debate in the case. Examining *June Medical* in wider historical and policy context, we can see how the Justices who denounce balancing as legislative rather than judicial are directing judges to defer to state

---

[19] *See infra* Sections II.B (examining national movement), II.C.1 (examining legislative record in Louisiana).

[20] *See infra* Section II.C.2.

claims about health. This adds the courts' imprimatur to modern forms of protectionism that inflict physical and dignitary injuries on poor women. The Justices who denounce balancing as legislative rather than judicial are engaged in a political project at the very moment they claim to be avoiding entanglement in politics.[21] Far from promoting democracy, judicial review of this kind undermines democracy by preventing robust debate over the constitutional, political, and human stakes of the questions raised by public power of this kind.

As we expand the frame on *June Medical*, we see courts, the very institutions we rely on to warrant facts amidst claims of fake news, promoting the confusion of facts and values in the abortion debate. Excavating the story of *June Medical* in the midst of debate about the 2020 election and the greatest pandemic in a century, I found that the distinction between background and foreground too often disappeared, as claims about truth, lies, democracy, life, and health ricocheted between them. In this story, the Roberts Court too often acts as the Trump Court in the ways it protects life.

Part I shows how President Trump's promise to nominate pro-life judges shaped the Supreme Court that decided *June Medical*, its membership continuing to evolve as President Trump replaced Justice Ruth Bader Ginsburg with Justice Amy Coney Barrett in the midst of the 2020 election. Part II expands the frame and situates the doctrinal debate in *June Medical* in historical and policy contexts. Part III returns to the terrain of doctrine and analyzes the Court's debate over balancing with attention to the kinds of pro-life lawmaking that federal judges will scrutinize or legitimate.

I close Part III by considering how the abortion question stands as Justice Barrett takes Justice Ginsburg's seat. Justice Barrett has already cast a vote in *Food and Drug Administration v. American College of Obstetricians*.[22] She was silent as the conservative majority allowed the federal government to enforce a TRAP regulation requiring women to travel to access medication abortion in the midst of the pandemic,[23] prompting Justices Sotomayor and Kagan to conclude their dissent in the words of Justice Ginsburg.[24] As an advocate and a Justice, Ginsburg understood the Constitution's guarantees of liberty and equality

---

[21] *See infra* Sections III.A, III.B.

[22] 141 S. Ct. 578 (2021) (mem.).

[23] *See infra* Section III.C.1; text accompanying notes 313–27.

[24] *See infra* text accompanying note 327.

to limit the ways that government can regulate pregnant women. By considering the limits on coercion that Justice Ginsburg long defended, we can begin to appreciate how the abortion decisions of Justice Barrett and other conservative Justices may change the meaning of constitutional principles and the forms of constitutional protection generations of Americans have looked to the Court to enforce.[25]

Courts do not always have the last word. As I show, frame expansion is now a regular part of the abortion debate and may enable the public to probe the logic of abortion restrictions when federal courts no longer will. The Conclusion reflects on the ways this debate about the meaning of pro-life law has exploded in the era of the pandemic.

I. The Question in *June Medical*

Change in abortion law is imminent. After promising "I am pro-life, and I will be appointing pro-life judges" who will return broad power over abortion law to the states,[26] President Trump seated three justices on the Supreme Court with the goal of weakening, or eliminating, a half century of law that protects women's liberty to decide whether to continue a pregnancy—a constitutional guarantee first announced in *Roe* and reaffirmed in 1992 in *Casey*. Through appointments battles that were each distinctively tumultuous, Justice Gorsuch took Justice Scalia's seat, Justice Kavanaugh took Justice Kennedy's seat, and Justice Amy Coney Barrett took Justice Ginsburg's seat.[27]

---

[25] *See infra* Sections III.C.2, III.C.3.

[26] Aaron Blake, *The Final Trump-Clinton Debate Transcript, Annotated*, Wash. Post (Oct. 19, 2016, 9:29 PM), https://www.washingtonpost.com/news/the-fix/wp/2016/10/19/the-final-trump-clinton-debate-transcript-annotated. During the campaign, Trump repeatedly promised to nominate Supreme Court justices who would overturn *Roe* and called this a "litmus test" for selecting nominees. *See* Press Release, Senate Democratic Caucus, *President Trump Wants a Supreme Court That Will Overturn* Roe v. Wade (July 5, 2018), https://www.democrats.senate.gov/newsroom/press-releases/president-trump-wants-a-supreme-court-that-will-overturn-roe-v-wade_thats-why-the-far-right-federalist-society-wrote-his-list-of-potential-high-court-picks (predicting the Court will overturn *Roe v. Wade* "automatically, in my opinion, because I am putting pro-life justices on the court"). In addition to these Supreme Court appointments, President Trump significantly changed the composition of the lower federal courts. *See* Rebecca R. Ruiz, Robert Gebeloff, Steve Eder & Ben Protess, *A Conservative Agenda Unleashed on the Federal Courts*, N.Y. Times (Mar. 16, 2020), https://www.nytimes.com/2020/03/14/us/trump-appeals-court-judges.html.

[27] *See* Amelia Thomson-DeVeaux, Laura Bronner & Anna Wiederkehr, *What the Supreme Court's Unusually Big Jump to the Right Might Look Like*, FiveThirtyEight (Sept. 22, 2020),

June Medical is a symptom of these shifts in the Supreme Court's composition. I first consider the question in *June Medical* as a question about the way a court functions through changes in its composition and then consider how the dispute over legal standards in the case is tied to the evolving shape of the abortion conflict.

A. WHICH COURT? HOW TRUMP'S APPOINTMENTS
   CHANGE THE COURT'S MIND

The question in *June Medical* was whether an abortion restriction the Court declared unconstitutional in 2016 in *Whole Woman's Health* would remain unconstitutional after President Trump replaced Justice Kennedy, who voted with the majority in *Whole Woman's Health*, with Justice Kavanaugh.[28] To determine whether the restriction imposed an undue burden having the purpose or effect of creating a substantial obstacle to abortion access under *Casey*,[29] the Court ruled in *Whole Woman's Health* that a judge should compare the benefits of the law to the burdens on access its enforcement posed.[30] In 2020, in *June Medical*, the four justices who voted to strike down the Texas admitting privileges law evaluated the Louisiana law under the same standard; Chief Justice Roberts, who dissented in *Whole Woman's Health*, concurred in striking down the Louisiana law on grounds of stare decisis but then joined the dissenters in attacking the plurality's "balancing" standard as requiring judges to make "legislative" judgments faithless to *Casey*.[31] "Nothing about *Casey* suggested that a weighing of costs and benefits of an abortion regulation was a job for the courts," Roberts objected.[32]

Debate about whether Chief Justice Roberts had changed the law had barely begun when President Trump seized the opportunity of

---

https://fivethirtyeight.com/features/what-the-supreme-courts-unusually-big-jump-to-the-right-might-look-like.

[28] Sheryl Gay Stolberg, *Kavanaugh Is Sworn in After Close Confirmation Vote in Senate*, N.Y. TIMES (Oct. 6, 2018), https://www.nytimes.com/2018/10/06/us/politics/brett-kavanaugh-supreme-court.html. This was not the first time a change in the Supreme Court's composition led to a change in abortion law. *See* GEOFFREY STONE, SEX AND THE CONSTITUTION 427 (2017) (discussing how shifts in the Court's composition led to the Court's decision in Gonzales v. Carhart, 550 U.S. 124 (2007)).

[29] Planned Parenthood of Se. Pa. v. Casey, 505 U.S. 833, 877 (1992).

[30] *See infra* Section I.B.

[31] *See infra* Sections I.B, III.B.

[32] June Med. Servs. L.L.C. v. Russo, 140 S. Ct. 2103, 2136 (2020) (Roberts, C.J., concurring).

Justice Ruth Bader Ginsburg's passing to appoint, in the midst of mail-in and early voting for the presidential election, Justice Amy Coney Barrett.[33] Vice President Pence pointed to Barrett as proof that his administration "stand[s] strong for the right to life."[34] Barrett had signed published statements making clear her strong opposition to abortion and "the Supreme Court's infamous *Roe v. Wade* decision" and calling "for the unborn to be protected in law," she had questioned the power of stare decisis to bind the Court, and she had voted to uphold abortion restrictions during her brief tenure on the Seventh Circuit.[35]

Several courts had already ruled that Chief Justice Roberts's opinion had modified the *Whole Woman's Health* framework[36] even before the nomination of Justice Barrett emboldened others to call for yet more dramatic changes in the Court's approach to health-justified restrictions on abortion. Only hours after Republicans on the Senate Judiciary Committee voted to approve Barrett's nomination to the Supreme Court, the Mississippi attorney general filed a supplemental brief urging the Court to review a Fifth Circuit decision striking down the state's 15-week health-justified abortion ban, "a case that directly challenges *Roe v. Wade* and has the potential to reverse the landmark 1973 decision."[37] The supplemental brief

---

[33] Joan Biskupic, *Amy Coney Barrett Joins the Supreme Court in Unprecedented Times*, CNN (Oct. 27, 2020, 11:09 AM), https://www.cnn.com/2020/10/27/politics/amy-coney-barrett-joins -supreme-court-unprecedented/index.html. In-person voting for the 2020 presidential election began in early September. *See* Sarah Almukhtar, Isabella Grullón Paz & Alicia Parlapiano, *2020 Presidential Election Calendar*, N.Y. Times (Sept. 21, 2020), https://www.nytimes.com/interactive /2019/us/elections/2020-presidential-election-calendar.html.

[34] Comm'n on Presidential Debates, *supra* note 5.

[35] *See* Adam Liptak, *Barrett's Record: A Conservative Who Would Push the Supreme Court Right*, N.Y. Times (Nov. 2, 2020), https://www.nytimes.com/article/amy-barrett-views-issues.html; Anna North, *What Amy Coney Barrett on the Supreme Court Means for Abortion Rights*, Vox (Oct. 26, 2020, 8:17 PM), https://www.vox.com/21456044/amy-coney-barrett-supreme-court-roe -abortion; *see also* Andrew Kaczynski & Em Steck, *Amy Coney Barrett Initially Failed to Disclose Talks on* Roe v. Wade *Hosted by Anti-Abortion Groups on Senate Paperwork*, CNN (Oct. 9, 2020, 10:53 PM), https://www.cnn.com/2020/10/09/politics/kfile-amy-coney-barrett-roe-v-wade-talks /index.html; Rebecca R. Ruiz, *Amy Coney Barrett Signed an Ad in 2006 Urging Overturning the "Barbaric Legacy" of* Roe v. Wade, N.Y. Times (Oct. 1, 2020, 12:50 PM), https://www.nytimes .com/2020/10/01/us/elections/amy-coney-barrett-roe-v-wade.html. For other sources, see Section III.C.

[36] *See* Hopkins v. Jegley, 968 F.3d 912 (8th Cir. 2020); EMW Women's Surg. Ctr. v. Friedlander, 978 F.3d 418 (6th Cir. 2020); *see also infra* Section III.B. *But see* Whole Woman's Health v. Paxton, 972 F.3d 649 (5th Cir. 2020).

[37] Kate Smith, *Mississippi Asks Supreme Court Again to Review Its 15-Week Abortion Ban*, CBS News (Oct. 29, 2020, 8:54 PM), https://www.cbsnews.com/news/mississippi-abortion-ban

pointed to the division of authority on how to read *June Medical* as raising the question "[w]hether the validity of a pre-viability law that protects women's health, the dignity of unborn children, and the integrity of the medical profession and society should be analyzed under *Casey*'s 'undue burden' standard or *Hellerstedt*'s balancing of benefits and burdens."[38]

B. BALANCING? THE QUESTION POSED BY WOMAN-PROTECTIVE ABORTION RESTRICTIONS

To understand the dispute in and about *June Medical*—that is, to understand why conservatives on and off the Court have attacked "*Hellerstedt*'s balancing of benefits and burdens"[39]—one has to ask a simple question: why restrict abortion? There is a stock answer to this question, so conventional in the abortion debate it passes without notice: states restrict abortion out of concern for unborn life.[40] But observe that states justified their admitting privilege laws in *Whole Woman's Health* and *June Medical* on the grounds that the laws protected women's health, not unborn life or its potentiality.[41] It is now common for states to defend burdensome and clinic-closing restrictions on abortion as health and safety laws that protect women rather than the unborn.[42] Is the claim to protect women's health

---

-supreme-court-considering-review; *see* Jackson Women's Health Org. v. Dobbs, 945 F.3d 265, 268–69 (5th Cir. 2019) ("In an unbroken line dating to *Roe v. Wade*, the Supreme Court's abortion cases have established (and affirmed, and re-affirmed) a woman's right to choose an abortion before viability. States may regulate abortion procedures . . . but they may not ban abortions. The law at issue is a ban.").

[38] Petition for Writ of Certiorari Supplemental Brief at 1, Dobbs v. Jackson Women's Health Org., No. 19–1392 (U.S. Oct. 22, 2020).

[39] *Id.*

[40] *See* Roe v. Wade, 410 U.S. 113, 159 (1973) ("It is reasonable and appropriate for a State to decide that at some point in time another interest, that of health of the mother or that of potential human life, becomes significantly involved. The woman's privacy is no longer sole and any right of privacy she possesses must be measured accordingly.").

[41] *See* Brief for Respondents at 31, Whole Woman's Health v. Hellerstedt, 136 S. Ct. 2292 (2016) (No. 15–274) ("Nothing close to clear proof of an unconstitutional purpose exists. . . . [Texas'] HB2 was enacted to 'increase the health and safety' of abortion patients and provide them with 'the highest standard of health care.'" (citation omitted)); Brief in Opposition at 9, June Med. Servs. L.L.C. v. Russo, 140 S. Ct. 2103 (2020) (No. 18–1323) (asserting "that [Louisiana] Act 620's hospital admitting-privileges requirement would address serious safety concerns relating to the lack of any meaningful credentialing review of doctors who provide abortions in Louisiana").

[42] *See* Linda Greenhouse & Reva B. Siegel, Casey *and the Clinic Closings: When "Protecting Health" Obstructs Choice*, 125 YALE L.J. 1428, 1446–49 (2016) (discussing targeted restrictions on abortion clinics).

credible? Why would it matter if, instead, the state sought to protect potential life, given that this purpose is generally thought to be benign, or even sacred?

This is the question lurking beneath the debate over doctrinal standards in *June Medical*. Writing for the *June Medical* plurality, Justice Breyer explained that the standard of review the Court employed in *Whole Woman's Health* derived from the Court's prior decisions in *Casey* and *Gonzales v. Carhart*:[43]

> In *Whole Woman's Health*, we quoted *Casey* in explaining that "'a statute which, while furthering [a] valid state interest has the effect of placing a substantial obstacle in the path of a woman's choice cannot be considered a permissible means of serving its legitimate ends.'" [*Whole Woman's Health*] at 2309 (quoting *Casey*). We added that "'*[u]nnecessary* health regulations'" impose an unconstitutional "'undue burden'" if they have "'the purpose or effect of presenting a substantial obstacle to a woman seeking an abortion.'" [*Whole Woman's Health*] at 2309 (quoting *Casey*)].[44]

To enforce *Casey*'s standard, the plurality explained, *Whole Woman's Health* directed courts to "consider the burdens a law imposes on abortion access together with the benefits those laws confer," and emphasized that courts "'retai[n] an independent constitutional duty to review factual findings where constitutional rights are at stake.'"[45]

Why does *Whole Woman's Health* (1) direct judges to enforce *Casey*'s standard by considering the burdens and benefits of a health regulation and (2) reaffirm *Carhart*'s direction that the courts "'retai[n] an independent constitutional duty to review factual findings where constitutional rights are at stake'"?

Much of this law is concerned with probing purpose.[46] Is a legislature using a health regulation to obstruct access to abortion in ways that *Casey* proscribes?[47] The framework *Whole Woman's Health* adopted for enforcing *Casey*'s undue burden standard enables a judge to determine, as *Casey* requires, whether a legislature enacted a health

---

[43] 550 U.S. 124 (2007).

[44] *June Medical*, 140 S. Ct. 2103, 2120 (2020) (plurality opinion) (quoting Whole Woman's Health v. Hellerstedt, 136 S. Ct. 2292, 2309 (2016) (quoting Planned Parenthood of Se. Pa. v. Casey, 505 U.S. 833, 877–78 (1992) (plurality opinion))) (citations partially omitted).

[45] *Id.* (quoting *Whole Woman's Health*, 136 S. Ct. at 2310, 2324 (quoting *Gonzales*, 550 U.S at 165)).

[46] *See infra* Section III.A.

[47] *See infra* Section II.A.

regulation with the purpose or effect of imposing a substantial obstacle to abortion without entering into potentially protracted and
inflammatory disputes about characterizing the purposes of legislatures that restrict abortion access.[48]

For empowering judges to enforce *Casey*'s undue burden standard
by means that avoided impugning a legislature's purpose, Justice
Breyer was attacked by Justice Thomas, who claimed in his *Whole
Woman's Health* dissent that "the majority's free-form balancing test
is contrary to *Casey*"[49] and asserted that the "Court should abandon
the pretense that anything other than policy preferences underlies its
balancing of constitutional rights and interests in any given case."[50]
Chief Justice Roberts joined other conservatives in a dissent arguing
that claim preclusion barred the Court's consideration of the case.[51]

In *June Medical*, Chief Justice Roberts voted to strike down Louisiana's admitting privileges law on the ground that the Court should
treat the Texas and Louisiana laws alike[52] but then incorporated into
his concurring opinion a critique of the *Whole Woman's Health* decision drawn from Justice Thomas's dissent in that case.[53] Chief Justice
Roberts invoked stare decisis as a reason for enforcing precedent
and as a reason for criticizing, and potentially revising, precedent:
"*Stare decisis* principles also determine how we handle a decision that
itself departed from the cases that came before it. In those instances,
'[r]emaining true to an 'intrinsically sounder' doctrine established in
prior cases better serves the values of *stare decisis* than would following'
the recent departure."[54] In Justice Roberts's view, stare decisis did not

---

[48] For an example of such an exchange, see *infra* text accompanying notes 377–79 (reporting
heated exchange in the Fifth Circuit between Judge Carlton Reeves and Judge James Ho).

[49] *Whole Woman's Health*, 136 S. Ct. at 2324 (Thomas, J., dissenting).

[50] *Id.* at 2328. Justice Thomas also proffered a reading of the abortion cases as governed by
rational basis review, but then attacked the tiers of scrutiny as a judicial graft at odds with the
original understanding. *Id.* at 2323–31 ("A law either infringes a constitutional right, or not;
there is no room for the judiciary to invent tolerable degrees of encroachment.").

[51] *Id.* at 2330 (Alito, J., dissenting).

[52] June Med. Servs. L.L.C. v. Russo, 140 S. Ct. 2103, 2134 (2020) (Roberts, C.J., concurring) ("The legal doctrine of stare decisis requires us, absent special circumstances, to treat
like cases alike. The Louisiana law imposes a burden on access to abortion just as severe as
that imposed by the Texas law, for the same reasons. Therefore Louisiana's law cannot stand
under our precedents.").

[53] *Cf. supra* text accompanying notes 49–50.

[54] *June Med. Servs.*, 140 S. Ct. at 2134–35 (quoting Adarand Constructors, Inc. v. Peña, 515
U.S. 200, 231 (1995) (plurality opinion)).

require "adherence to the latest decision,'"[55] but might be used as an instrument of its revision.[56]

Chief Justice Roberts employed his opinion proclaiming the importance of standing by *Whole Woman's Health* to attack the decision's direction to judges who are enforcing *Casey*'s undue burden standard to compare the burdens and benefits of a health-justified restriction on abortion:

> [C]ourts applying a balancing test would be asked in essence to weigh the State's interests in "protecting the potentiality of human life" and the health of the woman, on the one hand, against the woman's liberty interest in defining her "own concept of existence, of meaning, of the universe, and of the mystery of human life" on the other. [*Casey*] at 851. . . . Pretending that we could pull that off would require us to act as legislators, not judges, and would result in nothing other than an "unanalyzed exercise of judicial will" in the guise of a "neutral utilitarian calculus."[57]

In this remarkable passage, Chief Justice Roberts employed his opinion explaining the importance of the Court standing by its decision in *Whole Woman's Health* to argue that the direction *Whole Woman's Health* provided judges to consider burdens and benefits of a health-justified abortion restriction was not rooted in *Casey* and was beyond a court's competence because it was legislative rather than judicial in nature. The passage criticizing *Whole Woman's Health* for lack of fidelity to *Casey* itself mocked *Casey*[58] and raised questions about the scope of courts' authority to enforce constitutional law protecting women's decisions about abortion. Was the Chief Justice following *Whole Woman's Health* and *Casey*—or instead rewriting

---

[55] *Id.* at 2135 ("Stare decisis is pragmatic and contextual, not 'a mechanical formula of adherence to the latest decision.'" (quoting Helvering v. Hallock, 309 U.S. 106, 119 (1940))). *See* Melissa Murray, Comment, *The Symbiosis of Abortion and Precedent*, 134 HARV. L. REV. 308, 325 (2020) (arguing that "Chief Justice Roberts's respect for precedent depended entirely on identifying those aspects of past decisions that he wished to follow and those that he did not").

[56] This is not unprecedented in the Court's abortion cases, as Melissa Murray has observed. *See* Murray, *supra* note 55, at 327 ("In this politically pitched context, the Court has developed an approach to precedent that at once has generated important, and often incremental, doctrinal changes and simultaneously preserved the appearance of fealty to its past decisions. In these cases, the Court has distinguished and cabined earlier decisions, forging a line of jurisprudence that entrenches the abortion right while sharply limiting its scope."). For a close reading of the ways that Chief Justice Roberts' concurrence in *June Medical* sought to revise *Casey*, see *infra* text accompanying notes 247–53 and Section III.B.

[57] *June Med. Servs.*, 140 S. Ct. at 2135–36 (citations partially omitted).

[58] *See infra* text accompanying notes 249–51.

them? Commentators in the wake of the decision immediately divided about its meaning and portents.[59]

Even if changes in the composition of the Court have undermined Chief Justice Roberts's power to control the direction of its abortion decisions, it remains important to answer the questions he raised about law governing woman-protective abortion restrictions. His opinion channeled conservative objections to law governing health-justified restrictions on abortion under *Casey* and subsequent decisions and so promises to play a role in coming cases, given the many statutes restricting abortion in the name of protecting women's health that will be reviewed in federal and state courts.[60]

Is there a constitutional problem if health-justified restrictions on abortion in fact reflect concern about the unborn rather than women?[61] Is there a constitutional problem if laws restricting abortion reflect concerns about women as they claim to—but the claims about women's health instead express views about women's roles?[62] Are all reasons for restricting abortion equally benign, or are some constitutionally suspect?

II. *Casey*: Liberty, Equality, and the Turn to Health-Justified Abortion Restrictions

To surface the constitutional conflict lurking beneath arguments over balancing, I look back at the path from *Casey* to the

---

[59] As Dahlia Lithwick observed, initial responses to *June Medical* split along gendered lines. Dahlia Lithwick, *What's Left of* Roe v. Wade? *Exploring the Division of Opinion in June Medical Services LLC v. Russo*, SLATE (July 4, 2020, 6:00 AM), https://slate.com/podcasts/amicus/2020/07 /john-roberts-june-medical. *Compare* Noah Feldman, *Roberts Finally Makes His Position on Abortion Clear*, BLOOMBERG (June 30, 2020, 10:55 AM), https://www.bloombergquint.com/gadfly/su preme-court-abortion-ruling-will-loom-over-2020-election, *and* Jeffrey Toobin, *John Roberts Distances Himself from the Trump-McConnell Legal Project*, NEW YORKER (June 30, 2020), https:// www.newyorker.com/news/daily-comment/john-roberts-dissociates-himself-from-the-trump -mcconnell-legal-project, *and* Laurence H. Tribe, *Roberts's Approach Could End Up Being More Protective of Abortion Rights–Not Less*, WASH. POST (July 1, 2020, 2:24 PM), https://www .washingtonpost.com/opinions/2020/07/01/robertss-approach-could-end-up-being-more -protective-abortion-rights-not-less, *with* Leah Litman, June Medical *as the New* Casey, TAKE CARE (June 29, 2020), https://takecareblog.com/blog/june-medical-as-the-new-casey.

[60] *See infra* Sections III.A, III.B.

[61] *See* O. Carter Snead, *The Way Forward After* June Medical, FIRST THINGS (July 4, 2020), https://www.firstthings.com/web-exclusives/2020/07/the-way-forward-after-june-medical (reviewing *June Medical* and observing "[w]e have no choice but to continue to fight for the lives and dignity of these most vulnerable members of the human family").

[62] *See id.* (reviewing *June Medical* and observing "there is powerful evidence available that women have not, in fact, structured their lives around the freedom to choose abortion, nor does their flourishing depend on it").

admitting privileges cases. This retrospective serves at least two purposes. It revisits the Court's decision to narrow and to reaffirm the abortion right in *Casey*, identifying the constitutional reasons the Court adopted the undue burden standard. And it reconstructs how, in the years after *Casey*, arguments against abortion increasingly focused on protecting women.

I show how in the 1990s, abortion jurisprudence and antiabortion advocacy in fact evolved together in response to an emergent understanding of women as equal rights-holders in the American constitutional order. This account suggests why, in the years after *Casey*, a movement calling itself "pro-life" increasingly came to call itself "pro-woman" and to advocate women's-health-justified restrictions on abortion, and how *Casey* speaks to this body of law.

One can see the Court and the antiabortion movement grappling with the same currents in Americans' understanding of abortion twenty years after *Roe*. But one can also read in these developments the antiabortion movement's self-conscious efforts to reshape its arguments and tactics in response to the *Casey* decision in an effort to narrow and evade *Casey*'s constraints in a world where appearing to respect women's rights and welfare matters.

After showing why health-justified restrictions on abortion spread in the years after *Casey*, I demonstrate how these national developments shape the passage and defense of the Louisiana law at issue in *June Medical*. Tracing the development of the laws the Court reviewed in *Whole Woman's Health* and *June Medical* shows the many ways that pro-woman, pro-life laws violate *Casey* and the understanding of the Constitution's liberty and equality guarantees it vindicates. This encounter with pro-woman, pro-life law vividly demonstrates the constitutional, political, and human stakes of the fight over "balancing," which we will return to in Part III.

A. UNDUE BURDEN: THE CONSTITUTIONAL VALUES
THE CASEY PRINCIPLE VINDICATES

In 1992, the Supreme Court was widely expected to reverse its decision protecting women's decisions about abortion; instead, the Court's decision in *Casey* reaffirmed and narrowed *Roe*.[63] The framework the Court adopted in *Casey* was responsive to contending

---

[63] *See* Serena Mayeri, *Undue-ing* Roe: *Constitutional Conflict and Political Polarization in* Planned Parenthood v. Casey, *in* REPRODUCTIVE RIGHTS AND JUSTICE STORIES 137, 146–49

movement claims about the importance of protecting unborn life and about the importance of protecting women's decisions about abortion.[64]

Unlike *Roe*, *Casey* allowed states to restrict abortion in the interest of protecting potential life before viability,[65] but only so long as government protected potential life by means of persuading women, not obstructing or coercing them. This is the core principle that the undue burden standard enforces—why the undue burden standard is concerned with substantial obstacles to the exercise of free choice. The joint opinion defined an "undue burden" as "a state regulation [that] has the purpose or effect of placing a substantial obstacle in the path of a woman seeking an abortion of a nonviable fetus."[66] It explained: "A statute with this purpose is invalid because the means chosen by the State to further the interest in potential life must be calculated to inform the woman's free choice, not hinder it."[67]

Before viability, any constraints on a woman's access to abortion must be designed to "inform" and not "hinder" a woman's free choice—to persuade, not interfere, obstruct, or coerce. The principle that government could "inform, not hinder" a woman's choice meant that government could impose some regulatory burdens in the effort to dissuade a woman from ending a pregnancy but only insofar as the law's purpose was to persuade.[68] The joint opinion extended the same framework to health-justified restrictions on abortion: "As with any medical procedure, the State may enact regulations to further the health or safety of a woman seeking an abortion. Unnecessary health regulations that have the purpose or effect of presenting a substantial obstacle to a woman seeking an abortion impose an undue burden on

---

(Melissa Murray, Kate Shaw & Reva B. Siegel eds., 2019); STONE, *supra* note 28, at 415–20; *see also* Greenhouse & Siegel, *supra* note 42, at 1435 & n.34.

[64] Greenhouse & Siegel, *supra* note 42, at 1436.

[65] Planned Parenthood of Se. Pa. v. Casey, 505 U.S. 833, 873 (1992) (criticizing *Roe* as it "undervalues the State's interest in the potential life within the woman" in practice).

[66] *Id.* at 877.

[67] *Id. See also id.* ("Some guiding principles should emerge. What is at stake is the woman's right to make the ultimate decision, not a right to be insulated from all others in doing so. Regulations which do no more than create a structural mechanism by which the State, or the parent or guardian of a minor, may express profound respect for the life of the unborn are permitted, if they are not a substantial obstacle to the woman's exercise of the right to choose.").

[68] *Id.* at 878 ("[T]he State may take measures to ensure that the woman's choice is informed, and measures designed to advance this interest will not be invalidated as long as their purpose is to persuade the woman to choose childbirth over abortion."); *see also* Greenhouse & Siegel, *supra* note 42, at 1439–40.

the right."[69] The joint opinion defined *Casey*'s undue burden standard through a principle designed to preserve constitutional protections for liberty—for women's right to choose—at the heart of *Roe*.[70]

Yet the Court's understanding of liberty had evolved. Two decades after *Roe*, *Casey* informed constitutional protections for women's right to choose with an understanding of women's equal citizenship that was only emergent at the time of *Roe*.[71] The Court handed down *Roe* just before the Court extended equal protection to sex discrimination in *Frontiero v. Richardson*[72] and at a time when Justice Blackmun and his brethren on an all-male bench had difficulty understanding the sex-role stereotyping women faced when pregnant.[73] (The year after *Roe*, Blackmun voted against a pregnancy discrimination claim in *Geduldig v. Aiello*.[74]) Two decades later in *Casey*, Justice Blackmun, responding to advocates' arguments,[75] recognized that restrictions on abortion enforce traditional sex roles and so "also implicate constitutional guarantees of gender equality."[76]

---

[69] *Casey*, 505 U.S. at 878.

[70] *See* Roe v. Wade, 410 U.S. 113, 153 (1973) ("This right of privacy, whether it be founded in the Fourteenth Amendment's concept of personal liberty and restrictions upon state action, as we feel it is, or, as the District Court determined, in the Ninth Amendment's reservation of rights to the people, is broad enough to encompass a woman's decision whether or not to terminate her pregnancy.").

[71] Before *Roe*, advocates had argued that abortion restrictions enforced sex, class, and race inequalities; the Burger Court was moved to recognize women as rights holders, but not to ground the abortion right in the Equal Protection Clause. *See* Linda Greenhouse & Reva B. Siegel, *The Unfinished Story of* Roe, *in* REPRODUCTIVE RIGHTS AND JUSTICE STORIES 53, 56–57, 63–65, 68–69 (Melissa Murray, Kate Shaw & Reva B. Siegel eds., 2019). But women's rights challenges to abortion statutes plainly shaped the Court's reasoning in *Roe*, so that over multiple drafts of the opinion the Court came to recognize that "women's interest in retaining control over the decision whether to become a mother is of constitutional magnitude." Reva B. Siegel, Roe's Roots: *The Women's Rights Claims that Engendered* Roe, 90 BOST. UNIV. L. REV. 1875, 1894 (2010); *see id.* at 1894–96 (showing how impact litigation influenced the Court's understanding of the right).

[72] 411 U.S. 677 (1973).

[73] *See* Reva B. Siegel, *The Pregnant Citizen from Suffrage to the Present*, 108 GEO. L.J. 167, 191–94 (2020) (discussing opinions and papers of the justices discussing claims of pregnancy discrimination in the early 1970s); STONE, *supra* note 28, at 397.

[74] 417 U.S. 484 (1974).

[75] *See* Mayeri, *supra* note 63, at 150–52.

[76] Planned Parenthood of Se. Pa. v. Casey, 505 U.S. 833, 928–29 (1992) (Blackmun, J., concurring in part, concurring in the judgment in part, and dissenting in part) ("The State does not compensate women for their services [bearing and caring for children]; instead, it assumes that they owe this duty as a matter of course. This assumption—that women can simply be forced to accept the "natural" status and incidents of motherhood—appears to rest upon a conception of women's role that has triggered the protection of the Equal Protection Clause.") (citations omitted).

Just as Blackmun presented the abortion right as protecting women against state action enforcing sex roles, the joint opinion described the liberty interest in *Roe* as protecting women against state action enforcing traditional conceptions of "the woman's role, however dominant that vision has been in the course of our history and our culture. The destiny of the woman must be shaped to a large extent on her own conception of her spiritual imperatives and her place in society."[77]

In explaining how women relied on the right *Roe* protected—"[t]he ability of women to participate equally in the economic and social life of the Nation has been facilitated by their ability to control their reproductive lives"[78]—and in applying the undue burden standard to a law requiring women to give their spouses notice before they could end a pregnancy,[79] the joint opinion protected women's liberty on the premise that women are equal citizens who are entitled to protection from the forms of role-based coercion long employed to enforce and justify limits on their civic participation.[80] The joint opinion expressed "constitutional limitations on abortion laws in the language of its equal protection sex discrimination opinions, illuminating liberty concerns at the heart of the sex equality cases in the very act of recognizing equality concerns at the root of its liberty cases."[81]

But the most fundamental expression of these sex-equality commitments is *Casey*'s core principle: government can protect potential life by persuading and enlisting women but not coercing and instrumentalizing women as means to protect the unborn. *Casey* allowed "government to protect potential life by means that recognize and preserve women's dignity. . . . If government wants to protect unborn life, it has to respectfully enlist women in this project and cannot simply commandeer women's lives for these purposes."[82]

---

[77] *Id.* at 852 (plurality opinion).

[78] *Id.* at 835.

[79] *See id.* at 887–98; *id.* at 898 ("The husband's interest in the life of the child his wife is carrying does not permit the State to empower him with this troubling degree of authority over his wife.").

[80] Greenhouse & Siegel, *supra* note 42, at 1440–41 (discussing the sex-equality values the joint opinion invokes in holding that a spousal notice requirement is an undue burden).

[81] Reva B. Siegel, *Sex Equality Arguments for Reproductive Rights: Their Critical Basis and Evolving Constitutional Expression*, 56 EMORY L.J. 815, 831 (2007).

[82] Greenhouse & Siegel, *supra* note 42, at 1437; *see id.* at 1439–42 (observing that the different applications of the undue burden framework illustrate that the government must employ "modes of persuasion that are consistent with the dignity of women"). Constraints on

In short, by the time the Court narrowed and reaffirmed *Roe* in *Casey*, the Court had come to reason about state action regulating the conduct of pregnant women through the lens of the antistereotyping and antisubordination values of its equal protection cases, expressed so powerfully by Justice Ginsburg only a few years later in *United States v. Virginia*[83] and Chief Justice Rehnquist in *Nevada Department of Human Resources v. Hibbs*.[84]

B. WOMEN AS MOTHERS, WOMEN AS EQUALS: CASEY AND THE SPREAD OF WOMAN-PROTECTIVE ANTIABORTION ARGUMENT

Casey was a bitter disappointment for Americans United for Life (AUL), a key organization in developing strategies to erode political and legal support for *Roe*. The organization hoped to legislate and litigate *Roe*'s reversal; instead, *Casey* entrenched *Roe* and explained the abortion right as protecting women's liberty as equal citizens.[85] Several months later, the nation elected Bill Clinton, its first strongly pro-choice president.[86] Violent attacks on abortion clinics and providers, which had escalated during the 1980s, "ticked up dramatically in the 1990s" with a series of high-profile murders of clinic doctors, employees, and security personnel.[87]

---

the instrumentalization of women explain the joint opinion's requirement that government persuade by "the giving of truthful, nonmisleading" information. *Id.* at 1439 (quoting *Casey*, 505 U.S. at 882).

[83] 518 U.S. 515, 533–34 (1996); *see also* Siegel, *supra* note 73, 203–06 (discussing how *Virginia* reaffirms a heightened scrutiny standard for sex-based state action and addresses laws regulating pregnancy as containing sex-based classifications subject to heightened scrutiny).

[84] 538 U.S. 721, 736 (2003); *see also* Siegel, *supra* note 73, 206–09 (tracing evolution in Court's understanding of pregnancy discrimination). For nearly a half century, Justice Ginsburg understood the Constitution's equality and liberty guarantees to constrain laws regulating pregnancy, a view she espoused as an advocate and on the bench. *See infra* Section III.C.2.

[85] *See* Mayeri, *supra* note 63, at 139; *supra* Section II.A.

[86] *See* Gerald N. Rosenberg, *The Real World of Constitutional Rights: The Supreme Court and the Implementation of the Abortion Decisions, in* Principles and Practice of American Politics: Classic and Contemporary Readings 174–75, 185 (Samuel Kernell & Steven S. Smith eds., 5th ed. 2013) (describing President Clinton as "the first pro-choice president since *Roe*," recounting the numerous policies he implemented immediately after his election, and contrasting his positions on abortion to his predecessors).

[87] *See* Kimberly Hutcherson, *A Brief History of Anti-Abortion Violence*, CNN (Dec. 1, 2015, 7:51 AM), https://www.cnn.com/2015/11/30/us/anti-abortion-violence/index.html; Mireille Jacobson & Heather Royer, *Aftershocks: The Impact of Clinic Violence on Abortion Services*, Am. Econ. J.: Applied Econ., Jan. 2011, at 189, 220 ("In the 1980s and 1990s, radical anti-abortion activists unleashed a storm of violent attacks against abortion clinics and providers. Clinic arsons, bombings and even staff murders became widely-publicized tools in the anti-abortion effort to limit access to abortion services.").

Many in the antiabortion movement viewed these developments as exposing the limits of arguments that focused on saving babies and attacking women and doctors who put them at risk.[88] These confrontational and often violent tactics radiated hostility to women at a time when the nation professed commitment to the idea that women are equals whose dignity and welfare the law is obliged to respect.

After *Casey*, a growing number of antiabortion leaders began to respond to the views of women that shaped abortion rights jurisprudence in the decision. These antiabortion advocates shifted their arguments to focus on women and began to incorporate abortion rights frames into their attacks on abortion. A response of this kind is not uncommon in the midst of fierce conflict.[89] *Casey* recognized that "[t]he ability of women to participate equally in the economic and social life of the Nation has been facilitated by their ability to control their reproductive lives."[90] Seeking to respond to *Casey*—and to appropriate the political authority of feminism— antiabortion advocates increasingly began to argue that women's liberty, equality, and health required banning abortion.[91]

The antiabortion movement was responding to domestic and transnational expressions of women's equality. Harvard professor Mary Ann Glendon headed a Vatican delegation opposing abortion at the 1995 Beijing Women's Conference, reasoning on egalitarian grounds in an effort not to isolate the Vatican at the conference; Glendon's "appointment had been quietly urged by the Clinton Administration," the first time that a woman was named to head an official Vatican delegation."[92] As Glendon recounted Pope John Paul II's stance: "Not only

[88] Reva B. Siegel, *The Right's Reasons: Constitutional Conflict and the Spread of Woman-Protective Antiabortion Argument*, 57 DUKE L.J. 1641, 1660, 1664–68 (2008) (surveying advocates' writing during this era).

[89] *Id.* at 1650 ("The quest to persuade disciplines insurgent claims about the Constitution's meaning, and may lead advocates to express convictions in terms persuasive to others, to internalize elements of counterarguments and to engage in other implicit forms of convergence and compromise.").

[90] Planned Parenthood of Se. Pa. v. Casey, 505 U.S. 833, 835 (1992).

[91] *See* Reva B. Siegel, *Dignity and the Politics of Protection: Abortion Restrictions under* Casey/Carhart, 117 YALE L.J. 1694, 1724 (2008) (showing how the antiabortion movement developed arguments designed "to appropriate feminism's political authority and express antiabortion argument in the language of women's rights and freedom of choice").

[92] *See* John Tagliabue, *Vatican Attacks U.S.-Backed Draft for Women's Conference*, N.Y. TIMES (Aug. 26, 1995), https://www.nytimes.com/1995/08/26/world/vatican-attacks-us-backed-draft-for-women-s-conference.html (describing "efforts by the Vatican and the Clinton Administration to search for areas of agreement at the Beijing conference and to reduce attention to the

did the pope align himself with women's quest for freedom, he adopted much of the language of the women's movement, even calling for a 'new feminism' in *Evangelium Vitae*."[93] The Church opposed recognition of sexual and reproductive rights at the 1995 Beijing Women's Conference, while the Pope affirmed: "there is an urgent need to achieve *real equality* in every area."[94]

Leaders of the American antiabortion movement had already begun to employ woman-protective arguments to address audiences that increasingly expected expressions of respect for women's rights and welfare. In the aftermath of *Casey* and of President Clinton's election, advocates decided to foreground woman-protective arguments in an effort to persuade members of the public who supported abortion rights to support abortion restrictions and to explain to legislators and judges prepared to enforce abortion rights why they could nonetheless impose abortion restrictions on women.

1. *Woman-protective antiabortion argument in politics.* Woman-focused arguments for rejecting abortion had long circulated among women working at the antiabortion movement's crisis pregnancy centers,[95] and during the setbacks of the 1990s, the movement's male leadership began to draw upon these women-focused arguments for strategic reasons, to answer public concerns that the antiabortion movement cared only about babies and little about the women who bore and raised them.[96]

---

more emotional issues like abortion"); *id.* ("The United States Ambassador to the Vatican, Raymond L. Flynn, a former Mayor of Boston, lobbied heavily in recent months in favor of Ms. Glendon's appointment to lead the Vatican delegation."); *see also* Mary Anne Case, *Trans Formations in the Vatican's War on 'Gender Ideology,'"* 44 SIGNS: J. WOMEN IN CULTURE & SOC. 639, 642–43 (2019) (observing that Americans played roles on all sides of the debates in this transnational dialogue).

[93] Mary Ann Glendon, *The Pope's New Feminism*, CRISIS MAG. (Mar. 1, 1997), https://www .crisismagazine.com/1997/the-popes-new-feminism; *see also New Feminism*, WORLD HERITAGE ENCYCLOPEDIA, http://www.self.gutenberg.org/articles/eng/New_feminism ("New feminism is a philosophy which emphasizes a belief in an integral complementarity of men and women, rather than the superiority of men over women or women over men. New feminism, as a form of difference feminism, supports the idea that men and women have different strengths, perspectives, and roles, while advocating for the equal worth and dignity of both sexes. Among its basic concepts are that the most important differences are those that are biological rather than cultural.").

[94] *Letter of Pope John Paul II to Women*, LIBRERIA EDITRICE VATICANA (June 29, 1995), http:// www.vatican.va/content/john-paul-ii/en/letters/1995/documents/hf_jp-ii_let_29061995_women .html (discussing "personal rights").

[95] Siegel, *supra* note 88, at 1658–60.

[96] *Id.* at 1668–81.

Jack Willke—who in the 1970s developed antiabortion arguments that spread world-wide featuring pictures of the fetus in utero[97]— bluntly recounted the findings that led him to embrace woman-protective antiabortion arguments in the 1990s. As he recalled, in the 1990s, abortion rights advocates "changed the question. No longer was our nation arguing about killing babies. The focus, through their efforts, had shifted off the humanity of the unborn child to one of women's rights. They developed the effective phrase of 'Who Decides?'"[98]

Willke did market research and changed the focus of his arguments:

> We did the market research and came up with some surprising findings. . . . We found out that the basic problem in the minds of the general public was that, by their own evaluation, most were undecided on this issue. They felt that pro-life people were not compassionate to women and that we were only "fetus lovers" who abandoned the mother after the birth. They felt that we were violent, that we burned down clinics and shot abortionists. We were viewed as religious zealots who were not too well educated. Clearly, their image of us was one that had been fabricated and delivered to them in the print and broadcast media by a liberal press. After considerable research, we found out that the answer to their "choice" argument was a relatively simple straightforward one. We had to convince the public that we were compassionate to women. Accordingly, we test marketed variations of this theme. Thus was born the slogan "Love Them Both," and, in fact, the third edition of our Question and Answer book has been so titled, specifically for that reason.[99]

Willke reasoned that if the movement hoped to persuade Americans to support candidates, policies, and jurists to change the law of abortion, it would have to use arguments from the movement's crisis pregnancy centers: "We've got to go out and sing from the housetops about what we're doing—how compassionate we are to women, how we are helping women—not just babies, but also women."[100]

---

[97] *See* J.C. WILLKE, HANDBOOK ON ABORTION (1st ed. 1971), *reprinted in* BEFORE ROE v. WADE: VOICES THAT SHAPED THE ABORTION DEBATE BEFORE THE SUPREME COURT'S RULING 99 (Linda Greenhouse & Reva B. Siegel, eds., 2012), https://documents.law.yale.edu/sites/default/files/beforeroe2nded_1.pdf (excerpting first edition of Willke's *Handbook on Abortion*).

[98] Siegel, *supra* note 88, at 1670 (quoting J.C. Willke, *Life Issues Institute Is Celebrating Ten Years with a New Home*, LIFE ISSUES CONNECTOR (Feb. 2001), https://web.archive.org/web/20110305213857/https://www.lifeissues.org/connector/01feb.html).

[99] *Id.* at 1670–71.

[100] John Willke & Barbara Willke, *Why Can't We Love Them Both?*, 7 LIFE & LEARNING 10, 10–25 (1997), http://www.uffl.org/vol%207/willke7.pdf. For many other contemporary sources reflecting these developments, see Siegel, *supra* note 88, at 1664–69.

Willke was joined by other advocates of the woman-protective turn. David Reardon, a leader in developing empirical claims about abortion regret, put the point simply: "While committed pro-lifers may be more comfortable with traditional 'defend the baby' arguments, we must recognize that many in our society are too morally immature to understand this argument. They must be led to it. And the best way to lead them to it is by first helping them to see that abortion does not help women, but only makes their lives worse."[101]

Reardon claimed to show by empirical method that the interests of women and the unborn do not conflict.[102] "By finding this evidence and sharing it with others, we bear witness to the protective good of God's law in a way which even unbelievers must respect."[103] His claim of "no conflict" was a claim about sex roles—a religious and moral belief that a mother's interests are defined by the needs of her child:

> One cannot help a child without helping the mother; one cannot hurt a child without hurting the mother.
>
> This intimate connection between a mother and her children is part of our created order. Therefore, protecting the unborn is a natural byproduct of protecting mothers. This is necessarily true. After all, in God's ordering of creation, it is only the mother who can nurture her unborn child. All the rest of us can do is to nurture the mother.
>
> This, then, must be the centerpiece of our pro-woman/pro-life agenda. The best interests of the child and the mother are always joined—even if the mother does not initially realize it, and even if she needs a tremendous amount of love and help to see it.[104]

Reardon expressed these religious and moral beliefs about abortion in the language of public health.[105] In a 1995 article called "Is the

---

[101] Siegel, *supra* note 88, at 1672–73 (quoting David Reardon, *Politically Correct vs. Politically Smart: Why Politicians Should Be Both Pro-Woman and Pro-Life*, POST-ABORTION REV., Fall 1994, at 1, 1–3, https://afterabortion.org/why-politicians-should-be-both-pro-woman-and-pro-life.).

[102] *Id.* at 1674.

[103] *Id.* (quoting DAVID C. REARDON, MAKING ABORTION RARE: A HEALING STRATEGY FOR A DIVIDED NATION 11 (1996)).

[104] *Id.* at 1675 (quoting David Reardon, *supra* note 101).

[105] *See, e.g.*, Interview by Zenit News Agency with Dr. David C. Reardon, Director of the Elliot Inst., in Springfield, Ill. (May 12, 2003), https://www.afterabortion.org/vault/Zenit _News_PoorChoice_Interview.pdf ("Abortion is not evil primarily because it harms women. Instead, it is precisely because of its evil as a direct attack on the good of life that we can know it will ultimately harm women. While the research we are doing is necessary to document abortion's harm, good moral reasoning helps us to anticipate the results.").

Post-abortion Strategy a Moral Strategy?"[106] he called his method "Teaching Morality By Teaching Science" and described his method as "an alternative way of evangelizing."[107] On this view, emphasizing abortion's risks to women in the form of trauma, sterility, and breast cancer would reduce the ambivalence of voters who were otherwise reticent to criminalize abortion out of concern that it would harm women.[108]

In addition to arguing that access to abortion threatened women's health, Reardon also argued that access to abortion threatened women's freedom. Women were coerced into abortions that traumatized them.[109] In his 1993 article, *Pro-Woman/Prolife Initiative*, Reardon explained that candidates could "project themselves as both pro-woman and pro-life . . . by emphasizing one's knowledge of the dangers of abortion and the threat of women being coerced into unwanted abortions by others," and pointing out that "[t]his approach breaks down the myth that pro-lifers care only about the unborn while 'pro-choicers' care about women."[110]

In 1996, Reardon republished many of these arguments in a book taking its title from President Clinton's arguments for abortion rights, *Making Abortion Rare: A Healing Strategy for a Divided Nation.*[111] If

---

[106] David C. Reardon, *Is the Post-Abortion Strategy a Moral Strategy?*, POST-ABORTION REV., Summer 1995, https://afterabortion.org/is-the-post-abortion-strategy-a-moral-strategy.

[107] *Id.* Reardon continues:

> Whenever we cannot convince others to acknowledge a moral truth for the love of God, our second best option is to appeal to their self interests. If an act is indeed against God's moral law, it will be found to be injurious to our happiness. Thus, if our faith is true, we would expect to find compelling evidence which demonstrates that acts such as abortion, fornication, and pornography, lead in the end not to happiness and freedom, but to sorrow and enslavement. By finding this evidence, and sharing it with others, we bear witness to the protective good of God's law in a way which even unbelievers must respect.

> *Id.*

[108] *See* Siegel, *supra* note 88, at 1673.

[109] *See* Siegel, *supra* note 91, at 1722–23 (quoting Reardon in 1994 giving similar advice to pro-life candidates about making coercion claims).

[110] David C. Reardon, *Pro-Woman/Pro-Life Campaign*, POST-ABORTION REV., Winter 1993, https://afterabortion.org/pro-woman-pro-life-campaign (quoted in Siegel, *supra* note 91, at 1722).

[111] DAVID C. REARDON, MAKING ABORTION RARE: A HEALING STRATEGY FOR A DIVIDED NATION, *supra* note 103 at viii (1996) ("This book is about fundamentally redefining the abortion debate, redrawing the lines of battle to reemphasize our commitment to being both pro-woman and pro-life."); *see also id.* at xii (reasoning from the standpoint of "we, the Church").

Americans believed that abortion rights protected women's freedom, health and welfare, Willke, Reardon, and others would win over a resisting public by proving that banning abortion would protect women's freedom, health, and welfare. The appeal to traditional roles in the language of feminism was powerful, taking persuasive authority from each. Leaders of the antiabortion movement began to attack abortion in abortion-rights frames, arguing that laws pushing pregnant women into motherhood protected woman's health and freedom.

2. *Woman-protective antiabortion argument in law.* In the years after *Casey,* as antiabortion advocates in growing numbers embraced the arguments that abortion hurts women, Americans United for Life (AUL) set to work translating these new frames into a legislative and litigation strategy. In the wake of *Casey,* both AUL and the National Right to Life Committee elevated women to leadership positions to emphasize the organizations' woman-protectionist aims.[112] AUL lawyers focused on the importance of rebutting *Casey*'s assertion that "the ability of women to participate equally in the economic and social life of the Nation has been facilitated by their ability to control their reproductive lives."[113] The organization's records show that at an April 1993 board meeting, its new leader, Paige Comstock Cunningham, "announced 'a major shift in the rhetoric of AUL.' 'We must help people understand that abortion hurts women too'";[114] and the organization's director of public affairs urged that "only by focusing on 'the harm abortion does to the woman' could activists 'start changing hearts and minds.'"[115]

AUL leaders embraced arguments already circulating in the movement, but with an important difference. Lawyers would employ the claims about women funding woman-protective antiabortion arguments not simply to move public opinion but to enact laws and legitimate the use of state power against women and the doctors who sought to assist them.[116] Lawyers began to deploy the movement's

---

[112] *See* Mary Ziegler, *Some Form of Punishment: Penalizing Women for Abortion,* 26 Wm. & Mary Bill Rts. J. 735, 767 (2018).

[113] Planned Parenthood of Se. Pa. v. Casey, 505 U.S. 833, 835 (1992); *see* Mary Ziegler, Abortion and the Law in America: Roe v. Wade to the Present 143 (2020) (discussing AUL lawyers and James Bopp, lawyer for the National Right to Life Committee, responding to *Casey*'s claims about women's reliance interests in the immediate aftermath of the decision).

[114] *See* Ziegler, *supra* note 113, at 144.

[115] *Id.* at 144–45 (quoting Myrna Gutíerrez).

[116] In this account, I offer a brief review of AUL's use of the abortion-hurts-women to enact and defend legislation. For another example of influential woman-protective lawyering from

sex-role-based arguments—the pro-woman claim that the interests of mother and child never conflict, that what is good for children is good for women—to justify legislation restricting abortion rights and to defend the laws' constitutionality.

In 2001, *Mother Jones* published an article entitled *The Quiet War on Abortion* that showcased AUL's work advocating for health-justified abortion restrictions in the years after *Casey*.[117] By then, AUL had thoroughly embraced the tactical shift to emphasize woman-focused antiabortion arguments. AUL lawyers could draft laws restricting abortion that claimed to protect women's psychological and physical health and advocate for these public health measures through empirical claims that sounded credible and persuasive because they expressed religious and moral beliefs about women's traditional roles.

An AUL lawyer named Dorinda Bordlee (who would go on to play a central role in *June Medical*) explained the organization's new tactic for restricting abortion in the wake of *Casey*:

> The *Casey* decision started abortion opponents rethinking their tactics. Since direct assaults on *Roe* wouldn't fly, "there had to be a shift in strategy by regulation on the outskirts of abortion," says Dorinda Bordlee, staff counsel for Americans United for Life. That's when leaders developed a new approach: Couch the issue in terms of women's health. By claiming that abortions take place in dirty facilities and cause such illnesses as depression and breast cancer, right-to-lifers realized they could subtly move the focus of the debate. "For 25 years, the pro-life movement focused on the baby, and the abortion-rights movement focused on the woman," says Bordlee. "The baby and the woman were pitted against each other. What we have realized is that the woman and the child have a sacred bond that should not be divided. What's good for the child is good for the mother. So now we're advocating legislation that is good for the woman."[118]

In 2003, Clark Forsythe, then president of AUL, explained the movement's new legal tactic for restricting abortion to readers of the conservative Catholic journal *First Things*, emphasizing that those opposed to abortion need to "appeal to those who are currently

this era, consider the work of Harold Cassidy, another innovator and proponent of the coercion claim. *See* Siegel, *supra* note 91, at 1727–33 (tracing the influence of Cassidy's work in state legislation, and in court decisions, including Gonzales v. Carhart, 127 S. Ct. 1610 (2007)).

[117] Barry Yeoman, *The Quiet War on Abortion*, MOTHER JONES, Sept./Oct. 2001, https://www.motherjones.com/politics/2001/09/quiet-war-abortion.

[118] *Id.*

undecided or conflicted on the issue."[119] "If Americans come to realize that abortion harms women as well as the unborn, it will not be
seen as 'necessary,' and the 'necessary evil' may be converted into evil
pure and simple."[120]

In 2004, Denise Burke and Dorinda Bordlee, both then staff
counsel at AUL, contributed to a volume edited by Erika Bachiochi
entitled *The Cost of Choice: Women Evaluate the Impact of Abortion*[121]
designed to present a feminist framing of the argument that abortion
harms women. The editor and all the contributors were women.[122]
The volume included chapters by women law professors (including
Mary Ann Glendon), doctors, lawyers, and the president of Feminists
for Life; it profiled women's rights advocates who opposed abortion
alongside chapters that recount the alleged psychological and physical health harms abortion inflicts on women, such as the "Abortion-
Breast Cancer Link,"[123] and a chapter by Burke on AUL's new
campaign attacking abortion clinics as "the True 'Back Alley.'"[124]

The volume presented purportedly empirical evidence of abortion's
harms—numerous chapters cite the work of David Reardon, John
Thorp, Vincent Rue, and other movement authorities[125]—without
educating readers about the findings of the many psychologists,
psychiatrists, and government oncologists who have refuted these

[119] Clarke D. Forsythe, *An Unnecessary Evil*, FIRST THINGS (2003), https://www.firstthings
.com/article/2003/02/an-unnecessary-evil.

[120] *Id.*

[121] THE COST OF CHOICE: WOMEN EVALUATE THE IMPACT OF ABORTION (Erika Bachiochi
ed. 2004) [hereinafter COST OF CHOICE].

[122] *Id.* at 139–42.

[123] Angela Lanfranchi, *The Abortion-Breast Cancer Link*, *in* COST OF CHOICE, *supra* note 121,
at 72.

[124] Denise M. Burke, *Abortion Clinic Regulation: Combating the True "Back Alley,"* *in* COST OF
CHOICE, *supra* note 121, at 122.

[125] For information on the credentials of David Reardon and other movement authorities cited
in the book and offered as expert witnesses in support of woman-protective abortion restrictions,
see Pam Chamberlain, *Politicized Science: How Anti-Abortion Myths Feed the Christian Right Agenda*,
PUBLIC EYE (June 4, 2006), https://www.politicalresearch.org/2006/06/04/politicized-sciencehow
-anti-abortion-myths-feed-the-christian-right-agenda; and *False Witnesses—David Reardon*, RE-
WIRE NEWS GROUP, https://rewirenewsgroup.com/false-witnesses/#david-reardon. Vincent Rue
has been judicially chastised for organizing and ghost-writing expert testimony on the health
justification for admitting privileges laws, *see* Greenhouse & Siegel, *supra* note 42, at 1458–60,
and Judge Richard Posner pointed out evident problems with the testimony of John Thorp in
Wisconsin's case, *see infra* note 261.

abortion-harms-women claims in studies accumulating in the years
before the volume's publication and since.[126]

Current research confirms findings that were already reported at
the time of the *Cost of Choice* book but omitted from or minimized in
it. The American College of Obstetricians and Gynecologists reports
that "[n]umerous studies have found no link between abortion and
psychological trauma"[127] and that claims of a "purportedly heightened risk of mental health issues or substance abuse resulting from an
abortion" are "unsubstantiated."[128] A recent study compared the
health and wellbeing of women who had abortions with those who
were turned away because they were past a clinic's gestational limit
for care and carried the pregnancy to term. The study tracked nearly
1,000 women over five years and nearly 8,000 interviews and found
"no evidence that abortion causes negative mental health or wellbeing outcomes."[129] The interviews showed how ending a pregnancy
helped women negotiate financial, family, relationship, career, and
health difficulties, as well as the ways that women who sought an
abortion and were turned away coped with motherhood.[130]

Unsurprisingly, AUL was not interested in publicizing the facts
found by these scientists and social scientists. Over the ensuing decade, AUL developed models that translated the abortion-harms-
women frame into legislation that would encumber or shut down the
provision of abortion under the rubric of health and safety regulation,
including the passage of admitting privileges laws in numerous states;
the organization's annual publication, which provides model legislation, began publishing a whole section of model bills under the

---

[126] *See, e.g.*, Siegel, *supra* note 91, at 1719 n.81 (2008) (citing studies beginning in 1992 refuting claims of post abortion syndrome and citing 2003 studies of the National Cancer Institute refuting claims of association between abortion and breast cancer). For an update on the
breast cancer studies, see Stephanie Watson, *Abortion and Breast Cancer Risk*, HEALTHLINE:
PARENTHOOD (May 18, 2017), https://www.healthline.com/health/abortion-and-breast-cancer.

[127] Brief of Amici Curiae American College of Obstetricians and Gynecologists et al. in
Support of June Medical Services at 8 n.12, June Med. Servs. L.L.C. v. Russo, 140 S. Ct. 2103
(2020) (Nos. 18–1323 & 18–1460) (quoting E.M. Dadlez & William L. Andrews, *Post-Abortion
Syndrome: Creating an Affliction*, 24 BIOETHICS 445, 450, 452 (2009)), https://reproductiverights
.org/sites/default/files/documents/Major%20Medical%20Groups.pdf.

[128] *Id.*

[129] *See Introduction to the Turnaway Study*, ANSIRH 2 (Mar. 2020), https://www.ansirh.org
/sites/default/files/publications/files/turnawaystudyannotatedbibliography.pdf.

[130] *Id.* at 3–5 (summarizing findings); *see also* Joshua Lang, *What Happens to Women Who Are
Denied Abortions?*, N.Y. TIMES MAG. (June 12, 2013), https://www.nytimes.com/2013/06/16
/magazine/study-women-denied-abortions.html.

heading "Women's Protection Project."[131] The woman-protective arguments for banning abortion employed contested factual claims to advance a normative understanding of women's roles and family relationships.

Denise Burke, Vice President of Legal Affairs at AUL, explained the premises of the "health and safety" laws AUL promoted for state adoption through the Women's Protection Project, including the Texas admitting privileges law the Supreme Court was about to review in *Whole Woman's Health*. As she described the premises of the health and safety laws that AUL promoted, "the unique focus of [AUL's] mother-child strategy" was that it "recognizes that abortion harms both mother and child and demonstrates that the interests of women and their unborn children are inextricably intertwined. Simply, protecting and defending unborn babies also protects and defends women."[132]

Health-justified TRAP laws impose on abortion providers burdensome health and safety regulations not imposed on other medical practices of similar or even greater risk.[133] TRAP laws are not dissuasive in form; they do not contemplate dialogue with a pregnant woman but instead are directed at medical professionals and healthcare delivery systems, typically raising the cost of practice, sometimes prohibitively. The laws present as ordinary health and safety regulations but for the extraordinary burdens they place on abortion providers and their tendency to target or single out abortion providers for forms of

---

[131] AMERICANS UNITED FOR LIFE, DEFENDING LIFE 280 (2015) [hereinafter DEFENDING LIFE]; *see id.* at 16 ("Among the laws enacted over the last four years are abortion facility regulations and admitting privilege requirements which AUL has championed for more than a decade."); *id.* at 23 (discussing admitting privileges legislation enacted by 15 states); *see also* Erica Hellerstein, *Inside the Highly Sophisticated Group That's Quietly Making It Much Harder to Get an Abortion*, THINKPROGRESS (Dec. 2, 2014, 3:11 PM), https://archive.thinkprogress.org/inside -the-highly-sophisticated-group-thats-quietly-making-it-much-harder-to-get-an-abortion -9db723232471 (describing AUL role in passage of admitting privileges legislation); Janet Reitman, *The Stealth War on Abortion*, ROLLING STONE (Jan. 15, 2014, 2:00 PM), https://www .rollingstone.com/politics/politics-news/the-stealth-war-on-abortion-102195/ (tracing the shift to woman-protective arguments and the AUL's central role in translating abortion-hurts-women into TRAP legislation, describing the organization as "chiefly responsible for the most recent and highly successful under-the-radar strategy").

[132] Denise M. Burke, *Restoring Mother-Child Bonds That* Roe v. Wade *Damaged*, WASH. TIMES (Jan. 12, 2016), https://www.washingtontimes.com/news/2016/jan/12/denise-burke-restoring -mother-child-bonds-that-roe/.

[133] Greenhouse & Siegel, *supra* note 42, at 1446. Judges often find fault with the empirical claims of experts who testify in support of health laws singling out abortion. *See, e.g., infra* text accompanying notes 259–61 (describing Judge Richard Posner criticizing expert testimony in support of admitting privileges requirement).

regulation not imposed on other procedures of equal or greater risk. TRAP laws have focused on the licensing of clinics and clinicians and the regulation of telemedicine, admitting privileges, prescriptions for off-label drugs, and abortion clinic zoning.[134] As the laws spread, judges began to raise concerns about differential treatment of abortion providers as an indicator of the laws' potentially constitutionally suspect character.[135]

AUL is proud of the TRAP laws the organization worked to develop, enact, and defend. Its leadership openly discusses the organization's goals, as the interviews considered above suggest, at times discussing the laws' purpose to hinder women's access to abortion. An interviewer pointed out to Dan McConchie, then the group's vice president of government affairs, that AUL was promoting policies, like admitting privilege requirements, that meant "abortion clinics have become fewer and further between, and some women are forced to make two appointments in order to get the procedure." McConchie replied that "[s]tates can't outlaw abortion" but "[t]hat does not mean there's a constitutional right to abortion being convenient."[136] In 2012,

---

[134] For information on TRAP laws currently in effect, see *Targeted Regulation of Abortion Providers (TRAP) Laws*, GUTTMACHER INST., https://www.guttmacher.org/state-policy/explore /targeted-regulation-abortion-providers (last updated Feb. 1, 2021) (reporting that 23 states have passed laws regulating abortion providers that "go beyond what is necessary to ensure patients' safety").

[135] Greenhouse & Siegel, *supra* note 42, at 1446 & n.96 (citing cases); *see also* Bonnie S. Jones et al., *State Law Approaches to Facility Regulation of Abortion and Other Office Interventions*, 108 AM. J. PUB. HEALTH 486 (2018) (finding that while nineteen states had regulated abortion and other office-based surgeries, fourteen had only singled out abortion for regulation).

The COVID-19 pandemic has thrown into stark relief the differential treatment of abortion providers, as eight states attempted to categorize abortion as a "non-essential" procedure subject to COVID restrictions. *See Center Lawsuits to Protect Abortion Access During the COVID-19 Pandemic Are Working*, CTR. FOR REPROD. RTS. (May 5, 2020), https://www.reproductiverights .org/story/center-files-emergency-lawsuit-texas-protect-essential-abortion-access-during -pandemic; *see also* Joanna L. Grossman & Mary Ziegler, *Unconstitutional Chaos: Abortion in the Time of COVID-19*, JUSTIA: VERDICT (Apr. 15, 2020), https://verdict.justia.com/2020/04/15 /unconstitutional-chaos-abortion-in-the-time-of-covid-19. The Food and Drug Administration has singled out the drug used for medication abortion for a burdensome in-person distribution requirement; during the pandemic, it has refused to suspend this travel requirement. *See infra* text accompanying notes 313–27 (discussing Food and Drug Admin. v. Am. Coll. of Obstetricians, 141 S.Ct. 578 (2021) (mem.)).

[136] Olga Khazan, *Planning the End of Abortion*, ATLANTIC (July 16, 2015), https://www.theatlantic .com/politics/archive/2015/07/what-pro-life-activists-really-want/398297. McConchie currently serves as a Republican member of the Illinois Senate, where he has campaigned against abortion rights using women-protective frames. *See, e.g., McConchie Stunned Over Repeal of Provisions in Extreme Abortion Measure*, OFFICE OF SENATOR DAN MCCONCHIE (June 1, 2019), http://www .senatormcconchie.com/News/693/McConchie-stunned-over-repeal-of-provisions-in-extreme -abortion-measure/news-detail ("To make his argument, Sen. McConchie specifically pointed to

then-president Charmaine Yoest described the organization's aim in
enacting state legislation: "As we're moving forward at the state level,
we end up hollowing out *Roe* even without the Supreme Court. That's
really where our strategy is so solid."[137]

Admitting privileges laws proved especially effective in shutting
down clinics;[138] and their dramatic impact drew public notice. In 2013,
after the AUL-modeled bill at issue in *Whole Woman's Health* was
introduced in the Texas House, then-Lieutenant Governor David
Dewhurst tweeted a photo of a map that showed all of the abortion
clinics that would close as a result of the bill, announcing: "We fought
to pass SB5 thru the Senate last night, & this is why!"; then, as if to
qualify his admission of the state's clinic-closing purpose, the Lieutenant Governor immediately tweeted "I am unapologetically pro-life
AND a strong supporter of protecting women's health. #SB5 does
both."[139] The AUL-championed bill was openly discussed as clinic-
closing by legislators and abortion-ending by then Governor Rick
Perry (who thanked AUL for its assistance in drafting it).[140] In 2013, in
calling for the enactment of Texas's admitting privileges law, "Governor Perry himself declared that his goal was to 'make abortion,
at any stage, a thing of the past,' and that until we live in an 'ideal
world . . . without abortion,' Texas's aim should be to 'continue to pass
laws to ensure that abortions are as rare as possible.'"[141]

the fact that SB 25 repeals a number of provisions [regulating abortion] that currently protect
women's health. . . .").

[137] Emily Bazelon, *Charmaine Yoest's Cheerful War on Abortion*, N.Y. TIMES MAG. (Nov. 2,
2012), https://www.nytimes.com/2012/11/04/magazine/charmaine-yoests-cheerful-war-on
-abortion.html; *see also* Burke, *supra* note 132 (describing states like New York and California
at the bottom of AUL's Life List as "[b]elieving women must have unfettered access to abortion clinics" and "content to place women at the mercy of an increasingly suspect abortion
industry").

[138] Greenhouse & Siegel, *supra* note 42, at 1449–50 (describing the shutdown of clinics
in Mississippi, Texas, Wisconsin, Alabama and Louisiana after the enactment of admitting-
privileges laws).

[139] *Id.* at 1451–52.

[140] *See* Cary Franklin, Whole Woman's Health v. Hellerstedt *and What It Means to Protect
Women*, *in* REPRODUCTIVE RIGHTS AND JUSTICE STORIES 223, 230–31 (Melissa Murray, Kate
Shaw, & Reva B. Siegel eds. 2019) (describing AUL's multifaceted role in the Texas); Linda
Greenhouse & Reva B. Siegel, *The Difference a Whole Woman Makes: Protection for the Abortion
Right After Whole Woman's Health*, 126 YALE L.J. F. 149, 153 n.24 (2016).

[141] Franklin, *supra* note 140, at 231; *see also* Beth Cortez-Neavel, *Perry at Pro-Life Rally: Ideal
World Is One Without Abortion*, TEX. OBSERVER (Jan. 27, 2013, 4:51 PM), https://www.texas
observer.org/thousands-support-pro-life-legislation-on-40th-anniversary-of-roe-v-wade.

Opponents of the admitting privileges law argued "that if pro-life lawmakers were truly motivated by a desire to safeguard women's health, they would not single out abortion with unnecessary and even counter-productive regulation, but would instead direct their attention to the abysmal state of women's health and healthcare in Texas,"[142] emphasizing that "for all its purported concern about women's health, the Texas legislature had done little to address these statistics, and in fact had made matters worse."[143] None of these arguments moved the law's supporters and the state enacted the admitting privileges statute—which closed many of the state's abortion clinics—for the claimed reason of protecting women's health.

C. LOUISIANA RESTRICTS ABORTION TO PROTECT WOMEN'S HEALTH

While the Texas admitting privileges law was challenged in federal courts, an admitting privileges law substantially the same as the Texas law was introduced in Louisiana.[144] Rather than recapitulating debate over the statute in judicial decisions, I add to that record by demonstrating the many ties between the Louisiana statute and the history of woman-protective abortion restrictions we have just considered. I show that, for its supporters, Louisiana's admitting privileges law was a pro-woman, pro-life law of the kind the antiabortion movement began advocating in the aftermath of *Casey*. I then explore the understandings of its supporters with the questions prompted by these movement commitments in view.

I demonstrate that Louisiana officials discussed the TRAP law as a health and safety regulation during legislative debate but that once the official record closed, the law's supporters began openly to describe the admitting privileges law as a pro-woman and pro-life law or simply described the law's purpose as protecting unborn life.[145]

---

[142] Franklin, *supra* note 140, at 234; *see also id.* at 233 (describing opponents pointing out that the Texas law singled out the practice of abortion for regulation not provided to many other outpatient procedures when complications from abortion practice were lower by far than for dental work).

[143] *Id.* at 234. For an account of Texas's health care policy choices in the era that it was enacting and defending the admitting privileges law invalidated in *Whole Woman's Health*, see Siegel, *supra* note 10, at 214–15.

[144] Chief Justice Roberts observed that "the two laws are nearly identical." June Med. Servs. L.L.C. v. Russo, 140 S. Ct. 2103, 2139 (2020) (Roberts, C.J., concurring).

[145] *See infra* Section II.C.1.

With an appreciation of the kind of beliefs about women associated with support for pro-woman, pro-life health laws, I then examine what supporters of Louisiana's admitting privileges law meant when they described the law as protecting women's health.[146] In Louisiana, as in Texas, opponents of the admitting privileges law compared the state's interest in protecting women's health in the abortion context with its lack of interest in protecting women's health outside the abortion context. [147] While at least one pro-life advocate advocated to improve healthcare for pregnant women, most focused on protecting women's health by restricting abortion.

Expanding the frame, I show that at the same time the state restricted abortion through an admitting privileges statute asserted to protect women and the unborn, the state enforced policies contributing to the state's exceedingly high maternal mortality and infant mortality rates. Expanding the frame on the abortion debate shows how role-based judgments shaped laws protecting women's health and demonstrates the physical as well as dignitary harm such judgments can inflict, especially when focused, as they were in Louisiana, on poor women of color. Analyzed from this vantage point, Louisiana's pro-woman, pro-life law raises questions of liberty, equality, and life that the Justices never discuss in *June Medical*.

1. *The law's aims: protecting women or the unborn?*. Louisiana was a poster child for pro-life advocates at the time it enacted the Unsafe Abortion Protection Act[148]—and for many years beforehand. AUL, modeled on and affiliated with the American Legislative Exchange Council (ALEC), ranks states for their antiabortion advocacy in its annual publication *Defending Life*, which disseminates model anti-abortion legislation and profiles the accomplishments and short-comings of every state for its success in enacting abortion laws.[149] Between 2010 and 2014, AUL ranked Louisiana first of all fifty states. After passage of the admitting privileges law in 2014, AUL would award first ranking to Louisiana again, selecting the state's governor,

---

[146] *See infra* Section II.C.2

[147] *See infra* Section II.C.2. For discussion of this debate in Texas, see *supra* text accompanying notes 142–43.

[148] Act 620, 2014 Leg., Reg. Sess. (La. 2014) (enacted), https://law.justia.com/codes/louisiana/2015/code-revisedstatutes/title-40/rs-40-1061.10 (codified at La. Stat. Ann. § 40:1061.10–26 (A)(2)(a) (West 2020)).

[149] *See* Defending Life, *supra* note 131. For one account of AUL's relation to ALEC, see Franklin, *supra* note 140, at 229–30.

Bobby Jindal, to introduce the 2015 edition of *Defending Life*[150]– valuable publicity for Jindal's campaign for the Republican Party presidential nomination launched that same year.[151] In his short bid for the presidency, Jindal cited these antiabortion ratings frequently as one of his chief qualifications for the presidency.[152]

As the state's AUL ranking suggests, AUL was as influential in Louisiana as it was in Texas.[153] In Louisiana, the admitting privilege law was introduced with the assistance of Dorinda Bordlee, then counsel at the Bioethics Defense Fund. Previously, as counsel at AUL, Bordlee helped develop the organization's woman-protective restrictions on abortion, a strategy which in 2001 she described as based on the role-based belief that "[w]hat's good for the child is good for the mother."[154] To bring to Louisiana the admitting privileges law that was so successful in closing clinics in Texas, Bordlee drafted the Louisiana admitting privileges law using Texas language and worked with State Representative Katrina Jackson, sponsor of the Louisiana law, to introduce it.[155]

---

[150] *See* DEFENDING LIFE, *supra* note 131, at vii (featuring preface by Louisiana's governor Bobby Jindal); *id.* at 16 (reporting that Louisiana "has topped the Life List since 2010"); *id.* at 40 (2015 state rankings); *see also* Bill Barrow, *Bobby Jindal Touts Louisiana as 'Most Pro-Life' State*, ASSOCIATED PRESS (Nov. 2, 2016), https://www.postandcourier.com/politics/bobby-jindal-touts -louisiana-as-most-pro-life-state/article_8af7aca0-6f67-5ecd-b12a-2d7312159d0e.html (describing Governor Jindal's claims that Louisiana was America's most pro-life state); *Jindal Signs Hoffmann's, Jackson's Pro-Life Bills*, OUACHITA CITIZEN (June 18, 2014), https://www.hannapub .com/ouachitacitizen/news/local_state_headlines/jindal-signs-hoffmann-s-jackson-s-pro-life -bills/article_5a7800d2-f697-11e3-89f6-001a4bcf6878.html (same).

[151] Manny Fernandez, *Bobby Jindal Enters Presidential Race, Saying 'It Is Time for a Doer,'* N.Y. TIMES (June 24, 2015), https://www.nytimes.com/2015/06/25/us/politics/bobby-jindal -announces-bid-for-president.html.

[152] *See, e.g.*, Maya Kliger, *Jindal Touts Conservative Record, Bashes Obama*, DES MOINES REG. (Aug. 8, 2015, 10:08 PM), https://www.desmoinesregister.com/story/news/elections/presidential /caucus/2015/08/08/bobby-jindal-mason-city-iowa-falls/31362689 (documenting Jindal's campaign stops in Iowa and his claims "that his state has been rated the most 'pro-life' state in the country").

[153] *See supra* note 140 and accompanying text. Bordlee's ties with AUL continued. She filed an amicus brief defending the Texas law in the Supreme Court in *Whole Woman's Health*, which she wrote with Denise Burke of AUL. Bordlee and Burke have AUL ties. *See supra* notes 121–24 and accompanying text (describing Bordlee and Burke contributing to the *Cost of Choice* volume).

[154] *See supra* text accompanying notes 117–18, 121–26.

[155] Peter J. Finney, *State Rep. Katrina Jackson Is Pro-Life, Pro-Woman*, CLARION HERALD (June 3, 2014), https://clarionherald.org/news/state-rep-katrina-jackson-is-pro-life-pro-woman (noting that Bordlee crafted the bill, met with Jackson before the start of the legislative session to discuss it, and asked Jackson to be the lead sponsor); Sarah Zagorski, *HB 388 Passes Overwhelmingly in Louisiana Senate*, LA. RIGHT TO LIFE (May 14, 2014), http://archive.constant contact.com/fs191/1101796400807/archive/1117365764539.html (describing Bordlee as the

In 2014, as the Texas bill was being litigated in the lower courts, Representative Jackson introduced HB 388 as a woman-protective bill, a "commonsense"[156] health measure that "was not denying anyone an abortion."[157] Opponents of the bill offered extensive evidence that the bill was medically unnecessary[158] and would close three out of five existing outpatient clinics,[159] mirroring the effects of Texas's admitting privileges law.[160] The bill's proponents scarcely reacted.

To ensure that the Texas example was not overlooked, before the Senate committee hearing began, Dorinda Bordlee emailed Representative Jackson a story about the admitting privilege law's success in closing clinics in Texas.[161] Bordlee began the email by stating, "La HB 388 follows this model"; the remainder of the email consisted of a story explaining how a state could use even unconstitutional statutes to get around courts and close clinics.[162] The story Bordlee emailed Jackson

---

"principle architect of the bill" and Jackson as the "author[]"). Bordlee described the Louisiana law as based on Texas language. *See Factsheet on La. HB 388, Unsafe Abortion Protection Act*, BIOETHICS DEFENSE FUND (2016), https://bdfund.org/wp-content/uploads/2016/04/file_639.pdf.

[156] Defendant's Exhibit 119: Certified Transcripts of Legislative History of Act 620 at 38, June Med. Servs. L.L.C. v. Kliebert, 250 F. Supp. 3d 27 (M.D. La. 2017) (No. 14-cv-00525-JWD-RLB) [hereinafter DX 119]. DX 119 contains, in relevant part, a transcription of publicly available video of committee hearings. *See Hearing on HB388 Before the H. Comm. On Health & Welfare*, 2014 Leg. Reg. Sess. (La. 2014), https://house.louisiana.gov/H_Video/VideoArchive Player?v=house/2014/Mar_2014/0319_14_HW; *Hearing on HB388 Before the S. Comm. on Health & Welfare*, 2014 Leg. Reg. Sess. (La. 2014), http://senate.la.gov/video/videoarchive.asp ?v=senate/2014/05/050714H~W2014.

[157] DX 119, *supra* note 156, at 9 (transcribing testimony of Rep. Katrina Jackson) ("It's not denying anyone contraceptives. It's not denying anyone an abortion. It's not denying anyone the choice on whether or not to have one.").

[158] *Id.* at 15–16 (transcribing the testimony of Ellie Schilling, describing the heightened requirements that HB 388 creates for abortion providers). The district court subsequently found that "admitting privileges do not improve health outcomes in the event of complications" and therefore HB 388/Act 620 "is not medically necessary and fails to actually further women's health and safety." June Med. Servs. LLC v. Kliebert, 250 F. Supp. 3d 27 at 87 (M.D. La. 2017).

[159] DX 119, *supra* note 156, at 13. After an extensive factual inquiry, the district court vindicated this claim; it found that, if implemented, HB 388/Act 620 would "result in a drastic reduction in the number and geographic distribution of abortion providers, reducing the number of clinics to one, or at most two, and leaving only one, or at most two, physicians providing abortions in the entire state." *June Med. Servs.*, 250 F. Supp. 3d 27 at 87.

[160] Legislators heard testimony that "the same bill" in Texas led to the closure of "half of the clinics. . . . The Rio Grande Valley has been left with no abortion clinics." DX 119, *supra* note 156, at 28.

[161] *See June Medical*, 250 F. Supp. 3d 27, 55–56 (M.D. La. 2017); *see also* June Med. Servs. L.L.C. v. Kliebert, 158 F. Supp. 3d 473, 501–02 (M.D. La. 2016).

[162] Joint Exhibit 15: Email from Dorinda Bordlee to State Sen. Katrina Jackson, *June Medical*, 250 F. Supp. 3d 27 (M.D. La. 2017) (No. 14-cv-00525-JWD-RLB) [hereinafter Joint Ex. 15] (reproducing Bordlee's email to Jackson attaching the National Journal.com story). Bordlee also

was entitled "Texas is Permanently Shutting Abortion Clinics and the Supreme Court Can't Do Anything About It."[163] The report pointed out that when Governor Perry "signed a sweeping anti-abortion law in 2013, he did so knowing the measure faced an uncertain future" and could "land in the hands of the Supreme Court." But "back in the Lone Star State, the final judicial score won't much matter" because "[t]he law has already had tremendous success in closing abortion clinics and restricting abortion access in Texas. And those successes appear all but certain to stick—with or without the Supreme Court's approval of the law that created them."[164]

Yet the Louisiana legislature didn't talk about shutting down abortion clinics as officials did in Texas.[165] Before passage of the law, Louisiana legislators mostly stayed on message and talked about the admitting privileges law as protecting women's health, even as officials in Texas were openly defending that state's admitting privileges law as both woman protective and fetal-protective in the Fifth Circuit.[166]

Supporters did not always stay on message. Even before passage of the Louisiana admitting privileges law, the district court found that Governor Jindal and the state's health director were characterizing the law as protecting unborn life.[167] In public statements, Governor Jindal boasted about his state's AUL rankings[168] and observed that the admitting privileges law "will build upon all we have done the past six years to protect the unborn."[169] In heated exchanges with witnesses

---

tweeted out the story. *See* Dorinda Bordlee (@DorindaBordlee), Twitter (May 5, 2014, 4:46 PM), https://twitter.com/DorindaBordlee/status/463449659696889857.

[163] Joint Ex. 15, *supra* note 162 (annotating email containing text of Sophie Novack, *Texas Is Permanently Shutting Abortion Clinics and the Supreme Court Can't Do Anything About It*, Nat'l J. (May 5, 2014), https://www.nationaljournal.com/s/58245.

[164] *Id.* The AUL statute functioned as the story predicted. The Texas law forced over half of the state's abortion clinics to close, "and only a few have reopened. Texans in some metropolitan areas must travel as far as 300 miles one way for the procedure" and the state "now has 10 cities of more than 50,000 without an abortion clinic within 100 miles." Sophie Novack, *Texas Has the Most Cities More than 100 Miles from an Abortion Clinic, Study Finds*, Tex. Observer (May 15, 2018, 5:03 PM), https://www.texasobserver.org/texas-most-cities -more-than-100-miles-from-abortion-clinic.

[165] *See* DX 119, *supra* note 156. On Texas, see *supra* notes 139–40 and accompanying text.

[166] Greenhouse & Siegel, *supra* note 42, 1452 n.117 & 1470 n.203.

[167] June Med. Servs. L.L.C. v. Kliebert, 250 F. Supp. 3d 27, 56 (M.D. La. 2017) (detailing references to "unborn children" in the drafting of Act 620).

[168] *Id.* ("In a press release regarding Act 620 released on March 7, 2014, Jindal declared his position that Act 620 was a reform that would 'build upon the work . . . done to make Louisiana the most pro-life state in the nation.'").

[169] *Id.*

who argued that the law would harm women, legislative sponsors of the law briefly shifted off the ground of women's health and instead emphasized the law's importance in protecting the unborn.[170]

But after the admitting privileges law was enacted, its proponents were much more forthright in discussing its purpose in protecting unborn life. Governor Jindal said he was "proud" to support legislation that "will help us continue to protect women and the life of the unborn in our state."[171] His successor, Governor John Bel Edwards, who as a legislator voted in support of the legislation, defended the law as protecting "the dignity and sanctity of life."[172] The state's Attorney General, Jeff Landry, reacted to the Supreme Court's decision staying enforcement of that law, promising "[w]e will not waver in defense of our state's pro-woman and pro-life laws; and we will continue to do all that we legally can to protect Louisiana women and the unborn."[173] Landry used the expression "pro-woman and pro-life law" (or similarly "pro-life and pro-woman law") when discussing the law,[174] while his campaign website boasted that "our pro-life Attorney General, Jeff Landry, is working to protect the unborn . . . [by] [d]efending Louisiana's landmark admitting privileges law."[175]

After the admitting privileges law was enacted, the law's sponsor, Rep. Katrina Jackson, also began talking about it as protecting both women and the unborn. In a message Jackson provided for members of Louisiana Right to Life in the summer of 2014, Jackson, a

---

[170] *See infra* notes 191–99 and accompanying text.

[171] Emily Lane, *Bobby Jindal Signs Anti-Abortion Bill Thursday Likely to Close Clinics in Baton Rouge, New Orleans*, Times-Picayune (June 12, 2014, 7:25 PM), https://www.nola.com/news /politics/article_c2380d71-70b6-513a-b24d-416674e49289.html.

[172] *Gov. Edwards' Statement on U.S. Supreme Court's Ruling on Louisiana's Abortion Law*, Office of the Governor (Feb. 8, 2019), https://www.gov.louisiana.gov/index.cfm/newsroom/detail /1794 ("As a pro-life Catholic, I will always advocate for laws that protect the dignity and sanctity of life. I voted for the bill in 2014. I urge the Supreme Court to act quickly in this matter, so Louisiana may move forward.").

[173] Maria Clark, *Louisiana Reacts to Supreme Court Abortion Access Decision*, Times-Picayune (July 22, 2019, 2:13 PM), https://www.nola.com/entertainment_life/health_fitness/article_467c2c8c -46b4-55f7-9059-c19eee671243.html.

[174] *See, e.g.,* Adam Liptak, *Supreme Court Blocks Louisiana Abortion Law*, N.Y. Times (Mar. 4, 2016), https://www.nytimes.com/2016/03/05/us/politics/supreme-court-blocks-louisiana-abor tion-law.html.

[175] *Protecting the Unborn*, Landry for Louisiana, https://landryforlouisiana.com/protecting -the-unborn (last visited Aug. 9, 2020).

Democrat, wrote that HB 388 represented "[u]nity for [l]ife."[176] "God has created each of us, and He has called me to be true to my calling as a Christian and stand for life in the Legislature," she wrote.[177] By passing the law, she argued, "[w]e have overcome the lines that divide us to protect life."[178] Countering then-president of Planned Parenthood Cecile Richards's claim that the bill was enacted "at the expense of women's health and safety,"[179] Jackson argued that the bill was "drafted by women, authored by women, supported by women, and voted for by women."[180] Dorinda Bordlee also discussed the Louisiana law as protecting women and the unborn. After the Supreme Court declared the admitting privileges law unconstitutional, Bordlee described it as concerned with "the health and safety of women" and "legislation that is both pro-woman and pro-life."[181]

  2. *Pro-woman? the meaning of "health."* We have evidence about what "pro-woman and pro-life" means to Dorinda Bordlee. She has coined the term "holistic feminism" to describe her views.[182] Under the banner "Holistic Feminism: Abortion Harms Women & Children,"

---

[176] Katrina Jackson, *Unity for Life*, La. Right to Life Comm. (Summer 2014), https://myemail .constantcontact.com/Overcoming-Division-for-Life-August-15th-E-Newsletter.html?soid = 1101796400807&aid = XbEDcJ9ZvnU.

[177] *Id.*

[178] *Id.*

[179] Cecile Richards, Opinion, *Women Won't Stand for Abortion Rights Roll Back*, CNN (May 28, 2014, 7:55 AM), https://www.cnn.com/2014/05/28/opinion/richards-abortion-access -restrictions-south/index.html.

[180] Jackson, *supra* note 176; *see also* Kurt Jensen, *Pro-Lifers Hopeful For Outcome of Court's First Abortion Case in Four Years*, Am. Mag. (Mar. 4, 2020), https://www.americamagazine.org /politics-society/2020/03/04/pro-lifers-hopeful-outcome-supreme-courts-first-abortion-case -four (quoting Jackson as explaining at the time of oral argument in the Supreme Court that the Louisiana law showed "love for the women, for the unborn child, and for those we pass every day who unfortunately may make this decision (to have an abortion)").

[181] *Supreme Court Decision in* June Medical v. Russo *Is a Loss for Health, Safety of Women*, La. Right to Life (June 29, 2020), https://prolifelouisiana.org/supreme-court-decision-in-june -medical-v-russo-%EF%BB%BFis-a-loss-for-the-health-safety-of-women; *see also* Dorinda Bordlee (@DorindaBordlee), Twitter (June 30, 2020, 3:52 AM), https://twitter.com/Dorinda Bordlee/status/1277902847280123904 (tweeting that State Sen. Katrina Jackson "is a model of what it means to be pro-woman pro-life"); EWTN, *World Over - 2020-01-23 – Dorinda Bordlee with Raymond Arroyo*, YouTube (Jan. 24, 2009), https://youtu.be/A3mjVWmcfHo (describing Louisiana's admitting privileges law as a "common sense pro-woman pro-life law" and "what it is designed to do is to protect women" while speculating that a ruling on third-party standing could block 80 percent of abortion rights claims).

[182] *Holistic Feminism: Abortion Harms Women & Children*, Bioethics Defense Fund, http:// bdfund.org/stories/holistic-feminism-abortion-harms-women-children ("Holistic Feminism is a term coined by Dorinda Bordlee to discuss the reality of how abortion exploits women as sexual objects, and robs men of a meaningful life of loving care and respect for his family.").

the website of the Bioethics Defense Fund announces: "'Holistic Feminism' is a term that BDF uses to describe policy strategies that integrate the interests of the woman, the unborn child, and the often ignored interests and duties of men who can easily rely on abortion to shirk their legal and moral duties of child support and fatherly guidance"[183]—echoing sex-role-based views about abortion ("What's good for the child is good for the mother") that Bordlee expressed at AUL.[184] Bordlee has employed woman-protective arguments to justify a variety of restrictions on access to contraception and abortion.[185]

But what did "pro-woman and pro-life" mean to Jindal, Jackson, Landry, and others who led the way in drafting, enacting, and defending Louisiana's admitting privilege law?

In Louisiana, Texas, and across the nation, the coupling of "pro-woman and pro-life" openly announced a law's fetal-protective aims. But what did advocates mean by calling a law "pro-woman and pro-life"? The history we have examined shows that leaders of the antiabortion movement claimed concern about women because it was a useful way of moving resisting voters and judges to restrict abortion—which the antiabortion movement sought in order to protect unborn life.[186]

Were claims about women's health a ploy to protect unborn life in a way the public and judges willing to dilute *Casey* would accept? We can assume that there were differences among them. Undoubtedly, over

---

[183] *Id.*

[184] *See supra* text accompanying note 118.

[185] *See, e.g.*, Brief for Breast Cancer Prevention Institute as Amicus Curiae Supporting Petitioners at 2, Zubik v. Burwell, 136 S. Ct. 1557 (2016) (Nos. 14–1418, 14–1453, 14–1505, 15–35, 15–105, 15–119, and 15–191) (Bordlee as counsel of record) (arguing contraceptives "pose dangerous risks to women's health" in litigation challenging the ACA's contraceptive mandate); Brief for Charlotte Lozier Institute, March for Life Education Fund, and National Pro-Life Women's Caucus as Amicus Curiae Supporting Petitioners at 6, Nat'l Inst. of Family & Life Advocates v. Becerra, 138 S. Ct. 2361 (2018) (No. 16–1140) (Bordlee as counsel of record) (alleging harm to "vulnerable women and children" from a California statute that required covered facilities to provide information on comprehensive family planning services); Brief for Jérôme Lejeune Foundation USA et al. as Amicus Curiae Supporting Petitioners at 23–24, Horne v. Isaacson, 134 S. Ct. 905 (2014) (No. 13–402) (Bordlee as co-author) (arguing that sex-selective abortion constitutes discrimination on the basis of gender in litigation challenging an Arizona law that limited abortion after twenty weeks of gestation).

We cannot measure the influence of these briefs, which are read by the public and by judges, even when they do not cite them for support. *But see* Gilardi v. U.S. Dep't of Health & Hum. Servs., 733 F. 3d 1208, 1221 (D.C. Cir. 2013) (quoting Brief Amici Curiae of Breast Cancer Prevention Institute) (referencing an amicus written by Bordlee to justify a claim about the "increased risk for breast, cervical, and liver cancers" and "debatable science" of contraceptives).

[186] *See supra* Section II.B.

time, many who enacted and defended TRAP laws came to act on a sincere belief that a law pushing a resisting woman into becoming a mother was better for the pregnant woman herself. "Love them both," as Jack Willke came to argue, after market-testing the frame.[187] But better in what sense?

It is not sufficient to ask whether advocates manipulated their audiences into enacting woman-protective restrictions on abortion in order to protect unborn life or whether, instead, they sincerely believed that imposing health-justified restrictions on abortion was better for women. If the drive to limit women's access to abortion was based on a sincere belief about women's welfare, what kind of a belief about women was it?

On the face of it, advocating for "pro-woman and pro-life" laws because they are good for women is advocating on the basis of a sex-role-based belief that, as Dorinda Bordlee (and others) emphasized, "the woman and the child have a sacred bond that should not be divided. What's good for the child is good for the mother. So now we're advocating legislation that is good for the woman."[188] On this sex-role-based view, there is no conflict of interests between women and the unborn life they bear because, as Bordlee explained, what is good for the child is good for the mother. A state can restrict abortion to protect the unborn and it is good for women's health because what is good for children is good for women's health. The descriptive claim is also a normative claim about sex roles that are "good" for women.

The record, in Louisiana and elsewhere, shows that this belief, even when "sincere,"[189] was not a concern about women's health as we understand the term "health" outside the abortion context. It is not normal to adopt health and safety standards for the practice of medicine that eliminate risk by means that shut down the regulated practice—and then to act as if the standard's elimination of medical practitioners is of no consequence to patients' health and safety.[190] In

---

[187] See supra text accompanying note 99 (discussing polling that led him to change his argument for protecting unborn life).

[188] See supra text accompanying note 118. For similar views expressed by Denise Burke in 2016, see supra note 132.

[189] See ZIEGLER, supra note 113, at 145 (observing that "[m]any pro-lifers sincerely believed that abortion harmed women"). For women working in the movement's crisis pregnancy centers expressing these beliefs, see Siegel, supra note 88, at 1654–55.

[190] See supra Section II.C.1.

the ordinary case, further investigation and a likely adjustment of course is warranted; it might even be ethically required. But the supporters of the admitting privileges law appeared utterly unconcerned that the health and safety regulations they advocated would have nearly eliminated the practice of abortion in the state.

Evidence that officials advocating for admitting privileges restrictions on abortion were talking about women's health in a special, coded, sex-role-based way concerned with the wrongs of a woman ending a pregnancy—and not otherwise concerned with women's physical wellbeing—appears in the legislative debate over the admitting privileges law and outside of the debate.

In Louisiana, as in Texas, opponents of the admitting privileges law described in concrete detail the health harms the law could inflict on women in the state.[191] Not only would a law shutting down abortion providers push women into having later, more dangerous abortions; it would restrict women's access to the contraception that the clinics provided and it would push resisting women into bearing children under unsafe conditions, often without adequate healthcare.[192] Louisiana was among the most dangerous places to give birth in the nation, and, at the time the legislature enacted the clinic-closing admitting privileges law, there was a shortage of medical care for pregnant women in the state. Alice Chapman, the head of Tulane University's Medical Students for Choice, emphasized that "Louisiana ranks 44th in the nation for maternal mortality, 49th for infant mortality, and has only one OB/GYN for every 13,136 women."[193]

The bill's proponents brushed off warnings about the health injuries the admitting privileges law could inflict by pushing women into late or unlawful abortions—or by pushing women without access to medical care or health insurance into pregnancy. On several occasions, legislators leading debate over the admitting privileges law rebutted accounts of the health harms the law would inflict on women by reverting, fleetingly, to life-justified arguments for restricting abortion.

---

[191] For Texas, see *supra* text accompanying notes 142–43. For one example in Louisiana, see DX 119, *supra* note 156, at 18–20 (transcribing the statement of Alice Chapman, Tulane University Medical Students for Choice).

[192] *Id.* During the State Senate hearing, a witness urged the importance of addressing high rates of unintended pregnancy to bring down abortion rates. DX 119, *supra* note 156, at 64–66 (transcribing the statement of Autumn Fawn Gandolfi).

[193] DX 119, *supra* note 156, at 19.

In the most vivid of these exchanges, Representative Katrina Jackson, sponsor of the admitting privileges law, disparaged Alice Chapman and dismissed her concerns about the ways the law would injure women by announcing that abortion was genocide—a view she has elsewhere explained at greater length.[194] Jackson did not speak for all African Americans in the state.[195] Alfreda Tillman Bester, general counsel for the Louisiana State Conference of the NAACP, testified that the Louisiana state conference of the NAACP had voted to oppose the bill. Bestor gave impassioned testimony opposing the legislation as a threat to poor women's lives, health, and freedom,

---

[194] DX 119, *supra* note 156, at 20 ("I've heard it thrown around by the young ladies that were at the table today that this protects mostly minority women. . . . I'm not sure if you are aware, but the number one genocide right now in the African-American community . . . is because most of our babies are dying in the womb from abortions. Did you know that?"); *see also id.* ("But were you aware that more African-Americans die from abortions than any other illness? . . . I don't want people advocating erroneously for African-American women. . . . If we protect one facet of African-Americans, we protect all of them."). In other settings, Rep. Jackson speaks directly about these views, and is publicized by the antiabortion movement as holding them. Announcing that Rep. Jackson was chosen as a speaker at the 2020 March for Life (with the theme of "Life Empowers: Pro-Life is Pro-Woman"), Live Action quoted Rep. Jackson explaining her position on abortion: "I think it (abortion) mitigates our race's voting power, it hurts our race's power in the census. I really consider it to be modern-day genocide." Anne Marie Williams, *2020 March for Life to Showcase How Being Pro-Life Is Pro-Woman*, LiveAction (Dec. 13, 2019, 2:52 PM), https://www.liveaction.org/news/march-for-life-pro-life-pro-woman; *see also* Anna Reynolds, *Black Female Democratic Lawmaker Says Abortion Is "Modern-Day Genocide,"* LiveAction (June 6, 2019, 12:51 PM), https://www.liveaction.org/news/black-female -democrat-abortion-genocide.

LiveAction reports Representative Jackson's views selectively and does not discuss her beliefs as a "whole-life Democrat." *See* Lauretta Brown, *Pro-Life Democrat Katrina Jackson Marches for Life, Writes Louisiana Legislation*, Nat'l Catholic Register (Jan. 21, 2020), https://www .ncregister.com/news/pro-life-democrat-katrina-jackson-marches-for-life-writes-louisiana -legislation (reporting State Sen. Jackson identifying as a "whole-life Democrat" which she defines as "ensuring protection of human life from the time of conception to the time of death, which means we not only advocate for the birth of the child but we also advocate for that child to have a true chance at what we call the American Dream regardless of its parents' socioeconomic status, regardless of where they're from, regardless of their background"); *id.* (reporting Rep. Jackson asserting that "[p]ro-lifers and those who are pro-abortion . . . might not ever agree on the sanctity of life, but we can agree on the woman receiving proper health care during her pregnancy; and around this country and in the state of Louisiana we're having to address the high [maternal] mortality rate that has been developing"). Representative Jackson supported Medicaid expansion in Louisiana, as other supporters of the state's admitting privileges law did not. *See infra* text accompanying notes 201–05.

[195] To locate Jackson's views in the history of debates over race and reproduction before and after *Roe*, see Melissa Murray, *Race-ing* Roe: *Reproductive Justice, Racial Justice, and the Battle for* Roe v. Wade, 134 Harv. L. Rev. (forthcoming 2021). For a wide-ranging race-conscious de-bate among reproductive justice advocates about Jackson's pro-life views, see Bobbi-Jean Misick, *Black Advocates Take Different Views on What Louisiana's Anti-Abortion Amendment Means for Inequity*, Crescent to Capitol (Nov. 16, 2020), https://crescenttocapitol.org/2020/11/16 /black-advocates-take-different-views-on-what-louisianas-anti-abortion-amendment-means -for-inequity.

stating that "[s]ince this law went into effect in Texas, women have died because they self-induced and did not have access to clinics or hospitals that provided them with restorative care."[196] Representative Frank Hoffman, chair of the House Health and Welfare Committee, dismissed her testimony, countering: "I just want to make one point. You said women die in Texas. A person dies every day there's an abortion too."[197]

As Hoffman waved off the passionate testimony of two other opposition witnesses with the repeated retort that "someone dies,"[198] the third witness objected and emphasized that restricting abortion throughout Louisiana meant that *women* would die and urged the legislators to pursue their goal through policies that would actually reduce abortions and actually protect the lives and health of women. Bruce Parker, a community organizer with Louisiana Progress Action, emphasized that abortion restrictions would not in fact stop abortions but would lead to injuries and loss of life; he then identified the very different kinds of laws that Louisiana would have to enact to actually reduce abortion and protect life and health in the state:

> Restricting access to safe legal abortion does not mean fewer abortions, it means more unsafe abortions, more women having abortions later in their pregnancies, and more women's death[s]. Most women who have abortions are poor. Most are already mothers. If we want to be serious about wanting fewer abortions in Louisiana, that means giving women and girls access to reproductive healthcare so they can prevent unplanned pregnancies.
>
> It means guaranteeing that jobs pay a living wage and that women can access affordable child care, support policies that will actually decrease abortion in Louisiana and improve the lives of women and children, such as comprehensive sex ed, Medicaid expansion, raising the minimum wage, and expanding early childhood education.

---

[196] DX 119, *supra* note 156, at 26–27 ("This bill, in my opinion, reeks of interposition and nullification. We have a constitution in this nation. . . . And for this legislature to impose its religious opinions on women of this state is an absolute immorality, in my opinion."). While directly linking deaths to the passage of Texas's HB 2 is difficult, one study found that after HB 2 passed in 2011, deaths relating to pregnancy complications doubled in Texas. Marian F. MacDorman et al., *Recent Increases in the U.S. Maternal Mortality Rate*, 128 Obstetrics & Gynecology 447, 447, 454 (2016). Another study reported that 2 percent of Texas women report attempting to self-induce abortion, with 18 percent of those attempts occurring between the years of 2010–2015. Daniel Grossman et al., *Knowledge, Opinion, and Experience Related to Abortion Self-Induction in Texas*, 34 Contraception 360 (2015).

[197] DX 119, *supra* note 156, at 27.

[198] *Id.* at 29; *see also id.* at 25 (transcribing Chairman Hoffman's one-sentence reply to Dr. Alexis Lee, an opposition witness who discussed the dangers of pregnancy and giving birth).

If we are voting for this bill today because you believe it will save women's lives, I look forward to seeing you vote for those bills as well. You say you want to decrease the number of abortions, then do so.[199]

Where opponents reasoned about reducing abortion and protecting women's life and health as requiring coordinated policy choices, the bill's supporters steadfastly refused to discuss protection for women's lives and health in the broader policy context and enacted the admitting privileges law without addressing any of the concerns about the harms the law would inflict or discussing plans to mitigate them.

The silence of pro-life legislators aligned with their state's policy choices. At the time it enacted the admitting privileges law, Louisiana excelled in enacting abortion restrictions, enough for AUL annually to crown the state the most pro-life in the nation. But, outside the abortion context, the state did not have nearly the same appetite for promoting healthcare.

In a state where approximately 70 percent of women gave birth with the funding provided by the Medicaid program, Governor Jindal was in the news for cutting state budget contributions to Medicaid and lowering reimbursement to doctors and hospitals. (In 2011, an obstetrician reported being reimbursed by Louisiana Medicaid at 42 percent of the rate she was reimbursed from private insurance.[200])

In 2013, the year before Louisiana enacted its clinic-closing admitting privileges law, Governor Jindal made headlines for refusing to expand Medicaid, with some reports estimating that about 400,000 people in the state had incomes at 138 percent of the federal poverty level—or $26,952 for a family of three—which would have made them eligible for the health care coverage that the state refused.[201]

---

[199] *Id.* at 29 (transcribing the statement of Bruce Parker with Louisiana Progress Action). For another especially fierce expression of this argument, see *id.* at 27 (transcribing the statement of Carrie Wooten with Louisiana Progress Action) (arguing that "[b]y shutting three of our five abortion service providers in the state, you are forcing women into desperate situations, and they will act accordingly," predicting that "[l]ow-income women will suffer the most, women who are already mothers, women who work full-time at terribly low-wage jobs" and arguing that all who vote for legislation would be complicit in the desperation, illness and death enforcing the clinic-closing law would cause).

[200] *See* Robert Pear, *Cuts Leave Patients with Medicaid Cards, but No Specialist to See,* N.Y. TIMES (Apr. 1, 2011), https://www.nytimes.com/2011/04/02/health/policy/02medicaid.html ?searchResultPosition=2 (describing cuts to Louisiana's Medicaid program).

[201] Laura Maggi, *Sen. Landrieu Blasts Gov. Jindal, Says He's Spurning Federal Aid to Further Ambitions,* TIMES-PICAYUNE (Feb. 27, 2013, 4:14 AM), https://www.nola.com/entertainment_life /health_fitness/article_3cb1a179-7317-5356-8775-fecf85fda484.html#incart_m-rpt-2.

(Representative Katrina Jackson, a Democrat, co-authored the de-
feated Medicaid expansion bill.[202])

In his statement justifying the state's refusal to accept federal
healthcare for these families, Governor Jindal did not talk about his
interest in protecting life and in protecting women's health. Instead,
Jindal's statement refusing to accept federal support to expand Medicaid distinguished among citizens as more and less worthy of public
assistance, denigrating the dependent and praising the virtues of
limited government: "[W]e should design our policies so that more
people are pulling the cart than riding in the cart. . . . We should
measure success by reducing the number of people on public assistance. But the Left has been very clear—their goal is to transform all
health care in America into government-run health care. . . . It seems
that our federal government measures progress by how many Americans it can put onto public assistance programs."[203]

The state's decision to block Medicaid expansion harmed all low-
income Louisianans, but the consequences were especially severe
for pregnant people. According to Health Affairs, state Medicaid
expansions have closed devastating coverage gaps for low-income
women before, during, and after pregnancy.[204] Newborn children
benefited enormously too, as Medicaid expansions were linked to
higher rates of continuous perinatal care.[205]

Not only did Louisiana restrict access to abortion in 2014 while
refusing money from the federal government that would have provided healthcare to hundreds of thousands of uninsured people in the
state; the state restricted access to abortion without helping women
avoid unwanted pregnancies. At a time when the state had one of the
highest birth rates to teens between the ages of fifteen and nineteen,[206]

---

[202] Sheila V. Kuman, *Louisiana Health Committee Rejects Medicaid Expansion Bill*, TIMES-
PICAYUNE (Apr. 25, 2013, 5:30 AM), https://www.nola.com/news/politics/article_c00eb45f
-fbee-5797-9c1a-bfdd7e574709.html ("Monroe Democrat Rep. Katrina Jackson, one of the
six co-authors of the bill, said the expansion could bring over 400,000 currently uninsured
residents onto the Medicaid rolls, while saving the state money.").

[203] Bobby Jindal, *Why I Opposed Medicaid Expansion*, TIMES-PICAYUNE (July 23, 2013, 9:30 PM),
https://www.nola.com/opinions/article_c0155e08-f87b-5c8f-b4e3-092a5b095991.html.

[204] Jamie R. Daw, Tyler N. A. Winkelman, Vanessa K. Dalton, Katy B. Kozhimannil, &
Lindsay K. Admon, *Medicaid Expansion Improved Perinatal Insurance Continuity for Low-Income
Women*, 39 HEALTH AFFAIRS 1531 (2020), https://www.healthaffairs.org/doi/pdf/10.1377/hlthaff
.2019.01835.

[205] *Id.*

[206] *See* Kate Richardson, *Should Sex Education Be Required in Louisiana Public Schools: Voices
from the Listening Post*, VIANOLAVIE (Aug. 22, 2019), https://www.vianolavie.org/2019/08/22

the state allowed schools to offer abstinence-focused sex education for students above the sixth grade but otherwise lacked a standardized sex education curriculum.[207] In 2014, the legislature refused to redress the "the state's high rates of teenage pregnancies . . . by implementing 'age appropriate' sex education standards in public elementary and secondary schools."[208]

During the same session that the legislature enacted the admitting privileges law restricting access to abortion, the legislature declined to enact a bill that modestly expanded required coverage of developmentally appropriate sexual education in public schools.[209] Accurate sexual education including information about contraception has been shown to reduce teen pregnancy rates and reduce abortion.[210] Yet Governor Jindal and groups including the Louisiana Conference of Catholic Bishops and the Louisiana Family Forum opposed even this measure on the grounds "that parents should maintain exclusive control of their children's exposure to sex education."[211] Jindal once again opposed government involvement: "These are

---

/should-sex-education-be-required-in-louisiana-public-schools-voices-from-the-listening-post (reporting on program that aired April 10, 2014); *see also* Teddy Wilson, *Louisiana Committee Passes Bill to Ban Abortion Providers from Guiding Public School Discussion on Sex Ed*, REWIRE NEWS GROUP (Apr. 11, 2014, 4:01 PM), https://rewirenewsgroup.com/article/2014/04/11/louisiana -committee-passes-bill-ban-abortion-providers-guiding-public-school-discussions-sex-ed ("According to the federal Office of Adolescent Health, Louisiana has the sixth highest rate of teenage births in the nation and the eighth highest rate of teenage pregnancies.").

[207] *See* LA. STAT. ANN. § 17:281 (asserting that any public school "may, but is not required to, offer instruction in subject matter designated as 'sex education,'" and asserting that the major emphasis of such a course "shall be to encourage sexual abstinence between unmarried persons"). For a look at Louisiana's choices in comparative perspective today, see *Sex and HIV Education*, GUTTMACHER INST., https://www.guttmacher.org/state-policy/explore/sex-and-hiv -education (last updated Feb. 1, 2021) (graphing policy choices of all 50 states).

[208] Shadee Ashtari, *Louisiana Lawmaker Says Lack of Sex Education Is 'Really A Form of Child Abuse'*, HUFFINGTON POST (Mar. 17, 2014, 1:55 PM), https://www.huffpost.com/entry/louisiana -sex-education-patricia-smith-_n_4979641?guccounter=1.

[209] *Id.*

[210] See Leah H. Keller & Laura D. Lindberg, *Expanding the Scope of Sex Education and the Teen Pregnancy Prevention Program: A Work in Progress*, GUTTMACHER INST. (Feb. 27, 2020), https://www.guttmacher.org/article/2020/02/expanding-scope-sex-education-and-teen-preg nancy-prevention-program-work-progress (reporting that "evidence has long demonstrated that declining adolescent pregnancy rates are being driven by improved contraceptive use— not declines in sex (with no evidence that abstinence-only programs actually contribute to such declines)").

[211] *See* Ashtari, *supra* note 208. The sex ed bill asserted "abstinence is the most reliable way to prevent pregnancy" and directed that "no part of sex education instruction shall in any way advocate or support abortion." *Id.*

decisions that are best made by parents and local communities, not state government."[212]

But Louisiana did update its sex-ed laws during the same session it enacted the admitting privileges law. Governor Jindal signed into law a bill that Dorinda Bordlee helped draft prohibiting Planned Parenthood from having any role in sexual education.[213] (In opposing passage of the law, one witness warned against abstinence-only curricula, pointing out that in Mississippi, the curriculum "called on students to unwrap a piece of chocolate, pass it around class and observe how dirty it became."[214])

Questioning the values these legislative choices expressed, the director of Planned Parenthood in Louisiana located the state's 2014 abortion restrictions in the larger policy context: "When given an opportunity to expand Medicaid, ensure equal pay, increase access to health education and raise the minimum wage, the legislators refused to support Louisiana families." She asked: "If we don't provide access to health care or education to prevent pregnancy, how does eliminating access to abortion care make sense?"[215]

Those professing to restrict abortion in the interest of protecting women's health claimed concern about women's health of a kind that transcends the abortion context. Yet during the legislative hearings, those who called for passage of the admitting privileges statute as a health and safety, pro-woman, and pro-life law were unwilling to address, and even sought to silence, witnesses who raised questions

[212] *Id.*

[213] *See* Emily Lane, *Bill Bans Planned Parenthood, Other Abortion Providers from Instructing Schools on Sex Education*, Times-Picayune (Apr. 10, 2014, 12:18 AM), https://www.nola.com/news/politics/article_ad7e8c9a-2897-52fe-bdbe-9452870370fe.html (reporting that Rep. Frank Hoffman sponsored House Bill 306 prohibiting employees or representatives of providers from involvement in instruction or distribution of information in schools); Sarah Zagorski, *Governor Jindal Signs Bills to Protect Women and Children from Louisiana's Abortion Industry*, La. Right to Life (June 12, 2014), http://archive.constantcontact.com/fs191/1101796400807/archive/111 7626538741.html (identifying Bordlee "as principal architect of both bills" and quoting Bordlee detailing women's involvement and characterizing H.B. 388 as "by women and for women").

[214] *See* Lane, *supra* note 213 (citing recent article). The article linked to a report of a Mississippi class providing sex ed by circulating chocolate among children. *See* Alana Semuels, *Sex Education Stumbles in Mississippi*, L.A. Times (Apr. 2, 2014, 6:53 PM), https://www.latimes.com/nation/la-na-ms-teen-pregnancy-20140403-story.html ("'They're using the Peppermint Pattie to show that a girl is no longer clean or valuable after she's had sex—that she's been used,' said Barnard, who works in public health. 'That shouldn't be the lesson we send kids about sex.'").

[215] Melissa Flournoy, *Letter: Legislators Failed to Address Health*, Advocate (June 8, 2014, 12:40 PM), https://www.theadvocate.com/baton_rouge/opinion/letters/article_de65dc7f-08e0-5932-accc-7b3554f57f9c.html.

about the health risks the legislature was imposing on women by enacting a law that would dramatically restrict opportunities to end a pregnancy.[216] They did not discuss the health needs of citizens the state was pushing into motherhood as we ordinarily understand the meaning of "health."

If we consider the circumstances of pregnant women in Louisiana, we can better understand the different conceptions of women's health circulating in the legislative debate. Evaluating the public health data provides perspective on statements about women's health and safety expressed by supporters and opponents of Louisiana's admitting privilege law and sheds light on the values, priorities, and policy choices of a state that AUL long deemed the most pro-life in the nation.[217]

The United States has the highest rate of maternal deaths in the developed world, and the rate of pregnancy-related death is especially acute among black women.[218] And, five years after passage of its admitting privileges law, Louisiana's maternal mortality rate is among the highest in the nation.[219]

---

[216] *See supra* text accompanying notes 191–202.

[217] *See, e.g., Louisiana Ranked No.1 Pro-Life State*, LOUISIANA RIGHT TO LIFE (Jan. 23, 2020), https://prolifelouisiana.org/louisiana-ranked-no-1-pro-life-state; *Louisiana Number One: Americans United for Life Releases Life List 2020*, AMERICANS UNITED FOR LIFE (Jan 23, 2020), https://aul.org/2020/01/23/louisiana-number-one-americans-united-for-life-releases-life-list-2020.

[218] Nina Martin & Renee Montagne, *U.S. Has the Worst Rate of Maternal Deaths in the Developed World*, NPR (May 17, 2017, 10:28 AM), https://www.npr.org/2017/05/12/528098789/u-s-has-the-worst-rate-of-maternal-deaths-in-the-developed-world (reporting that the rate is rising in the U.S. as it declines elsewhere and observing that, in the U.S., funding is targeted at saving infants rather than focusing on the health of pregnant and post-partem women); *see also* Nicholas J. Kassebaum et al., *Global, Regional, and National Levels of Maternal Mortality, 1990–2015: A Systematic Analysis for the Global Burden of Disease Study 2015*, 388 LANCET 1775 (2016) (showing increasing maternal mortality in the US compared to similar countries); Pooja Mehta et al., *Racial Inequities in Preventable Pregnancy-Related Deaths in Louisiana, 2011–2016*, 135 OBSTETRICS & GYNECOLOGY 276, 277, 279 (2020) ("Non-Hispanic black women are three to four times as likely as non-Hispanic white women to experience a pregnancy-related death nationally."). Khiara Bridges has recently reviewed the literature on the sources of racial disparities in maternal mortality. *See* Khiara M. Bridges, *Racial Disparities in Maternal Mortality*, 95 N.Y.U. L. REV. 1229, 1248–67 (2020).

[219] *See* Laura Ungar & Caroline Simon, *Which States Have the Worst Maternal Mortality?*, USA TODAY (Nov. 1, 2018), https://www.usatoday.com/list/news/investigations/maternal-mortality-by-state/7b6a2a48-0b79-40c2-a44d-8111879a8336 (ranking Louisiana first out of forty-six states with available data); Emily Woodruff, *What Contributes to Louisiana's High Maternal Mortality Rate? The Distance to Care, Research Says*, NOLA.COM (Oct. 20, 2020, 10:45 PM), https://www.nola.com/news/healthcare_hospitals/article_c3cf355e-131f-11eb-851a-6b04dbf7e8d0.html ("Louisiana has among the highest rate of death for pregnant women in the U.S."). *But see* Marian F. MacDorman & Eugene Declercq, *The Failure of United States Maternal Mortality Reporting and Its Impact on Women's Lives*, 45 BIRTH 105 (2018) (reporting that because of inconsistencies in reporting and coding state data, the United States has only intermittently published data on

These health outcomes are not simply the expression of poverty. They are the expression of policy. A recent study identified as an important cause of Louisiana's high maternal mortality the absence of prenatal care in the state.[220] Over a third of the state's parishes lack "a hospital offering obstetric care, a birth center or any OB/GYNs or certified nurse-midwives."[221] More than one in four women in the state need to travel out of their parish for routine appointments, and they may not have the money, the ability to miss work, and the resources to secure child care. According to the study's findings, "women in these 'maternity care deserts' had a threefold higher risk for deaths directly related to the pregnancy, such as severe bleeding or preeclampsia, a dangerous complication involving high blood pressure."[222] The risk for pregnancy-associated deaths (deaths of any cause—such as homicide or suicide—up to a year after pregnancy) was dramatically higher as well.[223]

---

maternal mortality, and, citing Texas as an example, observing that this failure to report has allowed escalations in maternal mortality to go unnoticed and unremedied); Nina Martin, *Lost Mothers: The New U.S. Maternal Mortality Rate Fails to Capture Many Deaths*, PROPUBLICA (Feb. 13, 2020, 12:40 PM), https://www.propublica.org/article/the-new-us-maternal-mortality-rate-fails -to-capture-many-deaths.

[220] Low Medicaid reimbursement rates aggravate shortages, with the impact falling on the poorest, who are unable to find coverage for which they may be eligible, or unable to access a doctor until late in pregnancy. On the ways that low Medicaid reimbursement rates aggravate shortages, see Pear, *supra* note 200; and Elizabeth Renter, *You've Got Medicaid – Why Can't You See the Doctor?*, U.S. NEWS & WORLD REP. (May 26, 2015, 9:00 AM), https://health.usnews .com/health-news/health-insurance/articles/2015/05/26/youve-got-medicaid-why-cant-you -see-the-doctor. *See also* Karen N. Brown, *How Is OB/GYN Medicaid Reimbursement Impacting the Shortage of Doctors?*, VOLUSON CLUB: EMPOWERED WOMEN'S HEALTH (Jan. 17, 2019), https:// www.volusonclub.net/empowered-womens-health/how-is-ob-gyn-medicaid-reimbursement -impacting-the-shortage-of-doctors (reporting that "about 31 percent of physicians do not accept Medicaid, largely because its reimbursement is the lowest of all third-party payers. Many patients who have Medicaid have trouble finding a doctor and, therefore, wait longer to see one—which means that they are likely to need more care by the time of their appointment").

On the ways that Medicaid administration and lack of insurance affect pregnant women, see Julia Belluz & Nina Martin, *The Extraordinary Danger of Being Pregnant and Uninsured in Texas*, Vox (Dec. 19, 2019, 10:08 AM), http://www.vox.com/science-and-health/2019/12/6/20995227 /women-health-care-maternal-mortality-insurance-texas (describing, in a state that refused the Medicaid expansion, the large numbers of uninsured women as well as the brief and late Medicaid coverage provided pregnant women and relating the consequences of these health care deprivations in maternal and infant illness and death).

[221] Woodruff, *supra* note 219; *see also* Maeve Wallace et al., *Maternity Care Deserts and Pregnancy-Associated Mortality in Louisiana*, WOMEN'S HEALTH ISSUES (Sept. 8, 2020); Elizabeth Dawes Gay, *The Challenges and Solutions to Accessing Maternity Care in Louisiana*, EVERY MOTHER COUNTS (Nov. 30, 2017), https://blog.everymothercounts.org/why-louisiana-494cf0b487fc ("Almost half of Louisiana's counties do not have a single Ob/Gyn.").

[222] Woodruff, *supra* note 219.

[223] *Id.*

Women of color in Louisiana bear the brunt of the state's policy choices. At a time when Louisiana (repeatedly) decided to restrict access to abortion without significantly improving women's access to healthcare or to sex education, the "rate of pregnancy-related death among non-Hispanic black women was 4.1 times the rate among non-Hispanic white women," and "among non-Hispanic black women who experienced pregnancy-related death, 59% . . . of deaths were deemed potentially preventable, compared with 9% . . . among non-Hispanic white women."[224]

It should go without saying that these policy investments harm infants. The Department of Health and Human Services found that newborns whose mothers had no prenatal care are almost five times more likely to die than babies born to mothers who had early prenatal care.[225] In 2013, the year the state refused to expand Medicaid, the state ranked among the worst in infant health, one survey finding that "Louisiana performs worse than nearly every other state in the nation on measures of infant mortality, preterm birth, low birth weight, and caesarian sections."[226] Today, the Centers for Disease Control reports that Louisiana has the second highest infant mortality rate in the nation.[227]

Louisiana's decision to enact its admitting privileges law, obstructing women's access to abortion without making significant changes in the state's provision of Medicaid or sex education, compromised women's autonomy and women's health. The decision to enact the admitting privilege statute was not a benign expression of pro-life sentiment. It was an expression of antiabortion animus concerning women as well

---

[224] Mehta et al., *supra* note 218, at 276.

[225] *See* OFFICE ON WOMEN'S HEALTH, U.S. DEP'T OF HEALTH & HUMAN SERVS., *Prenatal Care Fact Sheet*, https://www.womenshealth.gov/a-z-topics/prenatal-care (last updated Apr. 1, 2019) ("Babies of mothers who do not get prenatal care are three times more likely to have a low birth weight and five times more likely to die than those born to mothers who do get care.").

[226] Vida Foubister, *Case Study: Louisiana's Poor Rankings Make Improving Birth Outcomes a State Imperative*, COMMONWEALTH FUND (Mar. 2013), https://www.commonwealthfund.org /publications/newsletter-article/case-study-louisianas-poor-rankings-make-improving-birth -outcomes.

[227] In 2014, when Act 620 was passed, Louisiana was tied for 4th in infant mortality. *See Linked Birth / Infant Death Records, 2007–2018 Results*, CTRS. FOR DISEASE CONTROL & PREVENTION, https://wonder.cdc.gov/controller/saved/D69/D96F850 (Nov. 30, 2020) (filtered set). By 2018, Louisiana had the 2nd-worst infant mortality rate in the country. *See Linked Birth / Infant Death Records, 2007–2018 Results*, *supra*.

as the unborn that threatened the lives and health of women and the children they might bear.

III. "Pro-Woman," Health-Justified Restrictions on Abortion in the Courts

Expanding the frame to consider *June Medical* in its larger historical and policy context brings into view the constitutional, political, and human stakes of the doctrinal dispute in the case. Expanding the frame explains why, in concurring, Chief Justice Roberts picked a seemingly technical fight over "balancing."[228] He was attacking judges who scrutinized the underlying logic of admitting privileges restrictions on abortion—assuming a stance toward the record not wholly unlike the committee chair who dismissed the testimony of opposition witnesses.

Integrating the accounts of *June Medical* in Parts I and II of this Article enables us to appreciate the role judges are playing in the political conflicts we have just examined. At the same time, the examination of doctrine serves the ordinary function of identifying forms of argument on which participants are drawing in the fight over revising and reversing *Casey*. The exercise identifies resources on which willing judges can still draw to scrutinize TRAP laws in the wake of *June Medical* and identifies the next points of conflict for judges seeking to legitimate TRAP laws.

It is no secret that conservative judges are weakening constitutional protections for the abortion right. At times, they shout out opposition to the right *Roe* recognized.[229] But where woman-protective abortion restrictions are concerned, judges often play another less appreciated role.

As opponents of abortion have come to package restrictions on abortion as protections for women, judges who oppose the abortion right embrace standards that insulate these legislative constructions from judicial scrutiny. In this role, judges are not shouting out moral, political, or jurisprudential opposition to the abortion right; they invoke a judge's commitment to democracy to enable a movement

---

[228] *See supra* Part I.

[229] Justice Clarence Thomas has reiterated that he "remain[s] fundamentally opposed to the Court's abortion jurisprudence." Whole Woman's Health v. Hellerstedt, 136 S. Ct. 2292, 2324 (2016) (Thomas, J., dissenting).

strategy that, as we have seen, in design and implementation avoids forthrightness about its aims.

Leaders of the antiabortion movement have adopted strategies to end abortion incrementally through TRAP laws that legislatures present as health and safety laws protecting women. Judges who make law requiring deference to legislatures not only uphold these restrictions; they insulate them from scrutiny, credit their woman-protective aims and justifications—and declare these modes of reasoning about and regulating women constitutional.[230]

It is a remarkable project for judges, whose logic seems more political than ethical or jurisprudential. Judges have voiced ethical and jurisprudential objections to *Roe* since the dissents in that case.[231] But more is involved if a judge acts on those objections by upholding abortion restrictions that push resisting women into childbearing for the announced reason of protecting women. It is one thing to reverse *Roe* and *Casey*; it is another to pursue that aim through forms of rational basis review that elude the public's grasp. What view of women, or democracy, does this reflect? These judicial moves invite a different ethical and constitutional dialogue.

Judges reviewing TRAP laws are reviewing laws that depend on indirection. Legislatures interested in restricting abortion can enact directive counseling mandates or reason-based bans on abortion, but these efforts to dissuade and to discredit do not prevent as many abortions as a woman-protective health and safety regulation of providers can. Yet as Part II suggests, enacting these laws requires obscuring their fetal-protective and abortion-restrictive aims for reasons that are political as well as legal. The incrementalist strategy seeks to decimate the remaining clinic infrastructure without triggering backlash from a public that expects at least nominal consideration of

---

[230] *Cf.* Korematsu v. United States, 323 U.S. 214, 246 (1944) (Jackson, J., dissenting) ("A military commander may overstep the bounds of constitutionality, and it is an incident. But if we review and approve, that passing incident becomes the doctrine of the Constitution. There it has a generative power of its own, and all that it creates will be in its own image. Nothing better illustrates this danger than does the Court's opinion in this case.").

[231] Justice Rehnquist asserted that the Court should have applied rational basis review and objected that the decision revived *Lochner. See* Roe v. Wade, 410 U.S. 113, 173–74 (1973) (Rehnquist, J., dissenting) (citing Williamson v. Lee Optical Co., 348 U.S. 483, 491 (1955) and Lochner v. New York, 198 U.S. 45 (1905)). Justice White, joined by Justice Rehnquist, raised concerns about protecting unborn life and expressed contempt for women who seek abortions: "During the period prior to the time the fetus becomes viable, the Constitution of the United States values the convenience, whim, or caprice of the pregnant woman more than the life or potential life of the fetus." *Id.* at 221 (White, J., dissenting).

women's interests and that, by large majorities, opposes overruling *Roe* and banning abortion. In 2019, a Pew poll reported that 70 percent of Americans oppose overturning *Roe v. Wade* and 61 percent believe abortion should be legal in all or most cases.[232]

Does an appreciation of these political constraints inform the reasoning of judges as well as advocates and legislators? Conservative scholars mercilessly criticized Chief Justice Roberts for engaging in political calculations in *June Medical* and elsewhere; in their view, his tendency to let political calculations shape his judgments sets him apart from judges they view as principled conservatives.[233] At the end of a Term Josh Blackman called "Blue June,"[234] Varad Mehta and Adrian Vermeule reported that "[c]onservatives . . . thought Roberts's invocation of precedent [in *June Medical*] was desperately unconvincing and served only to rationalize what appears to be a fear of signing on to more sweeping, and therefore more controversial, pro-life rulings."[235] Mehta and Vermeule blamed the Chief Justice for "the very politicization of the Supreme Court he sought to prevent" and concluded "Republicans' determination to install Barrett on the Supreme Court a week before a presidential election can be seen as a sign of conservatives' distrust of the chief justice . . . a political gambit designed to thwart a master of political gamesmanship."[236]

But is Chief Justice Roberts acting more politically than the conservative judges who would uphold woman-protective health-justified abortion restrictions on rational basis review? Once we read the doctrinal debate in *June Medical* as part of the story of woman-protective health-justified abortion restrictions this article recounts, we can better

---

[232] *See U.S. Public Continues to Favor Legal Abortion, Oppose Overturning* Roe v. Wade, PEW RES. CTR. (Aug. 29, 2019), https://www.pewresearch.org/politics/2019/08/29/u-s-public-continues-to-favor-legal-abortion-oppose-overturning-roe-v-wade.

[233] Josh Blackman, *Chief Justice Roberts Has Fallen into a "Truly Bottomless Pit from Which There Is Simply No Extracting [Himself]*," REASON: VOLOKH CONSPIRACY (Dec. 17, 2020, 6:24 PM), https://reason.com/volokh/2020/12/17/chief-justice-roberts-has-fallen-into-a-truly-bottomless-pit-from-which-there-is-simply-no-extracting-itself/?amp&__twitter_impression=true ("For Roberts, every decision has to [be] refracted through some bizarre political lens. His jurisprudential lodestar is the Gallup poll.").

[234] Josh Blackman, *The Ten Phases of Blue June*, REASON: VOLOKH CONSPIRACY (July 2, 2020, 7:30 AM), https://reason.com/volokh/2020/07/02/the-ten-phases-of-blue-june.

[235] Varad Mehta & Adrian Vermeule, *John Roberts's Self-Defeating Attempt to Make the Court Appear Nonpolitical*, WASH. POST (Dec. 17, 2020, 2:25 PM), https://www.washingtonpost.com/outlook/john-roberts-self-defeating-attempt-to-make-the-court-appear-nonpolitical/2020/12/17/d3d1df5a-3fd5-11eb-9453-fc36ba051781_story.html.

[236] *Id.*

appreciate the interlocking roles that advocates, officials, and judges have played in decimating abortion access over the years.

At the time the Court was to hear *June Medical*, there were six states with only one remaining abortion clinic.[237] With enforcement of its admitting privileges law, Louisiana would have joined their ranks, or, as a CBS News story announced, "Louisiana could become the first state not to have legal abortion access since the practice was legalized in 1973."[238] CBS reported that "the author of the law, Representative Katrina Jackson, denied the requirement was intended to shut down abortion access and called the regulation 'common-sense women's health care.'"[239]

Given the history of Louisiana's admitting privileges law we have considered, what kind of an answer is this? Is a judge considering a constitutional challenge to the law obliged to answer this question any differently than its legislative sponsor did? Observe that the Supreme Court nearly validated Representative Jackson's account of the admitting privileges law. In *June Medical*, four of the Court's conservative justices—including Justice Gorsuch, whom President Trump appointed to replace Justice Scalia, and Justice Kavanaugh, whom President Trump appointed to replace Justice Kennedy—voted to allow Louisiana to enforce the admitting privileges law to protect women's health and safety. Without Justice Kennedy, the last remaining justice who participated in *Casey* and who voted to strike down the Texas admitting privileges law in *Whole Woman's Health*, the Supreme Court, reshaped by President Trump's appointments, was poised to uphold Louisiana's admitting privileges law as a health and safety law adopted for women's benefit.

But with the approach of the 2020 election, in which debate over President Trump's judicial appointments and the decisions of the Court figured,[240] Chief Justice Roberts acted to protect the Court,

---

[237] Holly Dan, *These 6 States Have Only 1 Abortion Clinic Left. Missouri Could Become the First with Zero*, CNN (June 21, 2019, 12:48 PM), https://www.cnn.com/2019/05/29/health/six -states-with-1-abortion-clinic-map-trnd/index.html.

[238] Kate Smith, *Louisiana Could Become the First State Without Abortion Access as Soon as Next Year*, CBS NEWS (Oct. 18, 2019, 7:01 AM), https://www.cbsnews.com/news/louisiana-abortion -case-supreme-court-state-could-become-first-without-abortion-access-next-year-2019-10-18.

[239] *Id.* Before a conservative audience, Dorinda Bordlee predicted that a ruling on third-party standing could block eighty percent of abortion cases. *See* EWTN, *supra* note 181.

[240] *See supra* text accompanying notes 5–6 (reporting on argument about Supreme Court decisions and judicial appointments during the Vice-Presidential debate on the eve of the 2020 election); Mehta & Vermeule, *supra* note 235 ("Recently, as Democrats threatened to

institutionally and politically. Asserting that stare decisis required the Court to treat like cases alike, Roberts crossed over to vote with the four justices from the *Whole Woman's Health* majority in a concurring opinion in which he repeated some, but not all, of the objections asserted by the conservative justices who dissented in *Whole Woman's Health* and *June Medical*.[241] The "maneuver" avoided openly reversing *Whole Woman's Health* while voicing objections to the standard the Court adopted in that case, inviting lower courts discretely to narrow constitutional protections for the abortion right without outright overturning them.[242]

In what follows, I integrate the doctrinal dispute in *Whole Woman's Health* and *June Medical* into the history of TRAP laws we have just examined. Analyzed from this vantage point, we can see that conservative judges attacking balancing are embracing standards that will legitimate the woman-protective health justifications of TRAP laws and weaken the restrictions that *Casey* imposes on them. The standards conservative judges embrace do not preserve the distinction between law and politics;[243] they empower antiabortion advocates, validating their claim that TRAP laws protect women and eroding constitutional protections for the abortion right.

I take as a focal point of this discussion the concurring opinion of Chief Justice Roberts in *June Medical*. On the best view of the law, because Chief Justice Roberts' concurring opinion in *June Medical* diverged so greatly from the plurality, it did not modify *Whole Woman's Health*.[244] Yet there is keen interest in Chief Justice Roberts' opinion

---

pack the court if Judge Amy Coney Barrett were confirmed, left-leaning commentators urged Roberts to tack in their direction to 'save' the institution.").

[241] *See infra* Section III.B.

[242] *See* Mehta & Vermeule, *supra* note 235 (noting that "observers on both left and right have concluded that Roberts has engaged in strategic maneuvering: His goal appears to be to preserve what he takes to be the legitimacy of the Supreme Court, by disproving any suspicion that the justices vote ideologically or otherwise engage in political behavior" and calling out his decision in *June Medical* as avoiding "more sweeping, and therefore more controversial, pro-life rulings").

[243] *See supra* text accompanying note 57 (quoting Chief Justice Roberts in *June Medical*).

[244] In Marks v. United States, the Court reasoned that "[w]hen a fragmented Court decides a case and no single rationale explaining the result enjoys the assent of five Justices, 'the holding of the Court may be viewed as that position taken by those Members who concurred in the judgments on the narrowest grounds. . . .'" 430 U.S. 188, 193 (1977) (quoting Gregg v. Georgia, 428 U.S. 153, 169 n.15 (1976) (opinion of Stewart, Powell, and Stevens, JJ)). As expounded by an en banc panel of the D.C. Circuit, "the narrowest opinion must represent a common denominator of the Court's reasoning; it must embody a position implicitly approved by at least five Justices who support the judgment." King v. Palmer, 950 F.2d 771, 781 (D.C.

precisely because it signals the direction of a Court whose views are expected to evolve with its membership.

By reading the doctrinal debate in *Whole Woman's Health* and *June Medical* in light of the political history of the TRAP laws we have examined, we can better understand the path along which Chief Justice Roberts would incrementally move the law. The exercise shows the role judges play in constraining or enabling TRAP laws, and it allows us to inventory the constitutional limitations that remain on TRAP laws.

Once we decipher the path Chief Justice Roberts chose in *June Medical*, we can see that even if courts read his concurring opinion as changing the law, a willing judge *still* has authority and doctrinal resources to scrutinize TRAP laws.[245] Mapping the law in this way in turn identifies how the Supreme Court might next move to insulate TRAP laws from these forms of judicial scrutiny.

In short, reconstructing the debate over *Casey* that led to *June Medical* helps us understand not only the past but the future. It identifies choices that any judge—including Justice Barrett—unavoidably confronts in reviewing TRAP laws and other woman-protective abortion restrictions.[246]

A. THE TRAP STRATEGY AND THE JUDICIAL ROLE

In *June Medical*, Chief Justice Roberts argued that *Whole Woman's Health* was faithless to *Casey* because it directed judges to enforce the undue burden standard through a balancing test. He made this point

---

Cir. 1991) (en banc). *See also* United States v. Epps, 707 F.3d 337, 348 (D.C. Cir. 2013) (accord). In *June Medical*, members of the plurality did not support Chief Justice Roberts's dicta, including the Chief Justice's criticism of the balancing test. If there is a "common denominator" to be found between the *June Medical* plurality and Chief Justice Roberts's concurrence, it is that the "five justices who support the judgment" support adherence to *Whole Woman's Health*. *See* June Med. Servs. v. Russo, 140 S. Ct. 2103, 2133 (2020) (Roberts, C.J., concurring) ("The question today however is not whether *Whole Woman's Health* was right or wrong, but whether to adhere to it in deciding the present case."). *See also* Ramos v. Louisiana, 140 S. Ct. 1390, 1402 (2020) (rejecting the "new and dubious proposition" of a single Justice overturning prior precedent as "not the rule . . . for good reason" and noting this potential practice "would do more to destabilize than honor precedent"). For other approaches under *Marks* to read a fractured opinion like *June Medical*, see *infra* note 302 (discussing case law interpreting *June Medical*); *see also* Ryan C. Williams, *Questioning* Marks: *Plurality Decisions and Precedential Constraint*, 69 STAN. L. REV. 795, 806–07 (2017).

[245] *See infra* text accompanying notes 304–08.

[246] *See infra* Section III.C.

by invoking Justice Scalia's attack on balancing tests as endowing judges with discretion that rules, supposedly, do not.[247]

Of course, it is odd to object to balancing because it introduces discretion into a judge's determination of an "undue burden." But the appeal to Scalia clarifies the nature of the objection. Justice Scalia did not author *Casey*; he ferociously dissented from it.[248] Chief Justice Roberts also attacked balancing by invoking the "mysteries of life" passage in *Casey* that Justice Scalia famously mocked in his *Casey* and in *Lawrence v. Texas* dissents.[249] These signals at the very least suggest Chief Justice Roberts was establishing authority with those who revere the memory of Justice Scalia. They do not portend an altogether even-handed account of *Casey*.

We can get another perspective on the question whether balancing is faithless to *Casey* by consulting Justice Kennedy. Justice Kennedy, who coauthored *Casey*'s joint opinion, explained in *Gonzales v. Carhart*,[250] an opinion restricting abortion access, that *balancing was central to* Casey*'s core holding* and the undue burden test that enforced it:

> Before viability, a State "may not prohibit any woman from making the ultimate decision to terminate her pregnancy." It also may not impose upon this right an undue burden, which exists if a regulation's "purpose or effect is to place a substantial obstacle in the path of a woman seeking an abortion

---

[247] See *June Medical*, 140 S. Ct. 2103, 2135–56 (2020) (Roberts, C.J., concurring) ("Under such tests, 'equality of treatment is . . . impossible to achieve; predictability is destroyed; judicial arbitrariness is facilitated; judicial courage is impaired.'") (quoting Antonin Scalia, *The Rule of Law as a Law of Rules*, 56 U. Chi. L. Rev. 1175, 1182 (1989)).

[248] Planned Parenthood of Se. Pa. v. Casey, 505 U.S. 833, 980 (1992) (Scalia, J., concurring in part and dissenting in part) (arguing that the question is "not whether the power of a woman to abort her unborn child is a 'liberty' in the absolute sense. . . . The issue is whether it is a liberty protected by the Constitution of the United States. I am sure it is not."). When Justice Scalia balanced, for example, in limiting application of Second Amendment rights, he never drew attention to it. *Compare* Dist. of Columbia v. Heller, 554 U.S. 570, 634 ("We know of no other enumerated constitutional right whose core protection has been subjected to a freestanding 'interest-balancing' approach.") *with id.* at 628–33 (limiting Second Amendment rights in favor of the state's interest in regulating arms in a variety of settings).

[249] See *supra* text accompanying note 57 (quoting Chief Justice Roberts's opinion). For Justice Scalia's attack on Justice Kennedy's reasoning in *Casey*, see Planned Parenthood of Se. Pa. v. Casey, 505 U.S. 833, 980 (1992) (Scalia, J., concurring in part and dissenting in part); and Lawrence v. Texas, 539 U.S. 558, 588 (2003) (Scalia J., dissenting), which attacks "the dictum of [*Casey*'s] famed sweet-mystery-of-life passage" as "the passage that ate the rule of law." The Scalia attack is notorious amongst conservatives. *See, e.g.*, Joe Carter & Collin Hansen, *Anthony Kennedy's 'Sweet Mystery of Life' and the Self's Impossible Demands*, Gospel Coalition Council (June 29, 2018), https://www.thegospelcoalition.org/article/anthony-kennedys-sweet-mystery-life-selfs-impossible-demands.

[250] Gonzales v. Carhart, 550 U.S. 124 (2007).

before the fetus attains viability." On the other hand, "[r]egulations which do no more than create a structural mechanism by which the State, or the parent or guardian of a minor, may express profound respect for the life of the unborn are permitted, if they are not a substantial obstacle to the woman's exercise of the right to choose." Casey, in short, struck a balance. The balance was central to its holding.[251]

As this passage explains, *Casey* balances when it coordinates a woman's right to choose with the state's interest in protecting unborn life through the principle the undue burden standard vindicates: that, prior to viability, government may only protect potential life by informing, not hindering, a woman's choice.[252] This same concern about obstructing women's choices explains *Casey*'s holding that "[u]nnecessary health regulations that have the purpose or effect of presenting a substantial obstacle to a woman seeking an abortion impose an undue burden on the right."[253] Because balancing is central to *Casey*'s logic, balancing is required—and expressly built into—the standards the joint opinion directed judges to enforce. How would a judge determine whether health regulations are "unnecessary" or impose an "undue burden" without making judgments about weighing, comparing, or balancing of the kind Chief Justice Roberts attacked?

In short, by invoking Justice Scalia, who dissented in *Casey*, to attack "balancing" as unfaithful to *Casey*, Chief Justice Roberts was signaling positions in a fight over enforcing *Casey* that, as we will see, divided the Court in *Whole Woman's Health*—a case in which Chief Justice Roberts himself dissented.

If we look back to the first cases evaluating admitting privileges laws, we can see how judges fighting over *Casey*'s application to TRAP laws came to focus on the so-called "balancing standard" the Chief Justice attacks as faithless to *Casey*. This brief retrospective on the balancing debate throws into sharp relief competing claims about the judge's proper role—and inverts the story about law and politics that the Chief Justice tells.

When courts were first called upon to review the constitutionality of laws imposing admitting privilege requirements on abortion providers, they faced a question about whether to call out legislatures as

---

[251] *Id.* at 146 (quoting *Casey*, 505 U.S. at 877–79).

[252] *See supra* Section II.A.

[253] *Casey*, 505 U.S. at 878.

purposefully imposing obstacles to women's abortion access under the guise of protecting women's health. A purpose to impose a substantial obstacle violates *Casey*'s undue burden standard—and its underlying "inform, not hinder" principle—but were courts prepared to enforce *Casey* by determining whether legislators were hiding an unconstitutional purpose to obstruct women's access to abortion? The balancing standard that Chief Judge Roberts attacked allows judges to draw inferences about whether a legislature was obstructing access to abortion without requiring judges expressly to characterize the government's purposes.

It was Judge Richard Posner who first developed this approach in a case where the government's hostility to abortion was only barely concealed. In preliminarily enjoining Wisconsin's admitting privileges law, Judge Posner pointed out that the state gave doctors one weekend to come into compliance with a law that would have shut down two of the state's four abortion clinics.[254] The state justified the law as protecting women's health, Judge Posner observed, yet the state introduced no evidence in support of this claim, as *Casey* required: "The cases that deal with abortion-related statutes sought to be justified on medical grounds require not only evidence (here lacking as we have seen) that the medical grounds are legitimate but also that the statute not impose an 'undue burden' on women seeking abortions. The feebler the medical grounds, the likelier the burden, even if slight, to be 'undue' in the sense of disproportionate or gratuitous."[255]

The comparative standard Posner adopted provided a disciplined way of vindicating *Casey*'s "inform, not hinder" principle without directly accusing the Wisconsin legislature of misrepresenting its aims or concealing an unconstitutional purpose to deprive women of their constitutional rights.

But in a subsequent decision in Wisconsin's admitting privileges case, Judge Posner was a great deal more direct. He never used the term "balance" but repeatedly probed the question whether "the statute would have substantially curtailed the availability of abortion in Wisconsin, without conferring an offsetting benefit (or indeed any benefit) on women's health"[256] and he was blunt in explaining why. In

---

[254] Planned Parenthood of Wis., Inc. v. Van Hollen, 738 F.3d 786, 789 (7th Cir. 2013).

[255] *Id.* at 798 (citations omitted).

[256] Planned Parenthood of Wis., Inc. v. Schimel, 806 F.3d 908, 916 (7th Cir. 2015).

a passage of his opinion aimed at the nation and the Supreme Court, Judge Posner called attention to the distinction between legitimate moral opposition to abortion and the covert use of state power to obstruct the exercise of constitutional rights:

> A great many Americans, including a number of judges, legislators, governors, and civil servants, are passionately opposed to abortion—as they are entitled to be. But persons who have a sophisticated understanding of the law and of the Supreme Court know that convincing the Court to overrule *Roe v. Wade* and *Planned Parenthood of Southeastern Pennsylvania v. Casey* is a steep uphill fight, and so some of them proceed indirectly, seeking to discourage abortions by making it more difficult for women to obtain them. They may do this in the name of protecting the health of women who have abortions, yet as in this case the specific measures they support may do little or nothing for health, but rather strew impediments to abortion. This is true of the Texas requirement, upheld by the Fifth Circuit in the *Whole Woman's* case now before the Supreme Court. . . .[257]

Emphasizing the Wisconsin legislature's failure to provide the doctors adequate notice, Posner pointed to the legislature singling out abortion as evidence of a hidden purpose:

> Opponents of abortion reveal their true objectives when they procure legislation limited to a medical procedure—abortion—that rarely produces a medical emergency. A number of other medical procedures are far more dangerous to the patient than abortion, yet their providers are not required to obtain admitting privileges anywhere, let alone within 30 miles of where the procedure is performed.[258]

The state's principal witness, Dr. John Thorp,[259] submitted a report claiming that abortion was more dangerous than childbirth, which relied on a paper by David Reardon and Priscilla Coleman, which Judge Posner found, failed to control for many relevant factors; Judge Posner credited the study submitted by plaintiff's expert, which concluded "that the risk of death associated with childbirth is 14 times higher than that associated with abortion."[260] Judge Posner emphasized

---

[257] *Id.* at 920–21.

[258] *Id.* at 920.

[259] Dr. Thorp has repeatedly testified on behalf of admitting privileges laws for AUL, despite judges repeatedly questioning the accuracy and credibility of his testimony. *See* Imani Gandy, *When Does an Error Become Lie? The Case of the Missing Decimal Point*, REWIRE NEWS GROUP (Apr. 24, 2015, 11:07 AM), https://rewirenewsgroup.com/article/2015/04/24/error-becomes -lie-missing-decimal-point (discussing Thorp's pattern of inflating abortion complication rates when acting as an expert witness); *see also* Burke, *supra* note 132 (quoting Thorp).

[260] *Schimel*, 806 F.3d at 921–22.

that probing facts and determining credibility was critical to determining the state's purposes.[261]

In addressing the nation and the Court, Posner emphasized the rule-of-law values at stake in the government misrepresenting its "true objectives" for enacting the admitting privileges law: Neither legitimate ethical convictions nor passionate disagreement could justify using state power to surreptitiously and unlawfully deprive others of constitutional rights.[262]

Soon the technique of comparing benefits and burdens Posner introduced was adopted by other judges as an important technique (among many, including the singling-out test[263]) for drawing inferences about purpose in cases challenging admitting privileges statutes and other TRAP laws.[264]

But in 2014, the Fifth Circuit ferociously repudiated this approach in the cases that would become *Whole Woman's Health*. In these cases, the Fifth Circuit worked out the elements of a framework for legitimating TRAP laws and avoiding the rule-of-law questions that Judge Posner raised. Looking back at these decisions, we can identify the doctrinal elements of the framework that Chief Justice Roberts incorporated into, and omitted from, his *June Medical* concurrence.

In reversing a district court finding that the Texas admitting privileges law had no rational relationship to protecting women's health, Judge Edith Jones advanced a radically transformative account of the *Casey-Carhart* framework. Note the critical claims about rational basis and judicial factfinding:

---

[261] *Id.* (concluding that evidence of the law's benefits was "nonexistent," since Dr. Thorp "could not substantiate" his claim that the death rate for women who undergo abortions was the same as the maternal mortality rate or cite a single case where admitting privileges would have benefitted a woman who experienced complications from an abortion).

[262] In a fierce dissent, Judge Manion refused to engage with Judge Posner on these grounds and in a lengthy opinion which followed the Fifth Circuit, he insisted that rational basis governed the case and concluded: "There is no question that Wisconsin's admitting-privileges requirement furthers the legitimate, rational basis of protecting women's health and welfare." *Id.* at 935 (Manion, J., dissenting).

[263] *See supra* text accompanying notes 133–35 (discussing TRAP laws as singling out abortion for burdensome regulation).

[264] *See* Greenhouse & Siegel, *supra* note 42, at 1460–63 (discussing cases in the Eleventh and Ninth Circuit employing variants of this test). For discussion of other techniques courts have employed to draw inferences about purposes, see Thomas B. Colby, *The Other Half of the Abortion Right*, 20 J. CONST. L. 1043, 1092–100 (2018) (discussing inferences from face of law, comparison with the regulation of similar practices, bad fit between means and ends, foreseeable effects, legislative history and statements of legislators and others involved in the legislative process, historical background and specific sequence of events leading to enactment, departures from normal lawmaking procedures and discriminatory application).

Nothing in the Supreme Court's abortion jurisprudence deviates from the essential attributes of the rational basis test, which affirms a vital principle of democratic self-government. It is not the courts' duty to second guess legislative factfinding, "improve" on, or "cleanse" the legislative process by allowing relitigation of the facts that led to the passage of a law. . . . As the Supreme Court has often stressed, the rational basis test seeks only to determine whether any conceivable rationale exists for an enactment. . . . A law "based on rational speculation unsupported by evidence or empirical data" satisfies rational basis review.[265]

Judge Jones's characterization of the Court's abortion cases as all applying the rational basis test is wildly at odds with Justice Kennedy's own reading of *Casey* in *Carhart* itself.[266] Recall that it was the dissenters in *Casey*, Chief Justice Rehnquist and Justice Scalia, who asserted that the abortion right is an ordinary liberty properly subject to rational basis review of the most deferential kind.[267] Judge Jones then rejected Judge Posner's approach to applying undue burden, attacking his view that it was important for a judge to examine the facts justifying restrictions on abortion: "The first-step in the analysis of an abortion regulation, however, is rational basis review, not empirical basis review."[268]

Judge Jennifer Elrod next built the Fifth Circuit rational basis decision into an attack on Judge Posner's method of conducting the undue burden inquiry.[269] She admonished a district court for examining facts bearing on the question whether a health-justified restriction "would actually improve women's health and safety," and

---

[265] Planned Parenthood of Greater Tex. Surgical Health Servs. v. Abbott, 748 F.3d 583, 594 (5th Cir. 2014) (citations omitted). In criticizing the trial court's application of rational basis, Judge Jones cited many rational basis decisions but postponed invoking *Lee Optical* until a bit deeper into her analysis, where she sought to refute Judge Posner's singling out analysis. *See id.* at 596 ("States 'may select one phase of one field and apply a remedy there, neglecting the others'" (quoting Williamson v. Lee Optical of Okla. Inc., 348 U.S. 483, 489 (1955))).

[266] *See supra* text accompanying note 251.

[267] Planned Parenthood of Se. Pa. v. Casey, 505 U.S. 833, 966 (1992) (Rehnquist, C.J., dissenting) ("[W]e think that the correct analysis is that set forth by the plurality opinion in *Webster*. A woman's interest in having an abortion is a form of liberty protected by the Due Process Clause, but States may regulate abortion procedures in ways rationally related to a legitimate state interest." (citing *Lee Optical*, 348 U.S. at 491)); *id.* at 981 (Scalia, J., dissenting) ("I will not swell the United States Reports with repetition of what I have said before; and applying the rational basis test, I would uphold the Pennsylvania statute in its entirety.").

[268] *Abbott*, 748 F.3d at 596.

[269] Whole Woman's Health v. Lakey, 769 F.3d 285, 304–05 (5th Cir. 2014) (overturning the district-court injunction against the Texas ambulatory surgical center requirement), *vacated in part*, 135 S. Ct. 399 (2014).

announced that "[i]n our circuit we do not balance the wisdom or effectiveness of a law against the burdens the law imposes" and "[u]nder our precedent, we have no authority by which to turn rational basis into strict scrutiny under the guise of the undue burden inquiry."[270]

As Linda Greenhouse and I observed, the Fifth Circuit at times treated "only the question of whether an abortion restriction serves the interests of women's health as subject to rational-basis review," but elsewhere "the circuit makes a broader claim: that the entirety of the undue burden framework is a form of rational-basis review."[271] Both these claims are in direct conflict with many features of *Casey* and of *Carhart*, including *Casey*'s requirement that "the means chosen by the State to further the interest in potential life must be calculated to inform the woman's free choice, not hinder it"[272] and *Carhart*'s direction that "[t]he Court retains an independent constitutional duty to review factual findings where constitutional rights are at stake."[273]

When the challenge to the Texas law reached the Supreme Court, the justices divided between the approaches of the Seventh and Fifth Circuits. By revisiting this divide in *Whole Woman's Health*, we can better appreciate how Chief Justice Roberts positioned himself in *June Medical*.

Writing for the majority in *Whole Woman's Health*, Justice Breyer embraced Judge Posner's approach. Justice Breyer directed judges enforcing *Casey* to compare the benefits and burdens of an abortion restriction, and he directed judges to follow *Carhart* and independently review facts on which the law was premised.[274] His opinion for the majority expressly repudiated the Fifth Circuit's claim that rational basis of the *Lee Optical* kind was the appropriate standard of review for enforcing a constitutional right.[275] Justice Kennedy joined the majority opinion in full.

---

[270] *Id.* at 297.

[271] Greenhouse & Siegel, *supra* note 42, at 1466–67 (citations omitted).

[272] *Casey*, 505 U.S. at 877.

[273] Gonzales v. Carhart, 550 U.S. 124, 165 (2007). For a full account of the ways that the Fifth Circuit misreads *Casey* and *Carhart*, see Greenhouse & Siegel, *supra* note 42, at 1466–73.

[274] *See supra* text accompanying notes 44–46.

[275] Whole Woman's Health v. Hellerstedt, 136 S. Ct. 2292, 2309–10 (2016) (observing Fifth Circuit was "wrong to equate the judicial review applicable to the regulation of a constitutionally protected personal liberty with the less strict review applicable where, for example, economic legislation is at issue" (citing Williamson v. Lee Optical of Okla., 348 U.S. 483, 491 (1955))).

Justice Ginsburg joined the majority, but then, to clarify the stakes of the dispute, she wrote a brief concurring opinion that forthrightly discussed the relationship between the standard directing judges to compare a law's benefits and burdens and the majority's concerns about unconstitutional purpose. In her *Whole Woman's Health* concurrence, Justice Ginsburg repeatedly cited Judge Posner's opinion expressing rule-of-law objections to the surreptitious use of public power to obstruct the exercise of constitutional rights.[276] She observed that the Texas law singled out abortion, a relatively safe procedure, for burdensome regulation not imposed on other more dangerous procedures: "Many medical procedures, including childbirth, are far more dangerous to patients, yet are not subject to ambulatory-surgical-center or hospital admitting-privileges requirements."[277] Reviewing the record, she declared "it is beyond rational belief that H.B. 2 could genuinely protect the health of women, and certain that the law 'would simply make it more difficult for them to obtain abortions.'"[278] The state put the health and safety of poor women at risk,[279] she concluded, quoting Judge Posner's appeal to the nation, and observing "Targeted Regulation of Abortion Providers laws like H.B. 2 that 'do little or nothing for health, but rather strew impediments to abortion,' cannot survive judicial inspection."[280]

Remarkably, none of the Justices who dissented in *Whole Woman's Health* ever acknowledged, much less addressed, Justice Ginsburg's claim that the Texas admitting privileges law was obstructing women's access to abortion. Justice Alito (joined by Chief Justice Roberts and Justice Thomas) focused on claim preclusion, causation, and severability.[281] Justice Thomas then went on in a separate dissent, aligned with the Fifth Circuit, to eviscerate *Casey*'s purpose inquiry, arguing that "the majority's free-form balancing test is contrary to *Casey*"[282] and asserting that "the majority overrules another central aspect of

---

[276] *Id.* at 2320–21 (Ginsburg, J., dissenting) (citing four times Planned Parenthood of Wis., Inc. v. Schimel, 806 F.3d 908 (7th Cir. 2015)).

[277] *Id.* at 2320.

[278] *Id.* at 2321 (citing *Schimel*, 806 F.3d at 910).

[279] *Id.*

[280] *Id.* (quoting *Schimel*, 806 F.3d at 921).

[281] *Id.* at 2330 (Alito, J., dissenting).

[282] *Id.* at 2324 (Thomas, J., dissenting).

Casey by requiring laws to have more than a rational basis even if they do not substantially impede access to abortion."[283]

B. CHIEF JUSTICE ROBERTS, RATIONAL BASIS AND THE DRIVE TO TAME *CASEY*

Reading the various judicial opinions seeking to uphold TRAP laws and reverse *Roe* and *Casey* through rational basis review helps locate Chief Justice Roberts' *June Medical* opinion on that path. It shows that Chief Justice Roberts aligned himself with the attack on "balancing" under *Casey* yet held back from embracing the most ambitious of judicial efforts to reverse *Roe/Casey* by extension of rational basis review. In *June Medical*, it was not Chief Justice Roberts, but instead Justice Alito dissenting with Justices Gorsuch, Kavanaugh, and Thomas, who argued that Louisiana's admitting privileges law should be reviewed under the most deferential rational basis review.

A brief account of Justice Alito's dissent in *June Medical* clarifies what is distinctive in Chief Justice Roberts's position and forecasts claims about the Constitution that shifts in the composition of the Court could soon make law.

Speaking for the conservative justices in dissent, Justice Alito attacked balancing and urged "*Whole Woman's Health* should be overruled insofar as it changed the *Casey* test."[284] Instead of balancing, the dissent insisted, the true *Casey* test was "whether the challenged Louisiana law places a 'substantial obstacle in the path of a woman seeking an abortion of a nonviable fetus.'"[285] By selectively quoting *Casey*, it was the dissenters who "changed the *Casey* test," omitting mention of the purpose prong of the undue burden standard, as well as the "inform, not hinder" principle that the undue burden standard vindicates. These changes in the law would block judicial scrutiny of the health justifications of laws that single out abortion for burdensome regulation. But this was only part of the dissent's attack on *Casey*.

---

[283] *Id.* at 2325. Justice Thomas then attacked the tiers of scrutiny as a judicial graft at odds with the original understanding. *Id.* at 2329–30 ("A law either infringes a constitutional right, or not; there is no room for the judiciary to invent tolerable degrees of encroachment."). In *Whole Woman's Health* the rational basis claim was also presented to the Court in an amicus brief by written lawyers for AUL and the Bioethics Defense Fund including Denise Burke and Dorinda Bordlee. *See* Amicus Curiae Brief of More Than 450 Bipartisan and Bicameral State Legislators and Lieutenant Governors in Support of the Respondents and Affirmance of the Fifth Circuit, Whole Woman's Health v. Hellerstedt, 136 S. Ct. 2292 (2016) (No. 15–274).

[284] June Med. Servs. L.L.C. v. Russo, 140 S. Ct. 2103, 2154 (Alito, J., dissenting).

[285] *Id.* (citing Planned Parenthood of Se. Pa. v. Casey, 505 U.S. 833, 877 (1992)).

After arguing for a deferential approach to reviewing purpose, the dissent then argued for a deferential approach to reviewing effects. As part of their argument that clinics have no third-party standing, the dissenters suggested that clinics lack standing to invoke even their selective account of the undue burden standard. Once again, Justice Alito reasoned in ways that seem designed to confuse. Justice Alito suggested that "unless an abortion law has an adverse effect on women, there is no reason why the law should face greater constitutional scrutiny than any other measure that burdens a regulated entity in the name of health or safety."[286] Justice Alito then misdescribed an exchange in oral argument in order to hypothesize a case of a TRAP law with no burden on women[287] and began to discuss Louisiana's admitting privileges law as a garden-variety safety measure, emphasizing that many laws "justified as safety measures rest on debatable empirical grounds" and are subject to rational basis review of the kind employed in *Williamson v. Lee Optical.*[288]

In the fight over abortion rights, a judge's appeal to *Lee Optical* seeks *Roe*'s overruling; a judge's citation to the rational basis test recalls Chief Justice Rehnquist's dissents in *Roe*[289] and, joined by Justice Scalia, in *Casey.*[290] In calling for *Lee Optical*-style rational basis review, the *June Medical* dissenters were relitigating the Court's decision in *Whole Woman's Health.* The Supreme Court explicitly rejected this rational basis–*Lee Optical* reading of *Casey* when it reversed the Fifth Circuit in *Whole Woman's Health.*[291]

With this account of the dissent in *June Medical*, we can better appreciate how Chief Justice Roberts positioned himself in the case. We can begin by observing that the Chief Justice did not attack the passage in *Whole Woman's Health* that explicitly rejected rational basis as the standard for reviewing laws restricting abortion. Given the

---

[286] *Id.*

[287] *Compare id. with* Transcript of Oral Argument at 18–19, *June Medical*, 140 S. Ct. 2103 (2020) (No. 18–1323) (transcribing an interaction in which Justice Kavanaugh asks Julie Rikelman about a law that neither benefits nor burdens abortion access and she responds that the hypothetical "may pose a much harder question than this case," where "the district court . . . found that the burdens of this law would be severe").

[288] *June Med. Servs.*, 140 S. Ct. at 2154 (Alito, J., dissenting) (citing Williamson v. Lee Optical of Okla., Inc., 348 U.S. 483 (1955)).

[289] *See supra* note 231.

[290] *See supra* note 267.

[291] *See supra* note 275 and accompanying text.

citation practices of the most hostile judges, it is also noteworthy that in *June Medical*, Chief Justice Roberts did not invoke *Williamson v. Lee Optical*-style rational basis review, mandating deference to legislation if a judge can surmise any reason for it.

That said, the Chief Justice did offer resources to judges interested in weakening the *Casey* framework. In *June Medical*, the Chief Justice concluded his summary of *Casey* by quoting "reasonably related" language from the joint opinion: "Laws that do not pose a substantial obstacle to abortion access are permissible, so long as they are 'reasonably related' to a legitimate state interest."[292] This summary of *Casey* somewhat resembled the diluted *Casey* standard the *June Medical* dissenters proposed.[293] Like the dissenters, the Chief Justice selectively quoted *Casey* to legitimate judicial deference to the health justifications of TRAP laws.

Readers interested in the Chief Justice's practice of stare decisis (or the making of sausage) should compare his two-word quotation of *Casey* to the full sentence in its surrounding context. In *Casey*, the joint opinion held: "Unless it has that effect [*i.e.* imposing a substantial obstacle] on her right of choice, a state measure designed to persuade her to choose childbirth over abortion will be upheld if reasonably related to that goal."[294] The "goal" or "legitimate state interest" (Chief Justice Roberts's term) to which the state measure must be "reasonably related" is "persuad[ing] a pregnant woman to choose childbirth over abortion." In short, the language of "reasonably related" in the joint opinion does not mandate *Lee Optical*–style rational basis review of health-justified restrictions on abortion. The very page Chief Justice Roberts quoted ends in the observation: "Unnecessary health regulations that have the purpose or effect of presenting a substantial obstacle to a woman seeking an abortion impose an undue burden on the right."[295]

The Chief Justice again employed language out of context when he quoted *Carhart* to attack balancing as interference with the lawmaking process:

> Nothing about *Casey* suggested that a weighing of costs and benefits of an
> abortion regulation was a job for the courts. On the contrary, we have

---

[292] *June Med. Servs.*, 140 S. Ct. at 2135 (Roberts, C.J., concurring) (citing Planned Parenthood of Se. Pa. v. Casey, 505 U.S. 833, 878 (1992)).

[293] *See supra* text accompanying note 285.

[294] *Casey*, 505 U.S. at 878.

[295] *Id.*

explained that the "traditional rule" that "state and federal legislatures [have] wide discretion to pass legislation in areas where there is medical and scientific uncertainty" is "consistent with *Casey*."[296]

In this passage the Chief Justice quoted *Carhart* without explaining that the "medical and scientific uncertainty" to which Justice Kennedy referred in *Carhart* was established through independent fact-finding by two courts.[297]

That said, in *June Medical* the Chief Justice did rely extensively on the findings of the district court. In relying on the facts found by the trial court, the Chief Justice was sending a message about the value of judicial fact-finding, and he went out of his way to criticize the dissenting Justices for failing to respect the valuable fact-finding capacities of trial courts: "Clear error review follows from a candid appraisal of the comparative advantages of trial courts and appellate courts."[298]

Taking all the pieces together, what does this contextualization of Chief Justice Roberts's concurring opinion reveal? The Roberts opinion reasoned about *Casey* without ever mentioning the "inform, not hinder" principle guiding the undue burden test. In that respect, the Roberts opinion embarked on revising *Casey*'s undue burden test by disconnecting the standard from the principled statement of the constitutional values the standard was designed to serve.

A judge or Justice who is seeking to uphold TRAP laws would find resources to do so in the Chief Justice's opinion. Little more than a month after the Court handed down *June Medical*, the Sixth Circuit reviewing a TRAP law requiring abortion providers to have "transfer agreements" with a local hospital decided that the Chief Justice's concurrence constituted *June Medical*'s holding under *Marks v. United States*[299] and so provided the governing standard to follow.[300]

---

[296] *June Med. Servs.*, 140 S. Ct. at 2136 (Roberts, C.J., concurring) (quoting Gonzales v. Carhart, 550 U.S. 124, 163 (2007)).

[297] As Linda Greenhouse and I observed: "The medical uncertainty of which the Court spoke in *Carhart* was anchored in the factfinding of the two district courts whose judgments were on review," while by contrast in the Texas litigation, the Fifth Circuit "finds uncertainty by *rejecting* the factfinding of the district court." Greenhouse & Siegel, *supra* note 42, at 1468.

[298] *June Med. Servs.*, 140 S. Ct. at 2141 (Roberts, C.J., concurring) ("While we review transcripts for a living, they listen to witnesses for a living. While we largely read briefs for a living, they largely assess the credibility of parties and witnesses for a living." (quoting Taglieri v. Monasky, 907 F.3d 404, 408 (6th Cir. 2018) (en banc))).

[299] 430 U.S. at 193.

[300] EMW Women's Surg. Ctr. v. Friedlander, 978 F.3d 418, 433 (6th Cir. 2020).

The Sixth Circuit then read Chief Justice's concurring opinion as an invitation to reverse the trial court for following the balancing standard of *Whole Woman's Health*; and, relying on the passages of *Casey* and *Carhart* that the Chief Justice had quoted without discussion of their context, the Sixth Circuit then read the Chief Justice's opinion in *June Medical* as mandating the highly deferential rational basis review of *Williamson v. Lee Optical*, citing the same rational basis case that the *dissenters* in *Roe*, *Casey*, and *June Medical* invoked—and not Chief Justice Roberts.[301]

In short, the Sixth Circuit employed *June Medical* as an excuse to eviscerate abortion rights. The Sixth Circuit invoked the concurring opinion in *June Medical* as a cover to espouse views endorsed by the dissent.

The Sixth Circuit is not following the law. Under the best reading of the precedent that directs judges about how to enforce divided decisions, the portions of the Chief Justice's concurring opinion in *June Medical* that criticize *Whole Woman's Health* do not alter *Whole Woman's Health*'s authority as law.[302] And, crucially, even if a court decided that the Chief Justice's concurring opinion in *June Medical* modified *Whole Woman's Health*, the Chief Justice's concurring opinion does not mandate the Sixth Circuit's approach.

As we saw, in *June Medical*, the Chief Justice reaffirmed *Whole Woman's Health* while criticizing it. In his concurring opinion, the Chief Justice attacked balancing and offered a selective account of the *Casey* standard. Unsurprisingly, pro-life advocates read the concurring opinion as allowing states to enforce TRAP laws.[303] Yet, as we

---

[301] *See id.* at 437–38 (quoting Williamson v. Lee Optical of Okla., Inc., 348 U.S. 483, 487 (1955)).

[302] *See supra* note 244 and accompanying text (discussing United States v. Marks, 430 U.S. 188, 193 (1977), requiring a court to treat the "position taken by [the Justice or Justices] who concurred in the judgment[] on the narrowest grounds" as "the holding of the Court"). There is presently a debate over the application of the *Marks* rule to *June Medical*. *Compare* Hopkins v. Jegley, 968 F.3d 912, 915 (8th Cir. 2020) (holding that "Chief Justice Roberts's vote was necessary in holding unconstitutional Louisiana's admitting privileges law, so his separate opinion is controlling"), *and* EMW Women's Surg. Ctr. v. Friedlander, 978 F.3d 418 (6th Cir. 2020) (agreeing with the 8th Circuit's interpretation of *June Medical*), *with* Whole Woman's Health v. Paxton, 972 F.3d 649, 652 (5th Cir. 2020) (finding that the Chief Justice's test did not control under *Marks* and concluding "*June Medical* has not disturbed the undue-burden test, and *Whole Woman's Health* remains binding law in this Circuit." (citations omitted)).

[303] *See supra* Section II.A. After *June Medical*, Dorinda Bordlee described the "good news" that the Chief Justice's opinion returned the law to the undue burden standard "and that is something that means that our pro-life laws can stand, and the pro-life movement can continue to be creative in moving forward with policies that help women choose life." EWTN, *World Over – 2020-07-02 – Dorinda Bordlee and Carrie Severino with Raymond Arroyo*, YouTube (July 2, 2020),

saw, the Roberts opinion reasoned about *Casey* in ways that are significantly different from the dissenting judges in *June Medical*.

For this reason, even if a court concluded that the Chief Justice's opinion in *June Medical* modifies *Whole Woman's Health*, the Chief Justice's opinion in *June Medical* offers a willing judge authority and resources to review TRAP laws. To recall, the Chief Justice voted to reaffirm *Whole Woman's Health*; while Chief Justice Roberts criticized balancing, he did not mandate *Lee Optical*–style deference and left more than enough of *Whole Woman's Health* and *Casey* intact for a judge or Justice who is skeptical about the underlying purpose of a health-justified abortion restriction to probe the law. The judge could cite the *Casey* undue burden standard, which Chief Justice Roberts quotes in *June Medical*, that expressly prohibits laws serving the potential life or women's health interest that have the *purpose or effect* of imposing a substantial obstacle.[304] The judge could cite *Casey*'s "inform, not hinder" principle, which the Chief Justice did not criticize.[305] The judge could cite the repudiation of *Lee Optical*–style rational-basis deference in *Whole Woman's Health*[306] and appeal to the Chief Justice's emphasis on the important fact-finding role of a trial court.[307] Even if the judge avoided relying on the balancing standard, the judge could conduct singling-out analysis to probe whether the law was plausible as an ordinary health and safety regulation and employ the many tools judges use to "smoke out" hidden purpose.[308]

C. TRAP LAWS, JUSTICE BARRETT, AND JUSTICE GINSBURG

But now that Justice Barrett has replaced Justice Ginsburg on the Court, does this analysis of Chief Justice Roberts's concurring opinion even matter?

---

https://www.youtube.com/watch?v=ZY637UZ49Ng. Like Bordlee, David Reardon saw good news. As he read *June Medical*, the Chief Justice "signaled that *he will continue to entertain regulations that protect women's health*," and Reardon concluded, "[t]he good news for abortion opponents is that provisions in *Roe* allowing laws to protect health can be expanded to prevent 80% or more of all abortions." David Reardon, *Making Abortion Rare, the Chief Justice Roberts Way*, AFTERABORTION.ORG (Aug. 13, 2020), https://afterabortion.org/making-abortion-rare -the-chief-justice-roberts-way.

[304] *See supra* Section II.A.

[305] *Id.*

[306] *See supra* text accompanying note 275.

[307] *See supra* text accompanying note 298.

[308] *See supra* notes 263–64 and accompanying text.

In this simple sense, it does. As the Court presently interprets the Constitution, the Constitution directs judges to enforce its liberty and equality guarantees by scrutinizing restrictions on abortion that claim to protect women's health. There are sitting judges as well as judges yet to be appointed who are ready to do so. But as Justice Barrett's appointment signals, the Supreme Court might soon change that law.

There are many cases that the Court could choose as vehicles to change the law. Rather than speculate about how Justice Barrett and the other conservative Justices would reason in these different cases, I focus simply on the constitutional law governing health-justified restrictions on abortion. How will Justice Barrett's arrival on the Court alter the way the Court reviews the constitutionality of TRAP laws? What understandings of the modern constitutional tradition are at risk, now that Justice Ginsburg is no longer there to defend them? If the Court as currently constituted upholds a TRAP law, how might that decision transform its interpretation of the Constitution's liberty and equality guarantees?

There is much we know and yet much to learn. Before her Supreme Court nomination, Justice Barrett publicly attested to her opposition to abortion more clearly than any recent nominee. Justice Barrett's expressed opposition to abortion and her statements of a more limited commitment to stare decisis would seem to suggest she is likely to join the dissenting justices in *Whole Woman's Health* and *June Medical*.[309] That is what Vice President Pence signaled to voters.[310]

Yet unlike Justice Ginsburg, who answered questions about the constitutional basis of the abortion right in her confirmation hearing, Barrett was unwilling to answer questions about her constitutional views on abortion during her confirmation hearing.[311] For example,

---

[309] *See supra* text accompanying notes 35–36 (sources discussing her prior expression of opposition to abortion and her Seventh Circuit decisions on abortion). At the University of Notre Dame, Barrett was a member of the University Faculty of Life organization. *See* S. Comm. on the Judiciary, *Questionnaire for Nominee to the Supreme Court*, SENATE COMM. ON THE JUDICIARY (Sept. 29, 2020), https://www.judiciary.senate.gov/imo/media/doc/Amy %20Coney%20Barrett%20Senate%20Questionnaire%20(Public)%20(002).pdf (listing Amy Coney Barrett's membership in the University Faculty for Life from "approximately 2010–2016"). For an open letter that she signed attesting to her faith, see *infra* note 371 (discussing a *Letter to Synod Fathers from Catholic Women* Barrett signed).

[310] *See supra* text accompanying note 6.

[311] *Compare infra* text accompanying note 348 (quoting then-Judge Ginsburg answering a question in her confirmation hearings about whether she believed the abortion right was grounded in due process or equal protection), *with* North, *supra* note 35 (reporting that "[d]uring

Barrett's prior public commentary does not shed much light on how she would evaluate woman-protective abortion restrictions, other than a lecture she gave just before the 2016 election in which she briefly remarked that the Supreme Court was likely to allow states to impose more restrictions on clinics, a noteworthy way to respond to *Whole Woman's Health* and a result she seemed to support on federalism grounds.[312]

1. *Food and Drug Administration v. American College of Obstetricians in a changing court.* A recent decision of the Supreme Court adds to our understanding of Justice Barrett's views on the constitutionality of woman-protective abortion restrictions and highlights how differently Justice Ginsburg viewed the question. In January 2021, the conservative Justices voted to allow the Food and Drug Administration (FDA) to single out the drug used for medication abortion for burdensome health-justified regulation.[313] The FDA required patients to "go to a clinic in person to pick up their mifepristone prescriptions, even though physicians may provide all counseling virtually, women may ingest the drug unsupervised at home, and any complications will occur long after the patient has left the clinic."[314]

The Trump administration's FDA waived in-person requirements for other drugs during the COVID-19 pandemic but not for

---

her confirmation hearings, Barrett did not directly answer questions about how she would rule on abortion rights").

[312] *See* Nina Totenberg & Domenico Montanaro, *Who Is Supreme Court Nominee Amy Coney Barrett?*, NPR (Sept. 24, 2020, 2:02 PM), https://www.npr.org/sections/supreme-court -nomination/2020/09/24/915781077/conenator-who-is-amy-coney-barrett-front-runner-for -supreme-court-nomination (reporting that in 2016 then-Professor Barrett observed that "I don't think the core case, *Roe*'s core holding that women have a right to an abortion, I don't think that would change. . . . But I think the question of whether people can get very late-term abortions, you know, how many restrictions can be put on clinics, I think that will change"); *Hesburgh Lecture 2016: Professor Amy Barrett at the Jacksonville University Public Policy Institute*, YouTube (Dec. 5, 2016), https://www.youtube.com/watch?v=7yjTEdZ81lI&feature=youtu .be (discussing *Whole Woman's Health* just before the 2016 election and describing clinic regulation as a "who decides" question about federalism (without any mention of individual liberty or discussion of clinic closings) and observing that "[i]n the case out of Texas, after the Kermit Gosnell affair and all of that, states have imposed regulations on abortion clinics, and I think the question is how much freedom the Court is willing to let states have in regulating abortion").

[313] Food and Drug Admin. v. Am. Coll. of Obstetricians, 141 S. Ct. 578 (2021) (mem.). Before the COVID-19 pandemic, the American College of Obstetricians and Gynecologists supported removing the heightened regulations on mifepristone, finding them "inconsistent with requirements for other drugs with similar or greater risks." *ACOG Statement on Medication Abortion*, ACOG (Mar. 30, 2016), https://www.acog.org/news/news-releases/2016/03 /acog-statement-on-medication-abortion. *See also infra* text accompanying note 323 (discussing how the FDA singled out mifepristone).

[314] Food and Drug Admin. v. Am. Coll. of Obstetricians, 141 S. Ct. 578, 580 (2021) (mem.).

mifepristone.[315] The case presented a classic case of a TRAP regulation in action.

In *Food and Drug Administration v. American College of Obstetricians*,[316] the Court granted an application for stay of a district court opinion preliminarily enjoining enforcement of the FDA's requirement during the COVID-19 pandemic.[317] The conservative Justices voted to grant the stay but gave no account of their reasons.[318] Their silence about the constitutional stakes of the case was ominous, especially by contrast to cases involving pandemic policies they believed affected religious liberty, where a range of conservative justices felt compelled to express the particulars of their position.[319] Chief Justice Robert concurred in the decision to grant the stay, insisting that the case did not involve the question whether the FDA requirements for mifepristone impose an undue burden but instead concerned the question whether courts should defer to government's judgments about public health emergencies.[320] Justice Breyer voted to deny the application to stay enforcement of the district court's opinion.[321]

In a fierce dissent, Justices Sotomayor and Kagan agreed with the district court that the FDA regulation singling out mifepristone for burdensome regulation during the pandemic violated *Casey*, *Whole Woman's Health*, and *June Medical*.[322] The dissenters pointed out that "[o]f the over 20,000 FDA-approved drugs, mifepristone is the only one that the FDA requires to be picked up in person for patients to take at home"[323] and emphasized that "[t]his country's laws have long singled out abortions for more onerous treatment than other medical procedures that carry similar or greater risks."[324] They objected that

---

[315] *Id.*

[316] 141 S. Ct. 578 (2021) (mem.).

[317] *Id.* at 578.

[318] *Id.*

[319] *See* South Bay United Pentecostal Church v. Newsom, 141 S. Ct. 716 (2021) (mem.).

[320] Food and Drug Admin. v. Am. Coll. of Obstetricians, 141 S. Ct. 578, 578–79 (Mem.) (2021) (Roberts, C.J., concurring).

[321] *Id.* at 578.

[322] *Id.* at 581 (Sotomayor, J., dissenting). Justice Breyer indicated he would deny the application but did not join the dissent. *See id.* at 578.

[323] *Id.* at 579.

[324] *Id.* at 585 (citing Linda Greenhouse & Reva B. Siegel, Casey *and the Clinic Closings: When "Protecting Health" Obstructs Choice*, 125 YALE L.J. 1428, 1430 (2016)).

the record was "bereft of any reasoning": "The Government has not submitted a single declaration from an FDA or HHS official explaining why the Government believes women must continue to pick up mifepristone in person, even though it has exempted many other drugs from such a requirement given the health risks of COVID-19."[325]

Recounting the wide range of pandemic-related health harms and delays in treatment that the FDA travel requirement could inflict on women, especially low-income women who depend on public transportation, and the ways enforcement of the regulation heightened the risk of infection for communities already affected by health disparities, the dissenters called for the government to "exhibit greater care and empathy for women seeking some measure of control over their health and reproductive lives in these unsettling times."[326] In concluding, Justices Sotomayor and Kagan invoked Justice Ginsburg: "'[Women's] ability to realize their full potential . . . is intimately connected to their ability to control their reproductive lives.'"[327]

In this context, Justice Barrett's silence was telling. While it is widely assumed that Justice Barrett voted with the majority,[328] there is a possibility, however slim, that she cast a vote in dissent and chose not to reveal it.[329] But even if that is so, Justice Barrett's refusal publicly to object to a health-justified restriction on abortion that exposed women to myriad health harms spoke volumes, given the stakes of the constitutional controversy. Through this silence, Justice Barrett separated herself from Justices Sotomayor and Kagan, whose dissent invoked Justice Ginsburg to express how laws taking from women control of their reproductive lives injure women.

This split among women on the Court was almost a matter of design. Years before nominating her, President Trump spoke of Barrett

---

[325] *Id.* at 584–85.

[326] *Id.* at 585.

[327] *Id.* (quoting Gonzales v. Carhart, 550 U.S. 124, 172 (2007) (Ginsburg, J., dissenting)).

[328] Many reports describe it as a 6–3 decision. *See, e.g.,* Jaclyn Diaz, *Supreme Court Oks White House Request to Limit Abortion Pill Access During Pandemic,* NPR (Jan. 13, 2021, 2:56 AM), https://www.npr.org/2021/01/13/956279232/supreme-court-oks-white-house-request-to-limit-abortion-pill-access-during-pande; Alice Miranda Ollstein, *Democratic Lawmakers Push FDA to Lift Restrictions on Abortion Pill,* POLITICO (Feb. 9, 2021, 4:27 PM), https://www.politico.com/news/2021/02/09/democrats-house-fda-abortion-restrictions-467871.

[329] The order does not record the votes of the individual Justices. The Court does not always record the votes on its orders. *See* William Baude, *Foreword: The Supreme Court's Shadow Docket,* 9 N.Y.U. J. OF L. & LIBERTY 1, 14 (2015).

as his choice to replace Justice Ginsburg.[330] Conservative strategists reasoned that appointing a woman who opposed *Roe* would ensure that women on the Court would divide about abortion and that a woman's vote against abortion rights could be justified as a new form of women's rights. "I think the optics do matter. It's harder to make the case that a woman is against women's rights," Curt Levey of the conservative Committee for Justice explained. [331] Or as Ramesh Ponnuru put it, "If *Roe v. Wade* is ever overturned . . . it would be better if it were not done by only male justices, with every female justice in dissent."[332] Some depicted Barrett as a new kind of feminist. Erika Bachiochi, editor of *The Cost of Choice*[333] and a long-time critic of the sex-equality argument for abortion rights,[334] has explained that "Judge Barrett embodies a new kind of feminism, one that builds upon, while remaking, RBG-style feminism."[335]

---

[330] Jonathan Swan, *Scoop: Trump "Saving" Judge Amy Barrett for Ruth Bader Ginsburg Seat*, Axios (Mar. 31, 2019), https://www.axios.com/supreme-court-trump-judge-amy-barrett-ruth -bader-ginsburg-11d25276-a92e-4094-8958-eb2d197707c8.html (noting that before announcing Justice Kavanaugh's nomination for Justice Kennedy's seat, President Trump was reported to have said of then-Judge Barrett, "I'm saving her for Ginsburg").

[331] See Josh Gerstein, *"The Optics Do Matter": Trump Nudged to Pick Woman for Supreme Court*, Politico (June 29, 2018, 5:06 AM), https://www.politico.com/story/2018/06/29/trump -supreme-court-female-justice-abortion-685929.

[332] Ramesh Ponnuru, *In the Wings: Anthony Kennedy's Replacement Should Be Amy Barrett*, Chi. Trib. (June 29, 2018, 2:45 PM), https://www.chicagotribune.com/opinion/commentary /ct-perspec-vetting-supreme-court-replacement-kennedy-amy-barrett-0702-story.html. Recall Representative Jackson's effort to rebut the "war on women" charge by describing the Louisiana admitting privileges law as "drafted by women, authored by women, supported by women, and voted for by women." *See supra* text accompanying note 180.

[333] *See supra* text accompanying notes 121–30.

[334] In articles and talks, Bachiochi has challenged sex equality arguments for abortion rights. *See* Erika Bachiochi, *A Putative Right in Search of a Constitutional Justification: Understanding* Planned Parenthood v. Casey*'s Equality Rationale and How It Undermines Women's Equality*, 3 Quinnipiac L. Rev. 593 (2017); Erika Bachiochi, *Embodied Equality: Debunking Equality Protection Arguments for Abortion Rights*, 34 Harv. J. L. & Pub. Pol. 889 (2011); *see also* Erika Bachiochi, *Revisiting "Reliance Interests" in* Casey: *Does "Relying" on Abortion for Equality Actually Serve Women's Equality?* (Apr. 19, 2019) https://catholicwomensforum.org/erika-bachiochi -presented-susan-b-anthony-award (reporting title of talk at Harvard Law School co-sponsored by the Federalist Society and Harvard Law Students for Life).

[335] Erika Bachiochi, *ACB: A New Feminist Icon – at Politico*, Mirror of Justice (Sept. 27, 2020), https://mirrorofjustice.blogs.com/mirrorofjustice/2020/09/acb-a-new-feminist-icon-at -politico.html (announcing on a Catholic legal theory blog that Justice Barrett's feminism was about "remaking" "RBG-style feminism"). *See* Erika Bachiochi, *Amy Coney Barrett: A New Feminist Icon*, Politico (Sept. 27, 2020, 7:00 AM), https://www.politico.com/news/magazine /2020/09/27/amy-coney-barrett-supreme-court-nominee-feminist-icon-422059 (describing to a different audience Barrett's "new kind of feminism, a feminism that builds upon *the* praiseworthy antidiscrimination work of Ginsburg but then goes further"). For related commentary, see Anna North, *Why Republicans Keep Talking About Amy Coney Barrett's 7 Kids*, Vox (Oct. 13,

For her part, Barrett observed: "I have been nominated to fill Justice Ginsburg's seat, but no one will ever take her place." [336] The statement can be read many ways.

Together, *June Medical* and the FDA decision tell us that the law concerning abortion is about to change, and in ways that could reverberate beyond the abortion context. To what forms of sex-role–based coercion is Justice Barrett, or Justice Kavanaugh, or Chief Justice Roberts prepared to subject women in the name of protecting their health?

Justice Ginsburg opposed laws that impose traditional sex roles on men and women, including laws that bring government pressure to bear on their decisions about having children. A brief account of Justice Ginsburg's approach to laws regulating pregnancy identifies foundational understandings of the modern tradition that could be transformed by a decision upholding woman-protective restrictions on abortion.

2. How Justice Ginsburg understood liberty and equality limits on the regulation of pregnancy. Justice Ginsburg fought for rights of pregnant women for almost a half century.[337] She built her approach to equal protection with pregnancy at the core, not periphery. Ginsburg's second brief in the Supreme Court argued the case of a Catholic Air Force officer who challenged a regulation authorizing her discharge from the military on grounds of pregnancy or new motherhood—pressuring the officer to end her pregnancy to keep her job—while male Air Force officers who were about to become fathers were not similarly threatened with discharge from the military.[338] Officer Susan

---

2020, 5:40 PM), https://www.vox.com/2020/10/13/21514390/amy-coney-barrett-children
-kids-supreme-court ("[C]onservatives have applauded Barrett as the apotheosis of a new form of feminism.").

[336] Marianne Levine & John Bresnahan, *Barrett Praises Ginsburg Ahead of Supreme Court Hearing*, POLITICO (Oct. 11, 2020, 1:22 PM), https://www.politico.com/news/2020/10/11/barrett-ginsburg-supreme-court-428622.

[337] For Ginsburg's recollection of her personal experiences of pregnancy discrimination, see Siegel, *supra* note 73, at 182. *See generally id.* (tracing Ginsburg's efforts with other feminist advocates to challenge laws discriminating against pregnant women—arguing under equal protection, employment discrimination law, and the Equal Rights Amendment—and connecting this work to her judgments on the Supreme Court).

[338] *See* Brief for the Petitioner, Struck v. Sec'y of Def., 409 U.S. 1071 (1972) (No. 72–178), 1972 WL 135840. The *Struck* case, which was overlooked because it was mooted before argument in the Supreme Court, was very important to Justice Ginsburg. For more on the case, see Neil S. Siegel & Reva B. Siegel, *Struck by Stereotype: Ruth Bader Ginsburg on Pregnancy Discrimination as Sex Discrimination*, 59 DUKE L.J. 771 (2010), *reprinted in* THE LEGACY OF RUTH BADER GINSBURG (Scott Dodson ed., 2015). For a recent interview with the plaintiff and other

Struck, Ginsburg wrote in 1972, "was presumed unfit for service under a regulation that declares, without regard to fact, that she fits into the stereotyped vision . . . of the 'correct' female response to pregnancy."[339] (Ginsburg included in her brief, filed just before *Roe*, a due process challenge to the regulation as violating the plaintiff's right to sexual privacy and her autonomy in deciding "whether to bear . . . a child" and asserted Struck's right to free exercise of religion.[340])

And, just as Ginsburg challenged laws penalizing pregnant women who failed to conform to sex roles, she challenged laws that penalized men who engaged in care work rather than breadwinning[341]—arguing that women and men both should be free to choose care work and not coerced into proper sex-roles by the state because of the dignitary and status-based injuries coercion of this kind can inflict.[342]

As a Justice on the Supreme Court, Ginsburg wrote one of her most famous majority opinions in *United States v. Virginia*.[343] In *Virginia*, the Supreme Court for the first time discussed a law mandating the accommodation of pregnancy as classifying on the basis of sex and subject to heightened scrutiny. *Virginia* directs judges to look to history in enforcing the Equal Protection Clause to ensure that laws classifying on the basis of sex, including laws regulating pregnancy, are not "used, as they once were . . . to create or perpetuate the legal, social,

---

commentary on the case, see Dahlia Lithwick, Loretta Ross, Neil Siegel & Reva B. Siegel, *Body of Law: Beyond* Roe, WNYC: On the Media (Dec. 13, 2019), https://www.wnycstudios.org /podcasts/otm/episodes/on-the-media-body-law-beyond-roe.

[339] *See* Brief for the Petitioner, *supra* note 338, at 50–51 (citation and internal quotation marks omitted).

[340] *Id.* at 56–58. For Justice Ginsburg's remarks about the *Struck* case and account of a similar Air Force dismissal, see Nicole Flatow, *Single Mother's Air Force Dismissal Mirrors Justice Ginsburg's Dream Test Case—from 40 Years Ago*, ThinkProgress (Nov. 2, 2012), https://archive .thinkprogress.org/single-mothers-air-force-dismissal-mirrors-justice-ginsburg-s-dream-test -case-from-40-years-ago-c6a273a0e168.

[341] The same year as Ginsburg challenged the Air Force regulation in *Struck*, Ginsburg litigated Moritz v. Commissioner of Internal Revenue, 469 F.2d 466 (10th Cir. 1972), which struck down a tax deduction for the cost of a caregiver the IRS allowed only for women and formerly married men. She continued to challenge laws that enforced sex-role conformity around caregiving for both sexes. *See, e.g.*, Weinberger v. Wiesenfeld, 420 U.S. 636 (1975) (striking down a law denying social security survivor's benefits earned by a wage earner who died in childbirth to her widower who sought to draw on them to care for their infant son).

[342] For an account locating the *Struck* case in Ginsburg's efforts over the course of her career as advocate and as judge to challenge pregnancy discrimination, see Siegel, *supra* note 73, which discusses her arguments under equal protection law, employment discrimination law, and the ERA, both as an advocate and as a Justice.

[343] 518 U.S. 515 (1996).

and economic inferiority of women."[344]*Virginia* makes clear that the Constitution forbids the use of state power to enforce traditional sex roles, especially where the coercion subordinates women.[345]

Ginsburg approached abortion through the lens of the same commitments that guided her 1970s antidiscrimination work, whether on behalf of pregnant women or caregiving men, as the *Struck* case illustrates.[346] She continued to emphasize interconnections between the liberty and equality cases in lectures of the 1970s, 1980s, and 1990s[347] and in her Supreme Court confirmation hearing in 1993. Asked her views about constitutional protections for abortion, she answered forthrightly that the due process and equal protection guarantees each protected a woman's decision about pregnancy from government control: "[Y]ou asked me about my thinking about equal protection versus individual autonomy, and my answer to you is it's both. This is something central to a woman's life, to her dignity. It's a decision that she must make for herself. And when Government controls

---

[344] *Id.* at 534. *See* Siegel, *supra* note 73, at 204–06 (locating *Virginia*'s discussion of pregnancy in the Court's equal protection case law).

[345] *See generally* Siegel, *supra* note 73 (challenging the common assumption that the Court's decision in Geduldig v. Aiello, 417 U.S. 484 (1974), insulates the regulation of pregnancy from equal protection scrutiny and demonstrating, through an account featuring Ruth Ginsburg as advocate and judge, how the Supreme Court came to integrate the regulation of pregnancy into its equal protection sex discrimination framework, in cases including *Virginia*, 518 U.S. at 204–06, and Nev. Dep't of Hum. Res. v. Hibbs, 538 U.S. 721, 736 (2003)).

[346] In 2012 Justice Ginsburg recalled the *Struck* case:

Nonetheless, her choice was, you get an abortion or you get out. That's the reproductive choice case I wish had come to the Supreme Court first. Because what it was about was a woman's decision about her life's course. Would she bear the child or not? And perhaps the court's understanding of the issue would have been advanced if a woman took the position: I don't want the government to dictate my choice. Flatow, *supra* note 340.

[347] Ruth Bader Ginsburg, *Sex Equality and the Constitution: The State of the Art*, 4 WOMEN'S RTS. L. REP. 143, 143–44 (1978) ("Not only the sex discrimination cases, but the cases on contraception, abortion, and illegitimacy as well, present various faces of a single issue: the roles women are to play in society. Are women to have the opportunity to participate in full partnership with men in the nation's social, political, and economic life?"); Ruth Bader Ginsburg, *Sex Equality and the Constitution*, 52 TUL. L. REV. 451, 462 (1978) (hoping the Court would "take abortion, pregnancy, out-of-wedlock birth, and explicit gender-based differentials out of the separate cubbyholes in which they now rest, acknowledge the practical interrelationships, and treat these matters as part and parcel of a single, large, sex equality issue"). For the 1980s, see Ruth Bader Ginsburg, *Some Thoughts on Autonomy and Equality in Relation to* Roe v. Wade, 63 N.C. L. REV. 375, 386 (1985). *See generally* Reva B. Siegel, *Equality and Choice: Sex Equality Perspectives on Reproductive Rights in the Work of Ruth Bader Ginsburg*, 25 COLUM. J. GENDER & L. 63 (2013).

that decision for her, she's being treated as less than a fully adult human responsible for her own choices."[348]

It is therefore not surprising that Ginsburg's challenge to woman-protective antiabortion justifications for the Partial Birth Abortion Ban Act in *Gonzales v. Carhart*[349] expressed these same understandings—the same constitutional understandings that led her to challenge the Air Force regulation requiring Officer Struck to choose between her pregnancy and her job. The statute at issue in *Carhart*, which banned a method of performing abortions late in pregnancy, was enacted on fetal-protective reasoning, but Justice Kennedy added a woman-protective justification to the majority opinion upholding the statute, influenced by an amicus brief quoting abortion-regret affidavits in support of a suit reopening *Roe* and its companion case[350] (abortion-regret claims for which Norma McCorvey recently explained she was coached and paid[351]).

Justice Ginsburg began her opinion in *Carhart* by quoting the many passages of sex equality reasoning in *Casey*[352] and, on the basis of this authority, emphasized that "legal challenges to undue restrictions on abortion procedures do not seek to vindicate some generalized notion of privacy; rather, they center on a woman's autonomy to determine her life's course, and thus to enjoy equal citizenship stature."[353]

Then, invoking equality principles she had helped establish over a lifetime of litigating and deciding constitutional cases, Justice Ginsburg challenged the woman-protective justification for restricting abortion as violating women's dignity, safety, equality, and freedom. "[T]he Court deprives women of the right to make an autonomous choice even at the expense of their safety."[354] "This way of thinking

---

[348] *The Supreme Court: Excerpts from Senate Hearing on the Ginsburg Nomination*, N.Y. Times (July 22, 1993), https://www.nytimes.com/1993/07/22/us/the-supreme-court-excerpts-from-senate-hearing-on-the-ginsburg-nomination.html.

[349] 550 U.S. 124 (2007).

[350] For a movement genealogy of the abortion-regret claims in *Carhart*, see Siegel, *supra* note 88, at 1641–47.

[351] For McCorvey's end-of-life repudiation of her claims of abortion regret, see Jenny Gross & Aimee Ortiz, Roe v. Wade *Plaintiff Was Paid to Switch Sides, Documentary Says*, N.Y. Times (May 19, 2020), https://www.nytimes.com/2020/05/19/us/roe-v-wade-mccorvey-documentary.html, which recounts that "[b]efore dying in 2017, Norma McCorvey said she had supported anti-abortion groups only for the money."

[352] *See Carhart*, 550 U.S. at 171 (Ginsburg, J., dissenting).

[353] *Id.* at 172.

[354] *Id.* at 184.

reflects ancient notions about women's place in the family and under the Constitution—ideas that have long since been discredited,"[355] Justice Ginsburg emphasized, directing her readers to compare *Muller v. Oregon*[356] and *Bradwell v. State*[357] with *United States v. Virginia*[358] and *Califano v. Goldfarb*.[359] She then invoked the joint opinion in *Casey* expressing these core principles, quoting *Casey*'s direction that "[t]he destiny of the woman must be shaped . . . on her own conception of her spiritual imperatives and her place in society," and then its core "inform, not hinder" principle. "[M]eans chosen by the State to further the interest in potential life must be calculated to inform the woman's free choice, not hinder it."[360] In challenging woman-protective justifications for abortion restrictions, Justice Ginsburg invoked an understanding of women as equal citizens that is vindicated through cases interpreting both the Constitution's liberty and its equality guarantees.

3. *The constitution's liberty and equality guarantees in a changing court.* Let us assume, on the basis of the evidence we now have, that Justice Barrett would vote to uphold at least some woman-protective health-justified restrictions on abortion, as the rest of the conservative Justices have.[361] In choosing how she would justify such a vote, Justice Barrett would be taking positions about the meaning of the Constitution's liberty and equality guarantees—perhaps most dramatically if she joined Justice Alito in applying rational basis review to such a law, on the premise that the law burdens no constitutional rights.[362]

Would Justice Barrett even acknowledge that a pro-woman, pro-life law like Louisiana's raises concerns under *Casey*—or under *Virginia*? Given that the text of an admitting privilege statute like Louisiana's Unsafe Abortion Act addresses the pregnant woman as well as the

---

[355] *Id.* at 185.

[356] 208 U.S. 412 (1908). *See id.* at 421–22 (arguing that "as healthy mothers are essential to vigorous offspring, the physical wellbeing of woman becomes an object of public interest and care in order to preserve the strength and vigor of the race . . . legislation designed for her protection may be sustained even when like legislation is not necessary for men, and could not be sustained").

[357] 16 Wall. 130 (1873) (reasoning that the Fourteenth Amendment allows states to bar a woman from practicing law on account of her special family role).

[358] 518 U.S. 515 (1996).

[359] 430 U.S. 199 (1977); *see Carhart*, 550 U.S. at 185 (Ginsburg, J., dissenting).

[360] *Carhart*, 550 U.S. at 186 (quoting *Casey*, 505 U.S. at 869–70 (plurality opinion)).

[361] For some of this background information, see, for example, *supra* notes 309–12 and notes 328–35 and accompanying text.

[362] *See supra* text accompanying notes 284–91.

physician,[363] would Justice Barrett scrutinize the assumptions about women on which the law's claim to protect women from "unsafe" abortions rests? (Would Justice Barrett view these assumptions about women as "discredited,"[364] as Justice Ginsburg did when she compared woman-protective justifications for abortion restrictions to the views about women expressed by the Court in 1908 in *Muller v. Oregon*?[365]) Would Justice Barrett endeavor to distinguish *Virginia* on the ground that because pregnancy is a real difference, no sex-role stereotyping of pregnant women is possible—a position a majority of the Supreme Court rejected in *Virginia* and in *Nevada Department of Human Resources v. Hibbs*?[366]

Or would Justice Barrett avoid equal protection scrutiny under *United States v. Virginia* because her views about equal protection are closer to Justice Scalia's originalist dissent in that case (which she has discussed with some measure of approval)?[367] Do her originalist commitments lead her to reject the Court's cases holding that the Constitution prohibits sex discrimination, as Justice Scalia did,[368] or might

---

[363] *See* LA. STAT. ANN. § 40:1061.10(A)(2)(b) (West 2020) (directing the provision of information to the pregnant woman so that she can contact the physician with admitting privileges and locate the hospital at which the physician has privileges); *see also* Act 620, 2014 Leg., Reg. Sess. (La. 2014) (enacted).

[364] *See* Gonzales v. Carhart, 550 U.S. 124, 185 (2007) (Ginsburg, J., dissenting).

[365] *See id.* (citing Muller v. Oregon, 208 U.S. 412, 421 (1908)).

[366] *See* Nev. Dep't Hum. Res. v. Hibbs, 538 U.S. 721, 729 (2003). *See generally* Siegel, *supra* note 73, at 204–09 (demonstrating that the majority opinions in *Virginia* and *Hibbs* supersede Geduldig v. Aiello, 417 U.S. 484, 494, 496 n.20 (1974)).

[367] *See* United States v. Virginia, 518 U.S. 515, 568 (1996) (Scalia, J., dissenting) ("But in my view the function of this Court is to *preserve* our society's values regarding (among other things) equal protection, not to *revise* them. . . . For that reason it is my view that, whatever abstract tests we may choose to devise, they . . . ought to be crafted *so as to reflect*—those constant and unbroken national traditions that embody the people's understanding of ambiguous constitutional texts."); *see also id.* at 601–03 (celebrating and defending from constitutional challenge the "old-fashioned" gender code on which women's exclusion from VMI was based).

For Barrett's views, see Amy Coney Barrett, *Originalism and Stare Decisis*, 92 NOTRE DAME L. REV. 1921, 1923, 1926 & n.20 (2017), which discusses *Virginia*, sex discrimination case law, and Brown v. Board of Education, 347 U.S. 483 (1954), as "arguably nonoriginalist precedents." *See also id.* at 1943 (considering how Justice Scalia reconciled his commitment to originalism and to stare decisis and concluding that "[n]othing is flawless, but I, for one, find it impossible to say that Justice Scalia did his job badly").

[368] For Justice Scalia's most direct originalist challenge to sex discrimination law, see Stephanie Condon, *Scalia: Constitution Doesn't Protect Women or Gays from Discrimination*, CBS NEWS (Jan. 4, 2011, 5:33 PM), https://www.cbsnews.com/news/scalia-constitution-doesnt-protect-women-or-gays-from-discrimination ("Certainly the Constitution does not require discrimination on the basis of sex. The only issue is whether it prohibits it. It doesn't. Nobody ever thought that that's what it meant. Nobody ever voted for that. If the current society wants to outlaw discrimination by sex, hey we have things called legislatures, and they enact things

she practice a more dynamic brand of originalism[369] aligned with her writings recognizing that the Court decides cases responsively with public debate.[370]

In short, does Justice Barrett interpret the Constitution as allowing government policies designed to pressure women—especially poor women—into motherhood? If she does, is that because the injuries to women's dignity, health, and family that TRAP laws inflict are simply not of constitutional significance or instead because she believes that state action pushing resisting women into traditional roles protects "women's health"?[371] However she resolves these questions, would Justice Barrett acknowledge that there is fierce debate about the dignitary and physical harms that woman-protective abortion restrictions inflict? Or would she join with other conservative justices in deferential review that refuses even to recognize constitutional concerns about the dignitary and health impact of laws that pressure poor women into childbearing?

This is the critical juncture where we learn what Erika Bachiochi meant when she explained "Judge Barrett embodies a new kind of feminism, one that builds upon, while remaking, RBG-style feminism."[372] This is the critical juncture in which those conservative

---

called laws."). Justice Barrett clerked for Justice Scalia from 1998–1999. *See* S. Comm. on the Judiciary, *Questionnaire for Nominee to the Supreme Court*, SENATE COMM. ON THE JUDICIARY (Sept. 29, 2020), https://www.judiciary.senate.gov/imo/media/doc/Amy%20Coney %20Barrett%20Senate%20Questionnaire%20(Public)%20(002).pdf; Ruth Marcus, *Amy Coney Barrett's Alignment With Scalia Has Implications Far Beyond* Roe v. Wade, WASH. POST (Oct. 2, 2020, 6:51 PM), https://www.washingtonpost.com/opinions/amy-coney-barretts-alignment -with-scalia-has-implications-far-beyond-roe-v-wade/2020/10/02/d9278210-04e4-11eb-b7ed -141dd88560ea_story.html ("Speaking in the Rose Garden after President Trump announced his selection, Barrett invoked the 'incalculable influence' of her 'mentor,' Justice Antonin Scalia, adding: 'His judicial philosophy is mine, too—a judge must apply the law as written.'").

[369] *See, e.g.*, Steven G. Calabresi & Julia T. Rickert, *Originalism and Sex Discrimination*, 90 TEX. L. REV. 1 (2011).

[370] *See* Amy Coney Barrett, *Introduction: Stare Decisis and Nonjudicial Actors*, 83 NOTRE DAME L. REV. 1147, 1171–72 (2008); Amy Coney Barrett, *Precedent and Jurisprudential Disagreement*, 91 TEX. L. REV. 1711, 1723–24 (2013).

[371] *See supra* Part II (surveying beliefs about women espoused by advocates of pro-woman, pro-life laws). For a statement about faith, life, sex, and family, as well as views on poverty to which Justice Barrett has attested, see *Letter to Synod Fathers from Catholic Women*, ETHICS & PUB. POL. CTR (Oct. 1, 2015), https://eppc.org/synodletter. The open letter is of course best read in full. Among the many prominent Catholic leaders who signed this statement are Amy Barrett (signing as professor of law), as well as Erika Bachiochi and Dorinda Bordlee. Others include Carrie Severino, head of the Judicial Crisis Network, and Marjorie Dannenfelser, President of Susan B. Anthony List. It would take another article to consider how beliefs of this kind bear on constitutional interpretation.

[372] Bachiochi, *supra* note 335.

Justices who claim to respect women as equals demonstrate the beliefs about women and the Constitution on which that claim rests. As they change constitutional law in the midst of wide-ranging public debate, are the Justices forthright about the constitutional understandings they repudiate and embrace? This is the critical juncture in which the Justices will demonstrate their beliefs about the role of a judge in a constitutional democracy.

IV. Conclusion: What Expanding the Frame on *June Medical* Teaches about Pro-Life Law

For a half century, equal protection and due process cases have promised a pregnant woman freedom from the kind of government "protection" that deprives a woman of the ability to make decisions about her own health, family, and "life's course."[373] For a half century, the Supreme Court has interpreted the Constitution's liberty and equality guarantees to distinguish between an undertaking responsibly chosen and an undertaking that is government coerced. Constitutional protections for choice matter most when the undertaking coerced is one that the community disparages and disrespects, as the story of *June Medical* illustrates.

We see disrespect when government protects women's health by restricting abortion with a single-minded focus it does not devote to protecting the health of women who are bearing children, giving birth, and caring and providing for new life. Under *these* circumstances, antiabortion animus seems to concern control more than care.

Americans are now asking what values pro-life jurisdictions are enforcing when the government has a robust appetite for abortion restrictions—but notably less interest in choice-respecting policies that reduce abortion and support life in all its forms. Expanding the

---

[373] *See* Gonzales v. Carhart, 550 U.S. 124, 172 (2007) (Ginsburg, J., dissenting). For analysis of how woman-protective restrictions conflict with equal protection case law, see Reva B. Siegel, *The New Politics of Abortion: An Equality Analysis of Woman-Protective Abortion Restrictions*, 2007 U. Ill. L. Rev. 991. For analysis of how woman-protective restrictions conflict with substantive due process case law, see Siegel, *supra* note 73.

For analysis of how fetal-protective abortion restrictions conflict with equal protection case law, see Reva B. Siegel, *Reasoning from the Body: A Historical Perspective on Abortion Regulation and Questions of Equal Protection Reasoning*, 44 Stan. L. Rev. 261 (1992); Reva B. Siegel, *Sex Equality Arguments for Reproductive Rights: Their Critical Basis and Evolving Constitutional Expression*, 56 Emory L. J. 815 (2007); and Siegel, *supra* note 10. *See also* Reva B. Siegel, *The Nineteenth Amendment and the Democratization of the Family*, 129 Yale L.J.F. 450 (2020) (tracing claims for voluntary motherhood and the democratization of family care work from the decade before the Civil War to the present).

frame and pointing out inconsistencies in the policies of pro-life jurisdictions is another way of piercing the claimed justifications for these policies and exposing the status-based judgments antiabortion animus can express and the injuries to dignity, health, and life that antiabortion animus can inflict.[374]

As the Court unravels *Roe*, these frame-expansion arguments probing the meaning of pro-life will escalate in constitutional politics. Questions about pro-life legislators' inconsistent commitments to life and health arose in the fierce legislative debate over admitting privilege laws in Texas and in Louisiana.[375] And these questions shaped the Reverend William Barber's opposition to a near total ban on abortion in Alabama. Pointing to the state's high infant mortality rate and large numbers of uninsured people, Barber questioned "whether Alabama officials were really pro-life": "They won't support life by addressing poverty . . . They won't support life by addressing health care. They won't support life by pushing for living wages. And so their claim is immoral hypocrisy."[376]

Emphasizing these very inconsistencies, Judge Carleton Reeves called the woman-protective health justifications for Mississippi's fifteen-week ban "gaslighting"[377]:

> [T]his Court concludes that the Mississippi Legislature's professed interest in "women's health" is pure gaslighting. In its legislative findings justifying the need for this legislation, the Legislature cites *Casey* yet defies *Casey*'s

---

[374] Siegel, *supra* note 10, at 209 (observing that "many prolife jurisdictions lead in policies that restrict women's reproductive choices and lag in policies that support women's reproductive choices. Comparing state policies in this way makes clear that the means a state employs to protect new life reflects views about sex and property, as well as life").

[375] *See supra* text accompanying notes 142–43 & 191–99; *see also* Elizabeth Nash, *Louisiana Has Passed 89 Abortion Restrictions Since* Roe: *It's About Control, Not Health*, GUTTMACHER INST. (Feb. 11, 2020), https://www.guttmacher.org/article/2020/02/louisiana-has-passed-89-abortion -restrictions-roe-its-about-control-not-health.

[376] Brian Lyman, *At Rally Against Abortion Ban, Barber Denounces 'Immoral Hypocrisy,'* MONTGOMERY ADVERTISER (May 28, 2019, 1:58 PM), https://www.montgomeryadvertiser .com/story/news/2019/05/28/rally-against-abortion-ban-barber-denounces-immoral-hypocrisy /1257820001; *see also* Rev. Dr. William Barber II, *Exposing the Lie of 'Pro-Life' Politicians*, NATION (May 30, 2019), https://www.thenation.com/article/archive/alabama-abortion-william-barber.

[377] Jackson Women's Health Org. v. Currier, 349 F. Supp. 3d 536, 540 n.22 (2018); *supra* text accompanying notes 41–42. Mississippi's law justified the 15-week ban with a legislative finding that "[a]bortion carries significant physical and psychological risks to the maternal patient, and these physical and psychological risks increase with gestational age" and that "[t]he State of Mississippi also has 'legitimate interests from the outset of pregnancy in protecting the health of women.'" H.B. 1510, 2018 Leg., Reg. Sess. (Miss. 2018) (quoting Planned Parenthood of Se. Pa. v. Casey, 505 U.S. 833, 847 (1992)).

core holding. The State "ranks as the state with the most [medical] challenges for women, infants, and children" but is silent on expanding Medicaid. Its leaders are proud to challenge *Roe* but choose not to lift a finger to address the tragedies lurking on the other side of the delivery room: our alarming infant and maternal mortality rates.

No, legislation like H.B. 1510 is closer to the old Mississippi—the Mississippi bent on controlling women and minorities. The Mississippi that, just a few decades ago, barred women from serving on juries "so they may continue their service as mothers, wives, and homemakers." The Mississippi that, in Fannie Lou Hamer's reporting, sterilized six out of ten black women in Sunflower County at the local hospital—against their will. And the Mississippi that, in the early 1980s, was the last State to ratify the 19th Amendment—the authority guaranteeing women the right to vote.[378]

Expanding the frame revealed Mississippi's claim to protect women by banning abortion as a project of gender and racial control, not care, Judge Reeves objected. On appeal in the Fifth Circuit, Judge James Ho rebuked Judge Reeves, asserting that his opinion displayed "alarming disrespect for the millions of Americans who believe .. that abortion is the . . . violent taking of innocent human life. . . ."[379]

But increasingly, each side makes claims to protect life and looks to government to intervene in very different ways. Expanding the frame, the Reverend William Barber explained: "You can't be for life inside the womb and not be for life outside the womb."[380] Highlighting inconsistency in policy choices across contexts can identify the role that gender, race, and class-based judgments as well as beliefs about sex and property play in shaping pro-life policy.[381] When financial resources are among the most common reasons given for a women's decision to end a pregnancy,[382] when "[h]alf of all women who got an abortion in 2014 lived in poverty, double the share from

---

[378] *Jackson Women's Health*, 349 F. Supp. 3d at 540 n.22 (citations omitted).

[379] Jackson Women's Health Org. v. Dobbs, 945 F.3d 265, 277 (5th Cir. 2019) (Ho, J., concurring) (writing lengthy opinion criticizing Judge Reeves, never addressing his argument that the woman-protective rationale was "gaslighting," while objecting that "[t]he opinion issued by the district court displays an alarming disrespect for the millions of Americans who believe that babies deserve legal protection during pregnancy as well as after birth, and that abortion is the immoral, tragic, and violent taking of innocent human life").

[380] David Marchese, *Rev. William Barber on Greed, Poverty and Evangelical Politics*, N.Y. Times (Dec. 28, 2020), https://www.nytimes.com/interactive/2020/12/28/magazine/william-barber-interview.html (quoting Rev. William Barber).

[381] *See* Siegel, *supra* note 10.

[382] *See* M. Antonia Biggs, Heather Gould & Diana Greene Foster, *Understanding Why Women Seek Abortions in the U.S.*, 13 BMC Womens Health 29 (2013), https://www.ncbi.nlm.nih.gov/pmc/articles/PMC3729671.

1994,"[383] when "being denied a wanted abortion results in economic insecurity for women and their families, and an almost four-fold increase in odds that household income will fall below the Federal Poverty Level,"[384] why do antiabortion groups like AUL not list or advocate for redistributive measures as pro-life laws?[385] The organization's ethical opposition to abortion does not explain this silence. Or might it?

How exactly is it pro-life to coerce and forsake? The seeming inconsistency is resolved if government intervention is justified to prevent what is seen as intentional life-taking by women who should give themselves over to caring for life as others will not. Observe that this is an agent-focused, blame-centered account of the pro-life principle, not the only way of understanding the pro-life principle,[386] and one especially likely to become infused with status-based judgments precisely because it locates responsibility for care selectively on blameworthy agents rather than approaching responsibility for care as shared by the whole community.

What appears to be a universal theory of responsibility in the abstract turns out to involve judgments about poor women in practice. On this agent-focused, blame-centered account of the pro-life principle, government actors can assert commitments to life, private property, and

---

[383] Sabrina Tavernise, *Why Women Getting Abortions Now Are More Likely to Be Poor*, N.Y. Times (July 9, 2019), https://www.nytimes.com/2019/07/09/us/abortion-access-inequality.html.

[384] *See Introduction to the Turnaway Study, supra* note 129, at 3.

[385] *See* Defending Life, *supra* note 131 (detailing AUL's legislative advocacy in Louisiana and elsewhere). Also note AUL's long current list of model pro-life laws. *See Legislation*, Americans United for Life (Jan. 1, 2021), https://aul.org/what-we-do/legislation.

[386] For a debate about the proper application of the life principle, see Symposium, *Whole Life v. Pro-Life?*, 43 Human Life Rev. 21 (2017). Many Catholics understand the commitment to protect life to require action in a wide range of contexts. *See* Robert Christian, *What Is the Whole Life Movement?*, Millennial (Feb. 3, 2016), https://millennialjournal.com/2016 /02/03/what-is-the-whole-life-movement/ (explaining that "it is never permissible to intentionally and directly take an innocent life. But the wanton disregard for life present in unjust social structures and the dehumanization of others in ways short of direct killing are also incompatible with the whole life commitment to human life and dignity"); *Equally Sacred Priorities for Voters in the 2020 Presidential Election*, Network Advocs. for Catholic Soc. Just. (2020), https://networkadvocates.org/wp-content/uploads/sites/2/2020/08/EquallySacred Scorecard.pdf (describing the consistent-life ethic and the belief that protecting life is a seamless garment of "equally sacred priorities"); *see also* Brown, *supra* note 194 (quoting Rep. Katrina Jackson identifying as a "whole-life Democrat[]");Valerie Richardson, *'Whole Life Democrats' Seek to Redefine Party's Stance on Abortion*, Wash. Times (June 6, 2019), https:// www.washingtontimes.com/news/2019/jun/6/katrina-jackson-whole-life-democrat-abortion -posit/ (explaining that Jackson as a "whole-life Democrat" is concerned with a range of policy questions not limited to abortion).

the limited state—and so absolve themselves of responsibility for the lives of the women and children they have intervened in, whom they view as unworthy dependents, people who are "riding in the cart," not "pulling the cart."[387] As Judge Reeves explained, the apparent inconsistency in pro-life policy choices can be resolved if pro-life means control and not care.

Let's expand the frame again and return to the pandemic. An agent-focused, blame-centered account of the pro-life principle seems to explain the policy choices of those who call themselves "pro-life" where government action on abortion is concerned but who are unwilling to support government mask mandates[388] or to provide people health care and rudimentary means of support—even in a pandemic.[389]

Those opposing shut-down orders and mask mandates under the banner of "my body, my choice" are not announcing their sudden conversion in the abortion debate;[390] they are demanding that the government respect the liberty of those they view as especially deserving of freedom and respect—cart-pullers, not cart-riders—in circumstances where they recognize that human life is at stake, but, they believe, wrongful life-taking is not.[391]

---

[387] See supra text accompanying note 203 (quoting Governor Jindal explaining his refusal to accept federal health insurance for hundreds of thousands of people in Louisiana on the grounds that "we should design our policies so that more people are pulling the cart than riding in the cart. . . . We should measure success by reducing the number of people on public assistance.").

[388] See LLCoolJ (@llcoolj), TWITTER (Nov. 17, 2020, 12:45 AM), https://twitter.com/llcoolj /status/1328575048001744897 (asking "How can you be pro life but unwilling to wear a mask??").

[389] See supra text accompanying notes 5–10.

[390] See supra text accompanying notes 7–8.

[391] For example, Rusty Reno, editor of the conservative Catholic magazine First Things, made headlines as a pro-life leader who opposed public health shut-down orders and minimized the pandemic. These views focused attention on the limited pro-life principle to which Reno subscribes, and its distance from the care ethic. See Damon Linker, A Pro-Lifer Shrugs in the Face of Mass Death, THE WEEK (Mar. 25, 2020), https://theweek.com/articles/904580 /prolifer-shrugs-face-mass-death ("Abortion is about killing. Public health is about dying. That difference is everything for Reno. Ending a pregnancy is a great evil because it is the intentional taking of an innocent human life. But other forms of dying that happen by nature (a virus killing its victim is a natural process), like deaths that follow indirectly from social and economic structures that prevail in the United States, are matters of moral indifference."). See generally Dan McLaughlin, It Is Not Hypocrisy for Pro-Lifers to Accept a Risk of Death, NAT'L REV. (May 13, 2020, 6:28 PM), https://www.nationalreview.com/2020/05/it-is-not-hypocrisy-for-pro -lifers-to-accept-a-risk-of-death ("To the pro-lifer, looking at a particular person and taking their life away—actively, or by refusing life-or-death assistance — is a deliberate choice that is different in a morally meaningful way from simply adopting this or that public policy that is statistically projected to increase risks of death.").

Whatever pro-life means and whether the Constitution speaks to these questions through its liberty or equality guarantees or not at all, it is better to fight this out as a fight about constitutional values as Justice Kennedy, Justice Ginsburg, and Justice Scalia did than to bury the constitutional question in law jargon about balancing. Why is the Chief Justice of the United States Supreme Court mocking as un-judicial judges who are acting to protect the vulnerable from government coercion? Is it beyond the judicial role for a judge to smoke out inconsistency in the use of state power when state power inflicts the form of coercion and the kind of harms to dignity, health, and life that this use of state power does?

However painful it may be to make sense of this strange mix of policies as expressing pro-life commitments, it is worse still for judges to bury this mix of policies under cites to *Williamson v. Lee Optical*.[392] Attacking "balancing" allows judges to license double-speak about state action enforcing gender roles that can injure as well as degrade; to sanction without naming forms of government coercion that many Americans oppose; and to eradicate public contest over the Constitution's meaning while elevating white-washing into a practice of democratic principle.[393] The Trump Court has the power to practice constitutionalism this way. History will judge the constitutional vision and values it demonstrates.

---

[392] 348 U.S. 483 (1955); *see, e.g., supra* text accompanying notes 288–91.

[393] *See supra* text accompanying note 265 (quoting Judge Edith Jones explaining that abortion restrictions are subject to rational basis review "which affirms a vital principle of democratic self-government [that it] is not the courts' duty to second guess legislative factfinding"). *Cf.* Amanda Marcotte, *How Anti-Choice Propaganda Trained Republicans to Accept Trump's Coronavirus Denialism*, SALON (Sept. 2, 2020, 4:58 PM), https://www.salon.com/2020/09/02/how-the -anti-choice-movement-trained-republicans-to-accept-trumps-coronavirus-denialism.

MAGGIE BLACKHAWK

ON POWER AND THE LAW:
MCGIRT v. OKLAHOMA

Power and violence are opposites; where one rules absolutely, the other is absent. Violence appears where power is in jeopardy, but left to its own course its end is the disappearance of power.... To substitute violence for power can bring victory, but its price is very high; for it is not only paid by

Maggie Blackhawk (Fond du Lac Band of Lake Superior Ojibwe) is Professor of Law, New York University.

AUTHOR'S NOTE: Hannah Arendt famously eschewed the label of philosopher, because she was interested in the study of man as embedded within society and not in the study of "the essence of man in the singular." I aim to capture some small sliver of Arendt's perspective on embeddedness and pluralism in both the substance and practice of my own work. To that end, I am grateful for the collaborative engagement and sharp critiques offered by Greg Ablavsky, Monica Bell, Andrew Coan, Kevin Davis, Ryan Doerfler, Yaseen Eldik, Bill Eskridge, Bridget Fahey, James Hopkins, Larry Lessig, Daryl Levinson, Ellie Ochs, Farah Peterson, Robert Post, Martha Minow, Trevor Morrison, Adam Samaha, Reva Siegel, Joe Singer, and Rebecca Tsosie (Yaqui). This text owes its shape to particular audiences who were generous enough to offer their attention and energy to its co-construction, including the NYU Law Colloquium on Constitutional Theory, the Public Law Workshop at the University of Chicago, the Race and the Law Workshop at Yale Law School, the University of Houston Law Center faculty workshop, the University of Arizona faculty workshop, the Criser Distinguished Lecture Series at the University of Florida, and the National Constitutional Law Workshop Series. I owe a particular debt to Justin Driver for his editorial oversight and willingness to foreground a substantive area of the law that is often overlooked. Ned Blackhawk, gi-zaagi'in apane. Finally, it bears noting how much this particular essay sprung from my "embeddedness" within a particular community of students: I owe so much gratitude to Kate Bass, Emily DeLisle, Emily Galik, Sam Givertz, Emily Hooker, Hannah Pugh, Rebecca Wallace, Michael Weingartner, and Sam Whillans, as well as my federal Indian law students over the last three years. This essay is dedicated to them and the incredible accomplishments that await them.

The Supreme Court Review, 2021.

the vanquished, it is paid by the victor in terms of his own power.
(–Hannah Arendt, *Reflections on Violence* (1969)[1])

Almost every aspect of *McGirt v. Oklahoma* strains the imagination. On July 9, 2020, over two years after agreeing to resolve the question, the Supreme Court issued in *McGirt* a landmark ruling for federal Indian law.[2] In that opinion, the Court held that a "huge swathe of Oklahoma," including "three million acres and [] most of the city of Tulsa," was recognized by the United States as within the reservation lands of the Muscogee (Creek) Nation.[3]

Even *McGirt's* path to the Court was unorthodox: the Supreme Court had initially granted certiorari for its 2018 term in a related case with an identical legal question, *Murphy v. Sharp*.[4] It took the unusual step, however, of not resolving that case and instead scheduling it for reargument the subsequent term.[5] Then, the following December, the Court granted certiorari in *McGirt*. The case was identical in all operative respects to *Murphy*, save one: Justice Neil Gorsuch was not recused in *McGirt* as he had been in *Murphy*.

It seems likely that the justices would have preferred to ignore the legal question entirely. But *Murphy* forced their hand.[6] The Tenth Circuit had crafted an opinion that was correct as a matter of law but led to an unfathomable outcome.[7] It held that the lands at issue, including much of Tulsa, were within an Indian reservation—meaning that Oklahoma did not have jurisdiction over the case.[8] In order to reverse, the Court would need to do more than deadlock. A 4–4 opinion would leave many Tulsans under the jurisdiction of a Native

---

[1] Hannah Arendt, *Reflections on Violence*, 23 J. OF INT'L AFF. 1, 20–22 (1969) (original sentence order reversed).

[2] McGirt v. Oklahoma, 140 S. Ct. 2452 (2020).

[3] *Id.* at 2482 (Roberts, J., dissenting).

[4] *See* Murphy v. Royal, 875 F.3d 896 (10th Cir. 2017). Although the case began against then-warden Terry Royal, Tommy Sharp replaced Royal as warden during the litigation. *See* Sharp v. Murphy, 140 S. Ct. 2412 (2020).

[5] Scheduling Order, Sharp v. Murphy, 140 S. Ct. 2412 (2020) (No. 17–1107), https://www.supremecourt.gov/search.aspx?filename=/docket/docketfiles/html/public/17-1107.html. The Court had also requested and received supplemental briefing before scheduling the case for reargument. Order for Supplemental Briefing, *Murphy*, 140 S. Ct. 2412 (No. 17–1107), https://www.supremecourt.gov/search.aspx?filename=/docket/docketfiles/html/public/17-1107.html.

[6] *See Murphy*, 875 F.3d at 896.

[7] *Id.*

[8] *Id.*

nation and without the benefit of the Court's reasoning. Simply sitting on the sidelines to prevent the rule of law from becoming sullied by fundamental questions of power and violence was no longer an option.

Then, the unthinkable happened again. The Court in *McGirt* affirmed the Tenth Circuit's decision.[9] In a 5–4 opinion authored by Justice Gorsuch, it held that the state of Oklahoma had no power to apply its criminal laws to McGirt because the lands on which the crime was committed, lands including a large portion of Tulsa, were within the Muscogee (Creek) Nation reservation.[10] The implications of the decision could reach even further. Because Oklahoma is home to a number of Native nations situated similarly to the Muscogee (Creek) Nation, the decision could be read to apply to them also.[11] If so, nearly one-third to one-half of Oklahoma lands would be part of a reservation.[12]

McGirt offered Native people a rare victory before the Court—a sight seldom witnessed in the last fifty years as justices on the Supreme Court have grown increasingly skeptical of federal Indian law writ large.[13] The progressive legal academy has celebrated the decision as a win for Indian Country.[14] But the public and scholarly discourse has yet to capture *McGirt's* implications for broader theories of social and racial justice—in part, because the case is written in the technical language of jurisdiction and power rather than in the more legible language of rights.[15] Because deeper lessons about society are often revealed in the breach,[16] this article draws on the

---

[9] McGirt v. Oklahoma, 140 S. Ct. 2452, 2459 (2020).

[10] *Id.*

[11] *Id.* at 2482 (Roberts, J., dissenting).

[12] *Id.*

[13] *See, e.g.,* United States v. Lara, 541 U.S. 193, 214–26 (2004) (Thomas, J., concurring in judgment); Adoptive Couple v. Baby Girl, 570 U.S. 637, 656–66 (2013) (Thomas, J., concurring).

[14] *See, e.g.,* Ronald Mann, *Opinion Analysis: Justices toe hard line in affirming reservation status for eastern Oklahoma*, SCOTUSBLOG (July 9, 2020, 7:15 PM), https://www.scotusblog.com /2020/07/opinion-analysis-justices-toe-hard-line-in-affirming-reservation-status-for-eastern -oklahoma/.

[15] *See, e.g.,* Maggie Blackhawk, *On Power & Indian Country*, 2020 WOMEN & LAW 39 [hereinafter Blackhawk, *On Power*]; Maggie Blackhawk, *Federal Indian Law as Paradigm within Public Law*, 132 HARV. L. REV. 1787 (2019) [hereinafter Blackhawk, *Paradigm*].

[16] *See* PIERRE BOURDIEU, OUTLINE OF A THEORY OF PRACTICE 164–68 (Richard Nice trans., Cambridge Univ. Press 1977) (1972) (describing the need to examine and critique the taken-for-granted world when it is brought to the fore in order to grasp the power structures commonly accepted as "natural").

occasion of this highly unusual opinion to conceptualize how federal Indian law illuminates the relationship between power and law.

The following sections explore the ways that power and law intersect in *McGirt* and reveal the limited and often faulty presumptions we hold about how law and power work. Most notably, it was presumed from the start that the dominant ideology[17] would affect the outcome of the case by limiting the interpretation of the law. Most agreed that the case ought to be settled by precedent, and so the Tenth Circuit faithfully applied the governing rule—a rule which the Supreme Court had reaffirmed unanimously in its 2016 *Parker v. Nebraska* decision—to an almost indistinguishable set of facts.[18] Rule of law principles dictate that like cases should be treated alike, after all.[19] Yet even after the Tenth Circuit's ruling, scholars predicted that the Supreme Court in *McGirt* could not possibly hold that the lands were governed by the Muscogee (Creek) Nation, because it seemed unfathomable that a Native nation would govern a major city within the United States.

Even the parties arguing to the Court understood and relied on this presumption. In *Murphy*, the brief arguing for the state of Oklahoma opened not with argument from statute or precedent but with an aerial photo of the skyline of downtown Tulsa.[20] It was as if reality itself ought to resolve the case rather than legal argument. This approach gained traction at the Court. At oral argument, Justices Breyer and Roberts asked what the people of Tulsa might "think" if they awoke one day to the Court's opinion recognizing that they lived within an Indian reservation.[21] The belief that the country is ruled by predominantly white governments without any Native nations—or any other majority-minority government for that matter—had become so universalized and dehistoricized[22] that most presumed that

---

[17] Marx and Engels describe dominant ideology as the taken-for-granted world view or "superstructure" of society—comprised of "politics, laws, morality, religion, metaphysics, &c." Karl Marx & Friedrich Engels, The German Ideology 42, 395 (1932).

[18] 136 S. Ct. 1072 (2016).

[19] David Strauss, *Must Like Cases Be Treated Alike?* (May 18, 2002), https://papers.ssrn.com/sol3/papers.cfm?abstract_id=312180.

[20] *See* Brief for Petitioner at 3, Sharp v. Murphy, 140 S. Ct. 2412 (2020) (No. 17–1107).

[21] Transcript of Oral Argument at 50–53, *Murphy*, 140 S. Ct. 2412 (No. 17–1107).

[22] *See, e.g.*, Pierre Bourdieu, Language and Symbolic Power (John B. Thompson ed., Gino Raymond & Matthew Adamson trans., Harv. Univ. Press 1991) (1982); Michel Foucault, The Archaeology of Knowledge and The Discourse on Language (A.M. Sheridan

the power of that ideology would limit the operation of law. Most assumed that no matter what the law required, the Court could not possibly hold that the city of Tulsa rested within the borders of an Indian reservation; it was unthinkable.

Some of the lessons offered by this meditation are obvious: the fact that we presume that dominant ideology drives outcomes in the world, even against the force of law, will surprise only the most idealistic few. By breaching taken-for-granted presumptions about how power and law operate, *McGirt* laid those presumptions bare.[23] Yet, even more valuable lessons of *McGirt* are located not in that revelation but rather in how and why the case defied that expectation. The Court ultimately embraced the unthinkable in *McGirt* and did so because it claimed to be upholding the rule of law over power.

The body of law called federal Indian law is often considered sui generis and banished to a "tiny backwater" because of the counter-intuitive nature of the doctrine.[24] Federal Indian law is often viewed as counterintuitive because it does not comport with the general principles of public law—most paradigmatically, the federal government recognizes the sovereignty of Native nations to operate as enclave states within the territorial borders of the United States. *McGirt* could be considered yet another instance of its "exceptional" nature. But what if the field only appears counterintuitive because it successfully wields law in defiance of a contrary world view? Perhaps the most valuable lessons of federal Indian law rest in unthinkable moments like *McGirt*, when the unthinkable becomes not merely thought but is affirmed as the law of the land.

These unthinkable moments demonstrate that, rather than treating federal Indian law as sui generis, perhaps it is our presumptions about how public law operates that need to change. For example, social

---

Smith trans., Vintage Books 2010) (1969); ROLAND BARTHES, MYTHOLOGIES 164–68 (Richard Howard trans., Hill and Wang 2012) (1957); *see also* JOHN SEARLE, THE CONSTRUCTION OF SOCIAL REALITY 5 (2010) (detailing the relationship between "objective facts" and human institutions); John Searle, *What is an Institution?*, 1 J. INSTITUTIONAL ECON. 1, 1–22 (2005).

[23] *See* EDMOND HUSSERL, THE IDEA OF PHENOMENOLOGY: A TRANSLATION OF DIE IDEE DER PHÄNOMENOLOGIE HUSSERLIANA II 23 (Lee Hardy trans., Springer 1999) (1907) (describing the notion of "epoché" or a breach in the natural attitude that allows for bracketing and inter-rogation); *see also* ALFRED SCHÜTZ, THE PHENOMENOLOGY OF THE SOCIAL WORLD (George Walsh & Fredrick Lehnert, trans., Heinemann Educ. Books 1972) (1967); ALFRED SCHUTZ, ON PHENOMENOLOGY AND SOCIAL RELATIONS (Helmut R. Wagner ed., Univ. Chi. Press 1999) (1970).

[24] Philip P. Frickey, *Marshalling Past and Present: Colonialism, Constitutionalism, and Inter-pretation in Federal Indian Law*, 107 HARV. L. REV. 381, 383 (1993).

movement theory, like most theories of popular constitutionalism, has been crafted in the shadow of its paradigm case—that is, the civil rights movement that marched on Washington, transfixing the public eye and changing the public mind.[25] In generalizing from this specific case, these theories suggest that advocates must first change the dominant world view to effect enduring legal change. But what if, rather than aiming at the public mind, marginalized groups focused their advocacy strategies on changing the law through formal law-making institutions without ever tackling the dominant ideology? What if they exercised their power not to change the broader culture but to govern their corner of the world? Indian Country has long leveraged law to gain power.[26] Power in this instance is neither voice nor simply exit.[27] Native advocates use law to carve out jurisdiction and to govern—changing their own daily lives rather than reforming a

---

[25] *See, e.g.*, Lani Guinier & Gerald Torres, *Changing the Wind: Notes Toward a Demos-prudence of Law and Social Movements*, 123 YALE L.J. 2740, 2742–83 (2014); Robert Post & Reva B. Siegel, *Roe Rage: Democratic Constitutionalism and Backlash*, 42 HARV. C.R.-C.L. L. REV. 373 (2007); Reva B. Siegel, *Constitutional Culture, Social Movement Conflict and Constitutional Change: The Case of the De Facto ERA*, 94 CALIF. L. REV. 1323 (2006); Michael McCann, *Law and Social Movements*, *in* THE BLACKWELL COMPANION TO LAW AND SOCIETY 506, 509 (Austin Sarat ed., 2004); Michael McCann, *Introduction*, *in* LAW AND SOCIAL MOVEMENTS xii (Michael McCann ed., Routledge, 2006) (defining social movements as distinct from "more conventional political activities" and "as animated by more radical aspirational visions of a different, better society," framing radicalism and formal legal advocacy as mutually exclusive).

[26] *See, e.g.*, Mary Sarah Bilder, *Without Doors: Native Nations and the Convention*, 89 FORDHAM L. REV. 1707, 1749–53 (2021) (uncovering the influence of Native diplomats on the constitutional convention in securing the treaty power for the general government and away from the states, as well as ensuring an ongoing recognition of the sovereignty of Native nations by the United States); Greg Ablavsky, *Species of Sovereignty: Native Nationhood, the United States, and International Law, 1783–1795*, 106 J. AM. HIST. 591, 591–613 (2019) (documenting Native nations' use of international law to codify the recognition of tribal sovereignty into the laws of the fledgling United States); COLIN G. CALLOWAY, THE INDIAN WORLD OF GEORGE WASHINGTON 1–16 (2018) (describing the use of diplomacy by Native nations and their recognition as diplomats by President Washington following the Founding). Power here includes also the exercise of symbolic power or, as William Eskridge and Christopher Riano have de-scribed, *hermeneutical* dissent, or how a marginalized community creates and shapes interpretive tools to make sense of their own experience, despite an absence of legibility within the dominant social groups. *See, e.g.*, WILLIAM ESKRIDGE & CHRISTOPHER RIANO, MARRIAGE EQUALITY: FROM OUTLAWS TO IN-LAWS (2020); MIRANDA FRICKER, EPISTEMIC INJUSTICE: POWER AND THE ETHICS OF KNOWING (2007); Trystan Goetze, *Hermeneutical Dissent and the Species of Hermeneutical In-justice*, 33 HYPATIA 73 (Winter 2018). Notably, in the Native context, advocates codify these new vocabularies and new conceptual normative frameworks into law and the legal lexicon without introduction into public discourse.

[27] *See* ALBERT O. HIRSCHMAN, EXIT, VOICE, AND LOYALTY: RESPONSES TO DECLINE IN FIRMS, ORGANIZATIONS, AND STATES (1970); Daryl J. Levinson, *The Supreme Court, 2015 Term — Foreword: Looking for Power in Public Law*, 130 HARV. L. REV. 31, 33 (2016) [hereinafter *Looking for Power*]; Heather K. Gerken, *The Loyal Opposition*, 123 YALE L.J. 1958, 1963 (2014); Heather K. Gerken, *Exit, Voice, and Disloyalty*, 62 DUKE L.J. 1349 (2013).

recalcitrant nation-state. A doctrine that may at first appear as "incoherent" may instead offer an example of a different approach to legal change—and an inarguably successful example, at that. Instead of being "schizophrenic,"[28] as Justice Thomas has labeled the doctrine of federal Indian law, it could provide examples of marginalized groups fighting against dominant power structures—*unus multorum* rather than sui generis—only, in this case, the marginalized group succeeds in reforming the law without first confronting the dominant ideology.

With sovereignty as its heart and colonialism as its spine, the body of law that governs the relationship between Native nations and the United States known as "federal Indian law" provides legal scholars a case study in a generations-old power movement. The history of Indian Country advocacy teaches that scholars of social and racial justice ought to broaden theorization beyond their paradigm cases to incorporate the social movement strategy, history, and doctrine of Native nations. Rather than "reasoning from race," as did many other social movements of the twentieth century,[29] Native people have charted their own path toward what Native political theorist Vine Deloria considered a "power movement," as distinct from the rights movements that ultimately shaped the race doctrines.[30] Within this power movement, Native advocates have taken an approach distinct from movements organized around rights. This approach has allowed Native people to leverage the law in order to remedy historical injustice and subordination directly, rather than hope for antisubordination as a result of formal equality and integration.[31] Such antisubordination

---

[28] United States v. Lara, 541 U.S. 193, 219 (2004) (Thomas, J., concurring in the judgment).

[29] *See* SERENA MAYERI, REASONING FROM RACE: FEMINISM, LAW, AND THE CIVIL RIGHTS REVOLUTION 1–8 (2011); Reva B. Siegel, *She the People: The Nineteenth Amendment, Sex Equality, Federalism, and the Family*, 115 HARV. L. REV. 947, 953–56 (2002).

[30] VINE DELORIA, JR., CUSTER DIED FOR YOUR SINS: AN INDIAN MANIFESTO 168–96 (1969); *see also* CATHLEEN D. CAHILL, RECASTING THE VOTE: HOW WOMAN OF COLOR TRANSFORMED THE SUFFRAGE MOVEMENT 247 (2020) (describing the advocacy of Native women like Gertrude Simmons Bonnin, also known as Zitkála-Šá, in advocating for community control during the push for woman suffrage); NICK ESTES, OUR HISTORY IS THE FUTURE: STANDING ROCK VERSUS THE DAKOTA ACCESS PIPELINE, AND THE LONG TRADITION OF INDIGENOUS RESISTANCE 173 (2019) (describing the tactics of the Red Power movement in the long tradition of Native advocacy); KENT BLANSETT, JOURNEY TO FREEDOM: RICHARD OAKES, ALCATRAZ, AND THE RED POWER MOVEMENT 7–8 (2018) (detailing the history of Native nationalism, its centrality to the Red Power movement, and its growing significance after the occupation of Alcatraz).

[31] *See* Deloria, *supra* note 30, at 184 (describing the goals of the movement as "mutual respect with political and economic independence").

measures have included the ability to form their own governments and the creation and management of industries that supply social services to members, including health insurance, free electricity, Head Start education, and elder care.[32] These antisubordination measures have even made their way into federal and state governments, including the preferential hiring of Native peoples to staff the portions of the federal government that regulate Indian Country[33] and preferential placement of Native children within Native families when resolving their custody within the adoption and foster care systems.[34] *McGirt*, thus, can be understood to vindicate the doctrines shaped by Native advocates.

This article aims to translate federal Indian law and the success of *McGirt* in order to demonstrate the broad purchase of these lessons for understanding the relationship between power and law, as well as for theories of legal change more generally. Federal Indian law reveals the need to broaden the particular cases from which theories of regulation and legal change are formulated. In particular, it teaches that these theories should include power movements and that the strategies and histories of power movements could provide a deeper understanding of how power operates within society. Federal Indian law demonstrates how law can be harnessed for social change within the context of these power dynamics. Finally, in closing, this article offers some advice for Indian Country following *McGirt*. In particular, it aims to remind advocates to embrace the "unthinkable" nature of federal Indian law and to recognize that its power lies in its ability to change the world before changing minds.

I. On Law & Power in *McGirt*

McGirt is only a single case and a bit of an outlier at that. The line of doctrine to which *McGirt* belongs is unique within the broader body of federal Indian law. Yet, with those caveats in mind, it may still

---

[32] *See, e.g.*, Stephen Herzberg, *The Menominee Indians: Termination to Restoration*, 6 AM. INDIAN L. REV. 143, 158 (1978) (detailing the services provided to members by the Menominee Nation prior to termination as including health care, insurance for both medical and dental, employment, and free electricity and water).

[33] *See, e.g.*, Section 12 of the Indian Reorganization Act, 48 Stat. 986 (codified as amended at 25 U.S.C. § 5116 (2018)); *see also* Morton v. Mancari, 417 U.S. 535, 554 (1974).

[34] *See* Indian Child Welfare Act of 1978, Pub. L. 95–608, 92 Stat. 3069 (codified as amended at 25 U.S.C. §§ 1901–1963 (2018)).

offer valuable insights into how law can be leveraged to disrupt prevailing power structures. The Supreme Court in *McGirt* reached an "unthinkable" holding that shifted—or more properly, reaffirmed—power to a marginalized community, and it did so based on rule of law principles that prioritized formal legal texts. In so doing, *McGirt* offers a particularly legible example of the relationship between law and power because the rule applied by the Court explicitly placed the formal text of the law and historical arguments above the dominant ideology of the day. That rule, established by recent and unanimous Supreme Court precedent and known as the *Solem* test, ranked modern ideology as the least important factor for the Court to consider in determining whether Congress had diminished the borders of a reservation established by law. The test stated unambivalently that ideology alone could not overcome formal legal texts read in historical context.[35] In effect, the rule itself offered the possibility of historicizing Native erasure and allowed these arguments from history and formal legal texts to reveal the ahistorical and falsely universalized nature of the dominant ideology during the litigation. Briefs for the state of Oklahoma and members of the Court tried in vain to return more than once

---

[35] Professor Todd Henderson has offered a reading of *Solem* that discounts the role of textualism and "the analytical test" offered by the Court to support its holding that Congress did not diminish the reservation—a holding that Professor Henderson believes was driven by "the reality of the situation," which was that "two-thirds of the Tribe's enrolled members lived in the opened area." The outcome in *Solem*, Henderson believes, was instead driven by a concern over justice for the Native people living within the possibly diminished area. He discounts also the Court's decision in *Nebraska v. Parker*, the case that reaffirmed and strengthened the *Solem* test's commitment to textualism even with respect to an area with a predominantly non-Indian population and where "the tribe was absent from the disputed territory for more than 120 years" as "the perfect case to demonstrate [Justice Thomas's] fealty to textualism." *Parker*'s strengthened commitment to textualism, Henderson argues, is a misreading of *Solem* and its focus on whether classifying an area as within an Indian reservation or not might work an injustice against the population living there. *See* Will Baude, *Should Federal Indian Law be Textualist?: Todd Henderson on the Legal Status of Eastern Oklahoma*, The Volokh Conspiracy (Oct. 31, 2019, 4:56 PM) (publishing correspondence with Professor Henderson regarding the *McGirt* case).

Although *Parker* did state its textual commitments more clearly and firmly than did *Solem* itself, Professor Henderson's account is unpersuasive. It is difficult to discount the rule outlined in one opinion—a rule that did preference text above all other forms of evidence—and a unanimous opinion that reached the same outcome based on a consideration of the text—an outcome that the Court reached against opposite "facts on the ground." Moreover, a diminishment test based on the "Indian" or "non-Indian" character of an area contravenes the fundamental principles on which the *Solem* test was developed—that is, that Congress alone, not the actions of individuals, decides when the United States will violate treaty law establishing the borders of Native lands. A rule to the contrary would mean that not only is Congress given carte blanche to violate treaty law set by its own government, any citizen of the United States—so long as they operate en masse—would be free to do so also.

to the dominant ideology of Native erasure in the context of their briefs and oral argument.[36] But the structure of the *Solem* test and arguments from the rule of law appear to have lessened the power of ideology in deciding the outcome of the case.

Yet, *McGirt* was the exception to the general rule of federal Indian law outcomes before the Supreme Court. Likely because the Court is susceptible to the dominant world view, often even explicitly,[37] it has increasingly decided cases on the presumption of Native erasure and against the interests of Native nations. In a more central line of cases, which began with the Court's decision in *Oliphant*,[38] the Court developed a rule that values dominant ideology over arguments from formal legal texts. In the cases applying the *Oliphant* test, the Court took an affirmative role in stripping Native nations of the recognition of tribal sovereignty.[39] But the *Solem* test effectively turned *Oliphant* on its head. A comparison between the mechanics of these two doctrines lends further support to the theory that shaping a rule to formally exclude decisions based on dominant ideology could allow marginalized communities to better leverage law against the social dynamics of power. The following sections first explore the rule applied in *McGirt* and then conclude with its comparison to *Oliphant*.

A. *MCGIRT* & THE POWER OF PRECEDENT

Almost from the start, observers recognized that the law in *McGirt v. Oklahoma* was settled. In 2017, a panel of Tenth Circuit judges issued an opinion that granted the habeas petition of Patrick Dwayne Murphy and held that the state of Oklahoma, which had sentenced Murphy to death, had no jurisdiction over him.[40] The question of jurisdiction

---

[36] *See* Brief for Petitioner at 3, Sharp v. Murphy, 140 S. Ct. 2412 (2020) (No. 17–1107); Transcript of Oral Argument at 50–53, *Murphy*, No. 17–1107.

[37] *See, e.g.*, Obergefell v. Hodges, 576 U.S. 644, 660 (2015) ("Indeed, changed understandings of marriage are characteristic of a Nation where new dimensions of freedom become apparent to new generations, often through perspectives that begin in pleas and protests and then are considered in the political sphere and the judicial process."); *see also* Ronald Kahn, *The Supreme Court, Constitutional Theory, and Social Change*, 43 J. LEGAL EDUC. 454 (1993) (essay review); LARRY D. KRAMER, THE PEOPLE THEMSELVES: POPULAR CONSTITUTIONALISM AND JUDICIAL REVIEW 1 (2004).

[38] Oliphant v. Suquamish Indian Tribe, 435 U.S. 191 (1978).

[39] Montana v. United States, 450 U.S. 544, 564 (1981); Duro v. Reina, 495 U.S. 676, 679 (1990); Nevada v. Hicks, 533 U.S. 353, 374–75 (2001).

[40] *See* Murphy v. Royal, 866 F.3d 1164 (10th Cir. 2017).

turned on the application of a simple three-factor test.[41] The test had a long pedigree before the Supreme Court, which had issued the test's namesake opinion over thirty years earlier in *Solem v. Bartlett*[42] and had reaffirmed and clarified the *Solem* test only the year before in *Nebraska v. Parker*.[43] In establishing this particular multifactor test, the Court had taken the unusual step of articulating with precision how the factors related to one another, ranking them in order from most dispositive to least, and stating that the satisfaction of the final factor could not alone decide the case. The Court applied the multifactor test in *Parker* to hold that Congress had not diminished the borders of the Omaha Nation reservation and that those borders encompassed the small town of Pender, Nebraska. As it was formerly "Indian Territory," Oklahoma always seems to present a unique case within the field of federal Indian law. But the facts at issue in *Murphy* seemed eerily reminiscent of those in *Parker*.[44] One difference, of course, is that the small town of Pender, Nebraska, is not the bustling metropolis of Tulsa, Oklahoma. Regardless, the Tenth Circuit applied the *Solem* test in *Murphy* and reached the same conclusion as *Parker*.[45] A few months later, the panel declined to rehear the case and the Tenth Circuit also declined to review en banc.[46]

At first blush, *Murphy* should have ended there. But the Supreme Court granted certiorari.[47] The reissued Tenth Circuit opinion offers some indication as to why: in declining to rehear the case en banc, the chief judge of the Tenth Circuit and a member of the merits panel filed a concurrence in the denial of rehearing en banc.[48] Dissents from denials of rehearing are rare, although increasingly common as a signaling device in circuits, most notably the Ninth, where ideological splits are contentious and where judges aligned with the ascendant views of the Supreme Court wish to bring the matter to the Court's

---

[41] *Id.* at 1187–88.

[42] 465 U.S. 463 (1984).

[43] 136 S. Ct. 1072 (2016).

[44] *Murphy*, 866 F.3d 1215–18 (describing similar allotment efforts and a similar absence of tribal governance from the area in recent times).

[45] *Id.*

[46] *See* Murphy v. Royal, 875 F.3d 896 (10th Cir. 2017).

[47] Grant of Certiorari, Sharp v. Murphy, 140 S. Ct. 2412 (2020) (No. 17–1107), https://www.supremecourt.gov/search.aspx?filename=/docket/docketfiles/html/public/17-1107.html.

[48] *See Murphy*, 875 F.3d at 966–68.

attention.[49] Concurrences from denial are spotted even less frequently in the wild. But in *Murphy*, Chief Judge Tymkovich wrote separately to make clear that he agreed with the denial for rehearing en banc only because the "panel opinion faithfully applie[d] Supreme Court precedent."[50] Judge Tymkovich believed that the Court had tied the panel's hands "since Supreme Court precedent precludes any other outcome."[51] But he went on to flag the case for review, noting that the Court may want to revise the rule it had just reaffirmed unanimously in *Parker*. Judge Tymkovich offered an explicitly consequentialist reason for this proposed change in the rule: that "a substantial non-Indian population, including much of the city of Tulsa" might be encompassed by the reservation and "Oklahoma claims the decision will have dramatic consequences for taxation, regulation, and law enforcement."[52] Judge Tymkovich closed by suggesting that the Court might want to "enhance Steps Two and Three of *Solem*," the historical and demographic factors respectively.[53]

B. *MCGIRT* AT THE SUPREME COURT

The technical and complex nature of federal Indian law often makes the doctrine hard to follow, obscuring central disagreements and the lessons to draw from them. But this dispute over the *Solem* test is instructive. In *McGirt*, as in *Murphy*, the question of state jurisdiction turned on whether the crime was committed within an Indian reservation.[54] Because the area was designated a reservation by United States treaty, the question became whether the Congress had diminished the reservation since that time.[55]

The *Solem* test for diminishment has three factors, borne from a separation of powers "governing principle" rooted in the presumption that "only Congress can divest a reservation of its land and

---

[49] *See* Jeremy D. Horowitz, *Not Taking "No" for an Answer: An Empirical Assessment of Dissents from Denial of Rehearing En Banc*, 102 Geo. L.J. 59, 70–71 (2013) (documenting a rise of dissents from denials of rehearing en banc from circuits with polarization generally and from the Ninth Circuit particularly).

[50] *See Murphy*, 875 F.3d at 966.

[51] *Id.*

[52] *Id.* at 967.

[53] *Id.*

[54] McGirt v. Oklahoma, 140 S. Ct. 2452, 2459 (2020).

[55] *Id.* at 2462.

diminish its boundaries."[56] Thus, the factors are crafted with an eye to whether Congress evinced such an intent to diminish. The first and "most probative" factor considers the text of any laws Congress has passed with respect to the reservation and its borders.[57] Both *Solem* and *Parker* also included a clear statement rule requirement with respect to the first factor, in order to place the full onus of the decision to diminish borders—almost always in violation of the treaty law that established those borders—on Congress.[58]

The second factor considers history.[59] The breadth of acceptable historical argument is expansive. At the very least, the Court seems to invite historical argument that includes both the legislative history of any formal law as well as the conduct of the national government and the historical treatment of the area. The Court has also established a further hierarchy with respect to the forms of history it would accept as legitimate. It noted in *Parker* that the *Solem* test aims to correct for dominant ideologies of the past that may have infused the history of the time and so when properly applied should exclude evidence that would reinforce the mistaken "turn-of-the-century assumption that Indian reservations were a thing of the past."[60] In *Solem* and in *Parker*, the Court made clear that historical evidence of intent to disestablish the reservation must be "unequivocal" in order to be dispositive.[61] But as Judge Tymkovich noted in his concurrence:

> History . . . is not always well suited to provide the unequivocal evidence of disestablishment that *Solem* requires. Sometimes history is ambiguous, making it impossible to decide between competing narratives. Historians have been debating the Fall of Rome for millennia. Sometimes there will be unequivocal evidence one way or another. But sometimes not. When confronted with contemporaneous history that is far from unequivocal, *Solem* gives the edge to the tribes.[62]

History is a messy business, all the more so in the context of "intent," and so a presumption that ambiguous historical evidence cuts in favor of Native nations would seem to give tribal sovereignty quite the edge.

---

[56] Solem v. Bartlett, 465 U.S. 463, 470 (1984).

[57] Nebraska v. Parker, 136 S. Ct. 1072, 1079 (2016) (quoting Hagen v. Utah, 510 U.S. 399, 411 (1994)).

[58] *Id.* (citing *Solem*, 465 U.S. at 470).

[59] *Id.* at 1080–81.

[60] *Id.* at 1079 (quoting *Solem*, 465 U.S. at 468).

[61] *Solem*, 465 U.S. at 471; *Parker*, 136 S. Ct. at 1080.

[62] Murphy v. Royal, 875 F.3d 896, 967 (10th Cir. 2017).

Finally, the last factor of the *Solem* test considers "subsequent demographic history" of the area—defined by the Court to include "the contemporaneous and subsequent understanding of the status of the reservation by members and nonmembers, as well as the United States and the State [where the reservation is located]."[63] Chief Judge Tymkovich framed this factor as consequentialist—concerned not with the "understanding" of non-Indian settlers but with the impact on them.[64] By contrast, the Court in *Parker* described this step as one focused largely on "expectations" rather than requiring a finding of harm to non-Natives:

> Petitioners' concerns about upsetting the "justifiable expectations" of the almost exclusively non-Indian settlers who live on the land are compelling, but these expectations alone, resulting from the Tribe's failure to assert jurisdiction, cannot diminish reservation boundaries. Only Congress has the power to diminish a reservation. And though petitioners wish that Congress would have "spoken differently" in 1882, "we cannot remake history."[65]

The Court in *Parker* also made clear that Step Three of *Solem* could not alone support a case for diminishment.[66] *Parker* turned on the Court's treatment of this last factor, and the unanimous opinion concluded that satisfaction of the third factor could "'reinforc[e]' a finding of diminishment or nondiminishment based on the text. But this Court has never relied solely on this third consideration to find diminishment."[67] In its construction of the *Solem* test as a hierarchy from plain text to history to dominant ideology, the Court made clear that the law—as embodied within formal legal texts read within historical context—was distinct from and would prevail over contemporary ideology.

And so it was in *Murphy* and *McGirt* that the state of Oklahoma joined Chief Judge Tymkovich in calling for the Supreme Court to turn the *Solem* test on its head and decide the case based on dominant ideology alone.[68] The revised *Solem* test proposed by the state and

[63] *Parker*, 136 S. Ct. at 1079.

[64] *See Murphy*, 875 F.3d at 966–68.

[65] *Parker*, 136 S. Ct. at 1082 (first quoting Rosebud Sioux v. Kneip, 430 U.S. 584, 605 (1977); and then quoting DeCoteau v. District County Court for Tenth Judicial District, 420 U.S. 425, 449 (1975)).

[66] *Id.* at 1081.

[67] *Id.* (quoting Mattz v. Arnett, 412 U.S. 481, 505 (1973)) (citing Rosebud Sioux, 430 U.S. at 604–605).

[68] *See* Brief for Respondent at 29–30, McGirt v. Oklahoma, 140 S. Ct. 2452 (2020) (No. 18–9526).

ultimately championed by the dissenters in *McGirt* would place "contemporaneous and subsequent understanding" on par with the text of the formal law—thereby elevating dominant ideology to the level of law and eventually conflating the two.[69] Theorists of legal change would likely find this conflation familiar. Generalizing from their paradigm case, they have described in the past the conflation of law and ideology as a more accurate understanding of law than the simplistic and overly narrow conception of law as formal legal texts.[70] Contrasting themselves with legal realists, scholars of social movements have located the law in "particular traditions of knowledge and communicative practice" and reject "conventional positivist understandings of law largely limited to discrete, determinate rules and policy actions."[71] With a vision of law grounded in interpretive practice, these scholars would likely find the original formulation of the *Solem* test—which looks first to the text of a statute and next to historical context—as, at best, overly formalistic and, at worst, an inaccurate description of the process of legal interpretation. All texts, including "conventional positivist" legal texts, must be read against some context, and preferencing contemporary public discourse as context could empower the public, expand the range of available fora for legal change, and lend legitimacy to legal rules through ongoing accountability.

Yet, rather than adopting the approach suggested by Chief Justice Tymkovich and championed by the dissent, the unlikely alliance of Justice Gorsuch with the "liberal wing" of the Court—Justices Kagan, Ginsburg, Sotomayor, and Breyer—issued an opinion that "[held] the government to its word" and sounded in the register of textualism, formalism, and rule of law principles:

> To see the perils of substituting stories for statutes, we need look no further than the stories we are offered in the case before us. . . . If anything, the persistent unspoken message here seems to be that we should be taken by the 'practical advantages' of ignoring the written law. . . . But imagine what it would mean to indulge that path. A state exercised jurisdiction over Native Americans with such persistence that the practice seems normal.

---

[69] *McGirt*, 140 S. Ct. at 2482 (Roberts, J., dissenting).

[70] McCann, *supra* note 25 at xiv (defining social movements as distinct from "more conventional political activities" and "as animated by more radical aspirational visions of a different, better society," framing radicalism and formal legal advocacy as mutually exclusive).

[71] *Id*. at xii.

> Indian landowners lost their titles by fraud or otherwise in sufficient
> volume that no one remembers whose land it once was. All this continues
> for long enough that a reservation that was once beyond doubt becomes
> questionable, . . . even farfetched.[72]

As the majority began in *McGirt*, "[o]n the far end of the Trail of
Tears was a promise."[73] The Supreme Court ultimately upheld that
"promise" by embracing an "unthinkable" outcome and declining to
hold that the Congress had diminished the reservation borders of the
Muscogee (Creek) Nation.[74]

It bears some emphasis that, by rejecting the proposed revisions to
the *Solem* test and retaining the hierarchy which places formal legal
texts above ideology, the Supreme Court sanctioned in *McGirt* a vision of the world so radical as to be unthinkable. In so doing, it highlighted some of the inadvertent consequences of diminishing the
value of and even rejecting formal legal texts as law. The Court in
McGirt refused to allow dominant discourse and worldview to overcome the formal text of the law as it had been crafted by generations
of past Native advocates. Its decision thus preserved the power of a
marginalized community in spite of the broader public's conviction
that such an outcome was unthinkable. To do otherwise, according to
the Court, would be to permit "rule of the strong, not the rule of
law."[75]

Here, the rule of law empowered the marginalized community
that had, against all odds, shaped the text of those laws. Through a
process of hermeneutical dissent, Native nations had crafted a novel
vernacular to articulate their experience that centered power and
sovereignty—drawing on borrowed terms from international law.[76]
Then, advocates had forced that lexicon into formal lawmaking institutions and the formal legal texts of the United States. Initially, these
texts predominantly took the form of treaties, documents drafted col-
laboratively between the United States and Native nations. But Native
advocates brought their vernacular to all sorts of lawmaking fora and

---

[72] *McGirt*, 140 S. Ct. at 2470, 2474.

[73] *Id.* at 2459.

[74] *Id.*

[75] *Id.* at 2474.

[76] *See, e.g.*, Eskridge & Riano, *supra* note 26; Fricker, *supra* note 26; Goetze, *supra* note 26.

have successfully shaped all forms of legal texts over the last two hundred years.[77]

In the case of *McGirt*, the United States and the Muscogee (Creek) Nation had fixed the borders of the reservation through the formal legal text of a treaty that recognized the sovereignty of the Nation over those lands.[78] The Court held firm in *McGirt* that the text of the treaty—and any other subsequent formal legal text—determined the law that would decide the case.[79] Practices that aimed to usurp the sovereignty recognized by treaty law—like the practices of the state of Oklahoma's brazen application of its own laws or white settlers "flood[ing]" the jurisdiction in search of recently discovered oil—had not themselves made law.[80] These practices were simply unlawful in light of the legal texts that had been crafted through formal lawmaking practices and were not evidence of changing discourses and ideologies that should be read as law through the practice of interpretation. As the Court described:

> Unlawful acts, performed long enough and with sufficient vigor, are never enough to amend the law. To hold otherwise would be to elevate the most brazen and longstanding injustices over the law, both rewarding wrong and failing those in the right.[81]

The dissenters in *McGirt* took a different tack, placing power above formal legal texts in two respects. First, the power of dominant ideology played a subtle but powerful role in the framing of the dissent. The dissenters were forced by the historical arguments preferenced in the *Solem* test to confront the existence of Native nations and the history of majority-minority governance in the Indian Territory. They could not simply rely on the erasure of Native governance, because they had to confront both formal legal texts and historical argument that recognized Native governance as a central part of

---

[77] *See, e.g.*, Charles Wilkinson, *"Peoples Distinct from Others": The Making of Modern Indian Law*, 2006 UTAH L. REV. 379 (describing Native advocacy in legislatures and courts since the 1950s); *Ablavsky*, *supra* note 26 at 591–613; Kirsten Matoy Carlson, *Congress and Indians*, 86 U. COLO. L. REV. 77, 81 (2015); Kirsten Matoy Carlson, *Tribes Lobbying Congress: Who Wins and Why* (Nov. 4, 2016) (draft report presented at the 13th Annual Indigenous Law Conference), https://ssrn.com/ abstract=3043226 [https://perma.cc/H5LQ-CJ3C].https://ssrn .com/ abstract=3043226 [https://perma.cc/H5LQ-CJ3C].

[78] *McGirt*, 140 S. Ct. at 2459.

[79] *Id*. at 2462.

[80] *Id*. at 2469.

[81] *Id*. at 2482.

the history of the United States. Instead, the dissent resorted to historical argumentation of its own: In describing the facts of the case, the dissent drew upon American myths regarding western expansion and played off of stereotypical fears regarding majority-minority governments.[82] Sections of the dissent sound remarkably similar to the highly controversial "frontier thesis" described by historian Frederick Jackson Turner, who envisioned the settlement of the West as the practice that gave birth to the unique democratic ethos of the United States.[83] According to Turner, it was socialization through the pushing of the frontier line in the West—"the meeting point between savagery and civilization"—that caused settlers to become uniquely and exceptionally American.[84] The dissent takes an eerily similar tone to Turner's Manifest Destiny: "In the wake of the [Civil War], a renewed 'determination to thrust the nation westward' gripped the country. Spurred by the new railroads and protected by the re-purposed Union Army, settlers rapidly transformed vast stretches of territorial wilderness into farmland and ranches . . . . There to stay, the settlers founded '[f]lourishing towns' along the railway lines that crossed the territory."[85]

In contrast to the "flourishing" settler towns, founded by pioneers who tamed empty wilderness, the dissent describes Native governments as both racist and corrupt. Chief Justice Roberts emphasized the slaveholding practices of the Five Civilized Tribes and their alliance with the Confederacy—practices that held no relevance to the interpretation of the treaty that drew the disputed borderlines and which was signed after the events the dissent describes.[86] The nadir of the dissent's historical argument, however, is found in the description of allotment—a late nineteenth century policy of carving up reservation lands to sell to non-Indians, which the United States has itself formally repudiated as an abject failure—as necessary to stop corrupt Native governments from further exploiting Native

---

[82] *Id.* at 2483–85 (Roberts, J., dissenting).

[83] *See* FREDERICK JACKSON TURNER, THE SIGNIFICANCE OF THE FRONTIER IN AMERICAN HISTORY 1 (Penguin Books, 2008) (1893) ("The existence of an area of free land, its continuous recession, and the advance of American settlement westward, explain American development.").

[84] *Id.* at 3 ("The frontier is the line of most rapid and effective Americanization.").

[85] *McGirt*, 140 S. Ct. at 2484 (Roberts, J., dissenting) (first quoting COHEN HANDBOOK OF FEDERAL INDIAN LAW § 1.04 (2012) at 71–74; and then quoting S. REP. No. 377, at 6 (1894)).

[86] *Id.* at 2483.

people.[87] It bears further noting that the dissent drew its historical argument not from historical literature but from dicta in a 1915 Supreme Court opinion.[88]

Second, the dissenters offered a revised *Solem* test that elevated the power of the dominant ideology—both past and present—and the power of conquest above the formal text of the law and rule of law principles. They began by abandoning precedent and the three-factor test first described in *Solem* and later reaffirmed in 2016 in *Parker*.[89] Instead, they offered a return to first principles—that is, that Congress must evince an intent to disestablish reservation borders—and, from that principle, they advocated for a revised test.[90] In place of *Solem*'s hierarchy of factors, which positioned dominant ideology as the least valuable factor, the dissent's test considered "categories of evidence" that placed contemporaneous and subsequent understanding as both the "second and third" factors of the *Solem* test.[91] In essence, what the *McGirt* dissent proposed was that, in answering the bedrock question of whether Congress "evinced an intent to disestablish the reservation," the Court should jettison *Solem*'s hierarchy and should instead consider *all* the factors that make up that hierarchy as equivalently significant. The dissent's revised test would, in turn, allow dominant ideologies, both historical and contemporary, to erase Native people and governance and to overcome legal texts formally created by Congress—texts that recognized sovereign power of Native nations. To this end, the dissenters offered a revised Step One that included a deep contextual reading of formal legal texts that would "examine all circumstances surrounding the opening of a reservation" to find congressional intent to diminish the reservation borders.[92] The dissenters criticized the majority's search for words such as "cession" and "unconditional commitment to compensate" in formal legal texts as a brutish form of "magic words" literalism.[93] The distance between the majority and the dissenter's reasoning could

---

[87] *Id*. at 2484.

[88] *Id*. (citing Woodward v. Graffenried, 238 U.S. 284, 297 (1915)).

[89] *Id*. at 2482.

[90] *Id*. at 2485.

[91] *Id*. at 2482.

[92] Nebraska v. Parker, 136 S. Ct. 1072, 1079 (2016) (quoting *Parker*, 136 S. Ct. at 1079 (quoting Hagen v. Utah, 510 U.S. 399, 412 (1994))).

[93] *Id*. at 2489.

appear at first blush to be a dispute over interpretive methodology. The dissent described their differences with the majority as offering a more pragmatic rule that reads the text of the statute in historical context rather than a rule that looks to the sentence-level meaning of the text for intent.

But a closer look at the dispute between the majority and the dissent reveals more than a methodological dispute over the interpretation of text. Instead, the distance between the majority and dissent involved a more substantive disagreement about what forms of power ought to be legally cognizable. Not only did the dissent offer a rule that held the power of dominant ideology above formal law, but also the dissenters wanted the Court to recognize as law an exertion of power that was nonconsensual and even violent. As even Chief Judge Tymkovich observed in his concurrence to the Tenth Circuit's denial of rehearing en banc, the Supreme Court had in earlier cases rejected allotment as evidence of intent to diminish reservation borders.[94] The majority took this position because it reasoned that allotment was *unilaterally* imposed by Congress and the Court presumed that any act that diminished the sovereign territory of Native peoples and brought them further under the domain of the United States must be consensual.[95] The *Solem* test implicitly codified a rule that "law" could be created only through collective and collaborative action.[96] Thus, the Court held again and again that allotment could not serve as evidence of the intent to diminish reservation borders.[97]

In *McGirt*, the dissenters rejected the requirement of consent in determining whether the United States had brought under its jurisdiction a people swearing allegiance to a separate sovereign. They instead proposed that the Court interpret past acts of violence and domination by the national government and the states as legally cognizable

---

[94] *See* Murphy v. Royal, 875 F.3d 896, 966 (10th Cir. 2017).

[95] *McGirt*, 140 S. Ct. at 2463–65.

[96] Solem v. Bartlett, 465 U.S. 463, 417 (1984) (holding as probative evidence of intent "the manner in which the transaction was negotiated," including the offering of compensation and evidence of agreement by Native people). But *see Parker*, 136 S. Ct. at 1081 n.1 (2016) (noting in dicta that the probative nature of collaborative negotiations as evidence could be rooted in an understanding of the doctrine limiting unilateral congressional power).

[97] *McGirt*, 140 S. Ct. at 2464 ("To the contrary, this Court has explained repeatedly that Congress does not disestablish a reservation simply by allowing the transfer of individual plots, whether to Native Americans or others.") (citing Mattz v. Arnett, 412 U.S. 481, 497); Seymour v. Superintendent of Wash. State Penitentiary, 368 U.S. 351, 356–58 (1962); *Parker*, 136 S. Ct. at 1079–80)).

assertions of power. The dissent, that is, sanctioned "lawmaking" by conquest.[98] They argued that the Court should consider as legitimate means of lawmaking the breaking of treaty promises, criminalization of the governments of separate peoples, and imposition of government power on subordinated peoples at the margins of empire without their consent. Under this proposed rule, violence and lawmaking would be indistinguishable.[99] The justices support of conquest was not even thinly veiled. The acts of conquest offered by the dissent as evidence of disestablishment were not subtle. They included the abolishment of all Muscogee (Creek) courts; prohibition on the enforcement of any Muscogee (Creek) law not preapproved by the President of the United States; abolishment of Muscogee (Creek) tax collection, thereby stripping the Nation of revenue; and seizure of all Muscogee (Creek) resources by the Secretary of the Interior.[100] These acts, the dissent argued, were evidence of congressional intent to diminish the territory of another sovereign and were sufficient to subject the people of that sovereign to the power of the United States.[101] They reasoned that the state and national governments' violent conquest of the Muscogee (Creek) people and destruction of their government in violation of treaty law should not only be sanctioned by the Court, but that this violence should be legally cognizable as evidence for the Court to later hold that their reservation was diminished beyond all recognition.[102]

C. BEYOND *MCGIRT*

The Supreme Court's embrace of an "unthinkable" decision in *McGirt* stands in contrast to much of the doctrine developed in the field of federal Indian law in the last five decades. In its other federal Indian law cases, the Court followed a starkly different path. In particular, notable differences exist between *McGirt* and a sister doctrine that began in the 1970s with a question regarding criminal jurisdiction, *Oliphant v. Suquamish Indian Tribe*—a doctrine that the Court

---

[98] *McGirt*, 140 S. Ct. at 2490–93 (Roberts, J. dissenting).

[99] *See, e.g.*, Arendt, *supra* note 1 at 20–21 (distinguishing power as collaborative action from power as coercion and domination, defining the latter as violence).

[100] *McGirt*, 140 S. Ct. at 2490–93 (Roberts, J. dissenting).

[101] *Id.*

[102] *Id.* at 2493.

has since extended to encompass more and more areas of the law.[103] Both *Oliphant* and *McGirt* share common ancestry: an amalgam of the Marshall Trilogy and Justice Taney's later amendments to the Marshall Trilogy in *United States v. Rogers*.[104] Because of these origins, both cases are rooted in the same legal principle that the recognition of inherent sovereignty of Native nations can be expanded and limited by the "plenary power" of the political branches.[105] Given these shared origins, the starkly different approaches taken by the Court each merit further exploration.

In *Oliphant*, the Supreme Court was asked to decide "whether Indian tribal courts have criminal jurisdiction over non-Indians"—a question the Court answered in the negative.[106] In reaching that conclusion, the Supreme Court explicitly retreated from a textualist approach and noted without reservation that the operative formal legal texts—there, the 1855 Treaty of Point Elliot—"would appear to be silent as to tribal criminal jurisdiction over non-Indians."[107] With respect to historical argument, the Court looked less to historical evidence surrounding the specific treaty at issue in the case and instead examined "the common notions of the day" and "the assumptions of those who drafted [the texts]."[108] Relying on these "common notions" and "assumptions," the Court began with a weak-hearted attempt to draw from a provision in the Treaty of Point Elliot of 1855, where the Native nation "acknowledge[d] their *dependence* on the government of the United States" as likely restricting the criminal jurisdiction of the nation. Drawing on a few choice phrases in Chief Justice John Marshall's 1832 opinion in *Worcester v. Georgia*, the Court concluded that the "common notions" of 1855 lent term "dependence" greater meaning than it would typically denote in everyday

---

[103] 435 U.S. 191 (1978).

[104] 45 U.S. (4 How.) 567, 571–74 (1846).

[105] *See* Sarah H. Cleveland, *Powers Inherent in Sovereignty: Indians, Aliens, Territories, and the Nineteenth Century Origins of Plenary Power over Foreign Affairs*, 81 Tex. L. Rev. 1, 25 (2002); Michalyn Steele, *Congressional Power and Sovereignty in Indian Affairs*, 2018 Utah L. Rev. 307 (2018); Michalyn Steele, *Plenary Power, Political Questions, and Sovereignty in Indian Affairs*, 63 UCLA L. Rev. 666 (2016); Matthew L. M. Fletcher, *Preconstitutional Federal Power*, 82 Tul. L. Rev. 509 (2007); Blackhawk, *Paradigm, supra* note 15 at 1829.

[106] *Oliphant*, 435 U.S. at 195.

[107] *Id.* at 206.

[108] *Id.*

speech.[109] In the end, the Court admitted that the formal legal texts and historical evidence "would probably not be sufficient to remove criminal jurisdiction over non-Indians if the Tribe otherwise retained such jurisdiction."[110] The Court instead resolved the question over criminal jurisdiction by mulling over the meaning of sovereignty and whether one race could govern another race fairly without the particular requirements of due process offered by the United States.[111]

In contrast to *McGirt*, the Court in *Oliphant* turned away from formal legal texts and historical argument and turned instead toward general impressions and presumptions—to wit, "substituting stories for statutes."[112] These "stories" reflected a dominant ideology that erased the history of Native peoples and the United States's formal recognition of Native nations. In the end, the Court decided the contours of Native nations' ability to prosecute crimes committed within their borders, even crimes committed against their own police officers, based on the justices' own vision of United States history and structures of government.[113] This vision was not one informed by the realities of the long-standing interactions between the United States and Native nations but one rooted in a dominant ideology that raised Native erasure to a universal truism. *Oliphant* buffered this vision with nineteenth century precedent crafted by Justice Taney to justify the violence of the removal and reservation eras: "Indians are within the geographical limits of the United States. The soil and people within these limits are under the political control of the Government of the United States, or of the States of the Union. There exists in the broad domain of sovereignty but these two."[114] The Court

---

[109] *Id.* at 206–207.

[110] *Id.* at 208.

[111] *Id.* at 208–211 ("It tries them, not by their peers, nor by the customs of their people, nor the law of their land, but by … a different race, according to the law of a social state of which they have an imperfect conception …" (quoting Ex Parte Crow Dog, 109 U.S. 556, 571 (1883)).

[112] McGirt v. Oklahoma, 140 S. Ct. 2452, 2470 (2020).

[113] *Oliphant*, 435 U.S. at 210 ("[F]rom the formation of the Union and the adoption of the Bill of Rights, the United States has manifested an equally great solicitude that its citizens be protected by the United States from unwarranted intrusions on their personal liberty. The power of the United States to try and criminally punish is an important manifestation of the power to restrict personal liberty. By submitting to the overriding sovereignty of the United States, Indian tribes therefore necessarily give up their power to try non-Indian citizens of the United States except in a manner acceptable to Congress.")

[114] *Id.* at 211 (quoting United States v. Kagama, 118 U.S. 375, 379 (1886)).

in *Oliphant* placed "common notions" and "presumptions" above arguments rooted in formal legal texts or historical argument. By turning the Solem rule on its head, the Court reached the opposite outcome from *McGirt:* under the *Oliphant* rule, Native nations would lose power even when formal laws recognized that power—as their sovereignty was erased by the presumptions of a dominant ideology that did not recognize the existence of Native nations [115]

II. Translating *McGirt v. Oklahoma*

The implications of *McGirt* are still unfolding, but the case does not immediately present as raising questions of social and racial justice. Scholars of criminal justice might take notice that *Murphy* is a capital case[116] and *McGirt* involved a life sentence.[117] But both defendants, Jimcy McGirt and Patrick Dwayne Murphy, were indicted in August 2020 under federal charges for the same crimes for which they had already been sentenced by the state of Oklahoma.[118] The federal government had been unlikely to impose the death penalty—but, shortly after the date of the decision, the last administration once again embraced capital punishment and put another Native man to death.[119]

---

[115] Future cases, applying and extending the rule in *Oliphant*, reached similarly sovereignty constricting outcomes. *Montana v. United States*, most notably, extended the *Oliphant* rule from criminal jurisdiction to tribal civil jurisdiction of non-Indians. To the extent that the Court addressed formal legal texts at all, it began to read the content of treaties and statutes against the context of a presumption against the existence of tribal sovereignty. Rather than reading the treaties at issue *Montana* as documents that were created by two sovereigns that recognized each other and set the terms of their relationship, the Court began to plumb the treaties for language that would set the terms of tribal sovereignty within the borders of their own territory. Further, nothing in the opinion considered historical argument or reflected upon the long history of the United States recognizing the power of Native nations to exercise jurisdiction over non-Indians—including, and most notably, by the Supreme Court itself in the foundational case of *Johnson v. M'Intosh.*

[116] *See* Murphy v. Royal, 886 F.3d 1171 (10th Cir. 2017).

[117] McGirt v. Oklahoma, 140 S. Ct. 2452, 2501 (2020).

[118] Curtis Killman, *Feds file charges against two men whose state convictions were overturned on jurisdictional grounds*, Tulsa World (Aug. 1, 2020), https://tulsaworld.com/news/local/crime-and-courts/feds-file-charges-against-two-men-whose-state-convictions-were-overturned-on-jurisdictional-grounds/article_94e41a9d-3a2f-5ee2-8fc0-dba3c3dad3a0.html.

[119] Jessica Schneider, *US Government Executes only Native American on Death Row, Despite Calls from Tribal Leaders on the President for Clemency*, CNN Pol. (Aug. 26, 2020), https://www.cnn.com/2020/08/26/politics/lezmond-mitchell-native-american-execution-supreme-court/index.html.

Scholars of racial justice might observe that *McGirt* did not involve any obvious question of fundamental rights or discrimination
and that the undergirding doctrine also explicitly disclaimed consideration of "race," declaring the classification of "Indian" to be a
political status.[120] They might instead hope that *McGirt* would work
some magic of antidiscrimination in the daily lives of the powerless
in Oklahoma or prevent the further subordination of marginalized
communities, including communities of color, from equality of opportunity. But the briefs for McGirt, as well as for the Muscogee
(Creek) Nation as amici, spent page after page denying that a finding
in their favor would have any impact on the residents, Indian and
non-Indian alike, living on the lands at issue.[121] It is unclear how much
power the Muscogee (Creek) Nation actually gained from the win—
the federal government, not the Native nation, had jurisdiction over
McGirt's case following the decision, and the Court raised the possibility in *McGirt* that laches and other doctrines might bar the Muscogee
(Creek) Nation from exercising power in other contexts.[122]

So how, precisely, does *McGirt* implicate justice? The state of
Oklahoma's jurisdiction over McGirt turned on whether those lands,
as well as millions of other acres, are included within the borders of a
reservation.[123] The Supreme Court held that Congress had not diminished reservation borders that were established by treaty.[124] At the

---

[120] *See* Morton v. Mancari, 417 U.S. 535, 554 (1974) (holding that laws treating Native
people differently from others do not implicate race considerations because the classification
is closer to a political category like citizenship); *see also* Bethany R. Berger, *Reconciling Equal
Protection and Federal Indian Law*, 98 Calif. L. Rev. 1165, 1187 (2010); Bethany R. Berger,
Red: Racism and the American Indian, 56 UCLA L. Rev. 591, 593 (2009); Carole Goldberg,
Descent into Race, 49 UCLA L. Rev. 1373, 1390–93 (2002); Sarah Krakoff, *Constitutional
Concern, Membership, and Race*, 9 FIU L. Rev. 295, 296 (2014); Sarah Krakoff, *Inextricably
Political: Race, Membership, and Tribal Sovereignty*, 87 Wash. L. Rev. 1041, 1043 (2012); Sarah
Krakoff, *They Were Here First: American Indian Tribes, Race, and the Constitutional Minimum*,
69 Stan. L. Rev. 491, 543–47 (2017). *But see* Rice v. Cayetano, 528 U.S. 495, 514 (2000)
(rejecting, as an improper proxy for race, the government's use of ancestry and applying strict
scrutiny).

[121] *See* Brief for Petitioner at 39–43, McGirt v. Oklahoma 140 S. Ct. 2452 (2020) (No. 18–
9526) ("The Sky is Not Falling"); Brief for Muscogee (Creek) Nation at 41–45, *McGirt*
140 S. Ct. 2452 (No. 18–9526) ("The State's Exaggerated Arguments About Consequences
Provide No Support for Disestablishment").

[122] *McGirt*, 140 S. Ct. at 2481("Many other legal doctrines–procedural bars, res judicata,
statutes of repose, and laches, to name a few–are designed to protect those who have reasonably labored under a mistaken understanding of the law. ").

[123] *Id*. at 2460.

[124] *Id*.

very least, then, the Supreme Court in *McGirt* has refused by judicial fiat to dispossess further Native nations of land and sovereignty secured by treaty without the intervention of the political branches. The Court has held firm to its own stance—however compromised—that it is not the right institution to engage in imperialism—nor ought it decide on mixed evidence whether the United States has engaged in colonization of peoples at the margins of American empire. This slender reed of justice deserves to be celebrated in its own right.

But beyond that slender reed, a more nuanced story of social and racial justice can be glimpsed in *McGirt*: first, the case is the result of a long history of Native advocacy which has organized around the notion of power and sovereignty and which has relied on rule of law principles and formal legal change as the centerpiece of its advocacy strategy.[125] The case reflects a generations-long effort by Native people to resist subordination and colonization by leveraging and shaping law within formal lawmaking institutions. Relatedly, although it is true that the case does not implicate race or discrimination doctrines directly, the disaggregation of federal Indian law from this doctrine should be understood within the context of the broader organizing strategy of Native people.

The result in *McGirt*—that is, that millions of acres of land and a large portion of the city of Tulsa exist within reservation borders—reflects the result of power movement strategies. It highlights what recent social movement scholarship has termed "power-shifting."[126] In essence, the Supreme Court in *McGirt* reaffirmed the power of the Muscogee (Creek) Nation to make law, execute it, and enforce it over the lands and peoples within its borders. Within the borders of the reservation the Muscogee (Creek) Nation, a majority-minority government now governs. Does that mean that a Native nation may now

---

[125] *See* Bilder, *supra* note 26, at 1749–53; Ablavsky, *supra* note 26, at 591–613; CALLOWAY, *supra* note 26, at 1–16.

[126] *See, e.g.*, Jocelyn Simonson, *Police Reform through a Power Lens*, 130 YALE L.J. (forthcoming 2021); K. Sabeel Rahman & Jocelyn Simonson, *The Institutional Design of Community Control*, 108 CALIF. L. REV. 679 (2020); Jocelyn Simonson, *The Place of "the People" in Criminal Procedure*, 119 COLUM. L. REV. 249 (2019); K. Sabeel Rahman, *Policymaking as Power-Building*, 27 S. CAL. INTERDISC. L.J. 315 (2018); *see also* Levinson, *Looking for Power in Public Law*, *supra* note 27, at 33. It bears observation that much of this new literature draws its inspiration directly from the Black Lives Matter movement—some members of this movement have located its intellectual origins and its shape within the power movements of the 1960s and 1970s and those movements' call for "community control." Amna A. Akbar, *Law's Exposure: The Movement and the Legal Academy*, 65 J. LEGAL EDUC. 352, 356–60 (2015).

exercise limitless power over millions of acres in Oklahoma, including large portions of Tulsa? The short answer is "no," but it is important to reflect on where the limits on the Muscogee (Creek's) power come from and how *McGirt* offers the potential of a more just future. Like everything within federal Indian law, the power-shifting process is a bit complicated and requires an extra effort to translate. With broad contextualization, the doctrine provides valuable lessons to numerous theories of justice.

In federal Indian law, Native nations recognized by the federal government exercise power or "sovereignty" within reservation borders. The Supreme Court held in the "Marshall Trilogy,"[127] a series of three cases drafted in the antebellum era by Chief Justice John Marshall, that the sovereignty of Native nations within the territorial borders of the United States is limited inherently in two ways: Native nations cannot alienate their reservation lands except to the United States government, nor can Native nations treat directly with any nation-state other than the United States.[128] Except for those two inherent limitations, the Court held that the sovereignty of Native nations remained intact.

Although the Court also held that the recognition of this sovereignty could be restricted and expanded at the discretion of the national government, it held that the political branches alone could do so.[129] It may seem unthinkable, but federal Indian law demonstrates how the United States has sanctioned Native nations to operate as sovereign, enmeshed enclave states within its borders. Among its most radical possibilities, Native people could aim to reform the doctrine in order to return dispossessed homelands to Native communities, thereby expanding the current jurisdiction over which Native nations exercise sovereignty.[130] This future would allow not only majority-minority enclave governance but a more expansive and independent sense of sovereignty. The potential for radicalism in *McGirt* lies in the fact that the Court declined to participate in the restriction of lands over which the Muscogee (Creek) Nation could govern. The ruling, in

---

[127] Worcester v. Georgia, 31 U.S. (6 Pet.) 515 (1832); Cherokee Nation v. Georgia, 30 U.S. (5 Pet.) 1 (1831); Johnson v. M'Intosh, 21 U.S. (8 Wheat.) 543 (1823).

[128] *See Johnson*, 21 U.S. at 588–89.

[129] *See* United States v. Rogers, 45 U.S. (4 How.) 567 (1846).

[130] *See* THE LAND BACK MOVEMENT, https://landback.org/ (last visited Feb. 14, 2021) for a recent iteration of this movement. *See also 10 Point Program*, RED NATION, https://thered nation.org/10-point-program/ (last visited Feb. 14, 2021).

short, supported a broader jurisdiction for Muscogee (Creek) Nation sovereignty and a vision of potentially expanded sovereign power.

Skeptics of the potential of federal Indian law and the success of power movements within it would be right to point to the racism at the heart of the doctrine and to the many limitations placed on Native nations over the years.[131] Although the political branches have created a bevy of limitations on tribal sovereignty—largely in the context of criminal law—and the Supreme Court has ushered in even more restrictions,[132] the sovereignty of Native nations remains. Native people continue to maintain a culture of sovereignty and organize with power as a central guiding principle. By contrast to principles focused on rights, organizing around power and sovereignty motivates Native people to build spaces of governance that help give shape to their daily lives. Within reservation borders, Native people put into practice a culture of sovereignty that builds the collaborative construction of governments, hospitals, schools, and other infrastructure. Although many of these governments are built in the shadow of colonialism and reflect those limitations, some have allowed radical visions of community to take shape—including versions of democratic socialism; racial egalitarianism, the rejection of White supremacy; and restorative visions of criminal justice. At its fullest, federal Indian law could help cultivate a Native radical liberalism[133]—a project that confronts the racist history of America while adhering to the tenets of liberal egalitarianism in ways not seen within the history of the United States.

III. Lessons

The fact that the Court in *McGirt* reached an unthinkable decision by claiming to uphold law and rule-of-law principles has much to teach about the relationship between law and power. In

---

[131] *See, e.g.*, Robert A. Williams, Like a Loaded Weapon: The Rehnquist Court, Indian Rights, and the Legal History of Racism in America (2005); Elizabeth Reese, *The Other American Law*, 73 Stan. L. Rev. (forthcoming 2021); *cf.* Addie C. Rolnick, *The Promise of Mancari: Indian Political Rights as Racial Remedy*, 86 N.Y.U. L. Rev. 958, 967–68 (2011).

[132] *See, e.g.*, Oliphant v. Suquamish Indian Tribe, 435 U.S. 191, 209 (1978); *see also* Nevada v. Hicks, 533 U.S. 353, 374–75 (2001); Duro v. Reina, 495 U.S. 676, 679 (1990); Montana v. United States, 450 U.S. 544, 564 (1981).

[133] *See* Charles Mills, Black Rights/White Wrongs: The Critique of Racial Liberalism 201–15 (2017) (proposing "black radical liberalism" as an alternative to the failures of modern racialized liberalism in that it offers a form of liberalism "that draws upon the most valuable insights of the black nationalist and black Marxist traditions and incorporates them into a dramatically transformed liberalism").

particular, *McGirt* illustrates why scholars of law, legal change, and social movements ought to take notice of power movements like that of Native people and Native nations and of the social dynamics of power around which these movements navigate. The result in *McGirt* felt unthinkable and perhaps even impossible before the Court issued its opinion in July 2020. It was unthinkable even against a legal question that felt very settled under recent, unanimous Supreme Court precedent.[134] Yet rather than presume that the law would direct the Court's decision, sympathetic and less sympathetic audiences alike were convinced that the Court simply could not hold that portions of Tulsa rested within the borders of an Indian reservation because it did not comport with the public's taken-for-granted world view. This dynamic, and the dialectic it reveals, has much to contribute to our understanding of the relationship between law and power.

But *McGirt* also reveals the centrality of formal legal texts and historical argument to the possibility of unsettling the dominant ideology and provides a very visible example of how marginalized communities have long leveraged these strategies successfully to shift power. The following sections unpack these lessons in greater depth, offering at the close some thoughts on how Indian Country might further draw on these lessons when crafting their advocacy strategies in the future.

A. ON POWER

Theories of law and lawmaking would benefit by the inclusion of the study of power as developed within the social sciences—and of the social dimensions of power reflected in federal Indian law and other bodies of law shaped by power movements. Although reference to "power" often appears ubiquitous in both legal doctrine and scholarly literature, references tend to focus on the distribution of power between institutions and how particular distributions lend themselves to better or worse forms of governance.[135] Students of the law have developed an at times amorphous language to articulate the nature of those powers: police power, legislative power, executive power, judicial power, sovereignty, and jurisdiction. But that language betrays on its face the centrality of institutions to its analysis. The legal

---

[134] Nebraska v. Parker, 126 S. Ct. 1072, 1072 (2016).

[135] *See* Levinson, *Looking for Power, supra* note 27, at 33 (reviewing the literature).

academy—likely borrowing its vernacular from a long-lost theory of the science of government[136]—presumes that power is lodged within institutions like legislatures, courts, the executive, agencies, and the police and that it is shaped by its institutional form.[137] Weighty tomes have ruminated on the nature of "executive power,"[138] as if power owes its very character to the institution of its birth and not to the individuals who inhabit and wield power within that institution. The language of power within the legal academy offers even a means to articulate and mitigate harms caused to institutions by disempowerment: the "dignity" of sovereigns and branches provides immunity against another institution having power over them, and that dignity is harmed by the usurpation of power through coercion or other means.[139]

Despite the ubiquity of the reference to power, legal scholars seem to lack the language to fully articulate and explore the distribution of power between individuals and communities.[140] Studies of social justice rarely ask *"who* governs?"[141] in their quest to determine *how* governments can exercise their powers to best facilitate a just society. Theories of popular constitutionalism and popular sovereignty identify "the people" as the locus of power.[142] These literatures, however, rarely interrogate the "popular" of "popular sovereignty"—that is, scholars too rarely ask who "the people" are, how that category is constituted, and how power is distributed among them.[143]

---

[136] *See* James A. Robinson, *Newtonianism and the Constitution*, 1 MIDWEST J. OF POL. SCI. 252, 252–66 (1957); Harold A. McDougall, *Social Movements, Law, and Implementation: A Clinical Dimension for the New Legal Process*, 75 CORNELL L. REV. 83 (1989); Note, *Organic and Mechanical Metaphors in Late Eighteenth-Century American Political Thought*, 110 HARV. L. REV. 1832 (1997).

[137] *See* Levinson, *Looking for Power, supra* note 27 at 33.

[138] *See, e.g.*, MICHAEL W. MCCONNELL, THE PRESIDENT WHO WOULD NOT BE KING 1 (2020); ERIC NELSON, THE ROYALIST REVOLUTION 1 (2014); Michael Stokes Paulsen, *The Most Dangerous Branch: Executive Power to Say What the Law Is*, 83 Geo. L.J. 217, 217–346 (1994); ADOLPHE DE CHAMBRUN, THE EXECUTIVE POWER IN THE UNITED STATES: A STUDY OF CONSTITUTIONAL LAW 1 (1874).

[139] *See, e.g.*, Seminole Tribe of Florida v. Florida, 517 U.S. 44 (1996) (sovereign immunity); Shelby County v. Holder, 570 U.S. 529 (2013)(equal dignity principle); New York v. United States, 505 U.S. 144 (1992) (anticommandeering doctrine).

[140] Levinson, *Looking for Power, supra* note 27 at 38–39.

[141] *Id.* (quoting ROBERT A. DAHL, WHO GOVERNS?: DEMOCRACY AND POWER IN AN AMERICAN CITY (David Horne ed., 1961)).

[142] *See, e.g.*, KRAMER, *supra* note 37, at 8.

[143] Levinson, *Looking for Power, supra* note 27, at 38–39.

Recent years have witnessed a flurry of scholarship examining power in the context of social movements.[144] But these literatures tend to approach power through the lens of political power—often loosely defined as electoral power—or economic power.[145] *McGirt* stands as an example of how the social dimensions of power operate as distinct from power in the context of ordinary partisan politics. Both liberals and conservatives alike doubted that the Court would ever hold that the city of Tulsa was part of an Indian reservation not because their political leanings so dictated, but because such an outcome just seemed "absurd."[146]

Matters within federal Indian law often evade easy classification as either liberal and conservative, and cases rarely follow crude "counting to five" predictions based on the party affiliation of the president responsible for each justice's appointment. *McGirt* is, in this respect, certainly no exception. Given the unusual composition of the majority, with Justice Gorsuch as swing, joined by the so-called liberal wing of the Court, a vision of power as mere partisan politics might struggle to explain the outcome. In fact, each justice's approach to federal Indian law cases seldom maps neatly onto their broader jurisprudential patterns. Nor can each justice's approach be explained by the particular brand of liberalism or conservatism to which they subscribe. Some of the most anti-tribal sovereignty Indian law opinions were crafted by justices that many categorize as liberal, Justices Ginsburg and Stevens among them,[147] and these justices often shifted their position on Indian law issues over time. Justice Ginsburg, for example, joined the majority in *McGirt* after crafting distinctively anti-tribal sovereignty doctrines with respect to other legal questions.[148] A more nuanced legal realism might envision Justice Gorsuch's

---

[144] *See, e.g.,* Simonson, *Power Lens, supra* note 126; Kate Andrias & Benjamin I. Sachs, *Constructing Countervailing Power: Law and Organizing in an Era of Political Inequality*, 130 YALE L.J. 546 (2021); Rahman & Simonson, *supra* note 126; Simonson, *The Place of "the People" in Criminal Procedure, supra* note 126; Rahman, *Policymaking as Power-Building, supra* note 126; Akbar, supra note 126; *see also* Levinson, *Looking for Power, supra* note 27, at 33.

[145] Simonson, *Power Lens, supra* note 126, at 23; Rahman, *Policymaking as Power-Building, supra* note 126, at 315.

[146] *See, e.g.,* Baude, *supra* note 35; *see also* Mann, *supra* note 14.

[147] *See, e.g.,* Strate v. A-1 Contractors, 520 U.S. 438 (1997); Cotton Petroleum Corp. v. New Mexico, 490 U.S. 163 (1989).

[148] City of Sherrill v. Oneida Indian Nation of New York, 544 U.S. 197 (2005); *cf.* Carole Goldberg, *Finding the Way to Indian Country: Justice Ruth Bader Ginsburg's Decisions in Indian Law Cases*, 70 OHIO ST. L.J. 1003 (2009) (charting the development of a more pro-Native nation stance by Justice Ginsburg over her tenure on the Court).

experience as a westerner[149] as driving the outcome—other members of the Court certainly defied their usual procedural norms to afford him a vote on the case. But westerners appointed to the Court in earlier eras—Justices Kennedy and O'Connor, most notably—did not approach federal Indian law cases with such rigor, nor were they able to build and maintain coalitions among justices, liberal or conservative.[150] Power is branded on the face of the *McGirt* opinion, but its dynamics appear to defy the logics of how power is modeled in other contexts—political and economic alike.

Better understanding of how power operates within society could facilitate more nuanced models of how law and lawmaking institutions work. It could also offer a more comprehensive vision of how marginalized communities can and do navigate these dynamics in order to enact reforms and shift power to their communities. The following sections explore three lessons from federal Indian law and from *McGirt* on how the social dynamics of power are central to understanding law, lawmaking institutions, and theories of social movements and legal change—that is, that dominant ideologies often influence law, especially in courts; that movements can navigate power to enact enduring legal reform and that these movements are deserving of study; and that power movement led reforms could provide a framework that makes legally cognizable the disempowerment—not just the subordination—of marginalized communities.

1. *The power of dominant ideology.* The vision of "impossibility" that nearly drove the outcome in McGirt also seemed to transcend the usual predictive models for judicial decision-making—in fact, two of the last federal Indian law opinions issued by the Supreme Court were resolved in favor of tribal sovereignty and with the same unusual composition of justices.[151] Nonetheless, it remained impossible, absurd even, to believe that the Court would apply a unanimous 2016 opinion to resolve a very similar legal question in a similar manner.

---

[149] He was born and spent much of his life in Colorado, and he served as a judge on the Tenth Circuit before his appointment to the Supreme Court. *See* JOHN GREENYA, GORSUCH: THE JUDGE WHO SPEAKS FOR HIMSELF 11 (2018).

[150] *See, e.g.,* Matthew L.M. Fletcher, *Reflections on Justice Kennedy's Indian Law Legacy,* TURTLE TALK (June 29, 2018), https://turtletalk.blog/2018/06/29/reflections-on-justice-kennedys-indian-law-legacy/; Richard L. Barnes, *A Woman of the West, But Not the Tribes: Justice Sandra Day O'Connor and the State–Tribe Relationship,* 58 LOY. L. REV. 39 (2012).

[151] *See* Herrera v. Wyoming, 139 S. Ct. 1686 (2019); Wash. State Dep't of Licensing v. Cougar Den, Inc., 139 S. Ct. 1000 (2019).

The difference is, of course, the absurd idea that Tulsa could exist within an Indian reservation—an argument so persuasive that a highly experienced Supreme Court practitioner chose to open her brief with a photo of Tulsa rather than the text of legal argument.[152] The unusual procedural path of *McGirt*, the oral arguments in both *Murphy* and *McGirt*, and the experience of shock at *McGirt*'s ultimate outcome offer a prime teaching moment on the centrality of dominant ideology in shaping law—especially within the courts.

But what exactly is meant by "ideology"? At its base, an ideology encompasses a world view that is held universally by a society. Beyond partisan political preference, ideology is experienced by a society as the natural, taken-for-granted world. Professor John Searle's theory of "objective" or "institutional" facts helps to illuminate the nature of a view held seemingly as universal, without respect to demographics or political party.[153] Searle described a set of beliefs that are so taken for granted that to challenge them is absurd. It is to appear insane.[154] His most famous example is that of a twenty-dollar bill. An individual might disagree with the existence of the capitalist system.[155] That individual might protest the existence and use of money. But to doubt the fact that a twenty-dollar bill amounts to twenty dollars in currency that could be used to purchase items in a market is to appear insane. Those sorts of challenges are, to use a term from constitutional law, beyond "off-the-wall."[156]

Marx and Engels introduced the notion of a "dominant ideology," by which they aimed to capture and describe not just the worldview or "superstructure" of society—comprised of "politics, laws, morality, religion, metaphysics, &c"—but a worldview that made entrenched inequality and subordination appear natural.[157] They surmised that from this dominant ideology arose the "production of ideas, of

---

[152] *See* Brief for Petitioner at 3, Sharp v. Murphy, 140 S. Ct. 2412 (2020) (per curiam) (No. 17-1107).

[153] *See, e.g.*, Searle, *What is an Institution?*, *supra* note 22 (describing certain "institutional facts" as creating an objective, socially constructed reality through "collective intentionality" or "collective acceptance"); Searle, The Construction of Social Reality, *supra* note 22.

[154] John R. Searle, *Social Ontology: Some Basic Principles*, 6 Anthropological Theory 51 (2006).

[155] *Id.* at 52–53.

[156] Jack M. Balkin, *Constitutional Hardball and Constitutional Crises*, 26 Q.L.R. 579, 579 (2008). They are out of bounds.

[157] Marx & Engels, *supra* note 17.

conceptions, of consciousness."[158] The dominant ideology disguised as natural the material inequalities of society, but it also embodied the "ruling ideas" of society to justify those material inequities[159]—ideas that were "nothing more than the ideal expression of the dominant material relationships, the dominant material relationships grasped as ideas; hence of the relationships which make one class the ruling one, therefore, the ideas of their dominance."[160] Ideologies, according to Marx and Engels, legitimized those in power and obscured the violent subordination of the powerless through the logic of the ideology.[161]

Theorists of Native studies explore in depth how the power of the dominant ideology works to affect the "erasure" of Native people.[162] The dominant ideology of the United States includes a view of the nation as one comprised of immigrants drawn to North America seeking liberty and freedom, and willing to tame a vast—and empty—wilderness in order to do so.[163] Because the existence of Native people and Native nations problematizes this ideology, dynamics within the dominant ideology work to erase the history of Native people and deny their ongoing existence. Theorists have identified this erasure across a range of discourses, from literature to film to mapmaking to

---

[158] *Id.* at 42.

[159] *Id.* at 67.

[160] *Id.*

[161] *Id.* at 67, 92–94.

[162] For example, Lisa Kahaleole Hall argues that,

> The myth of a (mostly) empty North American continent waiting for (European) settlement and "development" is foundational to the origin story of the United States as a "nation of immigrants" developing an untamed wilderness. This continental origin story requires the denial of more than five hundred years of contrary facts beginning with the existence of millions of indigenous people inhabiting North America at the time of European contact and continuing through to the present with the struggles of more than 562 currently federally recognized tribal entities fighting to maintain their limited sovereignty and promised treaty rights in the context of complete public ignorance and complaints about their "special rights."

Lisa Kahaleole Hall, *Strategies of Erasure: U.S. Colonialism and Native Hawaiian Feminism*, 60 AM. Q. 273, 275 (2008). *See also* JEAN M. O'BRIEN, FIRSTING AND LASTING: WRITING INDIANS OUT OF EXISTENCE IN NEW ENGLAND (2010) (theorizing also that the presumption that Native people could not be modern was a fundamental aspect of the "disappearing Indian" and integral to the project of erasure); Patrick Wolfe, *Settler Colonialism and the Elimination of the Native*, 8 J. GENOCIDE RSCH. 387, 388 (2006) (describing erasure as the "logic of elimination" and as fundamental to the settler colonial project).

[163] *See* sources cited *supra* note 162.

art and have identified its power in myth-building as well as in supporting the development of a settler colonial state.[164]

Many legal scholars have internalized the dominant perspective
that Native nations have long ceased to govern within the borders of
the United States—ceased to exist, even—and that disempowered
minorities have always been disempowered. This worldview is deeply
troubling. It entrenches existing power inequities by holding out as
"natural" the perpetual disempowerment of racial minorities and
other subordinated groups.[165] It is also ahistorical. Although proffered
as a universal truth, it belies hundreds of years of history: subordinated
groups have wielded power only to have it wrested from them through
violence and lawbreaking.[166] This mistaken view nevertheless remains
surprisingly durable. Only very recently have legal scholars begun to
interrogate the impacts of erasure on the law.[167]

While it seemed predetermined that the Court could not possibly
hold that Tulsa existed, even in part, within an Indian reservation, it
did. In so doing, it has denaturalized the erasure of Native people and
Native governance and it has demonstrated the contingent nature of
the dominant ideology that appeared so natural beforehand. In the
last fifty years, theorists have begun to describe means by which
dominant ideologies, and the inequities they entrench, might be unsettled and reformed. Poststructuralists, most notably Foucault and
Bourdieu, abandoned Marx's "ideology" for terms like "discourse"
and "doxa"—terms that they theorized better capture the agency of
subordinated communities in internalizing and co-constructing a
worldview that entrenches inequities and justifies their subordinated
status.[168] Bourdieu theorized that it was in the moment of a breach of

---

[164] *Id.*

[165] Kimberlé Williams Crenshaw, *Race, Reform, and Retrenchment: Transformation and Le-
gitimation in Antidiscrimination Law*, 101 HARV. L. REV. 1331, 1370 (1988) ("Throughout
American history, the subordination of Blacks was rationalized by a series of stereotypes and
beliefs that made their conditions appear logical and natural.").

[166] *See infra* Part III.B.

[167] *See, e.g.*, Blackhawk, *On Power, supra* note 15, at 39–56; K-Sue Park, *This Land is Not Our
Land*, 87 U. CHI. L. REV. 1977, 1993–94 (2020) (reviewing the literature); *see also* Blackhawk,
Paradigm, supra note 15, at 1806–45 (2019).

[168] *See, e.g.*, MICHEL FOUCAULT, THE ARCHAEOLOGY OF KNOWLEDGE AND THE DISCOURSE ON
LANGUAGE 46 (1972); *see also* MICHEL FOUCAULT, DISCIPLINE AND PUNISH: THE BIRTH OF THE
PRISON (1975); BOURDIEU, *supra* note 16 at 156 (defining doxa as "a quasi-perfect correspondence between the objective order and the subjective principles of organization (as in
ancient societies) the natural and social world appears as self-evident.").

this taken-for-granted worldview—often by interrogation through historical argument or otherwise to reveal its contingent nature—that entrenched power relationships could be made legible and possibly unsettled.[169] In issuing *McGirt*, the Supreme Court breached the taken-for-granted world view that Native nations could not possibly govern a modern city and, in so doing, it offers the opportunity for the legal academy, as well as the public, to further interrogate and possibly unsettle the dominant ideology of Native erasure, should we choose to take advantage of it.

2. *Power movements and navigating the dynamics of power.* Although *McGirt* is the rare example of a win for Indian Country in the courts, it more closely resembles the success of Native advocates before administrative agencies and Congress. There, Native advocates have long focused their advocacy upon formal legal texts and have harnessed the power of those texts in order to prevent the dominant ideology from becoming law. Further study of the movement strategy of Native peoples and the law that they have shaped could expand understanding within the legal academy of law and social change. Because Native people and Native nations have organized around the notion of power—similar to the way that the civil rights movement organized around the notion of "rights"—their impact upon the law has been distinct, pressing the language of power and its machinations to the fore.[170] Organizing around power has also meant that the strategies used by Native movements have been distinct from rights movements. Rather than aiming for change within the broader society, they have focused instead on advocacy before formal lawmaking institutions. Advocates have focused instead on legal reforms that would not necessarily result in a substantive change in their daily lives but would leverage the law to shift power to their communities, enabling those communities to shape their own daily lives.

Social movement theory has, to date, often overlooked the advocacy of Native movements in its broader theorization of social and legal change.[171] It is likely that, like much of public law, this omission

---

[169] BOURDIEU, *supra* note 16, at 164 (describing the importance of interrogating the doxa, because "[t]he political function of classifications is never more likely to pass unnoticed than in the case of relatively undifferentiated social formations, in which the prevailing classificatory system encounters no rival or antagonistic principle.").

[170] *Blackhawk, Paradigm, supra* note 15, at 1845–76.

[171] *See, e.g.,* Guinier & Torres, *supra* note 25, at 2756–62 (distinguishing "social movements" from "interest groups" that "are more likely to engage in conventional politics by

is due to these theories reflecting most strongly the characteristics of their paradigm case—that is, the civil rights movement.[172] As was true in the context of the civil rights movement, as well as many movements that followed, these theories often presume that advocates must first change the dominant world view to affect enduring legal change. According to these theories, the law would then conform to this change, either because it arose directly from the social movement,[173] from the public as sovereign,[174] or because elite lawmakers would take notice of the change in public opinion.[175]

By contrast, Native movements have focused their advocacy strategies on direct engagement with formal lawmaking fora—predominantly Congress and the administrative state—and with the shaping of formal legal texts. These strategies have encompassed more traditional forms of engagement like treaty negotiations, lobbying, and petitioning, but also more radical strategies like land seizures, including the island of Alcatraz, and the occupation of offices of the Bureau of Indian Affairs. Most distinctively from the simple story we tell about the civil rights movement, Native advocacy strategies did not aim to change the broader culture but to shift power to Native communities[176]

---

trying to influence, in conventional ways, people who exercise state power" and not mentioning Native advocates); additional sources cited *supra* note 25.

[172] *See* Catherine L. Fisk & Diana S. Reddy, *Protection by Law, Repression by Law: Bringing Labor Back into the Study of Law and Social Movements*, 70 EMORY L.J. 63 (2020) (noting a similar exclusion from the social movement literature for another form of power movement, that of labor, and rooting that exclusion in the dominance of rights and the civil rights movement in social movement theory); Scott L. Cummings, *The Social Movement Turn in Law*, 43 LAW & SOC. INQUIRY 360, 365 (2018) ("[t]he story of how and why social movements have come to matter within contemporary legal scholarship takes off at the moment of crisis within progressive legal thought caused by *Brown* [*v. Board of Education*]."); Scott L. Cummings, *The Puzzle of Social Movements in American Legal Theory*, 64 UCLA L. Rev. 1554, 1556, 1556 n.4 (2017) (identifying the "zenith of social movements in American politics" as when "Martin Luther King, Jr. led civil rights protestors across the Pettus Bridge in Selma"); Catherine R. Albiston & Gwendolyn M. Leachman, *Law as an Instrument of Social Change*, *in* 13 INT'L ENCYCLOPEDIA SOC. & BEHAV. SCI. 542, 542 (James D. Wright ed., 2d ed. 2015) (gesturing to *Brown v. Board* as the origin story of the social movement literature).

[173] Guinier & Torres, *supra* note 25, at 2760; Reva B. Siegel, *Text in Contest: Gender and the Constitution from a Social Movement Perspective*, 150 U. PA. L. REV. 297, 320 (2001) ("While the authority of the Constitution is sustained in part through practices of veneration and deference, it is also sustained through a very different kind of relationship, in which citizens know themselves as authorities, as authors of the law.").

[174] *See, e.g.*, KRAMER, supra note 37, at 1.

[175] *See, e.g.*, 1 BRUCE ACKERMAN, WE THE PEOPLE: FOUNDATIONS 1 (1991).

[176] *See, e.g.*, Jocelyn Simonson, *Police Reform through a Power Lens*, 130 YALE L.J. 778 (2021) [hereinafter Simonson, *Power Lens*]; Kate Andrias & Benjamin I. Sachs, *Constructing Countervailing Power: Law and Organizing in an Era of Political Inequality*, 130 YALE L.J. 546 (2021);

through increased recognition of inherent tribal sovereignty, retaking of land over which Native nations could wield jurisdiction, and gaining power over the instrumentalities of the federal government that had usurped governance from Native people.

Leveraging positive law and rule of law principles has long been a tactic of Native people.[177] They had a hand in codifying tribal sovereignty into United States law by leveraging and repurposing international law at the Founding. They turned to treaties in the nineteenth century as tools of recognition, power building, and collaborative lawmaking, even as the United States constructed narratives of the disappearance of Native people.[178] And they have continued through the present day to use law to build new institutional forms to shift power to their communities, including through the construction of novel, and more collaborative, lawmaking institutions like the government-to-government relationship designed by the Indian Reorganization Act[179] and the compacting process that followed the passage of the Indian Gaming Regulatory Act.[180] Native people have, for example, seized, repurposed, and reshaped their very own title of the United States Code—Title 25, "Indians"—over the course of the twentieth and twenty-first centuries.[181] Title 25 of the United States Code and the extensive government-to-government interactions between Native nations, the national government, and the states over the last two hundred years belies a dominant ideology that perpetuates the erasure of Native people entirely.

McGirt, of course, presents a rare case of very high, very public stakes. But it is actually rather commonplace that the corpus of federal Indian law is leveraged to force lawmaking institutions to uphold the

---

K. Sabeel Rahman & Jocelyn Simonson, *The Institutional Design of Community Control*, 108 CALIF. L. REV. 679 (2020); Jocelyn Simonson, *The Place of "the People" in Criminal Procedure*, 119 COLUM. L. REV. 249 (2019); K. Sabeel Rahman, *Policymaking as Power-Building*, 27 S. CAL. INTERDISC. L.J. 315 (2018) [hereinafter Rahman, *Policymaking as Power-Building*]; Amna A. Akbar, *Law's Exposure: The Movement and the Legal Academy*, 65 J. LEGAL EDUC. 352, 356–60 (2015); *see also* Levinson, *Looking for Power, supra* note 27, at 33.

[177] *See* Bilder, *supra* note 26, at 1749–53; Ablavsky, *supra* note 26, at 591–613; CALLOWAY, *supra* note 26, at 1–16.

[178] *Id.*

[179] Act of June 18, 1934, ch. 576, 48 Stat. 984 (codified as amended at 25 U.S.C. §§ 5101–5129 (2012)).

[180] Act of October 17, 1988, 102 Stat. 2467 (codified at 25 U.S.C. ch. 29 § 2701 et seq. (1988)).

[181] *See* 25 U.S.C. §§ 1–5636.

rule of law against the power of contrary ideology. The dominant public narrative is one of erasure: Native people, once noble, are presumed extinct and Native governments have ceased to exist—if they ever were "governments" in the first place.[182] Yet, the laws of the United States are replete with recognition of Native nations, even in the shadow of this erasure, because Native people force that recognition into law. The strategy of Native people has long been to leverage what Professor Paul Mishkin described, in a phrase cribbed from the "father of Indian law," Felix Cohen, as "the normative power of the actual."[183] Professor Mishkin means "that which is law tends by its very existence to generate a sense of being also that which ought to be the law."[184] Formal law is, no doubt, subject to change. But those formal legal texts as the "actual law" possess a greater durability than the dominant ideology, because of the power of the status quo. Native advocates are then able to harness those formal legal texts through advocacy strategies typically wielded by the conservative legal movement: textualism, rule of law principles, precedent, and judicial restraint.[185]

These strategies are quite distinctive from those movement strategies that focus on changing the public mind, aiming to reform the dominant ideology directly. Marginalized and excluded from making meaning within the dominant ideology, Native peoples have long engaged in a process that theorists have termed "hermeneutical dissent" or the creation of new terms in order to make sense of their experience.[186] Generations of advocacy have aimed to codify this new vernacular into law—sovereignty, power, and conquest—thereby making the experience of Native people legible to formal lawmaking institutions. By contrast to advocacy strategies that aim to force the public to recognize the experience of Native people, advocating to

---

[182] *See, e.g.*, Hall, *supra* note 162, at 275; O'BRIEN, *supra* note 162, at 55–144; Wolfe, *supra* note 162, at 388.

[183] Paul J. Mishkin, *Foreword: The High Court, the Great Writ, and the Due Process of Time and Law*, 79 HARV. L. REV. 56, 71 (1965); *see also* Justin Driver, *The Constitutional Conservatism of the Warren Court*, 100 CALIF. L. REV. 1101, 59 (2012).

[184] Mishkin, *supra* note 183, at 71.

[185] *See, e.g.*, Frederick Schauer, *Formalism*, 97 YALE L.J. 509, 509–10 (1988); STEVEN M. TELES, THE RISE OF THE CONSERVATIVE LEGAL MOVEMENT: THE BATTLE FOR CONTROL OF THE LAW 145 (2008); Hon. Frank H. Easterbrook, *Do Liberals and Conservatives Differ in Judicial Activism?*, 73 U. COLO. L. REV. 1401 (2002).

[186] *See, e.g.*, Eskridge & Riano, *supra* note 26; FRICKER, *supra* note 26; Goetze, *supra* note 26.

alter the legal field directly allows advocates to fracture the law in order to lower the barriers to reform.[187] Unlike narrow discourses that form in pockets of a nation-state among dissenting communities, narrow legal texts offer to change outcomes in the world on nearly the same terms as their more general brethren. By prioritizing codification of these terms into formal legal texts rather than simply discourse, advocates have enabled those lawmaking institutions to recognize and, at times, remedy the harm caused by present and historical injustices. A focus on formal legal texts can also shift reform efforts away from the high-stakes game of having to unsettle an entrenched dominant ideology—a discourse that always seems to return to a state of erasure. The public is less familiar with the language of federal Indian law. Thus, the language of power and sovereignty of those doctrines feels unfamiliar, perhaps even otherworldly. But that feeling of otherworldliness is simply because the formal legal texts of the United States stand in opposition to a dominant ideology that we all take for granted—an ideology that erases Native people and elevates a vision of liberalism that excludes the recognition of historical wrongs like colonialism and slavery. Even beyond offering a more accurate picture of the law and a more complete picture of the dynamics of legal change, a greater fluency and familiarity with the language of federal Indian law could begin to supplement the principles of justice that we currently take for granted—principles that focus on rights and equality while overlooking the relationship between power, law, and justice.

The particular case of *McGirt* offers an example of how social movements can shape the law—by treaty in that case, a paradigmatic example of collaborative lawmaking—and then leverage that law to drive outcomes in the world, even when the public no longer believes those outcomes to be possible. Rather than simply allow the dominant ideology to drive the outcome in *McGirt*, in the end, the Court relied on "law" through formal legal texts, precedent, and rule of law principles to reach an outcome that shocked the public. A closer analysis of the *McGirt* opinion illustrates how advocates wielded these formalist strategies in order to guide the Court toward a holding that once appeared inconceivable.

---

[187] *See* Maggie Blackhawk, *Equity Outside the Courts*, 120 COLUM. L. REV. 2037, 2064–69 (2020); *see also* Pierre Bourdieu, *The Force of Law: Toward a Sociology of the Juridical Field*, 38 HASTINGS L.J. 805, 814–16 (1986).

McGirt held that Congress had never diminished the reservation borders of the Muscogee (Creek) Nation, established by treaty law in 1866.[188] The ruling required a deep dive into over one hundred and fifty years of legal history.[189] Formal legal texts like the Treaty of 1866 codified the borders of the Muscogee (Creek) reservation.[190] Similar to other treaties, the Treaty of 1866 demarcates nation-states and subnational political communities and delineates the material world over which the Nation may exercise sovereignty—a material world that encompasses millions of acres and portions of the city of Tulsa. No other formal legal text modified the 1866 treaty.[191] That one-hundred-fifty-year legal history further revealed additional instances where the federal government recognized Muscogee (Creek) sover-eignty—often against an oppressive effort by the United States to undermine the Muscogee (Creek) government.[192]

Native advocates argued from rule-of-law principles—precedent, textualism, and formalism—in order to force the Court to take their claims seriously. The *Solem* test, upheld and further articulated in *Parker* just years before the Court issued its opinion in *McGirt*, ex-plicitly preferenced formal legal texts above dominant ideology and later acts undertaken by individuals and the government of Oklahoma in accordance with that ideology. As Native advocates had in *Parker*, they again leveraged the power of precedent, along with the formal legal texts they had shaped over the last two hundred years, to force the Court to look beyond the dominant ideology for context. These texts made the existence and recognition of Native governance undeniable. At first, the Court in *McGirt* seemed poised to decide the case based on an ideology of Native erasure rather than the law—noted explicitly by the justices' line of questioning in oral argument that focused on what people in Tulsa might "think" if they were to wake up the next morning within an Indian reservation. But by an admittedly slender majority it declined to do so, and in a case that could impact some-where near 1.8 million residents in the bustling metropolitan area of Tulsa.[193] The durability of those formal legal texts—the "normative

---

[188] McGirt v. Oklahoma, 140 S. Ct. 2452, 2459 (2020).

[189] *Id.* at 2460–74.

[190] *Id.* at 2460.

[191] *Id.* at 2468.

[192] *Id.* at 2465–67.

[193] McGirt v. Oklahoma, 140 S. Ct. 2452, 2482 (2020) (Roberts, C.J., dissenting).

power of the actual"—created a counterweight to an ideologically driven outcome and resulted in a very visible shift of power to a marginalized community.

3. *Making empowerment and disempowerment legible.* The lessons of Indian Country—organized around sovereignty and crafted in the register of power rather than equality, antidiscrimination, and rights—are often illegible outside of a small community of specialists.[194] The lessons of *McGirt*—other than the celebration of a "win" for Indian Country—have been difficult to glean for scholars outside of the field. The ruling exposes the illegibility of harms caused by disempowerment, especially when those forms of disempowerment do not clearly implicate liberal concerns over rights, discrimination, and inequality of opportunity.

The structure of federal Indian law is, in many ways, in tension with notions of liberalism, and this is no more true than in the way that the doctrine engages directly with questions about how power is distributed between groups and the ability of one group to govern another fairly. Prevailing theories of justice presume that all of society participates equally in creating a just society.[195] Such theories, however, often overlook historical injustice like American colonialism and the dispossession of Native people. Thus, these theories do not correct for the injustice caused by unequal distributions of power and fail to reflect upon how certain distributions of power to non-compliant groups could facilitate or impede the formation of the ideal, well-ordered society.[196]

To date, prevailing theory within law has not fared much better at addressing the values at stake in the distribution of power within a society. At best, the Elysian turn in legal process theory may foster the

---

[194] *See* Frickey, *supra* note 24, at 383 (describing the field as a "tiny backwater").

[195] *See, e.g.,* JOHN RAWLS, A THEORY OF JUSTICE (1971); JOHN RAWLS, JUSTICE AS FAIRNESS (1985); JOHN RAWLS, JUSTICE AS FAIRNESS: A RESTATEMENT (2001). Scholars have recently begun to debate the applicability of "ideal theories" of justice, like that of Rawls, that are crafted with the presumption of full compliance of all members of a society and without deep consideration of the realities of human nature. *See* Laura Valentini, *Ideal vs. Non-ideal Theory: A Conceptual Map*, 7 PHIL. COMPASS 654, 654–64 (2012); Ingrid Roberyns, *Ideal Theory in Theory and Practice*, 34 SOC. THEORY & PRAC. 341, 341–62 (2008); Colin Farrelly, *Justice in Ideal Theory: A Refutation*, 55 POL. STUDIES 844, 844–64 (2007).

[196] *See* KATRINA FORRESTER, IN THE SHADOW OF JUSTICE 135–137 (2019) (describing Rawlsian egalitarianism and the liberal egalitarianism that formed in its wake as excluding reflections on historical injustices like colonialism and slavery, and instead allowing for a strictly presentist consideration of equality).

legibility of disempowerment by recommending heightened judicial review of substantive law that regulates less powerful communities.[197] But judicial review of this kind can only remedy the harm inflicted by illiberal substantive law enacted in the face of disempowerment; it cannot remedy the underlying disempowerment itself.[198] Disempowerment is rarely articulated as a harm in its own right, in part because many other areas of law—rights-based doctrines in particular—lack the language to articulate either the social dynamics of power or the harms caused by its improper distribution.[199] Without such language, the legal academy and establishment often lack the means to recognize the harms to individuals and communities wrought by disempowerment.

Federal Indian law generally, and *McGirt* in particular, makes legible and offers the language to articulate the harm inflicted upon subordinated communities through the deprivation of power rather than the deprivation of substantive rights. In contrast to social justice movements that organize around rights, federal Indian law speaks in the register of power directly. Generations of Native legal advocacy have forced that register into the law through language like sovereignty, recognition, and self-determination.[200] Cases can turn on whether the United States has affirmatively asserted its "plenary power" over Native peoples and Native governments and power is envisioned as zero sum—thus, depriving Natives of power in turn. This means that discussions of power are not obscured under the twin fig leaves

---

[197] *See* United States v. Carolene Prods. Co., 304 U.S. 144, 152 n.4 (1938); JOHN HART ELY, DEMOCRACY AND DISTRUST: A THEORY OF JUDICIAL REVIEW (1980).

[198] A notable, and ironic, result of an Elysian view of disempowerment is that once a marginalized community obtains power within the legislative process, the oversight could cut the other direction—effectively neutering the power of majority-minority governments under the guise of constitutional values. *See, e.g.* City of Richmond v. J.A. Croson Co., 488 U.S. 469 (1989) (citing explicitly the presence of a Black majority government in holding a piece of affirmative action legislation unconstitutional).

[199] Some literatures have tried to articulate the problem of disempowerment through the language of democracy—calling disempowerment "antidemocratic." *See* Simonson, *Power Lens, supra* note 126 at 783; Janet Moore, *Democracy Enhancement in Criminal Law and Procedure*, 2014 UTAH L. REV. 543; Dorothy E. Roberts, *Democratizing Criminal Law as an Abolitionist Project*, 111 Nw. U. L. REV. 1597 (2017); Jocelyn Simonson, *Democratizing Criminal Justice through Contestation and Resistance*, 111 Nw. U. L. REV. 1609, 1612, 1623–24 (2017). But this terminology does not fully capture the narrow harms to a particular community caused by disempowerment in a specific instance, rather than a systemic failure of an institution to an entire community. It also risks being remedied not by empowerment of a particular community, but by reform of an institution to make it more accountable to everyone.

[200] Blackhawk, *Paradigm, supra* note 15 at 1814; Blackhawk, *On Power, supra* note 15 at 41.

of interpretation and deference but rather take center stage. To provide just one example, the outcome in *McGirt* turned on which social dynamics of power the Court was willing to recognize as legally cognizable. The parties in *McGirt* each offered different accounts of how power operates in the social world—with one side embracing a vision of power that required consent and the other describing power in the form of violence and subordination.[201] Forced to confront and debate these visions of power directly, the Court in *McGirt* ultimately declined to codify into law a vision of power with violence and subordination at its core.[202]

Because the law recognizes the importance of power to justice in the context of Indian affairs, it also recognizes the harm in its deprivation. A better understanding of the strategies of these movements, as well as a greater fluency with their vernacular, could offer the opportunity to better articulate the harm that disempowerment has caused in other communities.

B. ON HISTORY

It has been said that history plays an outsized role within the context of federal Indian law,[203] and this has held true in the context of *McGirt*. Because of its centrality to the doctrine and to the case, the role of historical argument in guiding the Court away from dominant ideology and toward formal legal texts and rule of law principles bears further exploration. The *Solem* test, as strengthened by *Nebraska v. Parker*, invited a wide range of historical argument.[204] The test effectively created a space within the context of litigation for Native advocates to denaturalize and demythologize the erasure of Native people and Native nations through historical accounts of the long-standing existence and recognition of Native governance within the United States.[205]

---

[201] *See* Part II.A *supra.*

[202] *Id.*

[203] *See* Kathryn E. Fort, *The Vanishing Indian Returns: Tribes, Popular Originalism, and the Supreme Court*, 57 St. Louis. U. L.J. 297 (2013); Albert L. Hurtado, *Public History and the Native American: Issues in the American West*, Mont.: The Mag. of W. Hist., Spring 1990, at 58, 59 ("[V]irtually all historical writing on Indian topics has the potential to affect contemporary Indian life."); *see also* Williams, *supra* note 131, at xxiv–xxv; Frank Pommersheim, Broken Landscape 115–20 (2009).

[204] 465 U.S. 463 (1984).

[205] *See* Part II.A *infra.*

This section unpacks the mechanics of the relationship between historical argument and ideology, noting especially the use of history to reveal the contingent nature of the erasure of Native people. Beyond that, this section offers ways that history can be constructive as well as critical in nature—and describes how history could help us to envision a more just future.

Historical argument within the context of litigation serves multiple functions[206]—likely the most well studied and identified would be the historical contextualization of formal legal texts. Although history is often ambiguous and lacks definitive answers for questions of intent and meaning, there are examples where historical context does real work in unpacking the meaning of a text. A favorite example is one drawn from the work of Ronald Dworkin.[207] The example starts with a line from Shakespeare's *Hamlet*, where Hamlet "said to his sometime friends, 'I know a hawk from a handsaw.'"[208] The passage raises the question whether Hamlet intended the term "hawk" to denote a bird or a renaissance tool that goes by the same name.[209] In order to avoid an "extremely silly" reading of Hamlet's statement, Dworkin recommends resolving the question by turning to what the author of the text intended to convey at the time of its drafting—a reading in historical context—and "[i]f we apply that standard to Hamlet, it's plain that we must read his claim as referring not a bird, ... but to a renaissance tool."[210] In this way, historical

[206] *See* Samuel Issacharoff & Trevor Morrison, *Constitution by Convention*, 108 CALIF. L. REV. 1913 (2020); Jack M. Balkin, *Lawyers and Historians Argue About the Constitution*, 35 CONST. COMMENT. 345 (2020); Jack M. Balkin, *Arguing About the Constitution: The Topics in Constitutional Interpretation*, 33 CONST. COMMENT. 145 (2018); Jack M. Balkin, *The New Originalism and the Uses of History*, 82 FORDHAM L. REV. 641, 645–46 (2013); Trevor W. Morrison, *Presidential Power, Historical Practice, and Legal Constraint*, 113 COLUM. L. REV. 1097 (2013); Curtis A. Bradley & Trevor W. Morrison, *Historical Gloss and the Separation of Powers*, 126 HARV. L. REV. 411 (2012); J.M. Balkin & Sanford Levinson, *Commentary, The Canons of Constitutional Law*, 111 HARV. L REV. 963, 994 (1998); Mark Tushnet, *Interdisciplinary Legal Scholarship: The Case of History-in-Law*, 71 CHI.-KENT L. REV. 909 (1996); Cass R. Sunstein, *The Idea of a Useable Past*, 95 COLUM. L. REV. 601, 604 (1995); PHILIP BOBBITT, CONSTITUTIONAL INTERPRETATION (1991); Robert W. Gordon, *Critical Legal Histories*, 36 STAN. L. REV. 57 (1984); Robert W. Gordon, *Historicism in Legal Scholarship*, 90 YALE L.J. 1017, 1055 (1981).

[207] Ronald Dworkin, *The Arduous Virtue of Fidelity: Originalism, Scalia, Tribe, and Nerve*, 65 FORDHAM L. REV. 1249, 1251–52 (1997).

[208] *Id.* at 1251 (quoting WILLIAM SHAKESPEARE, HAMLET act 2, sc. 2).

[209] *Id.* at 1251.

[210] *Id.* at 1252.

argument lends clarity to textual meaning for a term that has shifted over time beyond the horizon of the linguistic community of its birth.

History also offers a powerful tool in revealing power relationships that are often taken for granted. Ideologies codify unequal distributions of power and tend to justify them by making the taken-for-granted world, including hierarchies of power, seem inherent in nature. Historical argument offers "a potent means of denaturalization, a way of uncovering the social that is concealed in the natural"[211] and a means "for breaking with received views that strike the uncritical observer as self-evident, commonsensical, and only natural."[212] Both Bourdieu and Foucault relied on history as a means of interrogating the taken-for-granted nature of ideology and of exposing the historically contingent nature of the world as it is. Bourdieu recommended an "epistemological break" with the taken-for-granted worldview and offered social history as a means to accomplish such a break.[213] Foucault offered the methodology of "genealogy" or "a form of history which can account for the constitution of knowledges, discourses, domains of objects...."[214] Beyond providing context to the texts of treaties and statutes at issue, historical argument in *McGirt* was conjured to challenge the dominant ideology that erased the existence of Native people and the governance of Native nations.[215]

A more full-throated recognition of the social dynamics of power and the role of historical argument in challenging these dynamics could allow future advocates for Indian Country to better leverage history toward future reforms. No doubt the historical argument in *McGirt* helped a great deal in unsettling erasure and in presenting evidence of how Native nations have governed in the past. Histories of majority-minority governance unsettle prevailing presumptions, held even by liberal theorists, that subordinated communities never wield power. These presumptions inadvertently naturalize those communities' powerlessness. Critical legal theorists and progressive movements

[211] Philip S. Gorski, *Maps, Mechanisms, and Methods, in* BOURDIEU AND HISTORICAL ANALYSIS 353 (Philip S. Gorski, ed., 2012).

[212] David L. Swartz, *Metaprinciples for Sociological Research in a Bourdieusian Perspective, in* BOURDIEU AND HISTORICAL ANALYSIS 22 (Philip S. Gorski, ed., 2012).

[213] PIERRE BOURDIEU & LOÏC J.D. WACQUANT, AN INVITATION TO REFLEXIVE SOCIOLOGY 224 (1992).

[214] MICHEL FOUCAULT, POWER/KNOWLEDGE: SELECTED INTERVIEW AND OTHER WRITINGS, 1972–1977, at 117 (Colin Gordon ed., Colin Gordon et al. trans., 1980).

[215] *See* Part II.A. *supra.*

look to simple versions of United States history that erase the empowerment and political agency of racialized minorities.[216] Based on these histories of ongoing subjection at the hand of the state, these theorists often assume that law as a tool of the state is inherently unjust.[217] But more recent, more inclusive social histories have begun to reveal the long-standing political agency exercised by marginalized communities. These histories teach instead the importance of power, sovereignty, and jurisdiction in opposing subordination and white supremacy. These recent, inclusive social histories also make legible the centrality of cases like *McGirt*—where Native nations retained power to govern—to envisioning social and racial justice beyond Indian Country. Embracing these histories and the plural functions of historical argument at work in advocating for legal reform could offer advocates not only a means to challenge dominant ideologies but to reveal the benefits of majority-minority governance and its contributions to a more just society.

A deeper dive into the history of Tulsa offers one such example of a more inclusive social history and one that illustrates the strengths of majority-minority governance. Although less widely known, the city and county of Tulsa, or Tallasi in the Muscogee (Creek) language when governed by Native nations as part of the Indian Territory, housed at the turn of the twentieth century two of the wealthiest communities of color in the country—the Osage Nation and the Greenwood District, colloquially known as "Black Wall Street." Some historians have speculated that the more racially egalitarian and socially democratic governance instituted by the Native nations in the Indian Territory may have contributed to the success of these communities.[218] Others have documented the ways that communities of color collaborated within these relatively egalitarian societies to unsettle some of the historical wrongs caused by United States' embrace

---

[216] *See, e.g.*, Robert Williams, *Taking Rights Aggressively: The Perils and Promise of Critical Legal Theory for Peoples of Color*, 5 Law & Soc. Inquiry 103, 118, 121 (1987) (describing Critical Legal Studies as largely derivative of "European critical social theory" and identifying its critique of legal discourse by communities of color as unmoored from the historical contexts where communities of color wielded these discourses to gain power and "ideological high ground" in the post-World War II era).

[217] *Id.*

[218] *See* Brian Hardinzki, *Why Indian Territory's All-Black Towns Prospered While Most of Oklahoma Territory's Faded Away*, KGOU (Aug. 3, 2015, 12:17 AM), https://www.kgou.org /post/why-indian-territorys-all-black-towns-prospered-while-most-oklahoma-territorys-faded -away.

of the colonization of indigenous peoples and the enslavement of Africans. These arguments raise important questions about the distribution of power and the importance of who governs in addressing questions of a just society.[219] This history could also possibly be our future—that is, that limitations enacted over the years on tribal sovereignty, although entrenched, are not unmalleable. Many of these limitations could be undone by simple statute.[220]

Recent work by David Chang and others documents how Native sovereignty over territory that became Oklahoma fostered the empowerment of racialized communities more generally and a more idealized egalitarian society—including both Black and Native communities that had settled into the Indian Territory in the late nineteenth century.[221] Here, Muscogee (Creek) sovereignty and majority-minority governance supported not just Native people, but also Black-majority towns and governments and eventually the wealthy Greenwood District that became known as "Black Wall Street."[222] The history of Native nations offers an example of how power movements have been able to establish alternative legal frameworks that ultimately led to a more egalitarian society. These alternative legal frameworks further inspired and supported a Black nationalist movement within the Indian Territory, a number of "Black Towns," and two of the most prosperous racialized communities during that period—"Black Wall Street" and the Osage Nation.

A broader historical retelling of the history of Native governance in and around Tulsa offers a stark rebuttal to the historical argument offered by the dissent in *McGirt* that presented Muscogee (Creek) governance as both racist and corrupt.[223] It also begins to reveal the promise of majority-minority governance in the realization of a more

[219] *See* QUINTARD TAYLOR, IN SEARCH OF THE RACIAL FRONTIER: AFRICAN AMERICANS IN THE AMERICAN WEST, 1528–1990, at 149–51 (1st ed. 1998); BARBARA KRAUTHAMER, BLACK SLAVES, INDIAN MASTERS: SLAVERY, EMANCIPATION, AND CITIZENSHIP IN THE NATIVE AMERICAN SOUTH (2013); MURRAY R. WICKETT, CONTESTED TERRITORY: WHITES, NATIVE AMERICANS AND AFRICAN AMERICANS IN OKLAHOMA, 1865–1907, at 33–34 (2000).

[220] *See, e.g.,* United States v. Lara, 541 U.S. 193 (2004) (upholding the statutory "fix" of the Supreme Court's *Duro* opinion that limited tribal criminal jurisdiction over non-member Indians (Duro v. Reina, 495 U.S. 676 (1990)).

[221] DAVID A. CHANG, THE COLOR OF LAND: RACE, NATION, AND THE POLITICS OF LAND-OWNERSHIP IN OKLAHOMA, 1832–1929, at 158–59 (2010); WICKETT, *supra* note 219, at 29–31.

[222] TAYLOR, *supra* note 219, at 149 (identifying Native Freedman as the earliest settlers in all-Black towns in the West).

[223] McGirt v. Oklahoma, 140 S. Ct. 2452, 2484 (2020) (Roberts, J., dissenting).

just society. Not only did the Muscogee (Creek) Nation empower their own citizens during this period, but their governments also supported other racialized and subordinated communities. Following the Civil War, the Indian Territory had garnered a reputation of being more egalitarian than other portions of North America and it began to draw a number of Black freedmen as recent émigrés from the South.[224] Racialization is such a powerful force that it would be a mistake to say that race did not operate within the Indian Territory. But the role of law in the construction of race did mean that race operated differently in Indian Country than within other jurisdictions where Native nations did not govern. The line between Black and Native—drawn forcefully in other contexts in order to construct and retrench the sharp boundary lines of the slave codes— had been blurred. Years of intermarriage, as well as the integration of Black people formerly enslaved by the Five Civilized Tribes, meant that the Muscogee (Creek) Nation included citizens of Native nations who presented as Black.[225] Jim Crow laws did not take hold of the Indian Territory after the Civil War as it did in the South, and so these individuals were not subject initially to as unequal forms of citizenship and as extreme forms of subordination as they faced elsewhere.[226] Within the Muscogee (Creek) Nation, citizens were extended property rights, the franchise, admission to public schools, and access to capital on more equal footing to others within the Territory.[227]

Often working in solidarity with Native freedmen, who had gained individual ownership in acres of land as the United States allotted

---

[224] CHANG, *supra* note 221, at 55.

[225] *See* KRAUTHAMER, *supra* note 219, at 149; TAYLOR, *supra* note 219, at 150; CHANG, *supra* note 221, at 67–69 (describing the often contentious, but steady rise of an "interracial nationhood" among the Muscogee (Creeks) in the years leading up to allotment).

[226] *See* Melissa N. Stuckey, *Boley, Indian Territory: Exercising Freedom in the All-Black Town*, 102 J. AFR. AMER. HIST. 492, 492–516 (2017).

[227] *See* GARY ZELLAR, AFRICAN CREEKS: ESTELVSTE AND THE CREEK NATION 90–91 (2007); WICKETT, *supra* note 219, at 13 ("When the 'surplus' Indian lands were opened to white settlement in 1889, the Five Civilized Tribes with the exception of the Chickasaw, had adopted their freedmen and granted them all the rights of citizenship. This profoundly influenced the course of race relations in the territories, for it meant that most ex-slaves of the Five Civilized Tribes possessed the vote, held a share in tribal lands to be divided according to the dictates of the Curtis Act, enjoyed access to the tribal educational system, and were granted equality in the judicial system. Clearly by the 1890s, then, territorial freedmen enjoyed far more privileges than blacks in the United States proper, either the South or the North.").

their reservations in the late nineteenth century, newly immigrated freedmen from the South established dozens of "freedom colonies," also known as "all black" towns, across the Indian Territory.[228] In the years following the Civil War, these towns became the sites of flourishing Black governments, businesses, farms, and schools.[229] The Greenwood District was formally organized in 1906 on land within the Muskogee (Creek) Reservation.[230] That land would later become known as the city of Tulsa.

The declaration of Oklahoma statehood in 1907 abruptly ended both Native governance and the relatively egalitarian legal framework offered by the Territory.[231] The state's first constitution began to construct formal legal categories around the racialized constructs of "colored" and "white," and mandated subordination through the segregation of those racialized groups.[232] The constitution also went on to explicitly codify into law a binary racial paradigm between "colored," defined as those of African descent, and "white," defined as "all other persons."[233] It was this "legal creation of blackness and whiteness" that further "encouraged black coalescence" between Native and southern freedmen, as they were forced to live together in segregated communities.[234] But the categories also became an integral mechanism for codifying additional subordinating measures into law. For the first few years following statehood, Black communities continued to wield a form of sovereign political power—through the franchise and otherwise—at the local level, and even more so within majority-minority geographies like the "all-black" towns. This came to an end, however, in 1910 when Oklahoma voters passed a ballot that amended the state constitution to include a "grandfather clause" that required a literacy test for all voters with the exception of individuals entitled to vote under any government in 1866 and their lineal

---

[228] See Stuckey, *supra* note 226, at 493.

[229] *Id.*

[230] See Ayana Byrd, *What SCOTUS Decision on Oklahoma Means for the Muscogee Creek Nation*, COLORLINES (July 13, 2020, 2:00 PM), https://www.colorlines.com/articles/what -scotus-decision-oklahoma-means-muscogee-creek-nation.

[231] CHANG, *supra* note 221, at 160–61.

[232] *Id.*

[233] *Id.*

[234] *Id.* at 161.

descendants.[235] Coalescence within the Black community, rather than building power through shared action, facilitated subordination. Over the next decade, disenfranchisement eroded the political power Black communities had previously built through local government and electoral power.[236] Ultimately, it was violence at the hands of white communities—violence that was leveled at the Black community through acts of mass violence like the Tulsa Race Massacre[237] and through systematic violence targeting Native people and their property[238]—not the failure of majority-minority governance that destroyed the power of majority-minority communities from the former Indian Territory.

C. ON INDIAN COUNTRY

The implications of *McGirt* are still unfolding, but the power of the dominant ideology continues to threaten to shape law in the wake of the opinion: soon after the Court issued *McGirt*, state, federal, and tribal officials negotiated to clarify the decision's impact but, in an effort to move away from "unthinkable" solutions, those discussions came dangerously close to bargaining away *McGirt's* promise. But the negotiations have not yet tamped down the tantalizing possibility of a radical outcome. In closing, this section offers a few thoughts on ways that the promise of *McGirt* could be better realized.

It is widely presumed that *McGirt* could have much broader jurisdictional impact in Oklahoma than just reaffirming the borders of the Muscogee (Creek) reservation.[239] Although *McGirt* addressed the explicit question of whether Congress had diminished the reservation of the Muscogee (Creek) Nation, the decision could also have implications for determining the borders of reservations belonging to four other Native nations located within Oklahoma that are similarly situated to the Muscogee (Creek).[240] These nations include the Cherokee, Choctaw, Chickasaw, and Seminole Nations and

---

[235] *Id.* at 163–65.

[236] *Id.*; TAYLOR, *supra* note 219, at 151.

[237] CHANG, *supra* note 221, at 195–97.

[238] *See* Margo Jefferson, *Books of the Times: Digging Up a Tale of Terror Among the Osages*, N.Y. TIMES (Aug. 31, 1994, at C16).

[239] McGirt v. Oklahoma, 140 S. Ct. 2452, 2484 (2020) (Roberts, J., dissenting).

[240] *Id.*

are known collectively with the Muscogee (Creek) Nation as the "Five Civilized Tribes." Beyond the reaffirmation of reservation borders, *McGirt* left ambiguous the implications of the decision for civil jurisdiction and left open the question of how to navigate the complex web of tribal, federal, and state criminal jurisdiction within reservation borders. But the Court certainly queued up the question, unsettling it from its previously taken-for-granted position, and brought the relevant parties to the bargaining table.

Immediately after the Supreme Court issued its opinion in *McGirt*, the Oklahoma Office of the Attorney General and the Five Civilized Tribes issued a working draft of an "agreement-in-principle" that proposed federal legislation for Oklahoma's congressional delegation to craft and usher through Congress.[241] The proposed legislation reached beyond the question resolved in *McGirt* to address both criminal jurisdiction and civil jurisdiction.[242] The only noncontroversial provisions codified and extended the holding of *McGirt* to reaffirm the reservation borders for all of the Five Civilized Tribes and requested funding to support tribal administration of criminal and civil matters.[243] The balance of the agreement-in-principle proposed that Congress codify into law the limited view of tribal sovereignty expressed by the Supreme Court in recent years and it even added additional limits to those imposed by the Court.[244] Most notably, the proposed legislation offered the most conservative reading of the Court's *Oliphant* doctrine, including the seep of the doctrine into civil jurisdiction in *Montana*—codifying into statute the Court's preferred dominant ideology and eschewing *McGirt's* elevation of formal legal texts and historical argument.[245] It also proposed to extend state criminal jurisdiction where *McGirt* had previously excluded it.[246]

Despite securing a rare win for Indian Country in the Supreme Court, the Five Civilized Tribes nearly bargained away their victory in order to return as quickly as possible to the taken-for-granted

---

[241] *See* Murphy/McGirt Agreement-in-Principle (2020), https://turtletalk.files.wordpress.com/2020/07/doc-2020-07-15-murphy-final-agreement-in-principle.pdf.

[242] *Id.* at 1.

[243] *Id.* at 1–2.

[244] *Id.*

[245] *Id.*

[246] *Id.* at 1.

world envisioned by the dominant ideology. Luckily, the agreement-in-principle was so widely panned by Native citizens and legal scholars that it never made it to the desks of the Oklahoma congressional delegation.[247] More recently, tribal representatives, including the Cherokee Nation attorney general and senior counsel for the Chickasaw Nation, have proposed instead that Congress create a system by which the Five Civilized Tribes and the state of Oklahoma can negotiate and form compacts with respect to criminal jurisdiction.[248] As proposed, such a system would resemble the compacting framework created by Congress under the Indian Gaming Regulatory Act in the wake of the Supreme Court's similarly sweeping decision in *Cabazon*—a case that held that there was no state jurisdiction over Native nations' gaming businesses.[249] Rather than codify a brief negotiation into a national statute, the proposed compacting framework would allow for ongoing negotiations between the Five Civilized Tribes and the state of Oklahoma—including allowing terms to be rewritten over time as circumstances change for each government. The governor's Special Counsel for Native American Affairs and the Attorney General for Oklahoma agreed with the compacting proposal but asked that it allow for compacting beyond the issue of criminal jurisdiction into questions over civil matters—most notably "taxation, regulatory affairs and zoning."[250] As of the date of this article, negotiations continue. But the issue stays at the forefront of Oklahoma politics. In January 2021, the governor for the state of Oklahoma,

---

[247] *See, e.g.*, Matthew L.M. Fletcher, *Commentary on the Oklahoma-Tribal "Agreement-in-Principle,"* Turtle Talk (July 19, 2020), https://turtletalk.blog/2020/07/19/commentary-on-the-oklahoma-tribal-agreement-in-principle/; Letter Re: Oklahoma's Agreement-in-Principle and Future Federal Legislation (July 21, 2020), https://aipi.asu.edu/sites/default/files/final_signed_letter_sent_to_tribal_leadership_-_final.pdf (petitioning Choctaw Nation of Oklahoma on behalf of a number of its citizens to ask their representative to "reconsider joining Oklahoma's Agreement-In-Principle"); Ray Carter, *Attorney General's Tribal Agreement Falling Apart?*, OCPA (July 17, 2020), https://www.ocpathink.org/post/mcgirt-chaos-continues-to-grow (reporting that two of the five Native nations had withdrawn support for the agreement-in-principle shortly after its release).

[248] Barbara Hoberock, *Tribes Want Congress to Allow Criminal Justice Compacts with Oklahoma in Wake of Landmark* McGirt *ruling*, Tulsa World (Jan. 15, 2021), https://tulsaworld.com/news/state-and-regional/govt-and-politics/tribes-want-congress-to-allow-criminal-justice-compacts-with-oklahoma-in-wake-of-landmark-mcgirt/article_fa214e92-56a1-11eb-ba66-d3ff7e9e662c.html.

[249] California v. Cabazon Band of Mission Indians, 480 U.S. 202 (1987). Compacting frameworks are also part of the Indian Child Welfare Act. Indian Child Welfare Act of 1978, 25 U.S.C. § 1919.

[250] Hoberock, *supra* note 248.

Kevin Stitt, called on the Five Civilized Tribes, including the Muscogee (Creek), to begin negotiations over the decision's implications[251] and he concluded his "State of the State" speech with a reference to *McGirt*, calling it "the most pressing issue for the state's future."[252]

It is possible that the reaction of the state of Oklahoma and its leadership could be mere rhetoric, designed for political theater. But it is also likely that the Supreme Court's willingness to embrace unthinkable outcomes, as demonstrated in *McGirt*, will illuminate other areas of the law that were presumed to be settled by dominant ideology alone. If the Court would recognize large portions of the city of Tulsa and nearly 2 million residents of Oklahoma as residing within an Indian reservation, what else could possibly become law? Shifts in the dominant ideology are often met with an initial concern that all absurdities have now become equally possible and a "parade of horribles" will soon follow.[253] It can be tempting when responding to breaches of this kind to offer the reaffirmation of the dominant ideology, perhaps even its most extreme version, in the hope that such a reaffirmation might preserve the incremental gains that caused the breach in the first instance. That temptation explains why the Tribes offered to give so much ground in their first round of negotiations.

A more thorough understanding of how dominant ideologies operate could provide some guidance on alternative approaches to the event of a breach or epoché moving forward. Dominant public discourse will often retrench status quo inequities in power. Native scholars have observed similar dynamics in the erasure of Native people from the dominant ideology of the United States. Rather than focusing concerns on resolving the destabilization of the dominant ideology, the history of Native advocacy and its successes teaches that advocates should instead focus on securing gains in formal legal texts and avoiding codifying into law those losses driven by dominant

---

[251] *See* Kaylee Douglas, *Gov. Stitt Calls for Tribes to Enter Formal Negotiations with State Following* McGirt *Ruling*, Okla's News 4 (Jan. 22, 2021, 11:47 AM), https://kfor.com/news/local/gov-stitt-calls-for-tribes-to-enter-formal-negotiations-with-state-following-mcgirt-ruling/.

[252] *See* Dillon Richards, *Tribal Leader Reacts to Stitt Calling* McGirt *Ruling the Most Important Issue for Oklahoma's Future*, KOCO News 5 (Feb. 2, 2021, 6:33 PM), https://www.koco.com/article/tribal-leader-reacts-to-stitt-calling-mcgirt-ruling-the-most-important-issue-for-oklahomas-future/35397898.

[253] *See, e.g.*, Ruth E. Sternglantz, *Raining on the Parade of Horribles: Of Slippery Slopes, Faux Slopes, and Justice Scalia's Dissent in* Lawrence v. Texas, 153 U. Pa. L. Rev. 1097, 1097–1120 (2005).

ideology in the past. A compacting framework could offer a law-making forum, even more so than litigation, away from public discourse infused with the dominant ideology—a forum that allows Native advocates successfully to raise arguments from formal legal texts and historical argument. At the very least, this approach would caution against the position taken by the Five Civilized Tribes in the agreement-in-principle—a position that would have ratified the Court's past efforts to codify dominant ideology into law. At best, this approach could guide Native advocates to embrace the unthinkable nature of federal Indian law and understand that its inconceivability is part of the struggle for power, rather than a reflection of some inherent truth. Instead of catering to or shoring up the dominant ideology against further transgression, Native advocates should focus on ways to shift power to their communities, build infrastructure around that power, and aim to change the world as it is. That way, the next time federal Indian law breaches the public's false consciousness, the world that is exposed as natural includes the fully realized promise of Native nations and of majority-minority governance.

RICHARD J. LAZARUS

ADVOCACY HISTORY
IN THE SUPREME COURT

The conventional wisdom within the legal academy concerning the meaning of a Supreme Court opinion seems both noncontroversial and unassailable. As evidenced by how law faculty routinely both write and teach, an opinion's meaning naturally depends exclusively on the written words of the official "opinion of the Court" published by the Court on the day the opinion is announced. Although law professors, prompted by conflict within the Court itself on the question,[1] have debated now for decades whether it is legitimate to consider legislative history in determining the meaning of otherwise ambiguous statutory text,[2]

Richard J. Lazarus is the Howard and Katherine Aibel Professor of Law, Harvard Law School.

AUTHOR'S NOTE: I am grateful to Gavan Duffy Gideon, Harvard Law School Class of 2020, and Samantha Neal, Class of 2022, for outstanding research in support of this article, and to Michael Dreeben, Jeff Fisher, Irv Gornstein, Richard Re, Charles Rothfeld, Cass Sunstein, Zack Tripp, Mark Tushnet, and Adrian Vermeule, for their insightful and appropriately skeptical comments on earlier drafts, which improved the article considerably. David Strauss provided a masterful edit of the final draft.

[1] See ANTONIN SCALIA, A MATTER OF INTERPRETATION: FEDERAL COURTS AND THE LAW 29–37 (Amy Gutmann ed., 1997); Stephen Breyer, *On the Use of Legislative History in Interpreting Statutes*, 65 S. CAL. L. REV. 845 (1992).

[2] *See, e.g.*, Victoria Nourse, *A Decision Theory of Statutory Interpretation: Legislative History by the Rules*, 122 YALE L.J. 70 (2012); James Brudney, *Confirmatory Legislative History*, 76 BROOK. L. REV. 901 (2011); John F. Manning, *Textualism and Legislative Intent*, 91 VA. L. REV. 419 (2005); Jane S. Schacter, *The Confounding Common Law Originalism in Recent Supreme Court Statutory Interpretation: Implications for the Legislative History Debate and Beyond*, 51 STAN.

The Supreme Court Review, 2021.

there has been a sharply contrasting absence of any legal scholarship examining whether there is a comparable official history to be consulted in resolving ambiguities in the text of the Court's opinions. It has been common ground that there is no "judicial history" analogous to legislative history.[3]

Hiding in plain sight from academic notice is the actual practice of Supreme Court advocates and, even more important, Supreme Court Justices. That practice has long made clear that such an official history does in fact exist and is regularly consulted by both advocates and Justices. It is not found in what many might assume to be the closest analogue: the personal papers of the Justices themselves. Those papers are not part of the official record of the case. Unlike presidential papers,[4] the papers of each Justice—bench memoranda, interchambers

---

L. Rev. 1 (1998); John Manning, *Textualism as a Nondelegation Doctrine*, 97 Colum. L. Rev. 673, 684–89, 710–25 (1997); William N. Eskridge, Jr., *Legislative History Values*, 66 Chi.-Kent L. Rev. 365 (1990); Frank H. Easterbrook, *What Does Legislative History Tell Us?*, 66 Chi.-Kent L. Rev. 441 (1990).

[3] I have found only two prior law review articles that incidentally touch on the role of underlying advocacy in understanding judicial precedent in the course of addressing distinct, but related, issues. But neither considers the issue head-on or the full extent to which the Justices rely on such advocacy to interpret their own prior handiwork. In *Judicial History*, published by the *Yale Law Journal* in 1999, Professor Adrian Vermeule, while addressing a different topic, refers briefly without analysis to how the "Court occasionally interprets its own opinions, and the rules it adopts, by reference to the briefs (including certiorari petitions), questions and answers during oral argument . . . and other materials generated in the course of judicial business before the issuance of an authoritative final text." Adrian Vermeule, *Judicial History*, 108 Yale L.J. 1311, 1328 (1999). Vermeule also describes one case, *Cantor v. Detroit Edison Co.*, 428 U.S. 579 (1976), in which a plurality opinion of the Court considered the advocacy underlying a prior ruling in trying to discern the meaning of that prior precedent for the *Cantor* case. Vermeule, *supra*, at 1330. Vermeule, however, never makes clear whether he believes that reliance on advocacy as an interpretive tool is legitimate and leaves the impression that he thinks it may not be, by equating the validity of its use with the use of internal judicial history, which he concludes should be out of bounds. *Id.* at 1354. He also quotes at length from Justice Stewart's dissent in *Cantor*, which took issue with the plurality's reliance on the briefs filed by the parties in the earlier case, arguing that "except in rare circumstances," advocacy "should play no role in interpreting [the Court's] written opinions." *Id.* at 1330–31 (quoting *Cantor*, 428 U.S. at 617–18 (Stewart, J., dissenting)). The other law review article is even more cursory in its treatment of the advocacy history issue than Vermeule's limited discussion. In *The Structure of Judicial Opinions*, a 2001 article published in the *Minnesota Law Review*, Professor John Leubsdorf addresses the issue of "[h]ow far should one go in extending the potential bounds of an opinion" and notes, without elaboration, that courts have sometimes "been known to rely on" prior arguments "to show what issues were before the court, and were therefore embraced by its opinion." John Leubsdorf, *The Structure of Judicial Opinions*, 86 Minn. L. Rev. 447, 492 (2001). What the Leubsdorf article more helpfully adds is a valuable reminder that the Reporter of Decisions used to include, along with the opinion of the Court in the published U.S. Reports, a summary of the arguments made by counsel. *Id.* Based on my survey of the Court's opinions, the Court appears to have discontinued that practice in October Term 1942, and the Court's opinion in *Alabama v. King & Boozer*, 314 U.S. 1 (1941), was one of the last times the Reporter included a summary of counsel's arguments.

[4] Presidential Records Act, 44 U.S.C. §§ 2201–2207 (2012).

memoranda, draft opinions, and voting records—are the exclusive property of the Justice and not generally publicly available.[5]

The comparable contemporaneous history is found instead in the advocacy underlying the Court's ruling—the written briefs and oral argument—all of which is part of the official record of the case that is made publicly available for all to see. In this respect, advocacy history of a case is singularly distinct from any of a host of outside, largely unknowable contextual factors external to the public record in a case that one might speculate influenced the votes of individual Justices and, accordingly, the Court's ruling itself.

To be sure, the Court's reliance on advocacy history has not always been without controversy. In 1976, several Justices sharply criticized Justice Stevens's reliance on such history in his plurality opinion in *Cantor v. Detroit Edison Co.*[6] In *Cantor*, Justice Stevens reviewed in great detail the precise arguments made by the prevailing party in determining the reach and meaning of a prior Court precedent.[7] Justice Stewart, joined by Justice Powell and then-Justice Rehnquist, argued in dissent that Justice Stevens's reliance on advocacy history as a basis for interpreting past rulings "would permit the 'plain meaning' of our decisions to be qualified or even overridden by their 'legislative history,'—*i.e.*, briefs submitted by the contending parties."[8] The dissenters contrasted that practice with reliance on "[t]he legislative history of congressional enactments," which they agreed was legitimate because, unlike advocacy history, that legislative "history emanates from the same source as the legislation itself and is thus directly probative of the intent of the draftsmen."[9]

---

[5] The practice of the Justices in releasing their papers is highly idiosyncratic. Some, like Justice White, ordered them mostly destroyed, while others allow for their release a certain number of years after their retirement or death, though current practice is for that period of time to be fifty years or more. *See* Kathryn A. Watts, *Judges and Their Papers*, 88 N.Y.U. L. REV. 1665, 1669–72 (2013) (describing ad hoc practices of the Justices). In his article *Judicial History*, Vermeule considers the extent to which draft opinions and internal memoranda circulated between the chambers of the Justices should be considered "as evidence of judicial intention or as interpretive context." Vermeule, *supra* note 3, at 1311. Vermeule ultimately concludes that the Supreme Court's exclusion of such judicial history is "justifiable on structural and institutional grounds." *Id.* at 1354.

[6] 428 U.S. 579 (1976).

[7] *Id.* at 587–91 & nn.18–20 (discussing Parker v. Brown, 317 U.S. 341 (1943)).

[8] *Id.* at 618 (Stewart, J., dissenting).

[9] *Id.*

The views of the *Cantor* dissenters on the use of advocacy history, however, have not prevailed, even while the use of legislative history has, by contrast, come under increasing attack. The Justices in their decision making regularly look to the advocacy underlying previously decided cases to glean precisely what the Court did and did not rule in a discrete set of circumstances. The best Supreme Court advocates all know this.[10] They scour the briefs and oral argument transcripts in prior cases in search of an argument to bolster their client's legal position.[11] As an advocate, before he became a judge, no less than Chief Justice John Roberts himself did so—a practice he has now continued on the bench.[12]

---

[10] *See, e.g.*, Email from Jeffrey Fisher, Fac. Dir., Stanford L. Sch. Supreme Ct. Clinic, to author (Jan. 19, 2020) ("[O]ne of the things we often preach in our clinic is the importance of reviewing the briefs underlying prior cases."); Email from Zachary Tripp, Assistant to the U.S. Solicitor Gen., to author (May 6, 2020) ("When I have a case that focuses on the meaning of a prior [Supreme Court] case, I virtually always look at the underlying briefs to try to understand what exactly the question was, how it was teed up, what the arguments were, etc.").

[11] *See, e.g.*, Transcript of Oral Argument at 15, Tull v. United States, 481 U.S. 412 (1987) (No. 85-1259) ("I certainly would ask that the Court consider the petitioner's brief in *Curtis v. Loether* against the government's brief in this case. They precisely mirror on all of the points that the government [makes here], and as we point out this Court unanimously rejected those positions.") (oral argument of Richard N. Nageotte); Transcript of Oral Argument at 26–27, Bray v. Alexandria Women's Health Clinic, 506 U.S. 263 (1992) (No. 90-985) ("As the *Griffin* case came to this Court, there was very little evidence of interstate travel. In fact, the Solicitor General's brief in that case . . . noted in footnote 6 that they believed there had been no allegations of interference with interstate travel.") (oral argument of Deborah A. Ellis); Transcript of Oral Argument at 18–19, United States v. Mead Corp., 533 U.S. 218 (2001) (No. 99-1434) ("Now, the tax counsel amici says no, that case was really about a regulation, not about a ruling. . . . When Justice Marshall was Solicitor General, he filed the Government's brief in the *Correll* case. His successor, Solicitor General Griswold, filed a reply brief. Neither of those briefs mention any regulation.") (oral argument of Kent L. Jones); Transcript of Oral Argument at 32, SEC v. Edwards, 540 U.S. 389 (2004) (No. 02-1196) ("[I]f you go back to the case the SEC has pointed to a number of times, the *Universal Service* case from 1939 in the Seventh Circuit, . . . its position in that case was stated in its brief in that case, and when you look at its brief in that case, it recognizes that it is not dealing with a fixed return. . . .") (oral argument of Michael K. Wolensky); Transcript of Oral Argument at 13, United States v. Georgia, 546 U.S. 151 (2006) (Nos. 04-1203, 04-1236) ("[I]f you go back to the Government's brief in [*Pennsylvania Department of Corrections. v. Yeskey*], when we were dealing with constitutional challenges to the application of Title II to prisons, the Government focused all its energy on defending it as valid Section 5 legislation. . . .") (oral argument of Solicitor General Paul D. Clement); Transcript of Oral Argument at 10, Woodford v. Ngo, 548 U.S. 81 (2006) (No. 05-416) ("Justice Ginsburg: . . . It's not clear, just from the—reading that opinion. [Jennifer G.] Perkell: Your Honor, I would respectfully dispute that, in that our reading of the opinion, as well as the Government's brief in that case, seemed to propose no unusual rule of exhaustion."); Transcript of Oral Argument at 15–16, James v. United States, 550 U.S. 192 (2007) (No. 05-9264) ("I think it can be read either way, although I think even the Government's brief in—or the Respondent's brief in *Taylor* talks about extortion and burglary being crimes that can be committed with no risk of physical injury to another person. . . .") (oral argument of Craig L. Crawford).

[12] *See* Transcript of Oral Argument at 37, United States v. Halper, 490 U.S. 435 (1989) (No. 87-1383) ("[I]t may be distinguishable. If you look back at the government's brief in the *Hess* case, for example, they had no doubt that—there that the penalty was, in essence,

The Supreme Court's October Term 2019 shows how both Supreme Court advocates and the Justices themselves use the advocacy underlying the Court's prior rulings. Advocacy history came up several times, including in two of the Term's highest-profile cases, which otherwise had little in common: *June Medical Services v. Russo*,[13] which concerned abortion rights, and *Our Lady of Guadalupe School v. Morrissey-Berru*,[14] which addressed the application of the First Amendment Religion Clauses to claims of unlawful employment discrimination by a religious elementary school. But even as the Court's use of advocacy history to determine what the Court previously ruled has largely been accepted, the Justices have disagreed about using advocacy history in other contexts. In particular, analogizing to the reasons why the Court has long declined to give stare decisis effect to its rulings by summary disposition, the Court has in recent years displayed an increased willingness to consider poor or otherwise inadequate adversary presentation in a past case as a justification for more readily second guessing that precedent. Some of the Justices question the legitimacy of that reasoning, which has taken on additional contemporary significance given the Court's increasingly intense internal debates concerning the role of stare decisis.[15]

To date, however, legal scholarship has not considered the role of advocacy history in Supreme Court advocacy and decision making in any of its iterations. This article seeks to bring out of the shadows the role advocacy history plays at the Court. In Part I, which is descriptive and historical, I examine the actual practice of the Justices in deciding cases and drafting opinions of the Court—how, in assessing the meaning of a prior opinion, the Justices consider whether a particular legal argument was made and, if so, whether it was accepted or rejected. Then I consider the more controversial proposition that the relative weakness of a party's argument in a particular case supplies a basis for giving that precedent less weight in assessing its entitlement

---

criminal.") (oral argument of John G. Roberts, Jr.); *see also infra* text accompanying notes 27 (discussing Chief Justice Roberts's opinion for the Court in *Parents Involved in Community Schools v. Seattle School District No. 1*, 551 U.S. 701 (2007)).

[13] 140 S. Ct. 2103 (2020).

[14] 140 S. Ct. 2049 (2020).

[15] *See, e.g.*, Ramos v. Louisiana, 140 S. Ct. 1390, 1404–07 (2020); *id.* at 1402–05 (opinion of Gorsuch, J.); *id.* at 1408–10 (Sotomayor, J., concurring); *id.* at 1410–16 (Kavanaugh, J., concurring); *id.* at 1421–22 (Thomas, J., concurring in the judgment); *id.* at 1432–40 (Alito, J., dissenting).

to stare decisis. In Part II, I focus on several of the highest-profile cases of October Term 2019, in which Supreme Court advocates, and sometimes the Justices themselves, relied on advocacy history.

In Part III, I discuss law teaching and legal scholarship; I offer an illustrative example of how one prominent Supreme Court ruling might be taught and written about differently by taking into account its advocacy history. The case is *Massachusetts v. EPA*,[16] decided in 2007, which is taught across the law school curriculum and is the subject of many law review articles. Perplexing, or even possibly indefensible, rulings by the Court can sometimes be more easily understood by looking at the case's advocacy history.

I. The Court's Reliance on Advocacy History

The best evidence of the actual relevance of the advocacy underlying a Supreme Court opinion in understanding the opinion's meaning is supplied by the Justices themselves. Although the Justices do not review the advocacy history of the Court's precedent in all or even most of their cases, they do so with sufficient regularity to make clear when, why, and how they believe such advocacy bears on a full and accurate understanding of their prior rulings. It might be tempting to dismiss the Justices' use of advocacy history as rhetorical window-dressing that is not truly outcome-determinative, and no doubt there are instances when such a characterization is accurate. But identifying when a reason given in an opinion is a mere make-weight for a predetermined outcome is a hazardous business: What might be a disingenuous make-weight for one Justice, including the opinion writer, might not be for another Justice whose vote was necessary to establish the majority.

Even more important, Supreme Court rulings are not just about the final judgment: a reversal or affirmance of a lower-court judgment. What makes the Court's opinion so important are the reasons the Justices give in support of their conclusions. Lower courts and the Justices in future cases take those reasons seriously, and when those reasons reflect reliance on advocacy history, advocacy history matters—no matter what an individual Justice's motivation might have been for invoking it.

---

[16] 549 U.S. 497 (2007).

The most common, and least controversial, use of advocacy history is when the Court considers whether certain arguments were made, or not made, and whether those arguments were made by the prevailing or losing party. All the Justices agree that such an inquiry is a fair basis for determining what the Court did and did not decide in a prior case, even when no ambiguity may otherwise be apparent from the text of the earlier opinion. Of course, that threshold agreement does not mean that they necessarily agree in specific cases whether certain arguments were or were not made.

There is, by contrast, far more contention within the Court about whether poor advocacy underlying a prior ruling is grounds for according that ruling less precedential weight and, accordingly, less stare decisis effect. Almost fifty years ago, Justice Lewis Powell first broached the idea that examining advocacy history was fair game in reassessing a case's precedential weight and susceptibility to being overturned. And the direction of the Court's decisions has since been in Justice Powell's favor, with poor underlying advocacy increasingly serving as a proxy for poor legal judicial reasoning—a factor the Justices regularly consider in assessing whether a past precedent warrants overruling.

A. ADVOCACY HISTORY AND THE MEANING OF PRECEDENTS

There are three typical situations in which the Justices look to the underlying advocacy to assess the meaning of their prior rulings. Significantly, the Justices do not just consider whether the earlier opinion itself refers to that advocacy; they consider the underlying advocacy so relevant to discerning the meaning of a precedent that they will examine its content even when the prior opinion itself makes no reference to that advocacy. In that way, they are willing to make certain assumptions about the relationship between the Court's opinion and the advocacy that preceded it.

First, there are cases in which the Justices consider the arguments affirmatively made by the *prevailing* party in a prior case in determining both the meaning and the current precedential weight of the Court's ruling in that case. In these cases, the Court applies the seemingly commonsense proposition that what it held in a prior case coincided with what the prevailing parties were arguing and, to that end, reviews those arguments for evidence regarding what the Court previously held. In some instances, however, such evidence about the meaning of what the Court previously held can, ironically, become a poison pill capable of eroding that same precedent's current weight should the strength of that prior legal argument now be called into question by intervening circumstances.

The second category of cases consists of those in which the Court considers the arguments made by the *losing* rather than by the prevailing party. Here, the Court is willing to assume, even in the absence of any express mention in the opinion itself, that the Court rejected the arguments made by a nonprevailing party. For the Justices, the existence of the argument in the briefs or oral argument of the unsuccessful party supports reading the Court's opinion as implicitly rejecting the argument. Based on this rationale, the Justices have frequently looked to past briefings and oral arguments and, upon discovering that the same argument being made today was made in a prior case, relied on its prior rejection as a conclusive basis for rejecting the argument anew.

The third and final category is the logical corollary of the first two: cases in which a prior argument was not raised at all. Precisely because previous arguments made, whether accepted or rejected, are relevant in determining the meaning of the Court's prior decisions, the Justices have frequently reasoned that the opposite may also be true: If an argument was not made when a prior case was decided, then it was *not* implicitly rejected by the Court and therefore cannot be so reflexively dismissed by the Court in a future case.

Cases in which advocacy history plays a role cannot always be classified as falling neatly into only one of these three categories. And, of course, in all three categories, the Justices routinely disagree, as they do about most anything else.[17] But, with very few exceptions, the disagreements are less about the merits of undertaking the inquiry into past advocacy than they are about whether arguments were raised, accepted, or rejected in the prior rulings under consideration. While one Justice may argue that a legal argument was raised and implicitly accepted by the Court in a prior ruling, a second Justice may argue that the argument was not raised at all or, if raised, was implicitly rejected.

1. *Prevailing arguments.* The Justices frequently disagree about precisely what they ruled in a prior case and will sometimes review the

---

[17] Similar disagreements arise when judges and Justices look to legislative history to aid in the interpretation of statutory language. Even when there might be threshold agreement that such history can be relevant, there can be sharp disagreement whether Congress intended to accept or reject a meaning of the language advanced by the legislation's supporters in the accompanying legislative history.

briefs and oral arguments of the party that prevailed in that case for relevant evidence. That is what Justice Stevens was doing in the *Cantor* case, which drew the ire of three of his colleagues on the Court in dissent.

In *Cantor*, the Court was considering whether the Court, in ruling in *Parker v. Brown* that actions by a state did not violate the Sherman Act, had also immunized from Sherman Act antitrust review private action approved by a state.[18] Justice Stevens's plurality opinion for the Court answered that question by looking at great detail at the arguments made by the parties in *Parker*.[19] Justice Stevens even included an excerpt from the index to the supplemental brief filed by the Attorney General of California (who was, as it happens, Earl Warren), as well as lengthy excerpts from the amicus brief filed by the US Solicitor General.[20] Based on that review, the plurality concluded that the Court's prior ruling in *Parker* did not control the legal issue raised in *Cantor*.

Another example of the Court's use of a prevailing party's argument is *Cannon v. University of Chicago*.[21] In *Cannon*, the Court relied on prior briefing to conclude that the notion that Title VI provided a private right of action was "implicit in decisions of this Court,"[22] namely, *Lau v. Nichols*[23] and *Hills v. Gautreaux*.[24] The Court acknowledged that neither case actually "address[ed] the question of whether Title VI provides a cause of action."[25] According to the Court, however, because "the issue had been explicitly raised by the parties at one level of the litigation or another"—a claim it supported by citing party briefs in the cases—the cases were "consistent . . . with the widely accepted assumption that Title VI creates a private cause of action."[26]

A more recent, higher-profile, and far more controversial example of the Court's reliance on advocacy history is *Parents Involved in*

---

[18] 428 U.S. 579, 581 (1976).

[19] *Id.* at 587–90.

[20] *Id.* at 588 n.18.

[21] 441 U.S. 677 (1979).

[22] *Id.* at 702.

[23] 414 U.S. 563 (1974).

[24] 425 U.S. 284 (1976); *see Cannon*, 441 U.S. at 702 n.33.

[25] *Cannon*, 441 U.S. at 702 n.33.

[26] *Id.*

Community Schools v. Seattle School District No 1,[27] decided in 2007. In *Parents Involved,* the parties' disagreement centered on no less than the meaning of the Court's ruling in *Brown v. Board of Education,*[28] universally regarded as one of the Court's most important all-time decisions.[29] *Brown's* core holding that de jure segregation in public schools violated the Fourteenth Amendment was of course not in question, but what was sharply disputed was how that ruling applied to student reassignment plans voluntarily adopted by public school districts in Seattle, Washington, and Louisville, Kentucky, in order to promote racial integration within those school districts.

The Court held those plans were unconstitutional, with Chief Justice John Roberts writing the plurality opinion for four Justices, and Justice Anthony Kennedy providing the decisive fifth vote in a separate concurring opinion. In his plurality opinion, the Chief Justice's defense of his reading of *Brown* relied heavily on the briefs filed by Thurgood Marshall, lead counsel for the NAACP Legal Defense Fund, and the other members of his team, and the oral argument presented by Robert Carter of the Legal Defense Fund. The Chief argued in effect that what the Court had ruled in *Brown* could be understood by looking at the legal arguments made by the prevailing parties:

> The parties and their *amici* debate which side is more faithful to the heritage of *Brown,* but the position of the plaintiffs in *Brown* was spelled out in their brief and could not have been clearer: "[T]he Fourteenth Amendment prevents states from according differential treatment to American children on the basis of their color or race." What do the racial classifications at issue here do, if not accord differential treatment on the basis of race? As counsel who appeared before this Court for the plaintiffs in *Brown* put it: "We have one fundamental contention which we will seek to develop in the course of this argument, and that contention is that no State has any authority under the equal-protection clause of the Fourteenth Amendment to use race as a factor in affording educational opportunities among its citizens." There is no ambiguity in that statement.[30]

---

[27] 551 U.S. 701 (2007).

[28] 347 U.S. 483 (1954).

[29] *See, e.g.,* Ramos v. Louisiana, 140 S. Ct. 1390, 1412 (2020) (Kavanaugh, J., concurring) (describing *Brown* as "the single most important and greatest decision in this Court's history").

[30] 551 U.S. at 747 (citations omitted) (first quoting Brief for Appellants in Nos. 1, 2 and 4 and for Respondents in No. 10 on Reargument at 15, Brown v. Bd. of Educ., 347 U.S. 483 (1954) (Nos. 1, 2, 3 and 5); and then quoting Transcript of Oral Argument at 7, *Brown,* 347 U.S. 483 (No. 8)).

In a concurring opinion, Justice Clarence Thomas quoted even more extensively from the briefs and oral arguments in *Brown* to support his assertion that "my view was the rallying cry for the lawyers who litigated *Brown.*"[31]

Some commentators critical of the opinion disputed the Chief's and Justice Thomas's characterizations of the Legal Defense Fund's argument in *Brown.*[32] Two of the lawyers who worked with Marshall on *Brown* were harshly negative, with one referring to the Chief's view as "preposterous."[33] But, for my purposes, what is relevant is the Chief Justice's and Justice Thomas's assertion of the significance of Marshall's and the Legal Defense Fund's arguments to the Court's understanding of *Brown*, rather than whether the Chief's actual portrayal of their argument was more or less persuasive. The latter dispute does remain relevant to the question whether their reliance on advocacy history in *Parents Involved* is best understood as a clear instance of its invocation as mere window-dressing for legal conclusions the opinion authors were already determined to reach rather than a factor that actually influenced their decision to any degree.

Finally, in *Marvin M. Brandt Revocable Trust v. United States*,[34] decided in 2014, the prevailing party in an earlier case was back before the Court in a later case, resisting the import of what it had previously, successfully argued. At issue in *Marvin M. Brandt* was whether the government had, as it was arguing, retained a reversionary interest in land that it had previously conveyed to a railroad after the railroad's subsequent abandonment of the land. In concluding that the argument lacked merit, the Court reasoned that "[t]he government loses that argument today, in large part because it won when it argued the opposite before this Court more than 70 years ago, in the case of *Great Northern Railway Co. v. United States.*"[35] During oral argument, Justice Samuel Alito, a former attorney in the Solicitor General's Office, took

---

[31] *Parents Involved*, 551 U.S. at 772.

[32] Goodwin Liu, *"History Will Be Heard": An Appraisal of the Seattle/Louisville Decision*, 2 HARV. L. & POL'Y REV. 53, 62 n.57 (2007) ("[T]he meaning the plurality assign[ed] [to the brief] is clearly not what the *Brown* lawyers intended."); James E. Ryan, *The Supreme Court and Voluntary Integration*, 121 HARV. L. REV. 131, 152 (2008) (characterizing the Chief Justice's description of *Brown* as "radically incomplete").

[33] Adam Liptak, *The Same Words, But Differing Views*, N.Y. TIMES (June 29, 2007), https://www.nytimes.com/2007/06/29/us/29assess.html.

[34] 572 U.S. 93 (2014).

[35] *Id.* at 102 (citing Great Northern Ry. Co. v. United States, 315 U.S. 262 (1942)).

the government to task for failing to fully acknowledge the extent to which it was departing from its prior arguments that had prevailed: "I think the government gets the prize for understatement with its brief in this case" by merely acknowledging that "the government's brief" in the prior case "lends some support to petitioner's contrary argument."[36] Alito pointedly read out loud at the argument "the subject headings of the government's brief in *Great Northern*."[37]

2. *Losing arguments.* The Justices also often consider, in deciding on the meaning of a precedent, whether the Court already considered and rejected a similar argument in that earlier case. Of course, the prior opinion itself can make that explicit. But when it doesn't on its own, the Justices do not hesitate to review the underlying advocacy to better understand the Court's earlier ruling. Their assumption is that the Court implicitly rejected arguments advanced either by a losing party or by a party who prevailed, but on another ground.

An especially high-profile example is *District of Columbia v. Heller*,[38] in which both the parties and the Justices looked to the briefing and argument underlying a prior decision. At issue in *Heller* was whether the Second Amendment confers on individuals a right to possess a firearm wholly apart from any service in a militia. The Court ruled five to four in favor of such an individual right. Front and center in the dispute between the majority and dissenting Justices was the import of the Court's prior ruling in *United States v. Miller*.[39] All sides tried to argue that the Court's treatment of the federal government's argument in *Miller* provided support for their respective positions.

The majority opinion, written by Justice Antonin Scalia, contended that *Miller* did not contradict the *Heller* majority's view in favor of an individual right: *Miller* ruled "only that the Second Amendment does not protect those weapons not typically possessed by law-abiding citizens for lawful purposes, such as short-barreled shotguns."[40] By contrast, Justice Stevens's opinion for the dissenters advanced a very different reading of *Miller*: "The view of the Amendment we took in *Miller* [is] that it protects the right to keep and bear arms for certain

---

[36] Transcript of Oral Argument at 24, Marvin M. Brandt Revocable Trust v. United States, 134 S. Ct. 1257 (2014) (No. 12-1173).

[37] *Id.* at 24–25.

[38] 554 U.S. 570 (2008).

[39] 307 U.S. 174 (1939).

[40] *Heller*, 554 U.S. at 625.

military purposes, but that it does not curtail the Legislature's power
to regulate the nonmilitary use and ownerships of weapons. . . ."[41]

Both the majority and dissent relied heavily on the briefing and argument in *Miller* to support their positions, as did respondents' counsel
in *Heller*. For instance, in *Miller*, the Solicitor General had argued that
the Second Amendment did not confer rights on individuals to bear
arms but established only a collective right to members of a state militia.[42] Justice Scalia's opinion for the Court in *Heller* referred expressly
to the Solicitor General's argument in *Miller* in reasoning that the
Miller Court, by declining to engage with the argument, should best be
understood as having implicitly rejected the collectivist theory. The
Heller respondents had argued the same to the Court in their brief:

> Petitioners' collective-purpose interpretation is . . . at odds with this Court's
> only direct Second Amendment opinion in *Miller*. In examining whether
> Miller had a right to possess his sawed-off shotgun, this Court never asked
> whether Miller was part of any state-authorized military organization. . . .
> Indeed, the government advanced the collectivist theory as its first argu-
> ment in *Miller*, but the Court ignored it. The Court asked only whether the
> gun at issue was of a type *Miller* would be constitutionally privileged in
> possessing.[43]

The Solicitor General's brief in *Heller* acknowledged the significance
of the federal government's brief in *Miller* in understanding what the
Miller Court ruled.[44]

What remains striking, of course, about the *Heller* Court's reliance
on advocacy history to read *Miller* so narrowly is that it sharply
contrasts with what had been *Miller*'s settled meaning over decades.
Either all those petitioners who had previously sought to challenge
their possession of firearms convictions failed to raise the advocacy
history argument to resist *Miller*'s assumed sweep or the Court had a

---

[41] *Id.* at 637 (Stevens, J., dissenting).

[42] Brief for the United States at 4–5, *Miller*, 307 U.S. 174 (No. 696) ("[T]he right to keep
and bear arms has been generally restricted to the keeping and bearing of arms by the people
collectively for their common defense and security. Indeed, the very language of the Second
Amendment discloses that the right has reference only to the keeping and bearing of arms by
the people as members of the state militia.").

[43] Respondent's Brief at 40, *Heller*, 554 U.S. 570 (No. 07-290) (citation omitted).

[44] Brief for the United States as Amicus Curiae at 19 n.4, *Heller*, 554 U.S. 570 (No. 07-290)
("Although the Court's decision (following the government's own brief in *Miller*) supports a
mode of analysis that interprets the Second Amendment in light of the relationship between
the regulated firearms and 'the preservation or efficiency of a well regulated militia' . . . the
Court did not express any holding on whether or to what extent the Amendment applies only
to 'militia related' activities." (footnote omitted) (emphasis added)).

change of heart about *Miller* and merely used that history to support
its new view.

There are plenty of other instances, like *Heller*, when the Justices
have looked to underlying advocacy to determine precisely what
arguments they had already considered and rejected when it was not
otherwise clear on the face of the previous opinion itself that the
argument had been rejected. Here are a few additional, illustrative
examples.

In *Preston v. Ferrer*,[45] the Court examined the written briefs to show
that arguments in favor of overruling *Southland Corp. v. Keating*[46] re-
lied on by respondent had already been "considered and rejected" in
Allied-Bruce Terminix Cos. v. Dobson.[47] As support for that claim, the
Preston Court directly compared arguments of respondent in his brief
to the arguments in an *Allied-Bruce Cos.* amici brief.[48] For the *Preston*
Court, the Court's prior rejection of the same argument supported the
Court's rejecting it again.

Jones v. United States[49] offers an especially effective use of advocacy
history because it was the same party (the United States) in both the
current and past cases. The *Jones* Court relied on briefing to demonstrate that *Russell v. United States*[50] had implicitly rejected a broad
construction of 18 U.S.C. § 844(i). The government in *Jones* argued
that 18 U.S.C. § 844(i), which makes arson of property "used in
interstate . . . commerce or in any activity affecting interstate . . .
commerce" a federal crime, applied to the arson of a private resi-
dence.[51] In support, its brief cited *Russell*, which held that the statute
applied to rental property;[52] the argument in *Jones* was that property
is "used" in commerce merely by, for instance, "receiving natural
gas."[53] The *Jones* Court, however, noted that the *Russell* Court "did
not rest its holding on [such an] expansive interpretation advanced

---

[45] 552 U.S. 346 (2008).

[46] 465 U.S. 1 (1984).

[47] *Preston*, 552 U.S. at 353 n.2; *see* Allied-Bruce Terminix Cos. v. Dobson, 513 U.S. 265
(1995).

[48] *Preston*, 552 U.S. at 353 n.2.

[49] 529 U.S. 848 (2000).

[50] 471 U.S. 858 (1985).

[51] *Jones*, 529 U.S. at 850–51.

[52] Brief for the United States at 19–23, *Jones*, 529 U.S. 848 (No. 99-5739).

[53] *Id.* at 855–56.

by the Government both in *Russell* and in this case."[54] The Court contrasted the government's brief in *Russell*[55] with the Court's holding.[56]

Finally, in *Maine v. Moulton*,[57] the Court similarly looked to the briefs to learn that the Court had already considered and rejected in *Massiah v. United States*[58] the same argument that the government was now making in *Maine*. Once satisfied by the briefs that the same argument had previously been raised and rejected in *Massiah*, the *Moulton* Court quickly rejected the government's argument that post-indictment statements by a defendant, recorded by a witness cooperating with the government, could be used at trial so long as the government had an interest in investigating crimes beyond those charged.[59] The Court cited the government's brief in *Massiah* to establish that the *Massiah* Court was "faced with the very same argument made by the Solicitor General in this case."[60]

3. *Arguments not made.* If the Court did not previously consider an argument that the Justices now consider important, that may provide a reason to conclude that the Court's previous ruling cannot be fairly read to have decided a particular issue at all. The most obvious example is when the Court, relying on the absence of legal argument by the parties on a particular issue, dismisses language in a prior precedent as mere dictum even if that language might otherwise appear to be central to the Court's reasoning. The absence of prior argument on the issue can be invoked as strong evidence that part of the Court's opinion was not necessary to the Court's ruling.

Sometimes the opinion itself may make clear on its own what amounts to the Court's ruling rather than mere dictum, but other times the opinion does not. In the latter cases, the best evidence of the actual legal issues before the Court may be found in the formally required "Questions Presented" in the petition for a writ of certiorari. As the Court's own rules make clear, the questions presented

---

[54] *Id.* at 856 n.8.

[55] Brief for the United States at 15, *Russell*, 471 U.S. 858 (No. 84-435) ("Petitioner used his building on South Union Street in an activity affecting interstate commerce by heating it with gas that moved interstate.").

[56] *Russell*, 471 U.S. at 862 (focusing on rental property as an activity *affecting* commerce); *see Jones*, 529 U.S. at 856 n.8.

[57] 474 U.S. 159 (1985).

[58] 377 U.S. 201 (1964).

[59] *Moulton*, 474 U.S. at 178–79.

[60] *Id.* at 179 n.15.

define the issues that the Court will consider. Unless the Court's own order granting review expressly provides otherwise, the questions presented as set forth in the petition and those issues "fairly included therein" formally define the legal issues before the Court,[61] except "in the most exceptional cases" where prudence warrants overcoming the "heavy presumption against" expanding the issues that the Court considers.[62]

No less than Chief Justice John Marshall explained the relationship between legal arguments advanced and the distinction between the Court's holding and dictum. In *Cohens v. Virginia*,[63] Marshall described the relationship between dicta and precedent by considering what counsel had argued in *Marbury v. Madison*:

> It is a maxim not to be disregarded, that general expressions, in every opinion, are to be taken in connection with the case in which those expressions are used. If they go beyond the case, they may be respected, but ought not to control the judgment in a subsequent suit when the very point is presented for decision. The reason of this maxim is obvious. The question actually before the Court is investigated with care, and considered in its full extent. Other principles which may serve to illustrate it, are considered in their relation to the case decided, but their possible bearing on all other cases is seldom completely investigated.[64]

On the "single question before the Court" in *Marbury*, the Chief Justice explained:

> The Court decided, and we think very properly, that the legislature could not give original jurisdiction in such a case. But, in the reasoning of the Court in support of this decision, some expressions are used which go far beyond it. *The counsel for Marbury had insisted on the unlimited discretion of the legislature in the apportionment of the judicial power; and it is against this argument that the reasoning of the Court is directed.*[65]

The Court has since picked up on this language from *Cohens* to measure precedential weight on the basis of arguments advanced by counsel: "For the reasons stated by Chief Justice Marshall in [*Cohens*],

---

[61] Sup. Ct. R. 14.1(a) ("Only the questions set out in the petition, or fairly included therein, will be considered by the Court.").

[62] *See, e.g.*, Yee v. City of Escondido, 503 U.S. 519, 535–37 (1992) (first quotation quoting Stone v. Powell, 428 U.S. 465, 481 n.15 (1976)).

[63] 19 U.S. (6 Wheat.) 264 (1821).

[64] *Id.* at 399–400.

[65] *Id.* at 400 (emphasis added).

we are not bound to follow our dicta in a prior case in which the point now at issue was not fully debated."[66]

Justice Owen Roberts used similar logic to try to explain why his famous "switch in time" during the New Deal—when he voted in *West Coast Hotel Co. v. Parrish*[67] in 1937 to overrule *Adkins v. Children's Hospital*[68] despite having voted just a year before to sustain *Adkins* in *Morehead v. New York ex rel. Tipaldo*[69]—was not the result of political pressure. Justice Roberts claimed that he voted to overrule *Adkins* in *West Coast* but not in *Tipaldo* because counsel in *Tipaldo* had not advocated overruling *Adkins*.[70] His explanation appears in a memo Justice Roberts wrote to Justice Frankfurter, which was published after the former's death:

> Both in the petition for certiorari, in the brief on the merits, and in oral argument, counsel for the State of New York took the position that it was unnecessary to overrule the *Adkins* case in order to sustain the position of the State of New York. It was urged that further data and experience and additional facts distinguished the case at bar from the *Adkins* case. The argument seemed to me to be disingenuous and born of timidity. I could find nothing in the record to substantiate the alleged distinction. At conference I so stated, and stated further that I was for taking the State of New York at its word. The State had not asked that the *Adkins* case be overruled but that it be distinguished. I said I was unwilling to put a decision on any such ground. The vote was five to four for affirmance, and the case was assigned to Justice Butler. I stated to him that I would concur in any opinion which was based on the fact that the State had not asked us to re-examine or overrule *Adkins* and that, as we found no material difference in the facts of the two cases, we should therefore follow the *Adkins* case. The case was originally so written by Justice Butler, but after a dissent had been circulated he added matter to his opinion, seeking to sustain the *Adkins* case in principle. My proper course would have been to concur specially on the narrow ground I had taken. I did not do so.[71]

---

[66] *See* Cent. Valley Cmty. Coll. v. Katz, 546 U.S. 356, 363 (2006).

[67] 300 U.S. 379 (1937).

[68] 261 U.S. 525 (1923).

[69] 298 U.S. 587 (1936).

[70] Though Justice Roberts focused on what he perceived to be the disingenuousness of *Tipaldo* counsel's argument, statements arguing more generally against the overruling of a decision where a party has not advocated doing so appear in other opinions. *See, e.g.*, City of Indianapolis v. Edmond, 531 U.S. 32, 56 (2000) (Thomas, J., dissenting) ("I am not convinced that [two precedential cases] were correctly decided. . . . Respondents did not, however, advocate overruling [the two cases], and I am reluctant to consider such a step without the benefit of briefing and argument.").

[71] Felix Frankfurter, *Mr. Justice Roberts*, 104 U. Pa. L. Rev. 311, 314–15 (1955).

Justice Roberts further explained that he later voted to overrule *Adkins* in *West Coast* because "the authority of Adkins was definitely assailed and the Court was asked to reconsider and overrule it. Thus, for the first time, I was confronted with the necessity of facing the soundness of the Adkins case."[72]

More than a half-century later in *Citizens United v. Federal Election Commission*,[73] Chief Justice Roberts used a similar argument in responding to the dissent's criticism of the majority for overruling *Austin v. Michigan Chamber of Commerce*,[74] a case the dissent asserted had been "reaffirmed" by the Court in three recent cases.[75] In a separate concurring opinion, the Chief disputed the dissent's characterization of the Court's recent precedent by pointing out that in none of those three cases, unlike in *Citizens United*, had "a single party" raised the question whether the Court's prior precedent should be overruled.[76] In the absence of anyone raising the issue, the Chief argued, the Court's prior precedent could not fairly be deemed to have been reaffirmed.[77]

B. ADVOCACY HISTORY AND OVERRULING PRECEDENT

The far more controversial use of advocacy history is when Justices decide that a prior ruling should be overruled because incomplete or otherwise poor advocacy led to a poorly reasoned decision. "'[T]he quality of the decision's reasoning'" is one of the most prominent factors the Justices consider in trying to decide whether stare decisis should be a bar to the Court's overruling a prior case,[78] and the quality of the advocacy may directly affect the quality of the Court's work.

The origins of the notion that inadequate legal advocacy undermines a ruling's precedential effect can be found in the Court's treatment of summary dispositions. The Court has long and frequently

---

[72] *Id.* at 315.

[73] 558 U.S. 310 (2010).

[74] 494 U.S. 652 (1990).

[75] *Id.* at 377.

[76] *Id.*

[77] *Id.*

[78] Ramos v. Louisiana, 140 S. Ct. 1390, 1405 (2020) (quoting Franchise Tax Bd. v. Hyatt, 139 S. Ct. 1485, 1499 (2019)).

acknowledged that because such rulings are not the result of full briefing on the merits and oral argument—for example, single-sentence
summary reversals or affirmances or even lengthier per curiam opinions based only on the Court's consideration of the jurisdictional
pleadings—they are less weighty even though they are nonetheless
binding precedent until formally reconsidered by the Justices.

The Court's stated justification for according less weight to such
summary dispositions—that they were not the product of the most
thorough briefing and argument—is what has led the Justices in yet
another thread of cases to embrace the more sweeping proposition
that weak advocacy in a prior case can likewise support giving prior
precedent less weight, even when the ruling was not the result of a
truncated process lacking the opportunity for full briefing and oral
argument. The Justices reason that the prior ruling is not entitled to
as much respect because the Court may have reached a different
result had the Justices had the benefit of better advocacy.

This reasoning has obvious intuitive force. But no less obvious is
its potential to undermine stare decisis. Especially with the benefit of
hindsight, it may prove not so difficult to identify arguments that
could have been raised, but were not, and to speculate that had they
been raised, the Court might have reached a different result. Such a
speculative inquiry, especially in the context of a prior decision that
has itself become over the years a settled part of law, could be fairly
viewed as an insufficient basis for overruling prior precedent.

1. *Summary dispositions.* The Court decides the vast majority of its
cases after full briefing and oral argument. But a handful of times
every year, the Court decides cases after considering only the jurisdictional pleadings, most often a petition for a writ of certiorari,
a brief in opposition, and the petitioner's reply to that opposition.
The Court does not take the next step of granting the petition and
requesting full briefing and oral argument by the parties. The Court
instead acts "summarily" by reversing or affirming the judgment
below based on the jurisdictional pleadings alone. The Court's action is based on the apparent rationale that the merits are sufficiently
straightforward, or perhaps of no anticipated precedential import,
and that the Court accordingly need not bother wasting its time on
the matter by ordering full briefing and argument. Quite often when
the Court acts in this fashion, it is to reverse a lower-court judgment,
but summary affirmances can also happen (if, for example, the Court
wants to resolve a circuit split but does not believe the issue warrants

full briefing and argument, or if the case is before the court on appeal, not certiorari, so the Court must decide the merits).

In some instances, the Court's only formal statement consists of a single sentence declaring that the judgment below is reversed or affirmed without any further explanation. In other instances, the Court's judgment is accompanied by an unsigned per curiam opinion, which may itself be no more than one or two sentences long, or may instead be many pages in length, offering a fuller explication of the Court's reasoning.[79]

The use of summary dispositions to rule on the merits has long been controversial on the obvious ground that the jurisdictional pleadings that serve as the exclusive basis of such rulings are not designed to provide the Justices with the kind of full ventilation of legal issues necessary for a merits ruling.[80] Individual Justices have not infrequently sharply criticized the practice,[81] though presumably they have on other occasions agreed to join such rulings in support of outcomes they personally favor. The Supreme Court Rules, moreover, expressly contemplate such summary rulings,[82] and there have been suggestions in recent years that the Court is expanding their use as an expeditious way to oversee the lower courts without the need for full briefing and oral argument.[83]

For my purposes, however, what is relevant is not whether summary dispositions are a wise practice, but that the Justices attach less precedential weight to such rulings because they appreciate that the underlying advocacy is less thorough. As the Court explained in

[79] Not all unsigned orders or per curiam opinions, however, are the result of such summary dispositions absent full briefing and argument. The most well-known counterexample is *Bush v. Gore*, 531 U.S. 98 (2000), resolving the dispute over the counting of ballots in Florida during the 2000 presidential election, though the rushed nature of the Court's consideration of the case—only five days transpired between the jurisdictional grant of review and the release of the Court's unsigned per curiam opinion following merits briefing and oral argument—makes the case little different from summary disposition as a practical matter. Another famous ruling that resulted in a per curiam opinion following full merits briefing and oral argument is *Buckley v. Valeo*, 424 U.S. 1 (1976). See *infra* notes 104–106 and accompanying text.

[80] Ernest J. Brown, *Foreword: Process of Law*, 72 HARV. L. REV. 77, 79–82 (1958).

[81] Alex Hemmer, *Courts as Managers:* American Tradition Partnership v. Bullock *and Summary Dispositions at the Roberts Court*, 122 YALE L.J.F. 209, 211 n.9, 223 nn.74–76 (2013).

[82] SUP. CT. R. 16.1.

[83] Hemmer, *supra* note 81, at 218–23.

Edelman v. Jordan in 1974,[84] although summary rulings are clearly of precedential value, "they are not of the same precedential value as would be an opinion of this Court treating the question on the merits."[85] In *Edelman*, the Court explicitly disapproved a series of one-sentence summary affirmances regarding the meaning of the Eleventh Amendment, "[h]aving now had an opportunity to more fully consider the Eleventh Amendment issue after briefing and argument."[86]

In 1998, the Court in *Hohn v. United States*[87] extended the reasoning of *Edelman* to discount the significance of the Court's prior per curiam opinion in *House v. Mayo*[88] that was several pages long, not a mere one- or two-sentence summary ruling. For the majority, it was not the length of the *House* opinion but the fact that the opinion was "rendered without full briefing or argument" that warranted its receiving diminished precedential weight.[89] During oral argument, Justice Ginsburg characterized the Court's prior ruling as "a rather skimpy opinion. It was per curiam and there was no opposition, and it wasn't a very well aired case, was it?"[90] Dissenting in *Hohn*, Justice Scalia expressed concern about the longer-term implications of the Court's willingness to discount the precedential value of all summary opinions in this manner:

---

[84] 415 U.S. 651 (1974).

[85] *Id.* at 671; *see also, e.g.*, Washington v. Confederated Bands & Tribes of Yakima Indian Nation, 439 U.S. 463, 476 n.20 (1979) ("Our summary dismissals . . . do not . . . have the same precedential value here as does an opinion of this Court after briefing and oral argument. . . ."); Tully v. Griffin, Inc., 429 U.S. 68, 74 (1976) (noting that a summary affirmance is not "of the same precedential value as would be an opinion of this Court treating the question on the merits" (quoting *Edelman*, 415 U.S. at 671)); Usery v. Turner Elkhorn Mining Co., 428 U.S. 1, 14 (1976) ("[The parties] direct our attention initially to [a summary affirmance that decided questions presented in the case] . . . , but having heard oral argument and entertained full briefing on these issues . . . we proceed to treat them here more fully."); Fusari v. Steinberg, 419 U.S. 379, 391–92 (1975) (Burger, C.J., concurring) ("[A]lthough I agree wholeheartedly with the Court's reasoned discussion of the tension between [a summary affirmance, on the one hand,] and [an opinion in another case, on the other], we might well go beyond that and make explicit what is implicit in some prior holding. . . . An unexplicated summary affirmance . . . is not to be read as a renunciation by this Court of doctrines previously announced in our opinions after full argument."); Allen v. Wright, 468 U.S. 737, 764 (1984) ("[T]he decision has little weight as a precedent on the law of standing. This Court's decision . . . was merely a summary affirmance; for that reason alone, it could hardly establish principles contrary to those set out in opinions issued after full briefing and argument.").

[86] *Edelman*, 415 U.S. at 671.

[87] 524 U.S. 236 (1998).

[88] *See* House v. Mayo, 324 U.S. 42 (1945).

[89] *Hohn*, 524 U.S. at 251.

[90] Transcript of Oral Argument at 37, *Hohn*, 524 U.S. 236 (1998) (No. 96-8986).

> The new rule that the Court today announces—that our opinions rendered without full briefing and argument (hitherto thought to be the strongest indication of certainty in the outcome) have a diminished *stare decisis* effect—may well turn out to be the principal point for which the present opinion will be remembered. It can be expected to affect the treatment of many significant *per curiam* opinions by the lower courts, and the willingness of Justices to undertake summary dispositions in the future.[91]

Justice Scalia proved prescient in suggesting that the *Hohn* rationale would have unanticipated results, though the Justice himself did not shy away from embracing that rationale when the occasion later suited his own jurisprudential ends.[92]

2. *Beyond summary dispositions.* Nor has the Court limited its willingness to discount the precedential weight of opinions that are, as in *Hohn*, the product of limited briefing and the absence of oral argument to summary dispositions. Both before and after *Hohn*, Justices have taken the lesson from their summary disposition rulings that incomplete advocacy undermines precedential weight and applied that lesson far more broadly to cases that were the product of full briefing and argument, but where the Court either reached out to decide issues not fully briefed or the advocacy itself was poor.

The former can be more fairly characterized as a self-inflicted wound,[93] while the latter underscores the extent to which the Justices

---

[91] *Hohn*, 524 U.S. at 260 (Scalia, J., dissenting).

[92] *See infra* text accompanying notes 100–102 (discussing Heller v. District of Columbia, 554 U.S. 570 (2008)).

[93] *See, e.g.,* Horne v. Dep't of Agric., 135 S. Ct. 2419, 2436 (2015) (Breyer, J., concurring in part and dissenting in part) (arguing for "full briefing" before deciding the issue); Glob.-Tech Appliances, Inc. v. SEB S.A., 563 U.S. 754, 774 (2011) (Kennedy, J., dissenting) (criticizing deciding an issue without "briefing or argument from the criminal defense bar, which might have provided important counsel"); City of Indianapolis v. Edmond, 531 U.S. 32, 56 (2000) (Thomas, J., dissenting) (declining to consider overruling earlier decisions "without the benefit of briefing and argument"); City of Boerne v. Flores, 521 U.S. 507, 546 (1997) (O'Connor, J., dissenting) (noting, in arguing that an earlier decision was wrongly decided, that the conclusion was reached "without briefing or argument on the issue"); Pounders v. Watson, 521 U.S. 982, 993 (1997) (Stevens, J., dissenting) (arguing it is "unwise to answer [a question] without full briefing and argument"); Missouri v. Jenkins, 515 U.S. 70, 140 (1995) (Souter, J., dissenting) (noting that "[n]o one on the Court has had the benefit of briefing and argument informed by an appreciation of the potential breadth of the ruling"); Batson v. Kentucky, 476 U.S. 79, 118 (1986) (Burger, C.J., dissenting) (advocating "reargument and briefing" on an issue before deciding it); United States v. Johns, 469 U.S. 478, 489 (1985) (Brennan, J., dissenting) (arguing "it is improper for the Court without briefing or argument to suggest how it would resolve this important and unsettled question of law"); Harris v. Rosario, 446 U.S. 651, 652 (1980) (Marshall, J., dissenting) (criticizing the Court for "rush[ing] to resolve important legal issues without

are aware of their dependence on outstanding advocacy in their decision making. The Justices may well be "Supreme," but that does not mean they are necessarily omniscient in identifying on their own all the potential pitfalls of ruling in a particular way. They are highly dependent on the insights provided by others, especially the lawyers who appear before them in their written and oral advocacy.[94]

In his concurring opinion in *Monell v. Department of Social Services*,[95] decided in 1978, two decades before *Hohn*, Justice Lewis Powell explained why he believed that it is appropriate to afford opinions based on inadequate advocacy less precedential weight. At issue in *Monell* was whether the Court should overrule its prior decision in *Monroe v. Pape*[96] that municipalities were not subject to suit under Section 1983.[97] In a separate concurring opinion, Justice Powell defended the *Monell* Court's decision to overrule *Monroe* partly on the basis that "the ground of decision in *Monroe* was not advanced by either party and was broader than necessary to resolve the contentions made in that case."[98] As further explained by the Justice:

> Any overruling of prior precedent, whether of a constitutional decision or otherwise, disserves to some extent the value of certainty. But I think we owe somewhat less deference to a decision that was rendered without

---

full briefing or oral argument"); California v. United States, 438 U.S. 645, 693 (1978) (White, J., dissenting) (criticizing the majority for "discard[ing] [precedential] holdings in a footnote" "[w]ithout briefing and argument"); Mapp v. Ohio, 367 U.S. 643, 677 (1961) (Harlan, J., dissenting) (arguing that, before departing from an earlier opinion, the Court should have sought out "that aid which adequate briefing and argument lends to the determination of an important issue"); *cf.* Citizens United v. FEC, 558 U.S. 310, 385 (2010) (Roberts, C.J., concurring) (noting the "careful consideration" given the issue: "two rounds of briefing in this case, two oral arguments, and 54 *amicus* briefs").

[94] *See* Richard J. Lazarus, *Advocacy Matters Before and Within the Supreme Court: Transforming the Court by Transforming the Bar*, 93 GEO. L.J. 1487 (2008); see *infra* note 163 and accompanying text. The other side of the same coin, however, is how the Justices might also reach poor decisions because of their vulnerability to particularly outstanding advocacy by counsel representing one of the parties before the Court. That unstated phenomena might explain the Court's unanimous decision in *Hudson v. United States*, 522 U.S. 93 (1997) to overrule *United States v. Halper*, 490 U.S. 435 (1989), a decision by the Court reached only eight years earlier, also by a unanimous Court. In *Hudson*, the Court concluded that its ruling in *Halper* was "ill considered" and had "proved unworkable." *Hudson*, 522 U.S. at 101–02. Who was the counsel in *Halper* who on behalf of his client managed to persuade the Justices to adopt such an "ill considered" and "unworkable" rule? An attorney with a private law firm making his first appearance before the Court: John G. Roberts, Jr.

[95] 436 U.S. 658 (1978).

[96] Monroe v. Pape, 365 U.S. 167 (1961).

[97] *Monell*, 536 U.S. at 662.

[98] *Id.* at 709 (Powell, J., concurring).

benefit of a full airing of all the relevant considerations. That is the premise
of the canon of interpretation that language in a decision not necessary to
the holding may be accorded less weight in subsequent cases. I also would
recognize the fact that until this case the Court has not had to confront
squarely the consequences of holding § 1983 inapplicable to official mu-
nicipal policies.[99]

In 2008, again in *Heller*, Justice Scalia's majority opinion for the Court
embraced Justice Powell's reasoning as a basis for discounting the
precedential weight of the Court's 1939 ruling in *United States v. Miller*
that the Second Amendment did not confer an individual right to bear
arms. Taking issue with Justice Stevens's argument that the *Miller*
ruling should be respected because the *Miller* Court had reviewed
"many of the same sources that are discussed at greater length by the
Court today,"[100] Justice Scalia's *Heller* opinion responded that this was
in fact not true, "which was not entirely the Court's fault":[101]

> The defendants made no appearance in the case, neither filing a brief nor
> appearing at oral argument; the Court heard from no one but the Govern-
> ment (reason enough, one would think, not to make the case the beginning
> and the end of this Court's consideration of the Second Amendment).[102]

Seven years later in 2014, in yet another high-profile case, *McCutcheon
v. FEC*,[103] the Court again embraced Justice Powell's reasoning in
Monell, agreeing that inadequate advocacy in a prior case is, by itself,
sufficient grounds to discount the case's precedential weight, wholly
apart from whether the prior ruling was at all summary in nature. And,
unlike in *Heller*, the *McCutcheon* Court was not faced with a prior ruling
in which one of the parties literally had not showed up to argue. In
McCutcheon, the Chief Justice, writing for the Court, discounted the
precedential weight of *Buckley v. Valeo*[104] based on the limited nature of
the legal arguments made in the case. Citing to *Hohn*, the *McCutcheon*
Court reasoned that the case could not "be resolved merely by pointing
to three sentences in *Buckley* that were written without the benefit of

---

[99] *Id.* at 709 n.6.

[100] District of Columbia v. Heller, 554 U.S. 570, 623 (2008) (quoting *id.* at 676–77 (Stevens, J., dissenting)).

[101] *Id.*

[102] *Id.*

[103] 572 U.S. 185 (2014).

[104] 424 U.S. 1 (1976).

full briefing or argument on the issue."[105] Although *Buckley v. Valeo* was nominally an unsigned per curiam opinion, it was rendered after full merits briefing and oral argument and the majority opinion alone was 144 pages long. The oral advocates included legal luminaries of the day: Deputy Solicitor General Daniel Friedman, former Solicitor General Archibald Cox, Lloyd Cutler, Ralph Spritzer, Brice Claggett, and Ralph Winter. Yet because, as the *Buckley* Court itself had acknowledged, the constitutionality of the aggregate individual campaign contribution limit at issue "ha[d] not been separately addressed at length by the parties,"[106] the *McCutcheon* Court discounted the prior ruling.

McCutcheon has, moreover, not proven out of the ordinary in evidencing the Court's willingness to extend the *Hohn* rationale to fully briefed and argued cases. In *Johnson v. United States*,[107] decided a year after *McCutcheon*, Justice Scalia himself authored an opinion for the Court that drew on the exact language he had repudiated in *Hohn* to deny stare decisis effect to two cases, *James v. United States*[108] and *Sykes v. United States*,[109] that had held the residual clause of the Armed Career Criminal Act was not void for vagueness:

> This Court's cases make plain that even decisions rendered after full adversarial presentation may have to yield to the lessons of subsequent experience. . . . *James* and *Sykes* opined about vagueness without full briefing or argument on that issue—a circumstance that leaves us "less constrained to follow precedent."[110]

The Court, however, decided both *James* in 2007 and *Sykes* in 2011 after full briefing and oral argument. The former opinion was forty-one pages long and the latter forty-nine pages long. Unlike in the Court's earlier cases in which it discounted summary rulings because the truncated procedures limited the nature of the advocacy provided, in *Johnson* as in *McCutcheon*, the Court chose to discount the weight of its prior precedent based on its view that the actual briefing and argument, while not formally limited as in a summary disposition, had nonetheless not provided for a full adversarial testing of all the issues decided in the prior cases.

---

[105] *McCutcheon*, 572 U.S. at 202.

[106] *Id.* at 200 (alteration in original) (quoting *Buckley*, 424 U.S. at 38).

[107] 135 S. Ct. 2551 (2015).

[108] 550 U.S. 192 (2007).

[109] 564 U.S. 1 (2011).

[110] *Johnson*, 135 S. Ct. at 2562–63 (quoting *Hohn*, 524 U.S. at 251).

Even more recently, in *Knick v. Township of Scott*,[111] decided in 2019, the Chief Justice's opinion for the Court justified overruling *Williamson County Regional Planning Commission v. Hamilton Bank*[112] in part because of the decision's "poor reasoning," resulting from the limited nature of the advocacy that the Court had received in the case.[113] According to the *Knick* majority, the Court had made the mistake of "adopt[ing] the reasoning of the Solicitor General" as expressed by an amicus brief for the United States, which had raised an argument even though "[n]either party had raised the argument before."[114] That was relevant, according to the majority, because "[i]n these circumstances, the Court may not have adequately tested the logic of the [*Williamson County*] state-litigation requirement or considered its implications."[115] The Court's reliance on the notion that *Williamson County* had been decided "without adequate briefing from the parties" was expressly invited by the brief filed by the petitioner and their supporting amici in *Knick*.[116]

Not surprisingly, now that the Justices have been making increasingly clear that they are open to these arguments, more advocates are making them—suggesting that it may soon become open season for the advocates of today to challenge the quality of advocacy of their forbearers. For instance, during October Term 2018, the *Knick* petitioner and her amici were not the only counsel making this kind of argument as part of their pitch that the Court should overrule longstanding precedent. The petitioner in *Gamble v. United States*[117] made a similar argument in contending that the Justices should overrule the Court's 1927 decision in *United States v. Lanza*.[118] At issue in *Gamble* was the validity of the so-called "dual sovereignty doctrine," which provides that the Fifth Amendment's Double Jeopardy Clause is not

---

[111] 139 S. Ct. 2162 (2019).

[112] 473 U.S. 172 (1985).

[113] *Knick*, 139 S. Ct. at 2174.

[114] *Id.*

[115] *Id.*

[116] Petitioner's Brief on the Merits at 22, *Knick*, 139 S. Ct. 2162 (No. 17-647); Brief Amicus Curiae for the American Farm Bureau Federation et al. in Support of Petitioner at 18, *Knick*, 139 S. Ct. 2162 (No. 17-647) ("Misled by this inadequate exploration of the issues, the Court in *Williamson County* inadvertently set a trap for property owners by failing to consider preclusion.").

[117] 139 S. Ct. 1960 (2019).

[118] 260 U.S. 377 (1922).

triggered where there are two sovereigns and two laws, and accordingly no double prosecutions for the "same offense." *Lanza* provided the foundational precedent for the dual sovereignty doctrine.[119]

In support of *Lanza*'s overruling, an amicus brief in support of petitioner in *Gamble* stressed that "[w]hen the case reached this Court, the defendants received abysmal representation."[120] Their brief was "meandering," presented arguments that were "quite hard to discern," and "inept counsel" failed to question the validity of the dual sovereignty doctrine.[121] The majority, however, declined to address this argument, and Justice Kagan left little doubt during oral argument that she found the claim unpersuasive. During her questioning of petitioner's counsel, Justice Kagan suggested that petitioner's argument that *Lanza* should be overruled because "the arguments weren't properly presented" before the Court decided the case wasn't especially convincing given that "it's an 170-year-old-rule that's been relied on by close on 30 justices . . . at one time or another."[122]

Justice Gorsuch, by contrast, was a fan of this argument. In dissent, he pointed out, like *Gamble* petitioner's counsel, that in *Lanza* "the defendants did not directly question the permissibility of successive prosecutions for the same offense under state and federal law."[123] According to Justice Gorsuch, that lapse of effective advocacy was why the "Court did not consult the original meaning of the Double Jeopardy Clause or consult virtually any of the relevant historical sources," which, he argued, rendered that aspect of the *Lanza* ruling no more than "dictum."[124] As described above, using prior advocacy to characterize an aspect of a prior Court opinion as "dictum" is a close cousin to using such inadequate advocacy to argue that the prior ruling should be overruled.

II. OCTOBER TERM 2019

The Court's October Term 2019 underscores the extent to which advocacy history has become a regular feature of Supreme

---

[119] J.A.C. Grant, *The* Lanza *Rule of Successive Prosecutions*, 32 COLUM. L. REV. 1309 (1932).

[120] Brief of Amici Curiae Law Professors in Support of Petitioner at 14, *Gamble*, 139 S. Ct. 1960 (No. 17-646).

[121] *Id.* at 14, 16.

[122] Oral Argument at 20, *Gamble*, 139 S. Ct. 1960 (No. 17-646).

[123] *Gamble*, 139 S. Ct. at 2007 (Gorsuch, J., dissenting).

[124] *Id.*

Court decision making. Advocates before the Court frequently relied on advocacy history in their arguments to the Court, and the
Court and individual Justices did the same in their opinions. Reliance on advocacy history was evident in a wide range of contexts:
from the seemingly most mundane matters such as denials of petitions for a writ of certiorari to the most significant—rulings on the
merits, including in two of the highest-profile cases of the Term.

Nothing is more routine at the Court than the denial of certiorari.
The Court does it thousands of times a year. The legal effect is plain;
the judgment below is left undisturbed and, in principle, a decision to
deny review says nothing about whether the Court believes the decision below was correct. No doubt for that same reason, it is highly
unusual for the Court or an individual Justice to offer an explanation
for why review is being denied.

Yet in *Patterson v. Walgreen Co.*,[125] Justice Alito, joined by Justices
Thomas and Gorsuch, did just that by publishing a statement concurring in the denial of certiorari.[126] In agreeing with the Solicitor
General, whose views on the jurisdictional issue the Court had invited, Justice Alito stated that the Court should, as the Solicitor General had recommended, reconsider the validity of its prior ruling in
Trans World Airlines, Inc. v. Hardison,[127] but that the Solicitor General
was also correct that *Patterson* did not present "a good vehicle for
revisiting *Hardison*."[128] Justice Alito supported his view that *Hardison*
should be reconsidered in a future case by citing what he described as
the limited nature of the briefing by the parties in that case: "the parties'
briefs in *Hardison* did not focus on the meaning of [the statutory] term"
interpreted by the Court in that case.[129] For Justice Alito and the two
Justices who joined his opinion, the absence of such argument by
counsel weakened the precedential weight of *Hardison* and invited its
reconsideration.

In April, Justice Gorsuch, dissenting in *Thryv, Inc. v. Click-to-Call
Technologies, LP*,[130] relied on advocacy history in a different way: to

---

[125] 140 S. Ct. 685 (2020) (mem.).

[126] *Id.* at 685 (Alito, J., concurring in the denial of certiorari).

[127] *Id.*

[128] *Id.* at 686.

[129] *Id.*

[130] 140 S. Ct. 1367 (2020) (Gorsuch, J., dissenting).

interpret the meaning of a prior decision in determining its impact on arguments being made in *Thryv*. In particular, Justice Gorsuch compared the arguments being made by the petitioner in *Thryv* to the arguments made by a nonprevailing party in a case decided by the Court just two years earlier. Upon concluding that what "Thryv argues today" was essentially the same argument, relying on the same language, made by the losing party in that earlier case, Justice Gorsuch concluded that the Court's controlling precedent required rejection of Thryv's argument too.[131] In rejecting Justice Gorsuch's reading of that precedent, however, the majority pointed out that the dissent's "view of our precedent" was not one that even the respondent advanced, further underlining the role that advocacy serves in the Court's reasoning.[132]

In *June Medical Services, LLC v. Russo*,[133] advocacy history was relevant to the arguments of the parties in one of the biggest cases of the Term. At issue in *June Medical* was whether restrictions placed on abortion providers by Louisiana amounted to an unconstitutional undue burden on a woman's right to access to an abortion. Front and center in the case was whether the Court's 2016 decision in *Whole Woman's Health v. Hellerstedt*,[134] striking down a similar set of restrictions in Texas, required invalidation of the Louisiana law. The U.S. Court of Appeals for the Fifth Circuit had upheld the Louisiana law in part by distinguishing *Whole Woman's Health* on the ground that the defenders of the Louisiana law were raising a legal argument not raised in the Texas case.[135] In response, those challenging the Louisiana restrictions, citing to the Texas brief,[136] argued that Texas had in fact made all those same arguments which the Court had rejected in *Whole Woman's Health* and therefore was bound by precedent to reject in *June Medical Services* too.[137]

---

[131] *Id.* at 1386.

[132] *Id.* at 1376 n.8.

[133] 140 S. Ct. 2103 (2020).

[134] 136 S. Ct. 2292 (2016).

[135] June Medical Services L.L.C. v. Gee, 905 F.3d 787, 806 (5th Cir. 2018) ("The benefit from conformity was not presented in *WWH*, nor were the reasons behind the conformity . . . directly addressed.").

[136] Brief for Petitioners at 35, *June Medical Services*, 140 S. Ct. 2103 (2020) (No. 18-1323).

[137] *Id.* ("But the Court in *Whole Woman's Health* was not moved by that argument, and in fact rejected the premise. . . .").

Petitioner June Medical stressed the same point in its oral argument. Its counsel began the argument by highlighting "two fundamental errors" made by the Fifth Circuit in upholding Louisiana's restrictions on abortion providers.[138] The second of those errors was its acceptance of "legal arguments that this Court rejected four years ago."[139] Justice Kagan, later in the argument, challenged counsel for respondent Texas on that same ground: "[I]t seems that Whole Woman's Health precludes you from making this credentialing argument, doesn't it?"[140] Texas, in its brief, had made the backup argument that, if necessary, the Court should overrule *Whole Woman's Health*—thus implicitly recognizing that rejected legal arguments are a basis for interpreting the meaning of a precedent.[141]

In one of the Court's most stunning rulings of the Term, the Court struck down the Louisiana law on the ground that, as dictated by its prior ruling in *Whole Women's Health*, the state law imposed an undue burden on a woman's right to obtain an abortion and therefore was unconstitutional. It was of course not at all surprising that the four remaining Justices from the *Whole Women's Health* majority reached that result, concluding that "[t]his case is similar to, nearly identical with, *Whole Women's Health*" and "the law must consequently reach a similar conclusion."[142] The headline instead was that the Chief Justice, who had dissented in *Whole Women's Health* and who made clear in *June Medical* that he still believed *Whole Women's Health* was wrongly decided, nonetheless concluded that stare decisis required him to vote to strike down an essentially identical law in *June Medical* that "imposes a burden on access to abortion just as severe as that imposed by the Texas law."[143] The Chief rejected the dissent's argument that factual differences between the two cases were sufficient to support a different outcome.[144] Those challenging the Louisiana law therefore successfully persuaded a majority of the Court by their

---

[138] Transcript of Oral Argument at 5, *June Medical Services*, 140 S. Ct. 2103 (2020) (No. 18-1323).

[139] *Id.* at 5.

[140] *Id.* at 43.

[141] Brief for the Respondent/Cross-Petitioner at 67, *June Medical Services*, 140 S. Ct. 2103 (2020) (No. 18-1323).

[142] 140 S. Ct. at 2133 (plurality opinion).

[143] *Id.* at 2134 (Roberts, C.J., concurring).

[144] *Id.* at 2139–41.

arguments, which included extensive reliance on advocacy history, that the case could not be fairly distinguished from *Whole Women's Health*.

Justice Alito's dissenting opinion in *June Medical* also used advocacy history, addressing a threshold issue raised in *June Medical*: whether the doctors possessed standing to challenge the constitutionality of the Louisiana law. In concluding that such third-party standing had been sufficiently established in *June Medical* notwithstanding what the dissent described as a possible conflict of interest between abortion providers and patients seeking abortions (whose protection was the ostensible purpose of the Louisiana law), Justice Breyer's plurality opinion relied on the Court's 1976 decision in *Craig v. Boren*,[145] which, Justice Breyer said, was similar in relevant respects to *June Medical*. In *Craig*, the Court permitted a vendor of 3.2 percent beer to challenge a law permitting females, but not males, to purchase beer at the younger age of eighteen; the law was justified partly on the ground that it would keep young men from driving while intoxicated. Justice Alito's response in dissent makes plain that he looked to the underlying advocacy to support his view that *Craig* failed to support Breyer's view: "Suffice it to say that there is no indication that this supposed conflict occurred to anybody when *Craig* was before this Court."[146]

In *Our Lady of Guadalupe v. Morrissey-Berru*,[147] argued on May 11, 2020, advocacy history was front and center in the litigation before the Court. The question presented in *Our Lady of Guadalupe* was whether the First Amendment's Free Exercise and Establishment Clauses barred a court's consideration of an employment-discrimination claim brought against a religious elementary school by a lay teacher at the school. In *Hosanna-Tabor Evangelical Lutheran Church and School v. EEOC*,[148] decided in 2002, the Court held that there was a "ministerial exception" to employment discrimination claims brought against religious schools but did not address the question whether that exception

---

[145] *Id.* at 2117 (plurality opinion) (citing Craig v. Boren, 429 U.S. 190 (1976)).

[146] *Id.* at 2169–70 (Alito, J., dissenting).

[147] 140 S. Ct. 2049 (2020). *Our Lady of Guadalupe* was one of two consolidated cases from the Ninth Circuit, both raising the same legal issue. The other case was *St. James School v. Biel*, 140 S. Ct. 680 (2019) (mem.) (granting certiorari). The respondent teachers in the two consolidated cases filed one joint brief with the Court. *See* Brief for Respondents, *Our Lady of Guadalupe*, 140 S. Ct. 2049 (2020) (Nos. 19-267 & 19-348).

[148] 565 U.S. 171 (2012).

applied to a lay teacher.[149] The party seeking to bring the employment discrimination claim in *Hosanna* was a teacher who was also an ordained minister.[150]

In *Our Lady of Guadalupe*, the respondent teachers contended that the Supreme Court in 1986 had already established binding precedent in *Ohio Civil Rights Commission v. Dayton Christian Schools*,[151] left undisturbed by *Hosanna-Tabor*, that a lay teacher at a religious school could file an employment-discrimination claim. The *Dayton* case concerned a lay teacher at a religious school who filed a complaint with a state civil rights commission, alleging that the school had engaged in unlawful sex discrimination in terminating her employment. The school sued in federal district court to enjoin the state administrative proceedings. The Court, in an opinion written by Chief Justice Rehnquist, held that the federal trial court should have abstained from adjudicating the case and instead allowed it to proceed before the commission, with review by state courts.[152] But the Court, in reaching that conclusion—in a passage of potential relevance to *Our Lady of Guadalupe*—rejected the school's argument that the federal court should have intervened because "the mere exercise of jurisdiction over it by the state administrative body violates its First Amendment rights"; on the contrary, the Court said, the state Civil Rights Commission "violates no constitutional rights by merely investigating the circumstances of [the employee's] discharge in this case."[153] On this point, the four concurring Justices agreed: "neither the investigation of certain charges nor the conduct of a hearing on those charges is prohibited by the First Amendment."[154]

Relying on the advocacy history underlying *Dayton*, the teachers in *Our Lady of Guadalupe* argued that the Supreme Court in *Dayton* had held that a "a lay teacher in a religious elementary school [can] sue her employer."[155] They asserted that the losing argument advanced by the Dayton Christian School in *Dayton* was "precisely" the "very same argument the Schools make here," which the Court in

---

[149] *Id.* at 190, 196.

[150] *Id.* at 177–78.

[151] 477 U.S. 619 (1986).

[152] *Id.* at 628.

[153] *Id.*

[154] *Id.* at 632 (Stevens, J., concurring in the judgment).

[155] Brief for Respondents, *supra* note 147, at 1.

Dayton "unanimously rejected."[156] And they buttressed their claim over multiple pages in their brief with detailed and lengthy verbatim excerpts from the briefs filed by the Dayton Christian Schools in *Dayton*,[157] which "stressed 'the *religious functions* carried out by every teacher at [Dayton Christian Schools],' including 'conducting devotionals, providing direct instruction in Bible study, integrating Biblical precepts into every subject taught, and giving witness to religious truth by examples and conduct.'"[158]

During the *Our Lady of Guadalupe* oral argument, however, the petitioner religious schools sought to turn the tables by enlisting advocacy history in support of their position before the Court. But instead of focusing on the advocacy history of *Dayton*, as the teachers had done, petitioners focused on the advocacy underlying *Hosanna-Tabor*. Petitioners' counsel commenced his oral argument by asserting that "[i]f Respondents' arguments give some members of the Court déjà vu all over again, that is because Respondents have recycled many of the arguments that Court unanimously rejected eight years ago in *Hosanna-Tabor*":[159]

> The pretext inquiry, the notice requirement, the idea that freedom of association makes freedom of religion entirely unnecessary all were raised in *Hosanna-Tabor* and rejected unanimously. Eight years later, Respondents' argument are not any more convincing.[160]

The Court sided with the petitioners.[161] But in this instance, the advocacy history debate that preoccupied the opposing counsel did not make it into either the majority or dissenting opinions. Consistent with petitioners' argument, but with no reference to their reliance

---

[156] *Id.* at 26.

[157] *Id.* at 24–26 (quoting Brief for Respondent at 19, 24, 31, Ohio Civ. Rts. Comm'n v. Dayton Christian Schs., 477 U.S. 619 (No. 85-488); Transcript of Oral Argument at 44, *Dayton Christian Schools*, 477 U.S. 619 (1986) (No. 85-488)).

[158] *Id.* at 25 (quoting Brief for Respondent at 31, *Dayton Christian Schools*, 477 U.S. 619 (1986) (No. 85-488)). Petitioners' reply brief in *Our Lady of Guadalupe* sought mostly to deflect respondents' argument rather than address it, claiming it "smacks of desperation." Reply Brief for Petitioners at 10, *Our Lady of Guadalupe*, 140 S. Ct. 2049 (2020) (Nos. 19-267 & 19-348). It contended, without citation, that the respondents in *Hosanna-Tabor* made the same argument (further embracing the relevance of advocacy history) and that the *Dayton* Court itself never indicated whether the teacher in that case was a lay teacher. *Id.*

[159] Transcript of Oral Argument at 6–7, *Our Lady of Guadalupe School*, 140 S. Ct. 2049 (2020) (No. 19-267).

[160] *Id.*

[161] 140 S. Ct. 2049 (2020).

on advocacy history, a seven-Justice majority held that the prior decision in *Hosanna-Tabor* was "sufficient to decide the cases before us." According to the majority, "[w]hen a school with a religious mission entrusts a teacher with the responsibility of educating and forming students in the faith," the First Amendment Free Exercise and Establishment Clauses bar the adjudication of an employment-discrimination claim between the school and the employee.[162] But the respondents' extensive reliance on the advocacy history underlying the *Dayton* case made no apparent impact at least on the face of either the majority or dissenting opinions. Neither opinion cited even once to the *Dayton* case, let alone its advocacy history.

III. The Use of Advocacy History in Law Teaching and Legal Scholarship

In prior scholarship, I have sought to demonstrate how the quality of Supreme Court advocacy—whether outstanding or poor—affects what cases the Court decides to hear on the merits as well as the outcome in those cases it decides to hear.[163] Advocacy matters to Supreme Court decision making, and, relatedly, seemingly anomalous decisions can sometimes be explained by looking at the underlying advocacy. This article takes the further step of demonstrating how Supreme Court advocacy not only explains *why* the Court has ruled the way it has but also *what* it has ruled. These relationships between advocacy and Supreme Court decision making provide rich pedagogical opportunities for law professors in how they teach Supreme Court opinions. And, for that same reason, legal scholars might stumble in their own efforts to evaluate a decision if they do not consider the underlying advocacy.

One prominent example, *Massachusetts v. Environmental Protection Agency*,[164] nicely illustrates these pedagogical opportunities and

---

[162] *Id.* at 2069.

[163] *See* Lazarus, *supra* note 94; Richard J. Lazarus, *Docket Capture at the High Court*, 119 YALE L.J.F. 89 (2009) [hereinafter Lazarus, *Docket Capture at the High Court*]; Richard J. Lazarus, *The National Environmental Policy Act in the U.S. Supreme Court: A Reappraisal and a Peek Behind the Curtains*, 100 GEO. L.J. 1507 (2012) [hereinafter Lazarus, *The National Environmental Policy Act*]; *see* Jeffrey L. Fisher, *A Clinic's Place in the Supreme Court Bar*, 65 STAN. L. REV. 137, 146–62 (2013); Joan Biskupic, Janet Roberts & John Shiftman, *At America's Court of Last Resort, a Handful of Lawyers Now Dominates the Docket*, REUTERS (Dec. 8, 2014), https://www.reuters.com/investigates/special-report/scotus/.

[164] 549 U.S. 497 (2007).

scholarly pitfalls. *Massachusetts* is widely considered by environmental scholars and practitioners to be one of the Court's most significant environmental law rulings of all time.[165] A five-Justice majority held that allegations of climate injury could satisfy Article III standing requirements, that greenhouse gases constitute "air pollutants" within the meaning of the federal Clean Air Act, and that the U.S. Environmental Protection Agency abused its discretion in declining to determine whether emissions of greenhouse gases from new motor vehicles could reasonably be anticipated by EPA's administrator to endanger public health or welfare.

But *Massachusetts*'s legal significance is not limited to environmental law. Because it is a leading Supreme Court case concerning both Article III standing and the scope of judicial review of agency action, the case is routinely featured and taught in administrative law,[166] constitutional law,[167] and federal courts[168] classes in law schools across the nation. But if those teaching the case in law school are unaware of the advocacy history underlying the Court's opinion, they are missing an opportunity to teach more fully about what the Court ruled in the case. The same is true for legal scholarly analysis of the Court's ruling. Scholars have written, debated, and theorized about the import of the Court's ruling, unaware that there are potential answers to their questions supplied by the readily available advocacy history.

A. SCHOLARLY COMMENTARY ON MASSACHUSETTS

In *Massachusetts*, the Court addressed three distinct legal issues: (1) whether the petitioners possessed the Article III standing required to bring the lawsuit in the first instance; (2) whether EPA had lawfully concluded that greenhouse gases were not "air pollutants" within the meaning of the Clean Air Act; and (3) whether, even if greenhouse gases were Clean Air Act air pollutants, EPA had abused its discretion

---

[165] *See, e.g.,* J.B. Ruhl & James Salzman, *American Idols,* ENVT'L F., May/June 2019, at 40.

[166] *See, e.g.,* STEPHEN G. BREYER ET AL., ADMINISTRATIVE LAW AND REGULATORY POLICY (8th ed. 2017); PETER STRAUSS ET AL., GELLHORN AND BYSE'S ADMINISTRATIVE LAW CASES AND COMMENTS (12th ed. 2018).

[167] ERWIN CHEMERINSKY, CONSTITUTIONAL LAW 53–59 (6th ed. 2017); NOAH FELDMAN & KATHLEEN M. SULLIVAN, CONSTITUTIONAL LAW 43–47 (20th ed. 2018); GEOFFREY R. STONE ET AL., CONSTITUTIONAL LAW 97–105 (5th ed. 2018).

[168] RICHARD H. FALLON, JR. ET AL., HART & WECHSLER'S THE FEDERAL COURTS AND THE FEDERAL SYSTEM 149, 283–86 (7th ed. 2015).

in postponing its determination whether the emissions of such pollutants by new motor vehicles endangered public health and welfare.[169] Although it was immediately clear when the Court announced its ruling in April 2007 that the *Massachusetts* petitioners had run the table, winning on all three issues, far less clear were the precise grounds of the Court's reasoning and therefore its precedential impact on future cases.

Most controversial of all for legal scholars seeking to assess the Court's ruling are its grounds for deciding that EPA had abused its discretion in deciding, in effect, not to decide the endangerment issue. Legal scholars have pointed out that the opinion is susceptible to many possible readings, from quite narrow to quite broad, the latter of which is "supported by important passages in the opinion."[170] According to two of the nation's leading administrative law scholars, Harvard law professors (and my faculty colleagues) Cass Sunstein and Adrian Vermeule, "the Court seems to hold that in deciding whether to decide, agencies *may consider only the same factors that would be relevant to the primary decision itself*"[171]—referring in the *Massachusetts* context to the factors relevant in deciding whether an endangerment was in fact presented by new motor vehicle emissions of greenhouse gases. As Sunstein and Vermeule correctly go on to point out, that would be "a puzzling holding, one that is flatly inconsistent with the larger structure of administrative law" because agencies legitimately defer decision making all the time because of their practical need to allocate limited agency resources among competing priorities.[172] As further described by Sunstein and Vermeule, the resulting confusion in the lower courts forced to wrestle with the implications of the *Massachusetts* Court's "absurd" conclusion has prompted legal scholars to dismiss it, "labeling *Massachusetts v. EPA* as wrongly decided or impossibly confused."[173]

Professors Sunstein and Vermeule proffered an alternative basis for the Court's ruling in *Massachusetts* that they contend would, unlike

---

[169] *Massachusetts*, 549 U.S. 497.

[170] Cass Sunstein & Adrian Vermeule, *The Law of "Not Now": When Agencies Defer Decisions*, 103 Geo. L.J. 157, 159 (2014); *see* Richard J. Pierce, Jr., *What Factors Can an Agency Consider in Making a Decision*, 2009 Mich. St. L. Rev. 67; Sharon B. Jacobs, *The Administrative State's Passive Virtues*, 66 Admin. L. Rev. 565, 611 (2014).

[171] Sunstein & Vermeule, *supra* note 170, at 160 (emphasis in original).

[172] *Id.*

[173] *Id.* at 175.

the one suggested by the actual language of the Court's opinion, have justified the result reached by the Court. They argue that although EPA could have lawfully deferred its endangerment determination for any of a host of reasons unrelated to whether an endangerment exists, including limited agency resources, "there is a legitimate concern underlying the broader passages in *Massachusetts v. EPA*, which is that the EPA was in effect circumventing the statutory scheme through inaction."[174] They accordingly propose that "even in the absence of a statutory deadline, agencies are subject to a general *anti-circumvention principle*: when deciding whether to decide, agencies may not circumvent express or implied congressional instructions by deferring action."[175] They then go on to argue that the anti-circumvention principle suggested by *Massachusetts* is still an "overly broad prophylactic approach" and suggest that an "anti-abdication principle" would be far preferable "by providing a standard, rather than a rule, and thus sweeping in fewer cases in which agencies genuinely do have good reasons to defer decisionmaking."[176]

In their self-described effort to "reconstruct" *Massachusetts*, Sunstein and Vermeule persuasively point out how the broader reading of the Court's holding suggested by the language of the opinion would lead to absurd results contradicted by the long-standing, settled background principles of administrative law.[177] They posit narrower and far more defensible theoretical bases for the result reached by the Court: an "anti-circumvention principle," and its close relative the "anti-abdication principle." They argue that while the anti-circumvention principle offers a good explanation for what the Court was trying to achieve prophylactically, the anti-abdication principle is better still because it offers a narrower ground, rooted in the impropriety of a federal agency deferring any decision because of its rejection of Congress's policy judgment. Their claim is not that the language of the Supreme Court's opinion actually evidences any intent to rest on either of these narrower theoretical bases they have identified for the first time. It is instead that the Justices in the majority could and should have rested the decision on these grounds.

---

[174] *Id.*

[175] *Id.* at 162 (emphasis in original).

[176] *Id.* at 189.

[177] *Id.* at 182–83.

B. WHAT THE MASSACHUSETTS ADVOCACY HISTORY REVEALS

What is missing from Sunstein and Vermeule's otherwise excellent analysis is any awareness of the availability of the advocacy history underlying *Massachusetts* to illuminate the Court's reasoning in the case. That advocacy history provides strong evidence that the majority opinion is best read to have in fact been narrowly based on the very anti-circumvention and anti-abdication principles upon which Sunstein and Vermeule fault the Court for not relying. That same history also leaves little doubt that the Justices were not endorsing the overly broad approach for which commentators have sharply criticized the Court, based on the supposition that the Court had absurdly held that agencies could not defer discretionary decision making on the basis of traditional background principles of administrative law, including the need to decide how best to allocate limited agency resources among competing agency priorities.

As described in Part I above, the Court regularly considers the arguments made by the prevailing party in determining the meaning of its prior precedent. In *Massachusetts*, not only were the arguments of the prevailing petitioners the source of the broad language in the Court's opinion that commentators and lower courts have since sharply criticized, but their accompanying advocacy makes abundantly clear that they did not intend the absurd meaning suggested by legal commentators and lower courts in reading that language. Nor should, for that same reason, that absurd reading be attributed to the Court. The most plausible reading of the opinion is that the Court, rather than adopting an obviously erroneous position, meant to embrace the approach urged by the advocates who prevailed, however inartfully the relevant passages of the opinion might have been phrased.

The offending language in the *Massachusetts* Court's majority opinion can be found in two sentences. The first is when the Court seems to announce the applicable test for evaluating the legitimacy of an agency decision to postpone a determination: "[O]nce EPA has responded to a petition for rulemaking, its reasons for action or inaction must conform to the authorizing statute."[178] The second is its conclusion, after reviewing the several policy reasons proffered by EPA, that EPA's reasons were arbitrary and capricious: "Although

---

[178] Massachusetts v. EPA, 547 U.S. 497, 533 (2007).

we have neither the expertise nor the authority to evaluate these policy judgments, it is evident they have nothing to do with whether greenhouse gas emissions contribute to climate change."[179]

Both the Court's test and its application of the test reflect almost exactly the wording and reasoning of the argument expressed in the brief filed by the prevailing *Massachusetts* petitioners. Petitioners argued that "EPA may not decline to issue emission standards for motor vehicles based on policy considerations not enumerated in Section 202(a)(1) of the Clean Air Act."[180] As further elaborated by petitioners in their brief: "The provision under which EPA made its decision, section 202(a)(1) of the Clean Air Act, is crystalline: EPA is to decide whether to regulate an air pollutant emitted by motor vehicles on the basis of its judgment as to whether public health or welfare may reasonably be anticipated to be endangered by the pollution, and not the grab bag of considerations EPA invoked in this case."[181]

But while making these arguments, which the Court accepted, the prevailing petitioners both freely and repeatedly conceded in their briefs and oral argument that EPA possessed the very kind of background discretionary authority to defer decision making that legal commentators faulted the Court for rejecting. In addition, the only basis the prevailing *Massachusetts* petitioners offered for why the Court should nonetheless rule that EPA had acted arbitrarily and capriciously in deciding not to decide the endangerment issue was the very anti-abdication principle that Sunstein and Vermeule seven years later proffered as what would have been a justifiable basis for the Court's ruling. And the petitioners had accordingly carefully crafted their concessions and legal arguments before the Court in order to maximize their odds of prevailing. For those same reasons, because these were the actual arguments made by the prevailing party before the Court, they provide a legitimate basis for interpreting the meaning of otherwise ambiguous language in the Court's opinion narrowly.

For instance, in their reply brief on the merits, petitioners did not dispute that under long-standing "background principles of

---

[179] *Id.*

[180] Brief for the Petitioners at 35, *Massachusetts*, 547 U.S. 497 (No. 05-1120), 2006 WL 2563378.

[181] *Id.* at 38.

administrative law," agencies might well be entitled to deference in the timing of their decision making based on factors such as "resource constraints" or "competing priorities."[182] But, as petitioners stressed, "[n]owhere did EPA assert that it was declining to regulate" for either of those reasons, and the federal government's contrary suggestion in its brief "ignore[d] the actual structure of EPA's decision."[183] Instead of relying on potentially lawful background principles, petitioners' reply brief argued, EPA had based its decision to defer a decision on an illegitimate ground: "the power to ignore statutes it does not like."[184] Although petitioners did not label this the "anti-abdication principle," that was precisely the point they were making.

Nor did either petitioners' concession about the availability of background principles of administrative law or the narrow basis of their anti-abdication argument escape the attention of the Justices during oral argument. Because petitioners knew that making such a concession about background principles of administrative law and relying on a narrow anti-abdication principle were their best, if not only, hopes of winning, petitioners' counsel stressed each during oral argument. And the Justices in response sharply questioned their counsel to make sure he appreciated the narrow nature of their argument, especially because of its potential to allow EPA to reach the same result on remand.

Massachusetts's counsel began his argument by expressly acknowledging that "EPA possesses a good deal of discretion in applying the statutory endangerment test"; its mistake was resting its ruling "on impermissible grounds."[185] For that same reason, counsel stressed, petitioners were not asking the Court to order EPA to regulate greenhouse gas emissions but merely "to visit the rulemaking petition based upon permissible considerations."[186] Counsel further identified the impermissible ground upon which EPA had instead expressly relied: "we disagree with the regulatory approach" laid out by Congress in the Clean Air Act.[187] "Rejecting mandatory motor vehicle

---

[182] Reply at 1, 19, *Massachusetts*, 547 U.S. 497 (No. 05-1120), 2006 WL 3367871.

[183] *Id.* at 19.

[184] *Id.* at 22.

[185] Transcript of Oral Argument at 3–4, *Massachusetts*, 547 U.S. 497 (No. 05-1120).

[186] *Id.* at 4.

[187] *Id.* at 19.

regulation as a bad idea is simply not a policy choice that Congress left to EPA," the *Massachusetts* counsel argued.[188]

In response to a question from the Chief Justice about precisely when EPA had abused its discretion by not deciding the endangerment issue and whether the *Massachusetts* petitioners were denying EPA had discretion "to deal with what they regard as the more serious threats sooner," petitioners' counsel freely acknowledged that EPA possessed just such discretion based "on background principles of administrative law."[189] But, counsel pointed out, in the record before the Court, "they do not rely on any of those grounds, they do not rely on lack of information, they did not rely on background principles of administrative law."[190]

At this point, Justice Ginsburg interjected to make sure that counsel for the *Massachusetts* petitioners understood the limited nature of the relief they were seeking with this argument:

> But if you are right and then it went back and the EPA said, well, an obvious reason also is constraint on our own resources, we have the authority to say what comes first, Congress—we couldn't possibly do everything that Congress has authorized us to do; so it's our decision, even though we have the authority to do this, we think that we should spend our resources on other things.
>
> Suppose they said that? You said they didn't say it this time around, but how far will you get if that's all that's going to happen is it goes back and then EPA says our resources are constrained and we're not going to spend the money?[191]

Counsel made clear petitioners understood and accepted all the implications of their narrow argument. He did not deny that EPA could on remand rely on "background administrative law principles," including "we just don't want to spend the resources on this problem," and, if EPA wrote such an opinion, there would only "be a narrow arbitrary and capricious challenge on that. But the point is here they relied on the impermissible consideration that they simply disagreed with the policy behind the statute."[192]

---

[188] *Id.* at 20.

[189] *Id.* at 19.

[190] *Id.*

[191] *Id.* at 20.

[192] *Id.* at 20–21.

It was completely clear at the time, moreover, why petitioners were willing to make such concessions and rely only on such narrow arguments: they had calculated that it was their only chance of winning the case on the third issue presented.[193] They were not alone in such an assessment. For that very reason, Justice Scalia, who had left no doubt during oral argument of his hostility to petitioners' position, sought to get their counsel to abandon the concession. As soon as counsel stood up for his rebuttal, Justice Scalia asked a seemingly humorous question: "Mr. Milkey, do you want us to send this case back to the EPA to ask them whether if only the last two pages of their opinion were given as a reason that would suffice? Would that make you happy?"[194] And, when counsel gamely responded that "It would not make us happy, your Honor," Justice Scalia quickly embraced that statement by saying "I didn't think so."[195] Although the Court's oral argument transcript indicates that the courtroom erupted in laughter in response to the exchange, Justice Breyer understood exactly what Justice Scalia was seeking to do, his humorous tone notwithstanding: to get the *Massachusetts* counsel to concede away what might be the petitioners' winning argument. So, when the *Massachusetts* counsel sought to move on, Justice Breyer interrupted and brought him back to his response to Justice Scalia:

> What is your answer to Justice Scalia? Because I thought you said before that you thought it was appropriate for us to send this case back so that they could redetermine in light of proper considerations whether they wanted to exercise their authority. . . . Am I wrong about that?[196]

The *Massachusetts* counsel, then realizing that he had unwittingly walked into Justice Scalia's trap, no less quickly seized the lifeline Justice Breyer was offering and walked back his earlier answer to Justice Scalia: "Your Honor, that is exactly what we want."[197]

In short, the advocacy underlying the Court's ruling in *Massachusetts* provides strong evidence regarding how best to address the issues otherwise created by the opinion's language in isolation, with which legal scholars and lower courts have struggled. There is little

---

[193] Richard J. Lazarus, The Rule of Five, 201-02 (2020).

[194] Transcript of Oral Argument, *supra* note 185, at 52.

[195] *Id.*

[196] *Id.* at 53.

[197] *Id.*

reason to suppose that the Court was "absurdly" overturning decades of background principles of administrative law that allow agencies in the absence of a prescribed statutory deadline to defer decision making because of resource constraints, given that the prevailing party readily conceded an agency could. And there was similarly good reason to conclude that the Court not only *should* have but *could* legitimately be understood to have granted relief on a narrowly tailored anti-abdication principle in ruling that EPA had acted arbitrarily and capriciously, when that was the only argument proffered by the prevailing *Massachusetts* petitioners for why they should win on that ground. Although the lower courts and legal scholars have so far neglected to consider the relevancy of that advocacy in reading the *Massachusetts* opinion, it is fair to expect that both Supreme Court practitioners and the Justices themselves will do so in a future case that raises the issue of precisely what the Court ruled in *Massachusetts*, as they have done for decades in analogous circumstances.

Conclusion

Advocacy matters a lot in Supreme Court decision making.[198] Advocacy frequently explains why the Court's docket reflects certain kinds of legal issues and not others. It explains why some cases are granted review and other cases are denied, and which legal questions are presented to the Justices when review is granted. Advocacy also frequently explains why the Court rules the way it does in those relatively few cases that it hears each year on the merits.

Advocacy history also matters. It can explain what the Court has ruled, especially in cases in which the opinion of the Court is otherwise ambiguous, but even in cases when the text of the opinion otherwise might seem clear. The Justices have for decades looked to the advocacy underlying a prior Court ruling to determine its meaning and, far more controversially, to assess its precedential weight. Knowing that, expert Supreme Court practitioners do the same in presenting argument to the Court.

Legal academics should take fuller account of the special role advocacy history plays in the Court's decision making both in their teaching and writing about the Court. There are rich pedagogical opportunities readily available in demonstrating to students the

---

[198] Lazarus, *supra* note 94; Lazarus, *Docket Capture at the High Court, supra* note 163.

relationship of advocacy to the "why" and "what" of Supreme Court opinions. What at first might seem absurd or wholly inexplicable can, upon revealing the relevant advocacy, quickly make sense to students in exciting ways and, no less important, underscore to future lawyers the importance of their role as legal advocates.

Finally, there is likewise untapped value available to legal scholars who invariably seek to understand both the "why" and "what" of Supreme Court opinions, but have to date not appreciated advocacy's significance in answering each of those questions. This article's primary purpose has been to bring the practice out of the shadows of Supreme Court advocacy and decision making. A secondary goal has been to invite further scholarly assessment of the legitimacy of the practice, including drawing distinctions between its invocation in differing contexts. For instance, could advocacy history be fairly deemed a weightier basis for concluding that the Court decided less than it might otherwise seem from the face of the opinion rather than more?[199] So too just because it may be legitimate to invoke advocacy history to determine what the Court previously ruled does not mean it is equally fair game to use such history to deny a prior decision stare decisis effect because its underlying advocacy was somehow deficient.[200] In these ways, among others, advocacy history seems to be especially important in the Court's increasingly prominent internal debates about the role of precedent. By examining how the Court relies on advocacy history, legal scholars can both enrich their own scholarship and offer the Justices the advantages of scholarly analysis regarding the merits and pitfalls of what they are doing.

---

[199] Professor Richard Re raised this and a serious of promising questions in comments made on an earlier draft of this article.

[200] Justice Kagan raised this important inquiry in comments she made during the oral argument in *Gamble*. *See supra* text accompanying notes 117–119.

DATE DUE